BY JIM NEWTON

Justice for All: Earl Warren and the Nation He Made

Eisenhower: The White House Years

Worthy Fights: A Memoir of Leadership in War and Peace
(with Leon Panetta)

Man of Tomorrow: The Relentless Life of Jerry Brown

*Here Beside the Rising Tide: Jerry Garcia,
the Grateful Dead, and an American Awakening*

HERE BESIDE THE RISING TIDE

HERE BESIDE

THE RISING TIDE

Jerry Garcia, the Grateful Dead,

and an American Awakening

JIM NEWTON

RANDOM HOUSE | NEW YORK

Random House

An imprint and division of Penguin Random House LLC

1745 Broadway, New York, NY 10019

randomhousebooks.com

penguinrandomhouse.com

Copyright © 2025 by James S. Newton

Penguin Random House values and supports copyright. Copyright fuels creativity, encourages diverse voices, promotes free speech, and creates a vibrant culture. Thank you for buying an authorized edition of this book and for complying with copyright laws by not reproducing, scanning, or distributing any part of it in any form without permission. You are supporting writers and allowing Penguin Random House to continue to publish books for every reader. Please note that no part of this book may be used or reproduced in any manner for the purpose of training artificial intelligence technologies or systems.

RANDOM HOUSE and the HOUSE colophon are registered trademarks of Penguin Random House LLC.

Photos on pages xiv, 42, 60, 86, 112, 122, 150, 176 (top), 202, 278, 306, 336, 366, 388, 416, 422 courtesy of Jay Blakesberg, Photos on pages 2 and 22 courtesy of Sara Ruppenthal Katz. Bottom photo on page 175 courtesy of Getty Images.

Hardcover ISBN 9780593447055

Ebook ISBN 9780593447079

Printed in the United States of America on acid-free paper

1st Printing

First Edition

BOOK TEAM: Production editor: Evan Camfield • Managing editor: Rebecca Berlant • Production manager: Richard Elman • Copy editor: Emily DeHuff • Proofreaders: Kristin Jones, Susan Gutentag • Indexer: Ina Gravitz

The authorized representative in the EU for product safety and compliance is Penguin Random House Ireland, Morrison Chambers, 32 Nassau Street, Dublin D02 YH68, Ireland. https://eu-contact.penguin.ie.

To the artists, musicians, radicals,
writers, thinkers, activists, teachers,
ministers, students, lawyers, journalists,
and Deadheads who demonstrate what
it means to live with purposeful joy.
And to Woody.

Nothing left to do but smile, smile, smile.

—ROBERT HUNTER AND JERRY GARCIA

CONTENTS

Introduction, xv

PART I: ORIGINS, 1

1. *"Utter Loss," 3*
2. *The Slingshot, 23*
3. *The Warlocks to the Dead, 43*

PART II: EXPERIMENTS, 59

4. *The Acid Tests, 61*
5. *Forces Collide, 87*
6. *The Gathering, 113*
7. *Summer of Love, 123*
8. *"Dark Star," 151*

PART III: DISCOVERIES, 175

9. *All Fall Down, 177*
10. *The End of the Beginning, 203*
11. *An American Music, 229*
12. *Now What?, 263*
13. *"Eyes of the World," 279*
14. *"On the Road Again," 307*

PART IV: LIMITS, 335

15. *Safe Harbor, 337*

16. *"The Answer to the Atom Bomb," 367*

17. *Bad Architecture and Old Whores, 389*

18. *"Any Other Day That's Ever Been," 417*

Epilogue, 423

Acknowledgments, 435

Sources, 441

Notes, 453

Index, 489

Summer Solstice. Golden Gate Park, San Francisco, June 21, 1967.

Elizabeth Sunflower/Retro Photo Archive

INTRODUCTION

JERRY GARCIA, SPIRIT-CENTER OF THE GRATEFUL DEAD, WAS onstage at Woodstock and Watkins Glen, the Carousel Ballroom in San Francisco, RFK Stadium in Washington, D.C., and Tivoli Gardens in Copenhagen. He mingled with fans and fellows at the Acid Tests in 1965 and 1966, played through a lunar eclipse at the Great Pyramid of Giza in 1978, and delivered what would turn out to be a struggling, soulful final performance at Chicago's Soldier Field in 1995.

Garcia liked to say he knew the Dead had achieved something when the number of people in the audience began to exceed the number of those backstage, a marker put down somewhere in the first year or so of the Dead's thirty-year run. By the time the Dead ended, which it did with Garcia's death, the band had played more than twenty-three hundred ticketed shows, not to mention scores of benefits, appearances, and free afternoons in parks. Garcia and his other musical collaborations—the Jerry Garcia Band, the Jerry Garcia Acoustic Band, the New Riders of the Purple Sage, Legion of Mary, Old & In the Way, his duets with David Grisman—produced hundreds of additional performances. From 1965 to 1995, Garcia's output was astonishing, obsessive, and, in the end, punishing. Time and again, music guided him away from tragedy—to safety, to community, to brilliance. It could not save him from himself, and it didn't, but it supplied his life with mythic consequence.

In December 1962, before there was even an idea of "the Grateful Dead," Garcia attended the Berkeley Folk Music Festival. He planted

XVI | INTRODUCTION

himself in the front row, raptly attentive, as Sam Hinton, master of the diatonic harmonica, held forth. That was a lean, twenty-year-old Garcia, two years after his ejection from the Army, long before he had come to the attention of his neighbors, much less the larger culture. The Garcia of that moment—intelligent, focused, absorbing—persevered. He would grow portly, then fat; he would drift in and out of rehabs, fighting diabetes, drug addiction, and a dangerous fondness for fast food. He would gain admirers and lose friends, retreating into painful isolation. But first he would interpret the culture that he inherited and reimagine it, taking along thousands, then tens of thousands of appreciative followers, breaking ground into new realms of consciousness, often with the aid of drugs, and reaching back to bring along others. Outwardly cheerful and avuncular, privately unsure and often irresponsible, he was, for many, a guide to new vistas.

Under Garcia's tutelage, bluegrass, folk, and jug music would merge with psychedelics, jazz, country, blues, and rock 'n' roll to produce the sound and band that were the Grateful Dead. Garcia was just one part of that band, but he was its essential ingredient, and its essence was connection. He played with others, bound up first with his bandmates, then with the larger communities of family, Deadheads, fans, the counterculture, and the culture at large.

If the 1960s felt like a swirl—and they often did—they were cycling around the Dead. From its early days as the Warlocks, the band created its own cultural phenomenon, notably more enduring than the sources it brought together. "They are their own greatest influence," *Rolling Stone* said of the Dead—and not in 1989 but in 1969, just four years after they began. That observation became only truer with time. The Dead's performances evolved over their decades together, building on the elements that defined the band: the blending of genres, a determination to soar, formlessness atop form. It was difficult to pigeonhole—hardly what critics meant by "acid rock," although that label was often applied to it. As Garcia pointed out, the songs themselves were often traditional and even old-fashioned. But when they were played under the influence of LSD, the results were distinctive—formlessness atop form.

Over time, the structure of a Dead show came to mimic an acid trip, or, perhaps more evocatively, a mythic quest: tight and perceptive at first, then off on a wander through thunder and dissonance, emerging to a gasp of revelation, landing at home. There was a thread of fear, of the danger that comes from full embrace of imagination, walking a high wire, exposed to the elements. And it was, over and over, night after night, a gathering, a communing of spirit among fans and band, a shared responsibility for ecstasy. Joseph Campbell, the great student and teacher of myth, grasped the connection to the eternal when he attended a show in the mid-1980s. "What it turns on is life energy," Campbell said later. "This is Dionysus talking through these kids."

As that comment suggests, a Dead show was more than a musical event. Accompanied by a traveling audience—stalwart Deadheads who would take in a string of concerts or even an entire tour—it was a circus, a ride on the rails of modern America. Each stop offered an immersion in values: integrity, creativity, humility, camaraderie, adventure, joy, love. These were the currency of the Dead, more than any solo or surprise inclusion in the night's lineup. Music was at the core, yes, but the event catapulted beyond. "We're in the transportation business," drummer Mickey Hart observed. "We move minds."

That ability suggests connections to the eternal, to mysteries and verities. And the Dead's relationship with their audience was also a matter of magic. As it happened, the Dead would find their way into the bloodstream of the culture at precisely the moment that the culture was prepared to receive it. It began, as so many things did in that era, in and around San Francisco.

ANGER, DRUGS, rebellion, dread, hope, and above all a heartfelt quest for freedom in all its guises ignited in the San Francisco Bay Area in the early 1960s and swept outward from there—from the burning shore where Golden Gate Park dropped into the Pacific Ocean to the rest of America and beyond. In broad strokes, that movement became known as the counterculture, though that term suggests more cohesion than was obvious at ground level. It was sometimes gorgeous, often chaotic, riven with contradiction, bound only by imagination.

The counterculture meant something very different to the Hells Angels, the Black Panthers, the Diggers, Weatherman, and the Student Nonviolent Coordinating Committee. It was lived differently in the communes of Quarry Hill and Olema than in the Haight or the East Village. The Merry Pranksters and Timothy Leary each experimented with LSD, but not with the same goals or experience. The Pranksters found Leary cold and self-important; Leary considered the Pranksters, at least some of them, irresponsible, unserious, even ridiculous. Lou Reed despised the Grateful Dead; Reed, unsurprisingly, was received coolly when he came with the Velvet Underground to San Francisco.

The thinkers of the movement were similarly diverse. They stretched from Huey Newton to Stewart Brand, from Jane Fonda to Theodore Roszak, from Tom Hayden to Peter Coyote, from Thomas Pynchon to Kurt Vonnegut. The counterculture attracted the cool appraisal of Joan Didion and the manic energy of Muhammad Ali. It bridged the wide gap between Herbert Marcuse and Hunter S. Thompson, and it traveled the short spaces between Miles Davis and Bob Dylan and Jerry Garcia.

Those varied people did not speak with one voice. Some wrote manifestos, others poetry. Some shouted, others proclaimed more softly. Some demanded change and others lived it. But all imagined a closer connection to the earth, a more respectful community of humans, an aversion to war, a rejection of mercenary capitalism, and an appreciation of fun. They made their cases in speeches and novels and performances. They created an alternative way of living and set an example for others to follow.

Longing united them. They sensed an absence, a conviction that society had gone terribly wrong and that it was time for something new—a life less rooted in reason, more accessible through vision, magic, perhaps faith. "The truth of the matter is: no society, not even our severely secularized technocracy, can ever dispense with mystery and magical ritual," wrote Roszak, who coined the phrase "counter culture" six years after attending Garcia's first wedding. "These are the very bonds of social life, the inarticulate assumptions and motivations that weave together the collective fabric of society and which require periodic collective affirmation."

Some marked the beginning of the movement and the era at the Human Be-In in San Francisco in 1967, though it had already been stirring before that. Some marked its end at Altamont in 1969, though it continued long after; indeed, it tickles our lives today. It seemed to some to spring from nowhere, a sudden eruption against the perceived repression of the 1950s into a full-fledged revolution of politics and culture. In another sense, however, it marked a stage in a progression—from Parisian bohemians to squares to Beats to Pranksters to hippies.

The counterculture's ambitions were as varied as its participants. Some sought the promise of sexual liberation or a way back to the land. Some practiced nonviolence, some built bombs in basements. The movement embraced technology—Deadheads were among the first to gather at the Well, a pioneering exercise in social media—and rejected it—nuclear weapons and nuclear power were among the movement's most hated foes. The counterculture was memorialized in clenched fists and hugged trees, long hair, yoga poses, and flaming draft cards. It brought vivid evidence of the power of mass action, and sad proof of the limits of political change. It ended the Vietnam War but failed to produce a reconsideration of war itself.

Today, the counterculture survives in immortal music, sparkling works of literature, lasting creations of art, and subtle changes in political consciousness. Happily left behind are short-lived skirmishes and regrettable episodes of recklessness—spiking punch with LSD, dangerous road trips, embarrassing moments of incoherence. It was not all good—some of it was downright awful. It left a mark.

And at the center of it all, for better and for worse, was Jerry Garcia—open, imaginative, and magnetic, only to become tragically withdrawn. What did his life mean to the counterculture? And what does the counterculture mean for us today? Those are big questions, with complicated answers, worthy of consideration at a time when so many feel a

xx | INTRODUCTION

loss of direction, when the country once again feels unmoored. Today, amid division and distraction, many wonder about the signs that were missed, the opportunities wasted, the gains achieved, the progress made, the lessons learned. It may not be too late. It is just possible that the counterculture may still suggest a path through the thicket, a twinkle in the darkness as we try to rediscover who we are and how we might be better.

PART I

ORIGINS

Jerry and Joe Garcia,
shortly before Joe's death by drowning. Northern California, August 1947.

CHAPTER 1

"Utter Loss"

JERRY GARCIA GREW UP IN WORKING-CLASS SAN FRANCISCO, and he grew up hard. The San Francisco of the 1940s is difficult to imagine today, viewed backward through the gauze of wealth and technology, but in those days, it was roughhewn, a city of labor and immigrants, of fishermen and shopkeepers. The city—no good San Franciscan would ever call it Frisco—radiated from its docks, where Fisherman's Wharf teemed with actual fishermen, streaming out into the Pacific in the morning dark, trawling the abundant seas, and jostling for position as they returned to sell their day's catch. The waterfront smelled of fish and salt air, rattled with the clatter of cleats and the thrumming of diesel engines, muffled by fog in the mornings, sharp and jangly in the clear afternoons.

The city was bracketed by bridges. Gray and functional, the Bay Bridge connected San Francisco to Oakland and to the vast American landscape to the east. The Golden Gate, meanwhile, decoratively presented the city to the west. Built as much for beauty as for any transportation purpose, the Golden Gate Bridge was grace and aperture, an opening to all that lay beyond. Within the city, cable cars cut across town, turned by hand at each end. They ran from the elegant stores on Market Street to the rougher environs of the waterfront, picking up passengers as the cars climbed through the hilly neighborhoods of Victorians—"painted ladies," as they later came to be called—and humble townhouses.

Nearly a quarter of San Franciscans came from someplace else. Its neighborhoods included émigré enclaves from England, Germany,

4 | HERE BESIDE THE RISING TIDE

Spain, Portugal, Mexico, and Ireland. Italians were a cultural force in the city, and they clustered in North Beach—the DiMaggio family lived there and ran a fishing boat, though the boys sneaked off to play baseball and proved pretty good at it. The city's many Chinese residents lived and labored in Chinatown, thought to be the largest Chinese community outside Asia. Tourists came from across the world for a peek into the Orient. The China Clipper restaurant offered eleven varieties of chop suey, most for under a dollar. A "preserved Dragon Egg" for dessert cost forty cents.

Garcia spent his early years in the Excelsior District, a tidy but tough Italian and Irish neighborhood south of the city's more picturesque environs, well off the path of tourists. The Garcia family lived in a tiny Mediterranean Revival home, living room above the garage, on Amazon Avenue, as nondescript as a San Francisco house could be. Jerry's father, Jose, a native of Spain who emigrated to the United States as a teenager and completed just two years of high school, was a musician—clarinet and saxophone. He owned Joe Garcia's, a bar on First Street in Rincon Hill at the base of the Bay Bridge, not far from the scene of the city's epic clash between labor and power in 1934, when the General Strike shut down the port. The echoes of that day haunted San Francisco for a generation, well into the lives of Jose and Ruth Garcia's burgeoning family.

Joe Garcia's catered to seamen. The bar had the hum of travel, the raucous energy of men eager to tie one on before setting out to sea. Ruth, who went by "Bobbie" and worked the bar, was eight years younger than her husband and had been a nurse prior to her marriage. Once married, she adapted her life to that of her husband. He was dexterous, a bit disorganized, handy with tools, and sporting. He was called Joe and made his living as a barkeep and proprietor of the family establishment. Long days and nights piled up into long years. A census taker in 1940 recorded that Joe had worked every one of the fifty-two weeks in the prior year, and that he had spent eighty-four hours at Joe Garcia's the week prior to the collection of the census data.

The Garcias' marriage was filled with work and family and was, by surviving accounts, pleasant. Their first son, Clifford, was born in 1937, soon after the bar opened. Cliff would pick up the nickname Tiff from his younger brother, who struggled to pronounce "Cliff" as a baby. When Cliff was four, he got that younger brother, Jerome John Garcia, named for the composer Jerome Kern and known, first to his friends and then to a growing legion of admirers and fans, as Jerry. He was born on August 1, 1942, at Children's Hospital in San Francisco.

Although the bar supported the young family, it was not the life either of the Garcia parents had set out to make for themselves. Joe's real love was music. He entertained at clubs and music halls in San Francisco in the 1930s, making a decent living as a musician and band leader. He fell back on the bar in 1937 after running afoul of the musicians' union—he'd allowed members of his band to play for free, an infraction for which the union fined him. And in San Francisco, to have been censured by the union was a mark of ostracism. The experience soured Joe on professional music, and he instead used his savings, along with help from his in-laws and a business partner, to open Joe Garcia's. Music remained as a family pastime but no longer as a living.

The family was culturally Catholic, but hardly religious, "loose Catholics rather than devout Catholics," as Jerry later put it. Tiff and Jerry attended mass weekly, toddling off to nearby Corpus Christi Church, Jerry a little overwhelmed by the solemnity of the ceremony and more impressed by the sound of Latin than by any theological insight. The brothers usually went on their own, shuttled off to church while their parents enjoyed the morning to themselves. Music made a deeper impression. Family dinners brought together the Garcias and Ruth's family, the Cliffords, in boisterous, loud, sometimes fractious gatherings. The adults would shout and disagree and then retire to sing, often accompanied by Joe on clarinet or sax. Dinners typically concluded with children and adults gathered around the dining room table singing for hours before heading back to their respective homes.

As a young boy, Jerry Garcia was quiet, a little impish. He smiles in early photos, diffident but engaging, with a distinctive sparkle in his eyes. He carried few memories of his very young life, though he did recall wearing out a record at his grandmother's, almost compelled to keep playing it on her wind-up Victrola. And he remembered being tossed into a pool by a drunk man and rescued by his father, who then knocked the drunk out cold. Though fragments more than memories, they hint at the residue of Garcia's childhood—his early obsessive behavior and his vulnerability, the relief of protection, though by a man who would not be there long to provide it.

When Jerry was four, the Garcias were vacationing in Lompico, a remote section of redwood forest north of Santa Cruz, where they escaped the city to a primitive house without electricity or running water, jointly built and owned by the Garcias and Cliffords. One morning, Jerry and Cliff, who was eight, were chopping wood, Cliff handling the hatchet and little Jerry placing the wood to be chopped.

"He was putting little pieces of twigs on the sawhorse," Cliff recalled, "and I was chopping them in half, making kindling. . . . He'd put his finger in and take it away, put it in and take it away. That happened a dozen times. Finally, I nailed him."

The ax drove a deep cut into the middle finger of little Jerry's right hand. Bobbie, the former nurse, jumped to the rescue, wrapping Jerry's hand in a towel as they rushed to the hospital. But it was a long drive, and Jerry's finger was badly injured. Efforts to reconnect it failed, and Jerry went home that night missing the end of his middle finger, severed just above the middle knuckle.

The loss of a middle finger—and the surrounding pain and anxiety— would affect any young boy, and it did Jerry, who forgave his brother but forever bore the scar of their game gone wrong. And yet the loss of Jerry's finger was dwarfed by the greater tragedy of his young life that took place the following summer. This time, the occasion was a fishing trip. Cliff was off with relatives in Lompico while Joe and Ruth took Jerry, who had just turned five, on a camping trip along the Trinity River in Six Rivers National Forest, a few hours north of San Francisco.

The couple and their little boy arrived on Sunday, August 24, 1947. The next day, Joe went off to fish the Trinity River near where Willow Creek flowed into the larger stream. Ruth and Jerry set up camp nearby.

As Joe fished the cool water on a cloudy afternoon, he slipped on a rock. He was sucked under by a strong current, perhaps dragged down by his waders as they filled with water. Witnesses saw him fall, but it took them fifteen minutes to extricate him from the Trinity. By then, Joe Garcia, forty-five years old, was dead.

In later years, Jerry would remember having watched his father's death, and some close to him believed the trauma of bearing witness to such a tragedy caused him lasting grief and confusion. Carolyn Garcia, the longest romantic partner of Jerry's life and the mother of two of his daughters, attributed some of his later uncertainty, even his addiction to drugs, to the events of that August day. There is no denying or minimizing a boy's loss of his father at such an age, but the pain that Jerry felt was almost certainly not the result of witnessing the event. Joe Garcia's death was unusual enough to warrant modest coverage in the Northern California newspapers, and no mention is made of Jerry's presence at the scene.

Whether Jerry witnessed the drowning or not, his father's death had a staggering impact on his youth. He soon effectively lost his mother, too, as she struggled to raise her two young boys by herself and ultimately turned them over to the care of her mother and father, their grandparents. The boys moved in with Bill and Tillie Clifford—and their pet parrot, Loretta, said to have been rescued from the smoldering ruins of the San Francisco earthquake and fire in 1906.

The Cliffords lived in a two-story house on Harrington Street, just a few blocks from the Garcia home on Amazon Street. They were, in Garcia's memory, "an odd couple. I mean, really odd." Jerry called his grandfather Pop, but that's as far as his affection went. Bill was quiet to the point of absence, an Irishman who "didn't have the gift of gab." Decades later, when Jerry Garcia jotted notes about his grandfather for a reflection on his own childhood, the memories strongly hinted at his anger. He referred to Bill Clifford as "dumb" and "So Dull." Summing up their relationship, Garcia wrote, "He was like oh, jeez . . ."

The opposite was true for Tillie. Beautiful, animated, political, tough, she was beloved by her grandsons. The room that Jerry and Cliff shared in their grandparents' house featured a portrait of a ravishing young brunette, hair pulled back, eyes blazing. Although Jerry never asked his grandmother about the picture, he believed it to be of her as a young woman. They called her Nan.

She was, Garcia wrote, "the super star of the family." Cantankerous and lively, she served as the elected secretary-treasurer of the local laundry workers union, and she was recognized wherever she went—in part because she was always decked out in public, sporting eye-catching hats and bright dresses. Tagging along, little Jerry would wait impatiently as she greeted friends and constituents. His memories of this time blended annoyance and admiration in a mixture that any child of a politician would recognize.

Bill and Nan's relationship was marked by a casual disregard for conventional marital mores. Nan had a boyfriend, and Bill accepted it. When she would travel on union business, it was not with Bill. He would stay home, puttering around the house, working with his tools, making improvements, while his wife and her boyfriend went about their affair. It was no secret, not even to her grandsons. Cliff knew his grandmother's boyfriend for more than twenty years.

By the time Cliff and Jerry came to live with them, Bill seemed to have been resigned to his wife's dalliance, but it had not always been so. One night in the spring of 1916, Tillie came home late, and Bill erupted. He was charged with beating Tillie and, when he appeared in court, was described as "contrite," explaining that he had waited up for his wife, growing more and more angry, and that he struck her when she finally returned home. The judge, Matt Brady, sympathized with Bill, but Tillie was having none of it: "You will run for office again," she told Judge Brady. "I shall see to it that you don't get some votes." For that, Brady threw her in jail, but then he relented, letting both Bill and Tillie go free after they had cooled off. Tillie was not done with it. She sued for divorce, charging her husband with cruelty. The episode passed, and Bill and Tillie patched things up. Their unconventional union survived, its differences long settled into silences by the time their grandsons came to live with them.

Jerry and Cliff would spend five years under their grandparents' roof. For most of that time, Jerry went to Monroe Elementary School, about six blocks from his grandparents' house. A third grade teacher, Miss Simon, encouraged his art, and he toyed a bit with a banjo. His mother remained present in his life, though day-to-day responsibility for raising him and his brother rested with Nan and, to a lesser degree, Bill.

The years with the Cliffords were alternately exciting and frightening, and though Garcia spoke of them lovingly later in life, they contained hardships as well. Jerry's health suffered. He developed asthma and spent long hours at home, taking up drawing. He loved comic books and television—Bill and Tillie had one of the first TVs in their neighborhood—and scary stories that extended to movies, with matinees on Market Street a special treat. For the rest of his life, he would recall seeing *Abbott and Costello Meet Frankenstein*, cowering in his seat at the scenes of the monster coming to life. Garcia had experienced real pain (the loss of a finger) and real fear (the sudden death of his father). Movie fright touched those nerves. He was shot through with energy and emotion, and his first consciously artistic experiences were visual.

Meanwhile, the larger canvas of his childhood was fragmentary, draped with uncertainty. The little boy who remembered his father pulling him from the pool as a toddler could no longer turn to Joe for safety or consolation. He recalled the mysteries of Catholic mass, along with early encounters with girls who would corner him in the neighborhood, force him to pull down his pants, and laugh at him. Struggle and humiliation, loneliness and mystery, all contributed to shaping his young life. He did not complain, at least once he was through it, but others sensed his confusion. His childhood, said Sara Ruppenthal, his first wife, was one of "loss. Utter loss."

But he had a sparkle. He asked questions, quietly probed. He took in images, heard the music in sound. Many years later, when Garcia was dead and his surviving friend and writing partner, Robert Hunter, was asked to sum up Garcia in a word, he started with "dead," then gave the matter more thought. "Inquisitive," he said. That was true from Garcia's first days to his last.

IN 1953, when Jerry was in grade school and Cliff in high school, their mother married a merchant mariner named Wally Matusiewicz. It was the chance for a new start, and Ruth took it seriously. She gathered up her boys from her mother and moved them out. Cliff and Jerry left everything behind. "She just wanted to start over," Cliff recalled. "A new life." The family moved to Menlo Park, a suburban town south of San Francisco that is now in the heart of Silicon Valley but then was a bedroom community for the city and a convenient middle-class neighborhood for professors and others associated with nearby Stanford University.

Attractive as the idea of starting over must have seemed to Ruth, it was yet another disruption for her sons. Cliff resented having to change high schools. Jerry lost the most loving figure of his youth, his glamorous, eccentric, and caring grandmother. Each of the boys acted out. Their stepfather tried without much success to discipline them, but since he was a sailor, he was often away. He tried to enlist Jerry in more physical labor, but Jerry passively resisted, sloughing off his stepfather's efforts. Cliff turned sixteen and secured a driver's license; he and Jerry would snag the family car and run up to San Francisco to be with old friends there.

Jerry scuffled around the edges of school. His more insightful teachers recognized his intelligence—upon entering middle school, Jerry was enrolled in the "fast learner" program at Menlo Oaks—and some saw potential in his art as well. But he was bored and distracted, and it showed. He was held back in the eighth grade while Cliff plodded through high school. And then Cliff jumped at the chance to be gone for good: After graduating from high school in the summer of 1956, he left home to join the Marine Corps. Jerry was alone.

While Cliff settled into life as a Marine, Ruth and Wally gave up on the Peninsula and moved themselves and Jerry back to San Francisco, plunging him once again into uncertain company—rough kids at Denman Junior High School and then rougher at Balboa High School. Jerry would later describe those as "razor-toting schools," inhabited by little gangsters patrolling their turf; Garcia, clean-cut and new, skirted the edges of that culture. And then, a break: He enrolled at the California School of Fine Arts (later the San Francisco Art Institute), first in a summer program and later for school-year classes at night. Unlike his normal studies, that made a difference. Garcia suddenly was amid beatniks.

GARCIA'S TIME at the School of Fine Arts placed him inside an artistic awakening. His first artistic voice would be that of the Beats.

It is worth taking a moment, then, to consider this cultural movement, one that would fuse the cultures of New York and San Francisco in midcentury America and that would alter the way many Americans approached literature, the visual arts, and music. It was, in a sense, the beginning of all that followed. It began in New York with a group of vagabonds and artists who found their way to one another and bonded over a blend of art and hardship, much of it self-imposed.

They arrived separately in New York. Herbert Huncke, slight, shifty, and fast-talking, was born in Massachusetts and discovered himself when he hitchhiked to New York in 1939 and settled into Times Square, a small-time street dealer and hustler with enough literary ambition to capitalize on his friendships and parlay a life of street prostitution into a literary adventure. Jack Kerouac, a Catholic French Canadian raised in Lowell, Massachusetts, came to New York in 1939, first to attend Horace Mann School and then to enter Columbia, where he played football until he was injured, then sneaked away to join the Merchant Marine. He returned to New York restless and searching. William S. Burroughs, raised Protestant in a wealthy St. Louis family, began visiting New York while studying at Harvard; he briefly served in the Army following Pearl Harbor but was allowed to leave after his father pleaded that his son's mental instability rendered him unfit for service. He made his way to New York in 1943. Lucien Carr, dashing, handsome, and two years younger than Kerouac, came to Columbia after Kerouac's departure and spent his time adhering himself to Lionel Trilling and attempting to craft a literary vision that borrowed from transcendentalism and amoral self-expression. Allen Ginsberg, a year younger than Carr, Jewish, son of Marxists, raised in New Jersey, was engaged from a young age in the troubles of the world. He published his first poem at age eleven and went on to study with Trilling. Huncke, Kerouac, Burroughs, Carr, and Ginsberg bonded in New York City, sharing drinks, nights, and close, grubby quarters.

One of Kerouac's contributions to his generation was unintended, for it was Kerouac who invented the phrase "the Beat generation." Despite the later associations with that phrase, Kerouac did not mean it to suggest a musical beat or anything so lighthearted. Kerouac's "Beats" were a beaten-down cohort of young people struggling to contest the conformity and dread of 1950s America, "down and out but full of intense conviction." A *New York Times Magazine* piece in 1952 credited Kerouac with the coinage and elaborated on the sense of being "beat," noting that it referred to "the feeling of having been used, of being raw. . . . In short, it means being undramatically pushed up against the wall of oneself. A man is beat whenever he goes for broke and wagers the sum of his resources on a single number: and the young generation has done that continually from early youth."

That original meaning, with all its weathered foreboding, quickly slipped into a lighter vernacular, derisive and superficial. "The Beat Generation" became "Beatniks" in the hands of the San Francisco newspaper columnist Herb Caen. In his version, "beat" went from meaning "beaten down" to something more like "keeping on the beat." Serious artists now were seen as wannabes, noticeable in their berets and goatees, guzzling red wine and snapping their fingers in lieu of applause. Kerouac, the godfather of the Beats, was repelled by the Beatniks—and even more by their cultural descendants, the hippies. As Lawrence Ferlinghetti observed: "Jack has nothing to do with Beat or beatnik except in the minds of thousands who read *On the Road* thinking he's some sort of crazy wild rebel whereas really he's just a 'home boy' from little ol' Lowell and certainly no rebel."

By the early 1950s, Kerouac had been jailed and married and had had one associate murder another. His first novel had been published, but years went by as he struggled to find a publisher willing to take his second. His words had been twisted and his identity as a "Beat" had moved from something serious to something close to laughable. Lost and lonely, he did what so many Americans in similar situations had always done: He moved west.

IT WAS natural that Kerouac would be drawn to San Francisco. As long as there had been a San Francisco, it had been a place of rowdy freedom, artistic and personal. Hub of the Gold Rush, inhabited by dockworkers, socialists, and activists, it was the home of the Bohemian Club, of Harry Bridges and the 1934 General Strike. In its early years, San Francisco had more prostitutes than housewives, more bars than churches, and though it had grown up by the 1950s, it retained its teenage pugnacity. It wasn't for everybody, but those who loved it loved it deeply. Kenneth Rexroth, its reigning poet, called it "one of the easiest cities in the world to live in." Contrasting San Francisco's Mediterranean feel with New Orleans's fake version of the same, complaining that a week in New York left him desperate for a doctor, that Seattle made him nervous, and that he felt he needed a passport just to travel to Berkeley or Oakland, Rexroth concluded that "if I couldn't live here I would leave the United States for someplace like Aix en Provence."

The city had been a temporary home to Kerouac before, and it figures in his travels in *On the Road*. This time, however, his return was followed by that of Ginsberg, who arrived in 1954 and brought with him a letter of introduction from William Carlos Williams. He presented it to Rexroth, and in that moment, the Beats were formally introduced to the San Francisco Renaissance.

As with the Beats, the Renaissance was loosely defined and yet rec-

14 | HERE BESIDE THE RISING TIDE

ognizably a thing. Leading figures included writers and visual artists, including Michael McClure, Philip Whalen, Wally Hedrick, Lew Welch, and Lenore Kandel. Ferlinghetti and Peter Martin were doubly influential, as writers and as founders of City Lights Bookstore (also known as City Lights Booksellers), which opened in 1953 on a wedge-shaped chunk of land in North Beach and added a publishing arm in 1955. Built on the ruins of a building destroyed in the 1906 earthquake, the store proclaimed itself a "literary meetingplace" and invited the city's literary community inside. They came. The Renaissance artists were in some ways different from the Beats who now joined them: Kerouac and Ginsberg found subjects in the urban underbelly—car thieves, prostitutes, bums—while the Renaissance group drew more sustenance from naturalism, the environment, and Eastern philosophy. But they found common ground in their alienation from the consensus moderates of the American 1950s. They jointly questioned form and structure in writing, painting, and music.

Ginsberg's arrival reunited him with Kerouac and provided the union of the Beats and the Renaissance with the spark that lit the chain reaction. Two cultures, East and West, bonded with the force of fusion. The specific moment of ignition, the night when the Beats and the San Francisco Renaissance combined their intensities and visions, occurred on October 7, 1955. The event took place at Six Gallery in North Beach. Kerouac was present but declined to read, instead serving wine in jugs. Ferlinghetti, Whalen, Gary Snyder, and McClure all were present. Snyder read from "The Berry Feast." The twenty-two-year-old McClure, reading in public for the first time, declaimed on animism, his developing notion of a unity of humanity and nature. The audience was rowdy and spellbound, "piffed" by California burgundy.

The highlight was Ginsberg's reading of his new poem, "Howl." Its opening lines proclaimed the arrival of the young and the pain of that birth:

I saw the best minds of my generation destroyed by madness, starving hysterical naked,

> *dragging themselves through the negro streets at dawn looking for an*
> *angry fix,*
> *angelheaded hipsters burning for the ancient heavenly connection to*
> *the starry dynamo in the machinery of night* . . .

As Ginsberg moved to the poem's more energetic passages, he sped up, young and wild-haired, eyes flashing and voice rising. He was a little drunk, and he gestured wildly, "arms outspread," chanting incantations to "Moloch," wailing of sobbing boys and weeping men, failed governments and war. The crowd chanted "Go, go, go!"

"It was," Kerouac recalled, "a mad night."

Luther Nichols of the *San Francisco Examiner* pronounced "Howl" a "poetic thunderbolt" and considered Ginsberg and Kerouac the preeminent young writers of the moment. Ferlinghetti agreed. He wrote Ginsberg the day after the Six Gallery reading, asking to publish the poem and referencing Emerson's historic overture to Whitman: "I greet you at the beginning of a great career."

McClure, on the other hand, initially thought the poem was "terrible," though he eventually came to see its power and regarded it as the moment when "we had gone beyond a point of no return." Trilling, mentor to both Ginsberg and Ferlinghetti (and Carr), told Ginsberg he thought the work was "dull." Other critics found it less dull than simply offensive. John Hollander called it the "ravings of a lunatic fiend." And John Ciardi extended his critique beyond Ginsberg to the larger group of writers he represented, labeling them all "not only juvenile but certainly related to juvenile delinquency through a common ancestry whose name is Disgust . . . little more than unwashed eccentricity."

Howl and Other Poems, the tiny paperback containing "Howl," "America," and "Sunflower Sutra," was copied by Ginsberg on mimeograph paper and then published by City Lights the following spring. From that point on, the book, with its recognizable black-and-white cover and its introduction by William Carlos Williams, would become a staple of every dorm room and coffee shop of the American art scene. One's opinion of the poems, and of Ginsberg more generally, would

16 | HERE BESIDE THE RISING TIDE

come to signal one's generational and artistic allegiances. It separated the Ferlinghettis from the Trillings.

A year after "Howl" came *On the Road*. It tells the story of Sal Paradise (Kerouac) and Dean Moriarty, who was modeled on Neal Cassady, soon to become a figure in his own right, through five sections chronicling trips across and around the United States and Mexico—San Francisco, Los Angeles, Denver, and Texas all feature prominently. They move relentlessly, if not exactly aimlessly, drifting through drinking and sex and drugs, sometimes through flights of ebullience and other times in nearly wretched despair. It is a story of friendship tested by circumstance, guided by the mesmerizing and perplexing person of Moriarty and observed by his friend, the wryly named Paradise. Released by Viking in September 1957, the book benefited from one of literary history's luckiest breaks. The regular book reviewer for the daily editions of *The New York Times* was on vacation, and another reviewer passed on the book, letting it fall instead to young Gilbert Millstein, who had already shown interest in the Beats. Millstein's review announced *On the Road* as a major contribution to American letters, "an authentic work of art." "There are sections of 'On the Road' in which the writing is of a beauty that is almost breathtaking," Millstein concluded. " 'On the Road' is a major novel."

With such a rave in the nation's paper of record, others could not ignore *On the Road*. Plenty of critics hated it. The *Times*'s regular critic was outraged when he read it, and the *Times* published a second, less glowing review a few days later. But Millstein's review—the result of exactly the kind of serendipity that book celebrated—meant that Kerouac's work would matter.

Kerouac's contributions to literature were mixed. The mythology of *On the Road* is that it was entirely a work of improvisation, written on a scroll in three weeks, fueled by Benzedrine, a work of "spontaneous prose," as Kerouac himself described it. That made a deep impression—Garcia was among those smitten by the book's seeming spontaneity—but it was largely fabricated. Kerouac labored over drafts and spent years refining the novel as he searched for an agent to represent him and a publisher willing to produce the book. The Dadaist myth that it grew out of a single binge encouraged a great deal of bad writing by those who failed to recognize the discipline and practice that created it.

Glorified and vilified for its excesses, the novel is stronger, sadder, and more grounded than is often recognized. *On the Road* widened the lens and expanded the range of American literature, no small feat. But its emphasis on tone and speed caused many to overlook its bleaker conclusions. The novel ends with Moriarty, homeless and reduced to a whisper on the streets of New York City, denied even a ride uptown in the narrator's Cadillac. Never mind. Excited readers seized on the novel's more rambunctious passages and its hell-bent commitment to movement, no matter the cost. Readers took to the road.

The book spoke most powerfully to those already engaged in Kerouac's project—the challenging of form, the expression of rage and bewilderment, the determination to live authentically. One group of San Francisco writers and artists who were experimenting with the same ideas formed a natural audience, and they took to it. And one of those was Wally Hedrick. After attending Pasadena Junior College near Los Angeles, Hedrick had migrated to San Francisco to take a position with the California School of Fine Arts, once home to Mark Rothko, Richard Diebenkorn, and Dorothea Lange. Hedrick was a painter who loved both the work and process. "It is in the act of painting that I find my keenest sense of self and of 'being,'" he wrote in 1956.

Two years later, he met a new student, a teenager with some talent as a visual artist and a burning sense that there was something more for him. Hedrick recognized something in the boy and gave him a copy of *On the Road*. "It became so much a part of me that it's hard to measure," Garcia said many years later. "I don't know if I would ever have had the courage or the vision to do something outside with my life—or even suspected the possibilities existed—if it weren't for Kerouac opening those doors."

The national reaction to *On the Road* helped draw attention to the literary stirrings in San Francisco, both because San Francisco figures in the story and because Kerouac was by then associated with the city (nothing helped validate West Coast culture in those days like its adoption by a New Yorker). The *Evergreen Review*, a new publication of Grove Press based in New York, devoted its second volume to "The San Francisco Scene." The issue, released in the spring of 1957, included "Howl," along with works by Kerouac, Snyder, McClure, Ferlinghetti, Henry Miller, Robert Duncan, and more, a blend of famed bylines and new talents that helped introduce the scene to those outside it, particularly in New York.

The issue captured a writing culture that was intellectually diverse and whose subjects reflected varied experiences while also conveying a shared set of literary understandings. Many wrote about San Francisco itself, finding within the city outlets for exploring naturalism, drugs, and music. Others considered the terrain beyond: the struggles of the priesthood, the tension of sexual energy, encounters with a dog. The pieces featured in the review included many poems—Snyder's "The Berry Feast," which he had read at Six Gallery, was a standout—as well as an essay by Miller and a column by Ralph Gleason, already the preeminent music critic of the region and on his way to being a formative figure in the cultural life of modern America. Gleason's piece sketched the state of the jazz scene in San Francisco and concluded: "The jazz fan, local or visiting, can find whatever type of jazz makes his pulse beat faster, intrigues his brain or merely causes his feet to tap. It's all here."

Struck suddenly by the possibilities, Garcia turned, not setting out deliberately on a firm path so much as giving himself up to it, a different kind of embrace and one that he would come to employ across all aspects of his life. These were days of enlightenment without organization, the idea of an artist dawning before the rigor of an artistic commitment had set in. It was more of a spark than a thunderbolt, but an idea flickered: Why not a life in art?

Under Hedrick's tutelage, Garcia was drawn to representational work rather than abstract expressionism, then in vogue at the school. He would continue to sketch and draw for the rest of his life, filling notebooks with figures and faces, birds, trees, landscapes. Hedrick inspired him in other ways, too: Although a visual artist by calling, Hedrick was also a banjo player, and one day he brought a record of Big Bill Broonzy to play for his class. "That's when I decided," Garcia said later, "I definitely do want a guitar."

He pleaded with his mom to get one for his birthday, badgering her relentlessly as the day drew close. Instead, for his fifteenth birthday, August 1, 1957, Bobbie gave Jerry an accordion. He was devastated—rare is the teenager dying to learn the accordion—and he let her know it. "I went nuts—'Aggghhh, no, no, no!,'" Garcia remembered. "I railed and raved, and she finally turned it in, and I got a pawnshop electric guitar and an amplifier. I was just beside myself with joy. I started banging away on it without having the slightest idea of . . . anything."

Knowing nothing had its advantages. Wally, Jerry's stepfather, tried to tune the instrument—a "good old Danelectro," Garcia fondly recalled many years and even more guitars later—but instead created an open tuning that forced Jerry to listen and allowed him to experiment. Jerry and Cliff had gathered up 45s and 78s from their parents' bar, and those records now became a source of learning. It started with Bill Haley, Dean Martin, popular tunes picked out through the stack of remainders. Then came Jimmy Reed, Gene Vincent, Bo Diddley, and especially Chuck Berry. Garcia focused on Berry, trying to follow his leads note by note, plunking away on his new instrument, teaching himself. Freddie King, a blues guitar player of the early 1960s, would later join Berry as a powerful influence, helping Garcia mold a specific style.

And then, at just the moment that Jerry Garcia was noodling with his new electric guitar, he discovered marijuana. It was floating around the jazz and art scenes in San Francisco. Sometime in the summer of 1957, Jerry and his friend Laird Grant managed to get their hands on two joints, and they cut out one weekend morning to the hills of San Francisco, getting high and laughing all the way. "It was just what I wanted," Jerry said. Eager for more, they bought marijuana joints for fifty cents apiece—"skinny pinners," as they were called. The two also happily swallowed handfuls of colorful pills without knowing what they were. Cliff came home from the Marines, and he, too, had discovered weed. Loneliness, dislocation, and boredom now had a new companion: fun.

The last years of the 1950s both literally and symbolically represented the end of Jerry's youth, and he spent them bouncing around Northern California. There were a few trappings of a conventional childhood: He joined the Boy Scouts and earned three merit badges—knot tying, compass reading, and lifesaving—hardly the work of an Eagle Scout, but an effort. He mowed lawns for spending money; one client was Y. A. Tittle, the great quarterback for the San Francisco 49ers. But most of Garcia's time in those days was devoted to smoking pot, popping pills, playing guitar, and making art. One Halloween, Grant and Garcia hopped a streetcar to North Beach and joined with other teenagers playing around, dodging cable cars. They ended up outside the School of Fine Arts just as a limo arrived. A woman stepped out in a long fur coat. She dropped the coat and stepped away, stark naked except for a raisin in her navel. One of the school's models, she had come to the costume party "dressed" as a cookie. It's easy to see how a couple of teenage boys would be attentive.

By the end of 1958, Garcia's behavior was careening out of his mother's control, from delinquency to worse, and she tried again to corral him—"a last attempt to pull me out of the trip," as Garcia recalled it. As she had been a largely absent parent during his childhood, her bag of tricks was limited, and she turned to the method she had tried before. She moved—this time to the town of Cazadero, north of San Francisco, hoping that isolation would change Jerry's behavior. The house was inviting—big windows opening onto the dark redwoods of Northern California—and Jerry tried to appreciate his latest change of circumstance. He did his best to find new friends, and he succeeded in one sense: It was in Cazadero that he joined his first band. They called themselves the Chords and played a couple of times, including for a high school dance. They even cut a demo, according to Jerry. It wasn't much, just kids playing around, easy-listening tunes, but it was fun. Still, Garcia resented the move and strained at his mother's yoke.

Ruth had once again underestimated Jerry's drive to resist and his ingenuity when it came to escape. Rather than enjoy the seclusion of the forests or settle in seriously with the Chords, he routinely "borrowed" his mom's car (without permission) to visit San Francisco and his old haunts and friends. He crashed for a while at Laird Grant's parents' home in Redwood City—Grant fixed up a chicken coop, and Garcia slept in that. Ruth wanted Jerry to finish high school but had lost any leverage over him.

"It was the time to leave it all," he said a decade later. "I wanted to just be some place completely different. Home wasn't working out really for me and school was ridiculous . . . I had to do something. At that time the only really available alternative was to join the Army, so I did that."

Robert Hunter, Dave Nelson, and Garcia (at right) play at the reception following Garcia's wedding to Sara Ruppenthal. Theodore Roszak and his daughter look on. Palo Alto, April 27, 1963.

Sara and Jerry walk down the aisle.

CHAPTER 2

The Slingshot

ON FEBRUARY 3, 1960, RUTH GAVE HER PERMISSION FOR JERRY, then still just seventeen years old, to join the United States Army. He was relieved to be leaving home, but he left angry, too, irritated at his mother's attempts to contain him and eager to be done with her and his old life.

His enlistment was finalized on April 12, committing him to three years of service. His enlistment papers record him at that moment: Jerome John Garcia was five feet eleven inches tall; weighed 170 pounds; had black hair and brown eyes; was missing part of the middle finger of his right hand; was a high school dropout with no criminal convictions. He denied membership in the Communist Party and a host of other subversive organizations. He was accepted into the Army. It is probably safe to say that few new recruits were ever less suited to the job.

Garcia was sent to Fort Ord in Monterey, California, for basic training, and he completed it. He graduated from a Basic Missileman Qualification Course and was awarded a certificate to prove it. He qualified on the range as a sharpshooter. Beyond that, his service was marked mostly by demerits and by the quick realization—shared by Garcia and his military bosses—that he did not belong there.

After completing basic training, Garcia was assigned to Fort Winfield Scott in the Presidio, next to the Golden Gate Bridge in San Francisco. He asked for training in electronics but was assigned to the motor pool. He grabbed at every opportunity to avoid duty, preferring to sneak off and practice on a guitar he'd smuggled onto the base. His personal

24 | HERE BESIDE THE RISING TIDE

billeting area within his barracks was unkempt, as was his personal grooming. And he took advantage of being close to home, slipping off the base to meet up with friends—in other words, going AWOL. On October 5, he was charged with willfully disobeying a superior and was confined to the base through October 19. Liberated from that punishment, he went AWOL five days later. Another fourteen-day punishment followed, as did another offense, this time on November 27. His superiors tried harder to get his attention: In addition to confinement, Garcia was fined $50 and given thirty days' hard labor, along with being busted from private back to recruit.

Captain John Downey met with Garcia in November to "determine whether he could be persuaded to make an effort." The answer was, simply, no. "He had no desire to improve himself as a soldier," Downey wrote. An Army psychiatric specialist weighed in, concluding that while Garcia was pleasant enough and had the capacity to make sound judgments, he also suffered from a "basic character behavior disorder of lifelong duration" and that no amount of counseling or persuasion would alter it.

In December, Downey threw in the towel. "I have found Garcia to be unreliable, irresponsible, immature, unwilling to accept authority, and completely lacking in soldierly qualities," he wrote. "Garcia's only interest appears to be getting out of the Army." No one agreed more heartily than Garcia, who waived his right to have his case reviewed and readily accepted his discharge. On December 12, he packed his things and left, to the mutual relief of himself and the United States Army.

He went to Palo Alto. Garcia had not spoken to his mother since joining the Army, and he was out of touch with Cliff, too. So when Garcia was discharged, all he had was mustering-out pay and a beat-up car, which he bought from an Army cook on his way out. Garcia drove it down the Peninsula, where it promptly died. He parked it and turned it into a place to live. Garcia had no job, no degree, and no real skills—there wasn't much work for a "missleman" in civilian life.

Fortunately for him, Palo Alto in those days was an easy place for a drifting young man to survive. With its magnolia-lined streets and ample parks, bike lanes, and libraries, Palo Alto was a quiet suburban town, but its proximity to Stanford gave it an air of sophistication as well. The local Peace Center was a gathering place for liberals and radicals, and Garcia could often pick up a meal from folks who gathered there. Meanwhile, a ramshackle building just off the Stanford campus known as the Chateau functioned as a cross between a commune and a flophouse. The three-storied Victorian on the edge of the Stanford golf course was a rambling hovel of dark and disheveled rooms. Every space was taken as young people rotated through, nabbing a bed, sleeping on the floor, camping in an outbuilding. It smelled of damp coffee grounds and stale wine. Music wafted from room to room. Garcia would eventually move in, but even before that, it was a place to be.

Afternoons were often whiled away at nearby Kepler's. Combination bookseller and meeting place, Kepler's allowed patrons to sit, talk, and play music as they browsed the cluttered metal stacks that ran the length and width of the building. Jerry settled in with an acoustic guitar, probably a cheap model lent or given him by a friend, attracting his first notices as a musical talent. He had an intense ability to concentrate—on his music when that was his focus, or on others when he was engaged in conversation. In the evenings, the Kepler's crowd often drifted over to St. Michael's Alley, a coffeehouse founded in 1959 and said to be the first of its type on the Peninsula. It did not serve liquor, so teenagers were welcome, and it became the gathering place for a generation of Beats and, later, hippies. Together, Kepler's and St. Michael's Alley anchored a community of young people who were busy finding themselves.

"When life looks like Easy Street," the Dead would sing years later, "there is danger at your door." It was late on the night of February 20, 1961. Garcia and friends had been partying at the Chateau, and a few of them piled into a Studebaker Golden Hawk after midnight. Lee Adams drove. At twenty-six, he was the house manager of the Chateau, the oldest of the group and the owner of the car. Garcia was in the passenger seat. In the back were a trio of friends, Jack Royerton, Alan Trist, and Paul Speegle. They raced through the quiet streets of Palo Alto, whip-

26 | HERE BESIDE THE RISING TIDE

ping by the Veterans Administration hospital on Junipero Serra Boulevard on their way to Speegle's mother's house in Los Altos Hills. Speeding along at perhaps 100 mph, Adams missed the turn at Fremont Avenue, lost control of the car, and crashed through a fence, flipping twice. Young men were scattered across pavement and an empty field.

Garcia was thrown so violently through the windshield that he was separated from his shoes. He landed hard and staggered away from the accident. He made his way back to the VA hospital, which did not have an emergency room. Finding a pay phone, he called for help.

Adams and three of his passengers suffered significant injuries. Royerton had a broken arm and a concussion; Garcia sustained a broken collarbone and head injuries serious enough to erase his memory of the accident. Trist had a fractured spine. Adams's abdomen was badly bruised. Only Speegle stayed with the car, and only Speegle died. His last words, uttered just before the car careened out of control, were "Wow, this is really beautiful."

It was just days before the young man was to turn seventeen, and his death on that early morning ended the life of a promising artist. Speegle, whose father, Paul Speegle, was the drama editor for *The San Francisco News–Call Bulletin,* was a gifted, hardworking teenager, earning money at the Stanford Law Library while developing as a painter, then at work on a dramatic series of oil paintings called "The Blind Prophet." Speegle also worked as an actor as part of the Teen Players at the Palo Alto Community Center and at the Comedia Theater in Menlo Park, and he played up his theatricality, dressing in "semi-Edwardian finery." His close circle of friends included Elaine Pagels, then taking the first steps of what would be her brilliant career as a writer and religious scholar. Although still a junior at stuffy Menlo-Atherton High School, Speegle was wise enough and interesting enough to be welcomed at the Chateau—fatefully, as it turned out.

The accident tore through Garcia's little community. Speegle's bright presence was extinguished, and the others in the car that night first had to recover from physical injuries and then from the trauma and guilt of having survived the crash. Close companions would recall Garcia's talking about that night for years afterward. It was at the same time a focusing moment. Garcia suddenly confronted the aimlessness of his life, which had spread through his years like a virus in the wake of his father's death—the wreckage of his family, his failure to graduate from high school, his failure as a soldier, his homelessness, his poverty, his uncertainty about adulthood. Shaken by the death of his friend, Garcia realized "I was idling."

The crash changed him. He slimmed down and grew a goatee. He looked, one friend recalled, "like Claude Debussy." He acquired an air of seriousness.

"That's where my life began," Garcia recalled. "That was the slingshot."

GARCIA WAS recovering from the accident—his arm still in a sling—when a friend invited him to go hiking one afternoon. He accepted, and she then asked whether she could invite another companion, a fifteen-year-old high school student named Barbara Meier. Garcia took one look at Meier, who went by the name of Brigid, and agreed. "Oh," he said, "tell her I love her." Meier, the daughter of literary parents and a young model already working for Joseph Magnin in San Francisco, was equally smitten, drawn by Garcia's dark hair and beard and his distinctly rebellious vibe. She was pining to be liberated from the confining straightness of her high school in Menlo Park, where she had been a year behind Speegle. Garcia, still just eighteen years old but with a stint in the Army behind him, the injuries from an accident still evident, and fired by a suddenly burning sense of purpose, seemed just the antidote.

At first their relationship was protective. Garcia and his friends were a few years older, and they took care of Meier. She always seemed to be arriving at parties just as the drugs or the booze ran out. But she was pretty and precocious, and the two struck up a sexually charged friendship that ripened into something more.

* * *

28 | HERE BESIDE THE RISING TIDE

PROPELLED BY the accident, infatuated with a pretty young girl, Garcia's primordial life now began to take shape. The next few years, at least in retrospect, had the feel of gathering up ideas and experiences. At the same time, these years exposed the holes in Garcia's upbringing—deprived of the security of family as a child, he struggled to create a family of his own. More broadly, this period witnessed the flourishing of tensions and contradictions that would define Garcia: the quiet craving for community against the joyful lust for freedom, the willingness to experiment along with the appreciation of structure, the embrace of classic form beneath the compulsion to improvise. It was a period of freedom and growth.

He turned to music with epiphanic intensity in the weeks and months after the crash. Even with his shoulder still braced in a sling, and equipped now with an acoustic guitar that Brigid had given him, Garcia's practicing became constant, almost obsessive. He played at the Chateau, in his broken-down car, in music shops, at Kepler's, at St. Michael's Alley—"from twenty-four to thirty-eight hours a day," one friend recalled. Garcia's concentration could be unnerving. He would wander around the Chateau with a guitar strapped on, approaching a person or a group of people and playing a bit for them, but if they tried to engage him in conversation, he would go blank. "You couldn't get him to stop," recalled his friend Sandy Rothman. "People would say 'Put that thing down,' and he would just keep going."

And just as Garcia urgently pressed forward, he met the man whose collaboration would define the rest of his life. Robert Hunter was also freshly discharged from the military—in his case, the National Guard. He was a year older than Garcia, but they shared more than an unhappy stint in arms. They were drawn to music and the arts, attracted by the culture of the Bay Area, and, in early 1961, pretty much destitute.

Like Garcia, Robert Hunter lost his father at a young age—in his case, to his father's alcoholism and emotional disarray. Robert's father was a Navy veteran, battered by the war, and had left his son behind when the boy was just seven. Robert remembered him, perhaps with some youthful embellishment, as a "soldier-of-fortune-slash-hustler."

His father's abandonment thrust the boy into foster homes and left him craving structure. He found it briefly in Catholicism, substituting the Church for the cohesion of home, but religion never held him firmly in its grasp the way books did. John Steinbeck was the first author who moved him, at age eight or so, and he set down fifty pages of his own first novel at age eleven. Howard Pyle, Robert Louis Stevenson, children's novels, then science fiction all held him for a while, as did Westerns. His mythos would later draw on those and other sources, mainly from literature, glancingly from religion, deeply from faith, as he constructed a landscape of Americana and lyrical values, populated with gamblers, outlaws, coal miners, and train engineers, set on beaches and in wilderness, on sand and stone, traversed by wolves and trains, dampened by whiskey and tea, home to Jack the Ripper and Jack and Jill.

Robert was born Robert Burns in Arroyo Grande, a small town on the central California coast just outside San Luis Obispo. His father's departure broke the family for a time, but his mother remarried, this time to Norman Hunter, giving her the stability to pluck her son back from foster care. Together with his stepfather, a bookseller and editor whose authors included William Saroyan, Robert and his mother moved to San Francisco and then, when he was eleven, to Palo Alto. He attended public school there, managing to shine and be an outcast at the same time. One teacher failed him on an assignment because she did not believe he could have done it himself, a source of pride for Hunter in later years. He was a member of the "free thinkers club," and at a high school divided between Elvises and James Deans, he styled himself an Elvis, more artistically rebellious than sullen. He remained a loner.

Hunter's family moved him from liberal Palo Alto to straitlaced Stamford, Connecticut, when he was in eleventh grade. He spent an unhappy senior year there, and another aimless period at the University of Connecticut, though he did win a spot as president of the Folk Music Club for a year, and then, after scraping together money from working at a local supermarket, made his way west again. He served six months in the National Guard and then turned up again in Palo Alto, familiar

30 | HERE BESIDE THE RISING TIDE

from his youth. He went to see *Damn Yankees* one night at the Comedia Theater, and there he was introduced to Jerry Garcia.

They discovered that neither had a regular place to stay, and that both were owners of beaten-up cars, so badly run down, in fact, that neither was drivable. They found an empty lot in East Palo Alto and parked the vehicles side by side, turning them into a makeshift dwelling. Hunter had nabbed a few huge tins of crushed pineapple when he left the Guard, and Garcia chipped in with a glove compartment full of plastic spoons. They ate pineapple, cruised coffeehouses, and played guitar.

Given their later division of labor, it is tempting to imagine that Garcia in those months was the musician and Hunter the wordsmith, but that too narrowly defines them. Hunter was himself a musician, playing alongside Garcia and others, albeit without Garcia's fanatic commitment to practicing. And Garcia was nimble with words, playfully enjoying long sessions with Alan Trist, a British friend and fellow survivor of the fateful car crash, in composing jabberwocky, tinkering with verbal tricks. Garcia and Hunter would come to be known for music and words respectively, but in those sunny early days, they each created both, searching for something artistic and feeling their way toward it.

Garcia was remarkable, as Hunter sized him up, less for his genius than for his personality. He practiced like Andrés Segovia, Hunter recalled. "However, he was *not* Segovia; he was Jerry. And the very act of being Jerry was, in his estimation, an excuse for almost anything. He had the easygoing self-assurance of a person who is used to being forgiven for any gaucheness he might choose to perpetuate on his contemporaries, so he committed them with an amazing regularity and a completely innocent conscience." Perpetually broke, Garcia haunted the local coffeehouse, where he and Trist and Hunter nursed refills all evening.

Within a few months, Garcia and Hunter were ready to perform for others. They played at a Stanford party and an event at the Peninsula School in Menlo Park. They played at Barbara Meier's sixteenth birthday party on May 26, celebrating their exciting young friend. In July, they took their show to San Carlos, at the Boar's Head Coffeehouse, upstairs from the Carlos Bookstall; it was an open mic event with Garcia on acoustic guitar and Marshall Leicester—an old friend of Garcia's who was home from Yale for the summer—on banjo, Hunter joining on vocals. The performance was small—the venue held only about thirty people—but it hinted at the talent behind it. Leicester opened the show on banjo and gave it a distinctive bluegrass feel, while Garcia, still just shy of his nineteenth birthday, sang with confidence and chatted with the audience between numbers. Hunter's vocals were weak and Garcia's more earnest than polished, but the trio displayed a devotion to craft.

Music by then had its hold on Garcia. But what kind of music, with what focus, remained very much in doubt. His location helped to direct that energy. Palo Alto—and the Bay Area more generally—at that moment sat at the confluence of at least two major musical traditions: folk and bluegrass. Garcia honed his early vocals on folk tunes. A few of those numbers suggested his eclectic taste and openness to ideas: "All My Trials" was an American folk song, "Rake and a Rambling Boy" of Irish origin, and "Oh Mary, Don't You Weep" a spiritual drawn from American slave history. He also picked up the banjo. Garcia's earlier dalliance with the instrument became a full-blown commitment when Leicester lent him his five-string, and Garcia dived into its complex picking.

It is a demanding instrument, but as before, he practiced. Relentlessly. Incessantly. "It was so fucking boring," said Meier, who was looking to Garcia for fun and excitement and instead found a young man content to spend hours laboring over banjo technique. Increasingly, Garcia's community was one of musicians. Folk musicians had a penchant for exactitude, and Garcia, who would later admit to a "puritanical" streak in his avidity, fell right in. "His idea of a party [was] to sit down and learn a new lick," Meier said of that period. She edged away. If the banjo was exhausting, however, there remained a spark between Meier and Garcia. In the fall of 1962, Garcia moved into the Chateau, or, rather, into a shed on the property of the Chateau. It was there that

Meier, still sixteen years old, lost her virginity to the twenty-year-old Garcia. When her father learned that she and Garcia had had sex, he forbade Meier to see him again—an order she evaded with all the creativity and determination of a driven teenager.

As for the annoying musical practice, even as it took a toll on Garcia's most intimate relationship—not for the last time—it paid off, too. Soon Garcia was regarded as the finest banjo player in Palo Alto's burgeoning bluegrass ecosystem.

David Nelson had heard of Garcia, "a legendary figure at the Kepler's scene," when the two first met. Nelson had been playing since he was in second grade, drawn to the steel guitar and ukulele. He found a kindred spirit in Garcia, and the two struck up a friendship that would follow them across all of their days. Decades later, Garcia's friends from the early years would agree that he liked nothing more than a day playing the guitar with Dave Nelson.

Meanwhile, Garcia outgrew Leicester's borrowed instrument and went hunting in the want ads for one to buy for himself. He found a seller in Palo Alto—and when he went to pick it up, he met the seller's son, Bill Kreutzmann, a talented young drummer whose life was about to intertwine with Garcia's.

ON OCTOBER 4, 1961, Lenny Bruce was performing the second show of a two-night stand at the Jazz Workshop in San Francisco's North Beach, just blocks from the scene of the historic Six Gallery reading six years earlier. Bruce's approach was comedic, not poetic (exactly), but he, too, slashed at conventions with crude, bracing language.

Already famous for a Carnegie Hall performance in February that highlighted his melding of forms—in Bruce's hands, the stand-up comedy routine pulsed with the spontaneity of jazz, the word association of Kerouac, and the defiance of Ginsberg—Bruce's San Francisco appearance was carefully monitored by authorities. His first night at the Jazz Workshop drew attention; the second night drew badges. Police watched as Bruce riffed through a routine in which he repeatedly used the word

THE SLINGSHOT | 33

"cocksucker" and toyed with the construction of "to come," leaning heavily into its sexual innuendo. The police allowed him to finish, then arrested him as he left the stage.

Six years had passed since "Howl" had drawn the ire of these same guardians of public decency, but time and experience seemed not to have imparted the lesson that bad words are difficult to control. In addition to his arrest in San Francisco, Bruce was busted in Philadelphia—where police focused on the sturdier charge of drug possession—and West Hollywood, where a sheriff's deputy hauled him in, again for obscenity, this time for using the word "schmuck."

As Bruce prepared his defense to the mounting list of obscenity charges, his lawyers needed help preparing transcripts of the comedian's remarks, which they hoped would provide a context that would exonerate him. Looking for help transcribing the rough tapes, a friend of a friend contacted Garcia, knowing of his keen ear. "I spent a lot of time listening to old-time records, and I was able to [listen to] indecipherable voices and tell what the words were," Garcia said. "I had an ear for it."

Bruce would take a snippet from the news, read it, and comment on it. "He used to do a bit where he would take a magazine. . . . He'd thumb through it, and then he'd riff off of some article," Garcia recalled. "It was real stuff. . . . It was incredible. I learned so much. What a mind. . . . It was like be-bop language, bits and pieces of language."

Garcia's job was to help Bruce defend himself against criminal charges. His takeaway was to see how language could layer, how it could build up from something solid into something freewheeling, experimental, brave, and exciting.

Experimentation. Structure and excitement. These concepts spoke to Garcia, reaching him through a musical idiom. In the winter of 1962, he headed to the Berkeley Folk Music Festival. Founded in 1958 and a staple of folk culture through the 1960s, the event gathered some of the nation's most celebrated—and, outside these circles, obscure—folk talents.

The festival was open to the public, so Garcia did not require special credentials to attend, but he did so with enthusiasm. He sat in the front row for a lecture by Sam Hinton, and attended workshops and panels with Ralph Rinzler and Jean Ritchie and the Georgia Sea Island Singers, among others. This was not the work of a casual musician hustling for dollar bills at bookstores and coffeehouses. This was part of a commitment to the history of this music, a devotion to deeper understanding and a reflection of Garcia's post-crash seriousness.

"Folk music provides a kind of home," said Michael Kramer, a leading scholar of the period and of the many ties that connect music and politics. Garcia was spongelike, imitating musicians who caught his ear, taking on their styles and observations, reconsidering songs—"stealing them," he joked—rather than what today might be called appropriating them. He gathered in musical ideas, just as he had learned from Bruce's monologues.

As for the larger community of folk music that took in Garcia, Kramer added: "It's a weird home," one that would come to house Garcia, Bob Dylan, the peace movement, and the Vietnam War in its many hidden rooms.

GARCIA'S YOUTH had been spent in motion. He yearned for a community of friends and fellows, for a larger family. In that, he was hardly alone. The atomized American 1950s heralded individualism—the family home replaced the crowded block of apartments, the subway gave way to the automobile. Suburbs connected by highways became the model for growth and development. That dislocation supplied an undercurrent for rebellion, the uneasy sense that society was pulling apart, that connections were fraying. It nursed new cravings—for connection, for authenticity, for direct experience.

In Garcia's case, it shaped not only the artist he was becoming but, more deeply, the person he was. His yearning for family was translated into his identity as an artist, steering him away from the lonely life of the solo musician or composer. He needed compatriots. Hunter and Leicester were the first, but Hunter had the qualities of a writer—dexterity with language, singularity with ideas—rather than of a performer. Leicester was a grand companion until it came time for him to go back to college. Garcia hunted for musicians, listening at Kepler's, taking a job as a teacher at Dana Morgan's music store in Palo Alto, picking up work where he could get it.

STEVE DUNNE was a boy of eleven when his mother brought him in to Dana Morgan's. It was a small instrument store on Bryant Street in Palo Alto, the place where parents brought a kid for a first guitar or an instrument to play in the school band. Dunne had been at summer camp in 1962 and came home wanting to play an instrument. His mother obliged him and took him to Dana Morgan's to sign him and his brother up for lessons. Jerry Garcia agreed to take on both—Steve for guitar, his brother for banjo—and did so with a calm and a degree of organization that left an impression on the youngsters.

Garcia would arrive with handwritten music notes, tablature to songs such as "Good Night, Irene," "Greensleeves," "Blowin' in the Wind"—classics and contemporary hits mixed in with pieces that Garcia himself was practicing. Garcia was particularly intent on teaching Dunne "Elizabeth Cotten style," a finger-picking technique in which the player picks the melody with his or her thumb and the bass line with his or her forefingers (Cotten was left-handed, so she fretted with her right hand and picked with her left). Dunne dutifully did his best. He showed up every week for a year, sometimes prepared for his teacher, sometimes not; Garcia hid his impatience well. "I'd start playing, and Jerry would say: 'Try this for a second, I'll be right back,' " Dunne said. With that, Garcia would leave his pupil to practice for a few minutes, and then return, "smelling like burnt rope," smiling gently and ready to listen to Dunne try it again. "Better," he would pronounce, "much better."

Years later, when Garcia was at the Keystone in Palo Alto for a performance of the Jerry Garcia Band, Dunne approached him at the bar and reminded him of his long-ago lessons. Garcia instantly remembered, adding: "I taught your brother banjo, too."

Garcia's work and musical ambitions were growing and being no-

36 | HERE BESIDE THE RISING TIDE

ticed. In February 1962, an engineer at radio station KPFA suggested that he would make a worthy guest on that station's midnight music hour. Garcia sat down for an interview, chatting about folk and bluegrass and playing a bit. His version of "Long Black Veil" captured some attention, and word began to spread. Garcia became "almost a regular," the engineer recalled. The engineer was Phil Lesh.

Garcia's romance with Meier reached its end. Desperate to draw her attention away from the shaggy Garcia, her parents introduced her to a dashing young writer, and she began spending time with him, only to be caught by Garcia one day on the Stanford campus with her new friend. It was, she recalled, "a very bad scene," nearly violent. Meier and Garcia bumped along awhile longer, but then, over the Christmas break that year, Meier and her family traveled to Mexico, where she had a fling with a young man named Mario. She told Garcia of the dalliance, and his jealousy overcame him. Their conversations went from strained to ragged. The two fell apart.

By February 1963, Garcia had found a new flame, a pretty young woman, willowy and gentle, blessed with an appealing singing voice. Unlike Meier, she was a part of the folk music scene, a Stanford student and friend of the already skyrocketing Joan Baez. Sara Ruppenthal first spotted Garcia at Kepler's, where Garcia, Dave Nelson, and Robert Hunter were playing and where Ruppenthal helped out Ira Sandperl, a manager, by busing tables. She had heard Garcia on KPFA, but now she got her first look at him. "I was just blown away . . . by his sense of humor and his musicianship and the virtuosity," she said, though she also found Garcia curiously detached from the issues of the day. Ruppenthal was deeply involved in the peace movement—Baez and Sandperl were at the center of it in Palo Alto—and all of them found Garcia's disinterest strange. "Ira," Ruppenthal recalled, "didn't like Jerry because Jerry wasn't political."

That was not enough to discourage Ruppenthal. Garcia, on the rebound from Meier, fell for her as quickly as she fell for him. Within a few weeks of their meeting, Ruppenthal was pregnant. Learning of it,

Meier was incensed—"I went nuts. I went crazy," she said. What was left of her relationship to Garcia crashed. Much, much later, Garcia would come to remember Barbara Meier as the true love of his life; by then, it would be too late.

Instead, he married Ruppenthal. They were wed on April 27, 1963, at the Unitarian Church in Palo Alto. Ruth Garcia, Jerry's mom, was present, as was his ailing grandmother, Tillie, though they were there mostly at Sara's insistence. Sara had not met Jerry's mother when they became engaged—Jerry himself had maintained his stubborn remove since leaving the Army—and she asked Jerry to introduce them. Instead, he took her to meet Tillie, who in turn insisted that the bride meet Ruth. It went well. Ruth "was just thrilled to see him again and impressed that he was marrying a college girl," Sara recalled.

Dave Nelson acted as best man even though he was skeptical of the marriage—selfishly imagining that it would interfere with his relationship with Garcia—and embarrassed that he had not gotten a haircut beforehand. Sara's friends and family regarded Jerry's with curiosity bordering on alarm. Sara's father was nattily dressed in suit and bow tie, and her guests crowded around the food table; Garcia's lined up for drinks.

Because Ruppenthal was studying at Stanford, some of the wedding guests were drawn from her circle there. In the small crowd was Theodore Roszak, the professor and pioneering intellectual whose writing would supply intellectual heft to the gathering of ideas of the early 1960s. Having Roszak present that day was roughly akin to having a young William F. Buckley at the wedding of a pair of young conservatives. One of the ceremony's most lasting images is a photograph of Garcia, Nelson, and Hunter, dressed for the occasion and playing their instruments. An uncropped version of that photo reveals that Roszak was standing nearby, cradling his daughter and smiling at the performance.

More traditional was the image that appeared in the paper. STANFORD STUDENT IS BRIDE read the caption in the *Palo Alto Times*, beneath a photo of the veiled, smiling Sara and her grinning husband with his neatly trimmed beard. Jerome John Garcia was described as an "instructor at the Dana Morgan Music Studio."

Their union was both marital and musical. Through much of 1963, the Garcias performed together, sometimes as a duet, other times in the company of other musicians. They worked well together, visually and musically, Sara's lissome figure and soft voice against Garcia's gruffer appearance. One of their numbers, "Deep Elem Blues," would find its way into the Grateful Dead's repertoire years later. Their daughter, Heather, was born on December 8.

TO COMMIT to music at the beginning of the 1960s was to dive into a culture. Elvis was fading, but his shadow was long. Sam Cooke and Ray Charles commanded the R&B charts, along with the Isley Brothers and King Curtis. The Beach Boys' "Surfin' USA" was the number one pop song of 1963, and Peter, Paul and Mary's "Puff, the Magic Dragon" fell somewhere between a kids' song and a sly ode to marijuana.

The new act was the one that would affect everything that came after it. It was born in Liverpool and made its first waves in 1963, tantalizing early audiences with "Please Please Me." Witty, catchy, and deceptively deep, the Beatles reinvented popular music, injecting it with meaning alongside melody and upending culture as they went. The Beatles' 1964 appearance on *The Ed Sullivan Show,* with their black suits, white shirts, black ties, and euphoric audience, signaled something unmistakably new. "Beatlemania," yes, but something larger, too, a shift of energy; an explosion of music as a vehicle for expression and, later, opposition; a breakout of youth from the 1950s. For an America still staggering from the assassination of John Kennedy, it was a shedding of grief, a roar of ebullience, heard from the studios in New York City across the expanse of the nation. More than one in every three Americans, some 73 million people, watched the Beatles on the night of February 9, 1964.

Not everyone was sold. The Beatles met with some skepticism among the folkies of Northern California, even more from the bluegrass players. The band that night projected a lighthearted exuberance—during the broadcast, when John Lennon appeared onscreen, producers put up a caption reading "Sorry girls, he's married"—that did not rise to the musical or cultural seriousness of those scenes. "Their first records," Garcia recalled of the Beatles, "were so sappy. I didn't really like them that much."

But infectious is infectious, and the Beatles won over the hardest, most studious hearts. For Garcia, it was the Beatles on film that converted him from self-serious skeptic to happy admirer. He caught *A Hard Day's Night* and was swept up. "It had such great flow to it," he recalled, "and such great style, and that thing of fun." That thing of fun.

It was, he added, "a chance to get back to yucks" for the bluegrass and folk players, the coffeehouse "denizens" who frowned their way through performances. As the Beatles' sound expanded and their lyrical sophistication deepened, the early hesitation melted away. A few years later, in 1967, *Sgt. Pepper's Lonely Hearts Club Band* would, according to Garcia, complete the Beatles' path to the far side; *Sgt. Pepper* and Dylan's *Blonde on Blonde* became the "anthem albums" of the Haight-Ashbury.

GARCIA WAS no more cut out for parenthood than he had been for the Army. He cried joyful tears when Heather was born but was afraid to hold her when she came home from the hospital. His contributions as a father vacillated between cheerful engagement and outright abandonment, in both cases a mirror of his upbringing. His drive was toward music and toward a more abstract community—a melding of like-minded men and women in search of identity and connection through music and literature—rather than the more traditional connections of home and family.

Heather had hardly been born before her father was off in search of the former at the expense of the latter. When Sara was released from the hospital on December 18—she was briefly hospitalized with an infection after giving birth—her husband was out of town, performing a bluegrass gig in Southern California. And when Heather was five months old, Garcia and his friend Sandy Rothman packed Garcia's '61 Corvair—it had belonged to Sara's father—with musical instruments and a bag full of blank audiotape and headed to the Midwest and the American South, then still remote and forbidding, the land of cotton and segregation, the deep thrumming of the spiritual and the hooded violence of racism. Garcia and Rothman were nervous about what they might find—Garcia shaved his goatee to avoid agitating rednecks—but went to capture the authentic voice of America and perhaps to impress Bill Monroe, the progenitor of bluegrass.

"We were searching for something big," Rothman recalled. They were gone for two months—traversing the Southwest and Midwest, with a side trip to Florida—and found moments of enlightenment. They even connected with Monroe, but it was too much for Garcia, who flinched at the chance to ask for an audition.

They made it up to Pennsylvania, where they met and jammed with a young acolyte of Monroe, David Grisman, who had come from New Jersey. That meeting made more of an impression on Garcia, who took note of Grisman because he was wearing a long raincoat, than it did on Grisman. Their friendship would blossom later.

Garcia returned home in July and quickly put his trip to use. Garcia formed and joined one musical ensemble after another, weaving together strains of folk, bluegrass, and jug band music, adapting those idioms as his prowess increased. He got good.

The Thunder Mountain Tub Thumpers, the Sleepy Hollow Hog Stompers, the Hart Valley Drifters, the Wildwood Boys, the Black Mountain Boys—lineups shifting as various musicians joined or moved on. Garcia's banjo as a member of the Wildwood Boys, captured in early recordings from the period, was stunning; less dramatic but notable was the band's easy relationship with its audience. Collected in a 2018 assemblage of tapes from the period and released as *Jerry Garcia: Before the Dead,* those early recordings feature a young Garcia, unmistakably brilliant, and it does not require hindsight to appreciate the blossoming sense of a career launching. Success almost certainly would have awaited Garcia as a folk or bluegrass musician had he stayed that course.

Instead, bluegrass, with its mathematical precision and emphasis on lightning-fast finger picking, morphed into jug band—a shift, as Ruppenthal put it, from "mathematical virtuosity" to "gutsy." What still hovered on the horizon were a few more entries into Garcia's musical lexicon—the soulfulness of the blues, the range and intelligence of classical composition, the embrace of jazz improvisation, and the raw power of electric music, which Garcia would describe as "finding my musical identity." Bandmates would bring those.

Early Grateful Dead, soon after dropping the name The Warlocks. The Matrix, San Francisco, 1966.

Ron Rakow/Retro Photo Archive

CHAPTER 3

The Warlocks to the Dead

THEY WERE FIVE FINGERS OF ONE HAND. ALTHOUGH JUST TEEN-agers and young adults, they brought their own musical backgrounds and inclinations—a blues singer, a rhythm-and-blues drummer, a jug-band-trained rhythm guitar player, a folk and bluegrass banjo picker turned lead guitarist, and a classically trained composer who made his chops as a trumpet player but converted to the bass at Garcia's suggestion. They had their idiosyncrasies: Their main singer didn't like to perform; their bass player was still learning his instrument; their leader hated to lead.

They were the Warlocks, though not for long.

Garcia was always at the center. He rejected the responsibilities of leadership—in the decades to come, he would spend almost as much time refusing to lead the Warlocks and then the Dead as he would spend doing exactly that. He liked to say that the perception of his leadership was a creation of the press, and that he was incorrectly seen as the leader of the band because he liked to talk. That's partly true. Garcia was in fact an appealing interview subject—candid, open, inviting. He charmed reporters precisely because he did not set out to charm them. But among his attractive characteristics was that he was self-deprecating, and his deflections papered over the obvious: The Warlocks and the Dead formed around him. Every member of the band felt that his principal connection to it was through Garcia. He recruited the musicians and set the tone. The early fusion of jazz, blues, and bluegrass mirrored Garcia's musical evolution; the band's place in the transition from Beat culture to the hippies followed Garcia's path. As the years went by and the Dead would consider whether a particular piece was "a Grateful Dead song," all eyes would look to Garcia.

But if Garcia's influence and musical sense defined the Warlocks and the Dead, it was not because he deliberately set out to lead the band. To the contrary, he refused to be its decision maker—of a piece in a life of avoiding responsibilities, or at least choosing to deflect them—and he attempted to stand outside its brightest spotlight, even as he literally commanded it onstage. Initially, the man at the center of much of the music, at least as received by the audience, was not Garcia at all. It was Pigpen.

RON MCKERNAN was born in the San Francisco suburb of San Bruno in 1945, making him three years younger than Garcia. His father, Phil McKernan, was a well-known disc jockey in the Bay Area. Phil McKernan was known as Cool Breeze, and he hosted a daily blues program at KRE, a Berkeley AM/FM radio station, one of the area's first to broadcast in stereo. His show ran for more than a decade, and his son grew up listening to Muddy Waters, Big Joe Turner, Howlin' Wolf, and, especially, Lightnin' Hopkins. The blues and jug wine informed Ron's early years—he began drinking at age twelve—and when Garcia met him in the early 1960s, he was holed up at home in East Palo Alto, grungy and practicing his harmonica. In those days, he was known as Blue Ron.

He was worse than indifferent as a student, though his charisma made him a popular fixture at Palo Alto High School. Classmates recalled him strolling the open-air corridors of the campus across the street from Stanford, a girl on each side. "The hallways would clear," recalled one fellow student. Charisma, however, went only so far. McKernan was expelled.

Beginning soon after Garcia's discharge from the Army and arrival in Palo Alto, the two began to hang out at the Chateau, at McKernan's East Palo Alto home, and around town. Garcia recalled him as an "Elvis Presley soul and hoodlum kid," lurking at the periphery of a folk and jug band scene, eager to find a point of entry into the blues. "He used to hang around," Garcia said of McKernan. "That's how I got to know him." Grubby and unkempt in public and onstage, though shy and gentle off it, "Blue Ron" became "Pigpen." The name stuck so firmly that his mother came to use it, too.

Pigpen played with a band called the Zodiacs, performing at frat parties, amusement parks, and the like, taking home twenty dollars for a show. As he and Garcia got to know each other, he persuaded Garcia to join the Zodiacs for a bit; Garcia, in a departure for him, played the bass. When Bob Matthews, Dave Nelson, and a high school student named Bob Weir decided to start their own jug band, Garcia jumped in and brought McKernan with him. That group was Mother McCree's Uptown Jug Champions—obliquely named for the character in a turn-of-the-century Irish American folk song—and the band played a little blues, a little jazz, a little Dixieland. Garcia played banjo and some guitar. Matthews held down the kazoo. Weir played the jug and improvised a washtub bass. Pigpen played harmonica and, reluctantly, sang. At one early show, Garcia introduced him by telling the audience: "Mr. Pigpen McKernan would like to sing a Lightnin' Hopkins song." Pigpen interrupted him: "I wouldn't like to, but I will anyway." He growled out an up-tempo take on "Ain't It Crazy." Pigpen brought the blues.

Pigpen fronted Mother McCree's and Garcia anchored it. But its youngest and most excitable member was Weir. Alone among the young men who would soon become the Grateful Dead, Weir grew up with money; much like most of them, however, his family life was scrambled. In Weir's case, he was adopted. His birth mother was a student at the University of Arizona in the 1940s when she met the man who would become Bob's birth father. She became pregnant but was in no position to raise a child, so she put her infant son up for adoption soon after he was born in San Francisco. Frederic and Eleanor Weir came to the baby's rescue, and his adopted parents, gentle, patient, and mild, were handed a handful. Unbeknownst to his parents or doctors, young Bob Weir was dyslexic, and one result was that his obvious intelligence clashed with his seemingly inexplicable inability to grasp written material. His parents made him take up an instrument—first piano, then trumpet—but they tired of the noise, and sighed with relief when he transitioned to guitar. Little Bobby inherited his adopted father's military posture, droll sense of humor, and style—"I dress like a Republican," he said in later years—but he was hardly a chip off that block. He was mischievous and tempestuous. He bedeviled teachers, was kicked out of the Cub Scouts, was often in trouble at school. The Weirs had the means to seek help, and they shipped him off to the Fountain Valley School, a progressive boarding school for boys in Colorado Springs. That was fortuitous in one sense—Bob there met John Perry Barlow, later to become a songwriting contributor to the Dead, a lyricist second only to Robert Hunter in terms of influence on the band's landscape—but not a great success educationally. He was jittery and distracted, one leg twitching in class; he did not impress his elders.

Doctors eventually caught on to his dyslexia, but by then Weir's reputation was established, built more on practical jokes and mild vandalism than grades. Weir lasted long enough to bond with Barlow, but the school rapidly tired of both. Finally, administrators agreed that one could stay if the other would leave, and Weir was expelled. He returned home to Atherton and enrolled at Pacific High School and later Menlo-Atherton High School, where Weir avoided schoolwork by obsessing over his thirteen-dollar Japanese-built guitar. Many days were spent cutting class and hightailing it a few miles south to Palo Alto and its music scene.

The story of the first meeting between Bob Weir and Jerry Garcia is a matter of lore to Deadheads, repeated in the expectant chatter before concerts a million times, dates and details hazy but essentially understood. It was New Year's Eve 1963, and Weir was wandering down the alley behind Dana Morgan's when he and a companion heard the sound of a banjo. They set out in search of the source and found a shaggy character practicing the instrument while waiting for a student to arrive for his lesson. "My friend and I apprised him that no one was likely to show up, as it was New Year's Eve," Weir remembered. Garcia, nonplussed, noted that he had a key to the shop's instrument room and invited Weir to join him there. "We played for hours and realized we had enough half-talent to start a jug band." Weir was young and impressionable. More than any other member of what was soon to become the Dead, Weir was open to being formed by it. He arrived with a jug, and he was ready to learn the rest.

That was the beginning of Mother McCree's. It was, Garcia boasted, "a fine jug band." Its early performances attracted some modest notice, and within a month or two, Mother McCree's was performing at the Top of the Tangent, a Palo Alto club. The audience one night included a dazzled young drummer. That was to prove lucky, as Mother McCree's was solid on banjo, vocals, guitar, and kazoo but weak on drums. "It was an amazing night," Bill Kreutzmann recalled. "Right then, I became the first Deadhead because I said, 'I'm going to follow this guy [Garcia] forever.'"

Kreutzmann was raised in a fairly conventional suburban home by a supportive mother and father. His father was a lawyer. His mother taught at Stanford. But that conventionality concealed a bohemian streak in the Kreutzmann household. His father also dabbled in art, and that work reached to a deeper place inside him than the law did. When a neighbor once complained about Billy Kreutzmann's drum playing, his father leaped from a chair in the backyard to confront the offending neighbor and defend his son's playing. And yes, his mother was a teacher at Stanford, but what she taught was dance, so she, too, was happy to encourage her son's budding musicality. When Billy was little, she would hand him a drum and ask him to keep time on it while she worked out dance steps in the living room. So, however accurate, "lawyer and teacher" does not quite do justice to the description of Kreutzmann's parents.

Kreutzmann's parents divorced when he was still young, and their split left him conflicted as an adolescent, torn by divided allegiances, sent for a time to boarding school, forced to repeat ninth grade, threatened with military school if he didn't improve. He returned to music, and that did not go well at first either. A school band teacher discouraged him by telling him he had no sense of rhythm, but rather than give up, he scoured Palo Alto's music shops in search of a teacher. He found Lee Andersen, a Stanford-trained physicist who was offering drum lessons—three dollars for a half hour—at his house on Perry Lane, just off the Stanford campus. Kreutzmann signed up for lessons every Saturday and lived for them, riding his bike over to Andersen's house, entering the scientist/drummer's Hawaiian-themed abode and bashing away, then spending the week pounding on his mother's pots and pans until it was time for another lesson. It took. His dad bought him a snare drum and hi-hat, and at a party one afternoon, Kreutzmann fell in with a friend who played guitar and another who played bass. They attempted a version of "Johnny B. Goode" and made it work. Some of the kids got up from a couch and danced. "It was," Kreutzmann said, "the first truly joyful moment of my life."

Then came the night at the Tangent. Kreutzmann had met Garcia when Garcia bought the banjo from his father, but now he saw him play, and he yearned to be part of his scene. Garcia didn't reach out to him right away after that night. It took a couple of weeks for the phone to ring. But it did, and Garcia asked: "Hey, you want to play in a band?" Kreutzmann accepted on the spot. He began rehearsing with the Warlocks right away, impressing Garcia and settling into a seat he would end up occupying for more than thirty years. Kreutzmann brought rhythm and blues.

That left one opening, and here the band, "led" by Garcia, opted for practicality. They needed at least two things: a bass player and instruments. Dana Morgan, son of the owner of the music shop where Garcia taught, offered both. Garcia once jokingly described the bass player as the worst guitar player in any band, so he settled for Morgan, who brought with him access to the store and its gear, if not exactly the inspired musicianship that Garcia might have wanted. They worked together for a while, but the other members were frustrated. "We tried to do some gigs and they were as disastrous as open mic night at the School for the Tone Deaf," Kreutzmann said. "The guy just couldn't play the bass."

They persisted, and they did make progress. The Warlocks' first real gig was an appearance at Menlo College, in Menlo Park, on April 1,

THE WARLOCKS TO THE DEAD | 49

1965. It created a bump, but not as much as the next, a month later, the first week of May, at Magoo's Pizza Parlor, also in Menlo Park.

A handful of people showed up the first night. A few dozen came the next. By the third, hundreds were crowded into the restaurant, overflowing its handful of vinyl booths and square-topped Formica tables, spilling into the street, where a chalkboard announced the band: "Warlocks." The pizza place didn't allow dancing but couldn't stop it that night. One young man came to the show because he'd met Garcia at a party and was impressed with his musicianship. That night, he caught the groove and was moving to it. He happened to be a classically trained composer at ease with instruments and blessed with absolute pitch. During the set break, Garcia approached him. "How'd you like to play the bass in this band?" he asked. Phil Lesh sensed that Garcia and this band were up to something special. "By God," he said. "I'll give it a try."

With that, the group had its final piece, a crucial one that would influence its musicianship and style almost as deeply as Garcia himself. Phil Lesh was odd and quirky and brilliant, classically trained and drawn to the avant-garde. Introduced to music by his grandmother, Bobbie, who had helped to raise him in Kensington, an East Bay community near Berkeley, Phil remembered the first time Bobbie invited him to join her in listening to the New York Philharmonic on the radio. It was a Sunday afternoon, and he was four years old. Bobbie found little Phil listening at her door. The Philharmonic played Brahms's First Symphony, and Phil felt he had "been carried into a familiar, half-remembered realm." It was an experience he never forgot, noting it in his memoirs, written more than fifty years after that Sunday.

Music never left Lesh. He took up violin, then trumpet, which spoke to him for its "brilliant and electrifying timbre," then harmony studies. While Jerry Garcia was digging through the discarded 78s from his parents' bar, Phil Lesh was just a few miles away, across the Bay, sifting through his parents' collection of big band jazz: "Glenn Miller, Tommy Dorsey, Harry James and the king of them all: Benny Goodman." He graduated from high school—an achievement that eluded most of his soon-to-be bandmates—but sputtered out at San Francisco State. He was turned away by the Army—whether for his eyesight (Lesh wore glasses) or his attitude, he was never sure—and then found a place at the College of San Mateo and, finishing there, transferred to UC Berkeley. Although he was never a dazzling student, his musical gifts attracted notice, and Lesh counted among his mentors the Italian composer Luciano Berio, who taught at Mills College in Oakland and who allowed Lesh to audit his course after Lesh, once again uninterested in academic success, dropped out of Berkeley. Lesh recorded some of Berio's work and absorbed Berio's adaptations of classical pieces, including a memorable outdoor performance by Lukas Foss of Mozart's Piano Concerto No. 25, which Lesh recalled as "a limpid stream of melody, happily accompanied by some twenty or so birds perched in the trees surrounding the seats."

Lesh's intellectual musicianship also drew him to jazz, especially improvisational jazz, so even as he composed a mammoth classical piece intended to be played by four orchestras at once, he was drawn to the work of John Coltrane. "Chords stacked upon chords," Lesh recalled, "phrases looping over the tiniest fraction of the beat, all with the most soulful inflections and passionate intensity." It was, to Lesh, entirely fresh, "solid and edgy."

As that assessment suggests, Lesh brought the Warlocks a far different orientation from those of its other members. It is all but impossible to imagine Pigpen reveling in Mozart's No. 25. But that was only one possible obstacle to his joining the Warlocks. Arguably more serious was the fact that Garcia wanted him as a bass player, but Lesh did not know how to play the bass. No matter. "I *knew* I could learn the instrument, and even play it differently than I had so far heard it being played," he wrote later. So when Garcia asked him to join the Warlocks, Lesh agreed, on one condition: that Garcia give him one lesson.

After the Magoo's Pizza Parlor shows in May, Garcia delivered. Garcia and his young family had recently rented a cottage on Bryant Court in Palo Alto, and he and Lesh went there that night, taking care not to awaken Sara and Heather. Garcia picked up a guitar, and, speaking quietly to avoid waking his wife and daughter, walked Lesh through the basics, emphasizing that the guitar's four heaviest strings were arrayed identically to those on a bass. He suggested that Lesh, who had received some early lessons on the violin, borrow a guitar and begin practicing scales with those strings. When he was ready, Garcia said, Lesh could join the Warlocks in rehearsal. Lesh got to work, guided by another piece of advice, this one from his roommate, who cautioned him "never play an open string unless you really *mean* it." Within a month, Phil had moved from San Francisco to Palo Alto.

Those early performances of the Warlocks were, for Garcia, a revelation. This was not the stiff, mathematical satisfaction of bluegrass or the self-serious soul searching of folk music. This had the potential to be something bigger. "We were going to be the next Beatles or something," he recalled. "We were on a trip, definitely. We had enough of that kind of crazy faith in ourselves." Even more than the prospect of becoming famous, though, was the realization that this group was on to something sublime. As Garcia noted: "We were always motivated by the possibility that we could have fun, *big fun.*"

Fun. Huey Lewis, another product of the Bay Area arts and music scene—though younger than Garcia and his bandmates—observed that most contemporary bands begin with a sound and then move to membership. A country music outfit searches for a pedal steel player who appreciates its ambitions; the jazz ensemble searches for the guitarist who gets phrasing and intricacy. The result is a harmonious, polished sound. The Warlocks formed differently. They began as friends with shared cultural appreciations—improvisation, experimentation, drugs—and developed their talents and style as a group. They came together, first and lastingly, to have fun. They were, as Lewis remarked in 2023, "a band that started as friends. That shaped what they did."

And now this group of friends was a band. The Warlocks were electric, experimental, enamored of folk, grounded in the blues, influenced by bluegrass, growing in sophistication with each performance—and getting louder, too. The Warlocks landed gigs at clubs and bars on the Peninsula through the summer and fall of 1965. They performed six nights a week, five sets a night, at the In Room in Belmont, where Garcia polished his electric guitar playing and Lesh learned the bass. They played off one another, trying out folk and pop melodies while under the influence of Coltrane's improvisation. They took advantage of the audience's indifference—it was a pickup bar mostly populated by divorcées, and the shaggy band onstage wasn't the center of attention.

They developed a sound. In those days, Kreutzmann's drumming was "brilliant and very fast," Garcia wrote to a fan in 1967. He set the beat, and Weir, though still so young that his bandmates nicknamed him the Kid, showed blossoming potential. Weir was, according to Garcia, a "hardworking young musician with fantastically good time."

They were mostly a dance band. Audiences, at least those not hitting on stewardesses and recently single patrons, moved to their music. And, once dancing, they did not care to be jolted to a quick stop. The Warlocks stretched out songs. "Gloria" was a particular favorite: Garcia would jam, Lesh and Kreutzmann would explore new directions in rhythm, and Weir began to experiment with chording variations. In the Warlocks' hands, "Gloria" ran to fifteen minutes and longer. And why not? Just because radio play or record company conventions dictated that pop songs be no more than four minutes long, why should that apply to a young band in a Bay Area nightclub? "The phonograph record is the thing that says, 'Hey, a song is three minutes long,'" Garcia said. "Not music itself, certainly not for dancing."

THE SUMMER of 1965 was notable in another respect. It was then that LSD, previously confined to government labs, Los Angeles hipster colonies, and a few isolated appearances elsewhere, made its way into the music scene around San Francisco—and dropped on the receptive tongues of the Warlocks, save Pigpen, who never warmed to it. And, as Garcia said, "The whole world just went kablooey."

The effects of LSD were both undeniable and indescribable. Acid is a hallucinogen, producing visual and auditory effects. It can slow a user's sense of time, focus attention, induce euphoria, and sometimes produce anxiety. It can be stressful and liberating, often in the same moment. Under its influence, a user can find galaxies in a linoleum floor, float through experiences with disembodied calm, or crash into imaginary barriers as solid as any wall. LSD brings new light to sunshine, new portent to shadow. It exaggerates, amplifies, coheres. Touch takes on new depth; sounds can present themselves visually, as floating notes or songbirds or lines of melody; colors, meanwhile, may take on sounds or smells—red as spicy or loud, blue as cool or melodic. The margins swirl into the center. LSD encourages inward thinking and outward connection, the simultaneous emancipation and evaporation of the self. To anyone who has experienced an acid trip, it is altogether clear that alternative realities are not imaginary. They are—or can be— as palpably real as any more widely shared reality, available to the person willing to expand his or her perception, to open that door.

LSD was invented, or discovered, in Switzerland in April 1943 by Dr. Albert Hofmann, who was working with some crystals in his lab when he began to feel dizzy. Leaving the lab on a spring afternoon and riding his bicycle home, Hofmann recalled feeling he was in "a not unpleasant intoxicated-like condition, characterized by an extremely stimulated imagination." Hofmann's trip home that day would forever be memorialized as Bicycle Day.

LSD found its way into psychological circles in the 1940s and 1950s as researchers—including Gregory Bateson and Margaret Mead—were drawn to the therapeutic possibilities of hallucinogens, tranquilizers, and antianxiety drugs that seemed to offer promising effects, perhaps even as chemical cures for psychiatric disorders such as schizophrenia. In one sense, that was nothing new. Drugs had long intrigued psychiatrists, as Benjamin Breen recounts in his thoughtful book *Tripping on Utopia*. As Breen writes, the philosopher Walter Benjamin had noted the "loosening of self" that accompanied some drug experiences, and many others had observed the ancient use of peyote and other drugs in native cultures across time and place, so the idea of drugs as a vehicle for discovery was hardly a novelty.

And yet LSD entered that debate in the 1950s as a new contributor

54 | HERE BESIDE THE RISING TIDE

to that history, something powerful and potentially liberating. Bill Wilson, founder of Alcoholics Anonymous, tried the drug and believed it might help break alcohol addiction. Psychiatrists imagined it breaking through barriers of self-protection. It at least seemed worthy of study and observation. In 1957, CBS broadcast a documentary series titled *Focus on Sanity* that featured a woman taking the drug for the cameras, filming her as she drifted through the first televised acid trip. Timothy Leary, a self-styled "existential psychiatrist" and dogged self-promoter, grabbed on to hallucinogens as a way to change humanity, starting with himself and setting out on a mission that would overlap with Garcia's soon enough.

LSD arrived in the San Francisco area under the malevolent auspices of the Central Intelligence Agency. Intrigued by the drug's psychoactive effects, the CIA began flooding the academic medical establishment with grant money intended to gin up research on the drug and its potential uses. Soon university departments and medical labs found that they could secure funding by creating experiments to test psychotropic drugs. One such series of experiments was run out of the Veterans Administration hospital in Palo Alto, to determine whether LSD and other drugs could be useful in interrogations. The experiments were conducted under the umbrella of a program known as MK-ULTRA, which often relied on dangerous, unscrupulous, and illegal tactics—snatching subjects off the streets of San Francisco, luring some to brothels, dosing subjects without their knowledge or consent. Others volunteered, however, and in some cases rather enjoyed it. Surviving records of MK-ULTRA include mentions of Ken Kesey and Robert Hunter as subjects, as the agency later sheepishly acknowledged that Kesey's "ingestion of LSD during these experiments led directly to his widespread promotion of the drug and the subsequent development of hippie culture" and that Hunter found the experience "creatively formative for him." When Garcia learned of their experiences, it is safe to say that it was only a matter of time.

The first time that Garcia dropped acid, he did so with Sara, and it began as a joyful romp around town, "bumping into each other and having these incredible revelations and flashes. . . . It was like another release, yet another opening." Joined by several friends, they made their way into the hills above Palo Alto. "We went up to Lagunitas to the Magic Circle, which was a huge redwood stump that was kind of hollowed out and covered with moss. It was a magic circle. And we just had a wonderful, wonderful, magical day."

There was, moreover, a discovery through LSD, one that united Sara's pacifism and Jerry's musicianship. LSD reveals, for many, a larger universality of things—an unmistakable connection that transcends ego and intertwines the individual with nature, whether at a physical, even atomic level, or in a more broadly spiritual sense. For Jerry and Sara, as for many others, the experience of tripping is often one of unity—the fundamental connectedness of all things that holds the planet together as a shared vessel. And in unity, there is something beyond even solidarity; there is indivisibility and all that it connotes. Once, while tripping, Garcia saw a 360-degree pattern, a winding process that combined "every kind of thought form somehow"; it revealed the word "All." And unity in turn suggests peace, for how can an organism be at war with itself? Sara felt that unity on LSD; Jerry did too.

"The plan was that we were going to change the world with acid because when you take acid, you can see everything is connected," Sara said. "It's like realizing the pacifist's dream. No more war, back to the roots, quite literally."

But LSD trips are long—four to twelve hours is the general range—and often complicated. At some point, Jerry got a glimpse of himself in a mirror, his face contorted. He became afraid, and Sara, too, was unsettled, fearful of what the drug was doing to them. They drove—yes, drove—to Hunter's house. Hunter seemed logical to turn to because he was experienced and because they remembered in that moment that he owned a copy of *The Tibetan Book of the Dead*, which popular wisdom of the time claimed might have something to offer under the circumstances. Hunter was patient and blunt, assuring them that it was just the drug and that it would pass. It did.

For Garcia, it had just begun.

56 | HERE BESIDE THE RISING TIDE

And for the culture, too. Acid dropped into the San Francisco Bay Area at precisely the moment that the area was ready for it.

On September 6, 1965, the *San Francisco Examiner* was reviewing a "new hip hangout" on Hayes Street in San Francisco. The Blue Unicorn was owned by twenty-five-year-old Robert Stubbs, amiable, bearded, helpful. Describing the atmosphere at the Blue Unicorn, the *Examiner's* reporter spotted a guy on a sofa, doodling on a *Harper's* magazine cover. The man, Dean Plapowski, was described as "30, elderly for a hippie," a new species which was described vaguely in the piece but seemed to suggest someone a little different from a beatnik or a peacenik, someone who embraced "causes from pacifism to planned parenthood," young people who began to find one another in places such as the Blue Unicorn, where they were offered pencils and paper, books, free meals, and a meeting place for the Sexual Freedom League. The press had just discovered hippies, and hippies had just discovered acid.

AS THE end of the year approached, the Warlocks were working at a strip joint in San Francisco called Pierre's. "I think that's where the uber-backbeat first lodged in our consciousness: Bump! Grind!," Lesh said. After wrapping one night, they took time off to record a demo for Autumn Records. Lesh had discovered another band recording under the name the Warlocks, so for this effort, they chose the name Emergency Crew. They put down a serviceable if unspectacular collection of six songs, mostly simple rhythms over a tambourine and snare drum and tinny electric piano—more early Beatles than blues, with one track closer to a James Bond sound—and nothing coming in at more than three minutes and twenty-five seconds. It did not sparkle with greatness, but it featured musicians who were coalescing as a band.

What, then, would this band be called? The Warlocks was now out. Emergency Crew was fine for the recording session, but no one liked it for a permanent name. Lesh liked Mythical Ethical Icicle Tricycle. Fortunately, it did not catch on.

Garcia dropped by Lesh's house one day while the search for a name

THE WARLOCKS TO THE DEAD | 57

was on the minds of band members. True to their shared love of language, the two were bouncing ideas off each other as Garcia thumbed through reference books—*Bartlett's Familiar Quotations* yielded nothing, and then he flipped open a handy copy of the *Britannica World Language Dictionary*. The thick volume opened to the G's, and Garcia's eye lit upon "Grateful Dead." Following the term was a brief definition of a widespread folk tale wherein a traveler comes upon a group of people who are refusing to bury the body of a man who died in debt. The traveler pays the debt, allowing the man to be buried and his soul to proceed into the afterlife. In appreciation, that soul returns the favor to his benefactor, granting him a wish, a fortune, or a bride, depending on the version of the tale. That recompense is known as "the gift of the Grateful Dead."

Lesh liked it right away; the others had to come around. Even Garcia, whose inspiration it was, had to consider it in its fullness. The name, Garcia said, was "repellent enough to filter curious onlookers" and off-putting enough that parents hated it. It juxtaposed ideas and words uncommonly linked. It was new and big and open-ended. From that day forward, Garcia was a member of the Grateful Dead.

PART II

EXPERIMENTS

Acid Test poster. Muir Beach, California, December 1966.

CHAPTER 4

The Acid Tests

WALLACE STEGNER DID NOT HAVE MUCH USE FOR HIPPIES. HE grew up with the work of Hemingway and Faulkner. He admired Robert Frost. He was a restrained writer, respectful of focus and discipline. Stegner's career-making novel, *Big Rock Candy Mountain,* tells the story of a family desperately scouring the American and Canadian West for stability in the face of influenza, economic depression, and war. Cast across vistas, it is a landscape novel and yet also embedded in the life and values of family. The novel struggles with American priorities, but far from rejecting them, it projects and incorporates them.

Published in 1943, *Big Rock Candy Mountain* established Stegner as a leading American voice and also pigeonholed him as a writer of the West, a niche solidified just a few years after the novel's release when Stegner founded a creative writing program at Stanford. He became "the Western writer," ensconced in the university that was then often called the Harvard of the West. A literary culture bloomed. Drawn by the chance to study with Stegner, some of the most promising young literary talents in the country came to Stanford. One was Ken Kesey.

Kesey was an Oregon native with the build of the wrestler he had been at the University of Oregon. He was brash and confident, alert to the possibilities of language and lured by the elasticity of culture. If Stegner constructed literature along architectural lines, Kesey enjoyed the challenging of form. He was ready to experiment, and he won a Woodrow Wilson National Fellowship after graduating from the University of Oregon. Kesey arrived at Stanford in 1958. He and Stegner did not hit it off.

62 | HERE BESIDE THE RISING TIDE

"Wallace Stegner had traveled across the Great Plains and reached the ocean and as far as he was concerned, that was far enough," Kesey recalled in later years. "Certain of us didn't believe that was far enough, and when we went farther than that, he took issue with it."

As the "certain of us" in that remark suggests, Kesey was part of a group of young writers in that period who were fired up by the emergence of new literary ambitions and who challenged Stegner's sensibilities. It was an extraordinary collection. In addition to Kesey, Wendell Berry, Larry McMurtry, Robert Stone, Ken Babbs, Ed McClanahan, and Gurney Norman were among the writers at work under Stegner's tutelage in the late 1950s and early 1960s.

At Stanford, Kesey was thrilled to study writing and to join a community of writers. He and his wife, high school sweetheart Faye Haxby, lived on a stretch of bungalows not far from the Stanford campus known as Perry Lane, just a modest walk away from the Chateau, where Garcia and his friends were bedding down in those days. Perry Lane had some of the Chateau's craziness but with a layer of sophistication. These were writers, not just teenagers and would-be musicians.

"We were part of the same world socially," Garcia said later; "that is to say, we lived in the same county." But Kesey and the friends around him were adult and accomplished in a way that Garcia and his circle were not. They eyed each other from a distance, at least for a while.

Although he was already the father of young children, Kesey's working attention was focused on his first novel, then still in progress. It was set in a psychiatric ward overseen by a forceful nurse who worked for "the Combine." The nurse confronted a garrulous, wisecracking gambler, fiercely unwilling to surrender to authority, and the manuscript explored their escalating conflict, sketching themes of rebellion and social control as well as probing the notion of what it means to be sane in a society that has reconciled itself to quiet insanity. In that last respect, the work fell into line with Joseph Heller's *Catch-22*, while Kesey's novel also examined the relationship between nurse and patient as proxy for establishment and rebel. Kesey wrestled with that conflict as he drafted

THE ACID TESTS | 63

and redrafted, convinced of the soundness of his novel but searching for a perspective to view its central tension.

Meanwhile, Kesey spotted an advertisement offering seventy-five dollars a day for students willing to be part of medical testing at the Veterans Administration hospital in Menlo Park. He signed up and got his first taste of acid. He discovered the "awful and unique logic" of a reality until then beyond his reach. It was revelatory and influential, "shell-shattering." "We were beautiful," Kesey wrote of his first few acid trips, all under the observation of researchers. "Naked and helpless and sensitive as a snake after skinning, but far more human than the shining knightmare that had stood creaking in previous parade rest. We were alive and life was us."

Mind opened, Kesey craved more. He went to work at a local psych ward, observing patients and pinching LSD and other drugs to share with friends. One night, under the influence of peyote, he imagined a Native American patient taking stock of the ward. That became Chief Bromden, and Kesey's novel had acquired its missing perspective. "With that Indian's consciousness to filter [the contest] through, that makes it exceptional," he realized. Kesey stitched his new character into the center of his story. The result was *One Flew Over the Cuckoo's Nest*, published by Viking Press in 1962.

Not all critics knew what to make of it, but those who appreciated *Cuckoo's Nest* loved it a lot. *Kirkus* called it a "thoroughly enthralling, brilliantly tempered novel." *Time* credited Kesey for his willingness to "tilt the reader's comfortable assumption about the nice normalities" and hailed the book as "a roar of protest against middlebrow society's Rules and the invisible Rulers who enforce them."

The royalties from *Cuckoo's Nest* opened up new opportunities, and LSD fueled a ravenous desire to experiment. Kesey had to fight off litigation related to the book, with Viking deducting $5,000 from a royalty statement to settle a lawsuit, but the young author shrugged that off and was suddenly flush. He bought a house in La Honda, a wooded area in the hills above and west of Palo Alto. He and his friends called themselves the Merry Pranksters, and Kesey's property became the clubhouse of their gang.

Kesey's second novel, *Sometimes a Great Notion*, was published in 1964. Denser and more digressive than *Cuckoo's Nest*, it, too, unfolded in Kesey's native Oregon, where he set the dramatic clash between old culture and counterculture in the logging rainforests. *Sometimes a Great Notion* was not a commercial success—Kesey's agent, Sterling Lord, lamented that "the book has not taken off in hardcover"—and it, too, drew mixed reviews. Orville Prescott called it "insufferably pretentious," in a *New York Times* review headlined A TIRESOME LITERARY DISASTER. *The New York Times Book Review* thought otherwise. There, Conrad Knickerbocker compared Kesey's first and second novels and preferred the second. Knickerbocker acknowledged the appeal of *Cuckoo's Nest* but added: "Such a beginning was insufficient to prepare us for the power and scope of the author's second novel. 'Sometimes a Great Notion,' a big book in every way, captures the tenor of post-Korea America as nothing I can remember reading."

Viking had prepared a celebration of *Sometimes a Great Notion*, and the Pranksters decided to attend. They would go together, and they would make a trip of it. Kesey bought a bus, a 1939 International Harvester that he found for sale in Atherton, south of San Francisco. He liked the idea of a school bus—a vehicle that transports young people to learning and then delivers them home—which he found both practical and specifically American. He was not content, however, to accept a school bus at face value. The artist Roy Sebern and the Pranksters painted it in bright primary colors and named it "Furthur," later corrected to "Further." They stocked up on LSD and speed and, with tips of hats to westward expansion and *On the Road*, they set out from California to New York, a self-consciously reverse migration.

Though the trip was not intended as a political statement, the Pranksters undertook it in the summer of 1964, the same months during which voters were sizing up the choice between Lyndon Johnson and his challenger, Arizona senator Barry Goldwater. To ease their passage through the South, the Pranksters scrawled a slogan on the outside of the bus that managed to seem both political and hallucinatory: A VOTE FOR BARRY IS A VOTE FOR FUN, the bus announced. It may have defused police through Arizona and the South; it was less well received when the Pranksters rolled into Manhattan.

The plan for the bus trip was to document the experience on film, and the Pranksters shot plenty of it. But they were high, of course, and the resulting project dragged across decades of fitful editing. And yet, despite themselves, they laid down a lasting cultural marker, primarily because their antics attracted the attention of a more disciplined chronicler, the journalist and author Tom Wolfe. Although Wolfe had his critics and the book has its failings, *The Electric Kool-Aid Acid Test*, published by Farrar, Straus & Giroux in 1968, may be more responsible for the lasting impact of the Pranksters than anything any of them said or wrote.

Wolfe's book traced the bus trip from its departure in La Honda on June 17, 1964, to the East Coast and back again. Neal Cassady, the same character fictionalized by Kerouac as Dean Moriarty in *On the Road*, was now at Kesey's side and usually behind the wheel. He drove as only Cassady could. Garcia would recall rides with Cassady through the streets of San Francisco as among the most terrifying experiences of his life—Cassady rampaging through intersections, playing with the radio, talking, never once seeming to look at the road. Robert Stone remembered Cassady as "the world's greatest driver, who could roll a joint while backing a 1937 Packard onto the lip of the Grand Canyon." Whether high on weed, tripping on acid, or speeding with Benzedrine—and sometimes on all of those—Cassady drove.

After stopping at Larry McMurtry's house in Texas, the Pranksters plowed through Houston and New Orleans, Biloxi and Mobile, and Florida, then shot north to Manhattan—which they liked to call "Madhattan"—and the Ninety-seventh Street apartment of the novelist Robert Stone, yet another alumnus of the Stanford writing program.

Kesey and crew rolled up to Stone's building and parked the bus out front. The cryptic Goldwater message, meant to smooth passage through the South, had the opposite effect in Manhattan, where Stone's

66 | HERE BESIDE THE RISING TIDE

neighbors flashed "Heil Hitler" salutes and middle fingers. Cassady was worn out by the trip, and his reunion with Kerouac was disappointing. The aging and alcoholic author, "out of rage at health and youth and mindlessness—but mainly out of jealousy at Kesey for hijacking his beloved sidekick, Cassady—despised us, and wouldn't speak to Cassady," Stone reported. The bus rolled on.

A short, unhappy stay in New York was followed by what was meant as a climactic crescendo of the journey, the much-anticipated meeting of America's two great LSD champions, the Merry Pranksters from the West descending on Timothy Leary and his band of Harvard outcasts and hangers-on from the East. It had the potential to be a hippie summit.

It was a dud.

The Pranksters rolled up to Leary's borrowed mansion in Millbrook, New York, in their psychedelic bus, music pumping from the speakers, Pranksters tossing smoke bombs and whooping it up. They were struck by the old-school clamminess of the place. "Psychedelics," Stone wrote, "had replaced tournament polo as a ride on the edge." But they blustered ahead, hoping to rouse Leary's crew from its torpor. No such luck. Ken Babbs tossed a green smoke grenade from the bus and watched the cloud blow into the windows of the mansion. No reply. "Oh man," one Prankster remarked as the bus ground to a halt. "It's like the Huns knocking on the gates of Rome."

Leary did not rush out to meet Kesey. Others made excuses for him: Leary was with a woman. Or maybe he had the flu. Instead, others wafted around the Pranksters, inviting them to the crypt, talking about "the loss of ego" and pointedly contrasting it with the flashy bus parked out front. When Leary finally appeared, he lectured.

"Some of the people here feel like you are making fun of us for being so formal," he said. "We can learn from your tribal nature."

The Pranksters hung around for an obligatory stay, then left, more than a little wounded by the condescension. They returned via the northern route—through Illinois and Wisconsin, on to South Dakota,

THE ACID TESTS | 67

up to Canada, back down through Idaho, over to the Esalen Institute in Big Sur, then Monterey, and finally home to La Honda.

The next night, Cassady was cooling his throat at St. Michael's Alley when he ran into a striking girl. Just eighteen years old and new to Palo Alto, Carolyn Adams was easy to notice. Open-faced, gregarious, thrilled to be in the breeze of the world, she was as vivacious as she was magnetic. "She was," Tom Wolfe observed, "one big loud charge of vitality." Adams had grown up in Upstate New York, where she was the daughter of not one but two scientists—her mom was a botanist and her dad an entomologist. She'd been kicked out of high school for a stunt she hadn't pulled and got her diploma in the mail. "It kinda hurt," she said, and she was looking for a change. Her brother offered her a lift. "I went in the VW van, at forty-five miles an hour, all the way to California." When they arrived, her brother lent her a motorbike and sent her on her way. She landed a job at Stanford, working in an organic chemistry lab and fending off advances from the night janitor.

On that warm night at the end of the summer of '64, Adams was on her way out of a boring relationship—her boyfriend's mother had come from the Midwest and snatched him home. Free of that encumbrance but facing the loss of her job and now her apartment, Adams was stretching her legs. She tucked a book into her bag and rambled over to St. Michael's on her Honda 50. She ordered a double espresso with a scoop of ice cream. In came two men, one wild-eyed and rambunctious and quite a bit older than the other, a wiry blond teenager. "They were giving me the eye," she said. Adams liked the look of the younger guy and made room for the two when they sidled up. The older man talked a lot and talked fast and asked if she'd like to go for a ride. Adams hesitated, and he sweetened the pot: "How'd you like to smoke a J?" Before she knew it, Carolyn Adams was in the front seat of his car, jammed in between a guy named Bradley and none other than Neal Cassady.

Cassady drove. Cassady always drove. In this case, he piloted the car onto the train tracks that ran just west of St. Michael's, separating downtown Palo Alto from the Stanford campus. He rattled along the tracks.

68 | HERE BESIDE THE RISING TIDE

Backward. Adams was thrilled and terrified, instantly cast under the spell of Cassady at full speed. They survived the tracks and sped into the hills, cavorting around the Peninsula until almost daybreak, when they came to rest at Kesey's place. Cassady proudly delivered Adams along with a cache of drugs.

She soon found her place among the Pranksters. Her looks made her easy to appreciate at first glance, and her wit held the attention that came her way. As with all Pranksters, Adams acquired a nickname. Stoic, sturdy, and domestically adept, she became Mountain Girl.

THINGS WERE happening, and close by. The fall of 1964 saw tensions rise across the Bay as students and other activists focused their energies on the campus of UC Berkeley. Civil rights demonstrations were gaining momentum, and as the war in Vietnam threatened not only the lives but also the liberties of young Americans, students protested. Press reports highlighted the role of outside groups on and around the campus, and the California legislature responded by prohibiting political activity, ordering a halt to fundraising and recruiting for outside causes. On October 1, an organizer for the Congress of Racial Equality named Jack Weinberg, who was not a registered Berkeley student at the time, set up a table on a little strip of land just outside the campus entrance at Sproul Plaza with literature on civil rights.

He was questioned by police and refused to answer or identify himself. He was arrested. As he sat in the police car awaiting transport to the local station, other demonstrators surrounded it and jumped on the hood. The police abandoned the car, and Weinberg remained inside, refusing to leave. He stayed there for thirty-two hours until the demonstrators and the school administration had hammered out an agreement under which students agreed to halt all "illegal" protests and the administration created a committee to consider political activity on campus. Weinberg was booked and released; police were at last able to recover their "sorry-looking car."

That cleared the plaza for the moment, but the deal did not hold, and more demonstrations followed, with clashes growing increasingly physical. Buffeted between protesters and the legislature, the Berkeley administration tried to carve a middle course, allowing on-campus activities to help outside causes but only if students could guarantee that the off-campus causes were legal. UC BRACES FOR MORE PROTESTS, the *Berkeley Daily Gazette* warned on November 7.

Mario Savio was a native of Queens who had set out to be a priest but found himself drawn to civil rights and to Berkeley. It seemed destined. Savio had a stammer that sometimes discouraged him from engaging in conversation. Magically, it subsided when he was called to speak to power.

By December, the struggle had grown pitched. Students called themselves the Free Speech Movement, and thousands rallied on December 2, occupying the main administration building. Police arrested 769 of them, later adding still more to what was the largest mass arrest in the history of California.

With no trace of a stammer, Savio delivered the words that would define his cause: "There's a time when the operation of the machine becomes so odious, makes you so sick at heart, that you can't take part!" he shouted through a microphone. "You can't even passively take part. And you've got to put your bodies upon the gears and upon the wheels, upon the levers, upon all the apparatus. And you've got to make it stop."

The effect was electric. "The student movement," the underground press reported, "is on."

WILLIAM WONG worked for the Narcotics Bureau of the Treasury Department. In 1965, he was attached to the San Mateo Sheriff's Department, which had jurisdiction in the hills where Kesey's land was located. As Kesey's reputation grew, Wong zeroed in on the renegade writer. In one sense, Wong's hands were tied: LSD, which Kesey and the Pranksters were so flamboyantly ingesting, was legal in 1965. That made an LSD bust impossible.

But it did not take much intuition to imagine that where there was legal LSD, there might also be illegal substances, namely marijuana. Under questioning from Wong, one young woman, a San Mateo College student named Kathy Nugent, said she had smoked a "cigarette rolled in brown paper . . . that she assumed to be marijuana." Other sources reported parties at the Kesey compound where marijuana was available, and specifically fingered Cassady and Page Browning. Cassady hardly needed a tipster: He'd been to prison and was, after all, the central character of *On the Road*.

Browning was less well known. A native of Ohio who had made his way west, Browning connected with Kesey and the Pranksters after they had returned from the bus trip. Soon to pick up the nickname Cadaverous Cowboy, the lean, cheerful Browning was running marijuana and making friends with those he supplied. It was Browning who first made the introductions that brought Kesey and the Warlocks together. He was, Carolyn recalled, "the liaison guy." Browning's connections to dope and to the Pranksters caught Wong's attention.

Wong and the sheriff's deputies crept in closer. They spied on the house from an adjacent hillside, sometimes so obviously that Mountain Girl would yell at them through Kesey's speaker system. They ignored her.

Still, the Pranksters enjoyed a sense of invulnerability—a false one, as it would turn out. They were under the protection of a famous writer, and they were hardly hiding their activities. Kesey had just returned from a cross-country trip in the tricked-out bus and had made it across America and back, high much of the time, without being arrested. Surely holing up in the hills above Palo Alto was no more an invitation to arrest than that? So the parties continued. On Saturday, April 17, yet another large gathering assembled in La Honda, and the antics went on well into the night. Wong was watching.

Just before midnight on the night of Friday, April 23, 1965, the agents and deputies showed up with a warrant, crossing the bridge over the creek to Kesey's house and setting off a mad scramble inside as residents and guests tried to flush drugs down toilets. The next day's papers treated it as a show-stopper, edging out news from the state leg-

THE ACID TESTS | 71

islature and the war in Vietnam: TOP NOVELIST KESEY, 13 OTHERS HELD
IN LA HONDA MARIJUANA RAID read the banner headline of the *San
Mateo Times.* The deck purported to clarify: "Biggest Haul in S.M.
County Since '59 Dope Arrest." Among those arrested were Babbs, Cassady, and Mountain Girl—all of whom gave Kesey's La Honda address
as their own. Reports indicated that some of those arrested "appeared
queasy"—understandable, given that Babbs realized as the police were
arriving that he had ten joints in his pocket. As the deputies rounded up
suspects, Babbs handed out joints, and various Pranksters chewed up
the evidence.

In the end, the bust was hardly the event that the headlines suggested. Deputies found a little marijuana—enough to warrant criminal
charges against Kesey but not enough to hold most of the others, who
were booked and held overnight only to have charges later dropped.

Meanwhile, the party went on, and grew through the summer. One
adventure bled into the next, an evolving, overlapping series of discover-
ies and enjoyments, sometimes intense, other times quiet. Among
them, one would acquire shocking notoriety as well as literary standing.
It was August 7, 1965. Hunter Thompson was among the guests, as was
the now regular contingent of Hells Angels. As Thompson wandered
the property late at night, he noticed activity in a cabin. Spying inside,
he came upon a "mad, mad scene": Angels surrounding a woman, her
dress hiked up. Thompson was repulsed and frightened, and his account of that episode, which he shared with Wolfe, appeared in *The
Electric Kool-Aid Acid Test.* "Pretty soon all the Angels knew about the
'new mamma' out in the backhouse and a lot of them piled in there,"
Wolfe wrote. The Angels circled the woman, "two or three would be on
her at once." Wolfe's rendering of Thompson's account stood out in the
book, a horrifying sequence that suggested far more than a party out of
control—rather, it presented a culture that had lost its bearings. Even
though Wolfe's account hinted that the woman willingly participated,
the grisly scene reinforced the Angels' reputation for predatory sexual
conquest and barbarism. And yet, as justified as that reputation was, it
seems not to have been at work that night. Anne Murphy, then Cas-

sady's girlfriend, later wrote her version of those events, reporting that she had been "joyously gang-banged by the Hell's Angels."

The night's other place in history was secured by a very different guest and in opposite fashion. Allen Ginsberg spent the same night at Kesey's place. He played finger cymbals and chanted, charming the Angels despite themselves. His account was written a few months later and appeared in a collection of his work in 1968. Titled "First Party at Ken Kesey's with Hell's Angels," it describes an unconventional evening but a tender one, a night in the redwoods with a fire in the fireplace, music playing, and dancing, with police hovering at the periphery, "red lights revolving in the leaves."

FOUR NIGHTS later and four hundred miles south, Watts first sputtered and then exploded into violence, as a traffic stop by the California Highway Patrol turned into a community confrontation and metastasized into a protracted and violent clash between police and residents, tearing at race relations in Los Angeles and beyond. The fabric was fraying.

With autumn, the Pranksters took their party on the road. It would be an exaggeration to say they had a plan—plans were not a hallmark of Prankster life—but Kesey wanted the party off his property. He was already facing trial on the marijuana charges stemming from his arrest in April; he hardly needed another bust. An idea took shape: a nomadic series of gatherings, happenings where music and art curled around LSD, where partygoers performed and performers partied, where sound and visuals collided and fused. The parties carried a whiff of outlawry— drugs, the Kesey bust, the Hells Angels—along with a gentle spirit that flowed from the LSD. Page Browning, who had seen the Warlocks play at Magoo's in Menlo Park, had another idea: a house band.

The first of these events was really a party at Babbs's home near Santa Cruz. The guests came in costume, and Babbs's living room was full of instruments that the Pranksters liked to play. This time, however, the guests included Jerry Garcia, Bob Weir, Phil Lesh, and Bill

THE ACID TESTS | 73

Kreutzmann. Still playing as the Warlocks that fall, they were just guests at this event, but they messed around with some instruments. "We played for about five minutes," Garcia said, "but it completely devastated everyone."

The party went through the night, musicians and others taking turns on the instruments, yammering lyrics, lying side by side on the floor. There was no act—no separation between performers and audience. Rather, it was a mingling and shared enjoyment. "Everybody there," Garcia said, "was as much performer as audience."

"Given a chance," Kesey said, "everybody has art in them."

And so it began. From the party at Babbs's place came another in San Jose, this one on December 4. Again, the atmosphere was more gathering than show. This time, guests were asked to contribute a dollar—mostly to help pay for LSD—and members of the band, playing publicly for the first time as the Grateful Dead, chipped in along with everyone else. Santa Cruz had been mellow and reflective; San Jose was crowded, drawing some four hundred people. And it was much more intense, more centered on the music—"one gigantic Animal House party on acid," as one history of the Acid Tests described it.

BOB DYLAN had made his way into American musical life in the fashion of so many before him, arriving in New York City and playing small gigs in Greenwich Village—twenty-minute sets at the Gaslight, where "you got the feeling that something, someone, was always coming to blow away the fog." He was a folk musician from Minnesota, drawn to the work of Woody Guthrie and awash in broad, deep reading. He found Faulkner difficult and preferred art to politics. "It's hard, what Faulkner does," a friend told him. "It's easier to write *Das Kapital*." A year older than Garcia, Dylan was swimming in the same river: shared references to Harry Smith's *Anthology of American Folk Music,* bohemianism and politics, culture and art. But Dylan and Garcia traveled different tributaries: Dylan had never been to California; he grew up in the Midwest and New York, had embraced *On the Road* but left it behind.

Dylan opened his vast career with a modest first effort, the eponymous *Bob Dylan*, released in 1962. It was not a conscious confrontation with the culture of the moment, but it spoke against it almost despite itself. "I just thought of mainstream culture as lame as hell and a big trick," Dylan later wrote. He felt himself at the cusp of something. "As for what time it was, it was always just beginning to be daylight."

The debut album was mostly covers, but it included two original Dylan songs, one of them his tribute to Woody Guthrie. Although the album did not sell well, it announced him as "the most unusual new talent in American folk music" and a "songwriter of exceptional facility and cleverness," according to the *New York Times* critic Robert Shelton, under the pen name Stacey Williams.

These were days for breaking—rules, traditions, expectations—and Dylan broke with his own community and culture. His fifth album, released in early 1965, opened with a bang. "Subterranean Homesick Blues" jumped off the vinyl, a couple of strums of acoustic guitar suddenly joined by an electric lick that announced Dylan's new direction. Folkie no more, Dylan was jumpy and excitable, as joyful as he was wry. "You don't need a weatherman to know which way the wind blows," Dylan sang, and history took note. The album's second side moved Dylan back to more familiar folk sounds, but that was just a tease. On July 25, 1965, he was appearing at the Newport Folk Festival and had performed a folk set already, but Dylan was ready to announce his autonomy. Backed by the Paul Butterfield Blues Band, he played three electrified songs to an astonished audience. These were folkies, and they were in no mood to be electrically lectured, even by Bob Dylan. Some cheered, but some booed.

"I ain't gonna work on Maggie's farm no more," Dylan sang. Not gonna work for Maggie, not for her brother, not for her pa, not for her ma. "I try my best to be just like I am / But everybody wants you to be just like them." Not Dylan. "I ain't gonna work on Maggie's farm no more."

* * *

CALLING THE Pranksters' LSD parties the Acid Tests brought together several ideas—the ancient test to determine whether a metal was gold, the exultation of discovery combined with the rigor of having to work for it. "Can you pass the Acid Test?" flyers asked. Guests were invited to search together, to discover, sometimes to wade through confusion and even fear. As the Tests took hold, the atmosphere evolved from one of a large house party to a bigger, sometimes frenetic feel. But they retained a hominess as well. They were not advertised beyond word of mouth and a few posters and handbills, some of which lacked specific locations or even a date—enthusiasts were expected to get that information from one another. The Dead were essential, though, and they showed for every Test after the first party at Babbs's place.

The festival moved north after San Jose. The next Test took place at the Big Beat in Palo Alto, with another the following Saturday night in Muir Beach, north of San Francisco. The Dead made a stop in between, playing at the Fillmore in San Francisco, where the San Francisco Mime Troupe, a radical band of street performers with a sharp political edge, was holding a benefit. Still brand new, the Dead did not make it onto the bill for that night's show, overshadowed by the Jefferson Airplane, the Great Society, the John Handy Quintet, the Mystery Trend, and the Gentlemen's Band. The Dead's setlist has not survived, but participants left with a memory of eruptive, barely controlled musical feedback. For many, that night would ring in their ears for decades.

Each of the Tests had its own identity. San Jose was big and boisterous and announced something new. Palo Alto closed early. Portland was homey. Muir Beach was sparsely attended, but Garcia considered it the first successful Test, since it was the first to integrate lights and sound. And each drew new people.

Owsley Stanley showed up in December and stayed for years. Grandson of a Kentucky governor and senator, son of a dissipated alcoholic father, expelled from a Maryland military prep school in ninth grade for doling out alcohol to his classmates, veteran of the Air Force, where he worked as an electronics engineer, Owsley—he always went by Owsley or, later, Bear—was intense, manic, brilliant, authoritarian, weird. After his on-again, off-again efforts to succeed in school petered out, Owsley came to Berkeley in 1963 and was offered a hit of LSD. Owsley was taken. He put his formidable but theretofore willfully ungovernable brain to work, and in less than a month of research—with the help of his chemist girlfriend—had taught himself how to make acid. His work immediately infused itself into the Bay Area music and arts scene.

At Bear's first Test, the music, combined with the acid, tore through him. "Garcia's guitar was like the claws of a tiger," he said. "It was dangerously scary." Owsley made up his mind that night to become a part of the Dead. He would remain a fixture of the band, its sound and its well-being—from where members lived to what they ate—for years thereafter.

Bear was at Muir Beach, and he contributed an annoying moment to it. He took to scraping a heavy wooden chair along the floor until George Walker gently coaxed him away from it. Mountain Girl recalled it as "an incredible exhibition of . . . making other people uncomfortable." Muir Beach also marked the arrival into the still nascent Grateful Dead family of a nineteen-year-old photographer, born Florence Nathan in Paris and raised in coffeehouses, who would later adopt the name Rosie McGee. She and Lesh met that night and struck up a romance.

Muir Beach came on the heels of the Big Beat Acid Test in Palo Alto—notable for the attendance of Robert Hunter and for its early close: The owner and bartenders shut it down at 2 A.M., leaving a bewildered and still high audience to straggle home. The next Acid Test, in Portland, took the Dead on a wild road trip—Cassady at the wheel, naturally. That event was quieter than most, perhaps the result of so many Pranksters having family in the house. One memorable moment, however, came when a friend of one Prankster, introducing himself only as Ace, joined the Dead onstage and proceeded to play the classical guitar. Garcia was impressed. "Man," he remarked, "that guy can really play . . . an amazing talent." After his number with the Dead, Ace hitched a ride home through a snowstorm and disappeared from history.

The Fillmore Acid Test on January 8 drew more than a thousand people, a "raging success," in the words of one historian of the period. That stoked the idea for something even bigger. The Pranksters were driving the bus, of course, and were enjoying the sense of mission that the Tests were coming to enjoy. Moreover, the Dead's performance at the benefit for the Mime Troupe had impressed a man who would come to play a central role in their expansion—Bill Graham. He, too, liked the idea of something big, something that would corral the excitement of the Acid Tests and bring that energy and the new music to a bigger venue. But the brains behind the Trips Festival, the man whose spark seems to have ignited it, was a lightning bug of imagination, a coiner of aphorisms, the kindler of many fires. He was Stewart Brand.

Brand was a graduate of Exeter and Stanford and an unhappy veteran of the U.S. Army. Tall and lean to the point of gauntness, quietly in command of himself, Brand could appear strikingly handsome or intimidatingly alert. He had an eye for photography and spent several weeks in early 1963 on the Warm Springs Indian reservation, meeting people and making photographs to produce a brochure. Returning to San Francisco after that assignment, he was given a copy of Kesey's *Cuckoo's Nest* and saw his own story—and that of American Indians—within it. Brand took note in his diary: "As Kesey writes it, the battle of McMurphy versus Big Nurse is identical to Indians versus Dalles Dam or me versus the Army."

He was hardly alone in connecting with *Cuckoo's Nest*. Many saw themselves in Kesey's book. But Brand's special blend of personal iconoclasm—he had a sensitive antenna for cults and groupthink—and keen sense of cultural trends would make him one of the signature participants in the counterculture and the technology revolution that it helped to spawn. In January 1966, what that meant was that Brand conceived of a gathering. He envisioned a multimedia onslaught— music, lights, cultural stimulants. Brand brought the vision. Graham found the venue. San Francisco hosted the Trips Festival at Longshoremen's Hall on the nights of January 21, 22, and 23, 1966.

Even before the doors opened, the festival made news. Shortly before 2 A.M. on January 19, Kesey and Mountain Girl were relaxing on a mattress on the roof of Brand's apartment building on Margrave Place, a few blocks north of City Lights. They were absent-mindedly smoking marijuana and tossing pebbles off the roof, annoying a neighbor below. The neighbor called the police. When they arrived, Adams and Kesey made no real effort to get away, assuming that the police had come for someone else. Instead, officers burst onto the roof and found the two—a married man with a nineteen-year-old girl—beneath a blanket. Mountain Girl got the best of the next day's coverage, as the *Examiner* described her as a "stunning brunette." But it also leeringly reported that the officers had broken up a "rooftop tryst," and she and Kesey were hauled to jail, where the author had to post a $2,000 bond; his teenage companion bonded out for $1,000. Mountain Girl insisted to reporters that there was "absolutely nothing romantic" between her and Kesey. That was, to put it mildly, a lie: Mountain Girl was already pregnant with Kesey's child.

For Mountain Girl, the arrest was an inconvenience, though not a small one, as possession of marijuana was a California felony in 1966. For Kesey, it was potentially devastating. Just a few days earlier, he and Page Browning had been sentenced to six months in jail and three years on probation from the April arrest in La Honda (Kesey was also fined $1,500). Kesey had yet to report to jail, and the judge who allowed him to remain free until that date had specifically directed Kesey not to associate with his drug-infatuated colleagues. Kesey thus faced the wrath of a judge who had been lenient with him. It was, as Wolfe reported in *The Electric Kool-Aid Acid Test*, a "beautiful mess and no two ways about it."

For the Trips Festival, however, it was all free publicity. Ignoring the pleas of his lawyer and probation officer, Kesey stumped around San Francisco on the afternoon of the first night of the festival, cajoling young people to join the fun that night at Longshoremen's Hall. There was music but also theater—the Mime Troupe, the city's Open Theater, and the Dancers' Workshop all participated—and Brand created a multimedia show for the event, "America Needs Indians!" At the center of the hall, the Pranksters erected a command tower from which they beamed images and pithy messages as if handed down from God. Ever resourceful, Kesey dressed as a spaceman, hiding his identity behind his costume's heat shield. The Loading Zone, a briefly popular soul fusion band, took the stage at around ten and played until the hall closed at midnight. The Dead were not billed for Friday night, and though they might have played anyway, they were thwarted by events. The bridge of Garcia's guitar broke in the confusion of the evening, and though Graham gallantly tried to fix it, the band was stymied.

By the next night, however, the event jelled, propelled mainly by the Dead, whose arrival was announced by blowing out the power as they took the stage. Once power was restored, the band plunged into a roaring version of "In the Midnight Hour," anchored by Pigpen, likely the only member of the band not on acid. Pigpen locked in to his microphone, "cajoling, exhorting, crooooning, rapping" to the spellbound crowd, by far the largest that the band had ever played for. And as Pigpen did his bit, the band was "howling around him," pumping out electrons, riding the electricity, threading it through the ocean of dancers, "oily swells moving on the vast deep." The recording of "Midnight Hour" has not survived that night, but early tapers did pick up a throaty, haunting version of "Death Don't Have No Mercy" highlighted by a sharp, penetrating Garcia guitar solo, proof that the work of the past year was paying off.

And in contrast to the haphazard feel of much of the weekend, the Dead's sound system was crystalline. Even in the tumult of light and sound—of thousands in masks and regalia, the messages being flashed through the audience and on the ceiling, the slides and film clips and tape-delayed voices in loops—the Dead's performance stood out.

Granted, the Trips Festival was not for everyone. The *San Francisco Examiner* described it as "three weekend nights of ear-splitting, headaching, eye-straining audio-visual bedlam," and posed the question "Is this Trips really necessary?" To Garcia, the answer was definitively yes. The festival, he recalled, was "magic, far-out, beautiful magic."

To the amazement of all involved, it also made money. The gross was $14,500 for the weekend. Graham took $900. The bands—the

Dead, Big Brother and the Holding Company, and the Loading Zone—each got a share, as did Brand. Much of the money went to the Pranksters, and Kesey promptly tucked it into the bus and fled the law, faking his suicide and ditching to Mexico with a few members of his merry band.

In the end, the Trips Festival was a thrill, a bore, and a dashing blast of creativity. It demonstrated that there was a culture that hungered for this sort of departure, for hitching up with craziness and music and drugs. It did not reveal deep appreciation for the American Indian story or the larger theatrical aspects, but the festival proved that the music moved people, that it spoke to them and satisfied them, that it transmitted values to and from the audience. It didn't just entertain; it transported. Reflecting on the weekend, Brand understood it best, as he so often did: "It was," he said, "the beginning of the Grateful Dead and the end of everybody else."

THE ACID Tests moved on, now heading south for a series of events in and around Los Angeles. That was unfamiliar territory—California, yes, but for all purposes, an entirely different state of being. It was a chance to take a look at the heart of the music business, but the Dead were already more music than business, and they hardly had a record up their sleeve, so they weren't pitching material. If the trip was meant to land a record deal, it was ill-conceived. Was it a chance to get away from the San Francisco scene, even just for a breather? Or an opportunity to evangelize the Acid Tests? Maybe. "In all honesty," Lesh wrote later, "I don't really remember."

Owsley made it possible. He was by now not just their acid supplier but an increasingly important contributor to their sound, for the simple reason that he was bankrolling it. Bear was devoted to pure sound, offended by hiss and distortion, and he dedicated his formidable, stubborn intellect to perfecting the amplification system of the Grateful Dead. The band, appreciative of his generosity if sometimes irritated by his personality, acquiesced. Their forbearance paid dividends. While in

Los Angeles, Bear rented a house for the Dead that doubled as a rehearsal space. He supplied as much LSD as the band could take and worked his magic on its sound. But his largesse came at a price: Owsley insisted on eating only meat and dairy, and he stocked the fridge with nothing else. Band members, along with assorted girlfriends, Pranksters, and guests, would sneak out for vegetables without telling Owsley, who would complain, even rage, to learn that residents had violated his "nutritional" guidelines.

The Los Angeles shows kicked off on February 6 with an Acid Test in Northridge. A *Los Angeles Free Press* account of that evening captures its joyful discombobulation: "Frightening, insane, chaotic? I suppose the answer depends on where you're at. To me, what went down was a recapture of an experience Man hasn't given himself the simple luxury of since he left his cave."

That was followed on February 12, 1966, by what became known, somewhat misleadingly, as the Watts Acid Test, since the event actually took place in a grubby warehouse in Compton. The Test got off to a rocky start, as someone took his eye off the punch and it ended up with two crowd-size doses of LSD, doubling the amount that most people ingested that night. It was that night's batch of acid that Hugh Romney, later to become known as Wavy Gravy, called "electric Kool-Aid," a phrase that came to stand for much more than just that night's punch. One young woman took so much that she was reduced to screaming "Who cares?" over and over, sadly enshrining her as the Who Cares Girl for eternity. So fried was Garcia that he is reputed not to have played at all, though he may have puttered on and off the stage.

It was after the Test concluded in the early morning hours, however, that two significant things happened. The first came during the cleanup after the show. Garcia found himself ambling around the room, absent-mindedly picking up debris and chatting with Mountain Girl, very pregnant and traveling with the Pranksters on their way to Mexico to reconnect with Kesey. She was lonely that night, a little tremulous about the future.

Garcia had reason to be out of sorts too. His marriage, just barely begun, was already ending. Sara had grown exasperated with his absences, the devotion he gave to his music in striking contrast to his neglect of his wife and young child. Distance worked mischief: He was unfaithful to her, and she was drawn to a member of the Pranksters. One night, when she was alone with Heather and their cat named Clyde, Heather finally fell asleep, and Sara dared to rush four blocks to the store—pushing an empty stroller with Clyde darting along beside her—to spend what little money she had on diapers, so that she could be ready when Heather awoke. Terrified that Heather would stir in the few minutes she was out, Sara ran as fast as she could. She returned to find Heather fine, still asleep, before dissolving with exhaustion. It was then that Sara knew she'd had enough. She spent part of the weekend discarding her husband's clothes and letters.

Jerry, meanwhile, was four hundred miles south, in a beat-up warehouse in Compton, too high to play. So it was that Garcia struck up a conversation with Mountain Girl as they swept the floors, far from home. It was, Carolyn said later, the first time she could recall a one-on-one conversation with Jerry, who until then had been at the edge of the Prankster community. She took note.

Then, when the band finally was packed up, the musicians piled into a car with their gear, and someone suggested that they swing by the Watts Towers. It was barely dawn, and Garcia was still swimming in the aftereffects of a heavy LSD trip and a long, confusing night. Suddenly before him were the perplexing structures.

The towers represent the life's work of Simon Rodia, an Italian American mason who began assembling the structures out of rebar and concrete in the 1920s and diligently added to them over a period of some thirty years. The resulting towers—the tallest tops out at almost 100 feet—are decorated with ceramics, porcelain, and glass, and form a durable expression of Rodia's painstaking work and singular vision. By 1966, the towers had survived a 1956 fire and a sustained effort by the city of Los Angeles to condemn and remove them. That morning, Garcia beheld them for the first time.

What struck Garcia in that moment was the folly, the struggle of the artist and art to become permanent, to withstand scrutiny and pressure and time. "If you work by yourself as hard as you can, every day, after you're dead you've left behind something that they can't tear down," he told an interviewer later. "I thought: That is not it for me."

In that moment, Garcia imagined an alternative vision for his own artistic expression. He would not work alone but rather with others—with a band, with an audience, as part of a community. And he would not erect an edifice but rather create an experience. "For me, it was important to be involved in something that was flowing and dynamic," Garcia said. Bob Weir distilled that idea further, if less elegantly: "Why not," Weir asked, "just have fun?"

The Acid Tests forged an identity for Garcia and the Dead that transcended their music. They established a relationship with their audience that would set the Dead apart from every other band of their era, that would help explain the band's ineffable bond with those who came to listen to them, to join them in enjoyment of the event—everyone a member of the audience but everyone a performer too. It was, Garcia said, "one of the few truly democratic art forms to appear in this century."

Over the course of the Tests, the Dead learned to listen, to feed off one another and to absorb and reflect the energy before and around them. LSD had a lot to do with that, of course, but so did the nature of the Acid Test events, with their shared sense of exploration that eroded the distinction between performer and listener. As Kesey put it, "you hear the Dead playing not just music but playing to the thing that's happening." In that sense, the Dead suggested a different energy exchange at the center of the experience: They were not a band giving energy to an audience, or even an audience reflecting it back to a band. It was a shared undertaking, art that prioritized immediacy over a more static idea of perfection, art that was fashioned by all those present, not merely those with microphones and amplifiers.

"Everybody," Garcia said, "was creating." And that became "the prototype for our whole basic trip."

As the participants in the Acid Tests veered in and out, they sometimes focused intently on the performance and other times drifted away or focused on one another. They erupted into ecstasy and sank into despair, often just a few feet from the stage. Somehow the Dead tracked and refracted all of that. "The people in the audience would know, 'Hey, they're playing this moment,'" Kesey said. "This is music that is different from any music that is being played anywhere in the world. It's changing constantly, and it's alert to what's going on."

The Dead, Kesey concluded, "were the best by far."

As for Stegner and Kesey, the rupture that split so many fathers and sons in that era—perhaps in any era—drove a deep wedge between teacher and student. It wounded both of them in ways that spoke to the larger divide under way in American culture. Kesey offended Stegner with comments in an interview, and Stegner cut him off (decades later, Stegner's official biography continued to list his most accomplished students but made no mention of Kesey). In an interview in 1993, Kesey acknowledged their break and said, his hurt on full display, "I read that he had said he found me to be ineducable."

Stegner recorded his thoughts as he usually did, fictionalizing events and expressing himself through his characters. And from that fictionalization emerges a glimpse of something bigger—the early implication of how what would become known as the counterculture would affect those outside it.

Later, in 1967, after the Acid Tests had run their course, after they had spun off the Grateful Dead and transformed Kesey from novelist to cultural emissary, Stegner put down his complicated response in a novel, *All the Little Live Things*. It is one of Stegner's saddest, most conflicted works, pitting a grouchy, retired literary agent, Joe Allston, against a hippie interloper, Jim Peck, who muscles his way onto Allston's land and into Allston's life. The elder man acquiesces to Peck's squatting on his property, resenting Peck and envying him at once.

When Allston and Peck first meet, the older man is struck by the younger man's stench, his motorcycle, but also "eyes which were brilliant and speculative." Allston imagines that Peck's saddlebags are full of books and fantasizes the full hippie collection: "Alan Watts on Zen

THE ACID TESTS | 85

snuggled up against Kierkegaard, Eugene Goodheart, Norman Brown, and Paul Goodman and maybe the hallelujah autobiography of Woody Guthrie. And a copy of *Playboy*."

Allston and Peck lock in an increasingly strained standoff, Peck converting a corner of the property into a campsite, then constructing a tree house, making noise, building campfires, generally ignoring Allston's attempt to enforce any rules. Meanwhile, their neighbor—a captivating pregnant mother named Marian Catlin—valiantly battles cancer, hoping to live long enough for her baby to be born safely.

Allston falls in love—the platonic and tender love of an older man for a brave, beautiful young woman—and when Catlin dies, Allston's despair curdles to glowering bitterness against Peck. Only then does Allston eject Peck from the property. In the stunned aftermath, Allston considers the course of events and describes them in language that could only draw upon Stegner's own heart and experience, his worried realization that the future, with all its flaws, was now at hand: "I disliked Peck because of his addiction to the irrational, and I still do," Allston notes. "But what made him hard for me to bear was my own foolishness made manifest in him."

The heat of the mid-1960s created collisions of all types.

Above: Jerry and Mountain Girl. Palo Alto, 1967.
Ron Rakow/Retro Photo Archive

Below: Demonstrators and police. San Francisco, 1967.
Elizabeth Sunflower/Retro Photo Archive

CHAPTER 5

Forces Collide

IT IS FREQUENTLY THE CASE THAT CULTURAL AND POLITICAL movements emerge, thrive for a while, and then produce backlash. Jim Crow can be seen as a response to the end of slavery, and civil rights to Jim Crow; the Moral Majority to *Roe v. Wade;* Donald Trump and "Make America Great Again" to Barack Obama and "Yes, We Can." Sometimes the backlash is long in coming, while other times it arrives quickly. In the case of the American 1960s, the backlash came even before the movement understood itself, even before it knew what it was. Over the course of one year, 1966, a new notion began to take shape and an old idea rose up to push the new back down—or at least to try.

The Acid Tests and their offspring were the new. They represented a suite of ideas—experimentation and improvisation; culture wrapped around politics; communalism and joy; drugs, sex, music, love; restless values in rebellion—against what, they did not quite yet know. The backlash came from discomfited adults, and it gravitated to the candidacy of one man in particular: Ronald Reagan. As the Acid Tests darted across California in 1966, Reagan ran for governor. The two campaigns, one improvised, the other studiously deliberate, circled each other, competing for adherents.

As the year opened, the Dead were returning to San Francisco. Reagan, after months of traveling the state, officially entered its politics.

"Ronald Reagan and A Need for Action!" the opening banner announced in the film released first to the California press on January 3 and then to the public on January 4. It included an exclamation point, but the presentation that followed was deliberately muted, a stern appeal from a reassuring man. Reagan was concerned about the condition of California, which had been reliably Republican, only to have riots and hippies put that history to the test. Now, Reagan was also here to make the case for old values, to make things right again. Old California was pioneers and visionaries, panners for gold, makers of movies. New California was rioters in Watts, spoiled kids at Berkeley, and drug parties featuring the Grateful Dead.

Reagan was the picture of conservative values. He strolled around his polished living room, complete with leather chairs and brass lamps, a grandfather clock next to a fireplace where a fire burned. Speaking directly into the camera, Reagan was poised and forceful but hardly alarmist. Yes, he was announcing his intention to depose California's incumbent governor, the garrulous and personable Pat Brown, but Reagan never mentioned Brown by name. His criticisms of "the executive branch" were severe but never mean.

When it came to discussing the children of the state, Reagan's demeanor noticeably hardened. It had taken effort and money, Reagan noted, for California to build a "great university," but that was not enough. "It takes more than dollars and stately buildings," he said, one hand on one of those leather chairs, the other in his pocket. "Or do we no longer think it necessary to teach self-respect, self-discipline, and respect for law and order? Will we allow a great university to be brought to its knees by a noisy, dissident minority? Will we meet their neurotic vulgarities with vacillation and weakness, or will we tell those entrusted with administering the university we expect them to enforce a code based on decency, common sense, and dedication to the high and noble purpose of that university; that they will have the full support of all of us as long as they do this, but we'll settle for nothing less?"

For Reagan, this was an appealing political situation. The reports from Berkeley were, at least to those of Reagan's generation and sensibilities, alarming. Radicals had somehow gained a foothold, outwitting their elders in an argument over what constituted learning, contesting even such notions as freedom and citizenship. Reagan's central argument was that California was being mismanaged by soft leaders. Parents wondered about the taxes they paid to send their students off to the nation's greatest public university system, only to have that system become a cradle of incivility and rebellion. Reagan understood. He pounded the university, knowing that it was the pride of his opponent.

Reagan entered the contest with other political winds at his back, notably in California's frayed race relations and growing white discontent with black demands for justice. The Watts riots back in 1965, still smoldering in California politics, were the other pillar of that case.

Those riots had begun shortly after 7 P.M. on August 11, 1965, when two California Highway Patrol officers pulled over Marquette Frye, a twenty-one-year-old black man suspected of drunk driving in Watts, a neighborhood south of downtown Los Angeles. The officers pulled Frye's car to a stop not far from his house. As they put Frye through sobriety tests, his mother and brother saw what was happening and defended him, loudly arguing with the officers. A crowd began to gather, and when the CHP took Ronald and Rena Frye into custody, the situation devolved. Within hours, a thousand people were in the streets, wrangling with police through the night.

That was just the beginning, a "prelude to Act I of a terrible tragedy," as the Los Angeles Times put it. Over the next two days, thirty-four people died as violence spread outward from Watts and throughout south L.A. Racism, redlining, police brutality, the grinding effects of poverty, all simmered beneath the surface of the riots, but polls afterward showed that white Americans overwhelmingly believed "that the riots were started and carried out by irresponsible Negroes." Those sentiments—resentment that blacks did not appreciate California's efforts at desegregation, anger that blacks would resort to violence—suggested a core of white discontent. Black activists would find common ground with the nascent counterculture. Whites, bewildered and self-righteous, would find their way to Reagan.

As Reagan well knew, Brown was vulnerable on both the events at Berkeley and the riots. The university was Brown's most beloved contribution to California, and he was conspicuously absent for Watts, vacationing in Greece when the riots broke out, so every reminder of the riots was a new reiteration of the charge that he was missing when it mattered. And that was, after all, Reagan's larger, only vaguely subtextual point: that adults had fled the scene, that teenagers—or blacks— were running wild.

Proof of that were the Acid Tests. The sight of young people, high on God knows what, dressed in weird clothes, their hair long and unwashed, resurfaced old images of *Reefer Madness* and disreputable Beatniks; it was enough to unsettle the most complacent parent. They seemed of a piece with protest and riots—part of the mounting sense that something was slipping away, some shared commitment to order, to American values. Something new was afoot, and to them it did not seem good. It felt to some like communism, not because most Americans knew much about communism but because, like communism, this new force, this growing energy, was threatening, subversive. People—voters—were afraid.

Reagan reminded them that they hadn't always felt this fear, that they had a right to security. These were *their* children in these schools. How could they sit still as their own children rejected their values? It was so obviously wrong, and surely it could not be their fault. They worked hard, paid to build the colleges that now threw their intellectual superiority back in their faces, paid for the social programs meant to show that they cared about blacks, who now rioted in response. How dare they? Reagan assured them that it was not their fault, that others— drug dealers, well-intentioned but misguided leaders, yes, even communists—were behind this unrest, and that he would tend to it.

As Reagan stalked Pat Brown, Garcia responded with what looked like indifference. Reagan denounced drugs and young misfits; Garcia and the Dead dropped acid and performed, every bit the misfits that Reagan made them out to be. Through the winter and spring of 1966, they moved up and down the coast, crisscrossing Reagan's campaign and ignoring the candidate's challenge to everything they stood for.

The Dead, as has often been noted, were not political, at least not in the sense in which we are accustomed to considering politics. They did not endorse Pat Brown or appear at benefits for him. They did not raise money for candidates or try to turn out young voters. But that defines politics too narrowly. These were inherently political days. Culture and politics swirled together. Getting high was political. Dancing was political. An Acid Test was an evening of fun and experimentation but, importantly, also an act of defiance. If one considers politics broadly—as protest, as the clash of values and ways of living—the Dead were at the center of California politics in 1966.

"In 1966, the world, and especially California, was changing fast," Robert Stone, a friend of the Pranksters, wrote. "The change was actually visible on the streets of San Francisco, at places like the Fillmore and the Avalon Ballroom. Political and social institutions were so lacking in humor and self-confidence that they crumbled at a wisecrack."

What was the Trips Festival but a wisecrack?

Kesey, then the artist most associated with the literature of experimentation, watched all this at first from afar. Having faked his suicide and hightailed it out of the country, he was hiding out in Mexico. Not many people had bought his suicide note, and the FBI was looking for him. He knew better than to poke his head over the fence. Instead, Kesey quietly sent word of his aliveness to the Pranksters, and in early March, Babbs led the Prankster contingent in Los Angeles on a journey south, decamping for "the edge of the world, poor and beautiful beyond belief." Mountain Girl came along too.

The FBI put out its feelers. On March 9, an informant told American authorities that Kesey had been frequenting a coffeehouse in the Puerto Vallarta area a week earlier. That sighting was confirmed by another informant, who said he'd seen Kesey twice in the area and that Kesey was living twelve miles outside town in a place he was calling Marijuana City. Kesey's friends and family were warned of the punishments for harboring a fugitive, but they didn't crack. Kesey's father said he was bewildered by his son's actions but did not know where he was. Babbs's estranged wife indicated that she believed him to be living back east, but the FBI clearly had its doubts. "Mrs. Babbs," one agent wrote, "was very evasive in her answers and is a 'beatnik.'"

92 | HERE BESIDE THE RISING TIDE

Kesey was content to hide out for now. For Mountain Girl, the situation was more complicated. She still faced the marijuana charges stemming from her rooftop arrest in January, and she was now seven months pregnant. So she returned to make her court date. Her lawyer pleaded that Mountain Girl's only addiction was "a perennial overdose of solicitude for persons who are far away." She was barely twenty, and the judge looked kindly on her. On March 22, he fined her $250 and sent her on her way. She promptly headed back to Mexico, where she gave birth to a little girl she named Sunshine. Kesey was the father, and his wife, Faye, was reluctantly accepting—these were the "no rules, good-time sixties," as Sunshine later said. Prankster George Walker agreed to be listed as the father on Sunshine's birth certificate.

AND THEN there was the war. On March 25, 1966, the Vietnam Day Committee sponsored events in San Francisco and Berkeley to express opposition to the war in Vietnam, where the ever-mounting conflict provided an energizing focus of dissatisfaction. Headlines that month announced a significant landing of Marines at the mouth of the Saigon River, where they established a six-mile beachhead without any significant enemy opposition. The war expanded. So did opposition.

It was Charter Day at UC Berkeley. Arthur Goldberg, the former Supreme Court justice whom President Johnson had persuaded to leave the court to take over the United Nations ambassadorship, was on campus to speak to students. Protesters had threatened to disrupt the ambassador's address, but a meeting of activists and sponsors of Goldberg's appearance struck a truce and their agreement held: A thousand to fifteen hundred students silently rose and departed when Goldberg was presented with an honorary degree; later, when called upon to register their views, about a thousand stood in support of the war, while seven thousand rose to oppose it. Goldberg was allowed to speak without interruption. Across the Bay, three thousand demonstrators marched down Market Street in San Francisco, bearing caskets draped with American flags.

The day of protests wound down toward an evening event—a "dance" sponsored by the Vietnam Day Committee in UC Berkeley's Harmon Gymnasium. The event was billed as a Peace Trip, an imitation Acid Test, though a powerful knock-off. Jefferson Airplane, then the biggest of the San Francisco bands, anchored the event, which featured the audiovisual stimulation that was the hallmark of the Tests so far. Flowers and a peace sign graced the flyer advertising the dance, which promised "flicks" and "magic lights."

The dance that night—and the reaction to it—cleaved California into camps. For hippies and peace activists, it went exactly as hoped. Loud, long music filled the gym until all hours. It was a place to unwind and connect after a day of registering outrage at the war, a chance to experiment with rebellion on a different level, a night of fun.

For Reagan, it was an outrage. Speaking at the Cow Palace in South San Francisco on May 12, Reagan delivered an address entitled "The Morality Gap at Berkeley." Introduced by the actor Chuck Connors and speaking to an adoring crowd, Reagan was in high dudgeon. He was mad about a lot in that campaign, but on this occasion, Reagan was particularly incensed by what he had learned of the Vietnam Day dance. "The incidents are so bad," he said, "so contrary to our standards of human behavior, that I couldn't possibly recite them to you here from this platform in detail, but there is clear evidence that there were things that shouldn't be permitted on a university campus."

This, Reagan emphasized, had been building for some time. The Free Speech Movement had blasted through tradition and authority, and it had led the way downward, coming to rest in the anarchy of the Vietnam Day escapade. As Reagan put it, "It began a year ago, when the so-called free speech advocates, who in truth have no appreciation for freedom, were allowed to assault and humiliate the symbol of law and order, a policeman on the campus. And that was the moment when the ringleaders should have been taken by the scruff of the neck and thrown out of the university once and for all."

The Cow Palace crowd loved that. It began clapping at the words "by the scruff of the neck" and was in full, enthusiastic support when Reagan demanded that the ruffians be expelled.

The Dead were not present for Vietnam Day, but it's safe to say they would have enjoyed it more than Reagan did. The band was still in Los Angeles, and on the night of the twenty-fifth they performed at Trouper's Hall. There, Pigpen enjoyed a signature evening, playing loud and forward on his Vox organ. The show featured Garcia in a background role, leaning into long, speedy guitar riffs on "Hey Little One" and "You Don't Have to Ask" and sly vocals on "I'm a Hog for You, Baby," as well as an early appearance of "Cold Rain and Snow," which found its way into the Dead's lineup in 1966 and never left it.

Two weeks after Vietnam Day, the Dead came back to San Francisco. Their months in Los Angeles had helped them as a band—they'd learned more songs, practiced together, performed for and with audiences— and they'd picked up a pair of managers as well: Rock Scully and Danny Rifkin, friends from San Francisco State whose early work for the Dead was passing out flyers in Los Angeles to drum up audiences for the band's performances in the still foreign territory of L.A. Both new to the business of managing a band—and tasked with the special challenges of managing a band as loosely organized and improvisational as the Dead were in those early days—they, too, improvised. Gradually, they fell into natural roles: Scully was the smooth talker and salesman; Rifkin, a sentimentalist with a gruff affect, would play the tough guy. It worked.

The Dead's growing prowess included the rapid expansion of their musical repertoire—the first steps of what would become their unrivaled songlist. At the beginning of 1966, the band's list of songs featured a few staples and several that they were trying out. Some would not last long: "Sick and Tired" and "Parchman Farm," for instance, got brief runs but were then dropped. By contrast, "Death Don't Have No Mercy," "I Know You Rider," and "In the Midnight Hour" each found a regular spot in the band's performances. Of them, "I Know You Rider" would express the Dead across the ages. The band first performed the number in 1965 and last played it in 1995, more than five hundred known live performances later. An old blues number of uncertain authorship, "I Know You Rider" began for the Dead with a pop feel—it had a peppy tone on the first known recording of the Warlocks, in November 1965—but it deepened over the years, with Garcia and Weir defining their vocal parts and Garcia building in a gentle guitar solo behind one of Weir's verses. What began in the 1960s as a boisterous pop take on an old blues piece would live as a powerful connector between band and audience, highlighted by the changing inflections of one verse, in which Garcia sang, "I wish I was a headlight / on a northbound train," delivered some nights with ebullience, other times with longing and even regret. "I'd shine my light," Garcia sang, "through the cool Colorado rain."

Meanwhile, "Good Lovin'," originally performed by the Olympics and popularized by the Rascals in 1966, caught the Dead's ear and jumped immediately into the band's lineup. The supremely danceable number was part of the Warlocks' sets at Magoo's Pizza Parlor in May 1965; it got an airing at the Big Beat Acid Test that December, and it was rarely out of rotation in the decades to come. And "Viola Lee Blues," an open-ended blues number by the songwriter and harmonica player Noah Lewis, who recorded the song with Cannon's Jug Stompers in the late 1920s, offered the Dead some of its longest, more experimental solo opportunities, with Garcia filling the role that Lewis's harmonica had long ago occupied.

The year had opened with an addition to the Dead's lineup that both highlighted Garcia's appreciation for the larger musical scene and hinted at what was to come. The Dead were booked at the Matrix Club in San Francisco for the nights of January 4–7 (a handbill for the gig advertises performances on the fourth and fifth, and setlists survive for the following two nights). Located on Fillmore Street, the Matrix was small and dimly lit and, in its early years, mainly known as the home of the Jefferson Airplane, in part because one of the club's owners was Marty Balin of the Airplane. For those January shows, the Dead took the stage, as usual, with only a rough idea of what they would perform, but the show one evening featured its debut presentation of "It's All Over Now, Baby Blue," written and recorded a year earlier by Bob Dylan. It was, Garcia said, "one of the prettiest things I'd ever heard."

The Dead's early interpretation approached Dylan's piece as an up-tempo bit, with Garcia cheerfully pumping out the Dylanesque rhymes over Kreutzmann's drums and Pigpen's organ. As the song matured in the Dead's hands, its moodier aspects would come forward, but the 1966 take was a crisp five-minute version. And with it, the Dead's work at interpreting Dylan, and the overlapping legacy of those two musical spirits, was launched—a golden spike of musical enterprises from opposite coasts but complementary ambitions. In the years to come, Dylan would supply the Dead with some of the group's most soulful and thought-provoking material. Robert Hunter delivered most of his lyrics to Garcia but also contributed to Dylan, and the Dead would help revive Dylan's career when it flagged in the 1980s. Long after Garcia died, Dylan would remain a faithful evangelist of the Dead's music. In the summer of 2023, Dylan surprised European audiences by delivering a rich, pensive rendition of the classic Hunter-Garcia ballad "Stella Blue." He performed it on the anniversary of Hunter's birth.

THOMAS PYNCHON published his second novel in 1966, the enthusiastically anticipated follow-up to his extraordinary debut, *V.* His second work, *The Crying of Lot 49,* was a trimmer tale, more of a television episode compared to the epic film that was *V.*

The Crying of Lot 49 is set in the nether regions of California politics and culture, poking at the movements and trends of the state at midcentury. Full of Pynchon's elaborate and byzantine turns, the novel is riven with mystery, foreboding, and revelation. Much of it takes place near San Narciso, a fictional California town near Los Angeles whose description reveals Pynchon's understanding of this landscape, "less an identifiable city than a grouping of concepts—census tracts, special purpose bond issue districts, shopping nuclei, all overlaid with access roads to its own freeway." Arriving in San Narciso, the central character, Oedipa Maas, perceives that she is at the precipice of revelation, one that "trembled just past the threshold of her understanding."

As she pursues Trystero, an ancient and shadowy postal service that threatens governments and social order (for reasons not quite clear), Oedipa follows clues up and down the state, glimpsing the post in its symbology and its durability. She debates the tension between individual invention and "teamwork . . . a symptom of the gutlessness of the whole society." She finds strange symbols on bathroom walls. She wanders the streets of Berkeley, where she secures a rare book from a Shattuck Avenue press, and she drifts through the scene of the campus's recent conflicts. "She came downslope from Wheeler Hall, through Sather Gate into a plaza teeming with corduroy, denim, bare legs, blonde hair, horn-rims, bicycle spokes in the sun, bookbags, swaying card tables, long paper petitions dangling to earth, posters for indecipherable FSM's, YAF's, VDC's, suds in the fountain, students in nose-to-nose dialogue." FSM's, of course, referred to the Free Speech Movement, YAF's to Young Americans for Freedom, and VDC's to the Vietnam Day Committee. Such were the crumbs that Pynchon scattered for diligent readers.

If Pynchon's most widely read novel—it is so, almost certainly, because it is his shortest and thus the one most often assigned to college students—was grounded in California as a place, it captured California's strange, elusive, combative sensibility at that moment in history. *The Crying of Lot 49* reeks with ominous portent, the chaos of drugs and the flaring of violence, the throbbing presence of deeper meaning, presented in symbols and whispers.

Bright, flourishing, inviting, elusive, dangerous: California, 1966.

THE DEAD'S work in 1966 was an expression of musical ambition and curiosity. It was also, perhaps less obviously, an experiment in freedom. As the band built the most eclectic musical signature in all of popular music, it followed its own tastes, largely free of the constraints of the music business or even its audience. It was a grand musical exploration by a band with little to confine it. They traveled light, played loud. They were free.

It was tempting to think of Garcia's brand of freedom as nothing more than license—the freedom to do whatever one wanted at any moment. To play and only to play. And yet that's not the case for freedom in music, which relies on structure and builds on tradition; the Dead were pushing the edges of tradition, but they were also a band grounded in blues and folk and bluegrass, each genre with its demands and histories. Garcia's interviews also could give the impression that he was simply in it for the fun, but his public expressions of mirth and self-deprecation occasionally receded. "There's been a lie about what freedom is," he told one set of interviewers, "and the big lie is that freedom means absolutely and utterly free, and it really doesn't mean anything of the sort."

Rather, Garcia understood that freedom came with responsibility, though he himself wrestled mightily with the obligations of duty—of family and parenthood, for starters. And yet he recognized the weakness of recklessness, even as he struggled to apply those ideas to himself. "For any scene to work," he said, "along with freedom there's implicit responsibility—you have to be doing something somewhere along the line—there is no free ride."

Although Garcia related freedom to responsibility, he considered those ideas outside the realm of politics. With his consciousness focused on questions of connection—that sense of interrelationship that courses through Buddhism and the I Ching, both of which caught Garcia's attention at various times, not to mention the experience of LSD—politics could strike Garcia as woefully irrelevant. He deplored the politics of war and Reagan, but also resisted the bossiness of the left. Garcia was determined to live his own way, not to obey the edicts of others, whether the stultifying cultural demands of the mainstream or the didactic orders of Bay Area radicals.

Still, he was aware of those forces, if only to resist them. Discussing politics with Charles Reich, the Yale professor whose writings on the environment and politics would give the period one of its most distinguished voices, Garcia framed politics in those terms—connection and balance. "Things have to get worse before they get better," he said. "I'm of that school of thought . . . the one where one side balances out another.

"You remember in the Fifties when things were kind of in the center," Garcia went on. "It's swinging over this way. And in the Fifties, it's in the middle somewhere. Sixties, swinging over this way. . . . It's operating in unison with the universe." The sense of "operation," of history in motion rather than the codifying of ideas, of experience rather than edifice, further amplified Garcia's sense of freedom: It was not an idea to be constructed or words to be hammered over. Freedom, lashed to the pendulum of historical progress, was to be experienced. Freedom was an experience, an Acid Test, not a structure, not the Watts Tower.

Not coincidentally, the quest for freedom became paradigmatically the ambition of the hippies and activists then finding their way as well. Some sought to change minds or politics or habits; others simply set off on their own and charted new ways of participating or surviving. That, too, tapped a profound determination to be free—free to live together according to rules adopted and accepted in small groups, in communes, in tribes.

It is worth noting, then, that some of the same impulse was at work in the other captivating California story of 1966. For Reagan's campaign was about freedom too. Reagan's invocation of freedom—his insistence that he understood freedom in a way that the blacks and the hippies and the radical students did not—cut to the heart of his thesis. The free speech advocates at Berkeley, in Reagan's view, had "no appreciation for freedom." To Reagan, hippies who found freedom in music or drugs were deranged or depraved, not enlightened. Reagan sought freedom from government too, but he found it in order, not in experimentation.

What, then, did freedom mean? Was it a positive right to explore or a negative protection against interference? Was it simply the right to experiment with drugs? Did it necessarily require some sense of duty to others? Or was freedom better understood as the right to attend a university without disruption? Or to protect a particular version of democracy or capitalism in Vietnam? Garcia and Reagan were using the same words, juggling the same ideas, and they sometimes found common quarter—in the notion of responsibility, for example—though that realization would have horrified both of them. For the most part, they were divided by their common language, championing "freedom" but signifying very

100 | HERE BESIDE THE RISING TIDE

different things by that word. The sparring over freedom between Reagan and the young left that began in the spring of 1966 would continue for decades—after Reagan rose to national prominence and the forces against him coalesced, fell apart, and regrouped under the umbrella of the Dead. Ronald Reagan and Jerry Garcia would take their fight from California to Washington and beyond. In a sense, they are fighting it still.

REAGAN'S BELLICOSE denunciations of hippies and antiwar activists and ungrateful blacks had precisely the desired political effect. He had entered the Republican primary as an underdog challenger to George Christopher, a moderate Republican with a solid record as mayor of San Francisco. But Reagan, aided by an intelligent campaign team and a restive California, chipped away. Christopher, in turn, was hobbled by the state GOP's acceptance of the so-called Eleventh Commandment, which prohibited—or at least discouraged—Republican candidates from speaking ill of one another. That left Christopher hamstrung when he fell behind Reagan and could not muster a reply without seeming to violate the norms of state Republican politics. By June, Reagan's momentum was unmistakable, and the results of the primary confirmed it. Reagan won nearly two-thirds of all Republican votes, polling better in his primary than Brown did in his.

Reagan did that without the support of young people. To many of them, Reagan represented the Vietnam War and the draft, both of which he wholeheartedly supported. He stood for stifled impulses and silence, stuffed leather chairs and fireplaces. He was on the side of repression and coercion. He was death. And the Dead, the name notwithstanding, stood merrily in contrast. "The music they played was so full of fun—*life!*" said Dan Wilson, a young man who attended a Dead show that year. "And I was worried already about the Army and the Vietnam War, and that was so dreary—it's death. And here was the Grateful Dead, just the opposite."

To prove the point, the Dead briefly decamped for Marin County, where they found a place to rent, an old mansion and property known as Olompali. They arrived in full entourage, reestablishing the group home they'd shared in Los Angeles. Jerry and Sara were apart by then, so he was solo. Kreutzmann, by contrast, was married, with a young daughter, so he got the best bedroom to share with his young family. Phil and his girlfriend, Rosie McGee, snagged another. This merry band settled into a historic property (it's now a state park) amid the spirits of ancient Native Americans.

Set in the rolling hills, Irish green in the spring when the Dead arrived, turned to gold and gray by summer, Olompali featured a swimming pool and a stately, twisted California live oak. The move-in itself marked a transition for the band. Owsley, accustomed by then to dominating in band matters—he was, after all, paying for much of it—claimed the biggest bedroom for himself but was overruled.

Olompali was a picture-perfect location to regroup, to simmer in the company of community and, as it turned out, in the history of California itself. It sat on land once occupied by Miwok Indians and was the site of the only battle in California's short-lived war of independence, the Bear Flag Revolt, which pitted a few dozen "American Bear Flaggers" against a small contingent of Mexican forces in the Battle of Olompali on June 24, 1846. The two sides shot at each other across long distances. One Mexican soldier was killed, and a few men on each side were wounded. That was the extent of the revolt, which evaporated when the United States declared war on Mexico, seized the territory, and, once gold was discovered, eagerly granted California statehood.

History oozed from the Dead's new home. High on acid, Garcia communed with the Indian spirits that wafted through the house and land. One afternoon, Scully found Garcia moving from the oak tree to the basement of the house, imagining himself being chastised by the spirits as the descendant of conquistadors. The party continued outside as Garcia, overwhelmed with guilt, hid beneath the dining room table. "The living and the dead mingle," Scully wrote. "It's hard to tell which is which."

The Dead's brief time at their storied rental property was blissful in part because they were together, communally, and apart, physically and psychologically removed from the main currents of society, from Reagan and Vietnam and Watts. The members of the Dead ventured forth for shows and then returned to Olompali, where they played host to a springtime house party—music on the lawn, men and women frolicking naked in the pool, connecting to history and spiritual vibes through the presence of the oak. Olompali was the getaway for the participants in San Francisco's coalescing musical scene. Grace Slick hung out by the pool, Janis Joplin lounged in the shade of an oak.

One teenage boy came to Olompali that summer in the company of his mom, and he gravitated to the musical instruments set up near the pool. He played the harmonica a bit, picked up some appreciative nods and suddenly realized he was naked. Glancing down at himself, he stopped playing the harp and melted back into the crowd, as seamless a transition from performer to audience as any could be. The experience never left little Huey Lewis.

OLOMPALI WAS a brief stop for the Dead, but it also tapped into a larger movement. California in the 1960s recaptured a bit of its native history by refashioning tribal living into the commune.

Drawn by their own version of separatism, groups of young people gathered in communities—some within cities, more often in the country—to connect to the land and one another, to reject what they saw as the stifling restrictions of mainstream culture. Most of these communities were scattered across the redwood forests and glens of northern California, but one of the first was the Hog Farm, founded by Hugh Romney (known as Wavy Gravy) in North Hollywood. At about the same time, Lou Gottlieb, a folk musician who created the Limeliters trio, used his music earnings to buy an egg farm near Occidental, an hour north of San Francisco. He opened the property to guests in 1965; it became known as Morning Star, and it survived as one of the longest-standing communal properties in California.

Others followed. The Friends of Perfection in San Francisco, Table Mountain Ranch in Mendocino, Struggle Mountain in Los Altos, Black Mountain and the Land in the Santa Cruz Mountains, Free Family in Olema. By the mid-1970s, these outposts would dot the land of California as delicately as had those of native peoples hundreds of years earlier. In that, Olompali was both heir to one history and leading edge of another. It was a community of searching souls, separate from society and a society unto itself. And though it was not precisely political, it refracted politics into a larger sense of self, connecting humans to one another and communities to the land.

Communalists would have their day, demonstrating that, to some, freedom and fulfillment were best achieved as part of something larger, not as a mere individual experience. Communal living was not easy, requiring "time, patience, and practice to resolve obstacles and create habitual responses that were based on community well-being rather than merely personal preference," Peter Coyote observed. There was a lot of chopping wood and fetching water. And once children were born, they focused the attention on the frailties of loose compacts and understandings. Indeed, the idyll of Olompali was nearly shattered one day when a child wandered off and fell into the pool, unnoticed at first in the melee of activity. Garcia helped rescue the youngster, but it took him back, briefly but shockingly, to the 1947 death of his father in the waters of the Trinity River. Drowning and the fear of it would never quite leave Garcia.

But communal living also highlighted such values as humility and coexistence. Some of those values found easy purchase in the 1960s, then dropped away for a time, resurfacing in yet another form once the home computer and internet presented another iteration of community. That iteration of freedom and its relationship to community would also revolve around the Grateful Dead and its followers.

Reagan was, of course, the opposite of communalism in all respects. He valued individualism and scorned collective action. He saw the land as something to dominate, not to revere. Speaking to the Western Wood Products Association, Reagan clarified the limits of his regard for wild things: "We've got to recognize that where the preservation of a natural resource like the redwoods is concerned, that there is a commonsense limit. I mean, if you've looked at a hundred thousand acres or so of trees— you know, a tree is a tree, how many more do you need to look at?"

Was living at Olompali a political act? Certainly not, at least in the conventional sense. The Dead did not drop acid or move to Marin County in order to support Pat Brown or oppose Ronald Reagan; they found a place to rent and enjoyed their time living there. And yet they lived there communally and so joined a movement of those doing the same. Lesh recalled the smell of barbecue, the naked people in the pool, the bright summer sun—"a true synergy of spontaneity and structure, created on the spot." The Dead's "commune," its Olompali sojourn, connected them to the larger communal movement, with all its manifold political implications.

"Politics belong[s] to a middle-aged, whiskey-drinking group," one writer noted after spending a Sunday afternoon at Olompali. "The new politics, which excludes civil rights marches and Viet Nam demonstrations, since these are within the framework, grows from a new psyche. Create a new people and inevitabl[y] the Johnsons, Nixons and Kennedys can be seen to belong to an age of unenlightenment. A new purity of insight as well as sensation is a consequence of a 'trip,' however mild, on LSD."

As for the day's music, the writer added: "The Dead assaulted the senses."

COMMUNITY EXTENDED not just to place—Olompali—but to the relationship between San Francisco's young bands, together sometimes misleadingly called the San Francisco Sound—misleading because they presented an array of musical styles and genres and are perhaps better thought of as a San Francisco Scene. The first to achieve real status were the Charlatans, whose Victorian garb helped establish hippie fashion. Next were the Great Society and the Airplane. Then, in a rush, came the Dead, Quicksilver Messenger Service, Big Brother and the Holding Company, and a host of others, many short-lived. To a remarkable degree, those bands saw themselves as part of a larger community, far more cooperative than competitive.

They supported one another, advised one another on musical styles and approaches. Garcia lent his talents freely. The Airplane's sophomore and breakthrough album, *Surrealistic Pillow,* would be released in early 1967, and Garcia was a major, if largely uncredited, contributor. His guitar work was featured prominently on four of the album's tracks—"How Do You Feel," "Today," "Plastic Fantastic Lover," and "Coming Back to Me"—and he contributed arrangements, acoustic guitar licks, and guidance throughout, interceding between the Airplane and the album's producer, Dave Hassinger. Even the title was said to have been his idea. In deference to his contract with Warner Bros., which prohibited him from recording with RCA, he was neither paid nor directly acknowledged for those contributions. On the album, he is credited as the Airplane's "Musical and Spiritual Adviser." Cooperation among bands made sense, Garcia said in an interview at Olompali, because the musicians all were working to discover new possibilities. The San Francisco scene was, as Garcia put it, all "a huge band. . . . We all play together in various combinations."

The bands abhorred the notion that they were part of an industry and preferred instead to think of themselves as an extended family. There was irony in that: Garcia never tended much to his biological family. Neither the Grateful Dead nor his extended Olompali "family" included his wife and daughter, living less than fifty miles away on the San Francisco Peninsula. But Garcia craved connection, and Olompali, as well as the San Francisco scene, supplied it.

If 1966 marked a year of growth for the Dead, it also supplied reminders that there was plenty of growing yet to do. In July, the Dead traveled to Vancouver for the British Columbia Trips Festival, a knock-off of the San Francisco scene in an area where it had yet to really catch on. The Dead headed north with anticipation, but things went wrong from the beginning. They were hassled at the border and almost late for their appearance. When the band was introduced on the night of July 29, the announcer declared with bravado: "The Grateful Dead!" Not a single person clapped.

106 | HERE BESIDE THE RISING TIDE

* * *

THE DEAD'S time at Olompali was brief. It came to an end when summer drew to a close and the lease expired. It was time to move, and San Francisco beckoned. In September, the band and their associated family closed up the mansion and kicked around for a bit before trickling into a house in the heart of Haight-Ashbury in the city. Near the panhandle of Golden Gate Park, it was located at 710 Ashbury Street. Tall and narrow, clad in white clapboard, the house was typical of the Victorians that gave the Haight its visual character.

A short flight of stairs led up to the front door. As you entered, the kitchen was to the right and a dining area to the left. Stairs inside led to the bedrooms, which various band members claimed along with their loved ones. Garcia took a room at the top of the stairs. Scully and his girlfriend, Tangerine, took another room, but she soon fled for cleaner quarters. Danny Rifkin had a spot. Many people came and went, some sleeping on the floor or in a chair.

Garcia, still just twenty-four, briefly reached out to his wife, thinking that perhaps his new place, a house in San Francisco rather than the temporary quarters at Olompali, might provide a suitable place for them to reunite and raise their daughter, Heather, then three years old. Sara visited but could not envision a life there together. "It wasn't a place I could do family," she said. "Although we both felt the pull to get back together, it just didn't seem like it would work." That was their last attempt at reconciliation. Their lives would intersect—Sara was there for the death of Jerry's mother in 1970, and Garcia resumed his relationship with Heather in the 1980s—but they lived entirely apart from that point forward.

Before the friendlier fans in San Francisco, the Dead recovered from their disappointing Vancouver gigs and got to work. They played the opening of a new ski store, the North Face, in San Francisco's North Beach. STILL HOT, BUT SKI NUTS OUT, the *Chronicle* reported, and though it misspelled the band's name—"Greatful Dead" would haunt them for years—it captured the weirdness of the affair. The shop, founded by a pair of mountaineers on a spot "150 feet above sea level," catered to the well-to-do ski crowd but was located next door to the Condor Club, the notorious San Francisco strip club where Carol Doda made her name as the "pioneer of topless entertainment." The opening attracted skiers and hippies as only San Francisco could. "People were dancing wildly amid the ski equipment displays," the *Chronicle* reporter wrote. "And what a collection of people. There were nattily dressed individuals rubbing shoulders with bearded, long-haired and sandal-clad beatniks from the neighborhood."

Until that fall, announcements of musical happenings around the Bay Area had almost always begun with the Jefferson Airplane. The Dead were lucky to get mentions in the major papers, and when they did, it was farther down in columns featuring the work of others. That began to change once the Dead were in the Haight. It was Pigpen who first won critical superlatives. Writing in September, the influential music critic Ralph Gleason of the *San Francisco Chronicle* pointed to greatness in the reluctant young front man. "He is one of the best blues singers of his generation," Gleason wrote. "Sunday night's performance was surely the equal even of the Mick Jagger vocal on 'Going Home.'"

The Dead's first record, known as the Scorpio Single, featured "Stealin'" on the A side and "Don't Ease Me In" on the B side. It was a rough production, recorded in a converted Victorian next to Buena Vista Park in the Haight. Only some 150 copies were pressed and distributed, almost entirely in San Francisco, so the record made scarcely a splash, but it captured a moment—a fleeting one, as it would turn out—in which Garcia was "less of a presence than Pig."

THE FINAL weeks of the political contest were close and testy. Brown simultaneously poked at Reagan's inexperience—if voters would be wary of having surgery from a "citizen-doctor" or flying on a plane under the command of "citizen-pilot," Brown offered, they might consider the implications of having their state run by a "citizen-politician"— and warned against his potentially dangerous extremism. It was a confusing, contradictory message: How could Reagan be both naïve and dastardly? The contradiction rang even more hollow against Reagan's personality. To many voters, the sunny and self-deprecating Reagan exuded a confidence that hardly seemed like the posturing of an amateur, and it certainly didn't feel threatening.

By contrast, Brown managed to be first lethargic and then desperate. He dismissed Reagan as an actor, then reminded voters that it was an actor who killed Abraham Lincoln, a joke that was more dark than funny. Brown seemed low on energy as the campaign rounded the Labor Day turn, and he performed adequately but unspectacularly in a joint appearance with Reagan on *Meet the Press* on September 11. Reagan, by contrast, nimbly handled that affair.

And then Reagan, who was often blessed by political good fortune, got a boost in the form of a riot arising from a police shooting in San Francisco. It was fall, and the city was clear of its cooling summer fog, so the afternoon was hot. Patrolman Alvin Johnson spotted a group of young black men and thought they were trying to steal a car. He yelled at them to stop, and they ran. Johnson fired, killing a sixteen-year-old boy named Matthew Johnson. The shooting touched off "San Francisco's worst race riot" as pent-up frustration rippled through the deadening heat. The violence prompted immediate comparisons to the Watts riots of the year before, perfect for Reagan's playbook. Brown rushed from Sacramento to San Francisco and summoned the National Guard, which restored order quickly. But the images of rioting blacks in the state's second-largest city just a year after similar images from its largest city refreshed Reagan's overarching message: California was out of control, and a return to traditional values was overdue.

Try telling that to the Dead. Although the band had no performances scheduled on the nights that the Guard patrolled San Francisco streets, the last of the Acid Tests was set for October 2. And this one featured the much-anticipated but still secretive return of Kesey and the Pranksters. Kesey remained a fugitive, but he and the rest had tired of Mexico, where their visas were expiring. In late September—the seventeenth, according to the FBI—they packed up their encampment and straggled north, "leaving house in shambles and considerable damage and rent unpaid," the FBI noted. Babbs, Stone, and Paula Sundsten, whose Prankster nickname was Fetchin' Gretchen, went ahead in a truck. The rest followed in the bus.

After a long, long ride, interrupted time and again by breakdowns, the Pranksters pulled up to San Francisco State University just hours before the Test was to begin. Mountain Girl stepped off the bus, baby Sunshine in her arms, and felt the cool, damp grass of San Francisco for the first time in months, relieved to be home.

Fearing arrest, Kesey secreted himself in the campus radio station and broadcast his rantings to the late night crowd, singing a song he had written in Mexico with lyrics taken from the judge who had sentenced him and Mountain Girl that spring. Kesey was, he acknowledged, a "tarnished Galahad," burdened with guilt and shame. He got away that night without the authorities' laying hands on him.

Hunted but irrepressible, he eluded the law for a few more weeks despite what the FBI described as an "intensive investigation." Kesey taunted his pursuers, dropping in at a dinner party in early October and speaking there with reporters from the *Chronicle*, which published a story about it on October 5—and which FBI agents copied and dispatched to Washington the next day as an "urgent" cable. Then, on the evening of October 20, three FBI agents were driving past Candlestick Park, home of the San Francisco Giants, when they observed a "beatnik-type individual and other occupant wearing dark glasses but observed to resemble captioned fugitive." The agents honked at the van and cut it off. When the van finally stopped, Kesey ran, jumping a fence and racing for five blocks before giving up. Acid's freewheeling evangelist had been brought to heel, his adventures in freedom curtailed. Kesey received a light sentence, a six-month stretch at a county honor farm.

The San Francisco State Test also marked Mountain Girl's reunion with Garcia, who had not seen her since she left for Mexico after the Watts Acid Test in February. "I jumped off the bus," she said, decades later, "and jumped onto Jerry." The moment had the feeling of transition—the prototypical Prankster girl was now with the Dead.

A few days after the San Francisco State Acid Test, the gubernatorial campaign took its most notable toll on the Dead and their circle. Brown, eager to demonstrate his commitment to law and order, had, on May 30, signed a bill to outlaw the recreational use of LSD. So eager was Brown to be associated with the new law that he staged a televised signing ceremony at his Los Angeles home, and then, when the governor of Nevada announced that he had signed a similar bill earlier that day, Brown insisted that he actually had signed his a few hours earlier. That made Brown officially the first governor to make possession of LSD illegal, though the law would not take effect until ninety days after the legislature recessed. The fateful date fell on October 6, ending the legal era of consciousness expansion, at least in California, where most of that expansion had been occurring.

The move made sense politically. Brown was being dogged by Reagan as soft on crime, and he was able to point to his action against LSD as evidence of the contrary. In October, Brown specifically cited his signature on the LSD bill as proof of his unwillingness to tolerate lawlessness of the type that Reagan was highlighting. Although Reagan would remain the most enduring foe of the hippies, it was Brown who took away the community's drug of choice.

On Halloween night, the Acid Tests, too, reached a zenith of sorts. Dubbed the Acid Test Graduation, the event was billed as a farewell to LSD. Among those permitted to attend, astonishingly, was Kesey. At a hearing on October 25, Superior Court Judge Francis McCarty dressed Kesey down, calling him "more jackass than dragon and more fool than knave," but he relented when Kesey's lawyer, the legendary Patrick Hallinan, pleaded for Kesey to attend the Acid Test Graduation so that he could use the occasion to urge young people to "move beyond" drugs. The judge, tiring of Kesey's being described with inflated importance—Hallinan compared him to Oscar Wilde—agreed to let him go on bond. "If he wants to flee," the judge said, "justice will not weep. If he wants to stay, this will be one step into adulthood."

The "graduation" was scheduled for Winterland in San Francisco, with Bill Graham, who held the permit, agreeing to let the Pranksters use the hall. Halloween fell on a Monday in 1966, and on Sunday, Graham abruptly announced that he was backing out, apparently fearing that Kesey and the Pranksters had another trick in mind, in this case smearing walls and surfaces at Winterland with DMSO-laced LSD that could be absorbed through the skin. That had the potential for mischief on a truly grand scale, given that Pat Brown and the state Democratic Party were planning a rally at Winterland the next day. The mind reeled. Though Graham did not give a public reason for withdrawing from the event, he said no. The Dead, pleading a conflict, backed out too.

Instead, the Pranksters moved the event to a garage—they called it the Warehouse—and music duties fell to the Anonymous Artists of America, a folk and rock group featuring none other than Sara Ruppenthal, still Garcia's wife though she was no longer sharing with him either a home or a life. The event was hastily cobbled together and a little obscure. Tom Wolfe described Kesey dutifully pronouncing that it was "time to move on beyond the old acid experiences," but, Wolfe added, "much of what he says is allegorical or metaphorical and people have a hard time following it."

The Acid Tests thus ended with a whimper, but they had already helped to launch a movement, and ending them did not sink the ship. The new year would begin with the announcement of a new society, a demonstration of a new force in the land, a new energy that fused music and drugs and storytelling, a synthesis of old culture, ancient values, and youthful optimism. A new epoch seemed at hand. The Dead would stand—or, rather, play—at its symbolic and physical center.

And yet even as that movement leaped upward, so, too, did the forces determined to bring it back to earth. On November 8, Ronald Reagan was elected governor of California. Reagan took the oath of office on January 2, 1967, in Sacramento. He addressed the state for the first time as its governor on January 5. "Freedom," Reagan said, "is a fragile thing and is never more than one generation away from extinction. It is not ours by inheritance, it must be fought for and defended constantly by each generation."

Allen Ginsberg at the Human Be-In. Polo Field, Golden Gate Park,
San Francisco, January 14, 1967.

Elizabeth Sunflower/Retro Photo Archive

CHAPTER 6

The Gathering

IT WAS HARD TO GUESS WHETHER ANYONE WOULD SHOW UP. The *San Francisco Examiner*'s weekend listings for events in Golden Gate Park found room to highlight an exhibition of eighteenth- and nineteenth-century engineering at the de Young Museum and a history of religion lecture at the Hall of Flowers. But the paper made no mention of the Human Be-In.

For those on the lookout, however, there were signs. There were posters in shop windows, loving coverage in the San Francisco *Oracle*, a front page article in the *Berkeley Barb*, a little talk in Los Angeles. Some of the event's organizers distributed a press release a few days prior, promising "to powwow, celebrate, and prophecy the epoch of liberation, love, peace, compassion, and unity of mankind." A Bay Area press conference identified it as a merging of two cultures, radicals and hippies, united behind their common distrust of government and leaders, most notably Reagan, California's brand-new governor. Still, those cultures were young and inchoate. Would they show up for a powwow? And what, by the way, was a powwow?

Still, it was intriguing. One poster, created by Stanley Mouse and published by *The Oracle*, featured a bearded man, dreadlocks dangling along his naked arms as he stared straight ahead, his head framed by a shaded triangle. The third eye on his forehead, combined with the beard and dreadlocks, suggested something far out, vaguely Eastern. The headline did not explain much: SATURDAY, JANUARY 14, 1967, 1–5 PM A GATHERING OF THE TRIBES FOR A HUMAN BE-IN. It was billed as free and featured the

114 | HERE BESIDE THE RISING TIDE

names of poets and writers: Timothy Leary, Allen Ginsberg, Michael McClure, Richard Alpert (later to be known as Ram Dass), Lenore Kandel, and Gary Snyder. The activists Dick Gregory and Jerry Rubin appeared on the bill, though Rubin's name was misspelled ("Ruben") and Gregory was unable to make it. For entertainment, the poster promised "All S.F. Rock Groups." It urged anyone interested in attending to "Bring food to share. Bring flowers, beads, costumes, feathers, bells, cymbals, flags."

The description of the Be-In as a "gathering of the tribes" suggested, of course, that there were tribes to gather. To those in San Francisco in 1967, that had a particular meaning: It referred to two camps of young people expressing their dissatisfaction with contemporary life. They divided roughly into the hippies and the activists. Their symbolic headquarters were San Francisco for the hippies, Berkeley for the activists. They were distinct, yes, even wary of each other, but overlapping, too, in their appreciation for drugs, and most especially in their abiding conviction that they were on the verge of changing the world. The Be-In was meant to introduce them to each other.

THE MORNING ARRIVED. The members of the tribes, bearers of traditions older than they knew—those who felt themselves a part of it without really knowing what they were a part of or who else was part of it—wound their way to the Polo Field in Golden Gate Park. They arrived in VW buses and caravans, cars and old school buses. They brought dogs and children, crunching along gravel paths beneath blue skies with barely any idea what they would find. They came from all directions, streaming through the botanical garden to the east or entering the park from the south at the light on Sunset Boulevard. They came from the Richmond District to the north, from the Avenues, from the Haight—especially from the Haight. The first arrived early, and by late morning, close-in parking spaces were filled, so most arrivals were making the long stroll from the Haight.

As they turned a bend or crested a rise, the first impression was color. Banners and flags snapped in the sunny breeze. Day-Glo paint and paisley, stencils of marijuana leaves in green and gray. Many people came in jeans and T-shirts, painting the field in faded blues. There were masks, capes, feathers, body paint, cowboy outfits, Victorian top hats, brocade vests. They carried tambourines and flutes and bells and penny whistles—and flowers, of course. One man wrapped himself in a red gunny sack. One woman came draped in an empty flour bag with USA printed on one side. Court jesters and clowns bore their "assorted vestments like priests of some strange religion." And there was Leary, dressed in white, luminous, a flower lei around his neck and a daffodil tucked into his breast pocket.

The day progressed. The sun traveled from across the Panhandle to its zenith, coming to life, shining brightly, piercing the bright alabaster of a midday San Francisco winter sky to the saffron hue of afternoon. Puffs of smoke arose from the crowd, drifting like fog above and through the throngs dancing with soap bubbles—a special treat for the many participants who dropped LSD before or at the Be-In. Most people stood, but some spread blankets and sat or lay on the grass, swaths of colored fabric draped across the green. Some stripped off their clothes and danced naked. The crowd grew and grew as the event approached, then commenced. By midafternoon, most estimates placed it at about twenty thousand people. "I'd never seen so many people in my life," Garcia realized.

"It was a medieval scene, with banners flying, bright and uncommitted," wrote Helen Swick Perry, a social scientist working in the Haight during that period. "The day was miraculous, as days can be in San Francisco at their best, and the world was new and clean and pastoral. . . . People sat on the grass with nothing to do, sometimes moving up near to the small platform where a poetry-reading might be going on, or where a band might be playing. There was no program; it was a happening."

Watching from his wheelchair at the edge of the field, one observer took it all in: "There's never been anything like it since the Persians," Ambrose Hollingworth remarked.

For Peter Coyote, the impact was instantaneous—and lasting. "I was gobsmacked," he recalled decades later.

The platform provided a stage, but it did not dominate the landscape, much less the day. Low and modest, with a small PA system connected to a generator through a vulnerable extension cord, it gave the speakers and bands a place to perform. Speakers were asked to keep their remarks short, a deliberate move to make sure the Be-In was not a rally. It was not meant to be the occasion for protest or declamation, and the stage was barely the center of attention for much of the day, in part because the amplification was inadequate for the space, making it hard for most people to hear.

For those who cared to listen and could make out the words, the speakers offered varied thoughts. Rubin disobeyed the directive to avoid politics and held forth about the goings-on in Berkeley. Rubin, who had spent the night before in jail, also put in a plug for his own defense fund, irritating Garcia, who found Rubin's stridency alarming; it evoked "every angry voice I'd ever heard," he remarked later. Abbie Hoffman, also there on the grass, was more appreciative.

San Francisco was no stranger to student protest. A demonstration against the House Un-American Activities Committee in 1960 was said by some to have launched the modern era of student activism. It ended with protesters blown down the marble steps of City Hall, drenched participants scattered like leaves by fire hoses. Two years later, a young activist named Tom Hayden steered the Students for a Democratic Society to their historic completion of the Port Huron Statement, an eloquent expression of a new generation and its discontents. Irish, impish, ambitious, Hayden could annoy—his second wife, Jane Fonda, herself a breakthrough activist, demanded during her divorce from Hayden that if she predeceased him, he not be allowed to speak at her funeral—but he was equally capable of inspiring, and the statement that bore his efforts framed the aspirations of the activist "tribe" gathered on the field that afternoon.

Port Huron went beyond expressing outrage at the House Un-American Activities Committee. It was a statement of purpose and resolve, delivered by and on behalf of those young people "looking uncomfortably to the world we inherit." It defined politics as "the art of collectively creating an acceptable pattern of social relations," and its

THE GATHERING | 117

poetry had helped launch the Free Speech Movement and the Vietnam Day Committee. It hovered above the crowd at the Be-In, hippies and activists alike.

Of the poets, Ginsberg was probably the best known, "Howl" already a staple and a connection back to Kerouac and the Beats. But Snyder was familiar to many, he at an early stage of his vast and dignified career. He was even then at work on *Mountains and Rivers Without End*, an epic examination of what he called "the play between the tough spirit of willed self-discipline and the generous and loving spirit of concern for all beings"—words that could well have summed up the Be-In itself.

McClure and Kandel bridged the shrinking space between art and politics, their work dancing with the forbidden and daring the authorities to act. Kandel, in fact, was at the center of controversy that January, facing condemnation from the Catholic Church and criminal obscenity charges from civil authorities over her sexually explicit poetry. Undeterred by her pending charges, she read from *The Love Book*, which included "God/ Love Poem" and "To Fuck with Love." Kandel turned thirty-five that day. When she finished, the crowd sang "Happy Birthday."

Ginsberg was brief: "Peace in your heart dear," he said, "Peace in the park here." And Leary delivered the message for which he was already becoming famous, though it was also proving exasperatingly vague. "The only way out," he said, "is in. Turn on, tune in, and drop out."

Smells and sounds wafted across the field. Incense and marijuana made their presence known. The scent of flowers complemented that of the bay trees that lined the park. The rumble of conversations, the hum of connection, the music. The Airplane performed, as did (as promised) a full complement of San Francisco bands: Moby Grape, the Freudian Slips, the Loading Zone, the Hedds, Earth Mother and the Final Solution, the Sir Douglas Quintet, the Chosen Few, Sopwith Camel, Big Brother and the Holding Company, Quicksilver Messenger Service, and the Grateful Dead. At one point, the power cable was cut, silencing the music as well as the speakers. The *San Francisco Examiner*, determined to treat the whole event as ridiculous (the day was described on the paper's pages as "a bizarre union of love and activism"), chuckled over the power outage. It "stilled the Quicksilver Messenger Service and grounded the Jefferson Airplane," the paper noted.

The Be-In was blissfully self-organized. "Nobody claims to be the leader," Ginsberg recalled. Snyder blamed the press for trying to identify a boss. "The press," he said, "has a leadership complex." Yes, there were people who put up posters, rented sound trucks, built a stage, but they participated rather than directed. "I prefer to call them foci of energy," Leary insisted. Alan Watts agreed. It was, he suggested, a "stirring among people . . . organically designed instead of politically designed."

That conception of order and responsibility would lead to many moments of confusion in the years to come, but it could bring out the best in people, too. At the Be-In, to cite just one example, the presence of the Hells Angels sent a stab of fear through those who spotted their threatening leather jackets. But on that Saturday, the surly outlaws looked out for children who had been separated from their parents. Periodically, one of the Angels would come to the microphone and announce that the bikers had a child in their custody. "When a call would go out for 'Timmie's mother,' we all smiled and watched until finally from the huge throng a young woman would be seen moving serenely toward the Hell's Angels caravan," Perry said, "whereupon we would all settle back to our task of being." Perry called the Angels' zone a "heavenly nursery." For a day, the Hells Angels were neither intimidating nor distracting. They were babysitters.

LSD was widely shared at the Be-In, despite its having become illegal in California the previous October, and participants enjoyed the defiance of taking it, the possibilities of the drug amplified by the assurance that it was tweaking the new governor. At the Be-In, Owsley's latest was easy to acquire, and distribution of it fell to the Diggers, a forceful presence at the Be-In and in San Francisco culture and politics at that moment. Committed to a wholesale rethinking of values, the Diggers were an outgrowth of the San Francisco Mime Troupe, which, in turn, borrowed from sixteenth-century Italian commedia dell'arte to lampoon convention and reimagine the relationship between performers and audience (it was the Mime Troupe that gave Bill Graham his start). The Diggers took all of that even further, urging participants to consider the conditions they wanted for their lives and then "create the condition you describe." They dismissed capitalism, even money itself, demanding that events in the Haight be free and opening stores in which anyone could bring or take anything without paying. They served free meals, held free gatherings. The Be-In was free, and the Diggers supported it.

They doled out tabs and salted them into bread, which they packaged around free turkey and distributed as sandwiches for anyone who looked in need of nourishment, "physically or spiritually," as Digger Emmett Grogan wrote. "I was one of the guys handing it out," Peter Coyote said years later. There was no shortage of takers.

For the Grateful Dead, the Be-In was a local gig, a Saturday afternoon in the park—their park—one of the regular appearances for which they already were becoming known. Garcia and Mountain Girl wandered over to the Be-In early that morning and watched others arrive. The Dead hit the stage in the afternoon.

They opened with "Dancing in the Street," and the crowd rose to their feet. From the stage, Lesh saw "brightly woven waves of dancing movement," swaying banners, conga lines, undulations of color across the green grass. The band kicked into a number it had just been rehearsing, "Morning Dew," their cover of Bonnie Dobson's aching walk through the landscape of a postapocalyptic world. "Where have all the people gone today?" Garcia sang, his voice strong and plaintive, amplifiers cranked to the edge of feedback. Weaving threads of naturalism—walking through morning dew—and foreboding—"I guess it doesn't matter anyway"—the performance that afternoon rested less on lyrics or message and more on Garcia's three-minute, forty-five-second guitar solo, building from slow, single notes into longer runs, speeding up and playing through and around Kreutzmann's crescendoing drums and Lesh's freewheeling bass.

In the middle of the Dead's turn onstage, a speck far above caught one person's eye, then another, until all heads were tilted upward—"a single ripple of turned heads and eyes," Perry recalled. Down from the blue sky came a man in a motorcycle helmet, carried earthward by a parachute. He landed in the middle of the field, gathered his gear, and trundled off. It seemed perfectly natural and utterly dazzling. "Was he really the Great Provider?" Gleason asked. Noted Perry: "We wanted to believe in magic."

The Dead were unfazed. A run of "Viola Lee Blues" followed "Morning Dew." "Viola Lee Blues" accelerated as the band played, riding the day's energy, eventually taking off on a whipsaw run, churning faster and faster, the drums speeding up, Lesh skating along the neck of the bass, Weir strumming almost frantically. And then, after more than nine minutes of jamming, the band abruptly downshifted back into a blues beat and barreled to a conclusion. One more number rounded out the thirty-minute set, a quick-paced shuffle through "Good Morning, Little Schoolgirl," featuring a flute solo by Charles Lloyd, whose piping and vocal improvisation ran across the top of the Dead's presentation and wandered in exotic directions.

One joyous dancer turned to a neighbor and remarked on the Dead's swing, a matter about which he knew plenty since he happened to be Dizzy Gillespie. Writing for the *Chronicle,* Ralph Gleason pronounced the Dead's performance "remarkably exciting."

The day drew to a close. Snyder blew a conch shell. Ginsberg led the participants in a chant—the "mantra of the Buddha of the future, *Om Sri Maitreya.*" He urged the members of the tribes to turn their faces upward and move toward the sunset. They did, absorbing. Before leaving, Ginsberg made another request: that they clean up the park. They did that too. "This is truly something new," wrote Gleason, "and not the least of it is that it is an asking for a new dimension to peace, not just an end to shooting, for the reality of love and a great nest for all humans."

It was, Gleason added, "a statement of life, not of death, and a promise of good, not of evil."

There were no arrests (a police melee in the Haight that night netted thirty-two people, most for failing to disperse, but that was hours after the Be-In shut down), no disturbances. The Polo Field was left as tidy as it had been that morning. Peter Coyote departed in wonder, unsure exactly what it all had meant but convinced that something had shifted; the vocabulary required to understand what had just occurred would come only later.

THE GATHERING | 121

* * *

COVERING THE BE-IN for *The Rag* out of Austin, the writer Larry Freudiger posed the question:

> Who really fired the first shot? Was it John Lennon or Mick Jagger? Was it Bob Dylan, perhaps, or Joan Baez? Was it Mario Savio? It could well have been Jeff Poland, who campaigned for the sale of contraceptives on campus at San Jose State in 1963. Or the now forgotten hero who lit a joint in the police station in San Francisco, initiating the first "Puff In." Or maybe even Jack Kerouac, now in hiding at his mother's house in the East, wondering just what is going on.
>
> I don't really know how it all started—and if I don't know, and you don't know, we certainly have nothing to fear from Ronald Reagan.

The energy evident at the Be-In drew from deep and different wells, from Savio, Hayden, and Kerouac, who were not there, and from Snyder, Kandel, Rubin, and Garcia, who were. It swept together currents—cultural, political, and pharmaceutical—that carried activists and hippies, poets and musicians. Together, they mingled and gathered and just *were* on the Polo Field on January 14, 1967. The currents swirled. The tribes united. When it was over, it was one culture that remained with the blowing of the conch shell and the setting of the sun. The varied strains of discontent—those fed up with calcified literature and art, with ghoulish and dishonest politics, with oppressive attitudes toward sex and drugs and freedom—had whirled through America, and especially California, before that afternoon, sometimes intersecting but often on their own trajectories. Unorganized, leaderless, and deeply affecting, the event that day touched Garcia. It was, he said, "really fantastic. I almost didn't believe it."

From the Be-In emerged a new, more cohesive notion, a set of understandings that bound the tribes into a larger movement. They would disagree on tactics, sometimes bitterly and disdainfully, but they were, from that point forward, parts of a whole. They were a counterculture.

The Dead's house at 710 Ashbury was a gathering place for the San Francisco Scene and counterculture. Here: Members of the Dead, Quicksilver Messenger Service, Janis Joplin and Big Brother, Jefferson Airplane, and the Charlatans pose for a photo on the front steps.

Ron Rakow/Retro Photo Archive

CHAPTER 7

Summer of Love

WHAT, THEN, WAS THIS COUNTERCULTURE? START WITH THE WORD, or words, since "counterculture" began as "counter culture." The phrase traced its origins to that guest at Jerry Garcia's wedding to Sara Ruppenthal. When Theodore Roszak joined that event with his wife and daughter, he experienced it as an observer, too. Six years later, Roszak published *The Making of a Counter Culture,* his attempt to make sense of the forces that coalesced during that period and the first to use the term "counter culture." Roszak's important book examined the ideas that young people were bringing to the struggles of the 1960s, and it explored them through a lens that was sympathetic but scholarly rather than with the giddy enthusiasm of a participant or the dismissive air of a skeptic.

For Roszak, "counter culture" began with opposition. If this new culture was "counter," the obvious suggestion was that it was against some other culture. Roszak dubbed that force, the entity being resisted, the technocracy. He characterized technocracy as the "social form in which an industrial society reaches the peak of its organizational integration. It is the ideal men usually have in mind when they speak of modernizing, up-dating, rationalizing, planning." Technocracy, then, was a force of dehumanization, sterilization—efficient and productive but at the expense of what he regarded as more fundamentally human: community, compassion, wonder, love. The rise of technocracy was not particularly ideological—it existed in both the United States and the Soviet Union—and it profoundly altered the essential power structure by elevating experts and degrading everyday people forced to defer to those who understood its workings "since it is universally agreed that the prime goal of the society is to keep the productive apparatus turning over efficiently."

Technocracy was at work in industry, where mechanization replaced people. It was at work in politics, where polling and advertising replaced human persuasion. It was tragically at work in government and military matters, where the Vietnam War churned on despite public ambivalence. And it was staggeringly at work in society's surrender to the logic of nuclear weapons, to the idea that safety was best secured by the principle of Mutually Assured Destruction. "The counter culture takes its stand against the background of this absolute evil," Roszak wrote, "an evil which is not defined by the sheer *fact* of the bomb, but by the total *ethos* of the bomb, in which our politics, our public morality, our economic life, our intellectual endeavor are now embedded with a wealth of ingenious rationalization."

And so dissent formed. Isolated at first, lone artists expressing their rebellion, as artists will. Small movements—Beats, Beatniks, the San Francisco Renaissance, communes—rose to challenge convention. Then the gathering politics—the civil rights movement, the Port Huron Statement, the Free Speech Movement, the Diggers. Then the music—the Jefferson Airplane and, yes, the Grateful Dead. By the end of 1966, there were enough forces to be seen as "tribes." By the end of the Be-In, there was a counterculture.

Roszak's work did not spring out of nothing. Herbert Marcuse, a favorite philosopher of 1960s activists and hippies, framed similar questions through the lens of Marxism, working with the concept of alienation and trying to square class struggle with Freudian psychology and the revolutionary role of art. Roszak found much to appreciate—along with some points of disagreement—in Marcuse. For Roszak, Marx was a "scholarly drudge," too bleak, too invested in social forces rather than human vitality, and Roszak admired Marcuse's valiant attempts to find joy in that work. It was, however, a task, and Roszak solved it by sidestepping it, moving around alienation and instead proclaiming that a new moment, outside the dialectical materialism at the core of Marxism, was at hand, and that it could place mankind "on this benighted side of liberation."

Roszak's main focus was the technocracy and the response it had provoked, so the "counter" in "counter culture" was preeminent. Later historians and social critics would compress that into a single word, the "counterculture," a move that both symbolized the movement's solidifying place in society and reflected some confusion over Roszak's initial formulation (lunch counter protests associated with the civil rights movement gave the word "counter" its own rebellious connotation). Those historians would project forward and backward, noting that some form of counterculture ran through histories of place, struggle, and ideas, from the Left Bank to the East Village, from the Paris Commune to People's Park and, much later, to the Oregon Country Fair and protests against the World Bank and fossil fuel industries. This broader counterculture comprehended poets, novelists, painters, journalists, and essayists; it included activists outside conventional politics and eventually inside as well. It stretched from eccentrics to activists to bohemians—from Wavy Gravy to Jane Fonda to Jerry Garcia.

Curtis White, a thoughtful writer on these issues, employed the single word "counterculture" to describe a history of dissent dating back some two hundred years "whose fundamental purpose has been to displace the violence and inequality of Western capitalist culture." Damon Bach concentrated on the American counterculture, narrowing the historic scope and broadening the counterculture's reach to include "hippies and cultural dissidents," many of whom were only tangentially concerned with the violence or inequality of capitalism. Other scholars and observers similarly reached in different directions, either closely on politics or more broadly in fashion, design, family structure, and, of course, music.

One thread of this tapestry ran brightly. The idea of bohemianism dates to the 1830s. It was born as myth. Cultural bohemians have no actual relationship to the region of Bohemia. The journalist Félix Pyat appears to have been the first to use the word in connection with an artistic, vagabond community, writing in 1834 of Parisian artists devoted to the conviction that "art itself is a belief and the true artist is a priest." A few years later, a portrait of "Bohemia," liberated from the strictures of mainstream culture, fascinated by drugs and apathetic or even hostile to such values as security and prosperity, took shape in the writing of Henry Murger. Murger's sketches of artistic life in Paris, published serially in the magazine *Le Corsaire* in the 1840s and then collected and published in 1851 as "Scènes de la vie de bohème," featured the sculptor "Jacques D——," the painter Marcel, the "Jew called Solomon," and other struggling artists living in the Latin Quarter.

Writers and artists were intrigued. George Sand lived as a bohemian and wrote of them. So did Whitman, Rimbaud, Baudelaire, and Picasso. Journalists and other writers founded San Francisco's Bohemian Club in 1872, initially refusing to allow wealthy members but relenting when the club needed money.

Were the bohemians a vanguard of politics, or were they outside those struggles? Even though bohemians and Marxists shared contempt for the bourgeoisie, Marx was famously dismissive of the artistic vagabonds, precisely because he did not see sufficient class cohesion among cultural bohemians for them to join with the proletariat in the coming class warfare. But the bohemians were forged in the same old-world class system as Marx, and their rejection of bourgeois values placed them at odds with ruling power. Even if their ambitions were not explicitly political, then, the implicit politics of their art often aligned them with the broader aims of countercultures through the ages. Bohemians were prominent in the Paris Commune and flirted with anarchism; Whitman weighed in on slavery, suffrage, and nativism; nineteenth-century American bohemians often drew close to the Communist Party.

Still, bohemians tended to see politics in local terms, in cities or neighborhoods, and mostly avoided geopolitics along with the machinations of political parties and electoral contests. That remove, as well as that entanglement, describes Garcia's place in the early phases of the 1960s American counterculture. In style and devotion to his craft, in his use of drugs for transcendence, his aversion to conventional politics and immersion in a community of like-minded artists, Garcia was a bohemian. And, by extension, so was the Dead. "We're part of a whole, huge community of head adults," Garcia said in 1970. "There's a lot of us . . . movie makers, musicians, painters, craftsmen of every sort, people doing all kinds of things. That's what we do. That's the way we live our lives."

So convinced was Garcia of the liberating power of art that he refused to recognize that the government had authority at all. To him, government power was a myth, a delusion made real only by acquiescence. "The government is not in a position of power in this country," he said. "The kind of power that they think they have is some pretty illusory thing and exists only as long as people continue to believe in it."

His unwillingness to accept or even acknowledge government power extended to those who wielded that authority. Discussing politicians, he asked: "What do they actually do that affects a person's life?" Answering himself, Garcia concluded: "Not much."

To be outside politics is not the same as to be removed from it. White's conception of the counterculture as seeking to "displace" capitalist violence and inequality is deliberately chosen. The counterculture did not always seek to replace capitalism, to knock it forcibly from its position of dominance. Rather, the counterculture often led by different means, and artists functioned as an "avant-garde," a leading edge. "Art suggests, 'Wouldn't you rather live in this way?'" White said in 2023. "Wouldn't you rather live in a world that was committed to beauty, to love, to the ecstasy of a Garcia extended, trancelike guitar voyage?"

Whatever its contours, its limits or points of disagreement, the counterculture that strode away from Golden Gate Park on the evening of January 14, 1967, comprehended certain attributes: It was arrayed in opposition to—or contempt of—the government, both in Sacramento and in Washington; it was opposed to the war in Vietnam; it was enthralled by drugs and committed to the present, to life in the moment; it was home to a largely leaderless collection of activists and artists; and it was committed to freedom and to a supportive communalism, at odds with what many would regard as American "individualism," the kind of freedom espoused by Reagan and the solid majority of Califor-

128 | HERE BESIDE THE RISING TIDE

nians who had just placed him in office. The counterculture's freedom, the freedom of Garcia and the Dead, was the freedom to be together in fun and exploration, to jointly reimagine the culture through experience and to do so outside the technocracy's conception of "efficiency" or even "reason."

THE TECHNOCRACY found the Dead in the form of Warner Bros. Signing the Dead to their first record contract was the work of Joe Smith, a straitlaced Army veteran and graduate of Yale University. Smith wore a blazer to his first Dead show, a 1966 gig at the Avalon Ballroom. His wife wore pearls. "No one my age had ever seen anything like that," Smith said. "People with painted bodies lying on the floor and smoking. And the light shows. And the band doing one of their forty-minute drone sets. It was kind of startling."

But Smith was there to break into the new sound, and he cheerfully offered the Dead a contract. The Dead received a $3,500 advance for the initial recording and were promised 5 percent royalties for the first year, rising to 8 percent for "Term 2" and beyond, with the advances escalating as well. The band received one unusual provision: Rather than pegging royalties to the song, as was common for popular music acts, they were paid by the minute, more typical for contracts with jazz artists and, in this case, a concession to the Dead's emphasis on long improvisation. In the contract, the members of the band were identified individually by name ("Kreutzmann" was misspelled as "Kreutz Mann") and collectively as "all adults, except Bob Weir." "They bought it," Smith said. "So the adventure began!"

The members of the band and their entourage trundled off to L.A. two weeks after the Human Be-In. Some of them were nervous—Lesh admitted to jitters in the face of this first brush with industry pressure—and came with drugs, of course, in this case a supply of Mountain Girl's diet pills. Although the scale of this was new to them, the Dead had recorded in a studio before, and Garcia had some sense of what he was doing, informed in part by his work on *Surrealistic Pillow*. Specifically, he asked for Dave Hassinger, whose work for the Airplane had been done for RCA but who had just signed on as a producer for Warner Bros. The company agreed.

Warner Bros. did not own its own music studio, so they met in RCA's Studio A, the same cavernous, barnlike room that the Airplane had recorded in months earlier—Lesh described it as "about the size of the Vehicle Assembly Building at Cape Canaveral." Unfortunately, RCA's rules for the use of Studio A required that the Dead use the company's engineers, so Hassinger, new to producing, would not be allowed to engineer the album, as Garcia had hoped. In a rare interview in 1985, Hassinger explained his approach to Blair Jackson: "I'd made two or three trips up to the Bay Area and seen them at the Fillmore, and I thought they were dynamite. What I was after on the album was to capture as much of the energy as I could."

The whole project took four days. In one sense, Hassinger succeeded. The tracks brim with energy, at times more manic than focused, but true to the Dead's early spirit, rough and freewheeling.

Predictably, the Dead's tracks did not include an obvious single, and Warner Bros. asked for another song, one that might get some airplay. The Dead returned to the studio a few weeks later, recording "The Golden Road (to Ultimate Devotion)" in San Francisco. It was a quick, two-minute, seven-second number, fast-paced and, by the standards of this album, an unusually layered piece. It satisfied Warner Bros. and ended up leading off the album, though to little commercial avail. Though it received Bay Area airplay, record stations elsewhere were no more interested in it than in the rest of the album.

For the most part, the album, eponymously entitled *The Grateful Dead*, exhibited more potential than mastery. Tracks included quick, professional takes on "Beat It On Down the Line," "Cold Rain and Snow," and "Cream Puff War," whose lyrics were written by Garcia; the song was catchy, but Garcia recognized his limits and would soon welcome the addition of a more profound lyricist. The band gave greater

130 | HERE BESIDE THE RISING TIDE

attention to "Morning Dew," already evolving from its Be-In performance to a more complex number, and capped the album with a ten-minute version of "Viola Lee Blues."

To Lesh, the album felt like "sound and fury buried in a cavern." Garcia at first seemed pleased with the results. "It even has mistakes on it," he said, and he meant that as a boast, not an admission. "It sounds just like us." Later, Garcia soured a bit, acknowledging that while it presented a kind of "crude energy," it struck him as "hyperactive" and "embarrassing."

It was released on March 17. Smith, proud of his foray into the counterculture but still sporting a Carroll & Co. blazer, hosted a release party on March 20 in North Beach, where the world of record company executives mingled with the world of San Francisco hippies, one camp nursing cocktails, the other passing joints. "I want to say what an honor it is for Warner Bros. Records to be able to introduce the Grateful Dead and its music to the world," Smith announced. Garcia retorted: "I want to say what an honor it is for the Grateful Dead to introduce Warner Bros. Records to the world." In their own way, each was right.

Writing for the *Chronicle,* Ralph Gleason said he liked what he heard. "The Dead's material comes from all the strains in American music," he wrote. He predicted national tours, gigs in New York and elsewhere, all part of a bright future the critic imagined for a band at the release of its first album. Of Garcia, Gleason wrote that he was "a learned and highly articulate man."

Gleason's influential attention helped to boost the Dead into a new musical orbit, introducing them to the world of publicity. Garcia immediately became the center of that effort. Whereas Pigpen could be sullen, Lesh obscure, and Weir spacey, Garcia was clever and quick. And nothing about him seemed manipulative. Even when promoting the Dead's work, he was self-effacing and refreshingly honest. He listened to questions and enjoyed conversations. He became the public face of the Dead.

On April 8, just weeks after the album was released, members of the Dead appeared on San Francisco's KPIX TV station. Gleason anchored the conversation, and he opened by noting the explosion of music in San Francisco and proclaiming that "one of the most exciting and interesting bands in San Francisco these days is the Grateful Dead.

"We're talking with the Grateful Dead," Gleason continued, "particularly to Jerry Garcia, the lead guitarist."

The interview that day was brief, a setup for the Dead to play "Cream Puff War," but it established their approach to interviews. All the members of the band were present in the studio, and various voices would chime in as Gleason posed questions. But the talk centered on Garcia and the repartee was lively, deflective, fun. "What kind of music does the Grateful Dead play?" Gleason asked. "Loud," Garcia replied. "Dance music, for dancers, at dances." "Where does it come from? Do you write all your songs?" Gleason asked. "No," Garcia responded, and Lesh chimed in: "We steal it from a lot of places." Appreciating that, Garcia elaborated: "We're clever thieves."

As Gleason had noted in his review, Garcia emphasized that the Dead's source material was varied—"old blues, new blues, jug band," "classical licks," jazz—and agreed with Gleason, who observed: "It doesn't sound like other bands. Why is this?"

"Because," Garcia said, "we're not other bands. We're the Grateful Dead."

MORE THAN any other group, it was the Diggers who supplied the Haight with thought-provoking politics. They were provocateurs, but their waters ran deep indeed, with all the seriousness and self-awareness of young spirits caught up in the possibility of change. They were, Coyote said, "an art project."

But the concept was hard to grasp. Coyote recalled the day he was keeping an eye on the store—to say that he was "managing" it would have been inappropriate, since it would have implied hierarchy—when he noticed a woman tucking items under her blouse. He approached her and gently told her there was no need to shoplift. At first she denied it, defensive at having apparently been caught. He assured her that he was not accusing her of stealing but rather giving her permission to take what she wanted. As the idea dawned on her, she collected what she needed. Two days later, she returned with a flat of day-old doughnuts and placed them on the counter.

"She understood a free economy," Coyote said. "Imagine how you'd like to live. Then act it out."

The Digger ethos infused life and imposed demands in the Haight. Outrageous and militant, the Diggers took issue not just with the obvious targets, the police department and city hall, but also with hip capitalists, the merchants and bands that sprang up in response to Haight-Ashbury's new sexiness. In that context, the Dead had a foot in each camp. To the outside world, they were a band, still young but promising—an attraction, its members budding rock stars. Within the Haight, however, that was regarded with some suspicion. They were less committed than the Diggers to making the Haight a laboratory for revolution, the Paris Commune of its day. They were of the Haight but also outside it—more emissaries than hip capitalists, they carried the message outward, but they understood that rent and food cost money, too.

"The Grateful Dead were the best among evils," Coyote said of the music scene and its connection to the larger Haight-Ashbury community. "They were the most like a family. They were the most like us."

Still, Coyote added, "if we went to them, and we needed money for one of our events, they'd say: 'What's the matter, man? Don't you have your money trip together?'"

True enough, though, as Coyote noted, the Dead also played for free, for Digger events and for the many community causes that found purchase in the Haight. And they were hardly strangers to privation. Garcia had been living out of his car barely two years earlier. In early 1967, the Dead had a record contract, but $10,000, even in 1967, went only so far once it was divided among members of the band and their managers; gigs got them a couple hundred dollars at most. The Dead had plugged in to capitalism, but it would take time—a long time—for that to bring them much security.

SUMMER OF LOVE | 133

* * *

THE BLACK Panthers were not bohemians. A bohemian wants to be left alone to pursue his art, but a radical wants something more. A radical wants to change the fundamentals, the basics. The Panthers were radicals.

Founded in October 1966 by Bobby Seale and Huey Newton, the Black Panther Party for Self-Defense began with six members based in Oakland, California, determined to "further our civil human rights and achieve real freedom and justice for all the people." Southern violence in response to civil rights demonstrations led the Panthers to reject nonviolence in favor of self-defense. The Panthers took up arms.

The Panthers' broader program extended well beyond armed provocation and self-defense. The party's "ten points" emphasized freedom, employment, housing, restitution for racist exploitation, exemption from military service for black men, an end to police brutality, liberation of black men from jails and prisons, and self-determination as sought by America's Declaration of Independence, which the platform quoted— but its impact reflected the party's startling embrace of arms and violence. With the force of performance art, Seale, Newton, and a growing cadre of party members carried weapons and publicly displayed them, shadowing Oakland police while defiantly exercising their right to do so.

Images of armed black militants tailing police were enough to startle California politicians into unaccustomed action. In April 1967, Don Mulford, a Republican from the Oakland-Berkeley area, introduced a bill to sharply limit carrying a weapon in public, a direct response to the Panthers. A group of Panthers drove to Sacramento to protest the bill. Some thirty members of the party showed up at the state capitol on May 2, the day Mulford's bill was scheduled for consideration. Led by Seale, who had a .45-caliber pistol strapped to his side, the Panthers strode through the Capitol and entered the Assembly chamber.

"You can't come in here," the guard told them. "We don't have a constitutional right to go in the spectator section to watch the State Assembly make legislation?" Seale responded. Startled by the appearance of an armed black man at the entrance to the chamber, reporters jumped up, knocking the guard over. Seale strode past him, trailing the rest of the Panthers, not into the spectator section but into the chamber itself. They carried rifles, shotguns, and handguns.

Members dived beneath their desks. Photographers leaped to their cameras. Although it was something of a mistake—the Panthers had not meant to enter onto the floor—the event was riveting. Newspapers across the nation featured photographs of Black Panthers "invading" California's capitol. Reagan signed the Mulford Bill. The Panthers had turned Reagan into a champion of gun control.

DAILY LIFE in the Haight was both chaotic and, at first, curiously placid. Mornings got off to a late start, but by the time the fog had burned away in the late morning, the streets began to rustle. Diggers set out on the morning rounds, shaking down restaurants and grocers for scraps, rounding up items for the store. Kids roused themselves from flophouses and made their way outside.

Culture radiated from the park. The nook where the larger Golden Gate Park narrowed into the Panhandle created the western edge of the Haight-Ashbury. Overlooking it from the park was a woody knoll nicknamed, of course, Hippie Hill. From it, looking east over about forty square blocks, lay the Haight.

The Diggers spread across it. The Free Store moved around a bit but eventually settled at 910 Cole Street, where large windows made the store's contents easily seen from the street. Free meals were available most days, and patrons lined up for food in front of the "Free Frame of Reference," an open wooden frame that invited those who passed through it to consider their social and physical context. Hungry men and women would do so eagerly, sometimes with a giggle, other times with a deep sigh. And then hold out their plates for stew.

Stores did brisk business. In Gear offered hip clothing across the street from the Psychedelic Shop, which sold LSD until it became illegal and then became a head shop and later added a "calm center" in the back where kids could come down from a bad trip. Hip fashion boutiques included the House of Richard, Blushing Peony, and Mnasidika, all on Haight, and Xanadu for leather crafts. There was plenty of food: Tracy's Donuts at 1569 Haight was a natural for the munchies. Pall Mall Bar, with its Love Burgers, and the Drugstore Café were local favorites. The I and Thou Coffee Shop, at 1736 Haight, was the place for aspiring writers. Far Fetched Foods sold health food, the first store in the area to stake that claim.

It was, of course, groovy. "There will always be at least one man with long hair and sunglasses playing a wooden pipe of some kind," Hunter S. Thompson wrote on visiting the neighborhood.

Most of those who came to Haight-Ashbury in 1967 arrived with little if any money, and work was scarce, but life was cheap. Money eked into the neighborhood through panhandling and support from home. Drugs provided income to some, more as the crowds got bigger. "Few hippies can afford a pair of $20 sandals or a 'mod outfit' for $67.50," as Thompson observed.

Services moved to the area, too. The Haight Ashbury Free Medical Clinic handled its share of drug cases and sexually transmitted diseases, as well as all manner of scrapes and bruises. Various legal services offered help; the most prominent was the Haight-Ashbury Legal Organization (HALO), which shared space at the Dead's house for a while. Teachers volunteered at Happening House; runaways found shelter at Huckleberry House; the Switchboard posted messages from worried parents to wandering children. *The Oracle*, beacon of the underground press, founded with the profits from a head shop and known for its busy typography and swirling color layouts, started off behind the Print Mint and then moved to 1371 Haight. *The Oracle* managed to please—and displease—everyone. To straight readers, it was the epitome of radical thinking and annoying imprecation, while to Digger Emmett Grogan, it was a mouthpiece of the hip capitalists, the "moneyed class," and freighted by its "pansyness."

The streets were lined with posters, swirling, colorful, enigmatic.

136 | HERE BESIDE THE RISING TIDE

The artists Alton Kelley and Stanley Mouse trolled the library for images and grafted them to the colors of LSD and their own formidable talents—Kelley on ideas, Mouse on visual specifics. They seized on photographs of Native Americans and Gold Rush prospectors, images of Smokey Bear and Winnie-the-Pooh. They found one etching in *The Rubaiyat of Omar Khayyam* drawn by Edmund Joseph Sullivan in the early twentieth century and used it to decorate an advertisement for the Dead at the Avalon Ballroom. That image, a skeleton surrounded by blooming flowers, would anchor the Grateful Dead's iconography for the remainder of its existence—and beyond. Kelley and Mouse opened a shop at 1711 Haight Street in 1967, where they hung out their shingle as the Pacific Ocean Trading Co.—POT Co., for anyone too slow to get the joke. The shop sold paraphernalia and posters.

Poster art was supported by the concert business, which was growing and competitive. Bill Graham's ambitions were hard to contain, and his innate sense of empire building led him to split with Chet Helms, who then founded a rival operation. Helms had been part of an original collective called the Family Dog, which put on shows at Longshoremen's Hall. In the fall of 1965, Helms hired Mouse and Kelley to produce posters; they were later joined by other artists such as Rick Griffin and Victor Moscoso. Wes Wilson, meanwhile, was Graham's principal artist for the Fillmore.

The artists played off one another, each with a distinctive palette and lettering style. Posters tended to be abstract—it was deliberately difficult to tell exactly when and where an event was being held amid the swirling letters, colors, and lines. Graham preferred a cleaner approach. Ever the businessman, he wanted to be sure patrons knew where to go and when the show would begin.

Joining the Avalon and the Fillmore in 1967 was an old fixture suddenly sprung back to life. The Straight Theater had been closed for a few years, but a $100,000 hippie renovation brought the old movie house back to life, and it reopened in 1967. Back in business, the Straight relied on the Dead. "They always came through for us," one of the founders recalled years later.

SUMMER OF LOVE | 137

The musicians lived where they performed. Janis Joplin settled at 122 Lyon Street, one block south of the Panhandle. The Airplane lived at 2400 Fulton, across the park but within walking distance. Members of Big Brother and the Holding Company were at 1090 Page Street. And of course the Dead were at 710 Ashbury, directly across the street from the Hells Angels, who holed up at 715 Ashbury.

As the Haight swelled with new arrivals, it became wilder. Kids running away from home now had a place to run to, and they streamed into the city, finding their way to the park and to the happening that was Haight-Ashbury. Many dressed as clowns or donned Edwardian coats and hats. They mingled with Hells Angels and musicians, real and would-be. Some slept in the park or found stoops or floor space in the Victorians that ran the length of the Panhandle. "A carnival seemed to be taking place on every block," Joel Selvin wrote. The trickle built for weeks, then redoubled in May, when Scott McKenzie's performance of John Phillips's "San Francisco (Be Sure to Wear Flowers in Your Hair)," a treacly but catchy ode to the happenings in the Haight, crashed the charts. "If you're going to San Francisco," the song offered, "you're gonna meet some gentle people there."

It was both lure and curiosity. Gray Line Tours opened a route through the neighborhoods, advertising it as a tour of "Hippieland." Hippies were irritated. One, John Connolly, asked city leaders to halt the buses and make tourists visit the area by foot. "Let them walk," he implored at one town meeting. "It might even help the United States in general." That got a rise from the crowd of five hundred, but the *Examiner* was less impressed. It noted Connolly's "beard and boots" and chastised him for failing to remove his hat when addressing the city commission. Frustrated, hippies responded by pelting the buses with water balloons—Weir got caught in the act of one such balloon bombardment—and holding up mirrors to reflect the onlookers back to themselves. Municipal buses ended service through the neighborhood on weekends after residents staged a series of "mill-ins," semiorganized wanderings in the street that ground traffic to a standstill.

Hijinks made light of what was going on, but problems were emerg-

138 | HERE BESIDE THE RISING TIDE

ing even in the early stages of the neighborhood's transformation. THE HAIGHT HIPPIES MEET THE FUZZ, the *Examiner* reported in February 1967, noting then that the hippies were "beginning to understand police problems." By March, the *Examiner* was reporting clashes between "crusading cops" and the "modern monks" of the Haight, by which the paper meant the Diggers. A town hall meeting in March addressed run-down housing, dirty streets, drug use, and "misunderstanding generated by some of the district's 'new community' or 'hippie' elements."

The young people who ambled into San Francisco in early 1967 did so without urging, magnetically attracted to the site of the Be-In and curious to be part of it. By April of that year, some of the Haight's more established figures, notably Chet Helms, had formed the Council of the Summer of Love to organize concerts in the park and other activities around the expected gathering. Word spread in underground papers and even some mainstream outlets. Young people began arriving in greater numbers. At first the atmosphere was gentle—flowers and face paint, outdoor concerts, camping in and around the Haight. Even in those early stages, though, there were worrisome signs.

Newspaper stories explored the "confusing world of drugs" and featured appeals for information about children gone missing. In April, one tormented mother paced the streets of the Haight posting pictures of her thirteen-year-old daughter. "She is a dependable and responsible little girl," the mother told reporters. She reached out to the Diggers for help.

More arrived. Hunter Thompson's piece for *The New York Times* in May labeled the area "Hashbury," which never caught on, but he captured the sense of a community groaning under its new appeal. "The Haight-Ashbury scene developed very suddenly in the winter of 1966–67," Thompson wrote, bursting from a "quiet, neo-Bohemian enclave" into "the crowded, defiant dope fortress that it is today."

Sinister forces gathered as well. Leslie Van Houten was seventeen when she and her boyfriend touched down in Haight-Ashbury. She would soon find her way to another resident of the Haight that year: Charles Manson rolled in from Los Angeles in 1967 and settled into an apartment at 636 Cole Street, two blocks south of the Panhandle. Storms were gathering.

JOAN DIDION visited the Haight in "the cold late spring of 1967" and found what seemed to her not so much new energy as lost people. "The center," she concluded, "was not holding." She had grown up in a California of steely pioneers, neighbors who looked out for one another by killing rattlesnakes—"to do less . . . was to endanger whoever later entered the brush."

In the Haight, she found dissipation and torpor, children who had left home to avoid their chores and were drawn to a district crawling with young people and drugs. These did not strike her as discoverers so much as prey. Those children lit upon drugs and found themselves victims. They believed consciousness to be something beyond words. Didion did not accept that. "As it happens," she wrote, "I am still committed to the idea that the ability to think for one's self depends upon one's mastery of the language." What she observed were children, "sixteen, fifteen, fourteen years old, younger all the time, an army of children waiting to be given the words."

One of those was Susan. Susan was five years old and had just gotten over the measles. She liked Coca-Cola and ice cream, wanted a bicycle for Christmas, and was a fan of the Grateful Dead, especially Bob Weir. And Susan, when Didion met her, was high on acid. Susan was attending what she called "High Kindergarten." To Didion, that was the tragedy of the Haight—the rattlesnake in the grass.

Along with such writers as Truman Capote, Hunter Thompson, Norman Mailer, Gay Talese, and Tom Wolfe, Didion would merge the techniques of novel writing with the demands of nonfiction reporting. With her cool discernment, she would help create what would come to be known as the New Journalism. Like the Beats or the artists of the San Francisco Renaissance, it was more of a school than a coherent movement, but its tenets included vivid storytelling, often in the first person, shrewd observation of human action, and a sense of purpose, of challenging norms. The New Journalism abandoned the notion of objective reporting and embraced the participation of the observer. It was correctly associated with the counterculture, which often served as its subject, and much of it took shape in the protests against the Vietnam War (Mailer's *The Armies of the Night* comes to mind, as does his *Miami and the Siege of Chicago*) and in the rising demand for America to live up to the obligations of its prosperity. In Didion's hands, it was a sharp implement.

MOUNTAIN GIRL moved in with Jerry, and they settled into life at 710 Ashbury. They were a striking couple—tender and affectionate, "very touchy, touchy, touchy," one friend recalled. They shared a room with Sunshine, unfortunately directly above Pigpen, who would keep them up with his singing until Mountain Girl stomped on the floor. When morning came, she pulled the day together. Jerry would rise surprisingly early—he was usually up by six-thirty—and would start his morning with a few hours' practice on his guitar. Mountain Girl had Sunshine to feed, so she would shuffle downstairs to the kitchen and make breakfast. Rosie McGee, living nearby with Lesh and Kreutzmann—all of whom found 710 cramped after living there for a bit—would arrive in the morning and chip in with household chores. Weir slept in, as did Pigpen.

Drugs were everywhere, of course, but not universally consumed. After the Acid Tests, LSD remained a fixture of the community around the Dead, and members of the band occasionally returned to it, but the days of performing while tripping gradually ebbed away. Pigpen avoided acid, sticking with alcohol, and Weir made a hard shift away from most drugs, plunging into a macrobiotic diet and the early phases of the health food movement, even though it gave him gas and flatulence.

The Dead family made no attempt at sexual equality. Women did almost all the housework, while band members played instruments and brought in money. But neither the men nor the women saw that as a particularly sharp gender line, much less an oppressive one. The vibe was communal. "We were a group of friends with very little money," McGee recalled. "If Jerry needed guitar strings, I went out and got them. . . . I was not contributing financially, so I contributed in other ways. I never thought of it as demeaning."

As their reputations grew, the members of the Dead held court, hosting journalists and others, welcoming the neighborhood inside. "Our place got to be a center of energy and people were in there organizing stuff," Garcia said. "The Diggers would hang out there. The people that were trying to start various spiritual movements would be in and out; our friends trying to get various benefits on for various trips would be in and out. There would be a lot of motion, a lot of energy exchanged."

However bohemian and apolitical they imagined themselves, the Dead were part of the politics of the moment. Benefit performances were a regular part of their appearances in 1966 and early 1967, as they would be in the years to come. In one six-month stretch, the Dead played the Festival for Peace (October 21, 1966); a benefit for the Student Nonviolent Coordinating Committee (November 20, 1966); the Benefit for the Council of Civic Unity (with Sly and the Family Stone and Moby Grape, on February 12, 1967); a benefit to protest the execution of Aaron Mitchell at San Quentin (April 11); a benefit as part of the Week of the Angry Arts–West Spring Mobilization to End the War in Vietnam (with Quicksilver Messenger Service, Big Brother and the Holding Company, and Country Joe and the Fish, on April 9); and a benefit in support of the San Francisco Mime Troupe (April 12). Hardly the schedule of an apolitical band.

They passed on the chance to appear in one of the Haight's biggest happenings that spring: The film *Petulia*, directed by Richard Lester—who had also directed the Beatles in *A Hard Day's Night*—and starring Julie Christie and Richard Chamberlain, was shooting in the neighborhood. The Dead appeared in bit roles, as did other San Francisco bands. When it came time to sign releases to allow their appearance to be included in the finished film, members of the Dead realized that in order for them to have even minor speaking parts in the film, they would be required to sign a loyalty oath to gain admission to the Screen Actors

Guild. That requirement, adopted by SAG in 1953, was thanks to none other than Reagan, who, as president of the guild, had pushed for a "voluntary statement of affirmation" in the 1940s and had supported the broader oath as a board member. Offered the opportunity to pledge their loyalty to the United States and to "repudiate" Communism in exchange for a speaking part in a Hollywood movie, the members of the Dead chose to skip the film. That cost them any chance at speaking roles, but Lester included a musical bit from them anyway. *Petulia* features a clip of the Dead performing "Viola Lee Blues."

But having political ideas was one thing, expressing them was another. Garcia regarded any attempt to draw him out on politics with allergic suspicion, confirming to many his aversion to politics, even when politics seemed to ooze from his work. His only recorded song lyric, from "Cream Puff War" in 1966, reprimands an unnamed set of adversaries in a fashion that suggests his disdain for conflict: "You're both out in the streets and you got no place to go / Your constant battles are getting to be a bore."

Interviewed in 1967 and asked "How is this war in Vietnam hitting you?" Garcia's first response was stunningly myopic. "Not directly at all so far, except that it's getting hard to buy things like cymbals and guitar strings because they're making bullets out of them." Saved by the interviewer, who followed up by asking about his previous military service and whether he would serve if it were not for that, Garcia grabbed the life raft: "Would I go? I would not go. I am totally against war. I'm against it not on any religious principles but just because I could never kill anybody. . . . It's anti-life, and I'm against anything that's anti-life."

It was hardly a sophisticated political analysis, but as Garcia continued, he displayed a more deeply felt compassion. "I don't see how anybody could drop bombs on rice paddies or little villages," Garcia said. "What I've seen has really horrified me. I don't understand why it's going on. . . . I don't feel like I'm any kind of subversive force. I feel like an American, and I'm really ashamed of it lately. I don't think the country has to do that. I don't think the people want it to happen."

Garcia liked to talk, and he could talk himself in circles. On this morning, however, his meandering led him at last to light upon a formulation that seemed to express a broader vision, really for the first time: "If everybody in the world could learn to be responsible to the extent of taking care of what's going on right around them, to seeing that nobody dies in front of them, to care a little, then the world's big problems would disappear."

As a tentative foray into the language and reasoning of politics, Garcia's observation was telling. He was not venturing a preference for candidates or policy, areas that would have struck him as hopelessly political. Rather, he expressed personal values—caring and responsibility as part of a larger pursuit of freedom—and gently projected them into a larger worldview. Those instincts would remain deeply felt throughout his life.

And as for politics and the Dead's music: "We don't want to change anybody. We just want to give everybody a chance to feel a little better. . . . The music that we make together is an act of love and an act of joy. And we like it. We like it a lot."

THE MONTEREY International Pop Festival started with a meeting in Los Angeles, not San Francisco. The idea sprang from a conversation in the office of Lou Adler, manager of the Mamas and the Papas and a record producer at the leading edge of rock music. Paul McCartney was there, as were members of the Mamas and the Papas. They were commiserating about the state of rock 'n' roll, which was captivating young people but still lacked critical appreciation outside places such as Los Angeles and San Francisco. Why, they wondered, should jazz enjoy so much prestige and rock 'n' roll so little?

One reason, they agreed, was that jazz had its gatherings, its festivals, where aficionados came together to share their admiration. One such festival was the Monterey Jazz Festival, held just a few hundred miles north of L.A. In that moment, the Monterey International Pop Festival was born.

Lou Adler was a standout figure in the music business, so it was natural that he should begin the work of recruiting performers. But his identification with Los Angeles made him suspect among the San Francisco bands, so the early plans for the festival leaned heavily on talent from elsewhere. Soon the list of performers made the event too big to ignore: the Mamas and the Papas, of course, as well as Simon and Garfunkel, Jimi Hendrix, the Who, and more. Setting aside reservations, some of the leading San Francisco bands—the Airplane, Quicksilver, Moby Grape, Big Brother and the Holding Company, the Steve Miller Band, and the Dead—agreed to participate.

Even then, there was some suspicion, reinforced by the news that Adler intended to film the performances and produce a movie. That struck the Dead's bohemian sensibilities the wrong way, and when they were presented with a rights waiver just before they took the stage, they refused to sign it. In the meantime, however, they accepted the chance to play and were awarded a prime slot, on Sunday evening between two of the festival's most highly touted acts, the Who and Hendrix. That placement proved both respectful and unfortunate.

The weekend kicked off on Friday, June 16, with a lineup of groovy and soulful acts, moving then into the singer/songwriters—the Association, the Paupers, and Lou Rawls, followed by the British folkie Beverley Martyn, the American pop singer Johnny Rivers, and Eric Burdon and the Animals, a bluesy British rock band. The night was capped by Simon and Garfunkel, already huge in 1967.

Saturday was broken into two segments, an afternoon and an evening lineup, and the crowd was treated to some of San Francisco's finest. Big Brother and the Holding Company wowed the audience, which got its first look at Janis Joplin. The Airplane played that night after Garcia introduced them, and the day ended with a set from Otis Redding, who closed the festivities with "Try a Little Tenderness," a fitting message from the San Francisco scene.

It was Sunday, though, that sealed the Festival's place in rock 'n' roll history. The music that evening began with a set from the Blues Project, a tempestuous and short-lived group from New York, then featured a second appearance from Big Brother and the Holding Company, bringing Joplin back to the stage. But the highlight section of Sunday's lineup was three bands: the Who, followed by the Dead, followed by Jimi Hendrix.

A recap of the event in *DownBeat* magazine detailed the scene. It began with the Who: "Let it be said that this British group exceeded all expectations," the writer made clear. Drummer Keith Moon thrashed away, tossing drumsticks into the crowd while anchoring the band's beat. "Meanwhile, Townshend commenced to strike the stage murderously with his guitar, chunks of which were flying everywhere. Drums soon were tossed around like beachballs."

The writer reported that Hendrix was even more flamboyant. His electrically charged set was "possibly the major event of the festival." Hendrix dazzled with speed atop blues, his guitar work, in a word, "amazing." Moreover, "he uses the instrument as a prop for a dazzling repertoire of visual dramatics, playing the instrument only with his right (fretting) hand, twirling it around in the manner of Lightning [sic] Hopkins and other predecessors, playing it with his teeth, and using it in a variety of postures that would make Bo Diddley blush."

Not to be outdone by Townshend's guitar bashing, Hendrix brought his set to a close by dousing his instrument in lighter fluid and setting it ablaze.

Between those acts came the Dead, just back from New York City, where they had been well received at a free show in Tompkins Square Park. At Monterey, they struck *DownBeat* as "a curiously down-homey bunch that has become enshrined as the king group of West Coast acid-rock." "Down-homey" was not exactly the vibe when the Who were done wrecking the place, and the Dead's set was further crimped by an interruption, as Peter Tork of the Monkees poked his way onstage at the end of the Dead's opening number, a fourteen-minute version of "Viola Lee Blues," to dampen expectations that the Beatles might appear; he implored anxious participants at the fence line to back down while Lesh taunted him by urging the same fans to come inside. Although *Down-*

Beat conceded that Garcia and Pigpen were "two of the coast's top freak-out musicians," the magazine treated the Dead's performance as "kind of a slipshod, lazy way to play music."

That was both true and somewhat unfair. The Dead's performance at Monterey was not its best, but it was never destined to stand out between the Who and Hendrix. Garcia laughed about it later. "We played badly there," he told an interviewer twenty years later, startling her to laughter with his candor. "That was one of our classic bad scenes. We came on the stage just after the Who just finished smashing their equipment for the first time in America. The audience is devastated." With the smoke still clearing and the stage littered with debris, Garcia added, "We come out and play our little set—ding, ding, ding. And then Jimi Hendrix comes out after us and annihilates."

Mercifully, the Dead's refusal to sign the film waiver meant that its gentle performance sandwiched between two towers of theatrics has largely been lost to history. Even more happily, one who did sign the waiver was Janis Joplin. Her dazzling, throaty appearance highlighted the film and launched her into public acclaim. Joplin's life would be brutishly short but brilliantly illuminated. The spark was struck in Monterey.

WHEN THE Monterey festival ended that Sunday night in 1967, bands and fans packed up. The San Francisco bands scooped up a bunch of amplifiers and loaded them onto a truck, leaving behind a note explaining their appropriation (and later telling the organizers where they could collect the gear). They headed north to San Francisco.

After months of building, the post-Monterey rush of young people put the Summer of Love over the top. The drugs moved from marijuana and LSD to speed and heroin. Sexual liberation tipped into sexual assault. There were too many people to feed, too many in need of medical care and legal representation. Even merchants, the short-term beneficiaries of the jolt to hip capitalism, were overwhelmed. When George Harrison visited in August, it was a moment of great hippie potential—

SUMMER OF LOVE | 147

an actual Beatle ambling through the Haight. But Harrison found it "horrible—full of ghastly drop-outs, bums and spotty youths, all out of their brains." He was repelled. "It turned me right off the whole scene." Harrison hightailed it out of the area.

Hippies were blamed for crime, including the brutal murder of a drug dealer whose right arm was severed in the homicide. Abandoned and sick babies were traced to young women ("hippie girls") drawn to Haight-Ashbury and then lost to drugs. A drop in San Francisco's resilient burlesque trade was attributed to the hippie invasion. "The topless thing has lasted longer than we thought it would," Police Chief Tom Cahill said, "but it's dying now." The reason: Topless hippie chicks were abundant, and "they don't charge $1.50 for a drink."

CBS weighed in on August 22. Harry Reasoner had come to San Francisco in April, and he returned with a shocking exposé on the city's unfolding experience with its "occupation" by hippies. "They represent a new form of social rebellion," Reasoner warned as the broadcast opened and film rolled of young people in a park, bongos in the background. The one-hour special examined "the temptation" and "the danger" posed by the hippies, especially with their "evangelical" advocacy of LSD, by diving into the "hippie capital of the world," San Francisco.

Reasoner's report was thick with contempt, disparaging hippie values and painting hippies as misguided narcissists, "saucy children" thumbing their noses at mainstream society and finding escape from their vapid lives by using LSD. *The Oracle* got a turn in the broadcast, as did the Diggers, "a hippie subgroup." And so did the Dead. "This is the house of a popular local band which plays hard rock music," Reasoner said as the camera panned 710 Ashbury. "They call themselves the Grateful Dead. They live together comfortably in what could be called affluence."

Reasoner's associate, Warren Wallace, gathered the members of the band together around a table and asked them about what the hippie movement was "trying to accomplish."

"What we're thinking about is a peaceful planet," responded Garcia, who wore a black bowler hat for his first appearance on national television. "We're not thinking about anything else. We're not thinking about any kind of power. We're not thinking about any of those kinds of struggles. We're not thinking about revolution or war or any of that. That's not what we want. Nobody wants to get hurt. Nobody wants to hurt anybody. We would all like to be able to live an uncluttered life, a simple life, a good life. And like, think about moving the whole human race ahead a step or a few steps . . . or a half a step."

The Hippie Temptation, as the program was called, went down in San Francisco as a joke, a silly moment of mainstream media misunderstanding the experience of the young, a kind of *Reefer Madness* of the Haight. It cemented Garcia's belief that the idea of "hippies" was fundamentally a media construct, an attempt by outsiders to categorize and dismiss the experiences of San Francisco.

But just because Harry Reasoner and the *San Francisco Examiner* were hysterical did not make them wrong. As Didion had sensed in the "cold late spring," the situation was sliding out of control. She reported on a flyer that recounted a gang rape of a young girl. Its violent tone rattled Garcia, as it did others. Lesh watched as the "love generation" became prey for darker forces, and though he credited the Diggers and the free clinic with trying to protect the vulnerable drawn to the Summer of Love, "it was like trying to hold back the tide with beach toys." Looking back decades later, Lesh saw in that summer the cracks beginning to show, "the influx of hard drugs, the increasing isolation from and indifference to one another, the resultant failure of communication and shared responsibility."

The Summer of Love was an inflection point in the life of the counterculture. For those who traveled to San Francisco in early 1967, the Summer of Love was revolutionary. Was it a failure? Of course—eventually. The quiet, lovely student-and-artist bohemian model worked for a time—say, from 1964 to 1966—but the sheer appeal of that life was its own undoing. Runaways and drugs, lunatics and criminals, overwhelmed the community's capacity for caring, even when that capacity was enormous. "It just put too much energy into too fragile a situation," Garcia said, "so that the energy was more than the capacity to absorb it.

"You could feed one thousand, but you couldn't feed twenty thousand," he added. "As soon as there got to be more than traffic could bear, then it was like an ecological upset."

But was it also a success? Yes to that too. Those months witnessed a flourishing of counterculture, of its evolution from the idea of a culture "counter" to technocracy or capitalism or square fashion into a "counterculture" with values and ambitions. It was a gathering of the tribes, a communion of hippies and radicals, a place of peace that could accommodate Hells Angels and hip capitalists and lost souls. It was led by artists and bolstered by activists—there was a role for the Dead and also for the Diggers. It did not require government support or participation— Ronald Reagan lent no hand, nor did the county supervisors or police of San Francisco. It did not last. By fall, the energy was ebbing, the lost children, most of them, trickling back home.

But that did not mean it was not worth living for. The Summer of Love was the Paris Commune reborn in the Panhandle of Golden Gate Park—extravagant, messy, meaningful. And temporary. Rather than a failure, perhaps it is best regarded as a brilliant but brief success.

Grateful Dead. Montreal, August 1967.
Ron Rakow/Retro Photo Archive

CHAPTER 8

"Dark Star"

ROBERT HUNTER HAD DRIFTED AWAY FROM GARCIA AFTER 1965. Their side-by-side cars and cans of pineapple had once sustained them, but as the Dead took off, Hunter was left without a place in the new band. Gifted as a writer, he was just so-so as a musician, below what Garcia and the Dead were creating. So he went in search of himself. He dabbled with Scientology for a while. He wandered to New Mexico and was sketching and writing—poetry, starts at novels, lyrics. He mailed one set of trial lyrics to Garcia in 1967, a batch that included "Alligator," "Saint Stephen," and "China Cat Sunflower." Garcia, rarely one to move quickly, jumped in response. "I got the first and only letter I ever received from him," Hunter said, "almost by return mail, asking me to come out and join the band." It took Hunter a while to get home, but when he did, he was treated to his own words, now put to music.

Hunter's first contributions to the Dead proved his range. "Alligator" was whimsical, a nod to a nursery rhyme, the quick tale of an anthropomorphic alligator, sleepy and creepy, threatening and personable. Put to music first by Hunter as a jug blues melody, "Alligator" grew in Pigpen's hands as he shaped it with Lesh and added lines that Hunter appreciated. Somewhere along the way, the band threw in a few kazoos, for reasons lost to time.

"Saint Stephen" was more richly human and serious. Its allusions were more complex than those of "Alligator," and its language more baroque ("Ladyfinger dipped in moonlight," "Several seasons with their treasons," "Talk about your plenty, talk about your ills / One man gathers what another man spills"). Old in its references and modern in its connections, "Saint Stephen" could have found its way into the work of the progressive rock bands of later years. Instead, it served as an early marker of the Dead's versatility and the suggestion of a musical path not taken.

And then there was "China Cat Sunflower." Hunter liked to say that "nobody ever asked me the meaning of this song." With good reason, since his lyrics were all sound and imagery; if there was a coherent through line, it has escaped generations of listeners. "Copper-dome bodhi drip a silver kimono," one line went. Another: "Comic book colors on a violin river crying Leonardo words from out a silk trombone." And so on. This was wordplay. Superb wordplay, filled with allusion, drawn from a literate and vibrant mind—and one influenced by the use of LSD. The song was introduced to the Dead's performances in early 1968 and remained with the band for the rest of its time, often setting up "I Know You Rider." "China Cat's" lyrics were a cheerful bit of Lewis Carroll nonsense, as Hunter himself playfully acknowledged. "It's good that a few things in this world are clear to all of us," he observed, approvingly.

This was Robert Hunter in 1967: intellectual, well read, deep, playful, mischievous. Time would change all the members of the Dead, but Hunter never lost those qualities.

HUNTER JOINED the Dead at a cabin on the Russian River in early September and was treated to a magnificent blast from his old friends. He heard them play "Alligator" and bore witness to the emerging Dead.

On September 3, they played a tiny dance hall in tiny Rio Nido. The signature piece of the evening opened with thunder—a big, loud explosion of electricity, heavy metal in its cacophony—and then almost as quickly dropped into a riveting groove. What followed was a thirty-one-minute take on "In the Midnight Hour," with Pigpen at his finest and the rest of the band in swinging syncopation. Lesh called it "perhaps the finest" version of the song the band ever played. It attested to their development at that still early juncture, powerfully growing from their debut album and combining the essential elements of the Dead—blues, jazz, improvisation, and, in those Pigpen years, a rough sexual energy as well. Garcia's guitar work was speedy and nimble, Lesh ventured up and down the bass without any conventional connection to a backbeat, and Weir skillfully laced in chords, while Kreutzmann was rock-solid on the beat, holding close even when Pigpen went afield with his harmonica and the music fractured into space at about the thirteen-minute mark. Returning to Kreutzmann's driving drums, Pigpen cajoled one person at a time to dance; Lesh thumped along, and Garcia and Weir caressed licks from their guitars. "Come on," Pigpen sang. "Get up and dance." Oh, did they.

It was a tour de force, one of Pigpen's most memorable contributions to the Dead. What's more, the night's performance included a tantalizing look at still another signpost in the band's development. The Dead's Rio Nido gig included an extended take on "Dancing in the Street," part of their repertoire for months, but revamped by the fall of 1967. Mellower and more thoughtful, the tune now had room for Garcia to stretch, and on September 3, he did. The center section, three minutes or so, showed off the band trying out something. In those minutes, Garcia and Lesh spoke to each other across the melody and toyed with a recognizably new idea, a musical fragment, really, but evidence of something on their minds. Only a handful of fans witnessed all this firsthand, but Hunter was one of them, and he channeled it into the work that would re-form the Dead in the years ahead—billowing outward from the iron foundation and wispy allusions of Rio Nido and into something even more grand and empyrean: "Dark Star."

If Hunter wrote his first trio of lyrics *for* the Dead, he wrote the next one *with* the Dead. What he heard that night and over those days along the Russian River, not far from the area where Garcia's mom had dragged him in a failed attempt to extricate him from the music and drugs of San Francisco during his high school years, was the sketch of a new number, the one tucked inside "Dancing in the Street" on September 3. The verses pushed back and forth between A and G, with

154 | HERE BESIDE THE RISING TIDE

Weir and Garcia experimenting around those chords, then dropped into a more complex arrangement for the chorus. Hunter heard fragments of it that night and worked on it as he listened, and later as he lay in bed in his cabin. He let his mind roam.

"I just started scratching paper," he told an interviewer in 1978. The first words he put down were "Dark star crashes, pouring its light into ashes," each syllable attaching to the melody line that the band was practicing. Garcia gobbled it up and asked for more. At first, Hunter could not find the rest. Then, back in San Francisco, Hunter woke up one morning at 710 Ashbury and went for a walk in the park. He had the lyricism of T. S. Eliot in his head, specifically Eliot's "Love Song of J. Alfred Prufrock," which includes the line "Let us go then, you and I, when the evening is spread out against the sky." A hippie in the park handed Hunter a joint, and he amended Eliot's rhythm to suit his own. Onto the page went "Shall we go, you and I, while we can, through the transitive nightfall of diamonds." It sounded like Eliot but also felt different, puzzling even Hunter: "I don't have any idea what the 'transitive nightfall of diamonds' means," he conceded. "It sounded good at the time. It brings up something that you can see."

And so, drawing themes and images, building them around chords and a sensibility more than a structure, Hunter completed "Dark Star."

The full song, with Hunter's lyrics, made its first appearance in Los Angeles on December 13, 1967. It would thereafter offer the Dead its signature improvisational vehicle, and it would anchor the Dead's reputation at the vanguard of musical experimentation. It was wide and open-ended, and its feeling oscillated with the evening—some nights gentle and meandering, other nights forceful, even frightening. It could shatter with feedback or whistle in the wind. It was, for Garcia and for early Deadheads, the preeminent expression of the Dead in the 1960s, and it grafted neatly onto what its audience believed itself to be, too. It was psychedelic—the movement of notes and ideas, fluid and improvisational. It owed much to LSD, to be sure, but just as much to the jazz cohort of Dead influences—Coltrane and Miles Davis are inside "Dark

Star" in the way the musicians listen to one another, free to go in their own directions while bound to the journey of the sound.

Woven into the Dead's image and iconography, the "dark star" stood for transformation and illumination, for duality and ambiguity, even for Garcia himself (Robert Greenfield's 1996 oral biography of Garcia was entitled *Dark Star*). And it found its way into the mainstream as well: In 1987, Harper's Index, the magazine's trademark collection of pop culture statistics, listed the number of times the Grateful Dead played "Dark Star" in concert (46) just after the number of visitors to listen to the Watergate tapes at the National Archives in an average week (12) and just before the "percentage decrease in the number of people arrested for possession of marijuana in 1986 (20)."

"Dark Star" defied easy description as a musical feat, and Garcia resisted attempts to pigeonhole it. Asked by Charles Reich to explain the song, Garcia deflected, insisting that it was less of a fixed object than an unfolding idea. "I have a long continuum of 'Dark Stars' which range in character from each other," he said. "'Dark Star' has meant, while I'm playing it, almost as many things as I can sit here and imagine, so all I can do is talk about 'Dark Star' as a playing experiment." He was consistent. When the musicologist Graeme Boone analyzed the song in a 1997 book on rock, he included the band's reaction—to a man, they rebuffed his attempts to pin it down.

The song was never the same, even on back-to-back nights. The Dead were known to perform it sublimely and then come back at the next show and deliver it with an altogether different musical and emotional emphasis. Some versions ran six or seven minutes, others a half hour. Some were circular and complete; others trailed off into something else, never to resume. Every iteration was different. The song was forever in the moment.

And that, as Garcia tried to explain to Reich, was the whole point—the playing experiment, the opening of possibility, the embrace of the moment. It was the act, not the product, that defined the Dead. And in that, of course, the Dead found its relationship to the counterculture.

Not only did it challenge convention; it challenged the idea that convention was a thing at all, to embrace or even to oppose. At its best, "Dark Star" stripped away capitalism and politics, yes, but also past and future. It was magic and ritual, and it existed now.

As the Dead emerged from the Summer of Love and brought Hunter into the fold, the "now" was transcendent.

That was the meaning of "Dark Star." In the moment.

LT. COL. J. EDWIN MCKEE, commanding officer of the induction station in Houston, called the name three times. Muhammad Ali, then still almost universally referred to by his birth name, Cassius Clay, refused to step forward. Ali was led away and warned, then returned to the room and called one more time. He again refused and was asked to memorialize his refusal on paper. "I refuse to be inducted into the armed forces of the United States," he wrote. He was placed under arrest and indicted. On June 20, 1967, an all-white jury in Houston voted to convict Ali of refusing induction. At Ali's request, the judge sentenced him on the spot: five years in prison and a $10,000 fine.

Ali was the winner of an Olympic gold medal in boxing, a heavyweight champion of the world. Young, electric, thrilling. No matter. He was vilified. "Champ turned chump," editorialists harrumphed. "Shame, shame, shame, shame on you Cassius (Muhammad Ali) Clay," *The Messenger* of Madisonville, Kentucky, lamented. "You are a disgrace to America."

Ali persisted. A devoted convert to the Nation of Islam, he stood on his religious objection to war, and to the Vietnam War in particular. "I ain't got no quarrel with them Vietcong," he said. "No Vietcong ever called me nigger."

THE DEAD made several trips to Los Angeles in 1967, playing the Santa Monica Civic Auditorium in January, the Ambassador Hotel in April, the Hollywood Bowl in September, and the Shrine Exposition Hall in November, with a few club dates and free performances along the way. At one of those, band members noticed an unusually tall teenager elbowing his way to the front of the crowd.

Still just fifteen years old and growing, Bill Walton already stood out. He and some friends had heard about the Grateful Dead from listening to FM radio in San Diego. They absconded with one of their parents' cars and scooted up the coast to Los Angeles one weekend to catch the new band out of San Francisco.

"We just went up there, parked who knows where. We just went in our shorts and our tennis shoes and a T-shirt. We didn't have anything," Walton said. "We got in free, somehow went right to the front."

It was, for Walton, the beginning of a very long journey. "Our lives," he said, "were never the same again."

MICKEY HART was the son of not one but two drummers. Born Michael Steven Hartman in Brooklyn in 1943, he was raised by his mother, who steered him to the instrument she and Hart's father both played. A misfit in the manner of his future Dead colleagues, Hart had little use for studies but plenty of enthusiasm for music. He skated around the edges of high school and then joined the Air Force in order to be a part of the drum and bugle corps. Discharged in 1965, he connected with his long-missing father, Lenny Hart, when the latter invited him to come to San Carlos, just south of San Francisco, and help run his music store. Their relationship was never easy—Lenny Hart was shifty, while Mickey was focused to the point of obsessive. But they muddled through, and together the two owned and managed Hart Music.

That meant that the younger Hart found himself in San Francisco during the Summer of Love. The city was abuzz, of course, and Hart's intense, manic energy felt at home in the charged circuitry of that summer. He cruised the concert scene, absorbing drum styles, and was on hand for a Bill Graham extravaganza at the Fillmore in August, when

Graham produced a series of concerts across musical genres—Count Basie with the Young Rascals, the Charles Lloyd Quartet, the Steve Miller Band, and Chuck Berry.

Shows such as these were Graham's great gift to the San Francisco scene—pairings that introduced patrons to new musical styles, inviting them to appreciate the connections between, say, Chuck Berry and Count Basie. Among those who got it was Hart, ravenously drawn to the universality and vitality of drums. And one thing that Basie and Berry had in common was a beat, anchored by great drummers—in the case of Basie, the one and only Sonny Payne. The Dead's drummer, Kreutzmann, was in the audience that night to learn from Payne, and while he was watching "in total awe," he got a tap on his shoulder from a wild-eyed San Carlos drum teacher, twenty-three-year-old Mickey Hart.

After the show, Kreutzmann, Hart, and a student of Hart's rambled through San Francisco, armed with drumsticks and imagination. "I knew how to play drums and all," Kreutzmann said, "but I sure didn't know how to do this stuff." Kreutzmann asked Hart to teach him, and over the next couple of weeks, Hart did, showing Kreutzmann something called a "false-sticking double paradiddle," multiplying beats and concentrating the accent on one hand. "It may sound simple, but it's tricky," Kreutzmann wrote. "The end result is that I became a better player."

And then a further notion struck him: Why not have Hart join the Dead?

Hart remembers that Kreutzmann invited him to meet the band at its rehearsal studio in Sausalito and that Hart got lost trying to find it. But Kreutzmann dogged him, and on September 29, Hart showed up to see the Dead at the Straight Theater.

It was the Dead's second performance at the Straight that summer, following a stream-of-consciousness evening on July 23, when they were joined onstage by an old friend, the ever-out-there Neal Cassady, who showed up at the Straight in full, florid expository form. Introduced by Garcia to a crowd familiar with him but undoubtedly mostly by reputation, Cassady settled into a scatting monologue, riffing on New York City and marijuana, Kerouac and sex and drinking and acid tests and suicide, dipping in and out of lucidity, breathing into the microphone as the Dead fell in behind him, Lesh setting the tempo with a modified bass line from the band's iconic "Turn On Your Love Light." Weir caught on and layered in his unique rhythm atop Lesh and the babbling Cassady. The music melted into feedback as Cassady rapped. "German pornography," he mumbled, and something about souls and "doing nothing," followed by a trip into the Rocky Mountains and a flat tire, wisecracks about "Stiff Doctor Dick" and cyclops and evolution.

For sixteen minutes, the audience was taken back—to the Acid Tests, to Kesey and the bus, to *On the Road*, a reach across time and space, a trip through the Beats and acid and home to the Haight. Not everyone knew what to make of it. A few young people in the audience jeered. But others got it, understood that they were being ricocheted through time and culture. And then the Dead piled back in. Time was malleable. The music held the moment.

A few weeks later, they were back again. As with most things in Haight-Ashbury that year, the events during the last week of September involved some sleight of hand. The Straight Theater did not have a permit to host concerts or dances, so posters advertised the shows that week as a "dance class," with a $2.50 "registration" fee. The regulations governing dancing did not extend to "classes," so the shows slipped through that loophole.

Hart showed up as requested but without gear. During intermission, he and Kreutzmann scrounged up a kit, and Hart joined the Dead for the second set. Hart fell in with the music—like "jumping into the jet stream"—and the result was notable. Lesh, for one, recalled it as "one of the highest-energy sets ever," and Garcia, ever unwilling to be seen as the band's leader but always recognized as such, gave Hart his blessing. "*This* is the Grateful Dead," he exulted after the show. "We can take *this* all over the world."

* * *

160 | HERE BESIDE THE RISING TIDE

FIRST, THOUGH, there was trouble at home.

Garcia, Mountain Girl, and Sunshine were out on a Monday afternoon, just kicking around the neighborhood, where the Haight was enjoying a cool fall day. As they turned the corner onto Ashbury, a crowd was gathered outside the house, and a neighbor waved to them from her window, warning them to come inside her house, which they did, and watched from the window as the San Francisco Police Department wrapped up its afternoon work at 710 Ashbury.

Acting on a tip—as if one were needed—the police knocked on the front door of the home of the Grateful Dead just after 3 P.M. on October 2, 1967. Denied entry, the police pushed their way indoors. As Garcia watched from across the way, the police hauled out evidence, having already dragged off Weir and Pigpen. Also arrested were managers Danny Rifkin and Rock Scully and equipment manager Bob Matthews, along with six women: Florence Nathan (Rosie McGee); Sue Swanson, the Dead's "first fan"; Veronica Grant (aka Veronica Barnard), who was dating Pigpen; Christine Bennett, who was dating soundman Dan Healy; Toni Kaufman, who worked for HALO; and Rosalyn Stevenson, identified only as a "girl friend." Five other people inside the house at the time of the raid were released. Of those taken into custody, Rosie McGee was particularly affected, as she attempted to cover the group's tracks by swallowing a handful of hashish to keep the police from seizing it. She was speechless for days.

Nathan's quick thinking notwithstanding, a search of a home belonging to the Grateful Dead in Haight-Ashbury in 1967 was pretty likely to turn up drugs, and in this case, police boasted of having discovered a pound and a half of marijuana and hashish. LOTS OF GRASS—GRATEFUL DEAD MOWED DOWN, the *Examiner* exclaimed. The paper's account was accompanied by a photo of members of the Dead and friends lined up on a bench at the police station. Pigpen was described as the band's "long-haired blues singer."

The eleven men and women pulled from the house that afternoon spent a few hours in jail before their lawyer, the city's estimable Brian Rohan, showed up to bail them out. They were charged with felony possession of marijuana. Once they were out, Rohan took over the criminal case and Rifkin spearheaded their public defense, calling a press conference at 710 Ashbury three days later and using it to attack California's marijuana laws generally—the law "classifies smoking marijuana along with murder, rape and armed robbery as a felony," Rifkin's statement noted—as well as its discriminatory application: "If the lawyers, doctors, advertising men, teachers and political officeholders who use marijuana were arrested today, the law might well be off the books before Thanksgiving."

After the press conference, the Dead served cookies, cake, and coffee to reporters and photographers. One reporter who asked a particularly stupid question—"How long did it take you to grow your hair that long, Danny?" he inquired of Rifkin—was threatened with a bowl of whipped cream in the face. By the following June, the hoopla had died down, and all of those arrested the previous fall pleaded guilty to misdemeanors and paid fines of $100 to $200 each—just $100 for Weir and Pigpen, who persuaded the court that they were not even smokers.

The arrests did nothing to affect drug use by members of the band or anyone else, but it did help solidify the Dead's place in the counterculture, where outlaws, rebels, and revolutionaries all had their place in the pecking order. The Dead, especially Garcia, fought attempts to draw them into the culture's revolutionary spirit and ambitions, but their cred as outlaws was bolstered by the city's attempt to treat them as such. They enjoyed it.

NEWS OF the Haight-Ashbury arrests got good play in San Francisco. It also found its way onto the pages of a brand-new music and culture magazine, born that fall not far from the Dead's 710 Ashbury home.

Rolling Stone published its first issue on November 9, 1967. It was the work of Jann S. Wenner, a former contributor to the *Daily Californian* at Berkeley and a protégé of Ralph Gleason. Raised in a well-to-do, nonobservant Jewish home and kicked out of a couple of schools as a kid, Wenner lit upon journalism early, drawn to Herb Caen's spirited column in the *San Francisco Chronicle*. Sometime around the sixth grade, Wenner decided to become an editor or publisher. "I have no clue where or how this odd notion struck me," he confessed later. Wenner worked his way into San Francisco journalism, covered the 1964 Republican Convention hosted by the city, became enchanted by the Beatles and Bob Dylan, and settled into the gyre of journalism, music, and politics that was the Haight in the mid-1960s.

Wenner was at Berkeley in 1964 for the Free Speech Movement and at the San Jose Acid Test in December 1965, where he first heard the Dead, later writing about them for the *Daily Californian*. He was at the Fillmore Acid Test and tagged along with the Pranksters to the Trips Festival, where he met Gleason, a vision of a reporter in a hat and trench coat. They shared a conviction that music mattered.

"We created *Rolling Stone* in Ralph's living room," Wenner wrote in his memoirs. Gleason chipped in $2,000 and Wenner $1,500; in total, Wenner said it cost $7,500 to launch the magazine, much of the balance coming from his parents. Its first issue carried the news of the arrests at the Dead's house on page 8. It featured a photo of the band members, all grins and mischief, on the steps and porch.

The magazine was never meant as part of the underground press and was not properly thought of as a journal of the counterculture. It was too flashy, too infatuated with the music business to stand outside it. It was interested in the currents of social change but almost exclusively in how musicians traversed them. It was, in those respects, a perfect vehicle for chronicling the life and history of the Grateful Dead.

But both also grew in ways that enlarged their place, sometimes despite themselves. *Rolling Stone* brought on Michael Lydon, Ben Fong-Torres, Lester Bangs, and Cameron Crowe, writers for whom music was a point of entry into the larger cultural ferment of the period. Though the magazine initially distinguished itself from the underground press by steering clear of political coverage, its rising prominence in the 1970s drew it beyond music and into bigger undertakings. Tom Wolfe covered Apollo 17, the last crewed moon mission, for *Rolling Stone*. Hunter Thompson brought his groundbreaking political cover-

"DARK STAR" | 163

age to the magazine, pioneering a whole new way of writing about drugs and politics. It covered the kidnapping of Patty Hearst, presidential elections, and the cacophonous cultural events that shaped and broke the counterculture in the 1960s and 1970s.

The Dead and *Rolling Stone* bridged worlds—fun and purpose, money and principle. They nibbled at the edge of politics and events, aloof from them yet identified with them. By the early 1970s, Wenner considered himself a "lapsed Deadhead," and the magazine's interest in the band waxed and waned. Nevertheless, *Rolling Stone* launched with the Dead on its pages and covered the Dead until its final days. Garcia and the Dead appeared on the cover of *Rolling Stone* in 1969, 1970, 1972 (twice, back to back), 1973, 1987, 1989, 1991, 1993, and 1995—with at least one cover story in each of four decades (Garcia also appeared in a montage commemorating *Rolling Stone*'s thousandth issue in 2006, and the magazine produced an "ultimate guide" to the Dead in 2021). Only Bob Dylan, the Beatles, and the Rolling Stones joined the Dead in being so prominently featured across that same expanse of time.

THE DEAD were eager to follow up their first album and to show off their expanding range. Already dissatisfied with their debut release, they resolved this time to bottle the psychedelic magic they were channeling live, that effervescent tincture of blues, improvisation, and trippiness that showed up in Rio Nido.

They re-upped with Dave Hassinger at Warner Bros., but this time they resolved to do it differently—to take their time and to explore the edgier, more experimental direction they were trying out live. They brought new music: "Alligator" was now a staple of their performances, and they were working up a new number, led by Weir, that combined churning chords and open musical space with an evocatively (if misleadingly) autobiographical lyric. The number did not have much of a name yet, so band members took to referring to it as "The Other One." It would go through modifications—it was called "That's It for the Other One" for a time—but its core musical line was on its way to be-

164 | HERE BESIDE THE RISING TIDE

coming a Dead staple. The Dead also brought their new drummer, Hart, and a second additional member, an especially abstruse musical addition named Tom Constanten, often known as T.C., son of a Vegas captain of waiters, friend of Lesh, admirer of John Cage.

They arrived in Los Angeles in November. The band rented an Egyptian-tomb-like residence across the street from Bela Lugosi's place, and Constanten, granted a week's leave from the Air Force, drove over from Las Vegas. They quickly settled into their surroundings. The Dead met with Maharishi Mahesh Yogi, who had advised the Beatles, and bumped into Donovan. "L.A.," Constanten said, "is really woven into that record."

The early results were positively weird. Constanten brought a new level of experimentation. Following the lead of Cage and Luciano Berio, he spun a gyroscope and pressed it to the sound board of a piano. He painted the piano's strings with a brush. He dragged a comb along the strings of a Hawaiian guitar. Garcia and Lesh were enchanted, the drummers less so. Constanten also added a layer of keyboard expertise (he had performed with, and composed for, the Las Vegas Symphony as a teenager), supplementing Pigpen and doubling up the Dead's virtuosity there in a manner not unlike Hart's contribution to their drum section. In this case, however, the two keyboard players brought almost diametrically oppositional styles, with Pigpen anchored to the blues and Constanten unmoored from all things conventional. "Mountain Girl said Pig was the black man's keyboard player," Constanten said, "and I was the white man's keyboard player."

The clash of sounds and ideas would soon become a source of unhappiness within the band, and although it eventually became a source of strength—even the Dead's hallmark—at first, in the studio, it did not go well.

Hassinger tried to adjust to the Dead's approach. After starting out in the same enormous studio where they had dashed off *The Grateful Dead*, Hassinger took the band to the San Fernando Valley and smaller quarters. He listened and struggled to translate to vinyl the sense of adventure already coming to characterize their shows.

The Dead had other ideas. Garcia suggested splicing together snippets from live performances and interspersing them with studio cuts, attempting to create whole, seamless songs out of scraps and interludes. It was an editing challenge that reflected Garcia's growing appreciation of the artistic freedom that the studio might offer. But progress was slow. They were not making much headway toward producing finished tracks, and Hassinger suggested that they might be better off working in New York, where the band was again headed on tour. There, attempts to capture the sound and shuttle their entourage—"family and children and friends and roadies and breastfeeding ladies and people sitting on the floor," as one studio owner recalled the shambling Dead collective—still proved elusive.

Moreover, they were difficult. Producers and engineers enjoyed Garcia. His easy disposition made up for his exactitude. But Weir could be spacey and indecisive, and Kreutzmann veered toward gruff. The new guy, Hart, though he was bubbling with energy, did not make many waves on this album. Lesh, however, was the object of outrage. Demanding, uncompromising, and short-tempered, he infuriated engineers and producers.

Executives begged the band to focus, but they simply would not. For the members of the Dead, no idea was too outlandish. At one point, Weir tried to explain the sound he was grasping for as that of "heavy air." Hassinger, bewildered, stared back at him. Weir remembered that as being the final straw, but Hassinger's recollection was that he was more puzzled than angered, and that he was even somewhat touched by Weir's sincerity. According to Hassinger, the final break came not over "heavy air," but rather after he questioned the quality of the vocal performances on two numbers, "Born Cross-Eyed" and "New Potato Caboose." To challenge any member of the band was to confront the whole of it in those days, Hassinger said, and his skepticism about those vocals left him at odds with all the musicians. Having antagonized the band he was there to produce, Hassinger realized his utility had come to an end. He quit. Dan Healy, already handling the sound for live Dead shows, took over.

166 | HERE BESIDE THE RISING TIDE

To the Dead—new at recording, self-conscious about their first album, aware of their galloping growth—this was simply the process of developing an album, one that mimicked their way of developing a song, slowly, organically, fitfully. To Warner Bros., it was unprofessional, expensive, and immature.

Joe Smith tolerated it for a while, then blew up. Writing to Rifkin two days after Christmas, Smith let the band have it. The recording sessions in New York, Smith said, had been hampered by "lack of preparation, direction and cooperation," the combined result of which was to have made "this album the most unreasonable project with which we have ever involved ourselves."

Smith singled out Lesh for criticism, blaming other members of the Dead and its entourage for failing to restrain Lesh into "anything resembling normal behavior." The bottom line, Smith added: "It all adds up to a lack of professionalism. The Grateful Dead is not one of the top acts in the business as yet. With their attitudes and their inability to take care of business when it's time to do so would lead us to believe that they never will be truly important. No matter how talented your group is, they're going to have to put something of themselves into the business before they go anywhere."

Not since the Army had anyone scolded Garcia quite that way. The band responded in kind, correcting Smith's grammar and writing "Fuck you" across the letter before posting it on the wall of the studio. The note was in Lesh's handwriting. So much for taking direction.

IT TOOK months more to get the album finished. Entitled *Anthem of the Sun,* it was released on July 18. Side 1 fused "Cryptical Envelopment" to "Quadlibet for Tenderfeet" to "The Faster We Go, the Rounder We Get" and, finally, to a sonic adventure by Constanten that went by the name "We Leave the Castle." Those four numbers were identifiably distinct but joined as "That's It for the Other One." "New Potato Caboose" and "Born Cross-Eyed" rounded out the side. Side 2 opened with "Alligator," now polished into an eleven-minute, twenty-second extended play that borrowed from live performances, and "Caution (Do Not Stop on Tracks)," an electronically adventurous meander inspired by the Dead's early sets at the In Room, where passing trains supplied a low, urgent rumble that the band chose to replicate rather than drown out. On *Anthem of the Sun,* "Caution" boiled along for a bit and then faded, as trains will, into a jumble of sound and echo.

The album's ambitions were as large as its soundscape. It was a tribute to the Haight and all its potential—and a eulogy for all of that, too, a farewell to that moment when it had all seemed possible, an expression of the bittersweet disappointment of its coming to an end. *Anthem* brought together the Dead's extensive, sometimes unfocused time in the studio and spliced it into sections of nineteen performances from September 1967 through March 1968. Hassinger received credit for his production work in Hollywood and New York. Bill Walker produced the colorful cover, an orange and yellow circle of flame and color surrounding stylized portraits of band members that resembled a mandala. It was an altogether original, if opaque, offering.

The album's impact rested largely with the receiver. *Rolling Stone's* reviewer, Jim Miller, was smitten with side 1, calling it "a masterpiece of rock," and it certainly caught the spirit of that year's adventures—chaotic, loud, exotic, and intense, it echoed life in Haight-Ashbury, with its easy afternoons of caring and its ominous shades of a world gone wrong. But even critics who respected the album had trouble loving it. Writing for *The Village Voice,* a very young Lucian K. Truscott IV found the music "searching, clinging, pulsing, fraught with hidden meaning," but admitted being lost in it. *High Fidelity* wondered about the Dead's drift from the blues into "a full-fledged (and by now somewhat anachronistic) acid-rock bag." The album, *High Fidelity* concluded, "is essential background music for pot parties (or methedrine or LSD)."

Lesh, the band's most enthusiastic advocate of the avant-garde, loved *Anthem* and considered it the Dead's "most innovative and far-reaching achievement on record . . . a temporal collage . . . a summation of our musical direction to date." For others, it was a striking bit of daring, more to be admired than enjoyed. For the Dead themselves, the album's impact was financial—the band's liberal use of studio time ultimately left it $100,000 in debt to Warner Bros.—and personal: It brought Lesh and Garcia together as the band members most comfortable on the edge, now the Dead's center of gravity. That left Weir and Pigpen somewhat on the outs, a rift that would soon widen into the band's closest flirtation with a breakup.

THE DEAD, along with the rest of the counterculture, struggled with their relationship to money. When Peter Coyote observed that the Dead were the best of the San Francisco bands because they most resembled a family—and thus had a more communitarian or shared sense of economics—he nevertheless emphasized that the band remained a money-making enterprise, and thus, if not exactly suspect, at least potentially compromised.

For the Dead, the perennial tension was one of values: How could they express themselves while also making a living and, as time went by, supporting the community that grew up around them? It was one thing to cover rent, quite another to support managers, sound engineers, lighting designers, road crews, and all their partners, spouses, and children. The Dead's work required that they intersect with the larger capitalist society—Warner Bros. wasn't in it for the values, and even Bill Graham, for all his devotion to music and culture, was a shrewd businessman. How, then, could the Dead be both a rock band and a counterculture institution?

The band's efforts to reconcile those identities began in 1968—during the period where the band was finishing *Anthem of the Sun*—when they decided that the solution was to create their own musical space in San Francisco. They decided to buy a theater.

Not "buy," exactly. Rather, they decided to lease a theater in partnership with other leading San Francisco bands, the Airplane and Quicksilver, doing business together under the corporate name Headstone Productions, guided by two men close to the Dead, manager Ron Rakow and criminal defense lawyer Brian Rohan, who had successfully dealt down the 710 drug bust charges from felonies to misdemeanors. The location they lit upon was not perfect. It was outside the Haight, at the corner of Market and Van Ness streets, four blocks south of City Hall. And it was above a car dealership. But it was big—it could hold some three thousand people—and it offered the chance for them to escape an already complicated relationship with Bill Graham. From the start, members of the Dead had admired Graham's intensity, though they deplored his preoccupation with money. They accommodated each other—Graham loved the Dead—but always with some reserve: He was afraid they would slip him LSD, and they were convinced he was ripping them off. Having their own venue allowed them to move beyond Graham, and on their own terms.

Rakow negotiated a deal for the space: Headstone would pay $9,000 a month in rent, plus 20 percent of the gate. Industry insiders arched an eyebrow at the price, but it set the musicians up to be their own bosses. They called their new home the Carousel Ballroom.

Management of the theater fell to Sat Santokh Singh Khalsa. Born Bertram Kanegson to a Jewish family in New York in 1939, Sat Santokh was an organizer, active with the War Resisters League and close to Bayard Rustin, the intellectual and spiritual guide for many drawn to nonviolence in that era. Sat Santokh arrived in San Francisco in 1964 and soon discovered psychedelics, which he regarded as "a possible gateway to transform our collective consciousness."

At the Carousel, Sat Santokh's role fell somewhere among the zones normally occupied by music promoters, community organizers, and camp counselors. Rakow "hired" him for the job, and his first task was to fix up the place; he turned to the Diggers, who cleaned it out and scrounged up bits of furniture, including "the most comfortable backstage that ever was," with couches, overstuffed chairs and even a balcony that allowed the musicians to watch as others performed. He hired North American Ibis Alchemical Co. to run nightly light shows. Committed to offering the Carousel as a community resource, the bands allowed local activists—Diggers, Black Panthers, and others—to have small spaces of their own to store materials and open tiny offices. Security was catch as catch can, with the Hells Angels sometimes manning the doors. Bands had liberal guest lists, always undermining the night's gate receipts.

It seemed a triumph of hip capitalism. The musicians would control their own venue and make their own money, without a promoter cut being siphoned off. They could play when they wanted and still build a reliable audience base. And, of course, they could attract other talents in precisely the same manner as Graham and Helms. They would, in other words, control their own destiny, the dream of every musical act since the advent of the music industry.

The Carousel opened in January. Days at the theater were busy—activists and hippies shuffled around the place, plotting strategy, talking, getting high. Afternoons turned to preparation for the night's performances. By early evening, the offices were empty, and the night crowd had begun to gather. And then the shows began. The scene at the Carousel was, one writer reflected, "a community of energy in celebration of life and consciousness in change."

The Carousel was an immediate hit. Just a few weeks after the bands took it over, Gleason lent his endorsement, writing in his influential *San Francisco Chronicle* "On the Town" column, "The Carousel is by far the best hall in San Francisco for rock groups in almost every imaginable way." Gleason's praise was the city's highest, and he gave it despite the air of disorganization that hovered about the place. In the same column in which he proclaimed it San Francisco's best rock venue, Gleason noted that one weekend's "dance" was not announced until Wednesday and that "there was considerable confusion" about who would play that Sunday and how much tickets would cost.

No matter. It was new and exciting. The Dead made the Carousel their main venue in San Francisco that winter and appeared at a highly anticipated show there on Valentine's Day. Then, just as they were preparing to open, they received crushing—if not altogether surprising—news from Mexico: Neal Cassady was dead. He had been visiting Mexico, where he met up with a girlfriend, Janice Brown, in San Miguel de Allende. On February 3, he had set off on foot from her house to a nearby railroad depot, where he had deposited his things. Along the way, he happened upon a wedding party and may have joined them for a drink. He was already taking barbiturates, and the combination pushed him toward oblivion. He was found the next day beside the tracks, unconscious, and he died shortly after that, never having regained his senses. The cause of death was listed as "generalized congestion," shorthand for a hard-lived but much-enjoyed life. He was forty-one.

With Cassady on their minds, the Dead delivered a limber, contemplative first set that featured much of the music soon to appear on *Anthem of the Sun*, including the new Hunter lyrics. Opening with "Morning Dew," Garcia sang in a soulful vibrato, his voice ringing clear, and he played hard, presenting the piece in all its mournful reflection. Behind him, Constanten's organ dripped across the vocal line, and then Garcia stepped back in, accelerating through his lead, throttling back to sing. They followed with "Good Morning, Little Schoolgirl," walking slowly into the number over Lesh's bass and Pigpen's loose harmonica and throaty vocal. "Dark Star" got a quick turn—a six-minute version that hardly plumbed the song's evolving potential but delivered it as a punchy dance number, followed by "China Cat Sunflower," performed a little fast that night. The set's highlight, however, was a fearless six-minute, twenty-seven-second bash through "The Eleven," the rhythmically complex number written by Lesh and the drummers. And then the band ripped into "Turn On Your Love Light," bringing Pigpen back to the microphone and closing out a set that showed off both the psychedelic and blues sides of the band in early 1968.

After a performance by Country Joe and the Fish, the Dead returned to the stage—their stage—to open the second set. Garcia dedicated the set to Cassady, and both the selection of "Cryptical Envelopment" and Garcia's delivery of it evoked Cassady's memory. The song's reprise— "You know he had to die"—carried special weight that night. Garcia sang it purposefully, clear and heavy with consequence. That segued, as it usually did, into "The Other One" and back to "Cryptical Envelopment." The suite, soon to appear on *Anthem*, owed much to Cassady— "The Other One" included Weir's lyric "The bus came by, and I got on.

That's where it all began / Cowboy Neal at the wheel, on the bus to never-ever land"—both as a figure in the music and as an inspiration for it. "New Potato Caboose," "Born Cross-Eyed," a twelve-minute "Spanish Jam," "Alligator," and "Caution" rounded out the night before the music tailed off into feedback and the band returned with "Midnight Hour" for an encore.

The version of "Alligator" that night warrants one other special mention. In addition to Hunter's lyrics and those added by Pigpen, the piece had an extra short aside: "Burn down the Fillmore," they sang together, led by Lesh, "gas the Avalon." That was out of place in the song—the otherwise allegoric tale of a personified gator—but it pointed to the moment. The Dead, slightly bitter but now liberated, were making a go of the Carousel.

"The Carousel," said Dead manager Jon McIntire, "was the epitome of anarchy at its finest." The Dead and the Airplane anchored the theater's short run, but they were hardly alone. Quicksilver recorded an album there on April 4, and Electric Flag put together one from recordings made later that month. The Santana Blues Band played five nights in April, and Dan Hicks and His Hot Licks opened for Johnny Cash on April 24. Thelonious Monk and the Charlatans played three nights in May. Big Brother and the Holding Company, with Janis Joplin, hosted a benefit for the Hells Angels on May 15—the bands charged one-dollar admission for Joplin, including unlimited beer. "It may have been the largest assemblage of Hells Angels in one place ever," McIntire recalled—and a June show that later became a live album. Fleetwood Mac opened for the Dead three nights. Chuck Berry, Steve Miller, and Buddy Guy all appeared there. Tuesday nights were jam sessions. Patrons would pay one dollar and would be treated to whatever musicians were on hand—Garcia was a regular, joined by Elvin Bishop and others, depending on the week.

On May Day, the Carousel served as the hub of the Free City Convention. There were, the *Berkeley Barb* observed, "hippies, blacks, Hell's Angels, servicemen. The anonymous organizers had apparently learned from the mistakes of past Be-Ins, whereat vast crowds were centralized around distant platforms of notables, participating passively via loudspeaker. This time it was decentralized for the first three hours, lots of little scenes and happenings."

It was a central point of excitement, a gathering place. "The Carousel, new as it is, radiates an important force in the community," one writer noted in June. "There's a great sense of participation there. We're all part of it."

Not for long.

Not because the Carousel was a failure. It was chaotic, to be sure. "The bands could never agree on anything," Lesh recalled. That was to be expected. Despite the chaos, the Carousel was magnificent, if only briefly. It connected divergent people and nurtured a sense of creative belonging. But its obvious strengths—community support, band engagement, consistent revenue—were undermined by programming mishaps and by a fatally bad lease that made it virtually impossible to break even. By May, Rakow complained that he was bleeding money, though he had no one but himself to blame, having negotiated the terms of the lease. Bill Thompson, who managed the Airplane, considered his counterpart a "rotten manager" and pointed to the Carousel deal as evidence of that. Gleason agreed that the deal was badly executed, calling it the "stupidest lease in show business."

In June, the owner of the building persuaded a Superior Court judge to bar the doors of the building until Headstone Productions made good on the rent, by then $11,000 in arrears. Rakow and the band slipped through that crisis, but legal wrangling continued. Headstone gave up at the end of June, and though the Dead briefly considered taking on the Carousel by themselves, band members thought better of it.

Graham spied his opportunity. He met with representatives of William Fuller, the owner of the property, and left the meeting with a lease of his own. On July 4, he shuttered his San Francisco venue, the Fillmore, and moved his business into the Carousel, which he renamed the Fillmore West. Graham now had Fillmores on both coasts. The Dead fell back into Graham's fold, newly appreciative of how difficult his job was.

174 | HERE BESIDE THE RISING TIDE

That ended the Dead's turn as theater operators. They had not built a lasting success at the Carousel, but they had tasted the fruit of counterculture cohesion, the merging of business and art into community. They never lost the feeling, even as those around them did.

As the Carousel was ending, so, too, was the Dead's residential life in San Francisco. Discouraged by the frenetic weeks toward the end of the Summer of Love, members of the band gave up on the city and trickled out in 1968, Garcia and Mountain Girl to Larkspur, Lesh and Rosie McGee to Fairfax, Weir and Hart to Novato, Kreutzmann to San Rafael—all small towns north of the Golden Gate. Only Pigpen remained in the city proper. A chapter closed.

Gleason put it best. Praising the Dead and the other bands for reaching beyond music and attempting to create a space for culture—a community center with rehearsal halls, offices, and galleries—Gleason acknowledged disappointment that the enterprise had fallen apart, doomed by naïveté and victim to bad leadership, overzealous policing, and especially "the hippie ethic of permissiveness." Still, he noted, it "was a fine dream."

PART III

DISCOVERIES

The war in Vietnam and the struggle for equality at home divided the counterculture between those who advocated for peace and those who took up arms.

Above: Antiwar protest. San Francisco, September 2, 1970.
Elizabeth Sunflower/Retro Photo Archive

Below: Black Panthers at the State Capitol. Sacramento, May 2, 1967.
Bettmann/Getty Images

CHAPTER 9

All Fall Down

THE SAME MONTHS OF EARLY 1968 THAT SAW THE DEAD ACquire, run, and lose the Carousel featured the country stumbling at war, buckling beneath assassination and riots, and lurching toward a political reckoning.

America entered the year with 486,000 soldiers in Vietnam, and the war became the galvanizing focus of the counterculture. Demonstrators had stormed the Pentagon on October 21, 1967, when a peaceful daytime rally on the National Mall fractured in the late afternoon as one contingent crossed the Potomac River to vent its anger at the Pentagon itself. Scuffling went on all night, and by daylight, marshals had arrested 682 demonstrators. Forty-seven people were hurt. A week later, Huey Newton was accused of shooting it out with Oakland police. Newton was hit in the gut and the leg, while Officer John Frey was killed. "Free Huey" became a battle cry of the growing underground. By the beginning of 1968, *The Oracle* reached a hundred thousand readers with every issue.

Rising anger lifted some boats and rocked many. Tom Hayden and SDS claimed leadership of the New Left, but impatience was tearing at their stewardship as more violent forces pulled away. Late in 1967, Hayden recognized that the left was hardening. "Resistance," he said, "became the official watchword of the antiwar movement."

Much of the same was true within the civil rights movement. Martin Luther King, Jr., defied many of his advisers and announced his opposition to the war in Vietnam at Riverside Church in New York City on

178 | HERE BESIDE THE RISING TIDE

April 4, 1967. "A time comes when silence is betrayal," King said. "And that time has come for us in relation to Vietnam." It was too much for Johnson, not enough for the more militant proponents of racial justice. Stifled by King's unwillingness to take up arms, they, too, itched for combat. Malcolm X was closer to the spirit of the moment. It was a time of Panthers—of guns and confrontation.

And so violence in Asia begat violence in America. The soft focus of the Be-In hardened and cleaved. To be silent was to be complicit. To act was to flirt with death. It was, one participant recalled, "a cyclone in a wind tunnel."

It would not take much for that mixture to boil over. The first twitch of the fateful year of 1968 came at the end of January, when North Vietnamese forces and Viet Cong launched a coordinated assault on South Vietnam. Known as the Tet Offensive, the strikes began on January 30 and 31, mostly small incursions that touched off protracted, difficult combat. One battle raged for twenty-five days. In the end, the assaults were repelled, and the Johnson administration claimed victory. That was arguable in purely military terms, but by 1968, the American public had been told for years that the end was near in Vietnam. As Hayden wrote, Tet "shattered any Pentagon illusions about a 'light at the end of the tunnel.'"

Instability seemed contagious. For restive Latinos, the emergence of Cesar Chavez, a magnetic champion of farm workers whose appeal in the Southwest rivaled that of King, supplied an organizing focus for long-standing grievances that stretched from fields to schoolyards. In 1966, Chavez marched from Delano to Sacramento—a page from the work of King and, before him, Gandhi—and devoted his organizing and spiritual energy to the United Farm Workers, whose iconic black eagle came to represent new possibilities for labor and Latinos, especially in California.

Energized by anger and hope, Los Angeles schoolchildren took their educational grievances into their own hands. Some fifteen thousand students walked out of their classrooms during the first week of March. The Walkouts, they called it, or the Blowouts. Fourteen years after

ALL FALL DOWN | 179

Brown v. Board, these students demanded the integration that *Brown* had commanded but that many had resisted and that California had managed to sidestep. Chicano students demanded bilingual education, representation among staff and faculty, an end to channeling them away from college opportunities and into vocations.

The nation teetered. And Johnson's ample, fragile ego faltered. He needed to be appreciated, even loved. Instead, he was abandoned, and not just by the hippies and commies and longhairs. He'd delivered civil rights legislation and still had lost King on Vietnam. He empathized with workers but faced dissatisfaction from Chavez. He'd been a teacher; now students were striking. He was losing James Reston and Walter Cronkite, Eugene McCarthy and Kennedy. Liberals.

On March 31, 1968, the president of the United States threw in his towel. "With America's sons in the fields far away, with America's future under challenge right here at home, with our hopes and the world's hopes for peace in the balance every day, I do not believe that I should devote an hour or a day of my time to any personal partisan causes or to any duties other than the awesome duties of this office—the presidency of your country," Johnson said, speaking slowly, eyes squarely on the camera, never glancing down at his notes. "Accordingly, I shall not seek, and I will not accept, the nomination of my party for another term as your president."

Three days later, Martin Luther King, Jr., left Washington, stopped over in Atlanta, and returned to Memphis, where he was supporting striking sanitation workers. The day ran late, and King was ninety minutes behind schedule when he arrived at the Mason Temple that evening, coaxed by aides to appear. With a violent storm raging outside, King, nursing a sore throat, bone tired, reflected on the long struggle. Wry, exhausted, and passionate, he built to his conclusion. "We've got some difficult days ahead. But it really doesn't matter with me now," he said,

> because I've been to the mountaintop. And I don't mind. Like anybody, I would like to live a long life. Longevity has its place.

180 | HERE BESIDE THE RISING TIDE

But I'm not concerned about that now. I just want to do God's will. And He's allowed me to go up to the mountain. And I've looked over. And I've seen the Promised Land. I may not get there with you. But I want you to know tonight, that we, as a people, will get to the Promised Land!

The next day, at 6:05 P.M., he stepped onto the balcony outside Room 306 of the Lorraine Motel. And then the shot. It ripped through King's jaw and blew his tie off his neck. He slumped to the ground, broken by the violence he had spent his life rejecting. Rioting erupted in 110 American cities.

"I was torn apart," Tom Hayden wrote, "with a grief that has not healed to this day."

THE UPRISING at Columbia University began on the afternoon of Tuesday, April 23, 1968, partly in response to the university's plans to build a new gym in Morningside Heights. Students staged a sit-in, ransacked the office of the president, and nervously took control of two buildings—later more—protesting not just the plans for the gym but also the university's relationship to the Institute for Defense Analyses, a think tank funded by the Department of Defense. By Thursday, the New York *Daily News* was reporting on the events at the "troubled campus," and student demands were expanding, though also dividing the student body, which cleaved into what the *Daily News* described as "Joe College types" on one hand and "long-haired, unkempt rebels" on the other.

Tom Hayden was neither a Joe College type nor an unkempt rebel. Clean-cut and sternly revolutionary, he was in New York when students rose up at Columbia. He took a subway uptown to get a look. "I had never seen anything quite like this," he wrote. "Students, at last, had taken power in their own hands." The FBI saw those events less sanguinely. Sizing up events at Columbia, J. Edgar Hoover concluded that Hayden was an outside interloper whose only reason for being on cam-

ALL FALL DOWN | 181

pus was to "furnish leadership and assistance to the student revolt." He directed the bureau to open an investigation into Hayden's finances, calling that "of prime importance."

The clash escalated over the next few days until, on April 30, Columbia president Grayson Kirk asked for help from the NYPD, which retook the campus. Columbia's student newspaper, the *Columbia Daily Spectator*, called the morning action a "brutal bloody show of strength" that resulted in 712 arrests and 148 injuries, including at least four faculty members who suffered head wounds. In response, students called a general strike. Their demands now included the firing of President Kirk.

Into this tinderbox galumphed the Grateful Dead. The Dead flew to New York at the end of April to perform at a series of venues—mainly medium-sized clubs. That itinerary put them in New York City just as Columbia boiled over. Organizers of the demonstration asked them to play for the student strikers. The Dead gamely accepted, showing up on Friday afternoon, May 3.

The day had been given over by the student strikers and their faculty allies to what they called "Liberation Classes," an afternoon of teachings on alienation, revolutions, imperialism and the like. The day's agenda went from noon to five-thirty, and it included just one nonacademic entry: Listed as "also" at 3 P.M. was "The Grateful Dead."

There is some difference in memory over how the Dead made it onto the campus. Legend has it that the Dead were smuggled into the university's main plaza in the back of a Wonder Bread truck. It's a charming story, originally and dubiously recounted by Rock Scully, whose gift for exaggeration was well documented. It's how Lesh and Kreutzmann recalled it in their memoirs, and how Weir described the arrival in an interview years later.

Outside participants remembered it differently. Bob Merlis, a Columbia student at the time (later to become a landmark music industry executive), was the one who reached out to the Dead through Scully, and he remembered the university's allowing the band to pass through the cordon—there had been enough trouble in recent days without a fracas over turning away the Dead—while the band's equipment arrived in a Ryder truck at 114th Street.

What is not in dispute is that the Dead took the stage that afternoon before an anxious, hyped-up student body frazzled by its ongoing conflict with the administration and excited at the support from a band already synonymous with the West Coast counterculture.

As the Dead finished setting up on the Low Library plaza, various would-be speakers crashed the stage, grabbing hold of the microphone to announce this event or that, or simply to pontificate. Weir took command. "I told five people in the space of one minute that 'No, man, these microphones were for the music and not for politics.'" Turned away, one speaker called him a "lame honky bastard." Another called him a "crass bourgeois son of a bitch."

The band's appearance hardly fitted that description. Kreutzmann wore a dress shirt with aviator sunglasses. Pigpen had on his leather hat, and Hart wore a furry Russian number. Weir pulled his hair back, Lesh sported a Fu Manchu mustache and a headband, and Garcia came in a striped T-shirt that set off his bold set of muttonchops. A crowd of several hundred students, most of them white, moved and clapped in sync as a speedy, energetic version of "Cryptical Envelopment" kicked off. Few danced, but they bobbed and gazed before the looming and embattled monuments of Columbia behind and above them.

Was this the Dead expressing a political stance? Kreutzmann argued that the Dead "weren't political hippies. We were the much more dangerous kind—fun-loving, peace-seeking, do-as-you-wish hippies." But Merlis, the student organizer, may have been in a better place to understand how the Dead struck the crowd. For him, the Dead were "vaguely apolitical, but it [was] political by dint of the fact that they so represented the alternative universe that many of us aspired to populate."

ROBERT KENNEDY came to California in 1968 on the heels of defeat. After winning primaries in Indiana and Nebraska, he lost to McCarthy in Oregon on May 28, an alarming setback. That made California pivotal, and pundits predicted a close finish. On Election Night, the results were as close as predicted, but a late surge of votes from Los Angeles County, specifically from districts with large numbers of blacks and Mexican Americans, edged Kennedy past McCarthy. Combined with an easy victory in South Dakota, Kennedy's path to the nomination was now open, the presidency itself in view.

Kennedy graciously accepted cheers just after midnight at the Ambassador Hotel in Los Angeles, then made his way from the stage toward the back of the hotel, passing through the kitchen. There a young man confronted the senator and shot him near the right ear before firing the gun several more times. He was grabbed immediately and later identified as Sirhan B. Sirhan, a twenty-four-year-old Jordanian angered by Kennedy's support for Israel. Kennedy never regained consciousness. He died Thursday morning, June 6.

Garcia was onstage on Election Night, part of an evening jam that also featured Elvin Bishop, Steve Miller, and others. Gleason was there for the *Chronicle*. He memorialized the spirit of the evening, the blunt contrast between the sway of the music and the dizzying events outside.

"At midnight Tuesday night it was a beautiful scene," Gleason wrote. "People came in off the street with late election news and inside there was a long jam session going on with all kinds of guitar players and saxophones and rhythm men and on the floor there was more dancing than I've seen anywhere in months.

"Throughout the ballroom an outstanding feature was the peacefulness and the joy as a wondrous assortment of people relaxed," Gleason added. "There were Hells Angels and hippies, many black people and many long-haired youth. It seemed for a moment like the hope of the future.

"And then I went outside, got into the car and punched the radio button only to hear a voice saying, 'When Senator Kennedy was shot tonight . . .' and the terrible real world came crashing in on me again."

* * *

184 | HERE BESIDE THE RISING TIDE

THE CHAOS of the moment seemed to reach the Dead itself in late 1968. With Lesh at the head and Garcia pushing from behind, the band, managers, and Bear met in August to discuss some simmering issues.

The band had been working hard all summer, practicing for four to six hours a day in their rehearsal space at the New Potrero Theatre. The Dead were comfortable with Scully and Rifkin as their managers and had recently recruited road manager Jonathan Riester to manage their road trips, along with Jon McIntire, who was attempting to sort out the band's books. But the Dead's musical apparatus was shifting, and the tensions that helped bring them expansive range were also worming their way into conflicting visions about where they were headed. Were they a rock band? An acid rock band? Was Constanten a full member of the group? And was the approach of Lesh and Garcia, whose experimentation with sound was plumbing new ideas for the group, pulling it away from songs and into formlessness, consistent with the blues and jug band grounding of Pigpen and Weir?

Those tensions came to a head, sort of, in an August meeting.

Scully, clearly designated to take the lead by Lesh and Garcia, went first. "The nature of the thing we have to talk about . . . musically depends on four guys," he said, nervously broaching the topic with the pointed reference to "four guys," since the band then included six. "The weight is on four cats in this band, not six as the band is now formed."

The issue, Scully continued, was stagnation. "It seems like the music is being carried to a certain level and then staying there. I notice it mostly from the way you guys respond to your own music. You guys tire of music that has much more potential, many more possibilities, too soon. I notice that we go through material, we devise and work up through arduous, tormentuous kind of days and agony, man. We finally get something together, and then you guys play it a few times, a very few times in relation to other bands, and it stays the same. It never gets any better. As a matter of fact, it begins to get worse. Very fast. Too fast for the material because the material is really complex and groovy and much further out than most music is these days. . . . And you guys that create it shouldn't tire of it so fast because so much creativity comes out of the stuff. You can hear it. It suggests things to me. I can't play it, but I can hear it in my head. I can hear further out things, and I'm disappointed when it doesn't get further out. The audience can feel that, too. This is a problem that's been inherent in the Grateful Dead for a long, long time."

That seemed to rouse Garcia. "All you gotta do is listen to the tapes there," he interjected. Lesh agreed, noting that much of the band's work fell short and that of the tapes Garcia was referring to, "I only like them with reservations." Again, Garcia supported Lesh, noting that "in the course of playing, you can hear stuff start to happen, and it don't make it, it don't deliver." Most damning, Garcia added, was that the band was arriving at venues to receive "screams before we started and then, you know, acknowledgment when we finished." The progress of a Dead set, Garcia, Lesh, and Scully all were saying, had become "downhill."

Lesh's frustration was clear. "After this weekend," he said, "that's the end of that. That is the end of that. No more."

Some startled chatter and uncomfortable silence followed. Addressing Weir directly, Scully demanded that he work harder. "You and Pig, Bob, have got to expand yourselves musically, a lot. And it means, I think it means, for now, getting more into your own things than you have been. And it doesn't seem like you do it for the band. . . . You don't seem to be playing any better. . . . For some reason, both of you have been having something going that hasn't allowed you to expand at a very fast rate, at least not at the rate of the other musicians in the band. You haven't kept up. You've fallen further and further behind."

Pigpen offered a few mumbled defenses, especially after Scully and Garcia praised him for quitting drinking and focusing on music. Weir remained silent, shocked and mortified.

The conversation drifted for a while to the band's efforts to hammer out the work on "St. Stephen," which it was attempting to get onto a record as an extended play offering. The difficulties around that project helped to underscore the divergent visions of how to move forward, now as a band of four rather than six, uncomfortably considering the song's elements while ignoring the bomb that had just gone off in the room. And it droned on, conspicuously avoiding the topic as midnight came and went.

Hart tried to cut it off. "I think it's time for me to make a motion," he said, "unless anybody else wants to talk about anything."

"A motion?" Weir asked. "What's that?"

"Split," Hart answered, "unless anybody wants to talk about anything else . . ."

That infuriated Scully, who had taken on the uncomfortable business of firing two of the founding members of the Grateful Dead, only to watch that topic drift away into late-night ramblings over how best to record an EP. "We haven't talked about anything more immediate than an EP and this record, really, in terms of Bob and Pig, and I think that you guys ought to make your intentions clear. You haven't to them so far. You were planning to, Mickey, but you are now making a motion to adjourn something that was started and not finished."

Hart tried to equivocate, but Scully refused to let him off. Scully reminded Hart that he and others had been complaining for weeks, and that now that the topic was broached, members needed to have it out fully, not cut off the topic before it was resolved. "We're not really saying it," Scully said, "not the way it's been said to me by some of you guys in the last month. And unless I'm wrong, I think we're avoiding saying ourselves out."

Lesh agreed, and Scully added that "I really want to go to work tomorrow knowing that everything's clear in everybody's mind, and I don't want it to be my interpretation."

Still another uncomfortable silence followed. This time, Garcia did attempt to exercise something almost like leadership. "Here is where it's at, man. You guys know that the gigs haven't been any fun. It hasn't been no good playing it. And it's because we're at different levels of playing. We're at different levels of music. We're thinking different thoughts, and we're just not playing together. It's not a question of values of one sort or another. It's just that there are four of us that can play together and pretty much agree on the kind of shit we're doing and pretty much understand where each other's at. And then there's you two guys, who are not alike particularly—you're both on different trips—and you're playing different music from each other and from us."

Garcia's next remark then hit the bone: "We can't do it. We just can't play that way. So you guys gotta find what you wanna do and do what you gotta do to play the music that you wanna play if that's what you want to do, if you want to play music and start getting your things together that way. And we gotta think also about the partnership and where that's at."

Garcia intimated that there might be other ways to work together musically—outside the Grateful Dead—and there might be chances to "get together on another level," but that was for the future. For now, the Dead as a six-man band was ending.

Lesh offered some vague words about musicians working together, the "tribe changing the world," but it was nervous filler. The boom had been lowered.

Silence. Twenty-two long seconds of silence. "But we're all still a family," Lesh said, breaking the quiet with a remark almost cruelly insulting. Still more uncomfortable patter then filled in—reassurances that work would be easy to find, that working with other musicians was the model, that each of the musicians could now work at their own speed.

Weir's refusal to engage through all of this seemed to elicit sympathy from Garcia, who balked when Scully reminded Weir that they had discussed some of these issues a week earlier and that Weir "had no words then," and "you still have no words." For Garcia, who had just delivered devastating news to his younger protégé, that was too much. "Asking him for explanations is not where it's at," he protested. "Conflict is not where it's at under any circumstances."

188 | HERE BESIDE THE RISING TIDE

"The idea of faction is not where it's at," Weir tentatively offered.

Sensing Garcia's displeasure, Scully backpedaled. He assured Weir that he owed the rest of the group no explanation, insisted he was just trying to "talk it out." Weir tried to offer something but stumbled. "That's more or less why I say I have no words," he said, mumbling.

"You'd never have to say a word if it was in your music," Scully responded.

To which Weir replied with a befittingly odd coda to his own firing: "I'd never have to say a word if it was in the way I tied my shoes."

And that was that. Whatever it was.

THERE ARE a few things worth noting about this pivotal meeting in the life of the Dead. There is the fact of the tape. This was a delicate gathering and one planned for some time, as the conversation makes clear. Still, it's strange to record a firing, more so to save a copy of such a freighted discussion.

There is also the poignant reminder of the youthful inexperience on display. Garcia was twenty-six years old when this meeting took place. Weir was twenty. It had been three years since the band first caught the attention of kids at Magoo's Pizza Parlor in Menlo Park, and they were at the beginning of a career—an adventure. Everything turned on this moment. Their conversation that night makes clear that they were frustrated at their progress—Garcia in particular felt hobbled. Enlarged by Hunter's return and the sonic opportunities that the Dead had dabbled with on *Anthem of the Sun,* Garcia and Lesh were able to see beyond the improvisational horizon. Energized by what they imagined, they were impatient and felt constrained by their roots, represented by Weir and Pigpen.

And there was Garcia himself, chronically torn between being the Dead's brilliant musical center and its unwilling administrative core. Garcia could have demanded more from his colleagues—could have insisted that they practice more, stretch their musical abilities further. He did not—could not, really. Prodded by Lesh and Scully, Garcia did

ALL FALL DOWN | 189

finally come close to making himself clear in their showdown, but it pained him to do so.

When finally forced to choose between music and friendship, he chose music. He dared to tell one of his closest friends, Pigpen, and a young man who very much looked up to him, Weir, that they could not keep up. He avoided it as long as he could, but Garcia fired his friends in defense of his music. But when Garcia at last exercised the authority that every band member ceded to him, he did it badly. In short, he was wrong, not just emotionally but musically as well. The band straggled out of the meeting into an uncertain future, broken up without an idea of where to head. They were lost.

Had the Dead succeeded in firing Weir and Pigpen for good that night, the future that would have lain before the remaining band—the foursome of Garcia, Lesh, and two drummers, Hart and Kreutzmann—would have been exceedingly strange. Weir and Pigpen may have felt like weights in the chaotic summer of 1968, but they were better described as ballast against the spacey tug of the band's experimentalists. Without those two, the band's relationship to musical earth might well have slipped away, propelling it into the world Lesh inhabited, of esoteric classicalism and acid-infused innovation, but it's difficult to imagine that music sweeping along the counterculture.

Fortunately, the firing didn't stick.

HOW BAD was 1968? The summer's only clear winner was Richard Nixon. Eisenhower's erstwhile and aggrieved understudy, Nixon had narrowly lost to John Kennedy in 1960, then seemed utterly defeated after his 1962 defeat for California governor at the hands of Pat Brown. But Nixon was nothing if not resilient, and he returned in 1968 with a harder edge. No longer the moderate heir to Ike's pleasant—and deceptively complex—stewardship, he was now the candidate of "law and order," the bulwark against American weakness and disarray, the counter to the counterculture.

The Republican National Convention assembled that year in Miami, and Nixon accepted his party's nomination on August 8. Beaming and breathing deeply as delegates chanted "We want Nixon," the candidate began by acknowledging that he had accepted the same nomination eight years earlier. "But I have news for you," he proclaimed. "This time, this is a difference. This time, we are going to win!" And with that, Nixon threw up his right arm, a stiff, rehearsed gesture that crystallized all of the uneasiness he so often projected.

"As we look at America, we see cities enveloped in smoke and flame," Nixon told the delegates. "We hear sirens in the night. We see Americans dying on distant battlefields abroad, we see Americans hating each other, fighting each other, killing each other at home."

Looking beyond Miami, Nixon appealed to the "great majority of Americans, the forgotten Americans, the non-shouters, the non-demonstrators." They would form his base—those non-shouters, those serious, quiet men and women who remembered, or thought they remembered, a simpler time, when children listened to their parents, when patriotism was a shared value, when blacks understood their place, when women were satisfied to be home raising happy, well-adjusted children. "The first requisite of progress," Nixon said, "is order."

Nixon paid lip service to some of the left's values—civil rights, peace in Vietnam, community—but he set himself apart, demanding that they take their place against what he saw as the fundamental norms of American society. Judges and courts had gone too far—this was Nixon's attack against his old adversary, Chief Justice Earl Warren—to protect criminals and activists. Real Americans needed help too, he insisted. Yes, civil rights deserved defending, Nixon said, but—with Nixon, there was always a "but"—"the first civil right of every American is to be free from domestic violence, and that right must be guaranteed in this country."

And to make his case for order, Nixon leaned heavily on the alternative, the frightening threat posed by the counterculture, with its grubby and ungrateful young people. To do that, he turned his attention specifically to Jerry Garcia. An ad directed at the issue of "American Youth" opened with a burst of fake acid rock and swirling images of concerts and young people. Up came Nixon's voice: "American youth today has its fringes . . ." And just as Nixon said the word "fringes," the image that flashed on the screen was none other than that of a smiling Garcia, sly grin and beardless face peering out from beneath a shaggy head of long hair and an American flag top hat. Nixon's narration then turned to the greatness of youth, and the images shifted to young people studying, working in labs and at drafting tables. The point was made: Nixon's America was one of hardworking young people; the "fringes" were the province of the counterculture, the home of Jerry Garcia and his ilk. To friends and a growing legion of fans, Garcia already was something of an icon; now that status was affirmed and extended—by Richard Nixon, no less.

The counterculture returned Nixon's contempt. His artifice, his awkwardness, his bluster about law and order, even his crabbed internationalism, fell so outside the ambit of the counterculture that he was not taken seriously as a person, much less as a president. Nixon was a caricature of repression, more worthy of contempt than opposition. Instead, the demonstrators, the shouters—as Nixon would have it—focused their ire on those who more acutely disappointed them. It was the Democrats who promised racial progress and peace—and whose promises had fallen so woefully short in 1968. It was the Democrats who would feel the force of that disappointment.

Tom Hayden arrived in Chicago in despair. Kennedy's death, he realized, had ended the chance for Democrats to nominate a candidate committed to peace in Vietnam. The opportunity to defeat Hubert Humphrey, Johnson's vice president, had "slumped to zero." The SDS, once Hayden's organization, had passed to the leadership of Bernardine Dohrn, a self-declared "revolutionary communist."

Abbie Hoffman and Jerry Rubin came with their following, the newly formed Yippies, a self-conscious attempt to unite the freewheeling spirit of the hippies with the militancy of the SDS, "a dope joke," a "half-cocked combination of hippie ethos and New Left activism," as the writer David Farber put it. Formally but almost never known as the Youth International Party, the Yippies were built specifically for the 1968 Democratic National Convention in Chicago. Rubin came to the idea with some experience. He was the one who had irritated Garcia with his stridency at the Human Be-In, and he was already a recognized veteran of the Free Speech and antiwar campaigns, including the 1967 march on the Pentagon. He was clever and provocative, and he saw Vietnam as the by-product of a lost society, one whose repair required more than new candidates for office. "Politics," he said, "is how you live your life, not who you vote for or who you support."

As 1968 unfolded, SDS and the Yippies both took aim at Chicago. Timothy Leary lent a hand, as did Allen Ginsberg. They envisioned a mass gathering, an "international festival of youth music and theater" that would juxtapose life and beauty against the "National Death Party," as they called the Democrats. Borrowing from the Be-In, they promoted their event as a gathering of "new tribes" and committed to a "politics of ecstasy." They announced a Festival of Life, complete with music, arts, and politics, to open on August 25, the day before the Democrats were to kick off their convention.

Mayor Richard Daley might have handled all of this with deftness or calm. He could have opened Chicago to three days of rowdy free expression, celebrating American democracy with Democrats inside the International Amphitheatre and protesters outside it. He could have encouraged camping in the parks and granted permits to march. But then he wouldn't have been Richard Daley. Instead, he summoned police and mobilized National Guardsmen and draped the Amphitheatre in barbed wire. He dragged his feet on the permits, then denied them. He forbade sleeping in the parks.

They were warned, to be sure. Daley wasted no chance to telegraph his contempt for protesters and their efforts. His office was in contact with "the hippies, the yippies, the flippies and everything else," Daley said. And yes, that included talks with members of the media, since "some of them are hippies and yippies." He was sued by the ACLU for refusing to grant demonstration permits; he ignored it. He was questioned about the city's readiness; he brushed it off. "There will be no trouble in Chicago," he boasted on August 16, days before the trouble began.

Todd Gitlin, writing for the underground *San Francisco Express Times* just days before the convention began, warned readers who were headed for Chicago to brace themselves for conflict. The city's police, he said, "deprived of their vacations, fat and mean, are everywhere." Gitlin's advice to those making the trip: "If you're going to Chicago, be sure to wear some armor in your hair."

The battle of Chicago began on Saturday, August 24, two days before the convention began. Protesters flowed in from around the country and concentrated in Lincoln Park. The Yippies trotted around their "nominee" for president, a pig named Pigasus. Ginsberg was chanting and urging good vibes. Daley had set an 11 P.M. curfew, and when the park was not clear at that hour, the police moved in, some on foot, others on motorcycles.

Each night thereafter, the confrontations grew larger, more intense, and more violent. The *Tribune,* in sympathy with police and order, reported on Monday that the police had repelled a "jeering mob of peaceniks." The next day, it reported that police had routed hippies and chased thousands from Lincoln Park. On Wednesday, the story was competing with the convention itself as 800 GUARDSMEN FACE HIPPIES IN PARK, AT HOTEL vied for space even on the *Tribune's* front page. Finally, on Thursday, the paper conceded the obvious: COPS, HIPPIES WAR IN STREET. Beneath that headline, a photograph of a smiling Hubert Humphrey seemed incongruous indeed. Watching the scene below from the upper floors of the Conrad Hilton Hotel, headquarters of the convention, delegates cried out in alarm. "Cut it out," some yelled at police. "Don't hurt [them]."

At the convention itself, Senator Abraham Ribicoff placed Senator

194 | HERE BESIDE THE RISING TIDE

George McGovern's name in nomination, a futile effort but one intended to give voice to the party's antiwar faction. "With George McGovern, we wouldn't have Gestapo tactics on the streets of Chicago," Ribicoff said. Daley was sitting up front. His reply: "Fuck you, you Jew son of a bitch, you lousy motherfucker. Go home."

Democrats limped out of their convention and into the maw of the New Nixon. On November 5, 1968, Nixon defeated Humphrey and third-party candidate George Wallace. It was a close race, and Nixon failed to win a majority of the popular vote. But the Republican's 43.4 percent was enough to edge out Humphrey's 42.7 percent and Wallace's 13.5. Wallace carried five Southern states, and Humphrey was confined mostly to the Northeast and Texas, while Nixon took the middle of the country, sweeping from California across the West and Midwest through Florida and the mid-Atlantic states.

That left Reagan in office in California, and Nixon headed for the presidency. If the counterculture was to change America, it would not be through the ballot, at least for now.

IN THE fall of 1968, with the world breaking down, Stewart Brand proposed a return to tools. Brand had been drifting a bit, wandering through the West in his VW bus. He visited communes and saw what the participants in those projects needed. He imagined servicing those outposts, offering staples. "What I'm visualizing is an Access Mobile (accessory?) with all manner of access materials + advice for sale cheap," he wrote in a note to himself.

He wound his way back to the Bay Area and found space in Menlo Park, not far from Kepler's, just around the corner from a new magazine, *Ramparts*, at the edge of what would become Silicon Valley. Brand looked up his old friend Kesey, and the two got an early look at the implications of personal computers. Kesey was bowled over. "It's the next thing after acid," he remarked.

Brand was excited at what lay ahead. "We are as gods and might as well get used to it," he wrote. Freedom was at hand—the old freedom from fear, the new freedom of drugs, the freedom to work together, the freedom to be alone. "A realm of intimate, personal power is developing—power of the individual to conduct his own education, find his own inspiration, shape his own environment, and share his adventure with whoever is interested."

With those stiff winds at their backs, Brand and Lois Jennings cofounded the *Whole Earth Catalog* and published the first issue in the fall of 1968. Anarchic and magical, it was a compendium of devices and ideas, listings, advice, musings. It was not in fact an actual catalog, at least in the modern sense. It recommended items, from books to house shells, but did not sell them; it merely steered readers to where they could buy them.

The front and back covers featured a picture of the earth, itself a product of Brand's vision. He had long imagined that a photo of the earth would have powerful effects on those who lived here, and when NASA captured such an image in 1967, Brand seized on its significance, a reminder that the inhabitants of the planet were both together and alone, surrounded by the dark of space. The catalog sold for five dollars, and its sixty pages were divided into sections including "Understanding Whole Systems," "Shelter and Land Use," "Industry and Craft," "Communications," "Community," "Nomadics," and "Learning." As those suggested, the "tools" offered in the catalog were of the broadest sort. Yes, it included conventional tools—an Alaskan mill for cutting lumber, kerosene lamps, tipis, hacksaws, files, scissors, a Hewlett-Packard 9100A Calculator (selling for $4,900 and weighing sixty pounds)—but also advice and contemplation.

It recommended and highlighted many books. The "Community" section offered *The Green Revolution, The Digger Papers,* and a list of "books on community" that ranged from *Animal Farm* to *Stranger in a Strange Land* to Plato's *Republic.* The section on Nomadics held up works on camping and woodcraft as well as *Survival Arts of the Primitive Paiutes.* And the "Industry and Craft" section posed a question undoubtedly on the minds of many readers: "Should sportsmen take dope?"

There was a crude roughness to the finished product. Page numbers were handwritten, typefaces mismatched, drawings interspersed with book covers and mysterious symbols. Despite that—or perhaps because of it—the catalog radiated a counterculture authenticity. In its organization and its spirit, the *Whole Earth Catalog* not only embraced technology but anticipated it.

Addressing a Stanford University graduation in 2005, Steve Jobs, the co-founder of Apple, reflected on the invention of the Macintosh, the freedom of being a beginner, the joy of discovery. Near the end of his speech, Jobs considered one of the influences of his early years. "When I was young," he said, "there was an amazing publication called the *Whole Earth Catalog*, which was one of the bibles of my generation. It was created by a fellow named Stewart Brand, not far from here, in Menlo Park, and he brought it to life with his poetic touch."

The catalog, said Jobs, was "sort of like Google, in paperback form, thirty-five years before Google came along. It was idealistic, overflowing with neat tools and great notions."

THE SHAPE of a Grateful Dead show would take a while to cohere, but its form drew from this period, from the experiences of drugs and society near the end of the 1960s. The starting point was improvisational: Like the sixties, the show was unpredictable, the product of whimsy and events, not plans. What that meant was that every Dead show was different, that the band arrived without a setlist or an album to promote. It was of the moment, creative and responsive—an allegiance to spontaneity that reflected one of the counterculture's ambitions, to live in the moment.

If there was therefore no such thing as a "typical" Dead show, the Dead's work did develop forms over time, reflecting the band's growth and life around it. In 1968, it was highly experimental and unstructured, with long stretches of feedback and free sound. In later years it would develop a certain architecture: The first set would be built around songs, picked from whatever was on the band's minds—or its collective mind—generally alternating between numbers sung by Garcia and those led by Pigpen or Weir. Those songs ended in a break, and the next set most often picked up where the first left off, only to drift further and further into the abstract and unformed. Garcia or Lesh might lead the way, until eventually every member of the band was experimenting with form and structure, listening to one another, leading, following, building, exploring. Those long sections, later slotted into "Drums" and "Space," wandered for a while, the mood reflecting that of band and audience, trading energy, playing off each other, coming upon new ideas, sometimes getting lost along the way. And then the musicians found one another and led one another home.

The musical arc was often compared to the experience of tripping on LSD: structure that yielded to formlessness, that could become scary or chaotic and then resolve to a kind of enlightened calm, the joy of the adventurer who has found new worlds and returned to tell of what he's seen.

If acid provided one analogue, culture suggested another—and 1968 supplied it. The year opened amid uncertainty but with certain assumptions: The end of the war in Vietnam was in sight. Lyndon Johnson would win reelection. Martin Luther King, Jr., would shoulder the burden of moral authority. One by one, those assumptions fell away. By the summer, King and then Kennedy were dead, and the counterculture's values—once grounded in participatory democracy, artistic and personal freedom, peace, love, community—had broadened to include fury and violence. Cities burned as the war ground on. The streets of Chicago were not just a conflict between hippies and vacation-deprived police. They were a battle of values waged by adversaries who were determined and grim and often armed. The nation improvised.

And it was the counterculture that was most affected. The cops in Chicago did not change because King was murdered or because the Tet Offensive exposed the folly of America's efforts in Vietnam. It was the protesters who grew more alienated, more frantic, more enraged. Fear begat fear, which begat violence. The freedom to experiment expanded into a broader license to confront and, finally, to fight.

In that maelstrom, the Dead's music grew, while they remained remarkably true to themselves. They did not retreat from the clashes of 1968, and though they vacillated, even faltered, as a unit, they held fast to their original values. The Dead treasured community and space. Their devotion was to living outside the strictures of politics, detached not only from the death culture of war but also from the incensed counterculture that took to violence in response. The band members sought not to change minds but to be allowed to live by their own values, and to insist that the broader culture not impose itself on them. It offered up those ideas as an alternative to the increasingly rigid and angry standoff of America in this moment. To use White's formulation, the Dead did not frontally challenge violence or inequity, but they served to displace those corrosive aspects of American life by offering themselves as an alternative—at the Carousel, at benefits, at Columbia, back home in San Francisco.

Yes, conflict insinuated itself into the Dead, too, and the band faced its closest brush with extinction during that fateful band meeting in August. But the Dead regrouped.

A young writer for the *Daily Californian* captured the Dead's resolute consistency in those years. "When a human being takes this course of action, when he faces and withstands the demands to mold himself to the social main-current, concentrating only on the realization of his constructive ideas, you call him by one word: artist," wrote Raymond Lang in May of 1969. "The Dead are artists."

Some of the artists close to the Dead were, of course, explicitly political. For Joan Baez, art was politics; her commitment to peace overarched her music and her life. So, too, with Country Joe and the Fish and other standout performers in San Francisco and beyond. But the intersection of politics and music was never sharply drawn. "Culture," wrote Mat Callahan in his study of what he called the "musical renaissance and social revolution in San Francisco" during those years, "was so closely interwoven with revolution that it became hard to distinguish where one ended and the other began."

Garcia's artistic and social vision clung to the idea that transformation was personal, that revolution, if it were to happen at all, would start with individual people, who would discover new selves through music. Emerging outside the confines of order, control, and violence, they would find themselves unbound, free in that deeply liberated sense of freedom. Garcia's artistic vision, similar to Dylan's, thus carried social implications even if it did not start as a message of confrontation or revolution—precisely in the area that Callahan suggested, where it was difficult to say where one began and the other ended. As Garcia noted to an interviewer from *Hard Road* magazine who asked what he thought of the "revolutionary moment": "I'm in the middle of it, all the different aspects of it. I just see it as a real slow revolution." What Garcia called the "old line revolutionary tack" had proven to be a "miserable failure," leaving artists and others to slog the long march to elevate consciousness. He was optimistic—"eventually the whole world will be a different place"—but it required patience.

That sentiment was shared by John Lennon, among many others. In "Revolution," which Lennon wrote, mostly in May 1968, and the Beatles recorded shortly thereafter, Lennon expressed his disdain for the political radicals of the period. Lennon argued that rather than change "the constitution" or "the institution," "you better free your mind instead." There was no use, he jabbed, "carrying pictures of Chairman Mao."

That did not endear Lennon—or the Beatles—to the more radical elements of the counterculture, but it placed them squarely within Garcia's worldview. One disappointed radical wrote an open letter to Lennon to complain about the song and to insist that the world required destruction in order for genuine rebuilding to take place. Lennon responded with a tart letter of his own, ending with a postscript: "You smash it—and I'll build around it."

On October 12, the Dead were back at the Avalon. Months earlier, they'd sung "gas the Avalon" in their playing of "Alligator," but that was from their stage at the Carousel. Now that the Carousel was the Fillmore West and under the control of Bill Graham, they were resigned to playing other people's venues, even in San Francisco.

They had been through a lot. After the meeting in August and the firing of Weir and Pigpen, the remaining band was left to consider what they had done, and as the new reality set in, it did not feel right. Lesh acknowledged later that he felt "confused and depressed" by the firings and his role in them, and he appreciated the value of his colleagues almost as soon as they were gone. He, Garcia, Hart, and Kreutzmann played a few dates as Mickey and the Hartbeats. That group produced some adventurous and memorable shows, but they realized that they were missing an ingredient—and that the loss of it was entirely their fault. "Eventually realizing our mistake, and thankful that we hadn't yet burned our bridges behind us, we quietly left the Hartbeats behind," Lesh wrote.

For their part, Weir and Pigpen worked harder, and when the Dead played their contractually obligated shows in October at the Avalon, it was as the full band—the Musicians Union contracts specified band members by name, so the Dead had no choice but to reassemble in full. Those performances went well, and Weir and Pigpen were reabsorbed. Weir introduced the band's opening tune. "It's a foxtrot, and it's also a ladies' choice," he said, his humor restored after his brief trip to the musical woodshed. And then Garcia and Lesh plunged into the densely woven fabric of "Dark Star."

"Dark Star" that October night, a cool San Francisco evening beneath a waning gibbous moon, was melodic and graceful, Garcia's voice clear and soft. As the band pushed into it, the music yielded, opening room for both clarity and anguish. Garcia sang quietly and played joyfully, Weir lending energetic support, Lesh lacing through his bass work, and the drummers in time. "Dark Star" could be light or whimsical or chaotic; some nights, it was all three. On this night, it was rich and deep.

One fan, reflecting years later, put "Dark Star" back into that moment. "This IS essential Dead," the listener wrote. "Yes, folks were crazy and fun-loving psychedelic children. But they also knew they were dancing on the edge of a dark abyss. And so they were warriors for the forces of light and love, had to be."

On that night, all of that, too, was the meaning of "Dark Star."

After Altamont. Altamont, California, December 7, 1969.
Elizabeth Sunflower/Retro Photo Archive

CHAPTER 10

The End of the Beginning

IF 1968 WAS A CONCENTRATED SPOONFUL OF CONFUSION AND collapse, 1969 seemed to offer hope, though in measured doses. It was the year of the moon shot and the year that John Lennon and Yoko Ono staged a bed-in for peace and recorded "Give Peace a Chance." The Beatles played their last public gig—on the roof of Apple Records—in January. Eisenhower died in March. Joe Namath, with his shaggy hair and playboy bravado, guaranteed a victory in Super Bowl III and delivered it, a dash of counterculture in football, no less. The Stonewall riots in New York announced the arrival of the gay rights movement in June. James Earl Ray and Sirhan Sirhan admitted their guilt in the murders that had reshaped America the year before, and the Chicago Eight, charged with their roles in disrupting the Democratic National Convention, went on trial, using the courtroom to mock their persecutors.

It was a year of beginnings and endings, validation for the counterculture and exposure of its fissures. Two festivals, six months apart, telegraphed its divergent directions. The Dead would be present for both.

FIRST, THOUGH, came a moment close to home that united those at odds with the government and the dominant conservative culture of the moment. One battle, fought in Berkeley, brought together the full range of American dissidents in confrontation with a common and familiar foe, Ronald Reagan, in the stylized combat that had become de rigueur in 1968.

In 1967, the University of California, Berkeley, had quietly acquired a 2.8-acre parcel on Telegraph Avenue (known as Lot 1875-2) with the intention of using it for dorms to relieve the campus's perennial shortage of student housing. But the university, short of funds and distracted by the Free Speech Movement, antiwar protests, and the replacement of Governor Pat Brown by Ronald Reagan, moved slowly to begin construction. It cleared the lot, then left it vacant, a muddy place to park a car or dump a load of trash. It was an eyesore.

An editorial in the *Berkeley Barb,* anchor of the counterculture in the East Bay, changed that. On the opening page of its April 18–24, 1969, issue, the *Barb* called for a "rural reclamation project" to transform the "mud flat" into a "cultural, political freak out and rap center for the Western world." It asked readers to come that Sunday and to "bring shovels, hoses, chains, grass, paints, flowers, trees, bull dozers, topsoil, colorful smiles, laughter and lots of sweat."

"The University has no right to create ugliness as a way of life," the paper announced. "We will show up on Sunday and we will clear one third of the lot and do with it whatever our fantasy pleases." The editorial was written by Stew Albert but signed "Robin Hood's Park Commissioner."

It worked. Some two hundred people turned out and within hours had turned the "desolate corner into a green haven," according to the *Berkeley Daily Gazette,* which noted that it was not quite sure whether the gathering was "entirely legal" but happily featured it across the top of its front page. The Black Panthers hailed it as "socialism in practice."

The response in Sacramento was less appreciative. The sine qua non of Reagan's 1966 election was his refusal to knuckle under to the pressures of the hippie left. One of Reagan's first moves in office had been to ratchet up his criticism of the university system's Board of Regents and to force the removal of the president of the university, Clark Kerr, whose offense was that he was, in Reagan's view, too gentle with student protesters. Now here they were again, challenging Reagan frontally, more of the "noisy, dissident minority" he had deplored as a candidate. It was a confrontation that Reagan and his administration, in this case under the supervision of Reagan's chief of staff, Ed Meese, had braced for, even welcomed.

And yet the vehemence over People's Park took Reagan by surprise. It took weeks to mount a response, but when local authorities, in the early dawn of May 14, ringed the park with chain-link fences and posted No Trespassing signs, the battle was joined.

A noon rally in Sproul Plaza drew some of the movement's most recognizable figures. Hayden, now living in Berkeley, was there. So was Mario Savio. It ended with Dan Siegel, another People's Park organizer, exhorting the crowd to "take the park." The crowd of several thousand surged in that direction, only to be halted by police. Rocks, bottles, and debris were exchanged for tear gas, birdshot, and buckshot. As the Panthers reported, "this was no normal Berkeley street battle." By nightfall, dozens had been hurt—more than fifty civilians were treated for injuries, many from bird- and buckshot, and many more were hit but treated their own wounds rather than risk arrest. Forty-eight were taken to jail. James Rector was shot by an Alameda sheriff's deputy; he died four days later.

That night, Reagan called in the National Guard. Berkeley was placed under martial law, any "meeting, assembly, or parade" prohibited by his order.

It was under tense oversight that a demonstration on May 20 was called to honor the fallen Rector. As protesters gathered in UC Berkeley's Sproul Plaza, guardsmen fixed bayonets and donned gas masks. Then, without apparent provocation, authorities fired tear gas from a helicopter. It wafted through the Berkeley hills, a stinging smoke cloud unleashed over a peaceful neighborhood. The comparisons to Vietnam were unavoidable as civilians reeled from gas dropped on them from above. Demonstrators tried to flee, but Guardsmen blocked their exit from the plaza.

Reagan later acknowledged that "innocent people suffered the distress that goes with tear gas," but he defended its use to avoid "hand-to-hand combat" between Guardsmen and demonstrators. Four hundred eighty-two people were arrested, many more doused with tear gas; charges against all of those arrested ultimately were dismissed. The *Daily Californian* called for the ouster of all the authorities involved, from the university's chancellor to Reagan himself, calling them "this despicable crew, the scum of public life." The Panthers deplored the display of American fascism. Assemblyman John Burton accused Reagan of turning Berkeley into "his own Vietnam."

The counterculture had no trouble choosing sides, and the Dead fell in with their natural allies. On May 28, after the gassing of Sproul Hall and surrounding neighborhoods, the Dead joined the Airplane, Creedence Clearwater Revival, and several other bands, including Santana, still enjoying the acclaim from its first album, to host a "People's Park Bail Ball."

Bail was the perfect lure for Garcia, who did not quite identify with the struggle but whose sympathies extended to those who had landed in jail. "To me," he told an interviewer as the People's Park episode was unwinding, "anything you're doing is okay as long as it's not making you uptight, or endangering you . . . unless that's what you wanna do. And why put yourself in a position of, you know, being about to go to jail? Jail's a terrible place, man."

The Dead did their duty at the Bail Ball, but they did not play especially well, and they struck at least one listener as grudging. It was for the politicos, he observed, another gig to help those whose causes the Dead appreciated but whose tactics often struck Garcia as barely scraping the edge of change.

As usual, Garcia envisioned revolution of a higher order: "We are trying to make things groovier for everybody so more people can feel better more often, to advance the trip, to get higher, however you want to say it, but we're musicians, and there's just no way to put that idea, 'save the world,' into music; you can only *be* that idea, or at least make manifest that idea as it appears to you, and hope maybe others follow. . . .

"My way is music," Garcia continued. "I've been into music so long that I'm dripping with it; it's all I ever expect to do. I can't do anything else. Music is a yoga, something you really do when you're doing it. Thinking about what it means comes after the fact and isn't very interesting. Truth is something you stumble into when you think you're going someplace else, like those moments when you're playing and the whole room becomes one being, precious moments, man. But you can't *look* for them and they can't be repeated. Being alive means to continue to change, never to be where I was before. Music is the timeless experience of constant change."

KURT VONNEGUT was too old to be a hippie. Born in 1922, he fought in World War II and was taken prisoner at the Battle of the Bulge. He was too temperamentally traditional, and a little too cranky, to be a full-fledged member of the counterculture. But he saw freshly, defied literary conventions, and wrote from a deeply held set of values, including a revulsion for war that he brought home from his service. Though he did not seek out the counterculture, it found him.

On March 31, 1969, Delacorte Press released *Slaughterhouse-Five or The Children's Crusade,* Vonnegut's sixth novel (and eighth book; he had also published two collections of short stories). It represented his deferred reckoning with his time as a prisoner of war in Dresden. *Slaughterhouse-Five* is correctly considered a World War II novel, but its release at the height of the war in Vietnam made it equally a novel about all war and one whose pointed, bitter observations on death and dying placed it at the center of the American debate.

Vonnegut's literary preoccupations were not those of Didion or Thompson or the New Journalists. He did not write about the Haight or drugs or wildness. He was closer in topic and spirit to Joseph Heller, whose *Catch-22* darkly satirized war and whose themes appear in Vonnegut's work, especially *Slaughterhouse-Five.* But Vonnegut wrote and published alongside the New Journalists, and *Slaughterhouse-Five* also reflects their influence. Whereas they absorbed the techniques of fiction and imported them into their journalism, Vonnegut brought those

208 | HERE BESIDE THE RISING TIDE

techniques back infused with journalistic insight, saturating his novel of the war with his own experience of writing it.

"All this happened, more or less," Vonnegut announced in the first sentences of *Slaughterhouse-Five*. "The war parts, anyway, are pretty much true."

He also employed the fanciful. He broke the novel free of chronology, soaring from the bonefields of Dresden to the end of the world to an airplane crash in Vermont to a collision between a Mercedes and a Cadillac sporting a REAGAN FOR PRESIDENT! bumper sticker. The novel's central character, Billy Pilgrim, is "unstuck in time" and tells the story of his crash, the loss of his wife, his own assassination in 1976. He lights upon a "black ghetto" in ruins, sidewalks crushed by National Guard tanks. "The people who lived here hated it so much that they had burned down a lot of it a month before," Pilgrim observes. "It was all they had, and they'd wrecked it." Martin Luther King, Jr.'s death is noted in the book, as is that of Robert Kennedy. "And every day my Government gives me a count of corpses created by military science in Vietnam."

Throughout this chronicle of death, Vonnegut pauses over and over, repeating the phrase for which *Slaughterhouse-Five* would always be remembered: "So it goes."

The novel takes place in time but also outside it. So, too, with form. *Slaughterhouse-Five* is a work of science fiction—it is populated by "Tralfamadorians," plunger-shaped beings who travel through time—but also of deep and personal pain, of irony but also seriousness. It was not "political," but its values were unmistakably in sync with those of the young people challenging Vietnam, their spirits enraged by the "count of corpses created by military science." The novel was beloved by the counterculture.

Garcia was among those moved by Vonnegut's work. He was especially taken with Vonnegut's earlier novel, the less acclaimed *The Sirens of Titan*. So appreciative was Garcia, in fact, that years later, he purchased an option on the novel and spent years trying to turn it into a movie. Garcia worked on that project with Tom Davis, friend and writing partner of Al Franken, both of whom Garcia got to know when the Dead appeared on *Saturday Night Live* in the 1970s. They fiddled with the project for years, enlisting the actor Bill Murray and pitching the film to Universal in 1984. Davis and Murray spent the pitch meeting goofing off, and the project ran aground, but not for lack of enthusiasm on Garcia's part. He was a devotee of Vonnegut, in whom he almost certainly saw a kindred spirit—a wry, playful experimentalist with roots in deeper traditions, an artist of his time and outside it.

WITH WEIR and Pigpen back in the fold by the end of 1968, the new year featured the reconstituted band, now with Constanten regularly holding down a keyboard spot onstage and in the studio. Performances could be frustrating—Constanten had trouble getting his equipment right—but the period was productive.

And strange. The Dead performed a weird gig on January 18, when the band taped an appearance with Hugh Hefner on the twenty-third installment of his television program, *Playboy After Dark*. The seven-member band—Garcia, Weir, McKernan, Lesh, Kreutzmann, Hart, and Constanten—were paid $1059.50 for their appearance, during which they played and Garcia, dressed in an orange and green serape, joined Hefner, who wore a tuxedo, for a brief conversation at the cocktail table on the sound stage. "Is the hippie scene changing now?" Hefner asked Garcia. "Yeah," Garcia chuckled. "We're all big people now." Their banter continued, Hefner struggling to be sensible while tugging on a pipe, Garcia dodgy and bemused.

It being the Dead and a decidedly strange event, rumors have swirled for decades that the coffee on the set was spiked with LSD. In his memoir, Kreutzmann repeated that as fact. "Everyone was dosed," he wrote. "Including Hugh Hefner." Perhaps, though notably the correspondence following the Dead's appearance, thanking them for being there, makes no reference to any incident. It seems more likely lore than true. Still, it was a trip.

On set, young women in miniskirts and men with sport coats over turtlenecks at first sat quietly as Garcia moved from the cocktail service to the stage. He led off with an acoustic version of "Mountains of the Moon," Constanten contributing a harpsichord-like counterpoint and Weir at the edge of camera range on rhythm guitar. That gave way to a jumpier number, "St. Stephen," and when the strobe lights kicked on, some of the show's fetching guests scrambled to their feet and danced. The show closed with "Love Light" and the audience in full motion— cameras veering from the band to the dancers and back. If nothing else, it was a reminder that the counterculture was a big tent.

Playboy was a kick, but the real work went on elsewhere. The band debuted "Doin' That Rag" in January; it presented the very trippy "What's Become of the Baby?" at its one and only performance in April; it unfurled the first offerings of "Dire Wolf" and "Casey Jones," both to become staples, in June. "Dire Wolf" and "Casey Jones" were stories, the former fancifully set in "Fennario," the mythical, wooded Western landscape of much of Hunter's work; the latter, part of a long tradition of American train music (in this case, a prominent reference to the conductor being "high on cocaine" managed to get the song barred from radio play, even though the song is better heard as a cautionary drug tale—the conductor loses control while under the influence).

"What's Become of the Baby?" by contrast, was wildly, almost incomprehensibly psychedelic. Its single public airing, in which the studio recording was played with the band accompanying it, was delivered on April 26 in Chicago. It was so suffused in feedback and sound effects that it drowned out Hunter's sweeping, literary lyrics. That was a shame, as Hunter anchored "What's Become of the Baby?" in the deep art of storytelling, peppering it with references to Kubla Khan, Odin, Muhammad, and Scheherazade. It tickled the *Arabian Nights* and hinted at some of history's most venerable writing. Putting all that to music was not helped by the presence of a nitrous oxide tank in the studio. Much babbling ensued. As a poem, it was transporting. As a recording, it didn't work.

The Dead were in the Midwest in January and February—Chicago, Kansas City, St. Louis—then over to Pittsburgh, Baltimore, and New

York City, where they hooked up with Janis Joplin, who had left Big Brother in a bid for her own stardom. The Dead opened for her on February 11 and 12 at the Fillmore East, reconnecting with her vivacious and troubled soul.

Back in California in late February, they recorded shows there from February 27 through early March that would become the core of their first live album, released later in the year. They also accepted an unusual invitation to perform at the Black and White Ball for the San Francisco Symphony on March 15—taking the gig because Weir's mother was in charge of the event—and filled out their spring and early summer with shows at college campuses, medium-sized venues, and benefits. Along the way, they jumped in and out of studios, first Pacific Recording and then over to Pacific High Recording, where they experimented with tapes and tracks and synthesizers. They released their third album, entitled *Aoxomoxoa,* in June.

The album underscored a dichotomy in the band's work. When Pigpen was in front, live and onstage, the Dead were a blues band, preeminently so on "Love Light." Churning through that number, the music was powerful and grooving, rooted in Pigpen's growly vocal. But Pigpen did not contribute to *Aoxomoxoa,* and when the music moved into wilder sounds and structures, away from a beat, the Dead became something else—an experiment. In that latter sense, *Aoxomoxoa* was, as Garcia described it, "a continuation of *Anthem of the Sun.*"

"The Grateful Dead is two bands," a reviewer for *Rolling Stone* observed in critiquing *Aoxomoxoa,* "the band when Pigpen is singing and the band when he isn't." On one hand, the reviewer was bowled over by the Dead, describing *Aoxomoxoa* as "the work of a magical band." But that same reviewer, Adele Novelli, identified Pigpen as a weight— "Pigpen 'fits' because the Dead choose to embody a generosity of spirit that won't tolerate throwing him out. But the band is more magical because [it is] unnamable, less definable, without him," Novelli wrote, a statement that was wrong on two fronts: The Dead *had* considered throwing him out. And the Dead was *not* more magical without him. The Dead's ultimate appeal would lie in the incorporation of diverse

212 | HERE BESIDE THE RISING TIDE

elements—from blues to experimental sound—not in the privileging of one over the other.

As Garcia noted, *Aoxomoxoa* could be best understood as a continuation of the Dead's experimental music that had led to this point. It featured "Doin' That Rag" and a crisp "St. Stephen" alongside "China Cat Sunflower" and the confused effort of "What's Become of the Baby?" The album's sound reflected its odd development as well. It was recorded initially on eight-track tape and then rerecorded once the Dead gained access to a new sixteen-track recorder that Ampex debuted in 1968. It was costly and time-consuming, running up the Dead's debt to Warner Bros.—the company allowed the band unlimited studio time, but the meter was running, and the fiddling, especially by Garcia and Lesh, pushed the band further and further into the hole financially. The Dead would end up owing Warner Bros. $200,000 for the time they took learning in the studio.

Moreover, by the time *Aoxomoxoa* was released, the Dead had already reached the end of the musical line that the album represented. Weir and Pigpen were back in the fold not just because they had redoubled their commitment to the work but also because Lesh and Garcia had seen what they were missing, that the band's future was not purely in the experimental but rather in the merging of forms, in the experience of the moment grounded in the structure. Given the band's rapid evolution, *Aoxomoxoa* felt daring—even its title, a palindrome suggested by artist Rick Griffin, was a challenge to pronounce—but also pretentious and in some ways immature, more a reminder of where the band had just left than a clue to where it was headed. By now, the trend was clear: The Dead were a transporting experience live, less compelling in the studio. Shows were drawing avid fans, while the albums barely sold.

WHEN THE Dead abandoned San Francisco, Garcia, Mountain Girl, and Sunshine had found a place in Larkspur, a "crumbly, two-story adobe house among towering redwoods." A creek gurgled nearby. It

THE END OF THE BEGINNING | 213

was a quiet home for a young family. Garcia and Mountain Girl would never have a traditional union—they were unmarried for years and often lived apart—but for some stretches they could seem almost conventional, sharing a home and daughters during Garcia's breaks between road trips. Larkspur was one such place, a nest of domesticity where Mountain Girl tended to hearth and home while Garcia practiced his instruments. In 1969, she became pregnant, and both looked forward to their first child together. Sara and Heather, meanwhile, remained at arm's length, living not far away but entirely apart from Garcia.

Enveloped by redwoods, Garcia dived into a new instrument, turning his attention to the pedal steel guitar, which had intrigued him for years and which he'd fiddled with a bit without fully embracing. The instrument is notoriously difficult to play; Garcia compared the experience to knitting. But he was nothing if not relentless. Garcia practiced day after day in the summer of 1969, and he progressed quickly. By the following year, when Crosby, Stills and Nash invited him to contribute a solo to "Teach Your Children," he delivered it in a single take. That solo gave the song its distinctive sound, capturing its sweetness and longing.

Garcia's compulsive musicianship, along with his growing mastery of his new instrument, led him to consider new outlets. And so, even as the Dead found new audiences beyond the Bay Area, Garcia tacked on another project, an ensemble that reached both backward and forward in his musical development.

A timeline—really, a genealogy—of the New Riders of the Purple Sage published in England's *Zig Zag* magazine traces the New Riders back to before the Dead, starting with the Pine Valley Boys in 1962 and working through the Wildwood Boys, the New York Ramblers, the Hart Valley Drifters, and Mother McCree's Uptown Jug Champions—the string of bands that had evolved into the Warlocks and then the Dead. That timeline also crosses into the history of Big Brother and the Holding Company, as that's where Dave Nelson was playing before merging with the New Delhi River Band. At the same time, John Dawson jumped from New Delhi to the Mescaline Rompers. Those intertwined roots, illustrated by the magazine's intentionally dense chart, demarked the interconnectedness of these bands and groups; they nourished one another with ideas and personnel, one of the many benefits of participating in a musical and artistic community.

In the spring of 1969, Dawson was feeling restless, and Garcia was trying out his new instrument. Grabbing a few days while the Dead were home, they performed together at some small venues near San Francisco, testing out bluegrass favorites in front of friendly, if slightly surprised, audiences. Enjoying that, Garcia then reached out to Nelson, his old friend from Palo Alto days. The nucleus of the New Riders was established.

From that point on, Dead shows would often open with the New Riders, who would perform their blend of folk and bluegrass with Garcia at the pedal steel. They would give way to a set of acoustic music by the Dead, who would follow that with an electric set, sometimes two. Garcia would be onstage for hours, moving from one musical style to another, one instrument to another. It was a remarkable display of Garcia's talents and tastes and a captivating presentation of American music drawn from every quarter of that heritage—not to mention a tribute to his stamina.

The Dead brought this new formula—country and bluegrass, pedal steel and acid—to New York in July. It worked. "It was not so much music then as gestalt," a critic for *The New York Times* declared. "They really did love everyone and they really did transcend showbiz. Merely by being themselves they projected an almost cosmic benevolence."

That writer, Robert Christgau, had been unimpressed by the Dead in 1967. But now he marveled at the Dead's New York appearances, at the "melting pot" of musical styles, at the fact that concertgoers left their seats and danced, at the clarity of Garcia's guitar and his versatility with the pedal steel. Of Garcia, he wrote: "He always got where he wanted to go, it was someplace new, and you were glad to ride with him."

* * *

THE END OF THE BEGINNING | 215

THE WOODSTOCK Music and Art Fair was the creation of four young men: Michael Lang, Artie Kornfeld, John Roberts, and Joel Rosenman. Lang, the twenty-four-year-old owner of a headshop in Miami, smitten by the power of music to change culture, began with the idea of a concert. He imagined the world's best bands coming together for a weekend in the New England woods, surrounded there by arts—painting, crafts, dance, theater, a kind of summer camp for hippies.

At first, tickets sold for six dollars. As the event grew, Lang and his colleagues raised the one-day ticket price to seven dollars and added options: two days for thirteen and the full three-day admission for eighteen. The venue was to be near Woodstock, New York, a small community with a distinguished musical history, where Bob Dylan and members of the Band had recently taken up residence.

The Dead were high on Lang's list of artists. He'd discovered the band a couple of years earlier, when he was planning a gathering of tribes in Florida and was looking to bottle the magic of the Human Be-In. For Woodstock, he wanted that San Francisco sound, and he was thrilled to sign up the Dead, along with Creedence Clearwater Revival, the Jefferson Airplane, and Janis Joplin. He even got a deal on the Dead, paying Joplin $15,000 and the Airplane $10,000, while nabbing the Dead for just $7,500.

The Dead hesitated at first. Woodstock was far away, and the scale of it—even in its early stages—was enough to give them pause. But they could hardly resist. Lang invited the Merry Pranksters, and though Kesey declined, Babbs piloted the bus, the now famous Further, across the country for the festival. Lang also reached out to Wavy Gravy— Hugh Romney—and asked the Hog Farm to help with crowds. Those were the Dead's compatriots, and their inclusion made plans for Woodstock a far cry from Monterey. And though Monterey had been a disappointment, the Dead had played many festivals since then. Woodstock was just bigger. Moreover, music was Garcia's yoga, as he said himself. It was his revolutionary expression. Lang's vision was of just that—the idea of a community founded on the revolutionary effect of music. Woodstock was made for the Grateful Dead.

216 | HERE BESIDE THE RISING TIDE

The Dead, however, were not exactly made for Woodstock. Lang saw that the band received a headliner's slot on the weekend's performance schedule, slated to play Saturday evening. They flew in a day or two before and came upon the mass of humanity that had wound its way up the New York State Thruway and into the dairy country of Sullivan County. Sat Santokh was living in western Massachusetts at the time, and he picked up the Dead from the airport and shuttled the band to a nearby hotel.

The Pranksters had set up a small stage near the Hog Farm operations at Woodstock and invited anyone to perform. Garcia took a spin, so did Joan Baez. Most were just visitors who happened to be carrying an instrument. "Line up on the left," Babbs directed them. "Walk to the middle, do your thing and go off to the right."

In that setting, away from the giant stage, Garcia was comfortable and at home, cozily surrounded by Baez and Babbs and the familiar faces of San Francisco. Mountain Girl skipped Woodstock—Annabelle would be born in February—so Sat Santokh, who had managed the Carousel, and Garcia shared a room at the nearby Holiday Inn. The next day, they rode together in a helicopter to the site, Garcia largely silent as he took in the mass of people below, cars pulled off and abandoned, willy nilly, in fields and pastures.

As Sat Santokh recalled it, the Dead arrived nervous, perhaps because "they made the mistake of watching the news," which was full of ominous reports that closed roads and deteriorating conditions were creating the seeds of a catastrophe, that food and water were running out and that people were "going to die."

As the Dead prepared to play their set, Sat Santokh could tell "they were not in a comfortable place." That dread deepened as night fell. The stage, hastily constructed in the weeks before Woodstock, relied on rotating turntables that allowed one band to set up as another was performing. But the Dead's equipment was heavier than others', and it was too much for the turntable; the wheels supporting their platform collapsed. That slowed the load-in. Meanwhile, rain had soaked the ground

THE END OF THE BEGINNING | 217

beneath the stage, rendering the electrical ground rod ineffective. An exasperated electrician sank a new rod—or perhaps tapped into the telephone ground—and the effect was alarming. The instrument circuit shorted out, and the guitarists got a shock every time they touched the strings. When Weir approached his mic, a "great big blue spark about the size of a baseball" smacked him so hard it knocked him off his feet and into an amplifier.

Bear, the Dead's resident expert, had the presence of mind to realize what was happening and lifted one of the grounds. But that created other problems. Now, the PA somehow tapped into nearby CB radios, and that chatter was mixed into the sounds from the stage.

High on acid, worried by the gathering darkness and howling wind, the members of the band tentatively launched into their set. The band opened with "St. Stephen," but the PA problems made it impossible to hear, so they backed up, launching into "Mama Tried," a Merle Haggard cover. A few more stabs at numbers, including an unfocused "Dark Star," followed before the band turned to Pigpen, probably the evening's least high person, and he guided his colleagues through a respectable version of "Love Light." With that, the Dead called it a night. Lesh remembered looking at Garcia and Weir. "An unspoken agreement passes between us: Let's cut our losses and blow this joint."

Garcia laughed it off. "Jeez, we were awful!" he said later.

Woodstock soared without them. Yes, it was a hassle—food vendors shut down, water had to be imported, long lines for porta potties and telephones kept patrons waiting for hours. Rain produced mud, heat bore down between showers, badly synthesized batches of acid sent some into waves of fear and discomfort. And yet adversity seemed to bond the crowd rather than dividing it. Thousands, hundreds of thousands, shared the weekend, dipping naked into lakes, passing food to one another, enjoying music and company. By Monday morning, most had departed, but those who remained were spellbound by Jimi Hendrix as he deconstructed "The Star-Spangled Banner" as a joyous, jarring, electric scream of defiance, a "blazing freak flag, a protective shield for eccentrics, oddballs, weirdos, outsiders, marginal people of every sort," one writer reflected. Once heard, it could never be unheard, a new anthem for a new generation swathed in mud and common purpose.

Not everyone got it. *The New York Times* passed judgment harshly and prematurely, declaring on the festival's final morning that it was a "Nightmare in the Catskills." It was, the *Times* intoned in full Establishment condescension, "a nightmare of mud and stagnation." It raised questions, the *Times* worried, about "what kind of culture . . . can produce so colossal a mess?"

That was just harrumphing. Even the *Times*'s stodgy editorial board faintly allowed that "the great bulk of the freakish-looking intruders behaved astonishingly well." Most of the weekend's troubles were well within the capacity of Wavy Gravy and the Hog Farm, which established itself at Woodstock as a cooperative band of hippies helping hippies. There were three deaths—two from drug overdoses and one young person run over by a tractor—but the toll paled beside that of most mid-sized American cities over any three days in 1969. One health officer who, unlike the *Times* editorial board, actually was present for Woodstock sized it up far differently: "At no time during the entire festival did any one of the one hundred fifty odd medical personnel who worked at the site treat any case, or see any incident, which involved the causing of personal or physical injury from one human being to another," Dr. William Abruzzi wrote. "Not a knife wound was sewed, not a punch wound was treated."

Abruzzi's compendium of medical issues at Woodstock confirms that observation. It lists hundreds of ailments—foot lacerations, sprains, seizures, and lots and lots of drug experiences, along with a couple of cases of laryngitis and a raccoon bite—but no injuries at all from humans hurting each other. It is hard to imagine any other gathering of four hundred thousand people, much less one over four days in inclement weather, during which so little human friction was observed. Abruzzi was more than just gratified by what he witnessed. He was moved.

"There was no fish or wine, but perhaps in that spirit, the bread went further, the water lasted longer," he wrote. "Christ would have smiled."

THE END OF THE BEGINNING | 219

* * *

THE BENEVOLENCE that Christ bestowed on Woodstock skipped Los Angeles that week. Just after midnight into August 9, at the home of the very beautiful and very pregnant Sharon Tate, a group of sadistic intruders broke in. Tate was stabbed sixteen times and slashed repeatedly. While she was still breathing, she was hanged from a beam and tied to her friend Jay Sebring. Tate, Sebring, Abigail Folger, Wojciech Frykowski, and Steven Parent all died that night. The house and gardens were left awash in blood. The word "PIG" was written in blood on the front door; the blood type matched Tate's.

The next night, just a few miles away, in the Los Feliz neighborhood, grocery store owner Leno LaBianca and his wife, Rosemary, were at home when the killers worked their way inside. The LaBiancas were found the next day by their son-in-law, heads covered in pillowcases, bodies bloody and riddled with wounds. They had been stabbed repeatedly with carving and steak knives, a bayonet, and a fork. "Death to Pigs" was written in blood on the wall of the living room. The assailants carved the word "WAR" into Leno LaBianca's stomach. On the refrigerator, also in blood, were the words "Healter Skelter," a misspelling of "Helter Skelter" that drew the Beatles into the horror of it all. The killers left a fork stuck in Leno LaBianca's chest.

CHARLES MANSON was thirty-five years old at the time of the Tate and LaBianca murders. He had spent the Summer of Love in San Francisco, hovering around the events of that season with his wild eyes and prison-honed ability to manipulate. He'd begun to assemble his followers that summer, drawing in wayward men and women—mostly women—as he constructed his horrific vision of the future.

He'd brushed up against the music scene as well. Dennis Wilson of the Beach Boys picked up a couple of hitchhikers in the spring of 1968. They turned out to be members of the Manson Family, and they proceeded to settle in at Wilson's Sunset Boulevard manse. They stayed for months, sponging off Wilson and availing themselves of his doctors to treat their sexually transmitted diseases. Wilson did not seem to mind. "Except for the expense," he later told Manson prosecutor Vince Bugliosi, "I got along very well with Charlie and the girls." That would change when Manson threatened the life of Wilson's young son.

In the meantime, Manson offered Wilson songs, most of which Wilson politely rejected but one of which made it onto a Beach Boys record. Manson had called it "Cease to Exist," but the Beach Boys tinkered with both music and lyrics. It appeared on the B side of a Beach Boys original, "Bluebirds over the Mountain," in December of 1968. "Cease to exist" became "cease to resist," and the title became "Never Learn Not to Love." Manson was outraged at the changes and uncredited on the single.

By the summer of 1969, Manson and Wilson had parted. Manson moved to an abandoned movie set on a property known as Spahn Ranch in the far reaches of Los Angeles County, where he and his followers settled in for what he imagined was the coming revolution. He spoke rhapsodically of the turmoil to come—he called it Helter Skelter, and the Tate and LaBianca murders were intended to light the match.

Neither Manson's name nor his role in the killings surfaced in the weeks immediately following the discovery of the seven brutalized bodies on back-to-back nights in the hills of Los Angeles. Manson waited for word of the uprising in Death Valley, and only after he was arrested on suspicion of stealing a car did he come under the control of the authorities. He was initially jailed in Independence, California, hundreds of miles from Los Angeles.

Once Manson was arrested and his "family" identified as the perpetrators, the killings took on emblematic significance. Rather than being characterized as the work of a madman or of deranged cultists, the killings were "hippie" murders, somehow the consequence of the license that had taken hold in California in the decade of the 1960s. The road led from the Haight through Woodstock, from free love to unmitigated violence, from disregard of one set of rules to disregard for all rules, from humanity to barbarism.

THE END OF THE BEGINNING | 221

That was nonsense. The values of Allen Ginsberg and Joan Baez and Jerry Garcia were no more antecedent to Manson than the writings of Thomas Mann or Bertolt Brecht were responsible for Hitler. Manson himself was contemptuous of hippies. He considered them weak and beneath his revolutionary mission. That did not dissuade some members of the counterculture, so blinded by their rejection of mainstream society that they imagined common purpose with Manson. Jerry Rubin met Manson, pronounced himself "in love," and said he was inspired by Manson's "words and courage." Bernardine Dohrn of Weatherman, soon to disappear into the underground, called it "far out" that Manson's followers had succeeded in "offing those rich pigs with their own forks and knives." The cover page of the underground paper *Tuesday's Child* from February 16, 1970, featured a drawing of Manson nailed to a cross. *Rolling Stone*, in its June 25, 1970, edition, published a long interview with Manson and described the killer in his cellblock "composing songs, converting fellow inmates to his gospel of love and Christian submission."

Bugliosi, who knew him better than most, flirted with the idea of Manson as a "right-wing hippie," but that, too, was glib. Manson was racist and anti-Semitic and sexist. His connection to hippies was coincidental—he happened into the Haight just before the Summer of Love and he shared a taste for drugs. In the end, he was, plainly and simply, a psychopath. "The madness he wrought did not reflect the soul of the late '60s," Bugliosi sensibly concluded.

As his prosecutor realized, Manson's crimes were not a product of the counterculture, and they did not end the sixties. But they rattled something. They shook the sense of moment. They reinforced the growing unease that something had gone deeply wrong, and that California was leading the nation off a precipice. The sentiments that brought Reagan to power in 1966 surfaced that same deep discomfiture. And one more event before the calendar turned would reinforce them yet again.

* * *

222 | HERE BESIDE THE RISING TIDE

THE DEBACLE that became Altamont began and ended with the Rolling Stones. They hatched the idea, they fouled the plans for it, and they went through it when the deteriorating situation on the ground made it clear to many of those around them, including Garcia and the Dead, that events had soured to the point of danger.

Rock Scully was close to both the Stones and the Dead in 1969. So when the Stones were planning their 1969 tour of the United States, Scully floated the idea of including a free concert in San Francisco.

Sam Cutler, a British rock promoter and manager who also hobnobbed with the Stones in that period, knew the Dead through Scully, "a kindred spirt," as Cutler called him. As the Stones set off to conquer America, the tour hit some bumps. There were complaints about ticket prices, confusion created by the lack of a central organizer, drug-induced distractions. Looking to change the tour's arc, Scully and Cutler met with Mick Jagger and resuscitated the idea of a free concert. Jagger was receptive, Cutler recalled, as a way "to try to give something back." Bill Graham also endorsed the idea, and initially the thought was that the Stones would conclude their tour with a free show at the Polo Field in Golden Gate Park, the now hallowed ground of the Be-In. The Dead would contribute their experience—and cachet—to the concert, serving as hosts. It was to be something of a rock 'n' roll summit, a Woodstock West to make up for the Stones' absence from the Catskills version a few months earlier.

The idea grew. It would be a free show. It would conclude the tour. And it would be filmed, the capstone of a documentary about the tour. All of that was coming together, but the parties were moving quietly, encouraged by officials in the San Francisco parks department, who worried about publicity drawing too many people for the park to handle. But secrets are hard to keep, and the *Los Angeles Free Press* broke the story in November. And then Jagger confirmed it, blurting it out during a news conference in New York. On November 24, Ralph Gleason took note and added details. The concert, he wrote, was planned for either December 6 or 7. Gleason reported that the Dead, the Band, and Ali Akbar Khan, among others, would be sharing the bill.

THE END OF THE BEGINNING | 223

Two other details stood out in Gleason's report: "Applications for permits to hold the free show apparently still had not been requested," he noted, calling that oversight "curious." In fact, Gleason appears to have been misled—permits had quietly been promised but only on the condition that no advance notice be given, a condition that Jagger had just broken. Another notable element of the forming plan, Gleason wrote, regarded one of the invited participants: "Plans currently call for the Hell's Angels to be a part of the day-long free show. They are to staff a truck with free ice and free beer."

Lack of coordination, misunderstandings, Hells Angels with beer. It was not hard to predict that something would go wrong.

Clouds began to gather. The practical issues were real—no permits meant no permission to play. The Stones themselves were hard to engage. Touring, they were in that strange remove from normal life, "traveling in a bubble," as Garcia put it. And the mood darkened as well. When Manson was identified in early December as the "cult leader" behind the Tate and LaBianca murders and the crimes were cast as hippie atrocities, it cast a shadow across the concert planning. The Diggers' Emmett Grogan dubbed the concert the First Annual Charlie Manson Death Festival. He tacked a notice to that effect on the Dead's office door in Marin. It did not augur well.

Within days of his first column, Gleason warned of trouble. Will the Stones appear next weekend? Gleason asked in his November 28 column. "Your guess is as good as mine," he answered himself. Commenting on the confusion over the permits and the race to find an alternative to Golden Gate Park, he added, "It has really been masterfully mismanaged."

For a brief moment, it appeared as if a convenient, if not particularly beautiful, alternate site might do the trick. Thinking they had solved the problem, organizers accepted an offer from the owners of the Sears Point Raceway, a half hour north of San Francisco, and dispatched crews, who began assembling a stage. The Diggers joined in. But when the owners heard about the movie, they wanted a piece. Jagger refused, and the deal fell through.

224 | HERE BESIDE THE RISING TIDE

Politics complicated the rushed search as well. Organizers feared how Reagan might react, wondered whether the pugnacious governor would make some political hay by shutting them down. People's Park was top of mind. But they dismissed the idea, banishing the "vibes" that it cast across their efforts. Sears Point was gone, and time was running out, but they kept pushing.

And then, suddenly, the owner of another speedway, this one in the dry, treeless terrain of southern Alameda County, east of Oakland, offered his place. He didn't want money, just the publicity that would come from hosting such an event. Desperate, Scully jumped into a helicopter that picked him up outside the Dead's offices, took a worried aerial tour of the scrappy property, and agreed. The concert was set for December 6.

People began arriving the night before. It was cold and bleak in the spare country, and the bare hills offered little shelter from the wind. Participants pitched tents and "huddled together around bonfires in the near freezing temperature," one journalist reported. The crowd grew all night and all the next morning. By afternoon, hundreds of thousands were on hand and more kept coming; the crowd topped out at about three hundred thousand.

In San Francisco, the Dead and Stones met at the Ferry Building, where helicopters were to shuttle them across the Bay and to the site. It was the first time Garcia and Jagger had met, "the jolly, messy San Francisco hippie and the cocky, aristocratic British rock star," as writer Joel Selvin described them. Jagger grabbed the first chopper. Arriving over Altamont, the scene already was bubbling. The site, said Scully, was "unimaginably appalling. Mini-Vietnam of garbage and old car wrecks."

On the ground, concert-goers pushed and shoved into place. In contrast to Woodstock, where a gentle sense of shared experience took hold, here the crowd felt "unfriendly, territorial, selfish," said the critic and writer Greil Marcus, who had also been at Woodstock. Fights broke out as sheriff's deputies, outnumbered both by the crowd and by the Angels, stepped back and let events unfold.

The Hells Angels were initially recruited to this event when it was planned for San Francisco. That was dicey enough, but the Stones had seen bikers at work elsewhere and liked the idea—the Stones imagined themselves outlaws and felt they understood the Angels. But the move to the East Bay changed the dynamics in ways the Stones never grasped. That last-minute course change meant that the Angels who turned up to help came from Oakland and San Jose rather than the City. The Angels in San Francisco had a more bohemian streak: They were friendly with the Dead, had a soft spot for hippies, and enjoyed the Haight scene, with its mellow tones. It was the San Francisco Angels who provided childcare—*childcare*—at the Be-In. Not so the Oakland Angels. They were meaner, more aggressive, and now empowered as security and juiced up on acid and beer. As the crowd grew and pressed toward the hastily erected stage, some brushed up against the Angels' bikes, a forbidden zone. The Angels flashed weapons.

Garcia retreated with Mountain Girl and Scully, cowering inside the bus they were using as a dressing room. "No way am I playing," he repeated over and over. Coaxed outside to watch the Airplane deliver its set, Garcia witnessed one of the day's more shocking moments, as an Angel who went by the name Animal clocked the Airplane's Marty Balin, knocking him unconscious while he was performing (Stephen Stills of Crosby, Stills, Nash & Young was stabbed repeatedly in the leg with a motorcycle spoke). Garcia and the rest of the Dead headed for the helicopters. "It wasn't just the Angels," Garcia said. "There were weird kinds of psychic violence happening around the edges that didn't have anything to do with blows . . . spiritual panic or something."

Altamont continued to spiral downward. Its most searing moment came that night, when Meredith Hunter tussled with members of the Hells Angels. Hunter, who was black, had a gun, and the Angels were by then thoroughly engaged in the battle. One of the Angels saw Hunter and plunged into the crowd after him. The Angel, Alan Passaro, stabbed Hunter to death just feet from the stage. The Stones played on. Tried for murder, Passaro acknowledged he had slashed and "stabbed at" Hunter, but said he could not be sure whether or how often his knife wounded the young man, who was stabbed five times and then beaten

226 | HERE BESIDE THE RISING TIDE

and stomped as he hit the ground. Passaro pleaded self-defense and was acquitted. When the verdict came down, he threw his head back and yelled "Yeow!"

While Woodstock is most happily remembered as a weekend without a single instance of "personal or physical injury from one human being to another," Altamont would go down as the opposite. It was where a man was killed in full view of the stage and the music went on, even as his body was dragged from the scene.

FOUR BORN, FIVE DIE AT ALTAMONT ROCK FEST read the headline in the local *Tracy Press*. The deaths would be reduced by one once the day had passed, but something terrible and dark had occurred at Altamont, something decidedly not Woodstock. *Rolling Stone* devoted its issue of January 21, 1970, to a comprehensive reconstruction of the concert, an early sign of the magazine's commitment to serious journalism. Its conclusions were unsparing: "Altamont was the product of diabolical egotism, hype, ineptitude, money manipulation, and, at base, a fundamental lack of concern for humanity."

The Dead were both vindicated and vilified—and both with good reason—for fleeing Altamont rather than taking the stage. They had done their best to pull this off, but the Stones, driven more by public relations than by a genuine feeling for their audience or their relationship to it, had insisted on going forward. The Dead tried, and failed, to prevent that calamity, but at least they could be proud of refusing to contribute to it. Still, leaving came at a cost, too. Staying might have altered the trajectory of that night. The Dead were revered in San Francisco and beyond by the end of 1969, and they might have been able to appeal to the crowd's better instincts. "The music might have been able to at least modify the rhythm of events," Lesh reflected later.

Mountain Girl recognized the tragedy for what it was, a clanging repudiation of what she called the "peace and love generation." "After it all went down," she said, "we all felt guilty." It was, Garcia said, a "hard, hard lesson."

And what lesson was it? Reflecting on Woodstock and Altamont, Garcia framed his observations in the language of freedom—and its relationship to anarchy. Both brought together large crowds without any effective control, "a huge number of people and no rules," as he put it in a 1970 interview with a reporter from the BBC. There are two ways such a combination can go, Garcia said, "One of the ways, obviously, it can go is a terrible bummer, like Altamont, and one of the other ways is into an immensely joyful scene, like Woodstock."

Gleason saw the deeper tragedy, beyond the mishaps and mismanagement that he had chronicled and warned of as the event took shape. It was not the deaths per se. Any gathering of three hundred thousand people—whether in a barren field east of San Francisco or in any medium-sized city any day of the week—involves some death, and, as with Altamont, some birth. And yes, it gave grist to those who saw this community as dangerous. "Altamont may be viewed by the Max Raffertys and the Ronald Reagans as further evidence of the sickness of the young," he wrote as the year ended.

Woodstock was the result not just of harmonic convergences or luck; it took months of planning. Altamont was a hasty money grab by the Stones. But Gleason's lament was not for mismanagement, haste, or ineptitude. It was not that Hells Angels acted like Hells Angels. It was not even that police stood by when they might have saved Meredith Hunter's life. Rather, it was that something ineffable slipped away in those moments when the Rolling Stones performed while a young man was murdered in front of them. "What started as a dream on Haight Street in 1965," wrote Gleason, "may very well have ended in Meredith Hunter's blood in front of the bandstand at Altamont on December 6 when Mick Jagger sang 'Sympathy for the Devil' as Hunter died."

The counterculture was not represented by Manson, and it did not end with the deaths of Sharon Tate or Leno LaBianca. The counterculture *was* represented at Altamont, and it did not fare well. But the counterculture itself continued, and it did so in no small measure because the Dead survived.

In 1970, the Grateful Dead released two albums that announced the band as an exemplar of American music. *Workingman's Dead* and *American Beauty* would stand as two of the band's finest recording achievements.

CHAPTER 11

An American Music

ALTAMONT SCARRED THE DEAD AND RATTLED THE COUNTER-culture. But Garcia, for all his frailties, could summon resilience. He had done it after his father had died, and again after the crash that killed Paul Speegle. He'd survived the Army, lived out of his car. And though he abhorred violence and abjured pain, he enjoyed a certain amount of chaos. The bitter aftermath of Altamont might have sunk some people, might have torn apart a less tested band. Instead, the Dead bolted out of Altamont and produced not one but two landmark albums in less than a year. In the process, they redefined themselves, moving away from their history as San Francisco's hippie band and laying a cornerstone for what would let them become the most consummately American musical enterprise of the era, maybe of all time.

First, there was some reflecting to do—and some bitterness to purge. Ralph Gleason had produced the most important contemporary accounts of Altamont. He'd warned that it was shaping up badly and he'd been ignored. His journalism, at the *Chronicle* and through *Rolling Stone*, supplied a thorough record—one of accountability and judgment—of that day and what went wrong.

But it bugged the Dead, especially Robert Hunter. Shaken and defensive, he wrote an uncharacteristically topical, if oblique, response. Hunter, who had not seen the day for himself—he'd skipped it to see *Easy Rider*—struck out against Gleason and the gathering wisdom around the debacle. Whereas Hunter could be elliptical—it was in fact something of a trademark—this was pointed. His notes accompanying

230 | HERE BESIDE THE RISING TIDE

his new song describe it as "a reply to an indictment of the Altamont affair by pioneer rock critic Ralph J. Gleason." No ambiguity there. And he wrote it fast. December had not even ended before the Dead first performed "New Speedway Boogie" (originally titled "New Speedway Blues"), the title a clear giveaway reference to the Altamont Speedway.

The inaugural performance of "New Speedway Boogie" was raw and clunky, laced with broken harmonies and dissonance, so far off that the band seemed almost uncomfortable with its own material. But there was no mistaking its intention. On paper, it opened with the lines "Please don't dominate the rap, Jack, if you've got nothing new to say," a broadside against Gleason's critique, though in its debut, Garcia opened with the lines, "One way or another, one way or another . . . this darkness got to give." The death of Meredith Hunter (no relation to Robert) turned up in the third verse: "Now I don't know, but I been told, in the heat of the sun a man died of cold."

If that were the sum of it, "New Speedway Boogie" could have been dismissed as a specific bit of social commentary—Garcia did find it a little on the nose, and Sam Cutler felt that the band became embarrassed by its directness—but Hunter's lyric considered Altamont in light of the era. "I spent a little time on the mountain, spent a little time on the hill," Garcia sang that December night. "I seen things that I don't understand, but I think in time we will." After a loping lead guitar section, Garcia returned to the song's fourth verse, picking up Hunter's admission of confusion, the dislocation that Altamont left with so many who were there. "You can't overlook the lack, Jack, of any other highway to ride. It's got no signs or dividing lines and very few rules to guide."

"New Speedway Boogie" was a philosophical reply and an admission of confusion, but it also contained a note of optimism. We might not understand today, but "I think in time we will." And it was on that note, that bittersweet affirmation of something better ahead, that the song tailed off. "One way or another, one way or another, one way or another, this darkness got to give."

"The poet suggests, the journey has just begun," wrote Prankster Ed

McClanahan in a profile of Garcia and the Dead. "The way is long and arduous and fraught with peril; Altamont is but one dark moment."

In its rawness and its commentary, "New Speedway Boogie" was an act of musical reporting. "It says more than anything I've read in five years," Hunter Thompson told Carey McWilliams at *The Nation*.

The Dead would perform the number, adjusting it as they went, through 1970, but as Altamont faded into history, so did Hunter's reply to Gleason. The song dropped out of the Dead's repertoire after 1970 and did not return for another twenty-one years. When the Dead next played it, in 1991, it was at the height of the first Gulf War, and its lyrics, now long separated from Altamont, took on a new spirit and perspective.

THE DEAD released their fourth album, *Live/Dead,* at the end of 1969. It was a success on several levels. Not only did *Live/Dead* help the band draw down its debt to Warner Bros., it also, at last, delivered what critics had been asking for since the band's first album: a glimpse of what made the Dead so special live. For the first time, really, the Dead on vinyl felt sentient, undulating and moving, listening to one another, experimenting, playing with and off the audience. *Live/Dead* was not the same as seeing the boys at the Carousel, but the album corralled the lightning into a bottle for the first time. For some, it would become the most treasured Dead album of all.

A double album spread over four sides of vinyl, it devoted the first side entirely to a twenty-three-minute version of "Dark Star," recorded at the Fillmore West in San Francisco on February 27, 1969. It opened with a gentle, almost tentative musical conversation between Garcia and Lesh, so soft and searching that it barely resembled a song at all. Then, after about a minute, they were joined by Weir, Kreutzmann, and Hart, and the expanding sonic space of "Dark Star" as experience. Constanten painted the edges with a light-fingered, tingly keyboard, and the piece wandered through a dream, or rather a union of dreams, as the musicians adjusted their temperaments and tempos to one another, building, holding, drifting, returning. After twenty minutes of playing to and for one another, departing on long flights of wonder, they cohered again just after the twenty-one-minute mark, and Garcia resumed the song's cryptic lyric, projected through Owsley's bell-clear speaker array. Side 2 continued the commitment to the avant-garde, blending "St. Stephen" into the rhythmically complex "The Eleven," with its challenging time structure. Those two merged songs, performed at different venues on different nights, occupied the entire second side in a percussive, powerful sixteen minutes and twenty-four seconds' worth of uncompromised musical power.

Just months earlier, some critics had suggested that the Dead were at a junction, forced to choose between a future of psychedelic experimentation or one of immersion in the blues. Weir and Pigpen had almost lost their jobs when their bandmates, for a moment, got caught up in that contest. But better thinking had prevailed. *Live/Dead* proved it.

Just as side 1 was devoted to "Dark Star," side 3 was a single piece of song, in this case "Love Light," every bit as grounded as "Dark Star" was a flight. Here was Pigpen, the antithesis of avant-garde, the voice of the blues, driving musical traffic with his grounded, mischievous vocal, powering forward, stepping aside for Garcia, stepping back to the center, rapping with his sly asides. If side 1 was acid, side 3 was whiskey. Lesh and the drummers curled up behind Pigpen with a backbeat, and the rest unfolded on its own. Choose between psychedelics and blues? *Live/Dead* said no. Emphatically, happily no.

So, too, with the album's final side, closing with "Death Don't Have No Mercy" and "And We Bid You Goodnight" with a dollop of "Feedback" in between. Side 4 rounded out the album's emotional valence, bringing an earnest solemnity to the proceedings. Death showed up here, peeking its head, as it so often did, into the work of a band named, after all, the Grateful Dead. Garcia wallowed in it, rolled it through the quiet, bluesy feel of "Death Don't Have No Mercy." "Death will leave you, standing and crying, in this land," he sang, ever so quietly, above the mournful organ, the sharp guitar. And then, cacophony and mystery, a long section of feedback and sound, the chaotic turbulence of LSD or the 1960s or what have you, and then home, with "And We Bid You Goodnight" an a cappella coda at the end of a long journey. "I love you, but Jesus loves you the best," the band sang, together. "And I bid you goodnight, goodnight, goodnight." Fade to silence.

This was the Dead as joy, and listeners got it. Some of the reception for *Live/Dead* was swamped by Altamont and its aftermath, but the album made its delayed impression as critics found their way to it. "The Grateful Dead are a family of diverse powers," one wrote, "but ecstasy is their chief calling." That critic, the UC Berkeley undergrad Raymond Lang, extolled the "earthy masculine ebullience" of "Love Light" and the "softness and color" of "Dark Star." He concluded with the reflective exhaustion familiar to anyone who had experienced a long, winding night with the Dead. "There is nothing left to say," he wrote. "It is all too sacred."

THE DEAD arrived in New Orleans during the last week of January. They flew in from Hawaii, and they were on the cusp of an important change. Tom Constanten had brought creativity, even brilliance, to the band's studio work, and he had tried, with mixed success, to project that contribution onstage. Moreover, he was in a different place psychologically from some of his Dead colleagues. Constanten was fascinated by Scientology and was trying to incorporate its teachings into his life—consuming work for one who took it seriously. Among other things, that meant he had sworn off drugs. He wasn't alone in that choice. Pigpen avoided LSD and most other drugs, though he drank heavily, and Weir had periods of sobriety as well. But it served to put a distance between Constanten and the rest of the band, a distance that only reminded all of those involved that he had come to the music later than the rest of them. He was not exactly an outsider—he was a full participant on *Anthem of the Sun, Aoxomoxoa,* and *Live/Dead*—but he felt at the edge of the band, his feelings occasionally hurt by offhand remarks from Lesh and downright aggravated by what he called "gamesmanship and power trips" from Owsley, who brushed off Constanten's complaints about his amplification by snottily retorting that "a good worker never blames his tools." By early 1970, he and the Dead had decided to part ways. He came to New Orleans, but he was packing to go.

The New Orleans shows were anticipated and worried over. The Dead were performing with Fleetwood Mac. And the Warehouse, where they were appearing, was a new venue, a converted coffee and cotton warehouse expanded into a performance space with room for thirty-five hundred people, determined to offer hippies a home on the banks of the Mississippi River. The owners liked to think of the Warehouse as "Fillmore South," and the Dead were the perfect band to kick off the new operation. But there was apprehension, too. The Airplane had come to town in May 1969 only to have five members of the band and crew arrested on charges of drug possession. The Airplane members were busted at the same hotel where the Dead were staying. And not only were the Dead easy arrest bait, but on this trip, they were traveling with Owsley, his own magnet for narcotics enforcement.

The Dead, along with Fleetwood Mac and a band called the Flock, played the Warehouse on the thirtieth. The Dead headlined the event and took the stage at around twelve-thirty in the morning, wrapping up about two forty-five. Garcia dropped by a friend's house on the way back to the hotel. By the time he got there, the place was crawling with police.

The officers of the New Orleans Police Department and the Federal Bureau of Narcotics turned up at the Royal Sonesta Hotel on Bourbon Street that morning because, they said, they had received an anonymous letter informing authorities that the Dead were coming to town and would "be carrying in their possession very large quantities of narcotics (of all types)." The letter was unsigned. "I cannot tell you my name because they would hurt me," the writer stated. "I used to date one of them." Armed with that tip, police and agents patrolled the halls of the hotel that evening and "smelled the odor of burning marijuana" outside several of the rooms.

New Orleans police were not famously scrupulous, and it's hard to believe that they smelled marijuana being smoked in those rooms at eleven-thirty that night, as they claimed in the General Case Report, since the Dead were at the Warehouse waiting to go on at that time. The Dead later famously alleged they had been set up "like a bowling pin." Between the anonymous tip and the shaky report, they had a point.

Still, it did not take much detective work to figure that the Grateful Dead and entourage might have drugs on them. The officers presented their findings—the letter and the suspicious smells they alleged to have whiffed—to a local judge, and they returned at three forty-five that morning to execute their searches. Shockingly, they found drugs. In room after room, the officers found cigarettes and "brown vegetable matter, vials of tablets and oils, jars of black, brown and white powders, a smoking pipe, rolling papers, Joss sticks, incense." When they knocked on the door of one room, "the officers could hear the sound of a toilet flushing." Occupants of each room, except for the one that Pigpen and Constanten were sharing, were rounded up and handcuffed. Garcia straggled in at five forty-five, and he, too, was cuffed and hauled off to the pokey.

DRUG RAID NETS 19 IN FRENCH QUARTER, the New Orleans *Times-Picayune* reported on February 1. The photograph was of Owsley Stanley, identified as "a technician for the Grateful Dead, a California rock music group." The article's subhead called him the King of Acid.

Garcia, Lesh, Weir, and Kreutzmann were all charged with drug possession (marijuana in Garcia's case, Lesh for LSD and marijuana, Kreutzmann for marijuana and barbiturates, Weir for marijuana and amphetamines). Mickey Hart was not identified in the arresting or charging documents, and his presence went unnoticed by the press, but that's because he gave a fake name, telling officers he was "Sumner Wind" (some of the documents called him "Sumner," others "Summer," further confusing the matter) and identifying himself as a "spiritual adviser for the band." It didn't work; "Wind" was charged with possession of marijuana. Members of the crew were nabbed too. Larry Shurtliff (universally known as Ramrod from his days with the Pranksters) was arrested, as were Jon McIntire, Rex Jackson, and John Hagen. The sweep also snared a few New Orleans residents and visitors—a saleslady at a local dress shop, an LSU student, a carpenter, a mechanic.

The arrest came at a particularly inopportune moment for Garcia. Even as he was being led off to jail, Mountain Girl was calling from California to let him know she was going into labor. The desk clerk at the hotel ruefully alerted Mountain Girl that Jerry was not reachable and suggested she try the police instead. Mountain Girl went through delivery by herself, and Annabelle Garcia was born on February 2, 1970, the first of two daughters of Jerry and Carolyn Garcia.

After a very long night, the Dead bailed out of jail and were back at the Warehouse. On February 1, they joined with Fleetwood Mac to perform a benefit—for themselves. The concert raised money for their legal defense and to help Owsley, whose legal troubles were of an order of magnitude more serious than those of the band members. They were all arrested on drug charges—felonies, to be sure, but run-of-the-mill possession cases. Owsley, however, was free on bail at the time of the New Orleans arrests. California authorities revoked his freedom in February, and Owsley was jailed to await trial. Eventually convicted, the "King of Acid" would end up spending two years at the Terminal Island federal penitentiary.

The New Orleans arrests did not cost the rest of the band nearly that much. Joe Smith at Warner Bros. said he resolved the charges by contacting the New Orleans district attorney, Jim Garrison, the notorious chief prosecutor best known for his deplorable grandstanding on the Kennedy assassination. Smith recounted the conversation for an interviewer years later: "Mr. Garrison," Smith remembered saying, "my name is Joe Smith and I'm with Warner Brothers Records and we admire the way you administer the law in your parish. We wish we had that kind of thing in California. We'd like to make a contribution to your reelection campaign fund.

"He said, 'That's wonderful, Mr. Smith. What do you have in mind?'

"I said, 'Fifty thousand dollars.'"

According to Smith, Garrison thanked him for the contribution, and

Smith reminded Garrison that the authorities in New Orleans had charges pending against his clients. Smith promised that they meant no harm and would not come back if they could just be allowed not to face those charges. The conversation, Smith said, "helped [Garrison] make that decision."

THE DEAD'S return to San Francisco in early February let Garcia meet Annabelle and gave the band a chance to put some of its new material onto a new record. This time, Garcia vowed to do it differently. In place of hours of tinkering, coins on piano strings, sounds played backward, and exotic instruments played in exotic ways, the vibe for this album would be, as the historian Blair Jackson called it, "stripped down and simplified."

As always, the work that the Dead brought into the studio had been developed live, and this time, some of it emerged from acoustic and country-inflected performances in 1969 and 1970. The Dead had not abandoned electric music—"Dark Star" was a staple of the period—but live shows picked up a hint of the Bakersfield Sound, cool country music with rock licks. Lesh's bass lines carried many of these pieces underneath a suddenly twangy Garcia guitar sound. Garcia's work with the New Riders of the Purple Sage and his embrace of the pedal steel guitar contributed too.

Those influences were finding their way into Dead shows by the summer of 1969. Gary Lambert, one of the Dead's most thoughtful fans, was struck by the folk and country feel of shows in the latter half of that year, when the Dead opened with "Green, Green Grass of Home" or "Old, Old House," and sets sometimes included "Silver Threads and Golden Needles" and "Long Black Limousine," classic country tunes that would have felt out of place in the Dead's repertoire a year earlier (in the case of "Silver Threads and Golden Needles," the song had been one of the first the Dead had played as a band, but they had done so only occasionally since 1966; it came back in a few acoustic sets in 1969 and 1970). "If you were used to the Grateful Dead being the most anarchic,

238 | HERE BESIDE THE RISING TIDE

psychedelic, weird-sounding band in the world, that could be a shock to the system," Lambert said.

The new direction—or, really, the new inflection—blossomed through late 1969 and early 1970. In January, the band was in Oregon and thumped through "Dire Wolf" with a distinctly homey feel. "I Know You Rider" also enjoyed a country turn. A bluesier take on Otis Redding's "Hard to Handle" followed, but the band slid back into a country groove with Hunter's evocative reflection on miners, "Cumberland Blues," and then "Me and My Uncle."

So when the members of the band piled into Pacific High Recording Studios a few blocks from the Fillmore West, formerly the Carousel, they came with country music in their ears, pressure to move quickly, and a host of fresh material that the extraordinarily productive Hunter-Garcia partnership was pumping out in that period. The result was *Workingman's Dead*.

The album consisted of eight tracks. That alone suggested a new approach. *Live/Dead*, after all, included just six songs and a long feedback section—and that was across two discs. *Workingman's Dead* would be songs—simply recorded and straightforwardly presented. Bob Matthews, who produced the album with Betty Cantor-Jackson, looked over the list of songs that Garcia and Hunter had written, and Matthews created a proposed lineup. "So when they came into the studio, there was a vision in everybody's mind about the continuity and the emotional feel of the project," Matthews said.

The band began its recording sessions for *Workingman's Dead* on February 16, and once they were in the studio, another aspect of the songs would assume greater importance: singing. In their early years, the members of the Dead were learning their instruments, and their albums reflected that focus, which came at the expense of polished vocals. But they'd gotten to know Crosby, Stills and Nash, who knew a thing or two about singing, and their work and guidance helped convince the Dead to focus more on harmony. "Nothing really communicates like the human voice," Garcia said in 1972, a discovery he attributed to "hanging out with Crosby." "I used to think of myself as a guitar player but hearing singing, and seeing it up close, has kinda made me want to sing a lot. . . . It's real satisfying to sing." Weir eventually came to enjoy singing even more than playing guitar. "Singing," he told David Gans in 1977, "is the most fun I know." *Workingman's Dead* would provide the first sustained vehicle for this developing aspect of their music.

"Uncle John's Band" led off the album, as Matthews had wisely proposed. It began with the strumming of an acoustic guitar, joined by a bass and then a melodic, controlled Garcia lead, more campfire than acid rock. Next, the voices, in harmony, chimed in. "Well, the first days are the hardest days," the band sang. "Don't you worry anymore." With one couplet, the album's tone was set: These are difficult times, the Grateful Dead, fresh from Altamont, acknowledged. And they'll get better, the Grateful Dead, brimming with ideas, reassured.

Here was freedom of a new sort. Not the freedom to play without limits, to follow every sound wave through its dimensions, volume, and tone, but the right to join and reinterpret long musical tradition, to respect what came before and create something new on top of it. To sing in harmony, not just to explore dissonance. This was no longer Ken Kesey coming to the edge of the Pacific and lifting off into space. This was digging deep into musical and American history and emerging with something fresh.

Hunter's lyrics were crafted in a distinctly American vernacular. He nodded to "Easy Street" and the "Buck Dancer's Choice," to walls "built of cannonballs," to a group whose "motto is 'Don't Tread on Me.'" Each of those communicated a history—fiddle players, railroads, the New Lost City Ramblers, the American Revolution. Hunter struggled with the chorus. He heard himself phrase the words "Goddamn, Uncle John's mad," but that seemed off, aggressive. Then it turned for him, morphing into "Come hear Uncle John's Band," the phrase now an inviting one, an opening to the album and to the band. "That's one of those little things where the sparkles start coming out of your eyes," Hunter said. He retained the "Goddamn," which moved to "Goddamn, well, I declare: Have you seen the like?" There, it was not off-putting; rather, it was exclamatory, excited. That wasn't enough to satisfy radio

240 | HERE BESIDE THE RISING TIDE

censors who objected to any use of the word, but it worked for the song. "Uncle John's Band" was an invitation, a welcome. And, without the archness of "New Speedway Boogie," it nodded to the moment, to the Dead's place in the larger counterculture taking shape around it, not driving that culture so much as riding it. "Here," Garcia and his band-mates sang, "beside the rising tide."

Garcia's music, meanwhile, drew upon his mythically diverse interests. The acoustic strumming, the gentle guitar line—those felt notably American, redolent of folk and country. But the melody moved beyond that. In fact, Garcia picked up a hint of it from an unlikely source. "I stole part of the melody from a Bulgarian women's choir record," Garcia told Vince Welnick in 1990, as Garcia was teaching him to play the song. "It's just one little phrase, actually, but I just loved the way it sounded." The song, "Shto Mi e Milo," as performed by the Pennywhis-tlers, bore little resemblance to the finished "Uncle John's Band," but it unmistakably included the phrase that lodged in Garcia's head while he was composing. And so the pieces came together.

What could be a more modern American project than the melding of a Bulgarian folk melody over country chords and American revolu-tionary themes in the hands of two midcentury musical wizards, bound together through visionary drug experiences? "Uncle John's Band" was a statement of freedom and tradition and the relationship between them. The song, Garcia acknowledged, "was a *major* effort, as a musical piece," but every bit of it worthwhile.

The balance of side 1 included "High Time," "Dire Wolf," and "New Speedway Boogie," a triumvirate of reflection and worry, dashes of humor, and that dark optimism that so specifically communicated the Dead—and the larger counterculture—at this moment. "High Time" had been part of the Dead's repertoire since the middle of 1969. "I'm having a hard time living the good life," the narrator confesses. Garcia was happy with the song, but a little disappointed in his vocal part. "I really can't do justice to that kind of song," he conceded years later.

The song was an ode to uncertainty and contradiction. "Nothing's for certain," the final verse concluded. "It could always go wrong." What did that leave? Living for the moment, making progress, accepting change, "come in when it's raining, go on out when it's gone." Serious stuff, but not gloomy. Moreover, despite Garcia's penchant for self-criticism, the song was poignantly delivered, Garcia's imperfections as a singer reinforcing its ambiguity.

So, too, with "Dire Wolf," which placed a ravenous wolf against a snappy, incongruous melody. It, too, dated from the summer of 1969. "Dire Wolf" was in part inspired by *The Hound of the Baskervilles,* which Hunter and Garcia watched together on TV, though the song bears scant resemblance to the film. The dire wolf of "Dire Wolf" was not just any wolf, but a card-playing, murderous beast, "six hundred pounds of sin." As Buzz Poole, in his authoritative examination of *Workingman's Dead,* observes, the song alludes to the Old and New worlds, the long extinct dire wolf (a smallish creature unlike the fearsome specimen in the song), red whiskey, and Lead Belly.

Its chorus suggests another preoccupation: "Don't murder me. I beg of you, don't murder me." This was a season of murder. The first performance of "Dire Wolf" predated the Manson murders, but the song grew and developed not just under that shadow but also that of Manson's horrifying San Francisco counterpart, the Zodiac Killer. "Popular culture forensics," Poole mused, reveal traces of the "Zodiac Killer's fingerprints" in "Dire Wolf."

The Zodiac Killer had struck first in Benicia, northeast of San Francisco, just before Christmas 1968 and continued to claim victims in the Bay Area throughout 1969, terrorizing the region and taunting authorities with his letters to local newspapers boasting of his killings and daring police to catch him. The Zodiac Killer dispatched victims through 1969, and on October 17, newspapers published his threat to target kids on their way to school. "School children make nice targets," the killer wrote in his distinctive block lettering, "I think I shall wipe out a school bus some morning. Just shoot out the front tire & then pick off the kiddies as they come bouncing out." That was meant to terrify, and it did. Among those unsettled was Garcia. On October 26, the Dead were in the middle of a low-key Sunday evening at Winterland in San Francisco when Garcia turned to "Dire Wolf." Uncharacteristically chatty, he introduced the number by saying, "This song is dedicated to the Zodiac cat and also to paranoid fantasies everywhere." He invited the audience to sing along.

Freedom and murder represented poles of a polarizing moment, but the Dead's response was something close to wry optimism. Certainly, that was true of "New Speedway Boogie," which, thoughtfully, ended side 1 of the album.

"Cumberland Blues" opened side 2 with a change of tone and outlook, an announcement as solid as "Uncle John's Band" had been for side 1. From the bleak, cold hillsides of Altamont, the Dead moved to the mining country of Appalachia, exact location unknown and unimportant. This was a labor song, a story of workingmen, as the album promised. So authentic was the number in its approach and sound that an actual miner once asked Hunter where he'd discovered the piece—as solid a compliment as the songwriter ever received. It also represented a broader band contribution. Lesh shared credit with Garcia for the music, and Weir contributed a rhythm guitar that was straight out of Bakersfield.

At one level, "Cumberland Blues" was pure fantasy. Hunter had never worked in a mine. But the lyrics rang true. The miner who couldn't win for losing, stuck collecting "five dollars a day," forced to walk a picket line "just to pay his union dues." The narrator shared those woes with Melinda, a high school friend of Hunter remembered more for her name than her person, and was ambivalent about it. "I can't help you with your troubles," he warned, "if you won't help with mine." But if the song read as ambivalent and anxious, it played boisterous—a trip into mining country through the eyes of a tough-minded scrapper.

The threat of death that ran through "Dire Wolf" found its mark in "Black Peter." Written by Hunter in the aftermath of a powerful acid trip and then radically reconsidered by Garcia, "Black Peter" was the album's most mournful song, as well as its most openhearted, expressing two congruent truths—that death is both tragic and universal. One of several Dead classics to experiment with a shifting point of view ("Wharf Rat" was another), "Black Peter" was sung by the narrator but also observed by the singer, hovering above his deathbed as his "friends they come around." The song was simple and sad, an old man lying in bed waiting to die. But the song's magic took flight in the bridge that Garcia composed for it, stepping away from the scene and finding its poignance not in the life of its central character but in the ordinariness of the moment. Everything leads up to the day of Peter's death, the lyrics observed, "And it's just like / Any other day / That's ever been. / Sun goin' up / And then the / Sun it going down. / Shine through my window and / My friends they come around / Come around / Come around."

Hunter wrote the lyrics of "Black Peter" to be sung at a "brisk" tempo, imagining a song more in the spirit of "Dire Wolf," but Garcia slowed it down and stretched it out. It was the longest song on *Workingman's Dead*. That was precisely what gave it definition. Garcia would perform "Black Peter" in many guises over the years, and as he aged, it could seem painfully autobiographical, verging on maudlin. Settled in this place, near the end of this album, it was positioned as the nadir of the tale.

Two final numbers, a nod to the Dead's past and sly appraisal of its moment, concluded *Workingman's Dead*. "Easy Wind" was a Pigpen vehicle, old-school blues written for Pigpen's voice and the only song not led by Garcia—as well as the only one for which Hunter wrote both words and music. Set in the Louisiana bayou—and first performed in Baton Rouge—"Easy Wind" felt older than it was. Like "Cumberland Blues," it spoke of blue-collar life—jackhammering rocks for "the great highway." The band had been playing the song since September 1969 by the time it put down the first of ten takes at the Pacific High studio. After some fumbling and corrections, they found it. "Easy Wind" stood out from the rest of the album for its origins and its voice, but it settled right into the idea of old American music freshly told. The song would not play a major role for the Dead in the years to come; the band played

244 | HERE BESIDE THE RISING TIDE

it through early 1971 and then let it go. But Hunter himself enjoyed it, playing it for another three decades in his solo performances, long after Pigpen had died.

Workingman's Dead concluded with a note of mischief. Even before the first chord of "Casey Jones" appeared, there was the unmistakable sound of a sniff. Given what followed, a tale of a train conductor at his post and under the influence—"Drivin' that train, high on cocaine" as the lyric announced—the sniff was not mysterious. Its origins, however, were. Buzz Poole dug deep into the sniff and discovered that it was, in fact, Garcia, but not Garcia hitting a line of cocaine. It was Garcia clearing his sinuses, preparing to sing. Too late. The sniff had its own life and meaning, and it would kick off the final entry of *Workingman's Dead* with a none too inside joke.

For a song that would often be cited as the Dead's tribute to cocaine, the lyrics actually conveyed nothing of the sort. If anything, the song was a cautionary tale insofar as it was about drugs. It warned Casey Jones of "trouble ahead" and "trouble behind." It even advised him to "watch your speed." But it followed a sniff, and it was sung by Jerry Garcia—neither of which suggested a warning to kids to avoid cocaine. "Casey Jones" was not a musical advertisement to refuse drugs, nor was it, as those who just heard the word "cocaine" assumed, an invitation to partake. It was, rather, one in a long history of cocaine blues numbers.

Beyond the references to coke, "Casey Jones" was a railroad song, crafted in the image of the famous engineer who, according to legend, hurried to make up for lost time but then, when the train was headed for a crash, stayed at the helm, pulling on the brake to slow the train and save the lives of his passengers at his own risk. Jones died in the crash, but his passengers survived. Casey Jones's heroism earned him a durable spot in the American songbook—and even in vaudeville—and Garcia imagined the Dead's "Casey Jones" to be their contribution to that history. "It's partly my way of expressing thanks to that whole tradition," he said in a 1971 interview.

"Partly" is worth a note because "Casey Jones" also reaches beyond the tradition it celebrates. The song documents, with a few historical interpolations, Casey Jones and his fateful accident in 1900, but it also wraps in the Dead's place in the American counterculture in 1969—when events were moving fast, when politics and art were colliding and intertwining, when drugs were potent, enlightening and distracting, when cocaine was new to that scene, jangly and foggy. "It's a pretty good musical picture of what cocaine is like," Garcia told Charles Reich in 1972. "A little bit evil. And hard-edged. And also that sing-songy thing, because that's what it *is*, a sing-songy thing, a little melody that gets in your head."

It was that. "Casey Jones," for all its jangly melody and musical roots, also left listeners with something to think about as 1970 rolled into view. At least, it did for those listeners who got to hear it. The song would be banned from many radio stations merely because of its references to cocaine, even though it explicitly warned of its dangers. It was a hard time to make sense of America. The Dead would not always offer clarity, but they could at least share in the attempt. "Trouble with you is the trouble with me," Hunter wrote and Garcia sang, "Got two good eyes, but we still don't see."

WITH *WORKINGMAN'S DEAD,* the Dead had made a genuine contribution to the history of American music built on ideas, melodies, and styles that were an expression of that larger culture as well as uniquely the work of these musicians and their lyricist. Arrestingly captured by Stanley Mouse's cover, featuring a photograph of the band sepia-tinted to give it an antique feel, the look of outlaws waiting for trouble on a street corner, the album sealed the Dead's place in a certain lineage. It did not, however, solve their most immediate problem. They were broke when they went into the studio to record *Workingman's Dead,* and they were broke—and betrayed—when they emerged.

* * *

246 | HERE BESIDE THE RISING TIDE

THE DEAD were famously difficult to organize, and the members of the band had reason to be unhappy with their management at the end of 1969. They were attracting national attention and touring relentlessly, and *Live/Dead* had received raves, and yet here they were, more than $100,000 in debt to their record company. By conspicuous contrast, the Rolling Stones, who had just made a shambles of Altamont but whose songs were staples of radio and record sales, made more than $400,000 from their American tour. *Each.*

Enter Lenny Hart. Hart was a preacher, a musician, and a con man. And he was Mickey Hart's dad. So Mickey Hart, delighted to be reconnected with his dad and eager to help out his new band, made a pitch for Lenny to join the Dead. Garcia and his colleagues, who knew almost as little about managing money as they did about coal mining, agreed to let Hart take on management responsibilities.

Hart's addition to the Dead family created as much confusion as it resolved. When Sam Cutler arrived on the West Coast to represent the Stones in the ill-fated discussions for a free concert, he couldn't tell who was in charge for the Dead. Hart took charge of the money. And then he stole it.

Working with a good-looking employee with a beehive hairdo at the Dead's bank, Hart took money as it came in, extending loans to Dead employees as advances, then pocketing the repayments. The Dead, used to being broke, did not notice at first, but as Hart's greed and confidence grew, his thievery became more brazen. Mountain Girl was waiting for a check—Garcia had recorded some music for Michelangelo Antonioni's *Zabriskie Point,* and MG was counting on the money. She heard that the check had arrived and went to pick it up, but Hart denied receiving it. Others began investigating, and Ramrod became convinced that Hart was stealing. "Either you gotta get rid of that Lenny guy or I'm quitting," he informed Garcia. It got worse: After a show one night, a couple of repo guys seized Pigpen's organ for failure to make payments. How could it be that the band was touring, raking in cash, and having its instruments repossessed?

It fell to Lesh and Mickey Hart to confront his father. "Phil and I asked to see the books," Hart wrote. "Lenny refused in a suave, bankerly sort of way and at that instant I knew: he had stolen our money."

That was the end of Lenny Hart's run with the Dead.

UNDETERRED, THE DEAD turned in a storied run in early 1970. A series of New York shows that February with the Allman Brothers Band cemented a relationship between the two bands and highlighted their surprisingly simpatico approaches. Yes, one was from Macon, Georgia, the other from San Francisco, but both were grounded in American themes and committed to exploring the outer edges of their crafts. Both even featured two drummers—something that Duane and Gregg Allman had seen, and admired, when they had played the Avalon at the heyday of the Haight. That February, the bands overlapped at the Fillmore East.

With members of Fleetwood Mac in the house as well, the Allman Brothers opened the evening with what Lesh recalled as a "blistering set." The Dead followed them to the stage, and Garcia invited Duane Allman to sit in during the Dead's "Dark Star." As the song unwound—formless and unscripted as always, band members listening to one another, tapping into the expectations of the audience, hearing and playing—other members of the Allman Brothers drifted onto the stage, merging the two bands as they wandered through some of the Dead's staples of the period, from "Dark Star" to "Spanish Jam" to "Love Light." Members of Fleetwood Mac found their way into the jam as well, and musicians played for hours, finally concluding in a "crashing finish."

"I walk outside," Lesh recalled. "It's daylight, and snow is falling gently on the streets of New York. The other musicians straggle out. We stand there, our breath steaming, and look east down the crosstown side street. A distended orange sun is rising between the buildings, casting lurid shadows in the fresh snow. I grab Bob and Jerry in a group embrace: *This* is what it's all about."

Two months later, on April 9, the Dead were home in San Francisco and back at the Fillmore West, with yet another iconic band opening for

248 | HERE BESIDE THE RISING TIDE

them in a pairing thrown together by Bill Graham, with his love of juxtaposing musical styles. This time, the artist was Miles Davis with his six-member band, fresh from *Bitches Brew*. Davis was touring for the new album and eager to introduce it to white audiences; the Dead were awed to share the stage with Davis, whose music all of them admired. Lesh watched in wonder, "my jaw hanging agape, trying to comprehend the forces that Miles was unleashing onstage." Garcia sought out Davis after the jazz great had finished his set and struck up a conversation. They enjoyed each other. The two "hit it off great," Davis said later. "Jerry Garcia loved jazz, and I found out that he loved my music and had been listening to it for a long time."

TWO EVENTS across eleven days in May rocked the counterculture and hardened even its most peace-loving participants. They were prompted—one directly and one indirectly—by an escalation of the war in Vietnam, specifically, Nixon's decision to expand the conflict into Cambodia, first with bombings and then with troops. Although the bombings were not officially acknowledged, *The New York Times* revealed them two months after they were under way, angering members of Congress and enraging the antiwar movement. Undeterred, Nixon went further, sending ground forces into Cambodia on April 28, 1970.

As Todd Gitlin wrote, "The dam broke." Students rose up at more than half the nation's universities. Almost a third went on strike, some closing for the rest of the academic year. Dozens of ROTC buildings were set on fire. A million or so students who had never before protested joined the ranks of those in fury against their government. "All in all, it was by far the largest number of students ever to demonstrate in a single spasm," Gitlin observed.

One of those demonstrations played out at the small Midwestern blue-collar campus of Kent State University, just east of Akron, Ohio. On the day after Nixon's address to the nation, protesters held an antiwar rally at the center of campus. The rally gave way to a turbulent night in the town of Kent, as protesters tangled with police and set upon police cars. The mayor called a state of emergency, and Governor James Rhodes, a Republican looking to burnish his law-and-order credentials, summoned the National Guard. A tense weekend followed, and on Monday, thousands gathered for a follow-up rally, again at the center of campus. With both sides girding for the demonstration, officials with the Guard concluded that the situation was too volatile to allow the rally to take place. They banned it and ordered the crowd to disperse. Refusing, some pelted the Guard and police officers with rocks, then scattered. With the Guard in pursuit and the two sides skirmishing, "more than 70 Guardsmen turned suddenly and fired their rifles and pistols," according to Kent State's reconstruction of the events. Approximately sixty-five shots were fired in thirteen seconds. Four students were killed and nine others wounded, including one paralyzed by a Guardsman's bullet.

Wars are fought on battlefields but won and lost in images. John Filo's photograph caught the moment when Mary Ann Vecchio knelt above the body of Jeffrey Miller, facedown on a sidewalk. Vecchio's face was twisted in despair, her arms raised, pleading. She was fourteen years old.

The nation recoiled. Nixon's war in Vietnam was now a war against students who objected to that war. Nixon did not address the killings himself, but his coolly worded statement deplored the "tragic and unfortunate incident" that he said "should remind us all once again that when dissent turns to violence, it invites tragedy."

Ten days later, students at Jackson State University in Mississippi were demonstrating, though not against the war per se. Their protest began over the behavior of white motorists who would speed through the campus on Lynch Street, tossing objects from their cars and shouting racial insults at the students. Black students demanded action, and as their grievances went unaddressed, they added others, including their anger over the Vietnam War. On the night of May 14, a dump truck in the area was set on fire. Police responded in riot gear and, finding no one at the scene, converged on a women's dormitory close to the burning truck.

They would later claim, falsely, to have been fired upon, though they were met with bricks and rocks. They responded by opening fire on the dorm, drenching it with more than four hundred rounds. Two young men, a junior at Jackson State and a high school senior, were killed.

The Jackson State killings slid beneath national attention. Not because the protest was smaller or less significant than the demonstrations elsewhere. Two young men were dead, and police were responsible. Those were compelling matters for public concern, but the victims at Jackson State were young black men, not a photogenic fourteen-year-old white girl in anguish over the death of a young white man.

The relative silence around the Jackson State shootings spoke to racism in America. The explosion of anger over Kent State testified to the public's exhaustion with a war that was turning on its own citizens. A collection of writings from underground newspapers of the period adorned its closing page with a full-page picture of the Kent State campus, Guardsmen taking aim at a young man with a headband and a flag. Kent State "brought repression home to white, middle-class America as only workers and blacks had known it before," the caption read.

Two demonstrations, 929 miles apart. Six dead, two the victims of racism, four of militarism.

Once violence begins, it is hard to stop.

MILES DAVIS, the Allman Brothers, Fleetwood Mac, Janis Joplin. These were some of the most adventurous and serious acts in popular music in 1970, and all were thrilled to connect with the Dead and their audience. No further evidence was needed of the Dead's increasingly firm place in the American popular music pantheon, at least within the counterculture. But while no other exhibits were needed, more were presented. That summer, the Dead were invited to join an epic musical tour, a trip close to the fulfillment of Garcia's dream of musical camaraderie. The setting was Canada, and the event was billed as the Festival Express.

The festival was designed as a rolling rock 'n' roll event, kicking off with a concert in Montreal and working its way across the country, the bands transported, together, by train. Acts included the Dead and the New Riders, Janis Joplin, the Band, Buddy Guy, the Flying Burrito Brothers, Delaney and Bonnie and Friends, and others.

The trip hit snags immediately. The Montreal shows coincided with a holiday there and were canceled. Instead, the tour kicked off in Toronto, where it was hit with a different problem. Calling themselves the May Fourth Movement—in honor of Kent State—twenty-five hundred protesters crashed the gates, clashing with police as they asserted their objections to the fourteen-dollar price of tickets. Music, they argued, belonged to the people; it should be free. The Dead worked with the protesters and played a free show to defuse the anger, but neither Garcia nor his bandmates bought the idea that the music they produced was owned by "the public."

Interviewed by Cameron Crowe in 1973, a grouchy Garcia unloaded on those who claimed a share of his craft. "In order to get so you can play music you have to sacrifice a lot of what would have been your normal life. You know what I mean?" he asked. "It's not a thing you just do. If that were so, everybody'd be making their own music and there wouldn't be professional musicians. There'd be no need for them. For someone to deny the fact that you spent a certain amount of your life working on some sort of discipline and learning how to play . . . that's the rip-off. . . . Anytime someone comes down on artists and claims their work on any level, I think that's pure bullshit. There's been too many great musicians who died poor."

As for the "people's music"—well, Garcia said, "It just ain't so."

That was Garcia in a mood. For the most part, he and the Dead were generous and conciliatory. They had helped spawn some of the radical energy they now confronted, and they handled the turnaround with grudging grace. The deal to play for free the next day quelled the uprising without accepting the argument. It set the Festival Express on its rolling way.

The express was fourteen train cars, strung together and rented by the promoters from the Canadian National rail service. Outfitted with amplifiers, drum kits, cameras, and a well-stocked bar car, the train departed Toronto and headed west. The jamming began the first day and never let up. "Before we'd cleared the Toronto city limits," Lesh wrote, "the monumental, historic, never-ending transcontinental jam was under way." At first, the musicians drifted to their natural sounds— country musicians in one car, blues in another. But the booze—there were not many drugs on the train, as the musicians were afraid of getting caught crossing into Canada—loosened boundaries. Garcia, who rarely drank, got in the spirit, wobbling through cars and plunging into the jam.

It was, for Garcia, one of the most enjoyable and memorable stretches of his life. He was allowed to play for days, and all to the rumble of a train. It was both fun and productive. Garcia played with Janis Joplin, Rick Danko, John Dawson, and more. They had the time and space to enjoy each other in ways that concerts rarely offered. It was, for Garcia, blissful.

The Festival Express contributed three signature works to the Grateful Dead. Noodling with his fellow musicians in the bar car, Garcia learned an old folk tune made famous by Woody Guthrie called "Goin' Down the Road Feeling Bad." It would become a Grateful Dead staple in the years to come. Garcia also put down the music for what would become "Ripple." Set to words that Hunter had drafted in a fit of inspiration just a few months earlier (Hunter wrote three memorable Grateful Dead lyrics in one two-hour afternoon at Alan Trist's West Kensington flat in May), "Ripple" would assume mythic status for the Dead, a moving hymn woven around a Zen meditation.

And finally, the trip produced a song that settled nicely into the band's running train mythology as well as one about the trip itself. "Might as Well" did not enjoy a very long run in Grateful Dead history, appearing first in 1976 and sporadically in live performances after that. But its chipper, upbeat tempo and unabashedly nostalgic lyrics made it stand out. It was, the song said, "One long party from front to end," set in boxcars to the tune of the rail. "Never had such a good time in my life before," Garcia sang at the song's bridge. "I'd like to have it one time more / One good ride from start to end / I'd like to take that ride again."

AN AMERICAN MUSIC | 253

* * *

LESH'S UPBRINGING was perhaps the most "normal" of any member of the Dead—two parents in the same household doing their best to raise a family. Still, Phil Lesh was a rebellious musician, a free soul who challenged his father's authority and set out to pursue a musical life. He was, after all, a leading member of a rock band by 1970. So it was with "guilt and apprehension" that Lesh absorbed word of this father's failing health, the result of prostate cancer. And yet those months were a time of repair, father and son rediscovering their appreciation for each other, Phil coming to realize that his father was genuinely proud of him.

As they bound up their wounds, Phil was fiddling with a tune, a chord structure and melody, a song in search of lyrics and an ending. He shared his work with Hunter, who returned with words. And not just any words. "Box of Rain" was one of the most generous, affirming lyrics to spring from Hunter's songbook. Its open spirit, its naturalism, its quiet appreciation for death and dying spoke tenderly in a way beyond even the most evocative Grateful Dead songs of that era. It was not so much a song about Lesh's father's dying as it was a tribute to eternity and ephemerality. "This is all a dream we dreamed," the lyric went, "one afternoon long ago." And as for the struggle of living and dying, well, "a box of rain will ease the pain. And love will see you through."

With Lesh tending to his father and *Workingman's Dead* still freshly being digested, the Dead decided to return to the studio—a surprising move in some ways. Most bands space out albums to maximize sales, touring behind the latest release and pitching the new product from city to city. That was so far from the Dead's approach, however, that releasing a second studio album in less than a year almost surely irked Warner Bros. more than it troubled any member of the Dead. What members of the band recognized was that they had new material—the products of this fecund period of collaboration between Garcia and Hunter. Hunter was living with Garcia and Mountain Girl at the time, giving them time to work out songs together, Garcia experimenting with melodies on piano or guitar while Hunter contributed ideas and phrasing. Music poured forth from them.

Their songwriting partnership was one of deep mutual understanding and also profound trust. They made light of it in interviews, but both understood that they were reaching for something bigger—and, in their best work, finding it. After Garcia's death, Hunter recalled a conversation in 1969, when the two were on a walk together in Madrone Canyon in Larkspur. Garcia noted that they were "creating a universe, and I was responsible for the verbal half of it." Hunter, no doubt taken aback by the scope of that project, countered that it was Garcia whose "way with music and a guitar" was "pulling it off."

"That's for now," Garcia responded. "This is your time in the shadow, but it won't always be that way. I'm not going to live a long time. It's not in the cards. Then it'll be your turn."

THE GRATEFUL Dead reentered the studio in August, this time at the San Francisco studio of pioneering audio engineer Wally Heider, who had recently set up shop. The Dead arrived with an armful of material and the recent experience of producing an album quickly and professionally. Over the next few weeks, they would bring the lessons of *Workingman's Dead* and the strength of the Hunter-Garcia songs as well as contributions from the rest of the band. The result was deliberate, considered, and warm, the Dead's most integrated and coherent album, from song selection to cover design. It was *American Beauty*.

The Dead had been scheduled to join the Great Medicine Ball Caravan, a bus caravan of acts that would cross the country, live in teepees, and play around for an accompanying movie crew in the summer of 1970. They backed out at the last minute, giving them a block of time back in San Francisco—and effectively stranding them there, since their crew, including sound engineers Bob Matthews and Betty Cantor-Jackson, were committed to the Medicine Ball. Still floating on the energy of *Workingman's Dead,* the band entered the studio on August 6.

Over the next six weeks, they recorded what many would regard as their studio masterpiece.

"Box of Rain" opened the album, setting a tone of reflection, fragility, and compassion—extensions of the emotional menu and western hue of *Workingman's Dead*. From its first notes, it was clear that this album would strike American chords too, but different ones, deeper and softer, more connected to the life of the country than to its history. It also meant that the album opened in Lesh's voice, another departure signaling that *American Beauty* was more than just leftovers from *Workingman's Dead*.

"Box of Rain" was followed by two songs that would come to define the Dead in the eyes of more casual fans. "Friend of the Devil" was an outlaw number, the ballad of a rascal, a bigamist on the run from the law and in debt to the devil. The song, which John Dawson of the New Riders helped write and develop, opened with a clean line of acoustic guitar picking. It spoke in the first person from the mouth of a man in the wind. "I lit out from Reno / I was trailed by twenty hounds," the narrator begins, with Garcia singing the lead vocal. The devil enters the chase in the second verse, as the narrator tries to outrun and outwit him and the sheriff, too. Jaunty and engaging, a little wistful, "Friend of the Devil" would enjoy a long and varied life in the hands of the Dead, who would speed it up or slow it down according to the mood of the evening. "Friend of the Devil" was covered by more bands than any other Grateful Dead song, and the Dead themselves played it more or less continuously, with three-hundred-plus iterations, from its debut in March 1970 through Garcia's death in 1995.

Weir followed with "Sugar Magnolia," and it hustled into its track with a bump. If "Box of Rain" was reflective and "Friend of the Devil" mischievous, "Sugar Magnolia" was buoyant, carried cheerfully on Weir's warm voice and growing out of a rare—and somewhat contentious—collaboration between Weir and Hunter.

Their conflict, which came to a head over "Sugar Magnolia," had its origin in differing understandings of Hunter's role as a lyricist.

Garcia edited Hunter's work, trimming and adjusting lines to suit his musical approach to a song and sometimes even making more significant edits—dropping a verse, substituting a phrase or idea. Their long friendship and almost mystical connection made such changes easy for Hunter to accept.

Not so with Weir. When Hunter delivered Weir lyrics for "Sugar Magnolia," the songwriter expected Weir to adopt them as written. Weir, restless and dyslexic, was more inclined to see them as a draft to be fiddled with. Hunter tolerated it for a bit and contributed the song's opening scene, setting the piece in the South and establishing its lighthearted tone—"blossoms blooming, Head's all empty, and I don't care." The rest of Hunter's lyrics continued in his fashion. Weir chose to insert thoughts of his own, and Hunter at first gritted his teeth. When Weir added the lines "She can dance a Cajun rhythm / Jump like a Willys in four-wheel drive," Hunter threw up his hands. Years later, Hunter published a collection of his lyrics, and he took pains to separate his contributions to "Sugar Magnolia" from those of Weir, demarcating Weir's with italics and adding a footnote to make clear that those verses "were written by Robert Weir."

More to the point, as Hunter and Weir haggled over the lyrics to "Sugar Magnolia," Hunter concluded that songwriting with Weir was not his future. Hunter turned to Weir's old friend John Perry Barlow, who happened to be visiting Weir at that moment and handed off the chore. "Why don't you write with him?" Hunter suggested. "At least you like him."

Still, that's a reminder that sometimes seeing the process does not help one appreciate the sausage. "Sugar Magnolia" may have exasperated Hunter—as well as giving birth to the songwriting team of Barlow and Weir—but it delighted audiences. Garcia contributed a coda, "Sunshine Daydream," and the hybrid piece was a happy romp, useful on the album for expanding the overall reach and furnishing a dance favorite in live performances. And it, too, contributed to the band's deepening Americana, with its magnolias and bluebells and even Weir's clunky nod to Cajun.

Two more songs, and one more change of voice, rounded out side 1. "Operator" was a Pigpen vehicle, a brisk two-minute, twenty-five-second telling of a wounded protagonist pleading with the telephone operator for help tracking down his errant lover. It was the only song that Pigpen would ever receive sole credit for writing, and it felt grounded in the landscape of the album. The singer asks the operator to search for his wayward partner, offering up sightings "down about Baton Rouge" or outside Portland, and he remarks on the flooding "down in Texas" and the "poles are out in Utah." Pigpen complemented his own singing with a catchy harmonica solo.

"Candyman" came next. A straight-up folk song, delivered in C major and 4/4 time, it brought the album back to Garcia's voice and did so in a fashion that felt old even while new. Like Casey Jones from *Workingman's Dead,* the Candyman is a character with a long story—in this case, a racy one. He appears in American music history, traveling about, gambling and luring women. He comes bearing candy, naturally, though not as shockingly as Mississippi John Hurt's candy man, with his "stick of candy just nine inches long." This Candyman, shady as a drug pusher, was less obvious, but still lurking—in the shadows of town and the crease of *American Beauty,* filling in country and blues with folk music, ending side 1 with a Western painting, more Stegner than Kesey.

And then came side 2, with its more complex ambition and more momentous achievement. The album showcased its influences: the adoption of the American landscape by the Band; the singing prowess of Crosby, Stills and Nash; and the immense vision of Bob Dylan, who moved between folk and electric instruments and who brought a storytelling style of songwriting. Garcia and Hunter were among the many artists of the period who admired Dylan. Here, it showed.

The second side of *American Beauty* opened with "Ripple," the lyrics composed by Hunter during his furious two-hour burst of inspiration in London, set to music by Garcia on the Festival Express as it made its way westward across Canada. "Ripple" was mystical, at times biblical, in its allusions, including several nods to the Twenty-third Psalm. And it was joyful and generous in its spirit—the ripple in still water, the mys-

258 | HERE BESIDE THE RISING TIDE

terious fountain, the admission of not knowing the path. It encompassed a modified haiku at its center ("Ripple / In still water / When there is no pebble tossed / Nor wind / To blow"), its lyrics the work of "a fantastic craftsman," as Garcia described his friend Hunter in reference to this song. "If I knew the way," Garcia sang at the end of the piece, "I would take you home." "Ripple" managed to be a sing-along rhapsody and a riddle, a quiet image of movement in water worthy of Gary Snyder, a tribute to hopefulness and an admission of helplessness. It was an ode to friendship. "There are some songs," Garcia said, "that sort of help you along."

What's more, the song was a testament to chance. David Grisman happened to be in San Francisco for the weekend in the summer of 1970 when he heard that the Dead were playing a softball game against the Jefferson Airplane. Grisman wandered by and ran into Garcia. "Hey, man," Garcia said. "I got some recording for you. I'd love for you to play on our record."

Grisman agreed and the next day recorded the mandolin track for "Ripple," lacing the song with the distinctive high tone of bluegrass. Rare is the piece of popular music that can claim such a broad sonic and literary landscape. Grisman's touch was its crowning glory.

After "Ripple" came a trio of songs that were individually moving and collectively even better. "Brokedown Palace" opened almost hesitantly, acoustic guitar, piano, pedal steel guitar, the thump of a bass and drum, then Garcia's clear, sad voice: "Fare you well, my honey. Fare you well, my only true one." Through verses and choruses, Garcia and his bandmates harmonized delicately in a slowly unfolding reminiscence, rolling alongside the singing river, sung as lullaby and lament. "Many worlds I've come," he sang, "since I first left home." The lyrics included a weeping willow—one of countless weeping willows that dot the American literary wordscape—planted by the river's edge, to be lain beside and contemplated. It would become the Dead's song of farewell.

And then, as the song receded, the mood of *American Beauty* shifted, and "Till the Morning Comes" snapped the attention back to the moment. "Till the morning comes, it'll do you fine," it opened, banging along. And off it went, jumping despite lyrics that played in cold and shadows, dark and snow. And then the trio of pieces resolved, concluding in the quietly beautiful "Attics of My Life."

With "Attics," Hunter displayed a virtuosity so complete as to be spellbinding. Dreamy and sweetly melancholy, "Attics" moved through sensations—"tastes no tongue can know," hearing the tune through a "bent" ear, "closed my eyes to see"—with a wafty serenity. It was arranged by Garcia, and "Attics" punctuated *American Beauty*, completing the song sequence of side 2 on an elegiac note. "When there was no dream of mine," it concluded, "you dreamed of me."

Tonally, that rounded out the Dead's American gift, but the band had one more song to offer, a joint production of a shared experience. It, too, was new, words and music written in the spring and summer of 1970, months after the Dead's New Orleans arrest and packed with the jangly irreverence of life on the road. Hunter traveled with the band during that stretch, getting his own look at the life that Garcia and his compatriots had sculpted for themselves.

"We wrote it from city to city," Hunter said in 1981. "And then we all finished it. We all gathered around a swimming pool in Florida on a hot day and set it to music."

Although the whole band contributed to the song and it told a story that the band was living, playing it did not come easily. "It wasn't natural," Garcia said in a 1972 interview. "It didn't flow, and it wasn't easy, and we really labored over the bastard, all of us together." Hunter had produced a rat-a-tat lyric, and Weir struggled to master it, practicing one line at a time. In its early performances, "Truckin'" rolled out slowly, rumbling rather than rushed; by the time the band hit the studio, Weir had performed it a few times and was getting more used to it. The Dead chose to speed it up for the album, and the words came in a tumble, a tongue-twister for Weir to sort out (try saying "Arrows of neon and flashing marquees out on Main Street" three times fast). Weir worked hard at it, and by the time the band was in the studio for *American Beauty*, the members of the Dead knew that "Truckin'" was something special.

260 | HERE BESIDE THE RISING TIDE

The song is part of a long history of American road music, thick with flash and glamor and the grit and contradiction—the ache to be on the road, the loneliness of actually being there. But this was the Dead's take on that tradition, and so "Truckin'" was seen through those eyes. Here the character at the center of the song found himself "sitting and staring out of a hotel window," as so many musicians have stared out of so many hotel windows. This time, however, the reverie was interrupted. "I'd like to get some sleep before I travel, but if you got a warrant, I guess you're gonna come in." And yes, Hunter's lyrics made clear, that did refer to just what audiences knew it did: "Busted, down on Bourbon Street. Set up, like a bowling pin."

In keeping with "Casey Jones," "Truckin'" featured a mention of cocaine. And, like "Casey Jones," it did so critically. The song mentioned "Sweet Jane" and worried about her. "She lost her sparkle, you know she isn't the same." Why? Because she's "living on reds, vitamin C and cocaine. All a friend can say is: 'Ain't it a shame.'"

"Truckin'" was sly and fun, rambunctious and mischievous. It was clearly by and about the Dead itself, and it came off with much of the band's worldliness, some of its weariness, and all of its joy. It even contained what would become likely the most recognized couplet in the Grateful Dead songbook: "Lately it occurs to me / What a long, strange trip it's been."

"Truckin'" wrapped up *American Beauty* and spun into its own orbit. Dozens of artists would cover it, interpreting it as a country ballad, a reggae ramble, and a spacey, synthesized beat. By the 2020s, there was a version to accompany yoga practices and two versions to put babies to sleep. For decades, it would explain the Dead to audiences who had never heard of Haight-Ashbury, to prep school kids who had never dropped acid, and to world-weary teenagers recording their high school experiences in their yearbooks, reflecting on what a "long, strange trip it's been."

When Garcia and Weir appeared on *Late Night with David Letterman* in 1987, their appearance was preceded by a bit between Garcia and Letterman. The two were playing Scrabble, and Garcia placed the letters IN to Letterman's TRUCK. "That's not a word," Letterman complained. "Truckin'," Garcia responded. The audience, well in on the joke, laughed appreciatively.

Of all the tributes that the song has received over the years, perhaps none was more welcome than its inclusion in Bob Dylan's 2022 book of sixty-six essays on musical pieces, *The Philosophy of Modern Song*. He saw the Dead as "a postmodern jazz musical rock and roll dynamo"— and he understood "Truckin'." "It conjures up something different from traveling," Dylan wrote. "It's arduous. But the Dead are a swinging dance band so it doesn't seem like hard work to go with them."

With the last notes of "Truckin'," *American Beauty* was in the can, but the album as a package got one more grace note. The Dead asked Alton Kelley to design the album's cover, and the title made him think of a rose. Working with partner Stanley Mouse, Kelley depicted the red rose in full bloom. He etched the image into a mirror, sandblasted it, and painted it deep red with an airbrush. He then framed the image and photographed it on his bedroom table. The resulting cover fused the transmuted musical themes into an enduring visual image that, like the album itself, wove together the universal and the American, the ancient and the present, the ineffable and the tangible—nature and beauty, longing, music, and a red, red rose. From 1970 on, the rose would join the skeleton (and later the bear and turtle) as icons of the Grateful Dead.

They were now the most American of all American bands, impressive to other musicians and absorbing to their growing legion of fans.

"If the Grateful Dead came to town," Hunter Thompson wrote to an editor at *Rolling Stone* in 1970, "I'd beat my way in with a fucking tire iron."

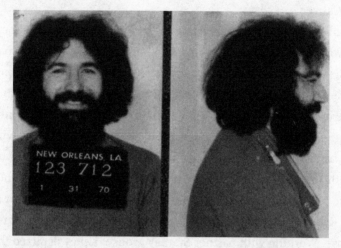
Garcia under arrest. Has there ever been a more cheerful mugshot? New Orleans, Louisiana, January 31, 1970.

CHAPTER 12

Now What?

THE RECEPTION FOR *AMERICAN BEAUTY* WAS EFFUSIVE. RE-viewers linked it to *Workingman's Dead* and discovered a new dimension in the Dead. Various critics called it "free-flowing," "delightful ear music," "good melody, good lyrics, and great music combined, a statement of philosophy and proficiency by a group of truly exceptional talent." *Rolling Stone* said *Workingman's Dead* was a "lovely album, lush, full, and thoroughly real in musical and lyrical content," and that *American Beauty* was a "joyous extension" of that work. More than one critic labeled it "a masterpiece."

It was Hunter, naturally, who identified the feeling that gave the album its depth. "There is an underlying tone of sadness to *American Beauty*," he said. It was at the center of "Ripple" and "Brokedown Palace." It was the essential feeling of "Box of Rain." Even some of the album's cheerier numbers had a solemnity to them. With some exceptions—"Sugar Magnolia," for instance—these were songs written in sadness and about sadness.

Garcia was in the studio in San Francisco when he received word that his mother, so long at the margins of his life, had been in a freak car accident. Always a shaky driver, Ruth Matusiewicz was in her Oldsmobile Cutlass in September. She had a puppy in the car, and the little dog managed to scramble beneath her feet as she was behind the wheel. She tried to brake, got her feet tangled up in the squirming pup, hit the gas by mistake, and plunged the car over an embankment and into the branches of a cypress tree. Driven by ambulance to San Francisco General Hospital, where she had long worked as a nurse, she received the best attention possible but slowly slipped away.

Garcia and his mother were not close. She had enjoyed the early flickers of his success, though she did not approve of his drug use. Sara Ruppenthal, who remained close to her even after splitting with Jerry, always suspected that Ruth preferred Cliff, the former Marine, to his younger brother, "the fuckup."

Garcia reciprocated her ambivalence, in ways that were both of a piece with the moment and specific to him and his mother. So many children of the era drifted from their parents—drugs were often an exacerbating factor—but in Garcia's case, his break with his mother was more deliberate. The scars of her abandonment after his father died never entirely healed. In a very private moment with Sara, he once shared a memory of Ruth leaving for work while he suffered from an asthma attack; he watched from his window, longing for comfort and getting none.

Their relationship had softened a bit since then, but he kept her at a distance, determined not to need her. She worked as a neonatal nurse in San Francisco and cut a dashing figure in the stiletto heels and fox stole she favored; Garcia lived across the bridge with Mountain Girl, Sunshine, and Annabelle, but rarely visited. At the time of Ruth's accident, she had never met Mountain Girl.

When Ruth was suddenly in peril, then, it was Sara, not Jerry, who rallied to her former mother-in-law's side. While Garcia labored in the studio, his ex-wife trundled up the Peninsula every afternoon to sit with his mother. It was a profound experience for Ruppenthal, whose relationship with Garcia was frayed but whose vast empathy swept into its embrace the mother-in-law connected to that marriage.

Garcia himself ducked out of the studio a few times to visit his mother, joined by his brother, Cliff, then living in their old San Francisco neighborhood. There were times, Cliff acknowledged, when it was hard to rely on his brother. "But he showed up for this," he recalled. Ruth lingered for two weeks, and when she died, it was again Sara, not

Jerry, who was by her side. She called her ex-husband and suggested that he come to the hospital to pay his last respects. Why? he asked. "She's already dead." Sara prevailed on him.

"There were issues with his mom that had not been resolved," Mountain Girl recalled in an interview years later. "Then he came to that moment when he knew they could never be resolved."

Garcia thereafter rarely spoke of his mother's life or death. He lived in the present, and in his art. He treasured the memory of her coming to see the Dead at a small San Francisco club in 1967 and chose to hang on to that.

FRIENDS OF the band left the earth as well, under circumstances that were becoming all too familiar. Jimi Hendrix died of a barbiturate overdose on September 18, 1970. Janis Joplin died of a heroin overdose on October 4. Her manager found her on the floor of her hotel room in Los Angeles, where she had just finished recording what would be her final studio album, *Pearl*.

Joplin's loss hit the band especially hard. She was more than just a fellow musician. She and Pigpen were lovers for a time, and she came to prominence alongside the Dead. She was on the Festival Express, the rare woman to crack that male cadre of musical talent. Her passing could hardly be called a shock—her drug and alcohol abuse were alarming even to seasoned veterans of the music scene—but her gruff singing voice disguised a fragile soul.

Hunter was moved to write a song in Joplin's memory, and his lyric dwelled on that gentle side of her, the trembling sparrow rather than the belting blues singer. "All I know is something like a bird within her sang," he wrote. "All I know, she sang a little while and then flew on."

Riding the success of their 1970 albums, which elevated the band in critical terms even if they had not yet eradicated its debt to Warner Bros., the Dead first performed "Birdsong" on a strange night in 1971, when they were joined in an ESP experiment from the Capitol Theatre in Port Chester, New York, transmitting images from their performance to another venue and testing whether others could receive them. The ESP results were mixed. The song was not.

From its first performance, "Birdsong" communicated the ephemeral essence of Joplin's short life and the beauty within it. The song placed her all around them. "Sleep in the stars," Garcia sang that February night, remembering his friend. "Don't you cry. Dry your eyes on the wind."

The season of endings also brought the denouement of the Lenny Hart affair. He would eventually plead guilty to two counts of criminal embezzlement and be sentenced to six months in jail after his lawyer argued that he was a "completely rehabilitated man." That same lawyer, in arguing for a light sentence, maintained that Hart had left the Dead because band members were getting "deeper and deeper into drugs" while he was finding religion.

That was hard to swallow. A handwritten note in the Dead's business files captured one reaction: "If Lennie Hart found God," it read, "he burned him too!" Hart repaid $55,000 of the money he stole while "getting more seriously into religion." The Dead moved on.

THE GRATEFUL Dead would never be mistaken for the Black Panthers. The Panthers' ten-point program emphasized grievance and demanded action. Their demonstration of arms at the California capitol in 1967 had turned Reagan into a supporter of gun control, but violence and violent speech never registered much with Garcia, who generally was as offended by the stridency of the left as he was by the repression of the right.

Still, the Panthers and the Dead occupied some of the same space. They were based in the Bay Area, of course, and their politics and priorities overlapped. The Panthers were about more than flashing arms, and the Dead were about more than performing music; their values intersected, even if their work largely did not.

"The Panthers are righteous," Garcia told one interviewer. "What they're doing is actual, practical things. They got a free breakfast trip, and they're starting a free shoes thing. . . . They're into action, and that's something we can understand 'cause we're from a place where talk is cheap. I mean, talk don't mean nothing, anybody can say stuff; the thing that counts is what you do."

Rare was the person who could find good in both the Panthers and the Hells Angels, but Garcia was just such a person. The same Garcia who was out of touch with his youngest daughter and could barely be persuaded to visit his dying mother craved community of a different sort, and he admired the Panthers and the Angels for creating it outside the structure of government. He appreciated fierce devotion to vision. And he did not like to be told what to do; he simply refused to acknowledge the government's right to do so. The Angels—and the Panthers—shared his appreciation for community, his rejection of government authority, and his obstinacy. Garcia approved.

On March 5, 1971, the Panthers hosted a Revolutionary Intercommunal Day of Solidarity for members of the party being held as prisoners. The event was held at the Oakland Auditorium Arena. The party charged $2.50 for admission, and the evening doubled as a belated birthday celebration for Huey Newton, the party's minister of defense and "supreme commander," who had turned twenty-nine two weeks earlier, on February 17.

Newton spoke at the event, and the Reverend Charles Bronson delivered an invocation, which he styled as a "revolutionary prayer." Reagan, the Panthers' chief nemesis, was on his mind.

"Oh Lord!" the reverend began. "Let the governor have seventeen car accidents on his way home. With a gasoline truck that's been hit with a match wagon over the Grand Canyon this evening. And if that's not bad enough for the governor, let the ambulance that takes him to the hospital have four flat tires. Let the motor crack. Let the block bust. Let the windshield crack this evening. Let the driver have a stroke with a hemorrhage, and run into a brick wall that's housing nuclear warfare and TNT this evening."

Amen.

The headliner for that night's music: the Grateful Dead.

268 | HERE BESIDE THE RISING TIDE

* * *

MUHAMMAD ALI fought his conviction for refusal to accept induction into the military all the way to the United States Supreme Court, where the justices at first evinced little interest in coming to his defense. After hearing oral arguments on April 19, 1971, Justice John Harlan was assigned the task of writing for what appeared to be a majority of the court to reject Ali's claim to have been improperly denied status as a conscientious objector. Harlan set to work, but he soon found himself struggling with that position.

To reject Ali's claim, the court needed to find that he had failed to meet a three-part test: that he was opposed to all war, not just the Vietnam War; that his objection was based on his religious training or deep beliefs; and that he was sincere in those convictions. In the initial stages of Ali's case, the board examining his case had rejected his claim to the status but had not specified on which of those three bases it had done so. In the course of his appeal, however, the government had conceded two of the three elements, acknowledging that Ali was in fact sincere in his beliefs and that they were part of his devotion to the theology of the Nation of Islam. That left the question of whether Ali refused to serve in "all wars," or whether the Nation's teachings permitted or even required participation in some holy wars.

The court could not quite bring itself to call him by his name—the case remained entitled *Clay v. United States*—but it upheld Ali's appeal, concluding that they could not be sure that the board had relied upon a valid basis for rejecting the boxer's claim. His conviction was reversed. Ali got his passport back and returned to boxing, eventually to regain his title as Heavyweight Champion of the World, not to mention his standing as an icon of the antiwar movement and the most famous man on earth, liberated to again "float like a butterfly, sting like a bee."

NIXON SEEMED secure as the 1970s opened. Although the war slogged on and public opposition mounted, American casualties peaked in

1968 and dropped thereafter, dampening some of the antiwar movement's intensity. Major demonstrations declined. And yet, as protest became more infrequent, it also developed a harder edge. Confrontation, as Hayden pointed out, became the watchword, and it ran a gamut—from nonviolence to "militance" to outright terrorism.

Weatherman—the radical group also known as the Weathermen and, later, the Weather Underground—conspired to break Timothy Leary out of prison in September 1970. Sprung, he relaxed on an Indian reservation en route to Algeria by smoking a joint and listening to a Grateful Dead tape. Weatherman set off a bomb in the Capitol in March 1971, causing property damage but no injuries.

A two-day protest aimed at shutting down the District of Columbia in May drew thousands to the streets with the promise of "militant nonviolent civil disobedience," as one poster proclaimed. "If the government won't stop the war, we'll stop the government." That event resulted in some twelve thousand arrests, more than at any other demonstration in American history. Caught between frustration and progress, impatience and anger, leaders of the Peace Movement debated how to move forward, "re-grouping and re-thinking," as a headline in the *San Francisco Chronicle* remarked in May.

The result was confusion. Even as Weatherman embraced violence, much of the left moved from deep, narrow commitment to shallower devotion yet wider acceptance—a broadening and flattening of the movement, which traded obsessive commitment for broader appeal, with new groups and ideas swelling the ranks of the counterculture. The Chicano Moratorium and the martyrdom of Ruben Salazar at the Silver Dollar Café in 1970 demonstrated the growing assertiveness of Latinos. Feminism stretched beyond the counterculture's free love tropes, graduating from the breakthrough critiques of Betty Friedan into a broader politics that swept in Gloria Steinem, *Ms.* magazine, the campaign for the Equal Rights Amendment, and the defense of reproductive and bodily freedom recognized by the court with *Roe v. Wade* in 1973 and fought over from that moment on.

Environmentalism could look back to John Muir, to Rachel Carson's

Silent Spring, Bob Dylan's "A Hard Rain's a-Gonna Fall," and Paul Ehrlich's *The Population Bomb*. But it found new adherents after the Santa Barbara oil spill in 1969. The sight of fouled birds and slimed beaches unified disparate elements of American politics around the idea that the earth had reached a desperation point. That trauma merged with the energy of the antiwar and civil rights movements in the creation of Earth Day, first celebrated in 1970.

New York shut down Fifth Avenue to cars, and in their place came "huge, light-hearted throngs" to the "ecological carnival." Students marched and petitioned and cleaned up parks and beaches in Los Angeles. The Lions Club in Bangor, Maine, cleaned up its parking lot. The second grade of Mary Troy's class at Bayside Elementary School in Imperial Beach, California, tidied up a square block near San Diego. Kids walked to school rather than ride in Iola, Kansas, and picked up trash in Parsons. In Montgomery, Alabama, where Rosa Parks had made her mark, two hundred students and faculty ate fried chicken on the campus of Huntingdon College and deplored the quality of their community's air.

So, too, in the arts, where new values widened creative lenses. The decade opened with explosive promise from the world of film. Steven Spielberg, George Lucas, Martin Scorsese (who had been at Woodstock), and Francis Ford Coppola were among the filmmakers whose work would redefine the medium in the 1970s. Raised in the ideals of the counterculture—whether embracing them, refracting them, critiquing them, or rejecting them—they would, in that decade and those to come, broaden the moral scope of film.

Literature, much of it also preoccupied with the concerns of the counterculture, found similarly rich earth. Didion released *Play It as It Lays*, her painful rumination on nihilism and meaning set in Los Angeles, in 1970. *The Joy of Sex* (1972) and *Fear of Flying* (1973) tested the expanding limits of sexual exploration. *Gravity's Rainbow* (1973) displayed Pynchon's abundant talents—as well as his barely contained paranoia—at their most vivid. *Jonathan Livingston Seagull* (first published in 1970, a bestseller in 1972) playfully set questions of freedom in the mind of a bird. *Zen and the Art of Motorcycle Maintenance,* by Robert Pirsig, finally found its way into print after more than a hundred rejections and then established itself by advancing deep questions of culture and aesthetics in the context of a westward trek by a father and son.

And as for the counterculture's most florid literary talent, Hunter Thompson? *Fear and Loathing in Las Vegas,* published in 1971, posed the essential question of what might happen if a journalist and his Samoan attorney set out from Beverly Hills for Las Vegas, across the desert landscape that Thompson called "the last known home of the Manson family," while toting "two bags of grass, seventy-five pellets of mescaline, five sheets of high-powered blotter acid, a saltshaker half full of cocaine, and a whole galaxy of multicolored uppers, downers, screamers, laughers . . . and also a quart of tequila, a quart of rum, a case of Budweiser, a pint of raw ether and two dozen amyls." It was a load, Thompson wrote, but "the only thing that really worried me was the ether. There is nothing in the world more helpless and irresponsible and depraved than a man in the depths of an ether binge."

PIGPEN'S HEALTH was failing, and Mickey Hart's mind was reeling. Pigpen had been drinking hard since he was a young teenager, and by the early seventies, it showed. Tired and drawn, he shrank from the energy of the band. And as the Dead's music evolved, it often seemed that Pigpen was at the edges of that, too. "Operator" was a signature number on *American Beauty,* but it served more as a reminder that he was still part of the Dead than as a signal of his resurgence. Through 1971, he hung on, losing weight, his cheeks hollowing, his energy ebbing.

And as Pigpen battled his depleting body, Hart fought his demons. Shaken by his father's treachery, Hart receded from the band, spending more time at the Barn, his ranch north of San Francisco. Bandmates were entirely forgiving—they recognized that Lenny Hart's duplicity was his own, not his son's, and they kept Mickey on the payroll—but he was racked with guilt and misgivings. He bumped along with the band through 1970, but his mental health was shaky. "I was confused, unbalanced," he wrote. "I wanted to flee and hide, bury my head and cry."

In February 1971, the band rolled into Port Chester, New York, where, over the course of four nights, it debuted "Bertha," "Playing in the Band," "Wharf Rat," "Loser," and "Greatest Story Ever Told" (on February 18), as well as "Deal" and "Birdsong" on the nineteenth. It was an extraordinary display of new songs, many of which would become staples and which ranged from the catchy "Bertha" to the structurally complex "Wharf Rat," a story ballad that unfolds on docks reminiscent of the San Francisco of Garcia's youth and that tells the tale of a broken-down drunk as he reflects on his life. He shares his story, pines for a woman he's lost, talks to himself, the narrative shifting points of view from one verse to the next. It is emotionally layered and highlighted by a plaintive hope strung across the song's bridge: "I'll get up and fly away, fly away." Together, the new pieces were sophisticated and varied. And all of that against a backdrop of period-specific craziness. This was the run that featured the ESP experiment—each night, audience members were asked to concentrate on a slide of an art print so that a recipient in Brooklyn, thirty-five miles away, could replicate it.

The display of new material was all the more astonishing in light of the turmoil going on outside the audience's view. As he performed on February 18, Hart was unraveling. He had been suffering for months, his anguish accelerated by his turn to drugs to find relief. That night, he was so lost, so addled, that Ramrod duct-taped him to his stool to keep him in place for the duration of the show. It is testament to how deeply drumming was at his core that Hart's travails were imperceptible to the audience and barely noticeable on tapes of the night's show. Nevertheless, at its conclusion, Hart left, with no plan to return. Agitated, sleep-deprived, strung out, he simply could not go on.

Hart's absence "left a big hole in the band's aura," Lesh recalled, but it did not interrupt its schedule or postpone the unveiling of its new music. In its first performance without Hart, less than twenty-four hours after he had departed, the Dead went back to one drummer,

Kreutzmann. They opened with "Truckin'," and though they seemed discombobulated at first, they settled into a romp through old favorites and new gems, including "Birdsong."

Hart's anguish got the best of him in a hurry. Pigpen's demise was slower and made more painful by its inexorability. Hart burned out; Pigpen faded away.

Word of his health troubles spread, and Donna Jean Godchaux, a singer who was working days at Union Oil and who had recently married a talented keyboard player, thought she had a solution. Her husband, Keith Godchaux, was, she felt, a perfect fit for the Dead's piano and organ needs. Initially a skeptic about the Dead, Donna Jean had gone to hear the band at Winterland with work friends and was converted. On hearing that the Dead might be looking for keyboard help, Keith and Donna set out to track down Garcia. They discovered that he was playing with his band at the Keystone Korner. They headed over.

As Garcia left the stage, Donna Jean corralled him. "My husband and I have something we want to talk to you about," she said. Garcia, she recalled, looked at her quizzically and invited her backstage. She and Keith were too shy to make their way to his dressing room, but Garcia came out and found them. "Here it is," she told Garcia. "Keith is your next piano player."

Bemused, but realizing that Pig's depletion was already weakening the music, Garcia invited Keith to try out. The band, including Pigpen, accepted him, and the two shared keyboard duties from that point forward.

Every change in Grateful Dead personnel would recast the music, and Keith Godchaux's addition to the lineup was proof of that. He brought a new delicacy to the keyboards, replacing Pigpen's soulful organ (and occasional harmonica) with a brighter touch, more twinkling and intricate, more in tune with the cosmos than with the blues. It was not a simple matter for Godchaux, whose light mastery of the keyboards was accompanied by a sad, brooding personality. But as Pigpen faded, Godchaux moved into the vacuum created by Pigpen's withdrawal. He began full-fledged rehearsals with the band in September, his confidence growing. Godchaux's first full performance came on October 19, 1971, and he arrived with a bang.

The Grateful Dead unveiled six new songs that night: "Tennessee Jed," "Jack Straw," "Mexicali Blues," "Comes a Time," "Ramble On Rose," and "One More Saturday Night." The show put Godchaux through his paces, moving up and down in tempo, cascading through some of the band's spacier numbers and then crashing back to self-contained songs. Godchaux struggled in places but held his own. He was, from that day forward, for as long as his disposition allowed him, a member of the Grateful Dead.

"WE CAN share the women. We can share the wine."

Those words opened "Jack Straw," heard for the first time at that October 19, 1971, show. The audience did not react strongly. That would change.

The song chronicles a roving band of criminals, drifting about the Southwest—Texas, Santa Fe, Tulsa, Wichita—as they settle scores and round up money. They jump a watchman for his ring and cash; they jump trains; they bury a man in a shallow grave. As a tale, it sits neatly within Hunter's Western anthology—it would have fit into Kerouac's too.

But the opening lines touched a nerve. As audiences grew to recognize the song, some would cheer for what became a classic Dead piece, a rambling, open-ended repository of some of Garcia's most extended and innovative solos. But less expected was the raucous cheer at the words themselves, a throaty appreciation of the mischief that some read into the lyrics, similar to the alarming roar that would sometimes greet another lyric, from "Candyman," when the band sang: "If I had me a shotgun, I'd blow you straight to hell."

In both cases, the songs could seem to celebrate depravity, or at least boorishness. Hunter was uncomfortable when he realized that was how his words were received. Complaining in 1981 to *Relix* about being misheard by some Deadheads, Hunter noted: "I bet they think 'Jack Straw' is about wife swapping. I don't think they listen very deeply."

It is the writer's lot to be misunderstood, but in this case, two aspects of the lyric invited that misperception. First, the lines opened the song, presenting them before the context—a conversation among outlaws bent on misdeeds—so the context that might have explained the words only came later. As first uttered, they seemed a declaration, not a snippet. Second, the Dead were less than enlightened on matters of sex and gender, and so an outsider might wonder whether those words did in fact reflect a tired sexist perspective. Jon Pareles, music critic for *The New York Times* and a fan of the Dead, wrote that its "view of women could charitably be described as pre-feminist, or perhaps prehistoric." He drew that conclusion from the opening lines of "Jack Straw."

That was not a fair reading of the song, but it was in many ways a reasonable critique of the band. The Dead were men, Donna Jean's presence in the band notwithstanding. Their routines and customs were forged when they were young, and they practiced a rough, barely postadolescent camaraderie on the road. Deprived of a loving mother as a boy, Garcia struggled to make and maintain meaningful attachments to women—"chicks," as he often called them. And he did not offer much to suggest that he was appreciative of women. The songs he sang, written by Hunter, largely avoided the subject of romantic love.

The members of the Dead's crew, if anything, were even more shaped by a machismo sensibility—hard-living, hard-working, hard-using. An atmosphere of gruff carnality prevailed. Comments about women's looks, innocent and lewd, were routine. Band members and crew members were hard on their comrades, and they were expected to take it—like a man, as it were.

"The Grateful Dead were, absolutely, sexist," McNally told an interviewer from National Public Radio. "They were victims of stock mid-century American male privilege and attitude. No question."

As usual, McNally was both blunt and truthful. But there was more. In fact, as McNally continued in the same interview: "They had . . . very strong, interesting and creative women who weren't shy about their opinions. . . . So they weren't dumb, and they weren't Neanderthals, and they learned things."

Two of the Dead's most valued talents were women. Candace Brightman was a brilliant lighting technician whose supple, layered designs— she described her work as "balance building to moments of musical intensity with lights, with an undercurrent of continuous change"— became as identifiably a piece of Dead shows as the music. And Betty Cantor-Jackson was a legendary sound engineer who directed the band's tone, volume, and shape from the soundboard at countless shows, going on to found a sound production company called Alembic with Bear and others, working to test and develop new equipment for the band. "Betty Boards" were treasured additions to any Deadhead's collection, clean, rich recordings of shows that memorialized the Dead's most historic appearances. Similarly, the Dead's business operations were directed by Eileen Law and their travel was managed by Frankie Weir, while merchandising and fan relations were run by Sue Swanson. Each of those women commanded a vital position in the Dead's organization and enjoyed the band's trust and confidence.

Still, it remains true that the Dead's social conscience—which turned up for the environment, for the Haight, for peace, for prisoners on Death Row, for Vietnam veterans, for Hells Angels and Black Panthers— did not extend to the cause of feminism. At one level, that's of a cultural piece. Casey Hayden rankled leaders of SDS and the Student Nonviolent Coordinating Committee with her pointed observations about the dearth of women in leadership positions, one of which was prominently held by her husband, Tom Hayden. Martin Luther King, Jr., surrounded himself almost exclusively with male advisers. Stokely Carmichael (later Kwame Ture) was said to have proclaimed that the only position for women in the liberation movement was "prone."

There is much to criticize in the failure of those who champion freedom only then to cabin their distribution of it. By what logic should some go free while others are held back? It does not pardon that offense to note that it is all too common, sometimes committed by the same people and groups who are later the victims of it. Earl Warren and Franklin Roosevelt freed, respectively, black schoolchildren and the people of Europe, but both worked to incarcerate 110,000 Japanese and Japanese Americans who committed no crimes. Poor immigrants in nineteenth-century America notoriously ignored the call of abolition, consumed as they were by their own struggles for recognition and living wages. The National Women's Rights Convention hissed Sojourner Truth for having the temerity to join the struggle of her race to that of her gender. Thomas Jefferson owned slaves.

History proves, time and again, that even the most visionary are bound by what they are capable of imagining in the times in which they are imagining it. They do not deserve absolution for such blindness, but they are entitled to our understanding. The Dead were visionary. Their work lifted hearts and souls, including those of women. And they appreciated the talents of the women around them, in whom they invested authority and trust.

But they were of a period and limited by their experience and the social imagination it supplied them. In that, too, they were creatures of their moment—of a culture and of a counterculture.

Garcia at rest, 1972.

Michael Dobo/Retro Photo Archive

CHAPTER 13

"Eyes of the World"

THE GRATEFUL DEAD LEFT FOR EUROPE ON APRIL FOOL'S DAY 1972. When the plane landed in London, the Dead's whole extended family poured out, pot fumes trailing. Band members, crew, spouses, girlfriends, former girlfriends, office managers, loyal friends—more than forty people in all. It was, recalled Rosie McGee, the fulfillment of a pledge from Garcia in 1967—that anyone from that time who was still around when the Dead made a full-scale assault on Europe could come along. McGee had by then broken up with Lesh, but she was working with Alembic and still part of the family. She jumped on board too. "Everybody goes," Garcia had announced at a band meeting. Everybody did, and on Warner Bros.' dime.

Over the next two months, they played twenty-two shows, starting with an April 7 performance at the Wembley Empire Pool and ending up back in London for four nights at the Strand Lyceum in late May. They gallivanted across the Continent, stopping in Denmark, Germany, France, and the Netherlands. They were greeted with excitement and curiosity, as visitors from the exotic land of San Francisco, bearing the word from the New New World, sharing folk tales from the outer reaches of consciousness and the exploding sounds of music, the much-imagined counterculture sailing in from across the Atlantic. "Everywhere they go," one writer noted, "they carry the magic of San Francisco."

They traveled by bus, sliding through various border crossings while hiding drugs in their equipment cases and bracing for the ax to fall. The band was in flux: Hart was off somewhere recovering; Pigpen was present but intermittent, slight and hollowed out but digging deep and delivering heartfelt soulfulness on occasion. Keith Godchaux came on fast, asserting himself at the keyboard, lacing his work across the backbone of the band; Donna Jean Godchaux found a place too. An accomplished singer whose credentials went back to Muscle Shoals, she struggled to master the Dead's sometimes overwhelming sound, but she had her nights. Even the equipment was in prime form—15,000 pounds of gear and a sixteen-track recording system anchored a state-of-the art live system with crystalline capacity for capturing shows on tape. "There's a sort of peak optimum," Garcia told an interviewer in London, "and right now we're at one of those peaks."

Europe '72 was both an album and an adventure—or, rather, an album that memorialized an adventure. As a business proposition, it fulfilled an obligation to Warner Bros., where Lenny Hart had re-upped the band's commitment even as he siphoned cash from its operations. But the tour succeeded far beyond its contractual requirements. It featured the Dead loose and happy, playing together, drawing on old material and producing new songs. In fact, one of those new songs was directed, at least in part, at Hart himself.

"Lost one round, but the price wasn't anything," Garcia sang, "Knife in the back, and more of the same." The chorus drew out the point most clearly: "He's gone, and nothing's gonna bring him back."

The Dead played "He's Gone" for an audience for the first time in Copenhagen that summer, in the splendor of that city's Tivoli Gardens. That first rendering was more up-tempo than the slower groove the band would eventually adopt for it. It came out clean and fast, edgy with defiance that suited its commemoration of a hurtful episode.

But, as with every other Hunter lyric that drew upon the life of the band, it spoke to events while also nodding to life beyond them. Hunter tipped a cap to Tennessee Williams and locomotives, to a composed character, "hot as a pistol but cool inside." As the Dead tried out the song and let it grow, the lyrics would resonate with parents seeing off a child, partners breaking up, loved ones dying; it would speak to the quest for serenity in a complicated, sometimes deteriorating world. The

"EYES OF THE WORLD" | 281

song's signature line, the one that would warm the hearts of Deadheads, at first was delivered quickly, almost perfunctorily. Only later would it assume anthemic proportions. "Nothing left to do," Hunter wrote and Garcia sang, "but smile, smile, smile."

And so they did. They romped through Europe, waging a battle of hijinks between the two tour buses—one group called themselves the Bolos, the other the Bozos—and delivering crisp, excited performances in one city after another. They broke to see the sights, dropping in to museums here and there, catching the castles of Denmark, a double rainbow above a Swiss mountainside, a ninth-century monastery and the Thingstätte amphitheater in Heidelberg, with its notorious place in Nazi history. They were young tourists, emissaries from the American counterculture and keepers of a faith.

"If the Grateful Dead family bond had been solid at the beginning of *Europe '72*, which it was, it's hard to describe what it became after nearly two months of concerts and adventures in foreign countries," Rosie McGee wrote. "It was an indescribable privilege."

THE DEAD returned from Europe euphoric. The shows were successful, and the community expanded, now to include European kids as well. The band's obligation to Warner Bros. was almost complete. It was a heady moment, and one that drew the members back to dreams of freedom, of independence from record companies and square executives. On July 4, Ron Rakow, the Dead's resident business genius and veteran of the Carousel and other projects, presented the members of the band with his vision for the future. It took the form of a ninety-two-page report that Rakow delivered to the band at a gathering at Kreutzmann's home, a document that became known as the So What papers.

Rakow's vision was nothing if not bold. He proposed that the Dead create their own record company, which they would use to produce, record, and distribute their own music as well as that of like-minded musicians and groups. He imagined creating whole new distribution networks, most memorably a chain of ice cream trucks that would tinkle up and down city streets summoning hippies from their homes to scoop up the latest offerings from the Grateful Dead. And he imagined that the government might help pay for it. This was, after all, the era of government support for minority business enterprises, and hippies seemed like a minority, sort of.

The proposal was a blend of fanciful and thought-provoking. Nothing came of the ice cream trucks or government subsidies, but the idea of creating a new label got their attention. Alan Trist, their British friend from the Palo Alto days, examined the So What options and weighed in with his own recommendations for the future. Trist did so methodically, laying out what he saw as the Dead's alternatives. He identified four: moving to another record company; cutting a deal with a discount distribution house; taking over distribution and mail order itself, as Rakow was suggesting; or creating a subscription service for Dead music, an idea first put forward by Owsley.

Trist laid out the philosophical and practical implications of each option, framing them not so much in the language of music but in terms of freedom and control—the more the band took on, the more it would be free of outside strictures. It would be entering unfamiliar territory, but the Dead's values could drive its business, too. Examining the implications of creating franchisees for Grateful Dead distribution, for instance, Trist wrote that the shift would create opportunities to explore "autonomy, open-system, flexible structure, adaptation, change." He presented a program of change and experimentation, launched first as a pilot project in San Francisco and then a possible expansion. "It will be," Trist wrote, "at the edge of our control."

The Dead's messy organization, tempted by ice cream trucks and small business loans, opted for something simpler but big and bold. It would break free altogether from the established music business, found its own record company, and run itself. Grateful Dead Records and its affiliated label, Round Records, would not try to create from whole cloth a national distribution network but would contract out that piece of the business, eventually turning to United Artists to manage production and distribution. Rakow sold foreign distribution rights to Atlantic Records for $300,000 and trundled off to Boston with Garcia to land a line of credit to help pay ongoing operating expenses. "It seemed as if being our own record company would be worth a try," Lesh said. "No one could see a downside."

THE DEAD family helped one another—and sometimes produced magic while doing so. A Prankster named Black Maria showed up on the Dead's doorstep in mid-1972 to let them know that the Kesey family business—a creamery owned and operated by Ken's brother Chuck— was struggling. The Dead considered how to help and on July 31 agreed to headline a benefit on the creamery's land, west of Eugene, Oregon. With just a month to prepare, the Dead and full entourage gathered for a "field trip." Only Pigpen stayed behind, his health failing fast.

The show took place on August 27, 1972, and was billed as a "potluck" that drew in neighbors from Eugene and Deadheads for miles, many from San Francisco. With Prankster Ken Babbs at the microphone, the New Riders opened that day, and then the Dead, playing on an outdoor field under a 108-degree sun, turned in a scintillating, hypnotic performance, highlighted by a dense, deep drive through the heart of "Dark Star."

That afternoon's concert, spiced by the presence of a nude man who perched high above the stage—forever to be known as "the naked pole guy"—would prove one of the Dead's most celebrated appearances, delivered before friends—soaring, searching, never mind the heat. It was a "spiritually immense journey," one group of Deadhead writers concluded, "the Grateful Dead experience at its best: kindred spirits gathered in harmony with Mother Earth to embark together in creating a transformational ritual that feeds the soul."

It also raised more than $10,000 for the Springfield Creamery, enough to keep it open. Given a new lease on life, the Kesey operation invested in its latest product, then novel probiotic yogurt, sending samples back to San Francisco with the Deadheads who had gathered

284 | HERE BESIDE THE RISING TIDE

for the potluck. Sales took off, and the creamery took a place at the head of yet another offshoot of the counterculture—the health food movement.

ON FEBRUARY 9, 1973, the Dead performed at Stanford University's Maples Pavilion, a show marked by another rollout of new tunes. "Eyes of the World" in particular wove together the threads of that period—its nods to Buddhism and gnosticism; its appeal to the homelands, evenings, and beaches of the heart; its evocation of consciousness, discovery, and awareness, seeing the world not just through one's own eyes but from all perspectives at once. "Wake up to find out," the song went, "that you are the eyes of the world." "Eyes" was written during the days when Hunter was living with Garcia and Mountain Girl in Larkspur, and it delivered a sweeping, open vision of connection. In Garcia's hands, it also supplied the Dead with an improvisational vehicle that would evolve over the years. From its first performance, when the Dead drifted into it from "Truckin'," it shimmered with excitement and vision; that iteration clocked in at nearly nineteen minutes, including long sections of Garcia nimbly flitting around the melody before fading into another of the new songs, "China Doll."

At Maples Pavilion that night, "Eyes" rolled out alongside the lulling "Row Jimmy," the bouncy "Loose Lucy," and "Here Comes Sunshine," with its Beatles feel. Together, the new music represented still another shift in the Dead's orientation, especially in the songs by Garcia and Hunter. The new pieces plumbed new musical styles—Garcia described "Eyes" as having a "samba feel . . . kind of a Brazilian thing," and the tunes collectively settled into a softer zone, away from what Hunter called the "cowboy space." It was not a dramatic shift for the Dead, but it was a noticeable one, signaling that the band's growth was ongoing, its adventure continuing to evolve rather than settling into the successful groove of *Workingman's Dead* and *American Beauty.*

One other song debuted the same evening, but its appearance was tentative. "Wave That Flag," even by its title, suggested something more overtly political than the Dead, certainly Garcia, generally set out to deliver. "Wave the flag, pop the bag," the song began, making clear that it was intended to interrogate patriotism rather than celebrate it. And yet it danced around the politics of the time. "Pull the tooth, stretch the truth," one verse went. "Feed the poor. Stop the war." After a few performances in 1973, Garcia took it back to the writing room and reemerged, in collaboration with Hunter, with "U.S. Blues," musically identical but with new couplets that were lighter and broader, no mentions of the poor or of war.

And yet, as always, the Dead lived amid the values of the time even as they resisted joining the politics directly. At the same show, they gave Wavy Gravy the microphone to speak to the crowd. "I was told to make this announcement short and not political," he told the crowd. "I'll make it short, but 'political' is weird, like, taking a shit is a political act, smoking it is a more political act. . . . World politics and a rainbow on a pole is where we're at." He proceeded to describe the bombing of a teaching hospital in Asia—"four times bigger than the one at Stanford"—and passed baskets for contributions to replace it. Asked decades later whether he still regarded "taking a shit" as a political act in 1973, Gravy laughed. "Still is," he said.

Pumping out this new lineup was the Dead's huge, expensive speaker system, with a $12,000 tweeter array that made its first appearance that night. It lasted less than a minute. Barely had the Dead hit the first notes of "Promised Land" than the tweeters blew out in a fizzle, dampening the top end of the music and making vocals and Godchaux's piano almost inaudible. Soundman Dan Healy had built the array and watched in horror as it crashed. "I smoked twelve thousand dollars' worth of speakers just like that," he ruefully recalled. For fans, those technical difficulties were made more confusing by the gymnasium's modern floor. Built to absorb the impact of leaping and falling athletes, it undulated when thousands of Deadheads rose to dance, rippling as the band performed. It was a show on rolling waters.

* * *

286 | HERE BESIDE THE RISING TIDE

PIGPEN DIED on March 8, 1973. The cause was a gastrointestinal hemorrhage, but drinking was really to blame. A neighbor who had not seen him for a couple of days went to inquire how he was feeling and found his body on the floor of his bedroom. He was twenty-seven years old.

His bandmates were braced for the news. Pigpen's health had been shaky in Europe, and though he had tried to rejoin the band, he'd been losing weight at an alarming rate—down 90 pounds from his fighting weight of 250. His final public appearance with the Grateful Dead was on June 17, 1972, shortly after their return from Europe, at the Hollywood Bowl in Los Angeles. After that, he retreated. "We were all prepared for it emotionally," Garcia said five days after his old friend's death.

Pigpen was laid to rest in a short, impersonal service at the Daphne Mortuary in Corte Madera. Afterward, members of the band gathered a few miles away to say their goodbyes, holding a wake at Weir's house. They spent the evening getting high and remembering their friend, sending him off "in a style akin to his own."

But the circumstances were lastingly morose. Pigpen had spent his final months alone, trying to put down some musical thoughts but far outside the small circle of love and music that had once enveloped him. He left a reel of unfinished songs and memories of long, happy nights exhorting men to "get your hands out of your pockets," to hit on the girl next to them, to "Turn on Your Love Light." He was a link back to the days of the Hells Angels and low-down blues. He could be lascivious and even profane. He was shy and yet came alive onstage. Pigpen would remain an enigma to his death, but not to Garcia. For Garcia, his friend's withdrawal first from the band and then from life would leave a vacant place in the music and in Garcia's soul. He carried a picture of Pigpen with him for years, tacking it up in dressing rooms from the Cow Palace to Cairo.

And yet nothing would slow Garcia's compulsion to perform. Less than a week after Pigpen's body was discovered, Garcia joined Peter Rowan, David Grisman, and John Kahn for a bluegrass performance at the Keystone Berkeley.

"EYES OF THE WORLD" | 287

* * *

OWSLEY STANLEY was fresh from prison in 1972, having served two years of a three-year sentence. The experience had hardened and chastened him. "He seemed completely changed, and not in a good way," Mountain Girl recalled. He rejoined his community sadder and a bit lost, "dark and dour." Bear quickly discovered that being an icon of the counterculture did not pay well. He needed to make money, and he remained committed to sound, specifically the sound of the Dead.

The Dead did not know exactly what to do with him. While Bear was away, Dan Healy had taken over as the band's chief soundman, and Bear returned to find himself with a job but not exactly a role. The Dead, meanwhile, still owed Warner Bros. one more record, so the two goals merged: Let Bear produce an album and let Warner Bros. figure out what to do with it.

History of the Grateful Dead, Vol. 1 (Bear's Choice) was released in July 1973. It was a trip back through the band's archives, and by the time it was released, it therefore felt like an artifact. It would prove an outlier—there never was a Vol. 2—but it delivered a tribute to Pigpen, who might otherwise have gone without memorial.

The album opened with "Katie Mae," and Pigpen could be heard flubbing the opening verse. But that was part of the Dead's magic, the looseness and easiness with experimenting live and being unashamed of screw-ups—willing, even, to include them on an album. And it seemed appropriate to Owsley to open the album with Pigpen, a decision he made just after Pigpen died in March and the album was in production. Pigpen's voice and instrumentals dominate the second side of the album—side 1 is acoustic, side 2 electric—putting him out front on covers of "Smokestack Lightning" and "Hard to Handle." The album features only one original Grateful Dead song, the Garcia-Hunter dirge "Black Peter."

The album also introduced a new character to the Dead's iconography, as the back cover featured a line of bears. Owsley was the inspiration for that image, though Bob Thomas, the graphic artist who also came up with the "Stealie," actually designed it. Thomas borrowed the bears from a printing press typeset block, and though the creatures became known as the "dancing bears," they are really marching, not dancing. Cheerful and colorful, they would appear on car bumpers and binders and later laptops in every corner of the world. Though some found them out of spirit with the Dead's deeper chords—best captured by the skull or rose—they contributed a lighter shading to the Dead's image, a signal of shared identity that captured some of the lighthearted spirit of a show.

The album also satisfied the Dead's remaining obligations to Warner Bros.

THE RUN-UP to Watkins Glen was stressful for Garcia. After a Philadelphia show in March, Garcia had been stopped while speeding on Route 295. The accounts varied slightly, but he was said to have been driving at 71 mph in either a 60 mph zone or a 40 mph zone, en route to either Massachusetts or Connecticut. In either case, the speeding ticket took a turn for the worse when the state trooper asked to look inside a suitcase that Garcia had in the car. He opened it to find Garcia's stash, initially described as one that "allegedly contained cocaine, heroin, marijuana and other drugs," bad news for a man arrested just three years earlier on suspicion of drug possession in New Orleans. Garcia was taken into custody, arraigned, and released on $2,000 bail when John Scher, the East Coast counterpart and rival of Bill Graham, came to spring Garcia.

Garcia's arrest deepened a fear that was rising around the band—that it was being used as bait. Lesh had been arrested in January after a young woman told authorities she'd been offered drugs at his house, though not by him. Then, as the band hit the road, trouble followed. Spring shows in 1973 drew large crowds, and those crowds often included police, sometimes undercover, who pounced on Dead shows as an easy venue for rounding up drug cases. Newspaper accounts tracked that work: nineteen arrested in Utica, seventy-five at the Nassau Coliseum; videotapes of a Dead show in Colorado were used to look for drug dealers. All told, it felt as though the law was closing in, trailing the Dead around the country, looking for easy marks.

As the plans for what was being called the Summer Jam: A Day in the Country were laid, Garcia faced a court date that could dramatically affect his future. Nevertheless, plans went ahead, propelled by a pair of young promoters and by the Dead's desire to demonstrate that they could play the big event—and that the experience of Altamont was an aberration, not some sort of cosmic evidence of the counterculture's collapse. Personal vindication was on the line, too: Sam Cutler, whose handling of Altamont on the Dead's behalf had earned him derision and worse, was eager to redeem himself.

By early July, promoters of the concert were finalizing the lineup and hoping to draw 100,000 to 125,000 people. The Dead and the Allman Brothers, whose fondness for one another had grown from the Fillmore East shows, were quick to agree. Initially, they were to be joined by Leon Russell, but Garcia pointed out that a concert of this size near the Canadian border should include the Band. The Band had stopped touring by then, so the invitation seemed perfunctory, but when the members heard that it came from Garcia himself, they reconsidered. Russell was dropped and the Band added.

The promoters assembled the venue. They had picked the eleven-hundred-acre Watkins Glen International Speedway, also known as the Grand Prix Racecourse, as the site, and they struck a deal with the owners. Plunging through local permits and permissions, they put together an epic gathering. They drilled wells for drinking water, ordered a thousand portable toilets, printed posters and tickets. Promoter Shelly Finkel gave his assurance that "another Woodstock won't happen here" and promised to cut off ticket sales at 125,000. Still, officials worried. "People in this community are willing to put up with nearly anything, but they want it orderly," the Watkins Glen mayor said. "We are sweating this one out."

They had reason for concern. Initial sales went well, and the promoters quietly upped the sales limit to 150,000, even as the local sheriff worried that as many as 200,000 people might show up. The Summer Jam was scheduled to begin at noon on Saturday, July 28. It was designed as a one-day concert, filling out the afternoon, evening, and night with the three bands. As the day approached, crowds began arriving, at first in a trickle, then a flood. The nearby village of thirty-five hundred braced, then surrendered.

"Clusters of barefooted, scantily clad girls and dirty, [bluejeaned] long-haired boys fill the sidewalk benches and shop doorways," one reporter observed. And though the *Niagara Falls Gazette* noted that "local residents are fighting to keep a lid on their worst fears," those fears seemed not to be materializing. The owner of one local dry cleaning store reported that the young people she had encountered were polite and "they're educated." "Why," Dorothy Chapman happily observed, "a lot of them are over in the library—reading."

While the behavior was encouraging, the numbers were alarming. Kids kept arriving, and those who got there early were in for a treat.

The Dead had insisted on controlling the sound system at Watkins Glen, which made sense given its unrivaled commitment to amplification and its recent leaps in that area. Owsley and Healy were both on hand for the event, and the Dead wanted to try out the speaker array specially installed to deliver music across vast swaths of land. With the crowd massing outside the venue, Bill Graham, whom the promoters brought in to help manage the stage, suggested opening the gates early, allowing fans to enter on Friday. And so, with hundreds of thousands taking their places from the stage to the horizon, the Dead conducted its "sound check" in the form of an unscheduled jam on Friday afternoon.

It started a little rough, but by the time the Dead had finished "Promised Land," the crowd could hear clearly and realized it was getting a free show. The Dead gave them ten songs that Friday afternoon, including a relaxed eighteen-minute "Birdsong" and a thirty-minute jam into "Wharf Rat" that devotees would remember for decades. The Summer Jam was under way.

"EYES OF THE WORLD" | 291

It was unfathomably big. By July 27, the day before the show, traffic was backing up, and officers were speculating that three hundred thousand might turn out. Cars were abandoned by the sides of roads five, then ten, then fifteen miles away; Route 17 was blocked by cars left behind as concertgoers undertook the rest of the trek on foot. By the morning of the concert, throngs were arriving over the hillsides and making the turn to the racecourse. "400,000 Jam Rock Site; More Coming," the UPI reported. "There are 95 acres of wall-to-wall people," one police supervisor said. "I don't know where we're going to fit them, but we can't stop them coming."

The actual concert opened promptly at noon on Saturday when the Dead, who had volunteered to go first, took the immense stage. It was hot and muggy, but with clear skies. A light rain fell later in the afternoon, bringing cool breezes and flashes of lightning that the crowd cheered. The bands played from noon until 3 A.M., leaving the crowd to wind down as the sun rose over the track and surrounding fields.

There were casualties. A couple of young people tried to parachute into the crowd, and one, a thirty-five-year-old "veteran parachutist," died when the flares he was toting apparently blew up on his way to earth, leaving him either snagged on a wire or caught in a tree—witnesses offered different accounts. Four died in traffic accidents going to or from the venue, and one person drowned. And there were arrests, of course, eighty in all, mostly for drug possession and illegal hitchhiking, but given that some six hundred thousand people eventually made it to the track, it had formed a city almost the size of modern New Orleans. In fact, Watkins Glen was far more noted for its civility than for its debauchery. "I've never gotten called 'sir' so much," State Trooper James F. Hicks reported.

Moreover, it marked a commingling of regional countercultures, a merging of West Coast hippies and their Southern counterparts, perhaps even a smattering of Canadians trailing the Band. The Allman Brothers and the Dead had been appreciating each other's music for years, sharing stages on both coasts, but never had so many of their fans met and shared a field. Their combined work shone at Watkins Glen, and their cultures basked in it, swirling together as effortlessly as hippies and radicals had enjoyed each other at the Be-In.

Lives changed that weekend. Steve Silberman would go on to a distinguished career as a writer, and he would become one of the Dead's most intelligent interpreters. He was a kid at Watkins Glen, there for his first show.

"I was 15, and I had just seen—well, I didn't know what I had seen," he wrote later, looking back on the morning after the show. "But I spent the next twenty-two years in the presence of that music, trying to figure it out."

Watkins Glen would be compared to Woodstock, sometimes thoughtfully, sometimes glibly, and often starting from the sense that Woodstock represented the 1960s and that Watkins Glen was an attempt to reclaim that spirit. Observers remarked on the contrasts: the Summer Jam was less political, more subdued, more broadly appealing—and less deeply felt. BIGGEST, BUT NOT WOODSTOCK, *The Des Moines Register* offered. *The New York Times*, which four years earlier had deplored the "Nightmare in the Catskills," found Watkins Glen wanting by comparison—and deplored it, too. "The post-Vietnam quietude of youth has been accepted," declared the *Times*, ever out of step with that segment of American life, "and the 'Summer Jam' is explained largely on hedonistic grounds, its participants merely desirous of being at the biggest party of all time."

That just demonstrated the Establishment's struggle to keep up with the changes unfolding before it. As Dylan famously noted, "Something is happening here, but you don't know what it is, do you, Mr. Jones?" By 1973, the counterculture was less fiery but bigger—as evidenced by Earth Day in 1970 and its successors. Those who were threatened or irritated by the counterculture failed to see that it, too, was changing— and growing.

For there was something to note about Watkins Glen. Not only was it bigger than Woodstock—it was the biggest rock concert of all time.

"EYES OF THE WORLD" | 293

* * *

GARCIA LEFT Watkins Glen first thing on Monday morning, boarded a helicopter and flew to Mount Holly, New Jersey, where he awaited sentencing for his March 27 arrest on drug charges. The judge, Herman Belopolsky, was uncommonly receptive to the appeal from Garcia's lawyer, who argued for dismissal of the charges in return for supervised release. The lawyer, Francis J. Hartman, had arranged for Garcia to meet with a psychiatrist, and the doctor told the court that Garcia was not a drug addict but rather "a family man and creative."

Based on that testimony and Hartman's argument that Garcia's only other brush with the law, his New Orleans arrest, had disappeared without an indictment (he did not mention, naturally, that Warner Bros. had helped ensure that outcome), the judge sentenced Garcia to a year's probation, requiring Garcia to meet with the psychiatrist every two months during that year. Assuming that Garcia met those conditions and avoided any other arrests, the charges would be dismissed.

Garcia, who appeared in court in jeans and cowboy boots, expressed happiness and relief at the result. He and Sam Cutler then got back on the helicopter and headed for Jersey City, where the Dead performed at Roosevelt Stadium on Tuesday and Wednesday nights.

NIXON COASTED to reelection. Buoyed by his Silent Majority and running one step ahead of the law in the Watergate scandal, he held off an earnest but overmatched challenge from South Dakota senator George McGovern, who secured the Democratic nomination after a wide-open Democratic primary, memorably covered by Hunter Thompson for *Rolling Stone*. Turning to Nixon, McGovern campaigned to end the war in Vietnam and with the affectionate support of the counterculture.

But nothing could save McGovern's effort against the better financed and solidly positioned Nixon. An underdog from the start, McGovern was set back by revelations that his vice presidential pick, Thomas Eagleton, had repeatedly been hospitalized for depression. Eagleton was dropped from the ticket, replaced by Sargent Shriver, but the campaign never regained momentum in what was already an uphill contest against the incumbent.

Thompson did his best for the Democrat. "I suggested that McGovern could pick up a million or so votes by inviting the wire-service photographers to come out and snap him lounging around on the beach with a can of beer in his hand and wearing my Grateful Dead T-shirt," he wrote.

The campaign turned down the idea, and Thompson thought later that "that was the moment" his relationship with McGovern's team "turned sour."

Nixon won more than 60 percent of the popular vote, leaving McGovern to carry only Massachusetts and the District of Columbia. Maybe he should have worn the T-shirt.

THE DEAD put in long hours to create *Wake of the Flood,* their sixth studio album. It was the first since the death of Pigpen and the first to feature Keith and Donna Jean Godchaux. Hart was missing, still recovering from his father's betrayal and his own troubles. The album was the first to appear on the band's own label, an exciting moment of emancipation from the studio system that they had bucked since the beginning. For all those reasons, the album represented a fresh start. "They had to reorganize," Donna Jean said later. "It really took place in the making of *Wake of the Flood.*"

Yes. And no. The album felt different in texture from what had come before—lusher, more layered, "ample, full and carefully rendered," as a reviewer for *Rolling Stone* put it. But, as with all their albums, many of the songs had been tested and refined on the road, so they were familiar to the band's audience long before the album was released in October 1973.

Some songs became classics. "Eyes of the World" was dreamy and alert, "Stella Blue" almost mournful in its deep sense of longing—one of many Dead songs that would grow and acquire new meaning over the years. Other songs tried new paths. "Row Jimmy" delivered a slow reggae beat, while "Let Me Sing Your Blues Away" was bright and engaging. Weir's contribution, "Weather Report Suite," extended the band's pastoral imagery and appreciation, and it did so with an ambitious, reflective collection of ideas, exquisitely captured by Rick Griffin's elegant cover art.

Not everyone loved the album. Robert Christgau gave it a B-minus, enjoying aspects of it but comparing the overall effect to the "ruminative, seemingly aimless part of the concert when the boogiers nod out." Still, it was, by Grateful Dead standards, a hit, selling some four hundred thousand copies and gathering more appreciation over time. And, since the Dead did not have to split revenue with a record company, it helped put the band back in the black.

ONE OF the alluring potencies of Robert Hunter's work was its ability to speak on varied levels, to grow with time and to reflect the interpreter. "He's Gone" could be heard as a blustery send-off to Mickey Hart's thieving father, a sad farewell to Pigpen, or a more general reflection on leaving and being left behind. Hunter's lyrics could feel topical and majestic at once, giving his best work immediacy and artistic elevation. That was certainly the case with "Ship of Fools."

First performed by the Dead at Winterland in February 1974, "Ship of Fools" took aim at ignorance and the ignorant, and it declared an unwillingness to aid their cause. "I won't slave for beggar's pay," the song went, "likewise gold and jewels / but I would slave to learn the way / to sink your ship of fools." As usual, Hunter's images and references could be read from deep sources, nods to Plato's *Republic*, myths from the Middle Ages, and a 1962 novel of the same title that chronicled the world's drift into World War II. It also felt strikingly contemporary. "Topical song, topical lyrics," as Garcia described it.

More of a polemic than a story, Hunter's "Ship of Fools" did not identify the ship or the fools aboard it. But events of early 1974 provided plenty of suspects. On February 4, 1974, just weeks before the song was first performed, a band of terrorist misfits calling themselves the Symbionese Liberation Army snatched nineteen-year-old Patty Hearst from her Berkeley apartment and followed the kidnapping up with demands that her wealthy and prominent family—owners of newspapers in California—pay ransom and sponsor food giveaways in order to secure her release. It would take nineteen months for authorities to bring her home, and by then she had taken on the name Tania and been photographed wielding an assault rifle and participating in a San Francisco bank robbery. The SLA's ship of fools was tragicomic in its boastfulness and its lethality.

And indicative of a counterculture consuming itself. As Vietnam persisted and Watergate eroded public confidence in Nixon, the counterculture's distrust of Washington had hardened, and the "resistance" that Hayden identified in 1967 had solidified into violence by the early 1970s. After Weatherman detonated its bomb at the U.S. Capitol in 1971, it followed with a bomb at the California Department of Prisons in San Francisco in August (protesting the killing of Black Panther George Jackson in San Quentin) and another at the Pentagon in May 1972 (to commemorate Ho Chi Minh's birthday). The Pentagon explosion, inside a women's restroom on the complex's fourth floor, touched off flooding that damaged computer tapes containing classified information. "The inner sanctum of the war machine had been attacked," one sympathetic account noted.

The group, variously known as Weather, Weatherman, Weathermen, and Weather Underground, bombed a New York police precinct in 1973, followed by bombings and fires at International Telephone & Telegraph offices in New York and Rome in September of that year (another bombing, at a federal office building in San Francisco, occurred almost simultaneously, but no one claimed responsibility for it); those attacks, attributed to Weather Underground, were carried out in protest of the company's attempts to help overthrow the government of Chile's Salvador Allende in 1970, information that became public in 1972 when congressional hearings revealed the company's role.

Weather called in the New York bomb twenty minutes before it detonated, and there were no injuries, though furniture and walls were destroyed and "five large window panels [were sent] to the street below." In its communiqué, Weather called on others to challenge ITT, as well as to study the writings of Latin American revolutionaries and poets.

All of this was violent and theatrical, of course, though to what end seemed unclear. Garcia had been alarmed at Jerry Rubin's tone at the Be-In when Rubin barked at the crowd with the fervor Garcia associated with political bosses. Now the counterculture had adopted the tactics of the culture it opposed, in theory as a tool to overthrow that culture while mimicking its most egregious violations. Was the violent wing of the counterculture the "Ship of Fools" that Hunter had in mind? He, of course, did not say, nor did Garcia nor the rest of the Dead. But the spectacle of wanton violence in the name of peace certainly made them candidates for the Dead's scorn.

Then there was Scientology. Hunter had dabbled in the goofball religiosity of Scientology. He'd even invited Garcia to join him for a meeting, though Garcia immediately took a dislike to it. "This was a brand-new thing at the time," Hunter later told David Browne. "This fellow came down and was telling us fantastic things, like you could get out of your body. All of that sounded great. But let's just say Scientology and I were not a very good match."

Bolstering the case for Scientology's being a possible target of "Ship of Fools" was the organization's fascination with naval regalia. L. Ron Hubbard founded the "Sea Organization" in the late 1960s, an inner circle of the group that dressed up in sailor suits as a display of devotion to the church and its founder. "Went to see the captain," Hunter's "Ship of Fools" opened, "strangest I could find." Hubbard fit that bill, and Scientology had both the ship and the fools of Hunter's lyric. "Ship of fools," Garcia sang, plaintive and slightly pleading, "sail away from me."

One other interpretation: the band itself. Robert Hunter was in England during this period, and he was in some dismay over the state of the band and its crew, who were dipping ever deeper into cocaine. Debates over the So What proposal and the Dead's new business ventures

298 | HERE BESIDE THE RISING TIDE

also agitated Hunter, who considered Rakow ruthlessly commercial. "Ship of Fools" could be seen as a meditation on the Dead itself, circa 1974.

But by far the ship and fools most associated with the Dead's new song in early 1974 were President Nixon and his crew—an interpretation seemingly in accord with Garcia's note that the song was "topical." By the beginning of 1974, the superstructure of Nixon's administration was crumbling. Under pressure from special prosecutor Archibald Cox to turn over recordings of White House meetings, Nixon ordered Cox fired in October 1973. Attorney General Elliot Richardson and Deputy Attorney General William Ruckelshaus resigned rather than carry out Nixon's order. Solicitor General Robert Bork complied. The "Saturday Night Massacre" left three professional corpses, and it sent Nixon into his final downward spiral.

A month later, Nixon met with newspaper editors in Orlando, Florida. The "nervous but self-assured" president insisted that he wanted the facts of Watergate to be made public because "the facts will prove that the President is telling the truth."

That truth, Nixon said: "I'm not a crook."

And then the public learned of an eighteen-and-a-half-minute gap on one of the tapes that Nixon was fighting to retain, an erasure as suspicious as it was emblematic of the gathering cover-up. Nixon entered 1974 wounded and bleeding, his ship adrift. Even his most devoted fools braced for the crash. "Though I could not caution all," Hunter wrote, "I still might warn a few: / Don't lend your hand to raise no flag / atop no ship of fools."

In 1974, there were plenty of fools to go around.

AT THE beginning of 1974, Garcia had two daughters, Heather with Sara and Annabelle with Mountain Girl. Warner Bros. had paid Garcia a $20,000 advance for a solo project in the early 1970s, and he and Mountain Girl made a stab at domesticity, using the money to make a down payment on a Stinson Beach home on a bluff overlooking the

Pacific. It was a gorgeous residence on 1.1 acres and the first home that either one had ever owned. They enjoyed it, but it did not usher them into a conventional life. Even with a wife, daughters, and a home, Garcia was restless, his relations untidy.

Some of the same could be said of the other band members. Kreutzmann married at age eighteen after getting his girlfriend pregnant, and though they had broken up soon after leaving Olompali, they shared a daughter, Stacy, born in 1964. Not long after settling in San Francisco, Kreutzmann met another woman, Suzanne Ziegler (she went by Susila), and after a charmed first date in the wine country, they struck up a romance and married. Their son, Justin, was born on June 10, 1969, "just in time to attend Woodstock," as Kreutzmann wrote. Bill and Suzanne would divorce ten years later.

Lesh and Rosie McGee were a couple throughout the Dead's early years, starting during the Acid Tests, but their relationship ended in the early 1970s. McGee stayed on as a member of the extended Dead family, working for Bear's sound company, Alembic, and even traveling with the band in Europe, where she acted as a translator—she spoke fluent French—and unofficial photographer. Back home, Phil retreated to his house in the redwood forest of Fairfax, where he "had several girlfriends but no serious relationship." He avoided cooking, instead eating in town and frequently visiting Hart at the drummer's Novato ranch, where the two collaborated on Hart's first solo album, *Rolling Thunder.*

Weir was the band's least attached member. One contemporary noted that he was the only member of the Dead who yearned to be a rock star, and he lived like one. Just a teenager in the early years, he relished the life in his own, inimitable, spacey way. He was notably the band's most handsome member, and thus a natural magnet for sexual liaisons. Weir eagerly played the part. "He was game for it all," Mountain Girl said later. Weir met a go-go dancer named Frankie Azzara in the late 1960s, and they were frequent companions for years after that. Dark-haired and lithe, she went by Frankie Weir but never actually married Bob.

And yet even Weir showed signs of growing up. In 1972, he bought

300 | HERE BESIDE THE RISING TIDE

his first home, including a studio that the Dead would soon use for their work.

WATERGATE CAUGHT up with Nixon, rocking his ship of fools in the spring of 1974. It was enough for even Garcia to take note. Interviewed earlier that year, he expressed amazement at Nixon's predicament—and in terms that spoke volumes about both Garcia and Nixon.

"Every morning, he wakes up with what must be a sense of total responsibility about everything in America," Garcia told interviewers Jim Ladd and Tom Yates. This from a man who abjured responsibility at every turn. "All this stuff is sitting there."

That was bad enough, in Garcia's view, but there was more. "Plus," Garcia said, "he's blowing it horribly. It must be horrible. It must just be amazing. I feel for the poor guy."

Garcia's sympathy for anyone forced to bear such responsibility went only so far when it came to Nixon, however. One night after a show in Berkeley, he was high with bassist John Kahn and manager Ron Rakow, wondering about the president of the United States. They lit upon a plan to save the Nixon presidency. Rakow memorialized it in a letter to the White House.

"Dear Mr. President," the letter began,

While we are of vastly different socio political persuasions, several of my associates and I had our first political meeting in our ten year history and we concluded that your involuntary removal from office would produce a decidedly negative result on the American life style; if, in fact, anything so diverse could be so collectively described.

Therefore, our focus was to arrive at a solution of what is now your problem and can be everyone's problem. We pass our solution along to you with only the remotest expectation that you will carry it out since, while it is brilliant, it is not extremely logical. We have concluded that the problems referred to above would disappear, as if by magic, were you to crome [sic] the entire Whitehouse.

"EYES OF THE WORLD" | 301

It was signed, "sincerely," by Rakow and sent on the stationery of Grateful Dead Records. Nixon did not reply.

BEAR'S CHOICE was just one of Owsley Stanley's contributions during his uncomfortable reunion with his old mates after his release from prison in 1972. The Grateful Dead that Bear rejoined was different from the band he'd left when he headed off to serve his time—bigger, more compartmentalized between musicians and crew, less inspired by acid and marijuana and more fueled by cocaine. But the band was always tinkering with its sound, and now it was looking to make a leap. Lesh and Garcia in particular trusted Bear's genius while tolerating his eccentricities. So with *Bear's Choice* released, Bear himself turned to the question of how the Dead sounded live.

Bear described his orders this way: "When the Dead said, 'Well, we want to go to bigger shows,' I [said that I] believe that based on what the speaker makers tell us now . . . we can build an integrated system where every instrument has its own amplification, all set up behind the band without any separate onstage monitors . . . a single, big system." That became the Wall of Sound.

Owsley worked at the problem for months, examining the demands of each instrument and innovating everywhere from microphone to speaker cabinets. The band experimented as it went, unveiling pieces of what was becoming the new array in late 1973 and then testing the whole apparatus at Winterland in early 1974. The Wall, as a recognized feature, got its first full look on March 23, 1974, at a show at the Cow Palace, a cavernous and acoustically challenging hall south of San Francisco.

The Wall of Sound was 40 feet high and 70 feet wide. The scaffolding into which it was set held 480 speakers, arrayed in columns, each column projecting the sound from a specific instrument—one for the bass, one for Garcia's guitar, one for Weir's, one for Godchaux's keyboards. The center section, a convex cluster of speakers that hung over the stage, was for vocals. McIntosh amplifiers drove the array, and each musician could control his own volume. And because this huge array had to be lugged from city to city and erected anew each time, Alembic, the company spun off from the Dead's sound operation, fashioned extra-sturdy cabinets for each speaker, helping to protect them from road wear and tear, though also adding to the overall weight of the system. One chart from that era charted the evolution of the Dead's sound by weight: In 1965, the Dead's gear weighed 800 pounds and fitted in Kreutzmann's station wagon; by 1973, it weighed 30,000 pounds and required a 40-foot tractor-trailer to haul it from place to place.

The show on March 23 was billed as "The Sound Test," and Owsley was on hand to gauge it. It was, smashingly, a success. QUIET! THE BAND IS PLAYING, the *Chronicle*'s headline read after the paper's reporter attended a tech rehearsal a day or two earlier. The band's control over the volume and distortion permitted the sound to carry without overwhelming the arena, allowing the sound to be clear and warm without being overwhelmingly loud. Intricate guitar work and hi-hat cymbals came through with equal precision, and Lesh's bass could be appreciated for its subtlety. So nuanced was the sound engineering that members of the audience at the back of the Cow Palace could hear each other at a whisper and still feel enveloped by the music. "The sound," Owsley proclaimed, "was simply phenomenal."

That was not just bragging. Nothing in all popular music compared to the Wall of Sound. It did, however, come at a price. The Wall of Sound was so enormous that it was a nightmare to move. And since life with the Dead was life on the move, that posed a problem: How could the band assemble and disassemble the Wall of Sound fast enough to keep pace with its touring schedule?

The short answer was that it could not. Even the Dead's famously efficient road crew simply could not move thirty thousand pounds of gear every night or two without accommodations. It required nine hours to set up the array and six to strike it; crew and equipment costs soared. The result was that the Dead were forced to build not one but two complete cabinet arrays to hold the Wall of Sound, so that while they were playing in front of one, the other was being erected at the band's next stop. The crew would then leapfrog the two sets of scaffolding and cabinets as a tour progressed—a triumph of acoustics but a near-doubling of the cost of touring.

The Dead, once a nimble rock band, became a lumbering, though brilliant and crystal-clear, monolith.

THE DEAD traveled widely with the Wall of Sound in 1974 and even made a brief return trip to Europe, with seven shows in London, Munich, Dijon, and Paris. It was rewarding but trying. The whole scene was getting so big, so fast, so fueled by cocaine, so demanding on performers and crew, that it wore out the Dead. At one point, band and crew together agreed to flush their stashes, but they quickly found more drugs, and the atmosphere grew darker, more paranoid. The Dead came home from Europe, looked ahead to the fall schedule, and imagined hauling all that gear around the country yet again. It was exhausting even to consider, let alone to accomplish.

Almost since the beginning, Garcia had been yearning for that perfect place, the zone where he could perform and record without compromising, without trimming his vision for the benefit of Warner Bros. or the industry, without sacrificing the freedom to experiment to fulfill the demands of the market or the media.

They continued to carve out studio time, though with mixed results. *From the Mars Hotel*, the Dead's seventh studio album, was recorded in March and April 1974 and released in June. "U.S. Blues" opened the album, which also featured such memorable tunes as "Scarlet Begonias" and "China Doll," as well as the egregiously bad "Money Money." The placement of "U.S. Blues" at the front of the album meant that *From the Mars Hotel* kicked off with a wry take on patriotism in the hands of hucksters. The album's final cut was "Ship of Fools," the thought-provoking renunciation of those whose hubris blinded them to reason and humility. As a collection, the album lacked the cohering vision of *Workingman's Dead* or *American Beauty*, but it contained gems.

Feeling stuck and unsure what to do next after returning from Europe in 1974, they elected to try a new way. By that point, Garcia, Weir, and Lesh each had ideas for solo work, and the Dead were ready to break from traveling and instead focus on individual projects and time in the studio. Doing so could, in theory, even give them time with family. Mountain Girl had stopped accompanying the band on tour after Europe in 1972, so she held down the home front.

Theresa Garcia, affectionately known as Trixie, was born on September 21, 1974, Garcia's third daughter and his second with Mountain Girl. Garcia missed her birth. As with his older daughters, Garcia parented remotely, but Trixie would remember his visits, his kindheartedness as well as his remove, resting after weeks on the road, then settling in for brief spells with his family. He would sleep late, then rouse himself to play with his girls, watch TV with them, and chat while running scales on his guitar. He was approachable but sometimes aloof. He had, Trixie recalled, a "grumpy bear" vibe.

The band's break from touring loomed. To mark it, the Dead planned a send-off, a set of shows at San Francisco's Winterland. The band played 111 songs over five nights, from October 16 through October 20, starting each night just after seven-thirty and winding up well past midnight. Their sets varied, of course, and ranged from old favorites to newer material, including "Scarlet Begonias" and the ambitiously complex "Weather Report Suite." Crews filmed the shows, laying the foundation for a movie that Garcia was excited to create about the band.

The final night also featured an overdue though somewhat awkward reconciliation. Mickey Hart had been away, but he knew that October 20 looked like the end, and he trekked over to Winterland with his drums. Kreutzmann was not happy to see him. "I was *not* cool" with Hart's sudden reappearance, he wrote later. "Personally, I was insulted that everybody else backstage rallied behind Mickey." He was overruled and went, grumbling, back out to play a second set—perhaps his last ever—with the Grateful Dead.

And with that, the Dead chugged through its final songs, delivered in the crystalline sonic envelope supplied by the Wall of Sound. The band opened with an extended feedback exploration, led by Lesh and

"EYES OF THE WORLD" | 305

his collaborator Ned Lagin, that came to be known as "Seastones." Out of that long wander erupted a couple of drum solos, a thumping thirteen-minute, forty-five-second "Not Fade Away," and a mix of dance numbers—"Good Lovin'" and "Promised Land"—and moodier pieces, including "Eyes of the World" and "Stella Blue." The Dead closed with a soaring "Sugar Magnolia" and cacophonous applause, and then returned to the stage. Graham honored the crew who had been with them for nearly a decade, bringing them onstage and introducing them one at a time—"Ramrod, Healy, get your asses out here, c'mon. Healy, Jackson, Ramrod, Joseph. Let's go. Everybody. C'mon. . . . This is the crew. For ten fucking years, they've done it."

As the band prepared to launch into its encore, Lesh explained Hart's presence: "Some of you folks might remember our old drummer, Mickey Hart, who's playing with us tonight."

Weir chimed in: "Fresh out of the mental institution and a brand-new man."

And then the band played a fast dash through "Johnny B. Goode" and a loping "Mississippi Half-Step Uptown Toodleoo" before closing with "And We Bid You Goodnight," quiet, short, serene.

"See y'all later," Weir said after the last notes faded. "Thank you."

As members of the audience trickled out, ushers stamped their tickets: "The Last One."

And that was it. The Dead, for all anyone knew, were finished.

Jerry on a camel. Egypt, September 1978.
Adrian Boot/Retro Photo Archive

CHAPTER 14

"On the Road Again"

"WE HAVEN'T BROKEN UP," GARCIA EXPLAINED. "WE'VE JUST stopped performing. We're going to keep on recording, and we probably will get back into performing, but we'll wait until we've had a chance to define how we want to do it."

There was a flaw in that logic, as the Dead soon discovered. The band had always existed mainly as a live act, as a gathering place for people and as a creator of culture; that sense of itself dated from the Acid Tests and marked a through line from there to the Be-In and the Summer of Love, the touring, the Carousel, even the Wall of Sound. As a business matter, the band did not make much money on its albums. *Workingman's Dead* and *American Beauty* were works of serious art, but the Dead were an experience, not an object. The notion of the band as a stay-at-home studio group did not make much sense.

The drugs were part of it. LSD still nibbled around the edges of the band and their entourage—the farewell shows at Winterland were awash in it—but cocaine had exerted its grinding influence. Touring had become work, and cocaine had become the way to get the work done. It was no longer much fun. As Mountain Girl said: "It had become chatty without being friendly."

In the spring of 1973, while the Dead were playing the Nassau Coliseum in New York, Garcia had met a young woman named Deborah Koons. Trim, dark-haired, intense, wealthy, she struck many of those around Garcia as distinctly outside the Dead's community, which tended to easygoing tribalism. Garcia was entranced, however, and Koons would soon become part of the Dead family, much to Mountain Girl's annoyance. Garcia and Koons rented a place in Bolinas, just a few miles up the coast from the home he shared with Mountain Girl in Stinson Beach. By the middle of 1975, Garcia had even managed to bring Koons onto the Dead's payroll, hiring her as an editor for *The Grateful Dead Movie*, which he was then struggling to complete.

"It was around that time," Mountain Girl said later, "that it really started to get to be a problem." She and Garcia would argue, he would leave and not return for days. Frustrated and unable to bring Garcia back to their home, Mountain Girl decamped with her daughters for Oregon. She had written a book—a cheerful guide to growing marijuana by one of the counterculture's most recognizable figures—and she used the money to settle herself not far from Ken Kesey and his family. She begged Garcia for child support, but he went silent, plunging more deeply into his work and avoiding, as was his habit, anything that smacked of personal commitment or obligation.

The Dead were on a touring break, maybe forever. Mountain Girl and his daughters were gone to Oregon, maybe forever. Garcia went on working.

THE BAND had two lives—a brief career together and then an album, released after the band had broken up, that outlived its members. The first of those lives began in 1973, when David Grisman, Peter Rowan, and John Kahn dropped by Garcia's house in Stinson Beach. "We could hear Jerry playing the banjo as we rolled up," Rowan remembered. Garcia, barefoot, greeted them at the door, and the group settled into playing. Over the next two months, they combed through old songbooks for fun. The idea of something more formal began to take shape: a bluegrass band, a return to those days in the 1960s when Garcia moseyed through one band after another, the Wildwood Boys, the Hart Valley Drifters, the Thunder Mountain Tub Thumpers. Those were golden months in the young life of Jerry Garcia, and these sounds, this bluegrass companionship, drew him back. The musicians realized that if they were going to be more serious about this, they needed a fiddle player, so they reached out to some friends. Richard Greene played with the group for a bit, but other commitments pulled him away. They eventually landed bluegrass great Vassar Clements, whose short hair and traditional roots made him seem an unlikely bandmate with the central figure of the Grateful Dead but whose musicianship and credibility in the tight, sometimes insular world of bluegrass made him a natural. He was delighted and accepted. Garcia suggested a name for the band: "Old & In the Way."

It was, Rowan said, "just four people who couldn't stop playing. We figured we could keep the demons at bay if we kept playing."

It was an unusual and not altogether easy collection of musicians. Grisman was exacting; Garcia was more casual. Kahn was an exemplary bassist—he and Garcia collaborated in other groupings as well—but, like Garcia, was drawn to drugs. Rowan had a freer style—his yodeling excursions were a signature—but he could grate on Grisman. Old & In the Way did not seem destined for a long life, and indeed it lasted barely a year as an enterprise. The goal was never to make a hit record, or really even to make a record at all. It was to enjoy one another's company, to tickle some audiences, to return to music that quickened the soul. "Old & In the Way had no ambitions," Rowan said. "Period."

The band toured a bit—all told, they gave forty-seven live performances, most of them captured on tape, with Owsley manically seeking the perfect sound. One of those recordings was made on October 8, 1973, at the Boarding House club in San Francisco. That recording sat unnoticed for a time, but then Owsley lit upon it—it seemed to him a night when the music clicked and the sound reflected it, capturing the musicians at their most harmonious, lifted by a lightness of spirit. By then, the band itself was largely defunct, never really having made the transition from side project to a fully operational band. The members went their separate ways in 1974, but Round Records, one of the Dead's labels, released the Boarding House shows as a live album in 1975. The album was entitled simply *Old & In the Way*.

It was more than just a hit. As measured by the music charts, *Old &*

310 | HERE BESIDE THE RISING TIDE

In the Way would become the bestselling bluegrass album to date (later surpassed by the soundtrack of the Coen Brothers' film *O Brother, Where Art Thou?*). It introduced the vast audience of the Grateful Dead to the music that undergirded the Dead itself, that explained the Dead's musical roots. There was a reason that the Dead felt distinctly different from the Rolling Stones or Bob Dylan or Led Zeppelin. This was it.

The album's success was an unexpected wonder, but it also left raw feelings. Because the album was an afterthought to the band itself, its release took the players somewhat by surprise. "The band had stopped playing, but there were these tapes, and they approached me with, 'Hey, let's put out these tapes,'" Grisman recalled. He agreed without thinking much about it, and he was paid $1,000.

But then the album was a sensation, and Grisman silently fumed as Round Records raked in profits. Too proud to alert Garcia to the injustice he felt, Grisman suffered. "These guys are playing Madison Square Garden, and I was driving around in a car that was falling apart," he said. "I just wanted my little piece of the action."

Years went by. As he did with most personal matters, Garcia paid no attention as his friendship with Grisman dissolved into bitterness. Only much later, after Garcia finally became aware of Grisman's situation, did the two musicians resume their abiding friendship.

FOR RONALD REAGAN, freedom was an expression of individualism, and groups, especially the government, were to be regarded with suspicion. For Joan Didion, life was too personal to be expressed in movements. For Garcia, the opposite was true. Life was to be lived together. He performed with others, he drew energy from the Grateful Dead's improvised family. He was part of a band that lived and thrived within a movement, a counterculture. Drugs were part of that community. The Warlocks and then the Grateful Dead found energy and inspiration in LSD. Marijuana opened them to hearing one another, gave them the patience to follow sound where it led them, to "case the music," as Weir liked to say.

"ON THE ROAD AGAIN" | 311

Cocaine was different. And then came heroin.

The Dead did not erect boundaries against drug use—an atmosphere of noninterference was central to its internal culture—but members of the band and their families frowned on heroin. Junkies were beneath them, zombie-like in their detachment compared to the Dead's more creative and inspiration-seeking drug adventures. And Garcia no doubt refused early opportunities to snort, smoke, or shoot heroin. It was available in San Francisco in the 1960s and was popular among jazz musicians. He could have had it if he'd wanted it, though Mountain Girl sternly policed it. She was known to check the arms of visitors to 710 Ashbury, looking for telltale needle tracks.

Garcia first tried heroin thinking it was "Persian opium," a powder and tar that showed up in Dead circles in the mid-1970s. Although it masqueraded as "Persian" or sometimes "Persian white" or "China white" (misleading, since the powder was usually brown), it was in fact heroin. He found that it calmed his rattling brain, helped him to focus in the studio on individual musical tracks. Like many a user before and since, he rationalized his use by refusing to shoot up. Garcia mostly smoked his heroin. "Within a week or so," Bear recalled, "he was addicted."

The precise moment when heroin got its claws into Garcia is difficult to pinpoint, no doubt because he hid it from those around him as long as he could. Scully recalls China white making an appearance during the band's 1974 Europe tour. Owsley places it in 1975 or 1976. But whenever that occurred, it did so with devastating, if delayed, effect.

Even as he began to use heroin, Garcia could still rouse himself to make music. He toured with a jazz group called Legion of Mary, which morphed into the Jerry Garcia Band after a few lineup changes. He helped create two bluegrass albums, *Pistol Packin' Mama* by the Good Old Boys and *Old & In the Way*. He played on other projects developed by members of the Dead and helped as an engineer and producer.

Of those side projects, the Jerry Garcia Band would prove the most durable, offering Garcia an outlet for recording and performance outside the cumbersome demands of the Grateful Dead. Oddly, given its focus on Garcia, he felt less pressure as a member of the Jerry Garcia Band than he did as a member of the Dead. JGB, as it was often known, gave their first performance in Palo Alto in September 1975 and remained intact through the rest of Garcia's life, moving through many lineup changes but always including John Kahn on bass and, for almost its entire tenure, Melvin Seals on keyboards. It had a looser, gospel-meets-reggae feel. It produced some heartfelt rhythm and blues, and it relied on covers more than original material.

JGB was mainly a performance vehicle, booking dates during the Dead's downtime, but it recorded one studio album, and it was one of Garcia's favorites. *Cats Under the Stars* featured "Rubin and Cherise," a shimmering and intimate song. For an obsessive who played music every day but could find the demands of the Dead too much to bear at times, JGB offered Garcia the best of two worlds: maximum creative relaxation with a minimum of logistical entanglement.

As the Dead's performing hiatus stretched through 1975 and into 1976, the other members of the band worked in close promixity while concentrating on their own projects, often with Garcia's help and in various combinations. Lesh and collaborator Ned Lagin turned the sonic explorations that they had performed at Dead shows in 1974 into an album of electronic music, *Seastones,* punctuated with appearances by Garcia, Hart, and David Crosby, among others. The project gobbled up studio time—one bill from January 1975 showed forty hours for $3,000 across four days that month—and the result was adventurous but abstract. Weir had released his first studio album, *Ace,* in 1972—although the album featured his songs, it was performed by the Dead and was, for all intents and purposes, a Grateful Dead album—and he now set about building a studio at his home and equipping it for his own use and that of the Dead. Hart, still at his Novato ranch and now thoroughly reabsorbed in the Grateful Dead family, followed up his 1972 release of *Rolling Thunder* with an album of Eastern-influenced rhythms called *Diga* while also dabbling in other work. Keith and Donna Godchaux recorded *Keith and Donna* at their Stinson Beach home and Wally Heider's San Francisco studios in 1975; Garcia helped produce it. All the while, members of the band kept afloat by drawing upon royalties and issuing themselves advances on future royalties. It was not a recipe for enrichment. In March 1975, Grateful Dead Records reported an operating loss of $80,198.94 for the previous nine months.

Still, the Dead managed, in a limited way, to continue being the Dead. Weir's studio construction occupied much of the early months of the hiatus, and purchase orders show a continual stream of deliveries—switches, buttons, wires, knobs, and "switch craft," all marked to "Weir project" or "Weir studio." It was there, in Weir's Mill Valley home and studio, that the Dead recorded *Blues for Allah*, the only studio album that was entirely created, recorded, and released during the band's hiatus from touring.

The songs were softer, more self-consciously poetic, and some of the music took on an international cast, one song in particular nodding to tunings and structures more Middle Eastern than rock 'n' roll. The album opened with one of Hunter's most evocative lyrics, "Help on the Way." "Paradise waits / on the crest of a wave / her angels in flames," Hunter wrote. He tried out other ideas, offering and striking out a verse built around the idea of a "beautiful lie" and wrapping in a phrase about the "slipknot jig," but he tossed out those ideas as he refined his lyrics. In what remained, Hunter moved through ideas—the angel, fire, blindness and vision—and resolved the piece with a statement that was apropos of the Dead and the culture from which it sprang: "Without love in the dream, it will never come true."

On the album and in performance, the Dead followed "Help on the Way" with an instrumental interlude called "Slipknot!" and then "Franklin's Tower," the three numbers interlocked, with "Help on the Way" and "Franklin's Tower" bridged by the instrumental "Slipknot!" which provided a jamming vehicle within the structure hammered out in Weir's studio, an ascending intensity that built, moved, opened up, and then settled into the rhythm that set the beat and feel of "Franklin's Tower."

Garcia had enjoyed Lou Reed's "Walk on the Wild Side," released in 1972, with its catchy doot-doot-tadoot riff, and it was bouncing around in his head in 1975. As the band fiddled in Weir's studio, that feeling—doo-wop above a reggae undercurrent (brought to the surface years later in Steel Pulse's cover)—gave Hunter's infectious lyric a solid grounding. Garcia sang of "wildflower seed on the sand and stone," transient, ephemeral, vulnerable to the slightest breeze. But that breeze was not to be feared: "May the four winds," Hunter wrote and Garcia sang, "blow you safely home." So, too, with the bell hanging in the tower, children growing to adulthood, the aimlessness of the moment. "If you get confused," the song advised, "listen to the music play."

The finished work of *Blues for Allah* reflected its interior approach, the itching of the band to put down something new and the confused central consciousness of its principal creator. From the haiku-set-to-reggae sound of "Crazy Fingers" to the extended, provocative Middle Eastern vocal of the title track, the album stood out among the Dead's works—its experimentation harked back to *Aoxomoxoa* while its professionalism was more of a piece with *American Beauty*. Complex and yet accessible, it accomplished what the Dead so often struggled to do—capture some essence of the band's vitality in the studio. And in this case it did so with wit, energy, and variety.

The album was guardedly received. Reviewing it for *Rolling Stone*, Billy Altman slathered it in faint praise, welcoming Hart's return to the fold and enjoying the Hunter-Garcia triptych that kicked off the album as well as side 1's more instrumental tracks. Altman, however, was unpersuaded by the chants and live crickets and other embellishments featured on "Blues for Allah" and the rest of side 2. That, he declared, was a "total washout." And yet he rather liked the album overall: "One good side of the Grateful Dead is more good Grateful Dead than I've heard since *American Beauty*," Altman wrote. "Keep your fingers crossed."

The release of *Blues for Allah* was enough to coax the Dead from its hiatus—a break from the break, as it were. The band shuttled across the Golden Gate to the Great American Music Hall to perform the new music to a select group of some six hundred friends, family, and radio station representatives. "The Grateful Dead cordially invite you," the invitations read, "to a rare and important musical performance." The event was set for August 13, 1975, at 9 P.M., ten months since the band had retreated from touring. The performance was recorded and broadcast on FM stations nationally two weeks later over the Metromedia Radio Network.

Bill Graham did not promote the show, but he kicked it off, explaining that he had won the right to appear after a series of coin tosses with Rakow and that he was being paid fifty dollars. Graham then introduced the members of the band one at a time, playing them in and culminating with Garcia, who nimbly dropped into "Help on the Way," opening the show just as the album itself unfolded, sliding into "Slipknot!" and "Franklin's Tower," the first public performance of that trio. As Garcia launched into a short, muscular, and focused jam that jumped off the fretboard immediately after the words "listen to the music play," the audience exulted, generating a warmth that carried through the polished evening, which ended with an extended, meditative, at times a cappella "Blues for Allah," complete with crickets. The performance mixed old favorites and new creations. And it made clear that whatever rustiness they might have felt, whatever distractions pulled them apart, whatever uncertainty or ambivalence undermined their foundation, the Dead were not done.

AND SO the Dead returned—not with great fanfare but rather a slow trickle back to visibility, four shows in 1975, forty-one in 1976, and sixty in 1977, widely considered a banner year in Dead history. Headline writers enjoyed the gift of it. BACK FROM THE DEAD, THE DEAD LIVE AGAIN, and variants thereof were among music publications' favorite quips for 1976. There were a few changes: The Wall of Sound, for one, was gone, mostly sold off in pieces.

The Dead reemerged into mid-1970s America. One foil of the counterculture, Nixon, had been dispatched, sent back to San Clemente to stew in his presidential pardon after resigning the office of the presidency under threat of impeachment. The war in Vietnam was over, its inglorious end itself a victory for that counterculture.

316 | HERE BESIDE THE RISING TIDE

Pundits liked to look for an "end" to the 1960s. The first wave of sixties "endings" had coalesced around Altamont or the Manson murders; another pegged the era's conclusion to the end of the war or the end of Nixon. No matter the date, by the mid-1970s, a change felt afoot. The music, for starters, no longer pulsed with the energy of a rebellious culture. The Captain and Tennille topped the charts, as did Elton John, Glen Campbell, Freddy Fender, and Frankie Valli. Movies, too. *The Towering Inferno*, thrilling and riveting but devoid of much cultural significance, was a box office hit, along with *Earthquake* and *Murder on the Orient Express*.

Books continued to channel the subversive power that now seemed to be waning, perhaps because books took longer to write. Robert Stone, an alumnus of Stegner's writing program who had welcomed Kesey and the Pranksters to New York on their legendary bus trip, published *Dog Soldiers*, his tough-minded passage through Vietnam and drugs and crime, in 1974 and won the National Book Award the following year. Edward Abbey's *The Monkey Wrench Gang* pushed the limits of environmental activism with Hunter Thompson–like fervor. Annie Dillard struck a softer tone but with no less urgent powers of observation with her eye-opening appreciation of her Virginia neighborhood, *Pilgrim at Tinker Creek*, as she and other Americans renewed their relationship to the land.

THE SONGWRITING partnership between Bob Weir and John Perry Barlow was an outgrowth of their childhood friendship, their freewheeling days under the disapproving gaze of teachers and staff at the Fountain Valley School in Colorado. Once they were reunited as adults, they experimented with a couple of tunes and then settled in to take the idea seriously. It was January 1972, and Weir visited Barlow at Barlow's Wyoming ranch, the Bar Cross. "We began with 'Black-Throated Wind,'" Barlow recounted in his 2018 memoir. Barlow sang that song's chorus— "Ah, Mother American Night, I'm lost from the light / Oh, I'm drowning in you"—which he'd written while riding a bus in Nepal. Weir promptly changed the melody, exercising the insistence on editing that had annoyed Hunter. Barlow was more patient. The process continued "like a dental extraction," Barlow said, but the two pushed on, drinking Wild Turkey and composing.

More songs followed over the years: "Looks Like Rain," "Feel Like a Stranger," "Estimated Prophet," "Let It Grow," and "Cassidy" would stand among the Dead's most beloved and frequently played numbers. Others—Barlow contributed some two dozen songs to the Dead's repertoire—stood out for their overt politics, surprising, perhaps, given that Barlow's own political views were more conservative than those of most of the Dead.

"Cassidy" was one of his first contributions, debuting at the same show as the Wall of Sound in 1974. As with much of the Dead's best work, "Cassidy" contained an intimate appreciation inside a larger vision. Barlow wrote it upon meeting one-month-old Cassidy Law, the newborn daughter of Eileen Law, the band's office manager. Encountering little Cassidy for the first time and armed with a chord pattern that Weir had written on the night of her birth—and also with thoughts of Neal Cassady in his head—Barlow put together one of his most moving lyrics. It was easy to imagine little Cassidy as the "child of countless trees . . . child of boundless seas." From there, the song took flight, envisioning the cleansing of scorched earth, the soaring of seabirds, the passing of Neal Cassady, life ending, life beginning: "There he goes, and now here she starts, hear her cry." And then the coda: "Fare thee well now / Let your life proceed by its own design / Nothing to tell now / Let the words be yours, I'm done with mine."

"Cassidy" first appeared on Weir's solo album, *Ace*. With its open and loving feel and a structure that easily accommodated space for a reflective jam, it quickly became a fan and band favorite, played hundreds of times from 1974 to 1995.

Once back on the road, the Dead regained its footing quickly. The early shows were mostly held in smaller venues, giving longtime fans a greater intimacy with the band, a closeness that large theaters had prevented and that the Wall of Sound, while a marvel, had never fully com-

318 | HERE BESIDE THE RISING TIDE

pensated for. Still, the pressure to go big was inexorable—and not just for the Dead. As the counterculture went from intensely focused to accommodating, from militant to more broadly appealing, so, too, did the Dead expand its reach, reluctantly yielding to economic logic: Popularity meant they had to play larger venues to reach their audience. Plus, they needed the money. *The Grateful Dead Movie* had become a money pit, with Garcia laboring for months to edit the film. Hiring the artist Gary Gutierrez to animate the opening sequence finally gave the movie its look—a seven-minute romp of skeletons, deserts, playing cards, spaceships, cops, jail cells, roses, and other Dead iconography that dissolved into the stage at Winterland with the Dead onstage, joyously performing "U.S. Blues" before an ecstatic audience. Gutierrez's magical animation would reverberate beyond the movie itself, expanding the band's visual vocabulary, but it was not until 1977 that the movie made it to theaters—a special and limited release with participating venues outfitted with sound systems capable of giving the music its due.

When it did, it was a hit with Deadheads, and deservedly, presenting the Dead in all its pre-hiatus excitement—the thrill of the crowd, the affection, the precision atop chaos. Donna Jean Godchaux was an eye-catching stage presence, and several sequences caught Rosie McGee, still twirling between the amplifiers, at stage right. The Wall of Sound and crew got their moment in shots taking the audience backstage into the work of loading the Dead into and out of halls, all to the music of "Goin' Down the Road Feeling Bad." At the center of the movie but never its star, Garcia anchored both band and adventure.

In 1976, the Dead played the Beacon Theatre in New York, the Capitol Theatre in Passaic, New Jersey, and the Tower Theater in Upper Darby, Pennsylvania. Back in San Francisco in July, the band played the Orpheum, a lovely, modest space with some two thousand seats. Some of those smaller spots were on the schedule in 1977, too, but they were interspersed with the Philadelphia Spectrum (seating for fifteen thousand plus), the Hartford Civic Center (sixteen thousand), and the Inglewood Forum (seventeen thousand). The spring events in 1977 achieved mythic status—the band's older songs had been reworked to bring Hart back into the lineup, and the sound was crisp.

A Cornell show on May 8 featured the band at a post-hiatus high, all systems firing. Although the Dead of this period did not have the open-ended experimentalism of the "Dark Star" days, there was a new gentleness—an expansiveness of spirit, a receptivity to change, and an appreciation for its own developing tradition. The performances that spring, of which Cornell was a perfect example (a show two weeks later at the Hollywood Sportatorium in Pembroke Pines, Florida, was another), found that warmth. The spring tour was arduous—it was extended more than once, and the promoter John Scher took to calling it the "Grateful Dead Endurance Tour '77"—but it produced a wealth of magic.

The run also restored the Dead to solvency, digging them out from the debt incurred by the movie and the long break from tour revenue. But few things were simple in the life of the Dead, and the ascent came to a screeching halt when Hart slid his Porsche off a dirt road in Half Moon Bay and wound up with a nearly severed ear, broken collarbone, and injured shoulder. Summer shows were canceled, and the Dead went home—Garcia back to solo projects—from June through August.

EVERY ARTIST knows that moment, that pause between the quiet and flash, the hesitation—it can even be a panic—when the brilliance might not be there for the asking. The writer feels it between the blank page and the written word, the painter between the canvas and the first stroke, the lyricist between the idea and the stanza.

"Light the song with sense and color / Hold away despair." Robert Hunter wrote those words while sitting in a vacant San Francisco house during a lightning storm. He asked for words to do it justice, and so he recorded the act of pleading—"a shameless invocation"—to his muse.

The Dead had long sung about themselves, directly or allusively. "Truckin'" was the story of the band on the road. "He's Gone" chronicled either Pigpen's death or Lenny Hart's crime, perhaps both. "New Speedway Boogie" expressed the Dead's conflicted feelings about Altamont and its aftermath. But this was something different. This was writing about the struggle to write, art about artistry.

Few subjects more elicited Hunter's intelligence than that quest, as he eloquently described it in perhaps his most evocative interview, a 1992 conversation with Steve Silberman in which Hunter described his translation of Rilke's *Duino Elegies,* his admiration for Lew Welch (the Beat poet who was, among other things, Huey Lewis's stepfather), and his appreciation for Wallace Stevens and James Joyce ("I was a stoned James Joyce head, *Finnegans Wake* head."). Hunter preferred life as a background character and often stood at the edge of the Dead's very bright limelight, but the Hunter of that interview—the Hunter of *Terrapin Station*—was fiercely, studiously literate. "This band is known for dense subconsciousness," Hunter explained. "A lot of it is the Muse."

Garcia was just a few miles away when Hunter's muse delivered him "Terrapin Station," and Garcia, too, was graced with a bright flash of inspiration. On the morning after the storm had passed, he and Hunter spoke. Hunter said he had a lyric. Garcia said he had music. They had simultaneously produced the suite of music that became the second side of the band's ninth studio album, *Terrapin Station,* released on July 27, 1977.

The album took its name from the terrapin, a turtle that is central to Native American mythology, connecting earth to life, bearing the weight of civilization with sturdy power. The album's cover, another product of the Kelley/Mouse Studio, delivered that concept with levity, as Heinrich Kley's drawing gave one dancing terrapin a banjo and the other a tambourine.

The second side suite was the album's showcase, complementing the solid contributions from Weir and Lesh on its first side, which also featured the band's studio cover of "Dancing in the Street," a Martha and the Vandellas tune that the Dead had been performing since 1966. Weir's "Estimated Prophet" described the mystics and spiritually overwhelmed followers bowled over by the times, a phenomenon he and

Barlow set close to home, most evocatively expressed in their description of California, aflame with magic, mysticism, and culture. "California, preaching on the burning shore," Weir sang above the song's complicated 14/8 time signature, which Kreutzmann helped him perfect. "California, I'll be knocking on the golden door."

Terrapin Station marked the Dead's return to the music industry, in this case Arista, having given their own label a try and having discovered that they were better musicians than record company executives. The album reflected that decision. It sold well and attracted followers—anything the Dead did by that point was assured of a solid reception, at least from its base—but it also was overproduced by Keith Olsen, who had worked with Fleetwood Mac. Olsen introduced an orchestra and choral singers to the *Terrapin* suite, replacing original tracks with the new orchestration. He did so without consulting the band, and they were stunned to hear the initial mix.

Betty Cantor-Jackson, the Dead's legendary soundmaster, was with Garcia when they listened to it for the first time. "I just looked at Jerry and went, 'What the *hell* was that?'" she recalled.

"Keith was real stoked on what he'd done," Weir said. The others were not. Hart called it "one of the most disrespectful things that has ever happened to me, musically." Garcia felt Olsen's additions "screwed up the feel."

Thus commenced a long and frustrating negotiation between the band and its producer. The final album incorporated that compromise, as Olsen dialed down the strings and choral sections, mollifying the band but never fully recapturing the "shuffle" that Garcia wanted for the suite. *Terrapin* was muddled, but then again, so were the Dead in 1977. The suite would find its truer expression in live performances.

ROBERT CHRISTGAU could lay claim—did lay claim—to being the dean of America's rock critics. His columns for *The Village Voice* spanned the rock era and imprinted it with his eloquent taste. He had enjoyed and supported the Dead early on; his 1969 piece for *The New*

322 | HERE BESIDE THE RISING TIDE

York Times had joyfully observed that the band "really did transcend showbiz," and he became a devoted fan. Christgau liked *Terrapin*, though he didn't love it. He called it "The Dead's best studio album since *American Beauty*" but conceded that "it runs a distant second."

But Christgau's faith in the Dead transcended any single album. He, better than most, saw the Grateful Dead's inextricable place in the larger culture. "The Rolling Stones is decadent. The Band doesn't boogie. The Faces are little guys. Grand Funk Railroad is passing crudity," he wrote in 1972, though it was just as true in 1977. "The Grateful Dead is the finest band in the land."

In 1972, Christgau added: "The Dead's gestalt embodied the fundamental Americanness of the so-called counter culture, and so did its music," he continued. "Picking from the melting pot of a collective heritage they then improvised on the pieces. Down-home boys and galaxy trippers, they combined black blues and bluegrass mountain highs, climaxing with long space jams off the tightest, most commercial soul-dance hits. Their devotion to their craft was fierce—they never stopped playing and the people never stopped dancing."

Some of that rapture had worn down five years later, but Christgau caught the Dead at the Palladium in May 1977 and found much of what he'd always loved. "I continued to admire the staunch communalism of Jerry Garcia's countercultural values," he wrote. Christgau worried that the Dead's time had passed, that those values no longer seemed relevant in a meaner culture, and that the band had never fully committed to the vocal part of its performance. He arrived prepared for the worst, and at first he was disappointed, but as the show went on, Christgau smoked a joint and was reinvigorated. "Clearly, not your textbook Great Rock and Roll Band," he acknowledged. "But even [their shortcomings] tend to merge into the Dead's version of the ultimate reality."

LABOR DAY marked the beginning of fall and return to touring, Hart still nursing his injured shoulder. Beaten up but relieved to be back at work, if not exactly at full strength, the Dead straggled into Englishtown, New Jersey. They had been preparing for this event for months, persuading reluctant town leaders to give their blessing, as the fear of "invasion" by rock fans and their drugs now became a predictable aspect of the run-up to any proposed festival, especially one headlined by the Dead. But despite threats of lawsuits and worried residents, the event, which also featured the New Riders and the Marshall Tucker Band, drew 107,000 ticketed audience members. It was the largest gathering in the history of New Jersey, and for many years it held the record for the largest number of ticketed attendees to any concert anywhere. The Dead delivered a thundering performance.

A few months later, in March 1978, Garcia was in the dressing room at the Capitol Theatre in Passaic, New Jersey, where the Jerry Garcia Band was performing. He was chatting with John Kahn and Maria Muldaur when someone knocked. "Come on in," Garcia shouted, and in came a twenty-two-year-old young woman, pretty and lost. Susan Klein was looking for a representative of the band and had stumbled into Garcia's space by mistake. He invited her to stay, and they slipped into conversation "about movies, books, the government, traveling," Klein recalled. Finally, it was time for Garcia to go—he was expected onstage—but he appreciated their talk, called it "the most intelligent conversation I've had in a long time."

That night ended with the flickering of a friendship, and it grew. When the Dead returned to play Giants Stadium on September 2, 1978, Klein was there. She had picked up a gift for Garcia, a dime-store trinket that alluded to their conversation in March. She persuaded a member of the crew to pass it along to Garcia, and a representative of the band came back out to tell her that Garcia hoped she would come backstage after the show so he could thank her for the gift. When she and a friend presented themselves, the gatekeeper stopped them. "No," he said, "just her," meaning Klein.

She and Garcia fell into conversation again, and Garcia marveled at her easiness. "You're not nervous around me," he remarked. "It's a relief."

One conversation led to another, from backstage to the Ramada Inn

324 | HERE BESIDE THE RISING TIDE

where the band was staying. And from there, a romance. They discussed movies and watched cartoons. She gave him a Gabriel García Márquez book, and she marveled at his memory for character actors and bits of art history. Drawn to him but coming from outside the Dead's circle, Klein was surprised and intrigued when he suggested that she move to the Bay Area to be with him. She agreed, and traveled to San Rafael, joining him in the in-law unit at Rock Scully's place.

And there Klein realized the extent of Garcia's drug use. "Rock would bring him heroin," she recalled. "He offered it to me once, and Jerry said no."

For weeks, she cooked and cleaned for Garcia, tending to him as he lived the shrinking life of the addicted. He would practice, record music, eat, doodle on pads and scraps of paper, watch television, sleep, and start again. Klein hovered, touched by him, worried for him, attracted to him. Their relationship would continue, off and on, through the early 1980s.

THE DEAD left East Rutherford, New Jersey, and the show at Giants Stadium for another world. For some time, Lesh and others in and around the Dead had imagined that a spiritual connection bound the American counterculture, especially the San Francisco counterculture, to ancient Egypt. There was a wizened serenity that reached from Bedouin desert to Golden Gate Park, a shared "nonlinear concept of time," as Richard Loren, then the Dead's booking agent, put it. What, then, if those cultures could come together? More to the point, what if the Dead were to play the Pyramids themselves?

To the amazement of the Dead's entourage, the Egyptian government was open to the idea. Egyptian president Anwar Sadat was engaged in peace talks with Israel's Menachem Begin, and Sadat was cultivating relations with the West. Moreover, his wife saw the chance to fundraise around the visit, and the Dead, in a shrewd bit of international diplomacy, offered to support an orphanage and antiquities museum she backed. With something in it for everyone, Lesh, Alan Trist, and Loren met with ambassadors and government officials. Carefully worded diplomatic exchanges followed ("For more than a decade, the Grateful Dead have been building an international reputation in rock and roll, and doing it with none of the antisocial posturing which has characterized much of their competition," Joseph Malone, president of the Middle East Research Associates, wrote to the Egyptian ambassador to the United States). Gradually the idea hardened into a deal. The Dead would play three shows, September 14–16, at the base of the Great Pyramid of Giza. The event would coincide with a lunar eclipse. Blown minds awaited.

The Dead asked Graham to produce the event, but he passed, electing to come merely as a guest. Instead, the band took charge of planning on their own. The Who supplied equipment so the band would not have to lug its gear across the ocean for such a short gig. And word circulated in the Bay Area that Deadheads could hop a plane and join the Dead in Egypt. A few hundred enterprising followers signed on, boarding in San Francisco and deplaning in Cairo.

"Animals roaming; cars honking; kids baksheering; adolescent sports waiting for Ali to regain his title," Ken Kesey, there to join the Dead and record events for *Rolling Stone,* wrote in a letter to his editors, "except for the three huge diesel semis parked in front of the Sphinx, unloading speakers and amps and sound stuff in piles to challenge the size of the big cat itself.

" 'What occurs?' the locals wanted to know.

" 'Rock and roll occurs, my friends. The Dead is going to play for three days in front of the Sphinx while Sadat and Begin wrangle on the other side of the globe and the moon does a full eclipse in the heavens above is what occurs!' "

Kesey and Graham were there. Bill Walton, too. Mountain Girl made the trip, and of course the Dead sound, lighting, and road crews. The Dead "footed the whole bill," as Kesey recalled, hoping to make back the money on an album of the shows.

But they played. On the night of the eclipse, the moon slipped behind the earth and went dark as musicians from nearby Abu Simbel

326 | HERE BESIDE THE RISING TIDE

performed. One by one, members of the Dead replaced them onstage and took over the music as the moon reappeared. Deadheads from California watched from the foot of the stage, Bedouins on camels gazed from the dunes beyond, their cigarettes glowing red in the darkness. It was not a clash so much as a merging of cultures, loud and joyful but also serene and serious.

The music was imperfect. The piano was out of tune, Kreutzmann's drumming was hampered by a cast on his wrist. But it had its sublime moments, as when the chanting performers of Abu Simbel sang out of "Ollin Arageed" and into the Dead's hypnotic "Fire on the Mountain." Garcia, swaying behind the clapping choir members and peering over the top of his glasses, patiently led the music from ancient rhythm to modern melody, from the sands of Egypt to the burning hills of California. It was a moment of cultural completion, "perfection personified," as the Dead historian David Lemieux described it.

Kesey gazed into the desert. "The Nubians are swaying and fading back into the same shadows," Kesey wrote. "Not a cough. The desert itself is entranced."

A correspondent from ABC was similarly moved. "The desert shook," he said, "from the shockwaves of three electric guitars." He signed off his report "in the once-silent desert."

Garcia took the time to consider his place at the foot of one of mankind's great achievements, the mysterious grandeur of the Pyramids. "They dwarf the horizon and they may dwarf us, but this is an event," he said. "Thousands of people, man, all helplessly stoned, all finding themselves with thousands of other people, none of whom any of them were afraid of. It was just magic, far-out, beautiful magic."

The Dead took a financial bath on the event, but not once did the members regret it. It was a triumph of mystery, a connection to the thrumming beat of the ancients, a twining of chords that ran through the ages, from Moses to the Haight. Weir recalled the feeling of stepping "outside the twentieth century," Kreutzmann connected to "the greater spirit of things." Lesh was overcome by the choreography of those nights, the rotation of members of the Dead with the singers from

"ON THE ROAD AGAIN" | 327

Abu Simbel. "Our performance lit a fuse," he wrote, "and myth descended into reality." Lesh then added a sly afterthought: "Let our chant fill the void, that others may know: In the land of the night, the Ship of the Sun is driven across the sky by the Grateful Dead." For years, observers had assumed the Dead got its name from the Egyptian Book of the Dead; now the Dead had reinforced that myth.

The performances themselves segued into a different celebration. Once the Dead had returned home, the band hosted a series of five shows at Winterland. Billed as "From Egypt with Love," the October performances were intended to give San Francisco fans who couldn't make the trip to Egypt a chance to share in the magic of those nights. At Winterland, the Dead played as slides from the desert rolled behind the band.

Garcia never got over it. "For me, it was one of those 'before and after' experiences," he said a few years later. "There's my life before Egypt, and my life after Egypt."

NBC'S *SATURDAY NIGHT LIVE* was the premier comedy and cultural touchstone for live television in the 1970s. *SNL* stood out even in an era of groundbreaking network offerings—Norman Lear's *All in the Family* debuted on CBS in 1971 and was followed by *Sanford and Son* the following year; *M*A*S*H* began in 1972, *The Mary Tyler Moore Show* in 1970. *Saturday Night Live* was in its fourth season in the fall of 1978, and it enjoyed an edgy, counterculture vibe; drugs lurked beneath the surface and swirled around cast members John Belushi, Bill Murray, Jane Curtin, Garrett Morris, Gilda Radner, Dan Aykroyd, and Laraine Newman. The show's humor darted around drugs and rebellion, and that season's lineup also included two "featured players" on the cast, Tom Davis and Al Franken, who were, among other things, devoted fans of the Grateful Dead.

Davis in particular had been lobbying *SNL's* producer, Lorne Michaels, to bring the Dead to the show as a musical guest, but Michaels resisted, saying he felt the Dead were passé, creatures of the sixties.

Davis kept after him, and Michaels eventually relented. Invited to appear, Garcia was nonplussed, having not paid much attention to the show, but Hart and Kreutzmann were thrilled and prevailed on the band to accept. The Dead's appearance was set for November 11, with the writer and comedian Buck Henry slated to host.

The Dead were both difficult and graceful guests. Franken enjoyed Garcia's deadpan humor and easygoing connection with cast and crew. Producers were less thrilled by his intransigent refusal to be impressed by television. During rehearsal, the show's director tried to plot out Garcia's movements so that the camera could track him. Garcia insisted on playing the song differently each time and wandered about the stage without concern for camera angles. "Don't you want to be on camera?" the director asked. "Not particularly," Garcia responded.

And yet, when the time came to go live, Garcia hit every one of his marks, stepping into the role and into a more national spotlight than the band had ever enjoyed.

The Dead performed "Casey Jones" with full-throated fun, and Garcia practically mugged for the camera. Donna Godchaux got her share of airtime, and Weir was at his full, handsome best. When the Dead returned for its second number of the show, the band performed a condensed combo of "I Need a Miracle" and "Good Lovin'." Rarely had the Dead turned in three such short songs before a live audience, but TV demanded brevity, and Garcia proved that even he could live within the strictures of NBC's rules. Their appearance was a hit.

Garcia stayed late at the afterparty, then made his way to Susan Klein's. As the sun rose in New York, they watched cartoons on TV.

THE SUMMER and fall of 1978 were rough for California. The state's political scene was forever punishing, and the early 1970s had seen the center of political energy move away from Reagan and toward the son of the man Reagan beat in 1966. The Brown this time was Jerry Brown, but he was no chip off his father's block.

Raised Catholic in San Francisco, little Jerry Brown grew up not far from little Jerry Garcia, but they moved in different worlds. While Jerry Garcia was roaming the San Francisco hills and experimenting with marijuana, Jerry Brown, four years older, was the son of the city's district attorney and dreaming of the priesthood. After graduating from high school, Brown attended Santa Clara University, then moved to a Jesuit seminary in Los Gatos. He took his religious studies seriously but eventually reconsidered. He dropped out in 1960 and headed straight for North Beach in San Francisco to get a glimpse of the world that had been coming alive without him.

Brown's iconoclasm would confuse pundits in later years, causing him often to be mischaracterized, either as a conventional liberal in the mold of his father or as a New Age counterculture figure more like Jerry Garcia. He was neither. His chosen field of politics was one of alliances and parties and relationships, but Brown was his own person, unmoored to the mainstream of the Democratic Party and unstructured by marriage, though his girlfriend for much of the 1970s connected him to the music industry, as he famously dated Linda Ronstadt.

Brown had no sooner landed the governorship of California than he imagined himself as president, and in 1976 he waged a flippant bid for that office, casually throwing his hat into the ring after the contest was under way. Brown did surprisingly well, but his presidential ambitions were thwarted by Jimmy Carter, and he returned to California to stand for reelection in 1978. He swept a hapless Democratic field on the June primary ballot, tallying 77 percent of the votes cast.

But the real story of that election was the passage of Proposition 13, the revolutionary tax initiative that reset the foundations of California's politics. Prop 13 reduced property taxes and kept them low—that was its lasting impact on California. Its message to the nation was of something larger and more portentous. It signaled an unhappy electorate, and it triggered what is sometimes known in politics as a "wildfire." California taxpayers were fed up. They acted outside the government and lowered their own taxes, a blaze lit by anger and self-interest. The

330 | HERE BESIDE THE RISING TIDE

1980s had not yet begun on the calendar, but the decade's politics, with its explicit rejection of the counterculture's values, was launched in 1978 in California.

An even more devastating blow came just months later. Communes were an important expression—and test—of the counterculture's values. They had always stood on the edge of the movement, a refuge and challenge for the truly committed. But the more tolerant members of the mainstream had found accommodation with them. The tolerance was so central to San Francisco's sense of itself from the 1960s onward that it extended to an unwillingness to confront exotic religious practices, effectively giving safe harbor to cults. One of those that flourished in San Francisco's atmosphere of political liberalism and religious tolerance was the Peoples Temple, under the leadership of the darkly engaging Jim Jones.

JONES HAD cut a swath through San Francisco politics in the mid-1970s, never directly engaging Garcia or the Dead, but traveling in overlapping circles and even venues—the temple was headquartered for a time at 1859 Geary Boulevard, next door to the old Fillmore, where the Dead often performed. Jones supported liberal politicians, backed liberal causes, offered his congregation in support of community projects.

Jones dreamed of creating a faraway sanctuary, a commune removed from the increasingly demanding questions of relatives whose loved ones had disappeared inside the Peoples Temple. He founded his commune in Guyana. He called it, of course, Jonestown.

Representative Leo Ryan, a congressman from San Mateo, visited Jonestown on November 17. The next day, twenty-six members of the temple accepted his offer to return to the United States with him. That touched off panic within the temple's leadership. One member jumped at the congressman, thrusting a knife at Ryan's throat and cutting himself in the process. Ryan's shirt was dotted with blood. The delegation hurried back to the airstrip with the defectors in tow, but Jones and his followers concluded that they could not afford to let them go. They attacked, killing Ryan and four others and wounding ten more. Jones then ordered the destruction of his temple.

Within days, the world knew the full horror of what happened: 913 Temple members—men, women, and children—died, most after drinking a cyanide-laced punch in an act of "revolutionary suicide" (a term pilfered from Huey Newton and distorted beyond recognition), others as the result of gunfire. Jones himself lay among the dead, killed by a gunshot, though who fired that bullet remains to this day a mystery.

The reverberations of Jonestown were international, and they hit most powerfully in San Francisco. The city shuddered in the days following it, riddled not only with grief but also with fear, as rumors of retaliation, of Temple repercussions, raced through the city's leadership.

Jonestown was a murder, a suicide, and a calamity at the outer edges of nightmare. It spoke to the terrifying power of a madman and to the alarming devotion of his flock. And in that, it accelerated the collapse of an idea: The very notion of peaceful communal living buckled under the weight of the bodies in the jungle. Once heralded by those who lived it and tolerated by those outside it, now the commune took on overtones of capture and death. A ribbon of history that stretched from native peoples through the communes of California, through the Dead's own summer home in Olompali, dissolved in the flavored punch of the Guyanese jungle.

It was no wonder, then, that the next tragedy would at first be linked to that one. The climactic event in San Francisco's season of grief—in California's year of struggle—unfolded in the early morning of November 27, less than two weeks after the mass murder-suicides of Jonestown. County Supervisor Dan White had resigned his position, complaining that he could not afford to devote time to it. White then thought again and decided he wanted to keep the job, placing Mayor George Moscone in the uncomfortable position of having to consider White's request to stay. For Moscone, White's departure was a political blessing, as it removed a conservative obstacle to Moscone's plans for change; bolstered by Supervisor Harvey Milk, a liberal ally. Moscone rejected White's request.

On the morning of the twenty-seventh, White was dropped off at

332 | HERE BESIDE THE RISING TIDE

City Hall by a friend, and he sneaked into the building through a basement window to avoid passing through a metal detector that would have picked up the loaded .38 special he hid beneath his jacket. White marched through the corridors to Moscone's office, brushing past Willie Brown, then a state assemblyman, as he left. Moscone invited White in despite the intrusion, and White shot him, first in the shoulder and chest and then, standing over him, two more times in the head. White then reloaded and headed for Milk's office. Supervisor Dianne Feinstein saw White in the hall and called for him, but he ignored her. He pushed his way into Milk's office and shot him five times, then fled.

Feinstein heard the snap of gunshots in the marble halls and rushed to Milk's office. She felt for a pulse, and her finger slipped inside a bullet wound. She knew. "There's no mistaking dead," she said decades later.

The dual assassinations sent San Francisco and California reeling. To many, it seemed that the Peoples Temple was to blame. The killings became even more unfathomable when it became clear that the perpetrator was a fellow supervisor. Feinstein's great contribution, the one that would seal loyalty to her across the years to come, was her calm comportment in those terrifying days. Succeeding Moscone as mayor, she firmly restored order to San Francisco, but it was a tenuous stability. It could seem in that fateful year that California was reaping some sort of karmic consequence, that the license of the 1960s was being repaid in anger and violence, that the social compact once hatched in the Haight—one of common purpose and kindness—was now defunct.

The frailty of that hard-won peace was highlighted the following year when, after White was convicted of mere voluntary manslaughter, violence erupted in San Francisco's gay community; police responded with their own pent-up fury. The White Night riots left more than a hundred people hurt and sealed the animus between San Francisco police and gay residents. It seemed the harbinger of a more hateful and dangerous era.

SAN FRANCISCO staggered through the holidays. Public gatherings were draped in fear and sadness, a hollow Christmas season in a city generally festooned with color and light at the holidays. Even the Dead's final performance of the year was one of farewell, of closing the timeworn, now shabby Winterland rather than opening something new. It took effort to summon joy, but the chance to celebrate was welcome.

The Dead were joined by the New Riders and their new *SNL* pals, the Blues Brothers, who opened the show and who introduced Graham for his New Year's entrance. "Ladies and gentlemen, yes!" Dan Aykroyd announced, his unmistakable bellow greeting the bearded figure of Father Time, suspended above the audience, gliding across the theater, tossing flowers from the cockpit of a long white tube with a glowing red dot where a headlight would be. "A momentous occasion!" Aykroyd continued. "As we cruise into the 1980s, here at Winterland in San Francisco, 1978 going on 1981, what you see before you is a ten—no, wait, twelve-foot-long burning ember of marijuana! Yes, let us begin the countdown: Five, four, three, two, two and a half, two minus one quarter, one. Happy New Year! Ladies and gentlemen! Happy New Year!"

Balloons dropped from the ceiling. Mirrored balls illuminated the audience in fractals. Graham disembarked from his gliding joint. The Dead kicked into "Sugar Magnolia" and then "Scarlet Begonias," which started bouncingly and then dropped into a thoughtful musical interpolation, Donna Godchaux scatting for a bit, Lesh wandering away on the bass, Garcia guiding with a light, jazzy lead. The hometown crowd delighted, and Garcia grinned broadly behind dark glasses and beneath an even shaggier than usual head of hair. "Everybody's playing," he sang, "in the heart-of-gold band."

The Dead gave Winterland the send-off it deserved that night, putting in three full sets, more than six hours of music. The band resuscitated "Dark Star" for the first time since 1974 and concluded with "And We Bid You Goodnight."

It was approaching dawn by the time they left the stage and Graham returned. He thanked the crowd and the Dead's crew, and he closed out the "wonderful love affair . . . with this building."

Before leaving, though, Graham served breakfast to all those who remained. "You can stay as long as you like," he said.

PART IV

LIMITS

The Reagan presidency ushered in an era of conservatism in Washington, while others took refuge. Here, fans rejoice. Greek Theatre, Berkeley, California, 1986.

Jay Blakesberg/Retro Photo Archive

CHAPTER 15

Safe Harbor

THE DEAD'S OLD SHADOW NEMESIS, RONALD REAGAN, WAS still kicking. By 1980, he had recovered from his narrow loss to Gerald Ford in the fight for the 1976 Republican nomination, and he was America's preeminent conservative, poised to claim the White House after Jimmy Carter had spent four years presiding over a nation that felt bad about itself.

Reagan's argument for himself plumbed deep American themes, thicker political blood than is spilled in most presidential elections. He reached back beyond Richard Nixon and Gerald Ford and drew on the energy of a movement that repelled Eisenhower; Reagan was cut from Goldwater cloth, and the concussive collapse of the party's center around Watergate had, in one sense, purified the brand. Extremism was abhorrent to Ike and tactically unsound to Nixon and Ford, but to Goldwater—and now Reagan—it was justified. In defense of liberty, it was "no vice," as Goldwater had insisted. Extremism survived the fall of Nixon and the ouster of Ford. It returned with Reagan.

As he clawed past the party's surviving moderates, notably George H. W. Bush, in 1979, the former governor of California advanced a narrower, older, harder view of the party and nation. He sought not just the rejection of a president but the discarding of an idea—that government was good and there to serve. No, said Reagan. "Government," he argued, "is never more dangerous than when our desire to have it help us blinds us to its great power to harm us."

Reagan's immediate task was to shove aside Carter, and Carter gave him plenty to work with. Although Carter had a slightly hip patina—the Allman Brothers were early and helpful supporters—his presidency had been rocky. He had presided over inflation and an oil crisis; the Soviet invasion of Afghanistan and subsequent American boycott of the 1980 Summer Olympics; and then, in its final year, the protracted hostage crisis in Iran. Reagan had dismantled Pat Brown as the failed head of a lost state; now he turned that same energy—and essentially that same message—against Carter. Reagan appealed to a new—or rather, an old—set of values that the counterculture had battered but clearly had not driven from the field. To Reagan, civil rights, the peace movement, and environmental protection, to name just three counterculture causes, were distractions from the reassertion of strength and individualism, the restoration of family, the recognition of hard work. Reagan spoke for those who were tired of hearing those notions questioned and belittled. He offered a return to them—even if that meant a return to a country that had never really existed at all, a cinema version of stalwart values extruded from movie Westerns and evocations of a mythic American past.

Accepting the Republican nomination in Detroit on July 17, 1980, Reagan accused Democrats of letting America down, of giving up on its future. "They say that the United States has had its day in the sun; that our nation has passed its zenith. They expect you to tell your children that the American people no longer have the will to cope with their problems; that the future will be one of sacrifice and few opportunities," Reagan, in full disapproval, intoned. "I will not stand by and watch this great country destroy itself."

If those sounded like the words of a man running against the Free Speech Movement and the Watts riots, that's because they were, even if some of the targets had moved. This was 1980, not 1960, and in the intervening generation, freedom—thanks in no small part to Jerry Garcia and the Grateful Dead—had become associated with licentiousness, freedom from care and responsibility. As Reagan accepted his party's nomination in 1980, he framed the idea of freedom in the language of escape—freedom from tyranny and persecution, not the positive freedoms of expression or action.

"Can we doubt," Reagan suggested, "that only a Divine Providence placed this land, this island of freedom, here as a refuge for all those people in the world who yearn to breathe freely: Jews and Christians enduring persecution behind the Iron Curtain, the boat people of Southeast Asia, of Cuba and Haiti, the victims of drought and famine in Africa, the freedom fighters of Afghanistan and our own countrymen held in savage captivity?"

Against the flailing Carter—and especially against the backdrop of the hostage crisis in Tehran—Reagan's freedom carried the day. He won a landslide victory in the fall of 1980, carrying all but a small handful of states and racking up the largest Electoral College victory by any nonincumbent ever to seek the office.

Reagan's America began on January 20, 1981.

But what of those who did not share Reagan's enthusiasm for individualism? What lay in store for those who treasured the environment or demanded racial equity and relied on the government to marshal those priorities? Or for those who drew nourishment from communities of love and kinship? Who abhorred nuclear weapons and life under their shadow? Or sought peace in Eastern religious practices or health in organic foods? Or, dare one ask, for those who found enlightenment or fun in drugs?

The counterculture had created space for those ideas, had allowed them to flourish and introduced them to one another. Now the mainstream culture not only turned away from those communities, it turned against them. Bond traders and real estate magnates were the new celebrities, pockets full of coke, disco their soundtrack as they piled into Studio 54.

For those appalled by that turn of values, the options were vanishingly small. One of them, however, was the Dead.

* * *

340 | HERE BESIDE THE RISING TIDE

THE DEAD had staggered to the end of the 1970s. The experiment with running their own music label having spent itself, the band was back to recording for others. *Terrapin* was successful, though compromised by Olsen and Arista. *Shakedown Street,* released near the end of 1978, was largely a disappointment.

More frightening was Garcia's deepening withdrawal into heroin, which pulled him away from company and contact. He would hole up at Rock Scully's house on Hepburn Heights Road in San Rafael and refuse efforts to draw him out, living "like a badger," one friend said.

Still, he surfaced and found joy in the world. He enjoyed movies and comics, and he could jump into any conversation about the Golden Age of Hollywood. He admired the films of Preston Sturges, spoke knowledgeably about the comedic character actors who patrolled the margins of great films. Franklin Pangborn, Eric Blore, and Alastair Sim were among his favorites. He considered *Duel,* an early Spielberg film, a dark classic, its themes of persecution and its setting on the road seeming to register with a man who spent so much of his life away from home. And he raptly, nervously absorbed Nicolas Roeg's *Don't Look Now,* which he watched with Susan Klein at Hepburn Heights one summer night in 1979. The movie opens with a drowning, which landed powerfully with Garcia, for whom the drowning of his father and the incident at Olompali rested heavy. It was "a theme and a trigger," Klein recalled. When the movie ended, Garcia breathed a heavy sigh.

Onstage and in the studio, Garcia's performances remained strong, and his compulsion to play pulled him in various directions and projects. As a result, it was hard to discern his troubles from afar, even as his personal well-being slipped away.

And Garcia was comparatively experienced. Less fortified to handle drugs along with the pressures of being in the Dead were Donna Jean and Keith Godchaux, whose troubles were mounting. They were often volatile on the road, openly fighting, smashing their cars during one episode, lighting a hotel room on fire during another. During the recording sessions for *Terrapin Station,* Keith sank deeper and deeper. Donna's singing, often a source of irritation to Dead fans, was growing increasingly shrill, and Keith's playing, once magical, was slipping away; his timing was off, his torpor sapped the energy from his sound, and he fell into the lazy habit of mimicking Garcia's leads, "a tic that began to irritate Jerry no end," as Lesh wrote.

Confrontation was never the Dead's strong suit—an aversion to authority that sprang from Garcia's almost pathological refusal to lead—but members of the band resolved to boot the Godchauxs. Luckily for them, the couple had decided on their own that it was time to go. A meeting of the band resolved the matter, as Donna and Keith agreed to leave. On February 17, 1979, the couple played their last show with the Grateful Dead, a Rock for Life benefit to address environmental pollution. Sponsored by the Campaign for Economic Democracy, it featured Tom Hayden and Jane Fonda, among others.

Donna Jean was subdued through the evening, even during "From the Heart of Me," the smallish, never popular number that featured her on lead vocals. At the edge of the stage, Keith was almost mute.

When the Dead returned to touring in April, it was with a new, young face at the keyboards. Brent Mydland, a native of Germany and son of a Norwegian Army chaplain, already knew Weir from playing with Bobby and the Midnites. With Keith gone, Brent slid into that spot and added his voice to the changing band. Keith and Donna formed their own group, the Heart of Gold Band, but its life was cut short along with Keith's. He died in a car accident the following year.

THE DEAD did not ask to be the oasis of the counterculture in the Reagan era, but that's what they became, by devotion and default. The music of the period was mixed. Michael Jackson was the decade's biggest musical star, and the popularity of heavy metal and New Wave did little to spark the imagination, though punk and the early stirrings of hip-hop suggested something more meaningful. Others brought energy, excitement, expertise, brilliance. Prince leaped to attention with his spellbinding guitar playing and fusion of funk and rock. Talking Heads and the Clash entered the 1980s with fan bases built in the previous decade. REM, Dire Straits, U2, Madonna, and the Smiths all attracted serious and devoted followings.

What set the Dead apart was that the Dead brought history and values as well. Some fans came to the Dead just to party, of course, but others arrived in search of connection, their hearts open and their irony parked. They found a community of like-minded souls. They discovered the music but also one another, sometimes only realizing how much they had craved connection once they had discovered it.

Politics moved in the opposite direction. It coalesced around Reagan, who not only animated the Republican Party but also defanged Democrats; soon, Washington wisdom solidified around the agreement that government had to get smaller, while the arguments turned to ways to accomplish that. The New Deal, the Great Society, the ambitions of an energetic common enterprise to relieve suffering, faded against the crass consensus that, in the lexicon of the era, "greed is good."

It did not greatly concern Garcia that many people rejected the music and life presented by the Dead. The Dead had their community, and that community knew what it liked. Garcia did not require mass acceptance, just room to play and support enough to do it. For that, devoted fans were more important than legions of them. As Garcia memorably put it in 1983: "Not everybody likes licorice, but the people who like licorice really like licorice."

And so those craving licorice found the factory. And, paradoxically, that catapulted the Dead to new heights of popularity, as those deflated by Reagan's vision of America found its antithesis in the Grateful Dead. The crowd grew and broadened, much like the counterculture itself. The road now was not just for young adults in minivans, sleeping outside and making their way by selling macrobiotic burritos. The Dead were playing at attractive venues, and old fans who had once seen them as students returned, staying in hotels, making shows into opportunities to reconnect. Some brought their children. A warm, appreciative air suffused the Dead's surrounding culture, as fans fled Reagan and were delighted to find the lights on at home.

SAFE HARBOR | 343

* * *

POLITICS IN the early stages of Ronald Reagan's presidency was hard and mean-spirited—and intentionally so. With Reagan only recently recovered from an assassination attempt in March 1981, the nation's air traffic controllers demanded raises. Reagan refused. On August 3, 1981, they went on strike. Of those members of the union who joined the walkout, Reagan announced, "They are in violation of the law, and if they do not report for work within forty-eight hours, they have forfeited their jobs and will be terminated." Two days later, Reagan, a lifetime member and former head of the Screen Actors Guild, fired 11,345 air traffic controllers. Reagan's hard-line cred was established.

For the Dead, it was a period of excitement. After the dispiriting saga of Keith Godchaux's decline, Mydland brought vitality and a voice to the band. He may not have had Godchaux's delicate keyboard mastery, but he projected a bigger personality. The band played more than eighty shows in 1980 and that many again in 1981, including fourteen performances in Europe—Amsterdam, London, Paris, Copenhagen, Munich, Rüsselsheim, and Barcelona. Shows consistently sold out.

In every respect, this was a musical ensemble that offered an alternative to greed and artifice. The Dead represented improvisation over formula, authenticity over artifice, deep water rather than the comfort of the shore. And though they avoided partisan politics, the Dead stood squarely in opposition to Reagan. Reagan proposed to build up American defenses; the Dead joined Joan Baez to "dance for disarmament." Reagan cut federal support for healthcare, education, and the arts; the Dead played for the Jack Kerouac School of Disembodied Poetics at Naropa University, the Marin Act of San Rafael, the Haight Ashbury Free Clinics, and the American Friends Service Committee. Garcia was beyond being opposed to Reagan. He was contemptuous of him. "We [are] embarrassed by the guy," he said. "He wasn't even a good actor."

Those who were drawn to the Grateful Dead did not imagine they were frontally challenging Reagan's America by attending a concert or even by traveling with the band. They were instead moving outside that America and inhabiting a country of their own. "Nobody ever said that that was going out of existence," Garcia said when an interviewer asked him about "the dark side, with Ronald Reagan."

"The world is still going along basically believing the same lame shit that it believed in the fifties and forties and whatever," Garcia said. "But that's their problem."

Not entirely. Garcia understood that the Dead was becoming more of an outlier and—by dint just of that—something of a threat. "I have a feeling this whole Reagan era means a tightening down from the top," he told one interviewer. "The world is still not that safe for people like us."

And yet the Dead remained steadfast. "Our reality and our continuity have been pretty much the same," Garcia said. The band's standing was built on a relationship with their audience that contained elements of trust and confidence, a shared embrace of formlessness. The Dead's musical commitment was to improvisation. Their core value, as always, was freedom. In and around the Dead, greed was deplored, showiness frowned upon, glibness regarded with skepticism. At a time when reality seemed sharp and capable of cruel caprice, the Dead dwelled in humility and was open to magic.

Even optimism flourished. "Anything you can believe in and focus your attention on and put your whole self into will work," Garcia said. "It's only a matter of time."

For Garcia, the essence of the Dead's place amid this cultural confusion was outside it. Arguing for something close to the idea that counterculture exists to displace, rather than replace, mainstream culture, Garcia recognized that the Dead stood apart. "We're really not quite in that whole world as it's presently constructed," Garcia told interviewers Blair Jackson and David Gans in 1981. "We're like the exception to every rule."

Asking about the Dead's place in the larger human experience, one cluttered with cults and politics, Garcia's interviewers suggested that the band deserved recognition as a "minor movement in the history of mankind." "Yeah," Garcia responded. "We're in there somewhere."

"You're more than a footnote," they persisted. "Oh jeez," he replied. "That's a relief. I thought I was going to have to go out and shoot a politician."

JERRY GARCIA and Mountain Girl had been together, off and on, for more than a decade by the time the 1980s rolled in. They loved each other, in their fashion, but lived almost entirely apart, she in Oregon with their daughters, he at Hepburn Heights in San Rafael. She visited him and worried at what she saw, his fraying edges, his worsening isolation. The formality of marriage had never mattered much to either of them, but Jerry's fragile condition alerted Mountain Girl to the possibility that she might soon be genuinely without him. She was blunt. "Look, you know you're probably going to croak here," she told him. "I would feel better if we were married."

He agreed, and the two formalized a relationship that had stretched from the humble cleanup of an Acid Test to the ever growing fame of the world-famous Grateful Dead. With tax issues also on their minds, they decided it was best to record the marriage before the end of 1981. They waited until the last possible moment.

It was backstage on New Year's Eve 1981. The Dead were joined that evening by Joan Baez, giving the event a family feel. Backstage, Garcia warmed up, Mountain Girl at his side. "He played this thing on the guitar for me," she said, "and it was so beautiful that it would have melted a stone."

Baez opened the show that night, with the Dead backing her. During the break, as the stage was being reset for the Dead to take up its New Year's duties, the band and others retreated to their dressing rooms. Mountain Girl was waiting. A Buddhist monk performed the marriage ceremony, delivering the vows in Tibetan. Mountain Girl laughed, unable to follow a word he was saying. Their daughters, now ages eleven and seven, looked on, bewildered but touched.

The Dead took the stage a few minutes later. Weir sang the first few numbers. Then it was Garcia's time to step forward. He led with "Cold

Rain and Snow." Its opening lines: "Well, I married me a wife, she's been trouble all my life / Run me out in the cold rain and snow." It rained that night and for several thereafter. When the weather cleared, Mountain Girl headed back to Oregon. Jerry would visit now and again, and she would come see him, but their separate lives resumed. "We got married," she said, "and it didn't make a damned bit of difference."

THESE TIMES summoned some to panic, some to surrender, and some to action. Popular musicians were beseeched to join this cause or another. The Dead were an appealing ask—their values identified them as the antithesis of Reagan, so his opponents often turned to them. They were besieged with requests to appear at one event or another, and they were torn between the impulse to help and the sense of being overwhelmed. That dilemma was crystallized in 1982, when the Dead joined Jefferson Starship, Country Joe McDonald, and Boz Scaggs at San Francisco's Moscone Center, named for the assassinated mayor, for an event to benefit the Vietnam Veterans Project.

Garcia happily accepted the invitation, which allowed the Dead and the other bands to draw a distinction between their opposition to the war and their support for those who fought it. "We were the soundtrack for the war," he said a few days before the event. "We all know Vietnam vets personally, and we're glad to do anything to help."

The Moscone Center had never hosted a rock concert, and planning the event was complicated. But it was the aftermath that was most distressing. Some twenty thousand people attended, so there should have been plenty of gate money, but many of the participants scrambled to cover their costs, and the cash seemed to disappear. The promoters later had trouble tracking down where the money had gone and how much had made its way to veterans. Big business was bad enough, Garcia fumed; big charity was even worse.

In 1983, the Dead squared their desire to give with their aversion to big charity by forming their own philanthropic arm, later naming it for Rex Jackson, a treasured member of the band's crew who had died in a car accident in September 1976. Prodded by its longtime adviser, manager, and spiritual goad, Danny Rifkin, the band funded the Rex Foundation by designating certain concerts as benefits and earmarking the money from those shows for a specific charity, which then identified recipients for its grants.

The foundation avoided politics as such and candidates altogether. Instead, it looked for recipients who offered promising ideas in culture, the arts, and community. Most recipients came to the foundation through the Dead family—band members, spouses, or friends would suggest an organization in need, and the foundation would consider it. Some of the choices were difficult and grew out of that family's diverse interests. "How do you choose between redwoods and blindness?" asked Cameron Sears, later to become the Dead's manager and, after that, executive director of the foundation.

Like the band, the foundation was grounded in the culture of San Francisco. Recipients worked in community improvement, respect for individual rights, ancient wisdom. Over time, the foundation grew and its work steadily expanded, extending the Dead further and further into the work of the world and the expression of values fundamental to the counterculture. The foundation would outlive the Dead itself, its work radiating across generations of men and women looking to make their society better, sometimes in the midst of a society getting worse.

THESE WERE days of dread—of the threat of nuclear war and environmental catastrophe, of conflict and uncertainty. The novelist Don DeLillo channeled that dread. His work scoured the depths of bleak humor, wasted possibility, and dark portent, themes and tones unacknowledged by Reagan but simmering beneath the nation's sunny political culture. DeLillo published *White Noise* in 1985, its story fictionalized from American life in the first part of the decade.

Its protagonist, Jack Gladney, is the founder of Hitler studies at the College-on-the-Hill. Gladney does not speak German, a fact he has hidden from his colleagues, and he is secretly taking lessons in preparation

348 | HERE BESIDE THE RISING TIDE

for a conference. Gladney and his wife, the "tall and fairly ample" Babette, live with their children, the collected offspring of various marriages, at the edge of campus. Seemingly guileless, Babette is secretly taking an experimental medication called Dylar to ward off the fear of death. Jack and Babette shop at the local supermarket, traverse their town and studies, see patterns, imagine themselves existing in codes and understandings, swim in streams of data and television.

And then a railcar derailment at the edge of town creates a spill. At first the radio describes it as a "feathery plume," then as a "black billowing cloud," and finally as an "Airborne Toxic Event." It bears down on their home.

At its most basic level, *White Noise* is a work of counterculture. Not because DeLillo was a hippie or a radical, but because he refused to accept the premises of his time and stood ardently in opposition to power. He skewered the pretensions of the academy and mocked the pablum and bland reassurances of the government. He asked the questions beneath the answers. Why should civilization live under a cloud of dread, an "airborne toxic event" borne on the breeze of a Canadian cold front?

DeLillo challenged society's acquiescence to that reality, as candidly and authentically as Vonnegut had done. DeLillo did not identify the source of that malaise as the "technocracy," as had Roszak, but the forces of rationalism created their own misshapen logic, just as Roszak had argued. DeLillo crusaded without the fanfare of a Hunter Thompson. He was more subtle, more incisive, and he dissected the assumptions of a society that preferred not to question them. In years to come, DeLillo would write of baseball and nuclear war, crowds and the Kennedy assassination. Through his work ran a cool contemplation of danger. He wrote of dread in a time of dread.

LIKE THE Reagan presidency, the Dead's decade was divided in two—Reagan's by his reelection, the Dead's by Garcia's crash. In the before time, the Dead performed some of its most sparkling shows; 1981 stood out for the freshness of Mydland's keyboards, Garcia's elegant guitar work, and Weir's increasingly assertive stage presence. Starting in September 1981, the band added the Greek Theatre on the UC Berkeley campus to its list of regular stops—after performing there once in 1967 and once in 1968, the Dead did not return until 1981, and then they played thirty-one shows there through 1989. It became an oasis within an oasis, a regular return to home and a cozy outdoor venue. For many followers of the band, it was a warm time, a feeling of closeness and community not just with the band but with one another.

It came through in the music, though sporadically. In the short run, Garcia's addiction seemed not to interfere with his musical communication. His voice grew more gravelly and more soulful, and his isolation removed the distractions of human life—to the detriment of his relationships but in some ways to the benefit of his artistry. He plunged deeper and deeper into guitar work, strengthening his technical command and expanding his range.

In 1981, the Dead marked the band's fifteenth anniversary and released a double set of double albums, *Reckoning* and *Dead Set,* recorded in the fall of 1980 at acoustic and electric sets at the Warfield Theatre in San Francisco and New York's Radio City Music Hall. From covering Elizabeth Cotten's "Oh, Babe, It Ain't No Lie," to embracing the audience with the unifying "Ripple," the acoustic sets were full and loving. During one of the Dead's performances of "Ripple" at the Warfield, Weir's dog walked across the stage. "That's Otis," Garcia said, a remark that made its way to vinyl on the *Reckoning* album. It was a family gathering.

The electric follow-ups featured a louder, more rambunctious Dead, and that, too, sent a signal—of indomitability, devotion to purpose, unwillingness to give up when so much around them had surrendered. The albums, together and singly, rang clearly of the Dead's integrity and resilience, a welcoming message to those in search of refuge.

Sadly, the shining performances and appreciative audiences of the early 1980s did not lift Garcia's spirits sufficiently to draw him out of his drug use. He was separated from Mountain Girl and his daughters.

350 | HERE BESIDE THE RISING TIDE

They would visit—or he would spend a few days with them in Oregon—and they would enjoy one another. But the drugs were never far away. Trixie, still a young girl, watched in puzzlement as he scraped bits of heroin off scraps of foil. Deeper and deeper he fell, shuffling through girlfriends and retreating to a dirty lair, nodding off to sleep as burning embers of heroin fell to his chest, singeing his beard and countless sweatshirts. He had not spoken with Sara or Heather in years. Klein saw him wither and could not take it anymore; she and Garcia separated for good. Garcia's finances fell into disarray as well. He was regularly paying $15,000 to $20,000 in penalties and interest on payroll and income taxes, a situation that dragged on year after year.

He had money, but it flowed through him without much discernible effect on his way of living. He and Mountain Girl sold the Stinson Beach house, and he holed up in the downstairs apartment of Rock Scully's home in San Rafael. That made drugs convenient—he and Scully used heroin together—and drew Garcia further away from the company of others. He and Scully were "easily doing $700 a day of this stuff. A gram costs $700, and it never sees the end of the day." On the road, Garcia despoiled hotel rooms, setting off smoke alarms when scraps of burning dope ignited seat cushions and blankets. Getting high went from a joy to a preoccupation to an obsession. As Scully put it, "Dope is now our major concern on the road."

People outside his closest circle began to notice. He was slovenly and smelled awful. His beard was pocked, his eyes sunken, his face swollen and puffy. His feet and ankles swelled to the point that he had to cut open the cuffs of his pants to get his feet through. "The Persian," Scully wrote, "obliterates everything from our lives."

By the middle of the decade, even audiences could see that something was wrong. One astute Deadhead, looking back on those years, called it the era of the "Desperate Dead," as the band could be sublime or ragged, sometimes veering wildly between those poles. Robert Greenfield, who wrote extensively about the Dead, recalled a benefit performance in September 1984 at the Marin Civic Center. "Jerry," he said, "looked awful that night. Not just dead but like a creature who'd returned from beyond the grave. His skin was so pale that in the lights, it seemed to glow a dull gray-green." Two months later, a critic in Boston was flummoxed by Garcia's playing, which he described as "perhaps the worst single performance this writer has ever witnessed in a major concert," faulting Garcia's voice, "wretched work on acoustic guitar," "mistaken notes," and "weirdly uneven" touch, all the work of a "listless troll." Bad reviews were hardly new to Garcia, but this was of another order.

Back home in the Bay Area, friends, including members of the band, tried an intervention. Garcia at first simply refused. "Fuck you," Lesh recalled his saying. He was particularly nasty to Kreutzmann, who tried to say something, only to have Garcia snarl, "You're only a drummer, what do you got to say?" But they hung together, and he grudgingly agreed to get help, promising that he would check himself in to a rehab facility in Oakland. He headed for it the next day, but chickened out, putting it off for two weeks.

Garcia eventually gave in. But not before one last fling. Garcia was driving his 1983 BMW and pulled it over near the Polo Field in Golden Gate Park, not far from the site of the Human Be-In eighteen years and four days earlier. Officer Mark Gamble of the San Francisco Police Department was on his regular patrol. He saw Garcia's car parked in the secluded area and checked the registration. Finding it expired, Gamble approached the driver and noticed a "strong burning odor." As the officer walked up to the window of Garcia's car, Garcia tucked something between the driver's seat and passenger seat; when asked to produce his license and registration, he nervously fetched the latter from the glove box but could not find his license. Gamble ordered him out of the car and then noticed a briefcase. It contained twenty-three packets of "brown and white substances."

Garcia was charged with possessing narcotics, in this case heroin and cocaine. Initially, charges included possession for sale, but that far more serious offense was dropped by the time of Garcia's arraignment. He was freed on $7,250 bail. Steve Parish and Lesh picked him up from the jail.

352 | HERE BESIDE THE RISING TIDE

Garcia was lucky to face his charges in his very understanding hometown. Though prison was clearly a possibility, Judge Raymond Reynolds instead ordered him to complete a month-long addiction program and perform a benefit concert for a food service operation based in the Haight. Garcia remained under the theoretical jurisdiction of the court for as long as two years, but he avoided jail. The *Chronicle* said Garcia "happily agreed" to those terms.

"I want to return something to the community," he said as he left court on March 19. "I'm from here, and this town has always been good to me."

GIVEN THE rush to embrace the Dead, both in tribute to its work and in escape from the darker forces around Reagan, it was natural that the 1980s would also see the formalization of the group's most ardent admirers. There had long been Deadheads, of course, the fans who traveled from show to show, selling T-shirts, food, and souvenirs to pay for gas and tickets. But that community contained many subcultures within the larger subculture of Deadheads. Fans congregated informally in spaces—the "Phil Zone," where fans of Lesh would sit or stand; the "Wharf Rats," a group of sober Deadheads who would gather to enjoy concerts without drugs or alcohol; "Deafheads," fans of the band despite profound hearing loss, who formed the "Deaf Zone," absorbing vibrations through balloons and following lyrics through sign language interpreters or computer screens.

More visible, and at times alarming, were the "Spinners," the ultra-committed dancers who picked spots away from the stage, beneath loudspeakers, often out of sight of the band, and then spun incessantly through shows, winding themselves into a meditative trance. Spinning seemed to arise spontaneously (not, as some have suggested, as part of a Sufi tradition) at shows in the 1980s, but the dancers discovered something deeper in the dizzying act of rotating wildly with the music, finding that the Dead opened "a portal into the sublime." Their commitment was so ardent—and, to many Deadheads, so off-putting—that they carved a niche of their own, not quite worshiping Garcia as a deity but regarding him as divinely inspired. Their fervor tested the limits of faith, as they came together under the banner of the Church of Unlimited Devotion, often known as the Family. The Church bought land in Mendocino, California, before eventually breaking apart amid accusations of sexual misconduct and abuse.

Of the Dead's various sub-subcultures, the one with the broadest and most lasting influence was the tapers. Fans began showing up for Grateful Dead shows as early as 1970 or so with taping equipment, initially handheld devices sneaked into shows, later more elaborate rigs, complete with boom microphones. It hardly bothered the band. In the early 1960s, Garcia himself had traveled with Sandy Rothman, recording the work of great bluegrass artists then unavailable outside the South and Midwest; Weir had taped local players in Palo Alto, especially Jorma Kaukonen. And the band religiously taped itself, a habit begun by Owsley, encouraged by the Pranksters' fondness for taping and extended by the Dead's sound technicians. Given his own history, Garcia was untroubled by seeing members of the audience tape the Dead. That squared with his view of the band itself: The band played the music in the moment for and with those present. What happened afterward was another matter altogether. A tape of a show was interesting, perhaps, but something altogether different than a show itself. "My responsibility to the notes is over after I've played them," he said. "They've left home, you know."

The music industry thought otherwise. To music executives, taping meant bootlegging. And bootlegs gave customers a free source of music that discouraged them from buying albums. And so, laboring under that set of assumptions, most artists prohibited taping to protect album sales. Again, that did not much trouble the Dead, who didn't make that much money on albums anyway.

The only real downside that the Dead saw for allowing their shows to be taped was that tapers themselves could be annoying. They shushed people around them, discouraged dancing near their gear, and generally tried to control space. Conflicts flared and subsided, but the growing complaints about tapers in the 1980s reached a point when some members of the Dead's entourage felt action was needed.

The matter first came under focused attention during a July 1984 meeting of the Dead and their managers. Between discussions of a radio station seeking to play tapes of Dead music and approval of a light show budget, someone suggested creating a "special 'tapers' section with higher priced ticket." A proposal was "to follow." It took a while to get the details right. The taper section (it was at first called the Tapester Section) initially was to be in front of the soundboard, but the boom microphones that tapers often used threatened to block the Dead's soundboard crew's view of the stage. Instead, tapers were allowed to set up behind the soundboard, where the taper section remained for the rest of the Dead's days.

As with most great ideas associated with the Dead, the decision to make room for taping ran entirely contrary to the grain of contemporary life, with its emphasis on scooping up every dollar, and of the music industry, with its concern for copyright enforcement. The Dead opted for openness and counted on Deadheads themselves to police the tapes they made—a solution rooted in community rather than rules. It was not the band's first gamble on values trumping strictures, but it was an especially successful one. Taping culture vastly expanded the Dead's audience and imbued it with a sense of shared purpose—its own set of rules (tapes could be traded but not sold), shorthand notes ("Fire on the Mountain" was usually just "Fire," "Eyes of the World" often just "Eyes," etc.), even its own symbology (tapes on which one song segued into another were marked by the use of a forward arrow, as in "China>Rider"). Tapers formed their own bonds, advertising for rare tapes, developing expectations about tape quality, and constructing identities around their work.

Rick Monture started taping in 1986, and as he lugged his Sony D5 and D6 decks to shows and timed the flipping of cassettes to avoid breaks in songs, he found himself drawn to the sound and the act of memorializing it. A member of the Mohawk Nation, Monture met like-minded enthusiasts from very different backgrounds, each committed to "capturing the moment." His was one of thousands of such tales. Taper culture, in fact, came to command a place outside the band itself, as tapers traded and collected shows with the fanaticism of baseball card collectors and the conviction of archivists. The Dead eventually would bring one of those collectors, Dick Latvala, into the band's fold, tapping him as its archivist and, after a while, putting him on the payroll.

"Taping is a creative art," taper Bob Wagner told Nick Paumgarten, *The New Yorker*'s great Dead scribe, in 2012. "It's analogous to writing nonfiction."

The impact of tapers is hard to overstate. Tapes and tapers would become a mainstay of the early internet and would command a place not only in music culture but also in broader debates over speech, expression, copyright, and intellectual property. Most remarkably, tapers breathed life into the music industry that once so feared them. When the internet made pirating music irresistibly appealing, the Dead had already lifted off from relying on easily duplicated albums for income. The band instead thrived on ticket sales, merchandise, and, later, releases of soundboard-quality recordings of bygone shows.

The Nobel Prize–winning economist and *New York Times* columnist Paul Krugman was among those who took note. "It turns out," he wrote, "that the Dead were business pioneers." Changes in the profitability of intellectual property would come slowly and unevenly, Krugman argued, but the Dead's decision to forgo money by not trying to control tapes of shows opened the way for a new business model built on other income streams. "In the long run," he concluded, "we are all the Grateful Dead."

Each of these groups—sober, deaf, religiously fanatical, electronically messianic—staked out sections of shows, arrayed across venue floors from the Philadelphia Spectrum to the Greek Theatre. Informally organized but driven by habit (corralled, in the case of the tapers), they gravitated to the same areas show after show, creating a patchwork of seating and dancing, a human mandala arrayed before and around the stage. Not everyone enjoyed everyone else—the tapers could be brusque with anyone who jostled their gear, the spinners could whirl without

356 | HERE BESIDE THE RISING TIDE

regard to whom they were crashing into—but the tenor of the experience was one of tolerance and acceptance. If a spinner wanted to spin, well, it was interesting to watch.

As the entire enterprise grew—larger arenas, bigger crowds—it also necessitated a barrier between band and audience, one that prevented the kind of contact that Garcia had once so cherished. If the Acid Tests were one model of the relationship between audience and performer, surely the Philadelphia Spectrum was another. It fell to the Dead's renowned crew to enforce that barrier, protecting band and music from those who loved them too much. Occasional audience members, overcome by rapture, would leap onto the stage or inveigle their way backstage, brushing up against Garcia or other members of the band. If so, they would find the gruff Dead crew waiting to repel them. In Garcia's case, that job fell to Steve Parish, a six-foot-five-inch New Yorker who first worked directly for Hart, only to have Hart fire him, after which he happily moved to Garcia. Once there, Parish imposed himself between desperate fans and the object of their reverence, a protective Praetorian Guard of one. Parish lived for the Dead—"from the vibration of a guitar string out to the back of the hall," he once told band historian Dennis McNally—and he took on his work with zealous devotion. There was no avoiding such barriers, but they did prevent much of the casual contact that had been so vital to the band's early sense of itself.

Outside the shows themselves, fans or the merely curious discovered a traveling marketplace, "Shakedown Street," as it became known. There were T-shirts and food, Frisbees, hacky sacks, pipes, hats, sandals, artwork, every shape and form of tie-dye—and, of course, drugs. The crowds swelled as many people came just to party or to soak up atmosphere. The gatherings would go from festive to alarming in the 1990s, but for the time being, the atmosphere was gently commercial, more farmers' market than mosh pit.

The growth of the Dead's community even gave rise to its own journalism, reporting on shows and members of the band, hints for Deadheads on the road, stories of those whose lives had been altered by their time with the Grateful Dead and other Deadheads. *Relix* was the first, debuting in 1974 as *Dead Relix,* a stapled fanzine aimed at tapers, before expanding into a more general-interest music magazine. In the 1980s, *The Golden Road,* created by Blair Jackson and Regan McMahon and written mainly by Jackson, released its first issue in the winter of 1984 and published quarterly thereafter. The first issue featured "complete show & set lists" for all of 1983, a methodical accounting that filled eight pages of the thirty-two-page magazine. Other features included "Roots: Under The Dead's Covers," an intelligent and far-ranging look at songs the Dead had covered, as well as photos from a Fillmore West show in 1970 and ads, including display ads, one of them for "Grateful Janitors," a cleaning service in Eugene, Oregon, and classified ads from tapers looking to expand their collections.

Dupree's Diamond News joined the traveling Dead journalism circuit in 1987, its editors announcing that "we are very serious about bringing you quality as well as quantity." Features included set analyses of every show from 1986, a list of tour dates for 1987, and extensive classifieds—ten dollars for twenty-five words—through which fans shared news and exchanged tapes. Issues were filled with loving commentary and tour stories, though also with critical appraisals. Mostly, it was a chronicle of awe. "I wondered how so much positive energy from these thousands of people could be confined to just this place," Associate Publisher Sally Ansorge wrote in Issue 2. "I was yet to discover that it wasn't confined then, and isn't now."

All of which was fascinating and a little perplexing to the band itself. "Deadheads aren't that easy to pin down," Garcia said in 1991. "They range from professionals doing hard scholarship to total street weirdos. That keeps it interesting because the feedback is amusing. At the same time, I feel guilty because I wonder, 'Isn't there something real to think about out there? Aren't there questions that people could be applying their valuable human energy to?' Getting involved with the Grateful Dead isn't going anywhere except onward."

* * *

358 | HERE BESIDE THE RISING TIDE

GARCIA'S ARREST interrupted the Dead's momentum of the early 1980s, but the band regained its footing even before his penance was paid. Two days after Garcia accepted drug diversion in San Francisco, the Dead was onstage in Hampton, Virginia, one of sixty-four more shows the band would play in 1985. The machine that was the Dead kept churning along.

It was, however, prone to seizing up. That year would combine bright performances with genuine clunkers, including what some regard as the worst Dead show ever, an August concert at Boreal Ridge near Lake Tahoe. It was billed as the "Highest Grateful Dead Concert in the World"—a sly reference to the altitude of the event (7,200 feet above sea level), though one that would be superseded when the Dead performed in Telluride, Colorado—and it came on a blisteringly hot and windy day. The heat and altitude knocked the guitars out of tune, and the wind disrupted the onstage monitors. Weir grew so frustrated at one point that he kicked an amplifier. The band played a discordant and disjointed "Friend of the Devil" and a ragged "He's Gone." The second set was a little better than the first, but even it could not rescue a bad afternoon. Deadheads chalked it up to the weather. "I have been to many dozens of Dead shows, from '72 to the end," one wrote, "and this one takes the prize as the all-around worst."

THE DEAD'S march through the middle part of the decade coincided with the nation's enthusiastic—and, to some, discouraging—affirmation of the Reagan presidency in 1984, when Reagan faced the Democratic challenger, former vice president Walter Mondale. Mondale beat out Senator Gary Hart and civil rights leader Jesse Jackson for his party's nod, but it was a halfhearted victory, as it left Mondale to face a popular president presiding over a recovering economy. Set up to administer a trouncing, Reagan faced just one roadblock, the question of whether, at age seventy-three, he was too old to competently perform the duties of the office.

Reagan's performance in the first presidential debate of the campaign stoked that question, as the president tripped over his words and seemed lost. Not for long. In the second debate, Reagan faced the age question directly. "You already are the oldest president in history, and some of your staff say you were tired after your most recent encounter with Mr. Mondale," the questioner, Henry Trewhitt of *The Baltimore Sun*, said. "I recall yet that President Kennedy had to go for days on end with very little sleep during the Cuban Missile Crisis. Is there any doubt in your mind that you would be able to function in such circumstances?"

"Not at all, Mr. Trewhitt," Reagan replied. "And I want you to know that also I will not make age an issue of this campaign. I am not going to exploit for political purposes my opponent's youth and inexperience." The camera caught Mondale laughing heartily along with the audience. Reagan carried forty-nine states, leaving Mondale with just Minnesota and the District of Columbia. And so the elderly archconservative, nemesis of the counterculture since 1965, returned for another four years.

Beginning in 1982 and then with increased vigor in his second term, Reagan ramped up the nation's so-called War on Drugs, increasing penalties for drug crimes, especially related to crack cocaine, and using the Department of Defense and the Drug Enforcement Administration to punish domestic use and to cut off foreign supply. Nancy Reagan then joined the fight. Inspired by an encounter with a group of schoolchildren who asked the First Lady what they should do if they were offered drugs, Nancy Reagan urged them to "just say no." Within months, more than ten thousand "Just Say No" clubs had sprouted around the country, heeding Nancy Reagan's campaign to create an "outspoken intolerance for drug use."

Few people were more publicly associated with the lighthearted and even wanton use of recreational drugs than Jerry Garcia. He never explicitly advocated drug use, skirting that question along with other pleadings for him to champion legalization, but he made no secret of his own use, and he did nothing to discourage others. "The worst thing

360 | HERE BESIDE THE RISING TIDE

about drugs," he had long contended, "is that they're illegal." Nothing in the intervening years, not his arrests, not his addiction, not the intervention of his friends and family, had shaken Garcia from that view.

It was hardly a surprise to find Nancy Reagan and Jerry Garcia on opposite sides of a debate about drugs, but the Reagan approach rankled. For young people already put off by Reagan's belligerence in foreign affairs or his glib dismissal of environmental concerns or his indifference to the growing plague of AIDS, Nancy Reagan's campaign was further evidence of Washington's contempt for what remained of the counterculture and its heirs.

It wasn't bad for business. In 1985, the Dead was the second-highest-grossing act in American music, bringing in more than $11 million in ticket sales, second only to Bruce Springsteen. And more was about to come.

STEWART BRAND was never far from the tip of the new, and in 1985 his creative spirit again crossed with that of the Dead. He helped launch the Whole Earth 'Lectronic Link, known as the WELL (later, less grandly, the Well), which fast became an early archetype of what would become social media.

The Well created one of the first "virtual communities." Its participants trumpeted communication and openness—anonymity was prohibited. They addressed one another on equal terms, and the effect was to democratize the growing neighborhood of interests. The motto "You own your own words" would greet Well participants when they signed on, and the ideas contained within that slogan—a happily sobering mixture of freedom and responsibility—defined the whole enterprise.

To run it, Brand and co-founder Larry Brilliant turned to Matthew McClure, who had worked for Brand at the *Whole Earth Catalog* and then moved to the Farm, a Tennessee commune, where he stayed for more than a decade. McClure launched the Well quietly in March 1985 and opened it to the public, boosted by word of mouth and advertising in Whole Earth circles, on April 1. Users connected via modem and joined in via the relatively new phenomenon of the home computer, Compaq or Macintosh being the favorites in those days.

The Well was built around "conferences," groups of similarly inclined participants who convened around a topic—socialism or California or hacking, say. Through the fall and winter of 1985, users found their way to the Well, signing up for this conference or that, weathering some of the community's technological growing pains. And then, in early 1986, they were joined by a new community: Deadheads.

The man who brought the Dead to the Well was David Gans, a Deadhead and writer whose work about the band is among the most insightful and who had published *Playing in the Band,* an elegantly thoughtful and brightly designed "oral and visual portrait" of the Dead, in 1985. In 1986, he was hosting a weekly radio show in San Francisco called *The Deadhead Hour,* and once he had discovered the Well, he used the show to promote a new conference for Deadheads which he co-founded with Mary Eisenhart and Bennett Falk, both of *MicroTimes* magazine. "You don't have to be a computer person," he said each week, "just a person with a computer." Few aphorisms better captured the new notion of computing, and few did more to launch the social media revolution.

"The Dead community was perfect for cyberspace," Gans said, "fanatics with lots to talk about who were not centrally located."

As Gans realized, Deadheads had plenty to discuss—tales from shows, arrangements for coming tours, tapes to trade. Many were already comfortable with technology; others bought their first computers just so they could join the Well. Many were based in the Bay Area, of course, but many also lived elsewhere around the country, so a technological link was a way to foster personal connection but also a way to create remote relationships. The Well spoke to their concepts of freedom and connection, community, responsibility, and fun. Deadheads electrified the Well. "It just took off," Gans said.

By 1987, nearly half of all traffic on the Well was about the Grateful Dead. The GD Conference split into multiple conferences—fans trading tapes, exchanging information about shows, making arrangements to tour—allowing the Well to turn the corner on profitability. And the values that the Dead's community brought to the conversation—sharing, authenticity, sincerity—helped soften some of tech's cynicism. The Well's experiment in social media and virtual community was rooted in the same soil that gave birth to the band, just miles from Magoo's Pizza Parlor and Kepler's bookstore.

The music historian Andrew Hickey, whose monumental *A History of Rock Music in 500 Songs* explores that history in exceptionally close detail, struggled to make sense of the Grateful Dead. But he was clear on the Dead's influence and their connection to the Well, along with their significance to the internet more broadly:

> Everything about the way that music technology, and entertainment technology more broadly, evolved—the growth of filesharing, the embrace by record companies of streaming as a way to provide music free at the point of listening to meet that demand, and the fact that where thirty years ago mid-level bands made a modest income from recordings and toured to promote them, while now they make a modest income from touring but release records to promote the tour . . . all of that comes back to the fact that it was Grateful Dead fans who were the first online, and who shaped the culture of the Internet in ways, good and bad, that we're still seeing today.

He added: "It may not be an exaggeration to say that the Grateful Dead have had a more lasting, and greater, cultural impact than the Beatles."

IN 1986, the Dead's influence and reach were at a mighty peak, a fact that drew the band to the attention of heretofore unlikely admirers. At *The New York Times,* the columnist William Safire, who had worked for Nixon and Agnew, noticed the Dead's attraction and was curious about the name. He dived into the Funk & Wagnalls *Standard Dictionary of Folklore, Mythology, and Legend,* emerging with an item that correctly unearthed the origins of the phrase "the grateful dead." "My question is," the tough-minded conservative writer asked, "how many other rock groups, or folk singers, use titles that have such deep cultural roots?"

If Safire represented one end of a cultural-political spectrum, surely Bob Dylan was closer to the other. He, too, was curious about the Dead.

For Dylan, the period was one of professional uncertainty. He had been fresh and inventive in the 1960s, reflective in the 1970s, but by the 1980s his place within a larger American music was vaguer. He had, one writer noted, "refused to remain static," but the other side of that was that he had "struggled to mature and express the lessons of age and experience." Dylan released *Empire Burlesque* in 1985 to tepid reviews; *Biograph*, which came out five months later, generated more enthusiasm, but that, too, was double-edged, since it was a retrospective, reinforcing the sense that his best days were behind him.

On top of that, some wondered about his core convictions. *Slow Train Coming* in 1979 placed Dylan as a born-again Christian, and though he refused to be pinned down about what that meant to him, it alarmed old fans in the counterculture and beyond. When Robert Hilburn, the great music critic of the *Los Angeles Times*, sat down with Dylan in late 1985, he was struck by Dylan's isolation. "I can't figure out sometimes if people think I'm dead or alive," Dylan said, adding: "The thing I really notice now is time."

As Dylan was considering his next musical move, the Dead were thinking about him too. At a band meeting in November, he was one of several acts the Dead considered offering a shared bill to in 1986 (the others were Huey Lewis, Eric Clapton, Dire Straits, and Sting). Dylan signed up in April for five shows and suggested that the Dead open for him in their first two shared billings, "then see how it works for the remaining three." The Dead would supply lighting and its PA system, Dylan would share additional sound costs for larger venues.

Dates and arrangements set, Dylan reemerged, recruiting Tom Petty and the Heartbreakers to serve as his backup band and setting out on a national tour. The highlights were the joint appearances with the Grateful Dead. The Dylan performances were a challenge—he tested the

364 | HERE BESIDE THE RISING TIDE

Heartbreakers by surprising them with different songs at every concert and by launching into numbers in different keys than they were expecting—but the overall effect of the joint appearances with the Dead was to suddenly and vastly expand Dylan's audience, sweeping in Deadheads and more casual fans.

By the time they reached Washington in July, the shows were a national phenomenon and hugely successful. They culminated with performances at RFK Stadium on July 6 and 7. The two shows grossed a combined $2,132,700, with more than $830,000 of that going to the artists. The Dead, by now staying at choice hotels, reserved forty-three rooms—and a suite for the Fourth of July fireworks—at the Four Seasons.

The RFK shows fell on two witheringly hot D.C. afternoons. Undeterred, Dylan appeared in leather pants, and he seemed energized by the huge crowd, bouncing amiably between numbers. No leather pants for Garcia, but the shows were grueling nonetheless. Perched high above the sweltering crowd, he soldiered through the two days and evenings, his strength ebbing. Worried crew and bandmates urged him to drink water, and he did, but by the end of the second night, nothing seemed to help. Although the crowd delighted in the event—made especially exhilarating by Dylan's joining the band for a ragged rendering of "It's All Over Now, Baby Blue" and a discombobulated "Desolation Row," two of his songs that the Dead had made their own—Garcia's condition was alarming. "He was red-faced and sweating," Lesh said. "I feared that he would blow a fuse." The Dead wrapped up with "Good Lovin'" and returned for an encore of the Rolling Stones' "Satisfaction," then hightailed it back to San Francisco.

Garcia barely made it back. The Dead were scheduled to have a couple of days off before heading south to Ventura County. Garcia spent the time at home, alone, and no doubt deep into using. He fell on Thursday, July 10, muttering nonsense and then collapsing. He was found passed out by his friend and housekeeper Nora Sage. She called for help and, once Garcia was at Marin General Hospital, alerted friends and family: Garcia was in a coma, suffering from diabetes—his eating habits and general disarray having taken their toll—and "general systemic infection as a result of an abscessed tooth and exhaustion." His chances of survival were uncertain.

Mountain Girl rushed back from Oregon and discovered, to her horror, that someone had given Garcia Valium, to which he was allergic. His heart stopped. Doctors shocked him back to life and had to repeat that twice, keeping him alive in the meantime with a respirator. Slowly, he shook off the effects of the drug but remained comatose. He was gray, sallow, unconscious. "I thought there was no way he would live," she said.

Fans massed outside the hospital. Thousands called the band's hotline or signed on to the Well, trading stories, looking for updates. The future of the Grateful Dead, and the life of Jerry Garcia, hung in the balance.

Joseph Campbell, Jerry Garcia, and Mickey Hart.
Palace of Fine Arts, San Francisco, November 1, 1986.

Jay Blakesberg/Retro Photo Archive

CHAPTER 16

"The Answer to the Atom Bomb"

WHEN GARCIA'S EYES FLUTTERED AWAKE AT MARIN GENERAL, he marveled. "I'm not Beethoven," he said, groggily. Mountain Girl understood. He was surrounded by people talking about him as if he weren't there, and he was flickering back to consciousness. He was saying "I'm not deaf," she recalled. "I can hear what you're saying." With that, he resumed living.

His family, such as it was, gathered around him. Cliff brought his wife and children. Sara came with Heather. Mountain Girl took command, and her daughters met Heather for the first time, gathering around their stricken but recovering father. For weeks, he regained strength, finding it, as always, in music.

As Garcia reentered consciousness and began the painstaking work of rebuilding his musicianship, he did not return to his childhood music, to the 45s he'd picked up at Joe Garcia's or the songs sung at family gatherings; nor did he resume, at least initially, with the songs of the Grateful Dead. He began again with folk and bluegrass and jazz, the American idioms that swirled in his American soul.

He worked his hands back into shape. Merl Saunders played with him, patiently coaxing him as he remembered, first the musical lines and then the shapes on the fretboard. "It was so bad," Saunders said. "He couldn't form chords."

Garcia moved back in with Mountain Girl, and she nursed him while his old bandmates taught him. His talents could not be suppressed, but it was slow, "just like teaching a baby," Saunders said. One step followed another. Chords led to short bits of lead guitar, which led to longer segments, then whole songs. Within a few months, Garcia was playing again. He made a quiet appearance with the Jerry Garcia Band in October, breaking hearts with his take on Dylan's "Forever Young." On November 21, he ventured out again, catching Los Lobos at a club in San Rafael and warming in the happiness of the crowd as he was recognized. Carlos Santana was in the audience, and he and Garcia made up for lost years. David Hidalgo, lead guitarist for Los Lobos, saw the two out front and invited them to join the band for "La Bamba." Garcia picked up a guitar and fell in comfortably. At Thanksgiving, Dave Nelson and Sandy Rothman joined Garcia and other members of the Dead for a celebration near San Anselmo. Garcia poured out lyrics from decades earlier, drawing them from recesses deep inside himself. Garcia was thrilled, friends and family relieved and overjoyed.

On December 15, in the comfortable setting of the Oakland Coliseum, the Dead got back to business. The first song that night, and Garcia's first appearance with the band since falling ill in July, was "Touch of Grey." It had been in their repertoire since 1982, so it was well known to the fans, but this time it carried new meaning. Hunter's lyrics spun out a litany of troubles—clocks running slow, falling behind on the rent, forgetting to feed the dog, an illiterate kid, a cow "giving kerosene"—but clung to optimism. "I will get by. I will survive," Garcia sang, his voice sorely missed. As he sang those words, the crowd roared with such love that even he was taken aback. And the band, as it always did, turned the chorus at the end of the song. "*We* will get by," band and crowd sang together. Tears rolling down thousands of faces, voices raised in uninhibited joy. "*We* will survive."

THE MONTHS following Garcia's return were exultant. His playing returned with zing. He lost weight—somewhere between 30 and 50 pounds—and he stayed clean. He settled his debt to the IRS and, at first, kept up the family connections created during his hospitalization. He spent some time with Heather, and they discovered their common

"THE ANSWER TO THE ATOM BOMB" | 369

love of music; growing up apart from her father, Heather had come to music on her own and now was an accomplished violinist. Her mother, Sara, watched in wonder as her ex-husband and daughter discovered ties that bound them—all three of them, really—across years and difficulties.

Deadheads appreciated the gift of Garcia's return, and they looked for lessons from it. "It sometimes takes a cataclysmic event—like Garcia's near-death—to shake us off our treadmills," Blair Jackson wrote in *The Golden Road*. "This break from touring has offered a good opportunity to slow down for a moment and move out of the hurricane." So uplifting was Garcia's return to health that many Deadheads took that moment to give up cocaine and change their lives. Dead shows for the next several years felt like a gift, one appreciated all the more tenderly for how fragile it was.

Garcia grew stronger. And with the return of his vigor came a familiar restlessness in his relationship with Mountain Girl. Garcia was soon living with another woman, Manasha Matheson, then a twenty-seven-year-old Deadhead who had been introduced to the band at Watkins Glen. The two had corresponded and visited after shows over the years, and now, as Garcia regained strength after his coma, their friendship deepened. He assured Matheson that his relationship with Mountain Girl was platonic, after which Matheson and Garcia became romantically involved. Matheson would have a daughter with Garcia, Keelin Noel Garcia, born on December 20, 1987. Keelin was Garcia's fourth daughter.

Garcia's return from the edge of death reinvigorated the Dead, as did an unexpected jolt from MTV, the new music video network. In August 1987, MTV held a "Day of the Dead," celebrating the Dead's music and their place in history. The telecast reached MTV's wide and growing audience, and Dead shows suddenly got yet another influx of curious visitors, young people intrigued by the story of the band and its connection back to a counterculture they barely knew.

Tour schedules for 1987 and 1988 returned to full throttle, and the band traveled in style, not just luxury accommodations but also a private jet—two, actually, one for the band and one for the crew. The Dead's twelfth studio album, *In the Dark,* was released in July 1987. The album included "Touch of Grey." Fully twenty-two years after that first performance at Magoo's Pizza, the Grateful Dead had a certifiable hit. The band's "Touch of Grey" video, released in June 1987, further cemented that connection to a new generation. Filmed at Laguna Seca and directed by Gary Gutierrez, who had animated *The Grateful Dead Movie,* it was a kick to make and a smash with viewers.

Dennis McNally delivered the update from the charts. "I have some imposing news to tell you," he announced to the band backstage at Madison Square Garden. "You've made the Top Ten."

"I am appalled," Garcia replied.

"Touch of Grey" and MTV brought new levels of fame and money. Garcia bought a new house, his first since Stinson Beach. It included a huge swimming pool, which he spent a fortune to heat. The house brimmed with television sets, on which he devoured old movies and lighthearted comedies. He bought a sleek BMW 750, replacing the one he'd been busted in while parked in Golden Gate Park. He drove this one poorly too. These were the trappings of wealth. Fame, however, seemed not to matter much to him.

Garcia had spent much of his life in a literal spotlight, and he had had plenty of opportunity to consider what it meant to be a celebrity. "I don't relate to that," he said in 1976. "I taught myself early not to believe that that's who I am. That's not me. . . . Luckily, the kind of fame that I'm involved in, such as it is, is low enough of a profile so that I'm not constantly being reminded of it."

He did not require adoration. When a British punk rock journalist put Garcia through an unusually contentious interview in 1981, Garcia enjoyed it. The reporter, Paul Morley, was openly contemptuous of Garcia, and he ventured the opinion that it was "absurd and disastrous" that the Dead had been "meandering along for sixteen years." Morley pushed Garcia hard, if self-consciously: "Does it disappoint you that . . . people like me can be disrespectful of you: think you are rusty, crusty, dusty and fusty?"

"No!" Garcia answered. "I don't give a damn. I would be afraid if everybody in the world liked us. The responsibility. I don't want to be responsible for leading the march to wherever. Fuck that. It's already been done, and the world hates it. Humans hate it."

In the years since his bemused run-in with Morley, Garcia's fame had only soared. Some punk rockers and, later, grunge rockers, despised the Dead for some of the reasons that Morley did, donning their hatred as a cultural fashion statement. Kurt Cobain, pioneer of grunge rock and founding member of Nirvana, famously wore a KILL THE GRATEFUL DEAD shirt and told *Melody Maker* magazine in 1992: "I wouldn't wear a tie-dyed T-shirt unless it was dyed with the urine of Phil Collins and the blood of Jerry Garcia." Overhearing that, Cobain's wife, Courtney Love, teased her husband: "How long have you been thinking about that one? . . . It's so boy."

Neither Morley nor Cobain got under Garcia's skin, but fame did have its downsides. By the end of the 1980s, he was recognized everywhere he went, and though the reception was almost always friendly, even fawning, he no longer enjoyed the luxury of anonymity. He lived in greater comfort, of course, but he sometimes hid from fans or grew annoyed with the demands on his attention. Fame, he said, was "the thing of constantly being forced to think about yourself all the time."

In the end, fame was just an idea, and one that did not interest him much. He was a working musician and a public figure; he relished the one role and rejected the other. "Fame is an illusion," he said near the end of his life. "I know what I do, and I know about how well I do it, and I know what I wish I could do. Those things don't enter my life, I don't buy into any of that stuff. I can't imagine who would."

For Garcia, the more frustrating side of worship was uncritical appraisal. Night after night, he would play, sometimes with the Dead, sometimes in his own band or with others. Without fail, fans would tell him he was perfect, that they were moved to tears of joy, that they could tell he was responding to them, channeling their energy. He knew when he'd been bad, but no one else seemed to. It could be infuriating, even maddening: What was the point of playing well if it made no difference to those who listened? Such is the price of adoration.

"I'll put up with it," he said, "until they come to me with the cross and nails."

THE CONTRAST between realities was stark. Inside the Dead, the band's fans were loving, bound by community and curiosity. Outside, the world seemed to have gone entirely mad. When the Reagan administration revived plans shelved by Carter for deploying a "neutron bomb" in Europe, the impeccably ghoulish logic of deterrence shocked many Americans. The bomb addressed what some planners considered a flaw in America's deterrence strategy: The only way to deter Soviet adventurism in Europe was to be ready to bomb Europe, but if America unleashed nuclear weapons on, say, West Germany, it would destroy the very country it was seeking to protect.

The neutron bomb entered that discussion by creating another option, one that would irradiate Soviet forces but leave European cities intact. Perfectly, then, deterrence led to a scenario in which buildings were protected while humans were annihilated. The neutron bomb, Reagan said, was a "moral improvement in the horror that is modern war."

By the terms of the Cold War, that made a certain sense, but that just made clear the lunacy of those terms. Old arguments about Vietnam, about razing a village in order to save it, resurfaced in the form of the nuclear freeze movement.

The campaign to halt nuclear weapons in their tracks gained energy and strength in the early 1980s, putting pressure on the Reagan administration through techniques perfected in the antiwar movement of the 1960s—demonstrations, rallies, allegiances with sympathetic officials and institutions. The Catholic Church supported a freeze, as did the Friends of the Earth and the U.S. Conference of Mayors. Senator Edward Kennedy backed the idea, and California senator Alan Cranston launched a presidential bid—unsuccessful—with arms control and the nuclear freeze at its center. Reagan perceived the movement as a threat to his emphasis on weapons development—"peace through strength"—and fought to hamstring it.

"I know that all of you want peace, and so do I," he told the American public in 1983. "I know too that many of you seriously believe that a nuclear freeze would further the cause of peace. But a freeze now would make us less, not more, secure and would raise, not reduce, the risks of war."

In his second term, however, Reagan pivoted as support for arms control continued to mount. He met with Soviet leader Mikhail Gorbachev on four occasions—Geneva in 1985, Reykjavik in 1986, Washington in 1987, and Moscow in 1988. Those sessions negotiated real achievements, including the signing of the INF Treaty, but they did not succeed in replacing the logic of armed rivalry. Rather, Reagan moved from the language of mutually assured destruction to the development of the Strategic Defense Initiative, a far-fetched concept of space-based weapons that could interdict nuclear missiles. Quickly dubbed "Star Wars," after the movie sensation of the era, SDI rattled the Soviets but never came to much.

The peace movement's role in ending the Vietnam War was undeniable. Its contribution to Reagan's policies was more ambiguous, but Reagan's advisers acknowledged its force. The Cold War concluded without an exchange of nuclear weapons, without deployment of the neutron bomb, and without the development of SDI.

THEY DID not come with crosses or nails, but they came. In the coldness of the 1980s, the Dead offered warmth. Under the threat of nuclear war, they offered places of peace. Small shows became big ones and then giant ones. Clubs became amphitheaters and then stadiums. The enterprise grew and grew. *Built to Last*, the band's thirteenth studio album, was released near the end of 1989. It drew mixed reviews and included what John Perry Barlow, Weir's usual writing partner, called "arguably the worst Grateful Dead song ever," the angular "Victim or the Crime." The lyrics opened with the line "Patience runs out on the junkie," which Weir would sing a few feet from Garcia, who didn't like the song but played it anyway.

Built to Last felt thin—"wimpy and soporific," the *San Francisco Chronicle* concluded—but nothing could slow the momentum now. Thousands would come to Dead shows without tickets, hoping to snag a "miracle" but willing, if necessary, just to spend the evening outside, mingling with other Deadheads, absorbing some of the counterenergy.

It got big. Then it got too big. And if the experience of the Haight in the aftermath of the Summer of Love had shown anything, it was that big was not always healthy for the counterculture. Here again, size began to take a toll.

"Too many people are showing up at our concerts," Weir said in 1989. In Hartford, police rounded up Deadheads who were camped in the rain. In Worcester, they were herded away from traffic. Some cities had had enough, refusing to allow the Dead access to venues. Two shows in Kansas were canceled after local authorities demanded an increase in security from twenty officers to 140. Seventy-nine people were arrested over three days in Irvine, California. Local authorities began to dread the band's arrival. The Dead tried pay-per-view, but it did not take the pressure off shows.

The good ship Grateful Dead took on passengers, plucking them from rough seas, offering them shelter and companionship. The eighties veered right. The Dead held steady, but it was getting tippy.

SAN FRANCISCO buckled in those years, crushed under the weight of an illness that was at first as mysterious as it was lethal. It started with a few cases in Los Angeles, a few in Europe, a few in San Francisco. Men turned up with purple lesions, succumbed to debilitating diarrhea. The patients were gay men, and the outbreak of Kaposi sarcoma for a while was known as "gay cancer." More cases followed. And more. By the early 1980s, gay cancer had become GRID, Gay-Related Immune

Deficiency. San Francisco had offered freedom and room to live for gay men; now it became the center of an epidemic.

In 1981, 270 cases of GRID were reported, and 121 of those suffering from it died. Reagan, now president, said nothing. GRID became AIDS and the cases multiplied. Tens of thousands were dead or dying. As the 1980s unfolded, San Francisco was laid to waste. In the Castro, home to the city's gay community, sexual license and freedom had been replaced by grief. Neighborhoods once alive with liberation now were dotted with empty stores and vacating homes. "So many people have died of AIDS that many residents say they can no longer count the number of friends they have lost," *The New York Times* reported. Health experts predicted that the death toll in the city would pass ten thousand by 1991—this in a city of 725,000 people.

On December 17, 1987, Garcia, Weir, and bassist John Kahn accepted an invitation from Joan Baez to appear at the Warfield Theatre for an AIDS benefit. The short acoustic set that night featured a spirited version of Dylan's "When I Paint My Masterpiece" and a pleading rendition of "Birdsong." But the night's highlight was when Baez joined her old friends for touching performances of "Turtle Dove" and "Knockin' on Heaven's Door," both of which cried out for the city's gathering dead. They also delivered a lovely "Dark Hollow," which Weir introduced after asking for "my own personal Christmas fairy to get my capo" and then described as "a cowboy version of 'Dark Star.'"

The announcer that evening, Scott Beach of KPIX, expressed it best. As he introduced Weir and Garcia, they entered behind him, taking their places on the darkened stage in front of a decorated Christmas tree. "I am absolutely convinced," he said, "if Jerry Garcia were to announce his candidacy for the presidency, Gary Hart would pull out again. And as president, Jerry Garcia's doctrine would surely include a few things that have been given precious little consideration: peace, equality and doing something to stop the spread of the worst public health problem of modern times."

"Forget it," Garcia muttered behind him. "Not going to happen."

376 | HERE BESIDE THE RISING TIDE

The musicians played for free, and the money from the event went to the Godfather Fund, the Rita Rockett hot meals program, Open Hand, and the Irene Smith massage team, as well as to the AIDS Emergency Program. It paid for rent and utilities and offered relief, however brief, for one of San Francisco's stricken communities whose suffering was recasting the city where Garcia had grown up.

DEADHEADS KNEW that one way to get into a show was to write to the band directly and to catch the eye of the person opening the envelope. So they enclosed gifts, poems, photographs, sometimes a little weed or other offerings. Or they decorated the envelope.

One such lavishly and lovingly designed entreaty arrived at the band's San Rafael headquarters in 1987. A red rose topped the envelope, sitting at the end of a long vine of thorns and filigreed leaves. Lightning bolts in red, white, and blue bracketed a mystic eye; delicate sketches of a moon and space dust sat beneath the postmark. "Preference of 2 tickets for New Years Eve," the author wrote. She included her return address in Malibu, California.

Gillian Welch was the "little Deadhead" who sent that note. She was a student at UC Santa Cruz in 1987, having set out to become a photographer but finding that she was repelled by the smell of the fixer chemicals in the darkroom. She had played the guitar since age nine and could mimic most anything. "People called me the human jukebox," she said. And then she found the Dead. Her first show was Chinese New Year 1987 in San Francisco. Listening to Garcia sing "Black Peter," she felt his angst in the music. "He was an incredible emotional connector," she recalled.

Welch moved from photography to music and launched a career of soulful songwriting and performing. The Dead's "Peggy-O" and "Oh Babe, It Ain't No Lie" spoke to her life and experience, moving her. She took in shows and left not just with musical clues but with values— individuality, personal freedom, community. "If you focus on it," she said many years later, "it rethinks your life."

Welch got her tickets and was there for New Year's with the Dead. She filed it all away, warm in the embrace of a community of music and caring. She followed the Dead for a while, taking in a memorable show in Telluride, Colorado, where she was swept up in the conga line that spontaneously took shape in the crowd. "Just a little Deadhead," she sang later, looking back at that time, "who is watching."

Welch's earnest musical project, undertaken with her partner, Dave Rawlings, unspooled in the years that followed and could be read as an extension of the Dead's example. It included wit, wisdom, and compassion; the embrace of American themes; and a songbook populated by American characters on their land, somewhere near the intersection of Hunter/Garcia and the poet Wendell Berry, another veteran of the Stegner writing program. The work of Rawlings and Welch was entirely their own, of course, but one could hear history and those early Dead shows sifting through the years.

So, too, for the basketball great Bill Walton, whose association with the Dead was almost as central to his image as his NBA championships, his days atop the NCAA, or his infectious basketball commentary. Walton wrote that he'd seen the Dead 869 times. Interviewed near the end of his life, he was asked about that total. How many shows had he actually seen? the interviewer inquired. "Not enough," he said.

GARCIA WAS usually a gracious judge of musicians, but there were exceptions. He found Jim Morrison stylized and unconvincing. He appreciated but had reservations about the Rolling Stones, whose violent lyrics and affect troubled him. Eddie Van Halen produced a deluge of notes but without what Garcia regarded as "rhythmic elegance." But for the most part he was eclectic in his tastes and generous in his appraisals. He could appreciate musicians as diverse as the Bulgarian Women's Choir and Elvis Costello, finding joy in work across a spectrum of genres and histories. It was strange, then, that his response to Bruce Springsteen was to be churlish.

Interviewed by Studs Terkel and Abe Peck in 1979, when Springsteen was an up-and-coming talent from New Jersey, Garcia shrugged him off as a regional phenomenon. "What Bruce Springsteen had to say to the kids of New Jersey didn't apply to the kids in California," he said.

Springsteen was puzzled by the Dead and initially dismissive as well. "In the 1970s I went to a Grateful Dead show at a community college. I watched the crowd swaying and doing its trance-dance thing and I stood very outside of it," he wrote later. "To me—sober, nonmystical, only half hippie, if that, me—they sounded like a not-very-talented bar band. I went home gently mystified."

But Springsteen came around. "Years later, when I came to appreciate their subtle musicality, Jerry Garcia's beautifully lyrical guitar playing and the folk purity of their voices, I understood that I'd missed it. They had a unique ability to build community and sometimes, it ain't what you're doing but what happens while you're doing it that counts."

Huey Lewis, both a student of music and a creator of it, thought he understood their shared mystification. He saw the two as approaching their craft from opposite poles. Garcia, he noted, came from a tradition of bluegrass and folk, where modesty was treasured, and of jazz, where "you make hard things look easy." Springsteen was a creator and creature of rock 'n' roll, "where you make easy things look hard." Springsteen pounded into chords, pleaded with the audience to join him in exuberant energy. He was a preacher delivering a nightly revival. Garcia was gentler; he pulled the audience with him, invited it to participate alongside his act of discovery. Springsteen called in thunder; Garcia walked in the rain.

Jon Pareles, the great rock critic for *The New York Times,* appreciated both men and their music, and he comprehended the extent to which Garcia represented something fundamentally different, something outside the normal understanding of a rock star, the land that Springsteen so fully inhabited. Garcia, he wrote, "simply wasn't interested in putting personality ahead of the music." If Springsteen's music could ricochet an audience into joy, Garcia's gift was that he could lead it there more quietly.

"There was no aggression in his solos, and even when he picked up speed, he phrased with the relaxed tickle of a bluegrass guitarist," Pareles reflected in 1995. "His most characteristic mannerism, sliding down a few frets, was the sonic image of someone slipping out of the spotlight. He played the way a dolphin swims with its school; his guitar lines would glide out, shimmer and gambol in the sunlight, then blend into the group as if nothing had happened."

As the counterculture migrated from the hyperactive ebullience of the 1960s and the 1970s, it traced something close to Garcia's path, a retrenchment into bohemianism. This was not a culture of radicals ready to take over the world; it was something smaller yet purer, a sliver of the committed, protecting one another from the rough politics of the world, finding solace in small company, a "gambol in the sunlight."

ALL OF this made the Dead of the 1980s something more than a curiosity. The Dead had been so outside the culture mainstream for so long—and were appealing for precisely that reason—that they naturally became the objects of deeper reflection. Surely this alternative way of living, grounded in creativity and caring rather than individualism and greed, had something to say to the larger culture, some lesson to impart.

The idea of studying the Dead was not exactly new. The ESP experiment that the Dead participated in during its Port Chester shows in 1971 grew out of the observation by Professor Stanley Krippner that there was something unusual about the "emotional intensity" of a Dead show that might lend itself to telepathic connection. The very idea for the experiment highlighted early intellectual fascination with the Dead and the devotion that the band inspired.

Eighteen years after Deadheads tried to transmit their thoughts from Port Chester, Rebecca Adams, a professor of sociology at the University of North Carolina at Greensboro, created a twelve-week course to study Deadheads and examine the question of whether they constituted a bona fide subculture. The course attracted a certain amount of ridicule—"Deadhead 101," it was called—but Adams was credentialed—

380 | HERE BESIDE THE RISING TIDE

she had a doctorate in sociology from the University of Chicago—and she talked reasonably about her academic ambitions for the course with reporters. Word got around quickly, and the course's first summer offering rapidly filled up.

By the 2000s, the Grateful Dead Studies Association was a recognized and reputable branch of the academy; its president and executive director, Nicholas Meriwether, brought intellectual appreciation for the Dead but also deep and exemplary scholarship of his own, helping to solidify Dead studies as a genuine discipline.

Meriwether was a graduate of Princeton and held an archival science degree from the University of South Carolina, as well as a love of the Dead beginning in his years as a college student—years that dovetailed with the Reagan presidency and all it entailed. "Unalloyed greed was writ large in the culture and celebrated. It accompanied a kind of right-wing Republicanism that repudiated every aspect of the 1960s," Meriwether said. "It came to power on a cultural warfare agenda that was all about denigrating the '60s, which never struck me as being particularly persuasive."

He went to his first Dead show in 1985. "And I knew I would think about it for the rest of my life," he said.

Enriched by dozens of scholars—and later encouraged by the creation of the Grateful Dead Archive at UC Santa Cruz—fascination with the Dead acquired another dimension: depth. Those long moved by the Dead's music and community discovered intellectual connections that helped explain the experience, fusing it to ancient spiritual and cultural movements. Dead Studies took the experience of a Dead show and linked it to history itself.

RECOGNITION ARRIVED in other unexpected ways. In February 1987, an ice cream company based in Burlington, Vermont, released a new flavor. The idea came from one Jane Williamson, a fan of the Dead and a lover of ice cream. She dropped a postcard to her favorite ice cream

"THE ANSWER TO THE ATOM BOMB" | 381

maker, Ben & Jerry's, suggesting that a merger of the company's ice cream and the Dead, with its values and community and joy for life, would be a "winning combination." Ben Cohen, the company's flavor developer and founding light, set to work. These were the days before focus groups and testing labs, so tinkering with the formula consisted of Cohen's trying out recipe ideas himself and sharing them with friends. In this case, he emerged with a blend of chocolate chunks, cherries, and vanilla ice cream. He called it Cherry Garcia.

The company shipped a sample of its new product to Garcia, but it did not appear to register with him. Told there was an ice cream flavor named for him, Garcia replied that he was glad it was not a motor oil.

With sixties bravado—or naïveté—the company distributed Cherry Garcia to stores across the country in February 1987 without ever securing Garcia's permission. And though Garcia seemed not to mind, the Dead's lawyers insisted that he make some defense of his name, recognizing that it had value and that failure to defend it could weaken Garcia's case if others sought to exploit it in the future. Garcia and Ben & Jerry's easily reached an accommodation—in return for the use of his name, Garcia received a royalty from sales—and the deal would turn out to be extraordinarily lucrative for both, as Cherry Garcia rocketed to the top of the Ben & Jerry's sales charts, holding down a place as one of its top-selling flavors to this day. Although the company did not disclose how much Garcia received from his namesake dessert, its CEO, Dave Stever, said in 2024 that Garcia's share would have been enough for most people to live on in the 1990s. With that, Garcia had gone from living out of his car and eating Robert Hunter's canned pineapple to being paid a handsome salary just so people could eat ice cream with his name on it.

FAME AND money came with a question: Would they ruin the Dead? Would Garcia or his bandmates leap at these new riches and compromise the core vision that they had been exploring for decades? Versions

382 | HERE BESIDE THE RISING TIDE

of the question had swirled around them for decades, as one band after another took the easy road of money and left behind some of the initial magic. Garcia understood the temptation but enjoyed playing with it.

Meeting with reporters in September 1987, one correspondent asked Garcia, "Has success spoiled the Dead?" Without hesitating, he answered: "Yeah."

The room laughed, and another reporter pressed. "How so?" she asked. "How has it changed you?"

This time, Weir responded for the group. "Well," he said, in his loose, comfortable drawl, "I was noticing the other night, for instance, that when I'm going through pistachios, opening pistachios, the hard-to-open ones, I don't bother with them anymore. Who's got time?"

That was the Dead as the 1980s closed. Loose and comfortable, famous but not overwhelmed. Relaxed and enjoying the moment, for its own sake and as a counterpoint to the center of the country, which had swung with Reagan into its harder shell. Greed was ascendant, and dread was its natural byproduct—the grinding sense that life had to mean more than that. Those in search of something else had, in fact, something else to gravitate to. Garcia and the Dead were there to supply it.

Not everyone likes licorice. But those who do, really like it.

AIDS TUGGED at the heart of the Grateful Dead. After the appearance with Joan Baez at the end of 1987, the band kept up the work on behalf of those who were suffering from the disease that Reagan refused to acknowledge. On May 27, 1989, they performed at an event known as In Concert Against AIDS, headlining a day at the Oakland Coliseum that also featured John Fogerty, Tracy Chapman, Tower of Power, Los Lobos, and Joe Satriani. More than thirty thousand people attended.

If AIDS was a hometown cause, the state of the world's rainforests was also much on the minds of San Franciscans, where environmentalism had been an animating issue since the 1960s. As the 1980s drew to a close, the Dead agreed to work with the Rainforest Action Network and Greenpeace to raise money and awareness for forest protection. The band hosted its first benefit in 1988—a show at Madison Square Garden with Bruce Hornsby and the Range, Hall and Oates, and Suzanne Vega—and followed that with a continuing commitment to the effort.

Garcia, Weir, and Hart traveled to the United Nations to make the case for protecting the rainforests, and the band's outspoken support for the cause drew national attention that reflected the Dead's wide-ranging audience. Among the outlets that carried interviews with members of the Dead: *Good Morning America*, MTV News, *Cashbox*, *Rolling Stone*, the *San Francisco Chronicle*, and *The New York Times*.

Garcia found the whole experience both exhilarating and a little disheartening. Why, he asked, should it fall to the Grateful Dead to address an issue of international urgency and significance? He asked that not out of resentment—despite his customary political reticence, he seemed happy to join the effort—but rather out of bewilderment.

"Of all the incompetent fuckups that have to end up dealing with this serious problem, why it falls into our hands, I'll never fucking understand," he complained, good-naturedly. "We can barely get onstage and play, so doing this other stuff is amazing to me! But as long as it keeps falling our way, I guess we have to deal with it. We have no choice really."

GARY HART did not get back in the presidential race in 1988 after dropping out over his dalliance with Donna Rice and his reckless display of it aboard a yacht perfectly named the *Monkey Business*. Instead, the race unfolded in the shadow of Reagan. On the Republican side, Vice President George H. W. Bush sought to succeed the man he had served with for eight years, though Bush was challenged for a while by the cantankerous Senator Bob Dole and the more wholeheartedly and religiously conservative Pat Robertson. Democrats pined for New York governor Mario Cuomo but were willing to settle for Hart, only to have Hart self-destruct. Senator Joe Biden withdrew after he was caught plagiarizing a speech from a British politician, and other big names took a pass. That left Massachusetts governor Mike Dukakis, who gamely pressed the case against Bush and the legacy of Reagan.

It was not enough. Not nearly enough, in fact. Bush beat him in all but ten states and the District of Columbia, amassing 53 percent of the popular vote and 426 electoral votes, a landslide.

George Bush promised America a subtle shift from Reaganism, a gentler version of the angry forces that Reagan marshalled in his presidency. He brought a different background and orientation to the office. Bush was the blueblood son of a senator, a graduate of Yale, a lifetime member of the American elite who had himself served in Congress, as ambassador to the United Nations, and as director of the CIA before becoming Reagan's vice president. Genial and decent, he seemed likely to stay the Reagan course, though with a softer touch.

Still, Bush was committed to the extension of the Reagan legacy. He switched his position on abortion to oppose it in order to join Reagan's camp. He famously committed to holding the line on taxes—a promise he promptly broke—and to extending the Reagan administration's commitment to "peace through strength."

For Garcia and many of those in the Dead's expanding orbit, Bush felt more like a continuation than a relief. "The government falls into the hands of the people who love power and who are bright enough to be rich, and that's the way it's gonna be here," he lamented soon after Bush's election. "It doesn't work, really."

As for the new president himself? "Bush," said Garcia, "is a total idiot."

IN THE long contest of values defined on one side by Ronald Reagan and his admirers and on the other by the Dead and theirs, the 1980s brought matters to something of a draw. Reagan's America would hold sway for a generation of politicians in Washington, who would interpret his legacy as one of small government and individual freedom—neither an entirely accurate reading of Reagan's record—and would often honor it in the breach. Those values aged unevenly, and would come to tatters in the Trump years, when the most obvious nods to Reagan would be record deficits and tax breaks for the rich, hardly hallmarks of individual freedom.

The Dead, meanwhile, worked a more alchemical magic. While Reagan and Bush shuffled off the American stage, the Dead held its place, drawing in those souls who imagined that safety was to be found in peaceful coexistence rather than under the threat of Armageddon, that comfort and support were to be found in community, that joy was the product of creativity and exuberance—and best experienced with others.

There are few winners in the marketplace of values. Notions wax and wane. Freedom, community, creativity—all have their place at all times, sometimes ascendant, sometimes in decline. But the end of the Reagan-Bush era offered clues as Americans voted with their feet. Although Americans rallied to him in his final months, the last years of Reagan's presidency saw his approval rating drop below 50 percent as the Iran-Contra scandal and questions about his cognitive decline haunted him. Bush did even worse, losing his reelection bid to Bill Clinton in 1992.

The Dead and their followers, meanwhile, clung to their community and continued their pursuit of freedom and creative improvisation when they were in fashion in the 1960s and 1970s and when they seemed to go out of style in the 1980s. A young person moved by those ideas in the 1960s might have joined the Black Panthers or participated in the Free Speech or civil rights movements, might have trailed around after Country Joe and the Fish or even attended Woodstock. In the 1980s, that person found the Dead.

The numbers, in this case, tell a story. In 1981, the first year of Reagan's presidency, the Grateful Dead sold about $7.4 million in concert tickets. By 1989, the last year of that epoch, the Dead had had a hit single, a popular album, even a music video. Garcia had slipped away and, miraculously, returned. In 1989, the Dead sold more than $29 million in tickets. The numbers for Reagan and Bush faded. Those for the Dead skyrocketed. People found something in them, something more than just rock 'n' roll.

JOSEPH CAMPBELL was a student of myth. His work was deep, and deeply rooted in the classics. *The Hero with a Thousand Faces* was his best-known treatise, a scholarly inquiry into the nature of myth and its resilient form across the ages—the "monomyth" that Campbell posited as the essence of storytelling and culture itself. In Campbell's formulation, the hero is lured into a journey and confronts a presence that blocks his way. Overcoming or evading that obstacle, he encounters new ideas or forces, eventually reaching a climax or nadir and emerging in triumph. He then returns, equipped with his new insights, and his world is reborn. That fundamental cycle is of departure, initiation, and return, and it appears, Campbell demonstrated, in literature across the ages.

Among Campbell's interested readers were members of the Grateful Dead. Garcia was intrigued by Campbell's *A Skeleton Key to Finnegans Wake,* Hart had read *The Way of the Animal Powers,* and Weir, dyslexia notwithstanding, had plowed through *The Hero with a Thousand Faces.* When Weir happened upon an associate of Campbell while jogging, a connection between the band and Campbell was struck. The Dead hosted a dinner for Campbell, and he attended a Dead show in Oakland in early 1986. He was enchanted.

On November 1, 1986, while Garcia was still recovering from his coma and hospitalization that summer, Campbell joined him and Hart for an event at San Francisco's Palace of Fine Arts. The program was entitled "Ritual to Rapture: From Dionysus to The Grateful Dead."

Campbell led the discussion, showing slides of artifacts from ancient Greece and beyond, describing mystery and cycles of time, tracing themes from the Temple of Apollo through the rise of Christianity under the Roman Empire. He warned of the "disheartening" history of "how a tradition of monotheistic, self-flattering confidence can come in and mutilate everything that was ever existing before it." The audience, appreciating the significance of that remark, laughed and applauded.

At the core of Campbell's address that day was his analysis of the tension between the form of the Apollonian and the whimsy and even destructive qualities of the Dionysian, the push and pull between structure and disruption. Art requires both, he noted, and he found Dionysus within the Grateful Dead and its devoted fans.

Neither the Dead nor Deadheads needed their experience to be validated by Campbell, but his scholarship placed that experience in a vast tradition, one as old as humanity, stretching from Greece and Rome through the celebrations of Greek Easter (Campbell called it Russian Easter), the worship of the Virgin Mary, and devotion to the Lord of the Living World. Those celebrations wound through cultures and epochs, from crucifixion to modern dread. What Campbell saw at a Dead show was a celebration of life, an affirmation of community, an expression of faith.

"It somehow involved everybody. There were kids there. There were old people there. And in other parts of the building, you could see that there were people just dancing and dancing," Campbell said of his visit to the Dead. "And that's what it is, the dance of life. . . . And they were not bound by any particular cultural or religious commitment to this group or that. It seemed to me, and I'm meaning this very seriously, a prime religious experience that transcended all the bondages and definitions of who and what that are the curse of the world today."

It was more than moving. It was, Campbell said, an antidote to dread itself: "This, I would say, is the answer to the atom bomb."

Mega Dead, filling stadiums. Silver Bowl, Las Vegas, Nevada, May 15, 1993.

Jay Blakesberg/Retro Photo Archive

CHAPTER 17

Bad Architecture and Old Whores

THE 1980S ENDED FOR THE DEAD ON JULY 26, 1990. BRENT Mydland had been struggling. Always insecure, Mydland wanted to feel at home within the Dead but found it difficult to relax in the rough camaraderie of the band. He would read mail from fans and feel slighted, wonder whether he was fully accepted by them or even by his bandmates. Garcia insisted that Mydland was never meant to feel like the "new guy," but Mydland couldn't help it. The road was hard on him, too. Married and with two young daughters, Jessica and Jennifer, he found that separation wore on him and isolated him. He drank heavily. Hard drugs followed.

By the late 1980s, Mydland was both mightily contributing to the Dead and painfully slipping away from them. He wrote two songs for his first album after joining the band—"Far from Me" and "Easy to Love You," which appeared on *Go to Heaven*, released in 1980—and two more on the next—"Tons of Steel" and his part of "Hell in a Bucket," a band effort, on the immensely popular *In the Dark*, released in 1987. Two years later, he was the band's biggest contributor to *Built to Last*, co-writing four numbers and singing all four, giving him the lion's share of the overall package. The album may not have impressed critics, but Mydland was clearly a full-fledged member of the band.

He was a vivacious, notable stage presence as well. His organ playing gave the band a new sound, and Garcia in particular appreciated his verve and originality, especially after weathering Godchaux's decline. Moreover, Mydland brought a tenderness to his work, an extension, perhaps, of his personal fragility but one that softened some of the band's more rowdy instincts.

And yet he suffered, retreating into the drugs that were all too available to a troubled soul in the center of the Dead's traveling universe. "From the beginning of his association with the Dead, it was obvious he was carrying a lot of pain around with him," Blair Jackson wrote in the pages of *The Golden Road*. He eventually took to heroin, then moved to shooting or smoking it or morphine with cocaine—the very dangerous practice of "speedballing." He was stopped more than once for driving under the influence, and by the summer of 1990 he was facing the possibility of jail time. Garcia might have offered counsel or support, but he himself was retreating as the 1980s ended.

The Dead were up and down in those months, some sloppy shows when Garcia's attention seemed to wander, but also sparklers, including a performance in March in which they were joined by Branford Marsalis, who lent his jazz talents to a version of "Birdsong," infusing it with a sublime saxophone line that the song did not know it needed until he supplied it. For Marsalis, an exquisitely trained jazz player, the opportunity to perform with the Dead was eye-opening. "They'd play the song, and then it would just take off," he said, adding that Garcia "was a marvelously gifted melody maker. . . . It was a joy to play with him."

The Dead completed the twelve-show run on July 23 after performances in Indiana and Illinois and headed for home, where a brief touring break awaited. Knowing he was back from the road, friends called Mydland at his home in Lafayette. He did not answer. They well knew of his despair and drug use and the unraveling of his marriage, so when he did not pick up his phone, they drove over to his house to check on him.

Still getting no response, they let themselves in and found Mydland, fully clothed, lying on the floor. By the time the police arrived, the place had been cleaned—evidence of drug use carefully removed—but toxicology tests confirmed what everyone suspected from the beginning: Mydland died from a drug overdose, "acute cocaine and narcotic intoxication" in the cold words of the coroner. He was thirty-seven.

BAD ARCHITECTURE AND OLD WHORES | 391

* * *

THE DEAD sang often of death and heartbreak; sadness hung about the music as surely as joy and brightness. But even in that welter of deep emotion, "Brokedown Palace" occupied a special place. It expressed the need to go on, to climb out from the wreckage, to "plant a weeping willow" and sing a lullaby. The song had been with the Dead ever since 1970. It appeared in the band's repertoire through the 1970s, and it held a place of quiet honor on *American Beauty*. As grief piled up in the years that followed, "Brokedown Palace" often touched those in mourning, including some whose ties to the Dead were profound. And in so doing, it united past and present grief, traversing time and distance.

On January 21, 1984, Ken Kesey's twenty-year-old son, Jed, was on board a bus with ten wrestlers and two coaches from the University of Oregon wrestling team. The bus slipped on an icy road, tore through a guardrail, and plunged over an embankment. One student, Lorenzo West, died before reaching the hospital; Jed was gravely injured. He lingered, unconscious, for several days.

His stricken father held Jed through his final moments, saw his face grimace in pain, saw the look of recognition, "the quick flickerback of consciousness, the awful hurt being realized," as Ken Kesey wrote in a letter to friends. Jed died on January 23, two days after the crash. "It was," Ken Kesey wrote, "the toughest thing any of us has ever had to go through."

A few months after Jed's death, the Dead were performing in Eugene, and Kesey went to see his old friends. "They were playing at our opera house," he recalled. "They did their usual stuff and got their big ovations and then, they started playing 'Brokedown Palace,' and they all turned toward me, and all our family was sitting up there. They all turned toward us and the guys in the audience began to turn toward us. And that song was sent from the Grateful Dead to our bruised hearts."

Six years later, the Dead were playing in Philadelphia on September 12, and for the first time since Mydland's death, they played "Brokedown Palace," choosing it as their encore that night. "Fare you well, my honey," Garcia sang, his voice tender and raw. "Fare you well, my only true one. / All the birds that were singing / Have flown except you alone." Mydland's name was not spoken, but his absence was heart-wrenchingly felt.

Decades later, Mountain Girl was sitting in her Eugene, Oregon, home and chatting on a weekday morning, sun streaming in the south-facing windows. Suddenly, Mydland's image and sound appeared on her television screen. Mydland's distinctively forceful falsetto wafted in from the past. Mountain Girl's memory was a little iffy by then, but the reminder of her old friend drew her back to earth, and she teared up. "When Jerry heard the news, he couldn't stop crying," she recalled. That was unlike Garcia. He tended to be stoic, and he'd lost friends and band-mates before—Pigpen and Keith Godchaux had already fallen away, the Dead's sad, strange history of losing keyboard players. This, though, hit him especially hard. Perhaps, Mountain Girl suggested, it pricked some guilt, some recognition that Garcia himself had seen Mydland's decline and was incapable of arresting it, if only because he, too, was slipping away.

HE WEPT in private. Publicly, the Dead soldiered on. "You don't cry around the Grateful Dead," John Perry Barlow wrote. The Dead's collective machismo did not allow it. Individually, members of the band might weep or reflect; together, they had the rough companionship of a ball club, what Barlow described as "emotional availability that ran the full gamut between spite and irony." Death takes many tolls.

With a fall tour planned and venues reserved, the band offered the keyboard job to Bruce Hornsby, a big name in his own right and a de-voted fan of the Dead. Joel Selvin of the *San Francisco Chronicle* broke the news of Hornsby's participation.

Hornsby had met Garcia in 1987 when he and his band opened for the Dead—he had asked for and received the Dead's permission to play "I Know You Rider." He and Garcia hit it off from the start, and Hornsby

BAD ARCHITECTURE AND OLD WHORES | 393

periodically opened for the Dead after that. Garcia seems to have considered replacing Mydland with Hornsby at the end of 1989, when Mydland's condition was worsening, but the two missed connecting, and the opportunity passed. Now, as a member of the band, Hornsby brought panache to some of its well-worn numbers, and his fresh take energized Garcia. But Hornsby had his own career—he had already sold six million records—and his participation with the Dead was understood to be temporary. Even as he agreed to step in, the Dead hired Vince Welnick to be Mydland's permanent replacement.

A Madison Square Garden run in September with Hornsby and Welnick sharing keyboard duties saw the Dead experimenting with new musical ideas and applying them to some of its classic work, including "Dark Star," which the band rarely attempted in the 1980s.

Welnick, previously of the Tubes, resembled Mydland in some respects—a skilled keyboard player who could handle the harmonies—but he arrived without much sense of the Dead's songbook, much less its customs and relationships. A rare recording of a Grateful Dead rehearsal features Garcia walking Welnick through some of the Dead's most recognizable tunes. When Garcia suggested practicing "Terrapin," Welnick responded, "That's deep, right?" Garcia laughed. "It's not really deep," he chuckled. "There's just a lot of parts to it." Welnick asked which version Garcia would recommend, and Garcia warned him off listening to the record, which was "stiff" and orchestrated. He suggested finding a live version.

Riffing through other milestones in the Dead's extensive repertoire, Garcia noted that Welnick would have to learn "Uncle John's Band"—"a simple song but lots of singing"—and Welnick tinkered with the piano part of "Fire on the Mountain." Garcia reassured him that "China Cat" was "basically simple" and sketched the transition to "I Know You Rider," arguably the oldest song in the Dead's history. " 'He's Gone.' It's easy," Garcia said. "This is an easy one." Welnick felt confident. "I'll get that eventually," he said.

The atmosphere that day was friendly and accommodating, Garcia patient and Welnick eager to learn. But it also made clear that Welnick was very much starting from scratch, making notes on songs he'd never heard as he joined a band that had been performing them for decades.

The early reviews were bad, very bad. WELNICK CAN'T KEEP PACE WITH THE GRATEFUL DEAD read a December headline in the *Alameda Times-Star*. The story was even worse. Welnick "proved himself unable to fill Mydland's shoes," his playing was "an awkward and unnecessary counterpoint" to Garcia. "He has no idea what he's doing up there," the critic, Dave Becker, wrote.

Welnick's performing would improve, but he never seemed fully to absorb the Dead's approach, preferring to linger at the edges of the sound rather than explore it himself. Which is not to say that the Dead suddenly went dark. The early 1990s found Garcia experimenting with a MIDI controller on his guitar, trying out new sounds that could feel fresh or overproduced depending on the evening. By the fall of 1991, Hornsby could feel the energy ebbing. And yet even the worst shows— in 1994 and 1995, there were many—had moments of brilliance, flashes of inspiration, glimpses of magic.

"For me, the experience is one of tremendous clarity," Garcia said in 1990. "I experience it as a kind of transparency, and it's very, very easy when you get to that place. It's impossible to make a wrong decision. In fact, the music is kind of playing itself in a way because I'm not making decisions about where I'm gonna be anymore or where I'm gonna end up or how long a phrase is gonna last or any of that. . . . It's like an invisible bridge across a huge chasm and if you don't look down, it'll be okay."

GARCIA HAD always been mercurial. He could be gentle and forgiving, and he was a famously attentive listener. When Steve Silberman sat down with him, he fell easily into conversation and was startled by how approachable Garcia was, only to realize, "Of course he's cool. He's Jerry Garcia!" But Garcia could be brusque and temperamental, too. Early in the Dead's career, he was furious with Lesh for spacing out during a show; he confronted him and shoved him so hard that Lesh fell down a flight of stairs. He had chronic stage fright, though he felt at ease once he began to play. And he could be sad, even morose. Leaving one Madison Square Garden show in the early 1980s, he complained to Susan Klein that he should have been a shoe salesman.

He ignored his health. He ate ice cream by the quart and let his appearance and hygiene disintegrate. When others complained about his smell, he brushed them off, suggesting that they wear cologne if they wanted to smell something different. In his final years, he skirted the edges of full-on heroin addiction, but he was rarely clean for long. His appearance and well-being would come and go depending on whether he was using or sober. The trend was downward.

A HALLOWEEN show in 1991 swirled together three strains of Grateful Dead cultural history when the Dead, including Hornsby, delivered a contemplative "Dark Star" to an appreciative Oakland audience. As the song unfolded, the band was joined by Ken Kesey, who took a microphone to eulogize Bill Graham. Graham, so long a pillar of the Dead's economics and performance, had died in a helicopter crash six days earlier, roiling the music community in the Bay Area and beyond. Kesey's extended riff was all Kesey, literary and absurd and deeply heartfelt. It evoked his own son, Mydland, the Dead's roots in the Acid Tests, their commercial success under Graham's stewardship, and the painful reminder of the losses that brought them to this moment and bound them together in the way that only grief can.

"I was in D.C.," Kesey began in old Acid Test fashion, rapping, "and when I got the message, I thought of two things. I thought of my son going over a cliff and Bill Graham spending a thousand bucks to put a thing up on the hill that points in all directions in Oregon so you can always find your direction from the top of that hill. And I thought of one more thing, and it's a little heavy, but that's what it's about. Nobody else preaches across the distance with their hand on your shoulder. . . . That's been true for a long time, reaching across. When you guys played

"Brokedown Palace" at that gig, I knew. Shit, this is the Grateful Dead telling me about my son! It's as big in time as it gets! And old Bill knew it! He knew it! He knew it!"

Kesey continued, kicking up dust about warriors and death and the state of the world, finally ending with a thunderous recitation of E. E. Cummings's poem "Buffalo Bill's," the Dead furiously playing behind him, his voice rising, the tempo speeding up to join him. And then it cooled back down. He left the stage. The jam faded into "Drums." "Drums" gave way to "Space." "Space" resolved back to "Dark Star," at first throaty and then lighter.

The set continued with a sprightly cover of "The Last Time" by the Stones; a wistful Jerry ballad, "Standing on the Moon," that flowed into Weir's "Throwing Stones"; and then a big, loud, emotion-purging "Not Fade Away," with Hornsby's keyboard giving Garcia's guitar a backboard. And finally, for an encore, the Dead trotted out its jocular take on Warren Zevon's "Werewolves of London."

It was a set that delivered the full range of history and culture, presented in spoken word and melody, in the Dead's own music and in what it clipped from the surrounding culture to give it meaning. All presented with the tenderness of the wildly popular, and deeply wounded, members of the Grateful Dead.

THE DEAD'S operation kept growing. A decade earlier, the Dead's earnings for the second half of the year had come in at about $825,000, but the band's bills—overhead, salaries, equipment—added up to $730,000 for the same period, leaving a surplus of just $95,000, out of which sound and lights still needed to be paid. By the mid-1980s, the band had a $250,000 line of credit and was swimming in ticket and merchandise revenue. The Dead paid $5,000 for catering alone during one set of Oakland shows. Band members braced for heavy tax bills.

And once *In the Dark* catapulted them to new fame, those numbers skyrocketed. The Dead put up the top tour of 1993, 81 shows in 29 cities, ticket sales of $45.6 million (second place went to Rod Stewart with $30.5 million, followed by Neil Diamond, Paul McCartney, and Bette Midler). The average Dead show in 1993 grossed more than $1.5 million. In one short 1994 tour, the band performed twenty-three shows in eight cities over six weeks, starting in Oakland on February 25 and ending in Miami on April 8. They sold 373,995 tickets; only 49 seats were not spoken for. The Dead pocketed a net profit of $511,390.42—on ticket sales alone.

But what had so long worked for the Dead as a modest band of traveling souls and even as a successful act of the 1980s began to unravel as the crowds went from big to immense, especially as they began to generate their own weather—crowds gathering for the sheer fun of being part of a crowd, building on themselves. Thousands of people without tickets began to descend on venues where the Dead was scheduled to play, either hoping to pick one up there or planning just to spend a day or two drifting in the culture without any real hope of seeing the band itself. At first the band ignored the gathering mass, but it kept growing.

LOCAL POLICE had always been present at Dead shows. By the end of the 1980s, *The Golden Road* and *Dupree's Diamond News,* chroniclers of Deadhead life, regularly featured letters and articles about the "overabundant numbers of cops," complaints about police overreacting to crowds or drugs, even the occasional presence of the National Guard at shows. Undercover officers were present as well. The July 1990 issue of *Dupree's* featured a letter from a twenty-four-year-old Deadhead arrested in Cincinnati after selling a half sheet of acid to undercover officers for fifty dollars; the magazine also published a letter from a prison inmate serving twenty-one months and noting the rising number of Deadheads among the prison population.

Interviewed by the *Los Angeles Times* in 1992, DEA administrator Robert C. Bonner called LSD "a potential problem drug of the future" and acknowledged that the DEA was increasing its efforts to thwart the sale and use of the drug. From arresting about a hundred dealers a year in the latter part of the 1980s, the agency made 243 arrests in 1991 and more than three hundred in 1992.

Although Bonner denied a specific program to target Deadheads, he confirmed that the DEA had embarked on what it called "Operation Looking Glass" and acknowledged that "it is true that we have had some investigations that have led us to some Grateful Dead concerts."

LSD prosecutions were particularly striking because of federal drug laws that relied upon the weight of so-called "carriers" in measuring the amount of LSD to be calculated for the purposes of sentencing defendants to prison. Thus, a defendant who impregnated sheets of paper with LSD would be sentenced based on the combined weight of the paper and the drug. A defendant who put the same amount of LSD into sugar cubes or a pitcher of orange juice could do exponentially more time.

The results were stark and manifestly unfair. An LSD dealer with one hundred doses of pure LSD inside a bottle (which did not count for sentencing purposes because it was not ingested) would face ten months in jail; the same amount of the drug spread onto blotter paper would earn that defendant five years; if impregnated onto sugar cubes, federal guidelines called for a sentence of at least fifteen years.

As DEA agents found targets at Dead shows, the Grateful Dead found itself the unwitting agent of drug enforcement—and irrational, mean-spirited drug enforcement at that.

A FRESH observer of the American culture and politics, a modern Alexis de Tocqueville, in the final decade of the twentieth century could have been forgiven for overlooking signs of the counterculture. The passions and urgencies of the 1960s—and even the 1980s—seemed far beneath the surface. Reagan and his anti-Soviet bellicosity were gone, and with them the mass demonstrations against the neutron bomb or in favor of a nuclear freeze. The poignance of Reagan's refusal to confront AIDS and the thousands of deaths that ensued faded as the government at last shelved its moral judgments and rallied to address the disease as a health crisis. Nelson Mandela came to power in South Africa, ending apartheid and the international demands for its dismantlement. The fall of the Berlin Wall in 1989 was followed by the disintegration of the Soviet Union, which eventually collapsed of its own weight in 1991, ending the superpower struggle that had defined and shadowed American lives since the end of World War II. In 1992, the political scientist and historian Francis Fukuyama declared victory for Western liberal democracies, "an unabashed victory of economic and political liberalism," and argued that its ascendance marked *The End of History and the Last Man,* a book-length take on an essay he had written three years earlier, when he raised the idea as a question, namely, "The End of History?"

Fukuyama's much-misunderstood piece and book suggested a conclusion, and, with it, the end of struggle and progress. Its triumphalism— "there are powerful reasons for believing that [liberalism] will govern the material world *in the long run*"—negated the premise of any counterculture: that alternative ways of living are necessary to challenge the dominant social and political consensus. But, to bastardize Twain, the reports of history's death were exaggerated. Neither counterculture— nor, for that matter, Marxism—ended in the early 1990s. They were, rather, coopted and amended, absorbed into mainline politics and academia, where they bubbled and simmered.

Witness Jane Fonda. The same activist once pilloried for visiting North Vietnam during the war matured into an effective advocate with the ability to join old radicals with new liberals. She turned increasingly to environmental causes, highlighting the accelerating dangers of climate change and fighting to remedy social injustices associated with environmental pollution. It was, she would say later, a return to her heart, to memories of feeling at peace near the ocean and its creatures, far from the violent activism around the war or even Tom Hayden's voyages into the vicissitudes of capitalism. The earth brought Fonda home.

Meanwhile, hippies no longer massed in the Haight. Earth Day settled into a quiet annual ritual rather than a giant show of force. The

Dead stayed at the Four Seasons, dined at the U.S. Capitol, and played for tens of thousands. Any memory of the band from the days when the number of people onstage eclipsed the number in the audience had long faded into a haze of addled memories.

As part of that larger dynamic, Bill Clinton's rise to power was confusing for the counterculture and the left generally. Because he was young by presidential standards, forty-six at the time of his election, he had grown up with the counterculture and shared some of its values. He cared about the environment. He valued education and community. He radiated empathy and was never more compelling than in moments of national distress. He played the sax. Even his sexual license, the source of many of his troubles, and his brush with marijuana—Did he inhale?—were reminders of his youth in a changing America. But authenticity also stood at the heart of that culture's value system, and Clinton's phoniness, so central to who he was and with its shady reminders of Nixon, always inserted a note of wariness.

The ambivalence of the left toward Clinton crystallized almost immediately. As a candidate, Clinton had supported the repeal of the military's long-standing ban on gays serving in the armed forces. He framed the question as one of freedom—in this case, the freedom of gay men and women to serve their country without retrograde discrimination. As a young and enlightened representative of a new generation, Clinton was well suited to end the archaic restriction. Except that Clinton was also cautious and inclined to half-solutions. No sooner had he been elected in 1992—a narrow victory in which the participation of third-party candidate Ross Perot held Clinton to just 43 percent of the popular vote—than Clinton equivocated. Senior military officials warned against dropping the ban, which they argued would undermine "unit cohesion," and senior Republicans on Capitol Hill warned against moving too quickly. Clinton agreed to studies and delay, and then, in the middle of 1993, announced what became known as "Don't Ask, Don't Tell," under which gays could serve in the military so long as they hid their sexual orientation.

Was that progress? Gays could now serve, after all. Or was it offensive? Gays had to hide who they were in return for the privilege of risking their lives for their country. It was both, of course, wrapped around the codification of lying as a matter of national policy. "Don't Ask, Don't Tell" set a tone for Clinton's presidency. It would be marked by progress muffled by caution, secrecy, and lies.

That did not prevent him from producing a presidency of enormous success and consequence. Even as scandals dogged him, Clinton strengthened the economy, lowered federal deficits, and recalibrated basic assumptions of American politics.

"Self-reliance and teamwork are not opposing virtues," Clinton said. "We must have both."

GRATEFUL DEAD lyricist John Perry Barlow got a call from the FBI in May 1990. Apple was furiously demanding to know who had stolen a section of source code that helped to drive its breakthrough product, the Macintosh computer. The FBI's search for a possible hacker brought the bureau to Barlow, who had attended a hackers' conference in San Francisco and whose facility with tech—and whose contact with some of its leading figures—were well known. The agent gingerly poked at Barlow, who lectured him about how source code and hacking worked.

The encounter plunged Barlow into an extended rumination on free expression and the internet. "Cyberspace," wrote Barlow, becoming the first person to apply that term to the new field of computer-based communications and community, "has a lot in common with the 19th Century West. It is vast, unmapped, culturally and legally ambiguous. . . . It is, of course, a perfect breeding ground for both outlaws and new ideas about liberty." That observation aptly described the early days of LSD in the hills south of San Francisco, not to mention the larger Grateful Dead project, so Barlow had some experience to draw upon.

Cyberspace was not a perfect replica for personal community, but it appealed to some of the same yearning that had once powered the communes that dotted the American landscape in the 1970s. Olompali was not a chat room, nor a "conference" on the Well, but they all drew people of like or similar minds together, physically or otherwise. "Welcome to Cyberspace," *Time* magazine, of all places, announced. The magazine commissioned a piece from Stewart Brand, "We Owe It All to the Hippies."

"Newcomers to the Internet," Brand wrote, "are often startled to discover themselves not so much in some soulless colony of technocrats as in a kind of cultural Brigadoon—a flowering remnant of the '60s, when hippie communalism and libertarian politics formed the roots of the modern cyberrevolution." Fred Turner's history of the period was aptly titled *From Counterculture to Cyberculture*. Even the devices that linked the new communities—home computers—spoke to a new iteration of freedom. The world's information was now available from home, unrestricted by even such institutions as libraries. As Brand famously aphorized: Information wants to be free.

Angered by the persecution of hackers, whom Barlow regarded with a mixture of curiosity, skepticism, and parental pride—he described himself as something of their Scout leader—the songwriter for the Dead helped to create the Electronic Frontier Foundation, intended to patrol freedom on the internet. Barlow acknowledged that computers were unsettling. They redistributed power along with information, offered users new vision, and exposed them to new vulnerabilities. Barlow called on those "who are comfortable with these disorienting changes" to do "everything in our power to convey that comfort to others." As Garcia had been to LSD and its new landscape, so Barlow was to the computer.

And thus it was especially poignant that just as Barlow peered into the beyond, one where computers and communications would pry open new expanses, limited only by the imagination, freedom as limitless as the Great American West, Garcia bumped up against the boundaries of what he had once imagined as limitless. Drugs had opened Garcia's perception, had placed his ego in check, had squashed the notion that reality was dull or small. But the magic wore off. By the 1990s, drugs had come all the way around for Garcia, from aperture to freedom to the tight grip of ownership.

It was August 1993, and the members of the Dead were home, taking a couple of weeks off between an East Coast summer tour that ended with two shows in Washington at the end of June and a short run of shows slated for Eugene, Oregon, and Mountain View, California, in August. It was a rare opportunity to regroup and replenish, a break in the punishing schedules of the 1990s, when concerts piled on top of each other and the crowd could seem an undifferentiated mass. Now they were home, free to sleep in their own beds, bask in the warmth of family, feel the cool breezes of Marin County and San Francisco. They had the chance to breathe.

Garcia's days did not allow for much of that. He spent this August day visiting automatic teller machines in the Richmond District in San Francisco five times, withdrawing $200 here, $300 there. By day's end, he'd taken out a total of $1,200. Such is the freedom-depriving tether of the addict—a rich addict, to be sure, but an addict nonetheless.

WHAT WAS left of Garcia's personal life fell apart. He tried to be a husband to Manasha, though he was still married to Mountain Girl. He spoke of enjoying time with Keelin, then still a young child. But he was unmoored. He reached into his deep past, even before his marriage to Sara, searching for a feeling that he had lost many years before. He reconnected with his teenage girlfriend, Barbara "Brigid" Meier.

Garcia first wrote to Meier in early 1990. She had remained in touch with Hunter but had not heard from Garcia in years. Garcia asked Dennis McNally to set up a meeting with Meier. McNally suggested that Meier, a practicing Buddhist, interview Garcia for *Tricycle,* the then new journal of Buddhist teachings. Meier was living near Boulder in 1991, and when the Dead stopped in Denver, it provided the occasion for Garcia and Meier to reunite. Using the guise of the interview, they did. They discussed Buddhism—and the interview duly appeared in the magazine—but also their lives. Garcia confessed that a part of him was still "very much in love with you."

For a few giddy months, it seemed that their old love had returned.

They vacationed in Hawaii, where Garcia introduced her to scuba diving—having taken up scuba in the late 1980s, Garcia became an enthusiastic devotee, plunging into a colorful world where he could float, freed from the baggage of his cumbersome weight, surrounded by color and motion and the sound of air flowing through the regulator. She encouraged him to work on his health, and he did, which seemed to ignite his creativity as well, as Garcia and Hunter delivered three new songs. Two were charming. "Liberty" was a gently political excursion, a paean to antiauthoritarianism that sketched the periphery of a libertarian worldview. "Lazy River Road" picked up themes of moonlight and rail cars, another trip through the Dead's long habitation of the American West.

The third was majestic. Hunter and Garcia, friends for three decades and granted a moment for reflection, were feeling their age and suddenly reminded of their youth, there in the person of Barbara Meier. They retreated to a pool house on Hunter's property and went to work, Hunter feeding Garcia one verse at a time, while Garcia put together the melody on an electric piano. Complex emotions—nostalgia, age, wistfulness, regret—poured into the song. "Summer flies and August dies," Hunter wrote, "the world grows dark and mean." And yet there were days, and days between, "polished like a golden bowl, the finest ever seen." "Days Between," as McNally observed, was the last masterpiece of the Grateful Dead.

Garcia's flirtation with Meier ended badly. Advised that he was using heroin again, Meier attempted to raise the subject delicately with him. It was after a show one night, and they were back at the hotel. Gently, nervously, she pressed her point: "I said, 'I just want you to know that I know that you're using. And that's fine. That's okay. That's cool. You do what you want to do. I'm not going to try and stop you. I just really don't want any secrets between us. I just don't want any secrets.'"

The room, she said, "went cold." Garcia responded: "I think it's time for you to go now. You know, I can't thank you enough, but this isn't going to work."

With that, Meier was gone, never to see Garcia again. In the mean-

BAD ARCHITECTURE AND OLD WHORES | 405

time, their reunion had hurt Manasha Matheson. Long suspicious of Garcia's attachments to other women, Matheson had at first been shielded from his infatuation with Meier. Once he had decided to commit to Meier, however, he'd broken off with Matheson in a letter, leaving her and Keelin behind as he tried to exhume the peace of his youth. Coldly, Garcia's lawyer let Matheson know that she had thirty days to vacate his house. "That broke my heart," she said.

Meier and Matheson had been sent packing. Garcia did not wallow for long. Deborah Koons reappeared, and their romance resumed.

BEGINNING IN 1992, the Dead performed "So Many Roads," a Hunter-Garcia composition that took age and experience as its subject. "It's Hunter writing me from my point of view," Garcia noted, adding that Hunter's lyrics "express the emotional content of my soul." The roads it considered had led him around the world, but "All I want," he sang, "is one to take me home."

"So Many Roads" cast "home" as San Francisco or a place of soulful quiet. For the Dead, meanwhile, the idea of home expanded in the 1990s. They were welcome everywhere, and in company that once would have shunned them.

Case in point: When Clinton won the presidency, the Grateful Dead were invited to perform at his inauguration. The band did not appear per se, but various members joined with other musical icons on January 18, 1993, on the Washington Mall, a venue inconceivable in the long years of Nixon, Reagan, and Bush (or even Carter). On Inauguration Night, a trimmed-down version of the band—including Weir, Garcia, and Hornsby—played the Tennessee Ball, surely one of few times that "Hail to the Chief" has been followed by "Proud Mary" and the "Beer Barrel Polka." Later, when the Dead were invited to Vice President Al Gore's official residence, they showed up with full entourage in tow and were charmed by the Gores' hospitality, though Garcia was not overcome by deference. He managed to sneak off for a toke, the better to appreciate the strangeness of the event.

406 | HERE BESIDE THE RISING TIDE

The Establishment received the Grateful Dead. Garcia dined on Capitol Hill with Vermont senator Patrick Leahy. The Dead were featured, along with Ben & Jerry's, Patagonia, Celestial Seasonings, and several others, in a study of "companies with a conscience." Garcia unveiled a line of neckties. Selling for $28.50 each, they were an overnight success: Phil Jackson, a fan of the Dead, wore one on the floor of a Chicago Bulls game; Bloomingdale's sold fifteen hundred in the first few days; retailers ordered a hundred thousand nationwide. The Dead were inducted into the Rock and Roll Hall of Fame, though Garcia skipped the ceremony—he wasn't fond of honors, and his addiction inclined him to avoid events other than shows. He was represented by a life-size cardboard cutout of himself.

The band even inserted itself into geopolitics, when the Dead made a modest donation to the Lithuanian national basketball team and the team competed in the 1992 Olympics in tie-dye shirts and shorts, beating the Soviet Union for the bronze medal while flying the colors of the Dead—a cheerful act of rebellion that combined liberation and the band's love of basketball, one of Walton's many contributions to their history.

Musicians registered their admiration as well. Etta James had enjoyed the Dead ever since she appeared with the band for a New Year's show in 1982—backstage after the show, she exulted: "This is the church's music, healing music. . . . Who would have fuckin' thought? From a bunch of stoned hippies." Within a decade, the word was out. Clarence Clemons of Springsteen's fabled E Street Band joined the Dead for five performances in 1988 and 1989 and floated the idea of joining the band, though it never came to pass. More successful were gigs with Branford Marsalis and Ornette Coleman, whom Garcia had long admired and had collaborated with. The great experimental jazz player caught his first Dead show in 1987 and forged a friendship with Garcia. In 1993, he sat in with the band in Oakland on February 23, thrilling musicians and audience alike with his powerful improvising during "Space," his respectful, painterly contributions to "Stella Blue," and his swinging spirit on "Love Light."

These were among the most recognized and admired musicians in the world, and they came from outside what might be considered the Dead's orbit. Their attraction spoke to the Dead's growing cross-cultural appeal. So, too, did the Dead's choice of an opening act in 1993, when Sting, one of the most popular performers of the early 1990s, warmed up for the Dead on an eleven-show run. Sting said he accepted the invitation because he wanted to see for himself what the fuss was about.

Perhaps the Establishment's most fun overture came in 1993, when the band was invited by the San Francisco Giants to sing the National Anthem for the team's Opening Day. Granted, it was an invitation in their hometown and extended by the Giants, whom Garcia had loved since childhood. Nevertheless, it marked some kind of change: The Grateful Dead were not exactly a marching band nor known for their patriotism.

Garcia, Weir, and Welnick agreed to represent the band at the ballpark on the afternoon of April 12, 1993, the Giants' home opener of the season. Once they were signed up, Garcia pooh-poohed practicing for the occasion. "I know the words," he insisted to McNally. But the anthem is a notoriously difficult song to perform, and McNally was worried that Garcia would slough it off only to be embarrassed in front of a stadium full of baseball fans, many of them less forgiving than Deadheads.

Rather than confront Garcia, McNally suggested to Welnick that someone needed to get Garcia to take the event seriously. Welnick understood, and he told Garcia that he was nervous about the event and wanted to rehearse. Garcia could hardly say no to a fellow musician, and so he agreed. The three members of the Dead set to it, writing out the lyrics and practicing their harmonies.

The day came. The members of the band did a sound check that morning and were introduced to several Giants greats. Willie McCovey was gracious, as he always was. Weir fawned over Gaylord Perry, whom Weir had idolized since childhood. The notoriously cranky Willie Mays, by contrast, was offered the chance to meet the members of the Dead but turned it down, maintaining he'd never heard of them (Mays had met Garcia at least once before, at a benefit event in 1975, but he'd clearly forgotten). Mays's brushoff amused Garcia. "Finally," he said, "someone who doesn't give a shit about the Grateful Dead."

They took the field in the afternoon. A color guard of Vietnam veterans from San Francisco's Presidio—the last stop in Garcia's brief military career—presented the American flag in center field as 56,689 fans rose to their feet. "And now," the announcer continued, "may we direct your attention to in front of the pitcher's mound, to honor America in the singing of our National Anthem: Jerry Garcia, Bob Weir, Vince Welnick—San Francisco's own, the Grateful Dead!"

The sight of Garcia in a San Francisco Giants jacket warmed thousands of hometown hearts, and the crowd roared its approval. The three nodded to the camera and then took tone and tempo from Welnick. They delivered a pitch-perfect anthem and trundled back across the infield, grinning. "Play ball!"

Backed by their new superstar, Barry Bonds, the Giants won in eleven innings. RECORD CROWD SEES GIANTS WIN HOME OPENER, the next day's *Chronicle* proclaimed. "The Dead sing, Bonds homers, foghorn blows."

Garcia found the whole experience exhilarating and amusing. Asked about what it meant for the Grateful Dead to perform the National Anthem, he replied, as only he could: "We're like bad architecture and old whores. Eventually, you get respectable if you're around long enough."

THE HARD feelings between David Grisman and the Dead lasted years, but eventually melted. In 1990, Grisman received the Rex Foundation's Ralph J. Gleason Award, a much-deserved acknowledgment of his musical and cultural contributions. Grisman heard that Garcia had pushed for his consideration, and their friendship resumed. Happily so, as Garcia's reconnection with Grisman in the 1990s would allow both to produce some of the most beloved music that either ever recorded.

When Garcia was home from touring, he would often beeline to Grisman's house, where the two would flip through old songbooks and pick out favorites. Playing with Grisman was, according to Garcia's daughter Annabelle, "the one thing that I know made him supremely happy." Grisman recorded those sessions, casual musical conversations between friends, sometimes joined by others. In the meantime, Grisman and Garcia joined for a number of performances, most in the San Francisco area. Their first album, *Jerry Garcia/David Grisman*, showcased not just their musical partnership but also the warmth of their friendship. It featured their take on "Friend of the Devil," reprising and expanding the mandolin line that Grisman had played on the original, and also a spellbindingly original instrumental composition written by Grisman entitled "Arabia."

The Garcia/Grisman collaborations continued through the early 1990s, with some of the results of their work released only after Garcia's death. These sessions not only supplied Garcia with a respite but also served to reintroduce that roots aspect of his musical repertoire to a new generation of admirers.

Those who discovered the Dead in the 1980s and 1990s came for many reasons, and to many of them the band's music seemed cut of whole cloth from the 1960s. It was "San Francisco" and "psychedelic." The Dead were a "jam band." The Grisman collaborations presented something far different. This was a music grounded in the full range of American musical history, as affecting on acoustic instruments and small stages as on full display in giant arenas. It was a reminder for some—and a revelation for others—that the Dead were always deeper than some imagined.

GUESS WHO'S GETTING MARRIED? the *Marin Independent Journal* asked on its front page on Saturday, February 12, 1994. Credit Paul Liberatore, the enterprising reporter for the *Independent Journal* who had long covered the paper's hometown band. The Dead were neither confirming nor denying rumors, but Liberatore's sources gave him the scoop: Garcia was marrying, again, and "the location of the wedding is the most closely guarded secret in the Bay Area rock community."

Guests were given a number to call on Monday morning and told they would get the location then for the ceremony that evening, Valentine's Day.

Two days later, Garcia and Deborah Koons were married at Christ Episcopal Church in Sausalito. A priest presided over the traditional affair, attended by fifty or so guests, including Heather, Annabelle, and Trixie, and of course the members of the Dead, including Hornsby. Grisman performed—Liberatore described it as a "Gregorian chant," which seems unlikely; Blair Jackson said it was the "Ave Maria." Garcia dressed in a dark suit, no tie. Koons wore white. After the small ceremony, some two hundred guests joined for a reception at the Tiburon Corinthian Yacht Club. Noted one guest: "There was no tie-dye."

How mainstream was Garcia? The event was covered by *People* magazine, which incorrectly credited Koons with having helped Garcia regain his health after his 1986 coma. "Judging from the good vibes on Valentine's Day, she brought him some happiness as well," *People* concluded.

Garcia was married again, but no more conventionally than before. He had bought a home outside Tiburon, and he held on to it, living separately from his new bride. He often spent the night at John Kahn's place in San Francisco or would make his way back to Tiburon, where TVs and computer games occupied him. He enjoyed Myst. Alone.

THE DEAD'S nine-city, fifteen-show East Coast tour in the summer of 1995 would become known as "the tour from hell." It included belligerent audiences, overreactive policing, strange turns of events, and plain bad luck.

The tour opened with a tumultuous bang in Highgate, Vermont, where at least ninety thousand fans, twenty-five thousand more than ticketed, began arriving days before the show, which had Dylan warming up for the Dead. Fans pressed to get inside the venue, and police opened the gates rather than try to hold the line. Forty-two fans were

BAD ARCHITECTURE AND OLD WHORES | 411

injured, one thirty-one-year-old man died of a heart attack. A week later, the Dead rolled into Albany to play the Knickerbocker Arena, a favorite venue in a favorite part of the world—Upstate New York regularly produced some of the band's more memorable shows. Not this time. Garcia's blood sugar was soaring; he was "in alarming health," McNally recalled. And his energy was flagging. The Knickerbocker shows were lackluster and disappointing.

Just as band and audience had long reflected and energized each other, now they dragged each other down. The energy exchange first discovered in the Acid Tests fizzled. The physical divide between stage and field was bad enough. Now the psychic space widened too. Audiences came demanding to be entertained rather than eager to share an evening. Long renowned for their quietude, Deadheads, or at least some of those who arrived at these shows, became insistent, unyielding. Size took a toll, altering the experience of the Dead just as it had the counter-culture more broadly.

A few miles from the Knickerbocker, two Albany police officers moved to arrest a fan for selling psychedelic mushrooms. The crowd would have none of it. The officers were swarmed and beaten. A group of Deadheads pelted officers with bottles from the roof of a parking garage, knocking one from his horse. Five fans were arrested. Dozens more were rounded up in other incidents. Some seventy-five were in jail by the time the Dead left town. The Deadheads in Albany were "not the same this year," police told the Albany *Times Union*.

On June 25, the Dead played RFK Stadium in Washington, D.C. That afternoon, as fans worked their way to the stadium, a lightning storm blew through. Three fans took shelter under a tree, only to have lightning strike it. Two were conscious when paramedics arrived, but the third was critically injured. That night marked Hornsby's final appearance with the Dead, as he returned to his own career.

Stops in Auburn Hills, Michigan, and Pittsburgh were unremarkable; at least no one was struck by lightning. Then, in Deer Creek, Indiana, events took yet another turn, a double turn, really, toward weirdness

412 | HERE BESIDE THE RISING TIDE

and instability. First was the death threat. A man under the misimpression that Garcia had stolen his girlfriend left messages threatening to kill Garcia in Deer Park. Security suggested canceling the show, which Garcia rejected, but the band played with the house lights on. Recordings of the band members speaking to one another over their headsets capture the evening's strangeness. "Weird when all those cameras," one says, "look like guns . . . gallows humor." In between songs, Lesh asks about a smell in the auditorium. "Is that the smell of fear?" he asks. Whereupon Garcia launches into "Dire Wolf," whose chorus pleads, "Don't murder me." An inside joke, but a dark one.

Meanwhile, thousands of fans without tickets had massed outside the venue, and they rushed the fences as the Dead began to play. They refused police orders to back down, and the throng hurled rocks and bottles, cheered on by fans on the other side of the fence, a spectacle that astonished Cameron Sears, the band's manager. Local officers called in the state police for help. They arrived in riot gear and used Mace to regain control of the scene. "How did we let it get this crazy?" Lesh asked himself from his vantage point onstage. No one was seriously injured, but seventeen were arrested, and the night's events—inside the arena and out—left band members, crew, and fans shaken.

McNally drafted a statement on behalf of the Dead commending the officers and condemning the band's fans, the first time the band had ever so directly criticized its own base. "Want to end the touring life of the Grateful Dead? Allow bottle-throwing gate crashers to keep on thinking they're cool anarchists instead of the creeps they are," the statement read. "The spirit of the Grateful Dead is at stake." Garcia, badly rattled, overcame his reluctance to tell others what to do and signed it. The Dead canceled the next night's show, the first time in its history that actions by its fans had forced the band not to play.

And then, on July 5, as a group of those fans took shelter from the rain at a campground outside St. Louis, the wooden deck where they were huddled collapsed under their weight, injuring more than a hundred.

No one blamed the Dead for that, any more than the band could be

BAD ARCHITECTURE AND OLD WHORES | **413**

blamed for a lightning strike at RFK. But the sense of embattlement deepened as arrests and injuries piled up.

The band could have stopped, but the momentum—the money, the many people who depended on them, the fervor of the fans—all pushed in the direction of continuing, and Garcia had neither the energy nor the inclination to resist. Lift-off moments still occurred, but they were dwindling. He knew it. The rest of the band knew it. But they could not muster the strength to change course. "Everyone was hanging on for dear life," Sears recalled. "It was a spiritually challenging time."

They did what they'd always done. They kept going. As they had sung for years, "The wheel is turning, and you can't slow down."

The final shows of the Summer Tour were held at Chicago's Soldier Field on the nights of July 8 and July 9. At first, it looked as though these shows might go the way of the summer. "Given the string of unfortunate events that has plagued the Dead's recent stops," one report noted, "some anxiety surrounded the band's trip to Soldier Field to close out the tour." And those fears were stoked when five or six thousand people turned up outside the stadium without tickets, hoping to catch the band before they headed back to California.

Fans milling about in Shakedown Street compared notes on the events of recent weeks, some blaming them purely on bad luck and coincidence, others noting the changed tenor of the audience, the sense of entitlement and desperation, the new belligerence. Some blamed it on alcohol, some on young people drawn to the band purely for the party of it, unschooled in the norms of the band's devotees. McNally sought to ease fears. Asked whether the Dead were considering quitting, he denied it. "There's never been a thought to do that," he said.

With the tour ending, the band, even Garcia, dug deep for those shows. Disinterest and distress gave way to memory, to old instincts, worn down by drugs and weariness and recent events but still there in flashes.

On Sunday night, the Dead opened with "Touch of Grey," stumbling into the number, Garcia's voice thin and unconvincing. Weir did his best to prop up his old friend, and the drummers kept things moving.

Even the song's triumphant chorus, "We will get by," could not rouse Garcia. He tried to belt it out, but the words seemed caught in his throat, a reedy little voice at the edge of a big sound.

The show developed mostly without Garcia's contributing much, but even the weakest Dead shows had their moments, and this one came in the second set, rolling out of an unspectacular version of "Samson and Delilah." It began with a few soft notes from Garcia's guitar, a tinkling of the keys from Welnick. "Thought I heard a blackbird sing up on Bluebird Hill," Garcia sang, his voice nothing close to strong but plaintive now instead of merely tired. He gathered a little energy over the opening lines of "So Many Roads," and its deep sadness and concentration found its way through him. "Born where the sun don't shine, and I don't deny my name," he sang. "Got no place to go, ain't that a shame?"

He sang of the "KC whistle" and the sound it brought of trains; of "Kokomo"; he told of the "jug band playing," rich with its memories of Palo Alto—the days he had shared with Barbara Meier and Robert Hunter and that now seemed so very long ago. In the years since, he had crossed "mountains high," "rivers wide."

Garcia dropped gently into his guitar solo, and the rest of the band quieted around him. And there it was: the pure moment that had eluded him—and them—in recent days, recent weeks, maybe recent years. But there it was again, in the sound of one guitar, notes almost visible over the heads of thousands of fans, themselves rapt and attentive. In the vast space of Soldier Field, nobody yelled or made demands or pushed. Nobody asked him to answer for rowdy fans or drug users. He played. And one note led to the next, droplets in a fountain, stones along a riverbed.

Returning from his solo, Garcia stumbled through the remaining verses. He forgot some words, mumbling, but then he found himself again. He was drifting but searching still. He played another sad and simple solo and came back to himself, to the road at the center of his song. "New York to San Francisco," he sang, "All I want is one to take me home."

At that moment, he found something in himself, something that

BAD ARCHITECTURE AND OLD WHORES | 415

had been alive in him since he was a boy, since he lost his father, since he bounced around San Francisco as a kid, since he slept in his car in Palo Alto and "blue-light cheap hotels," since he played the Acid Tests and Woodstock and Watkins Glen, since he stood at the Pyramids, since he built a band and anchored a culture and flinched at responsibility and neglected his family and produced the music that had moved and touched and changed so very many people, some of whom surrounded him in that moment, his hair and skin gray, his chin down almost to the chest of his dirty T-shirt, oblivious to the rapture directed at him but not disconnected, not in that moment, no, in that moment it was all there, all at once. It had not left him or abandoned him, nor he it. It could recede, but now it returned, all at once, and there he was, in a bluish spotlight on a stage thousands of miles from home but maybe the essence of home.

"So many roads to ease my soul," he sang, his voice suddenly loud and pleading, even demanding, breaking at the heart of it. "To ease my soul." He sang the phrase over and over, hitting it a little differently each time, sometimes in pain, sometimes in reflection, sometimes in gratitude or wisdom. "So many roads. So many roads. So many roads to ease my soul. . . . Lord, so many roads to ease my soul. So many roads. I've been down the road. Lord, I've been walking down the road. So many, so many roads."

He played, just a little longer. "So many roads to ease my soul."

It was Garcia's last performance.

Near the end. Shoreline Amphitheatre,
Mountain View, California, June 4, 1995.

Jay Blakesberg/Retro Photo Archive

CHAPTER 18

"Any Other Day That's Ever Been"

JERRY GARCIA DIED ON AUGUST 9, 1995, EIGHT DAYS AFTER HIS fifty-third birthday. Two days earlier, he had checked in to a single room at Serenity Knolls, a rehab facility in Marin County, down the road from a place the Dead had rented early in the band's life. A nurse doing early morning rounds passed by at about 4:20. The room was quiet, which was strange, since he was a loud snorer. The nurse checked on him and found no pulse and no breathing. Paramedics were called, but they could not revive him. Garcia was pronounced dead at 4:23 A.M.

The news was shocking to all who heard it, though perhaps least surprising to those who knew him best. It came at the end of a long decline and steep final descent. In the weeks leading to his death, after the band's return from the "Tour from Hell," even Garcia accepted that his health was precarious—heart disease, diabetes, poor diet, and drug abuse had combined to leave him weak and fading. He agreed to seek help, and Deborah urged him to get it at the Betty Ford Clinic near Palm Springs. He checked in in mid-July, expecting to stay for four weeks.

Two weeks later, he was out again, tired of the routines, tired of the food, irritated by the heat of Palm Springs. Deborah sprang him and, with the ever-faithful Steve Parish, brought him home.

His conversations with a few intimates, at least in retrospect, suggested that Garcia could feel the sand trickling through the hourglass. He ran into Alan Trist at the Dead's San Rafael offices, and Garcia regaled Trist with the work he was doing to create an illustrated memoir of his youth, later released as *Harrington Street*. "He launched into this

418 | HERE BESIDE THE RISING TIDE

forty-five-minute rave about it," Trist said. "My feeling is that he was trying to get out something before he died, that he knew he didn't have long."

Garcia called Hunter, wistful. "He had been into rehab again, and he called me up and he was out, and he was going to come over and we were going to get writing again," Hunter remembered. "He said some wonderful stuff that was very uncharacteristic of him. He said, 'Your words never stuck in my throat.' Jerry didn't tend to talk like that, and there was something possibly, slightly alarming about it."

His autopsy suggested that Garcia had relapsed. There were traces of heroin in his blood—almost certainly from the days between Betty Ford and Serenity Knolls—but he died of natural causes, if heart failure in a fifty-three-year-old man can be seen as natural. Garcia traveled the world in those fifty-three years, and it took its toll. He looked eighty by the time he died, just thirty miles from where he was born.

Garcia had sung about death for decades. "Brokedown Palace" opened Ken Kesey's heart after the death of his son; "Box of Rain" marked the death of Lesh's father, "Birdsong" the loss of Janis Joplin. In "Black Muddy River," Garcia sang of the time when the "last bolt of sunshine hits the mountain," the moment when he would "sing me a song of my own." And in "Stella Blue," Garcia had anticipated an ending, a moment when song and time and existence, "all rolls into one." Now death had found him.

The world he'd traversed and the audiences he'd moved responded to his death, culture and counterculture coalescing in memory of one now claimed by both. President Clinton called him a "genius" who "also had a terrible problem." Bob Dylan was more elliptical—no surprise there— recalling Garcia as "the very spirit personified of whatever is muddy river country at its core." Wavy Gravy composed a haiku that imagined Bill Graham waiting for Garcia's entrance into heaven: "The fat man rocks out / Hinges fall off heaven's door / Come on in, says Bill." *The New York Times*, the *Los Angeles Times*, and *The Washington Post* all noted his death, as did the *Mount Vernon Argus*, the *Stuart* (Florida) *News*, and *The Aquarian Weekly*. In Los Angeles, reporters covering the murder trial of O. J. Simpson quietly shared the news as they passed through metal detectors for the day's proceedings. In New York, Wall Street traders rushed to their Bloomberg terminals to confirm reports of Garcia's passing; the demand for access to news from the terminals crashed the system and forced the market briefly to suspend trading. The death of Jerry Garcia halted the New York Stock Exchange. That was something to ponder.

Deborah Koons presided over the funeral, which was held, fittingly, at St. Stephen's Church in Belvedere. Two hundred family and friends attended. Cliff was there, as were members of the band. So were David Grisman, Bill Walton, and Ken Kesey. A few members of the press were invited, but Koons went to great lengths to keep the event private, arranging for invited guests to gather at a parking lot in Tiburon and then be shuttled to the church. That kept Deadheads away, but it also imposed a barrier around her union with Garcia, a protectiveness that would breed much resentment once Garcia's estate became a matter of contention. Among other things, Koons barred Mountain Girl from attending the service (she waited it out at Hunter's place). Sara Ruppenthal and Barbara Meier did attend but chafed at Koons's exercise of control. Bad feelings set in quickly.

Koons spoke at the service, recounting her brief marriage with Garcia and declaiming on the love they shared. Mourners exchanged glances as she spoke; one later called it a "me-logy" for how much it centered on Koons rather than Garcia. When Koons noted that Garcia had told her that she, and she alone, was the love of his life, Meier chimed in from her pew that he'd told her that, too. Ruppenthal shouted out that he told her the same. The parishioners enjoyed it.

Annabelle Garcia reflected fondly and clearly on her father, drawing appreciative chuckles when she acknowledged him as a great man while adding that he was a "shitty father." The comment was offered with laughter and received that way, though with the obvious pain that it was true.

Grisman played "Amazing Grace." Steve Parish gruffly remembered his friend for his connection to working people; Weir paused to consider the man who had served as bandmate and big brother; later, at a public memorial, Weir imagined Garcia as lifted to the clouds and asked mourners to raise their faces and reflect joy skyward. In "Black Peter," Garcia had, in character, imagined the sun coming up and going down, and had foreseen a deathbed: "Shine through my window and my friends they come around." It did, and so did they.

The service was coming to an end, and the minister prepared to wrap it up, when Hunter called out from the back. "Wait," he said, "I've got something!"

Of course he did. Hunter stood before the congregation, hands shaking, voice trembling. He read from a poem he had composed the day before. In it, he begged for help from the muse who gave him and Garcia so much. He asked her to guide his friend onward: "May she bear thee to thy rest," Hunter read, the congregation quiet before him. The bright afternoon sun poured through the stained glass in the Marin hills, painting the congregation in bright colors, somber and picturesque. The afternoon was quiet and serious and luminous.

Hunter continued: "The ancient bower of flowers / beyond the solitude of days, / the tyranny of hours— / the wreath of shining laurel lie / upon your shaggy head, / bestowing power to play the lyre / to legions of the dead."

Garcia at home. Mill Valley, California, September 2, 1993.

Jay Blakesberg/Retro Photo Archive

Epilogue

THE GRATEFUL DEAD DIED WITH JERRY GARCIA. THE MEMBERS of the band would go on, individually and in various combinations, but they would not replace Garcia as they had Pigpen or Keith Godchaux or Brent Mydland.

The weeks and months after Garcia's death were rattling. Tensions from the funeral carried over to the scattering of Garcia's ashes into San Francisco Bay. When Mountain Girl arrived at the dock, Koons refused to allow her aboard the boat; appalled guests watched Mountain Girl attempt to wrestle her way onboard before being led away in tears. And then came the fights over money. Garcia died without a professionally drafted will, setting the stage for a protracted and ugly battle over his estate that locked Mountain Girl and Koons in extended litigation and forced members of the band and others to testify, often reluctantly.

The members of the Dead, meanwhile, struggled through uncertainty about life after the departure of the band's central figure. For a while, they entertained the notion of creating a San Francisco museum called Terrapin Station, possibly in the Fisherman's Wharf or China Basin neighborhoods. Big ideas came to nothing. Welnick struggled financially and emotionally, never really regaining his footing after Garcia's death. He attempted suicide soon after but recovered, only to resume his turmoil. Eleven years later, he cut his own throat and died. The toll was less severe on other members of the band, but they, too, were lost for a time before eventually falling into surprising riches, as they mined their archives and struck out on their own careers.

But if the Dead ended with Garcia, the music did not. The Dead scoured their history and produced gems. Under the guidance of the archivist David Lemieux, who succeeded Dick Latvala, recordings of long-ago concerts were produced intelligently and sold briskly. In 2024, the Dead landed their fifty-ninth album in the Top 40—breaking a record held by Elvis Presley and Frank Sinatra. Of those fifty-nine albums, forty-one had been released since 2012, well after Garcia's death. A collection of Madison Square Garden performances from the early 1980s won a Grammy in 2023 for "Best Boxed or Special Limited-Edition Package." It was the Dead's first album to win a Grammy.

And as the music went on, the culture most certainly did as well. The counterculture—that broad band of dissidents that included political radicals, student protesters, environmental activists, and bohemian artists—existed before the Grateful Dead and after it. The Dead's role across much of its period was neither to lead nor follow but rather to act as what Mountain Girl called the "rennet," comparing them to the catalyzing agent that activates cheese, in this case, the triggering mechanism that galvanized so many elements of American society into something recognizably a culture.

That culture flourishes today, sometimes exactly where one would expect to find it and sometimes in unexpected corners of the nation's political, intellectual, and cultural life. It most often contributes to the health of this society, though sometimes it does not.

The counterculture of the 1960s was not an unvarnished success. It failed in much of what it imagined. American capitalism survives, as does the idea of war as a method of resolving international conflict. Drugs infused the counterculture, and the effects of widespread drug use in America today can hardly be regarded as innocuous. Garcia's insistence that most of what was wrong with drugs was because they were illegal has some merit, but opioid use underscores the inherent danger of many drugs. Users, legal or illegal, suffer and die. The counterculture's celebration of marijuana and LSD does not imply its endorsement of fentanyl, but hippies and radicals joined in viewing the War on Drugs as a war on them. They weren't wrong, but drugs have exacted a toll on America and the world. Garcia did not die because the government persecuted him for his drug use. Garcia died because he had easy access to drugs for many years, and he destroyed himself by using them.

But it is unfair to those who participated in the counterculture of the 1960s, or who have joined it since, to argue that simply because the movement did not achieve all it set out to do, it was inconsequential. In fact, the counterculture influences our lives today in profound, broad, and specific ways. Peter Coyote, the member of the Diggers who now serves as a narrator of American history, argues that the hippies and their allies failed in much of what they attempted politically—Nixon was elected and reelected, Reagan too, and then Donald Trump—but succeeded in much of the cultural mission. Eastern religious practices, organic foods, respect for the environment, the long work toward a more equitable and open-minded society—not all Americans subscribe to or accept those ideas today, but they are largely agreed upon, at least in principle. Trixie Garcia, herself a thoughtful observer of the state of the world, adds a note: "This," she said of those principles, "is wholesome." It is indeed, but it was not always thought of that way. That it is now is evidence of lasting cultural change.

The counterculture today lives in politics as well. It flares in protest and skepticism. When Trump took office in 2017, more than three million Americans marched in anguished demonstrations that harked back to those against the war in Vietnam. Three years later, George Floyd died gasping for breath in Minneapolis, and Americans rose up in numbers that again invited comparisons to Vietnam War protests or the antinuke rallies of the Reagan years. In the summer of George Floyd, more than fifteen million Americans took to the streets of more than five hundred cities, defying a pandemic that made such gatherings dangerous. Black Lives Matter stenciled its message on millions of American hearts, and though the government did not topple, it shuddered, as President Trump retreated to a bunker beneath the White House and emerged spouting nonsense and flashing an upside-down Bible. BLACK LIVES MATTER MAY BE THE LARGEST MOVEMENT IN U.S. HISTORY, *The New York Times* concluded.

426 | HERE BESIDE THE RISING TIDE

As happened during the 1970s and 1980s, the outrage over police brutality and government mismanagement of the pandemic morphed into more conventional political action, especially once Trump was defeated in 2020. His reemergence four years later, criminal convictions notwithstanding, brought old activists back into the fray.

"Deadheads for Kamala" was among the early expressions of support for Vice President Kamala Harris's presidential bid. David Gans, chronicler of the Dead and formative figure in the creation of the Well, was one of the conveners of that effort. Two days later, Jane Fonda announced "Elders for Kamala." She co-hosted that call with Vermont senator Bernie Sanders.

But not all protest is equal. For if the counterculture helped decry police violence and create "Deadheads for Kamala," it also powered the antigovernment uprising on January 6, 2021, when Trump exhorted his followers to walk up the hill from the White House to the U.S. Capitol to stop the certification of the 2020 presidential election. Once unleashed, skepticism is a difficult principle to contain. It is one thing to doubt the government's body counts in Vietnam, another to doubt its scientific conclusions about the transmissibility of COVID-19 or its tallying of presidential ballots. Those subtleties can be missed—and sometimes are deliberately obfuscated. Painful as it is to admit, there is a line that connects the Weather Underground's 1971 bombing of the Capitol and Trump's aggrieved assault on that same Capitol fifty years later.

Happily, most of the counterculture's contributions to contemporary life are more constructive, more intimate, and more deeply affecting. That counterculture, with its continuing capacity to displace the violence and hatred that pervade so much of modern life, finds purchase in small encounters, in every corner of the country, in lives gently moved, in small gatherings of joy and fulfillment.

It lives at the Oregon Country Fair, where revelers gather annually to celebrate life outside the strictures of twenty-first-century America. There are jugglers and artists and reggae musicians, and more than a few posters and images of Garcia. There are booths offering guides to organic farming and solar and wind power. The festivities take place at the edge of the Kesey family creamery's land, just a few hundred yards from where the Dead played on a blistering afternoon in 1972. Today, the fair, which prohibits the use of drugs or alcohol, resembles nothing so much as an issue of the *Whole Earth Catalog* come to life.

It presents itself in the meetings of the Grateful Dead Studies Association, exploring new meaning in the life of a band that ended decades ago. The association gathered in Chicago in 2024, celebrating a respite in the COVID pandemic. Scholars traveled from around the country to present papers and share ideas. Jesse Jarnow discussed his *Good Ol' Grateful Deadcast*, a favorite podcast of many of those in attendance. Michael McClure recounted the history of his podcast, *Guess the Year*, in which contestants hear a clip of Grateful Dead music and try to identify the year it comes from (they succeed to a remarkable degree). Others delivered papers on the Dead's *Playboy After Dark* appearance, the persistence of the spinners at Dead shows, the culture of tapers, and more. Cheerfully and expertly overseen by Nick Meriwether, the gathering replicated some of the joy of a Dead show with a deeper, self-conscious intellectual inquiry that has lifted the Dead from their musical moorings and acknowledged a clear truth: The Dead touched, and continue to touch, the imagination.

It persists in the work of conscientious companies, those who devote their energies not just to profit but to good. Look no further than Ben & Jerry's, which so brazenly unveiled Cherry Garcia and only later cut its namesake in on the action. In the decades since, Cherry Garcia has been almost as popular as Jerry Garcia, and the Vermont ice cream company has pioneered not just treats but values. Ben & Jerry's practices the "playful pursuit of joy and justice in all its flavors," CEO Dave Stever noted. Many other companies have taken note, and the idea of responsible investing has spread, not enough to overthrow mercenary capitalism but plenty to offer options for living more thoughtfully.

It shimmers in the music of untold thousands of musicians who adapt and perform the work of the Dead every night, in every style known to the imagination. Of those, perhaps the best known is Dead & Company. That band, with John Mayer taking over on lead guitar and some of Garcia's vocals, picked up the Dead's musical mantle in the 2020s, tapping into the Dead's ever loyal following and shifting Weir into the limelight that Garcia once occupied. That, too, felt inspired— Mayer spoke of the music finding him and rekindling his excitement in sound; Weir gamely took the torch of his old friend and carried it forward, now the object of adulation so long lavished on Garcia. The shows were musically fulfilling—cleaner, more deliberate, if somewhat less inspirational, than the Grateful Dead. And they drew an audience that combined aging Deadheads with newer fans, too young ever to have seen Garcia play live but now treated to a new iteration of the Dead's songbook. That alone suggests a durability in both the music and experience of the Dead, a longing for it that reaches beyond fond memories or trips back through childhood, a reaching for connection that is bigger than the band or the audience of the moment, a yearning that may be more powerful now than ever.

After a moving and commercially successful run, Dead & Company announced that it was concluding touring in 2023 with a set of shows back at the Dead's birthplace, San Francisco. The shows that summer weekend were both nostalgic and altogether new—familiar music but far removed from the Carousel or Avalon. They took place in majestic Oracle Park, home of the San Francisco Giants, nestled up against San Francisco Bay and a reminder of just how far this band had come. Former Speaker of the House Nancy Pelosi, a fan, attended along with tens of thousands who swarmed the field and filled the seats of the graceful venue.

Dead & Company delivered three shows that weekend, the last on Sunday night. "Never miss a Sunday show," went the old Deadhead proverb, and it was affirmed on this cool San Francisco evening. Mayer's guitar work shone. His turn on "Althea" dazzled. Garcia's memory haunted many of the numbers, but the band did not specifically acknowledge him until it came to "Truckin'," a loping version delivered as the first of three encores. "Busted, down on Bourbon Street," Weir sang, as he had a thousand times before. This time, the giant screen behind him lit up with Garcia's mug shot from the 1970 New Orleans arrests. It stayed onscreen just long enough for thousands of eyes to take him in, to register the tribute, and to draw his spirit home to San Francisco. When the show concluded, an army of drones launched over the stadium's right field fence. Lit up, they flashed images of the skull and lightning bolt, of dancing bears and roses. Then the drones spelled out a parting message to supporters of the band, some of them loyally absorbing this music, these values, for fifty years. "Please be kind," the skylit message read. Filing out, parents guided their children, teenagers twirled, and fans of all ages clutched their merch and scattered onto the streets of San Francisco.

It works across time and generations. The intergenerational appeal of Dead & Company is as undeniable as it is provocative. Why, it seems fair to ask, do this music and the larger values it presents continue to resonate with fans far too young to have experienced the original? One hint comes from Meriwether, who notes that both a Dead show and the counterculture itself relished the idea of individual transformation experienced collectively. It is about the music, of course, but also something more, "not just the songs but the small-group improvisatory spirit that made those songs new every time," as Meriwether put it. That's an experience that many today associate with the 1960s, but it is not limited to a point in time. It is, as Joseph Campbell appreciated, one that stretches across the annals of civilization itself, from the Dionysia to Dead shows. There is no reason to expect that young people today have lost the taste for communal joy.

It thrives in generosity, specifically in the work of the Rex Foundation, in the gifts to community organizers and doctors and artists that the foundation annually bestows. In the summer of 2024, the foundation gave grants to Camp Daniel, which provides services and summer camp for those with disabilities and their families; to the House of Blues Radio Hour for interviewing blues greats and preserving their contributions to American history; to ANARDE, Advocates for Natural Resources & Development, for the guidance it offers to Ugandan communities confronting the pressures of development. To date, the foundation has awarded grants of more than $10 million, a living testament to the Dead.

It sparkles in poetry and literature. On a Thursday evening in May 2024, the great Gary Snyder was joined by admirers to share and discuss his poetry. "Be affectionate to your tools," the poet advised. Others reminisced about Snyder's love of fun and his determination to live humbly in the world, to see eye to eye with rocks and creatures. Coyote, a student of Snyder in Buddhism and a clear-eyed reader of his poems, remarked on the impermanence of freedom and the essential equality of all things. Those values and Snyder himself reach back through time, to the Beats, to the whole earth—planet and catalog. For Snyder's poems carry the elegant weight of substance across the ages; one hears in him not just the babbling of creeks but also the eloquence of Ginsberg, the adventure of Kerouac, the serenity of Zen. In Snyder's poetry, so long admired by the counterculture and beyond, masculinity is smoothed by wind, leaving a gnarled sense of place, of worn handles and careful words.

It peeks through the bleak landscape of Las Vegas. In the summer of 2024, Dead & Company, having previously pledged to give up touring, elected to take up residence at Vegas's vaunted Sphere. Deadheads viewed that with some suspicion—Vegas and the Dead were always an odd fit. But if the Sphere does not offer up the Dead at its most soulful, it gives something else in return: The venue's soaring technological opportunities mesh with the Dead's vast visual library and history. Spellbound audiences swoop through 710 Ashbury, above San Francisco, and into outer space. The band, surrounded by its own history, seems small in the space. But the overall effect is vast and enveloping, even overwhelming, something approaching the fulfillment of Owsley's ideas for sound and artistry. Fans leave with glassy eyes and mouths agape. It is "big fun," as Garcia most certainly would have said.

It even surfaces in the Establishment's ever expanding embrace of the Dead. Near the end of 2024, the surviving members of the Grateful Dead were awarded Kennedy Center Honors. Lesh had died just weeks earlier, at age eighty-four; his absence was keenly felt, as was the ever elongating shadow of Garcia. Hart, Kreutzmann, and Weir were all that were left, and they appeared for the band. They received their medals at the State Department the night before the Kennedy Center gala, donning them on a shimmering evening of gold décor and warm tributes, including one from President Biden. Al Franken introduced the band and quoted Garcia on the topic of licorice. Hart then spoke of the power of music, and Kreutzmann recounted the magical effect that hearing the band had had on one gravely ill hospital patient, who recovered despite all odds after having the Dead played for him on headphones.

Resplendent in tuxedo and finery, his medal dangling from a colored ribbon, Weir was his earnest self, observing American history from his distinctively off-kilter angle. He began by thanking the Founding Fathers, then reconsidered. "I'm not sure exactly if thanks are due," he continued, "but I want to recognize them anyway." Weir spoke a bit about the melding of cultures that gave America its music, though at the high price, he noted, of slavery. Weir looked forward to the work of the Dead being studied for hundreds of years. "That's a legacy," he added, "and I have a strong suspicion that Jerry Garcia and Phil Lesh's names will be part of that discussion as well."

And it dreams on the banks of the Ohio River, deep in the state of Kentucky. There, in the spring of 2024, the Bluegrass Music Hall of Fame and Museum opened its Jerry Garcia Exhibition. For three days, tie-dye and flannel filled conference rooms where panels of musicians and artists reflected on Garcia and on the connections between bluegrass and the Dead. Over the course of those days, musicians and fans and others searched for words to describe what all of this had meant to them, what it meant for musical styles to bind them in common values. They talked about the Acid Tests and the music business, about *Old & In the Way* and *Shady Grove*, about what money makes possible and what money corrupts, about Cherry Garcia ice cream, about the difference between appropriation and appreciation. In the evenings, musicians performed, and audiences set aside their preconceptions about this idiom or that, sharing joy.

432 | HERE BESIDE THE RISING TIDE

It was, unsurprisingly, Sara Ruppenthal (now Ruppenthal Katz) who best summed up her ex-husband's place in all of this. "We are all connected," she said as members of the audience sat quietly, the river rolling behind them. "We are all individual expressions of the Big Wow."

"I would say that Jerry's legacy to us," she continued, "is to be the best that . . . you can be. Don't try to be somebody else. Don't worry what other people think of you. Just go for it. Be as caring, compassionate and conscious as possible. We're all in this together. And we're looking at even rockier times than we were in the 1960s. It's going to require each of us to be patient and joyful."

That legacy, of Garcia and the Dead and the counterculture, lives in stories and histories large and small, but it may endure most poignantly in the small tales, the individual moments and people that the counterculture reached, that Garcia's music touched. It lives in Gillian Welch and Huey Lewis and Joan Baez and Cameron Sears; in Nick Meriwether and Peter Coyote and Blair Jackson and David Gans. It lives in the memory of Steve Silberman. It lives in all the good people, men and women, whose lives were made a little brighter because they were presented with the music of the Grateful Dead and the kindness and community that gathered around that music. Those varied souls carried their time with the Dead into the arts and law and journalism and activism—and, radiating outward, to colleagues and friends, siblings and children. Each holds an ember lit at Red Rocks or Telluride or the Greek Theatre or the Philadelphia Spectrum or even RFK Stadium. From their hands to those they touch, that web of shared experience, that embrace of compassion and kindness, grows into something larger, something like a counterculture.

"If I knew the way, I would take you home." Robert Hunter wrote that in 1970, and Jerry Garcia sang it for years. The line, from "Ripple," can be heard as a statement of futility—I would take you home if only I knew the way—or of generosity—I'm offering to take you home. But it also stands as a statement of acceptance, of community and love—I am here to help. Garcia sang that with conviction, with the self-awareness to realize that he did not know the way. He had no plan, no charted path. Instead, he let the currents of meaning flow through him. He gave up some piece of his ego, and he allowed the universe to work through him, to magical effect.

Perhaps that is where the counterculture comes to rest as well. At its most instructive, a culture that challenges authority and celebrates beauty does not teach us how to overthrow a government. It guides rather than directs. It offers another way. It demonstrates that we have the freedom to explore the world, to give proof of the fact that humans need not attack one another to discover ourselves; that we need not hate or denigrate to be fulfilled; that we may act with compassion and care for one another; that we may feel rather than merely reason; that we may be part of something larger; that we may be free and that music may help us to get there. And that when we surrender ego, even a bit, magic is at the door.

It doesn't work for everyone, and it doesn't always work even for those who come to accept it. It doesn't have to. Like a Dead show, it works in moments. And it's magnificent when it does.

Garcia did not know the way, and he was often lost. But he took us home.

ACKNOWLEDGMENTS

Over the past few years, I've often been asked how long I've been working on this project. There are several ways to answer that question, and each one suggests a different group of people to whom I am indebted for making it possible.

One answer is that it's been four years. It was in 2021 that I signed with Random House to write a biography of Jerry Garcia, and I am especially grateful to Ben Greenberg for all that has come since then. Ben's appreciation for the subject and for the book's duality—as both a biography of Garcia and a larger appraisal of the counterculture—made him something closer to a collaborator than an editor, though he is a fine editor. I'm honored and pleased that a book that mattered so much to me ended up in Ben's capable, considerate, and intelligent hands. I'm so very grateful to know him.

Ben's colleagues at Random House, individually and as a group, have given their all to this project, earning my deep appreciation. Emily DeHuff delivered a thoughtful and painstaking edit of the manuscript, while Evan Camfield skillfully oversaw its production. Emily Kimball vetted the manuscript for legal issues—no small task in this work of many characters with complicated histories. And Leila Tejani conscientiously did more work in more areas than I could keep track of, including the selection and presentation of the book's photographs, the bulk of which come from the incomparable Jay Blakesberg. And, speaking of photographs, my thanks to the extraordinary Annie Leibovitz for the portrait of Garcia on Stinson Beach that graces the book's cover. My

436 | ACKNOWLEDGMENTS

friend and former student Lauren Munro did a magnificent job of fact-checking, and the great Hilary McClellen then followed with a detailed scrub of her own. It gives me great confidence to know that Hilary back-stopped this project, and I am especially indebted to her for sticking with it even as she juggled other issues in her life.

Another answer to the question of how long I've been at this is something more like five or six years, since that's when I first began shaping the idea of Garcia's story into a book about him. My greatest thanks over that period are owed to Tina Bennett, my agent and advocate and most sharp and strategic reader. Tina understood both the promise and the risks of this book, and she worked diligently to help me produce a proposal that balanced the story correctly. One of the luckiest days of my life was the day I met Tina some twenty years ago. In the decades since, she has given me a life as a book writer. I am enduringly and deeply grateful to her for that, and for her friendship. Every writer should have a Tina.

In the course of writing this book—whether the four-year version or the six-year version—a number of people have lent me their time and expertise, and they deserve special appreciation. First and foremost is Nick Meriwether. Nick is the model of a public intellectual, deeply rooted in the fundamentals of archival research and academic excellence. He's also startlingly knowledgeable about the Grateful Dead. Many of my happiest evenings in working on this project have been spent with Nick at roadhouses in and around Santa Cruz, talking about Garcia and the Dead and the larger history around them. Nick also did me the invaluable service of reading a draft manuscript of the book, improving every page, from concepts to footnotes. I am indebted to him for all of that and delighted that our friendship, born in this project, continues.

Similarly, Blair Jackson contributed to me and to this project at many levels. His *Garcia: An American Life* is the best straight account of Garcia's life. His extensive contributions to chronicling the Dead include his collaborations with David Gans, another essential Dead scribe, and his work with *The Golden Road*, which he founded and which I have

ACKNOWLEDGMENTS | 437

extensively relied upon. His thoughts and ideas thus run through this book, and that was even more deeply enhanced by his careful review of the manuscript. Blair's generosity was essential to this project and is emblematic of who he is—a living testament to the kind and generous spirit of Deadheads.

It should go without saying, but just in case: Although I'm grateful to Nick and Blair for reading these pages, I alone am responsible for what's on them, and any errors or oversights are mine and mine alone.

Two others who contributed directly to the research of this project deserve special thanks. Dennis McNally is the Dead's official historian and the author of the definitive band biography, as well as a groundbreaking work on Jack Kerouac. He generously gave me several interviews, as well as countless leads and tips to pursue. His copious memory and willingness to share were immensely helpful, as were the many interviews that he conducted himself, now on file at the UCSC archives. The other was Steve Silberman, a great and giving man whose intelligence has helped many Dead scholars, including me. Steve died in 2024, shocking the community of the Grateful Dead. I'm honored to have known him.

Much of the work of any book is conducted in libraries, and I thank the librarians, archivists, and researchers who answered every request, suffered every frustration, and guided me to resources I did not even know existed. The lovely and helpful staff at the University of California, Santa Cruz, were foremost in that work. Thanks to Maureen Carey, Debra Roussopoulos, Mathew Simpson, Alix Norton, Zoe MacLeod, Kate Dundon, Jessica Pigza, Teresa Mora, Becca Rapp, Wyatt Young, Alessia Cecchet, Gabriel Mindel, Sue Chesley Perry, Angelika Frebert, and Scott Campbell. And to Luisa Haddad, public services coordinator for the library's special collections, great thanks for helping plan my many trips to Santa Cruz.

One unexpected joy of this project has been meeting so many people whose lives were touched and affected by Garcia and the Dead. Chief among those are the many members of Garcia's family who took time to speak with me and to share memories, many quite personal and not

438 | ACKNOWLEDGMENTS

all of them pleasant. Two deserve special note: Carolyn Garcia and I struck up a lively conversation at her pretty Oregon home in 2022 and have returned to it often in the years since, over meals and even a trip to the Oregon Country Fair. And Sara Ruppenthal Katz welcomed me into her life and memories in 2023. She has unfailingly weathered my questions while also supplying me with photographs and inviting me to join in her warm and embracing spirit. Not only is this book better for my knowing Sara; my life is, too.

Still another way of thinking about the gestation of this book is to go back more than a decade, when I began weaving this notion into my body of work on politics, culture, and California, three themes that intertwine here. That's a long time, and it covers a period of great change in my life. I am fortunate to have been surrounded by old friends and new during those years. They include Tom Holler, Kathleen McCarthy, Darren Glaudini, Lou Egerton-Wiley, and Miki Athay, each a source of support and inspiration. Jeff and Sally Farnum are dear to me and treasured additions to my life; Jeff's knowledge of music also is woven through these pages.

Reaching back still further are the loved ones whose intelligence, affection, and wholeheartedness are central to my life. Brad Hall and Julia Louis-Dreyfus have been there through all the years of my marriage (Julia even gets an endnote in the book for her interview with Jane Fonda as part of her wonderful podcast, *Wiser than Me*); their goodness, integrity, and resilience are models for me and mainstays of my life. Carol Stogsdill and Steve Stroud have graced my adulthood; their steadfast friendship has given me and my family so very much, from the quiet of Wisconsin lakes to comfort in difficult times. Henry Weinstein and Julianna Roosevelt are beloved friends of many years. Henry has enriched my life since our first meeting in 1991, when I joined him in the downtown newsroom of the *Los Angeles Times* and was lucky to be seated behind his imposing stack of papers. We've shared trials, baseball games, birthdays, and trips—and, sadly, a few funerals—over the years. Henry remains a polestar of integrity, friendship, exemplary journalism, and conscience.

ACKNOWLEDGMENTS | 439

Other friendships bridge time, distance, and new undertakings and have become more precious over the years. Fran Schwartzkopff and Eric Guthey, now comfortably outside America's mayhem in Denmark, have been essential to my life for decades, as have Beth Shuster and Michael Healy, thankfully closer to home. My UCLA colleagues, most notably Rhea Turtletaub, Jenn Poulakidas, and Duane Muller, have given me and my magazine, *Blueprint*, a welcome home, and my old friend and role model, Rick Meyer, has joined me in producing ten years of the magazine. I'm beyond lucky to rely on Rick and my friends at UCLA—for support, insight, and safe harbor from the collapse of daily journalism. Ah, but that's another story.

Dear friends Marshall Goldberg and Anne Roarke are loving supporters of this project and of me. And Mark Z. Barabak, my friend and colleague, was such an enthusiastic advocate that I imagined him as the book's model reader. He gets the first copy.

There's still another way of thinking about the life of this book, one that dates back to my time in college attending Dead shows as often as time and money allowed. My fellow passengers on that good ship Grateful Dead included Edward Sweeney, Mark Kamin, Dave Lenrow, Ted Hampton, Julie Craven, James Evans, Thalia Gould, and Nancy Hart. We had plenty of Big Fun. Those adventures left a lasting sense of wonder, possibility, and kindness. We live in different parts of the country today, and we lost Nancy many years ago, but I hope that some of the feeling that we shared in those years has found its way onto these pages.

One more slice at this book's history goes back even further ("Furthur"?), to my high school years in Palo Alto. While I was interviewing Sara Ruppenthal Katz for this book, we discovered that we graduated from Palo Alto High School exactly twenty years apart, she in the class of 1961, me in 1981 ("Raising hell and having fun, we're the class of '81"). My tiny bedside turntable in those years included worn, scratchy copies of *Workingman's Dead* and *American Beauty*, so perhaps that's where this book really begins—on the Paly campus, at Kepler's bookstore, and at St. Michael's Alley, which I haunted twenty years after Garcia and friends did. From that vantage, I owe another dollop of thanks

440 | ACKNOWLEDGMENTS

to my two best friends from those years, Bill McIntyre and Jeff Elder. We have shared many, many times together, and they have given me such basics as the loves of writing and music. Since that's this book in a nutshell, I thank them for all of that and all of this.

There are, of course, a few people who knew me even before I had heard of the Dead. Special thanks to those I have known and loved the longest: my brother, John Newton (and his husband, Marc Perrotta); my mom, Barbara Newton; and my late dad, Jim Newton, who had a little bit of Deadhead in him.

Finally, there are two souls who give me everything. My son, Jack, overwhelms me with pride and love. The path of sons and fathers is unique to every pair, and ours is ours. As I complete work on this book, I do so with the deep love for Jack that is matched only by my admiration for him and all he is achieving. Jack helped me talk through many of this book's story lines, but his real gift to me is the life that he's leading.

And then there is my wife, Karlene Goller. She is on every page of this book, which she improved directly with her editing and legal expertise and indirectly by her limitless willingness to talk with me about Jerry and the Dead. This book is suffused with her insights, uncredited but essential, into American politics, law, and culture. Her patience is also manifest here: Signing up to write this book gave me license to play the Grateful Dead on every car trip and to fly off to shows in San Francisco and Vegas and beyond; it was, after all, "work." Karlene has tolerated all that and maybe even—dare I say it?—come to like it a bit? I hope so. It's made me who I am, and I am, happily, hers.

SOURCES

BOOKS

Allen, Scott W. *Aces Back to Back: A History of the Grateful Dead*. Self-published: Produced with Outskirts Press, 2014.

Alpert, Richard (Ram Dass). *Be Here Now*. St. Cristobal, N.M.: Hanuman Foundation, 1978.

Babbs, Ken. *Cronies, a Burlesque: Adventures with Ken Kesey, Neal Cassady, the Merry Pranksters and the Grateful Dead*. Eugene, Ore.: Tsunami Press, 2021.

Bach, Damon R. *The American Counterculture: A History of Hippies and Cultural Dissidents*. Lawrence: University Press of Kansas, 2020.

Baez, Joan. *Am I Pretty When I Fly? An Album of Upside Down Drawings*. Boston: Godine. 2023.

———. *And a Voice to Sing With: A Memoir*. New York: Simon & Schuster Paperbacks, 1987.

Barlow, John Perry, with Robert Greenfield. *Mother American Night: My Life in Crazy Times*. New York: Three Rivers Press, 2018.

Barnes, Barry. *Everything I Know About Business I Learned from the Grateful Dead: The Ten Most Innovative Lessons from a Long, Strange Trip*. New York: Hachette, 2011.

Benson, Jackson J. *Wallace Stegner: His Life and Work*. New York: Viking Penguin, 1996.

Benson, Michael. *Why the Grateful Dead Matter*. Lebanon, N.H.: ForeEdge, 2016.

Berlin, Leslie. *Troublemakers: Silicon Valley's Coming of Age*. New York: Simon & Schuster, 2017.

Bernstein, David W., ed. *The San Francisco Tape Music Center: 1960s Counterculture and the Avant-Garde*. Berkeley: University of California Press, 2008.

Blakesberg, Jay. *Jerry Garcia: Secret Space of Dreams*. San Francisco: Rock Out Books, 2019.

Bloom, Joshua, and Waldo E. Martin, Jr. *Black Against Empire: The History and Politics of the Black Panther Party*. Berkeley: University of California Press, 2013.

Boot, Max. *Reagan: His Life and Legend*. New York: Liveright, 2024.

Boyle, Kevin. *The Shattering: America in the 1960s*. New York: W. W. Norton, 2021.

Brand, Stewart. *The Clock of the Long Now: Time and Responsibility; the Ideas Behind the World's Slowest Computer*. New York: Basic Books, 1999.

Brandelius, Jerilyn Lee. *Grateful Dead Family Album*. San Francisco: Last Gasp, 1989.

Breen, Benjamin. *Tripping on Utopia: Margaret Mead, the Cold War, and the Troubled Birth of Psychedelic Science*. New York: Hachette, 2024.

Brett-Smith, H.F.B., ed. *Peacock's Four Ages of Poetry; Shelley's Defense of Poetry; Browning's Essay on Shelley*. Boston: Houghton Mifflin, 1921.

Brinkley, Douglas, ed. *The Gonzo Letters*, vol. 2, *Fear and Loathing in America: Hunter S. Thompson*. New York: Simon & Schuster, 2000.

———, ed. *The Proud Highway: The Fear and Loathing Letters*, vol. 1, *Saga of a Desperate Southern Gentleman, Hunter S. Thompson*. New York: Villard, 1997.

442 | SOURCES

Brook, James, Chris Carlsson, and Nancy J. Peters. *Reclaiming San Francisco: History, Politics, Culture*. San Francisco: City Lights Books, 1998.

Brooks, David. *Bobos in Paradise: The New Upper Class and How They Got There*. New York: Simon & Schuster, 2000.

Brown, David Jay, and Rebecca McClen Novick. *Voices from the Edge: Conversations with Jerry Garcia, Ram Dass, Annie Sprinkle, Matthew Fox, Jaron Lanier, and Others*. Freedom, Calif.: Crossing Press, 1995.

Browne, David. *So Many Roads: The Life and Times of the Grateful Dead*. Boston: Da Capo Press, 2015.

Brownstein, Ronald. *Rock Me on the Water: 1974, the Year Los Angeles Transformed Movies, Music, Television, and Politics*. New York: Harper, 2021.

Bugliosi, Vincent, with Curt Gentry. *Helter Skelter: The True Story of the Manson Murders*. New York: W. W. Norton, 1974.

Burke, Patrick. *Tear Down the Walls: White Radicalism and Black Power in 1960s Rock*. Chicago: University of Chicago Press, 2021.

Callahan, Mat. *The Explosion of Deferred Dreams: Musical Renaissance and Social Revolution in San Francisco, 1965–1975*. Oakland: PM Press, 2017.

Cannon, Lou. *Governor Reagan: The Rise to Power*. New York: Public Affairs, 2003.

———. *President Reagan: The Role of a Lifetime*. New York: Public Affairs, 1991.

Capote, Truman. *In Cold Blood*. New York: Random House, 1965.

Carlsson, Chris, ed. *Ten Years that Shook the City: San Francisco, 1968–1978*. San Francisco: City Lights Foundation Books, 2011.

Carmichael, Stokely (Kwame Ture). *Stokely Speaks: From Black Power to Pan-Africanism*. Chicago: Lawrence Hill Books, 2007.

Cassady, Carolyn. *Off the Road: Twenty Years with Neal Cassady, Jack Kerouac, and Allen Ginsberg*. New York: Overlook Press, 2008.

Cassady, Neal. *The First Third: A Partial Autobiography and Other Writings*. San Francisco: City Lights, 1981.

Cleaver, Eldridge. *Soul on Ice*. Menlo Park, Calif.: Ramparts Press, 1968.

Conners, Peter. *Cornell '77: The Music, the Myth, and the Magnificence of the Grateful Dead's Concert at Barton Hall*. New York: Cornell University Press, 2017.

———. *White Hand Society: The Psychedelic Partnership of Timothy Leary and Allen Ginsberg*. San Francisco: City Lights Books, 2010.

Constanten, Tom. *Between Rock and Hard Places: A Musical Autobiodyssey*. Eugene, Ore.: Hulogosi, 1992.

Covach, John, and Graeme M. Boone, eds. *Understanding Rock: Essays in Musical Analysis*. New York and Oxford: Oxford University Press, 1997.

Coyote, Peter. *The Rainman's Third Cure: An Irregular Education*. Berkeley: Counterpoint, 2015.

———. *Sleeping Where I Fall: A Chronicle*. Berkeley: Counterpoint, 1998.

Cutler, Sam. *You Can't Always Get What You Want: My Life with the Rolling Stones, the Grateful Dead and Other Wonderful Reprobates*. Toronto: ECW Press, 2010.

Davis, Angela. *Are Prisons Obsolete?* New York: Seven Stories Press, 2003.

Davis, David A. *The Economic History of the Grateful Dead: A Look Inside the Financial Records of America's Biggest 20th Century Touring Act*. Self-published, 2024.

Davis, Tom. *Thirty-Nine Years of Short-Term Memory Loss: The Early Years of SNL from Someone Who Was There*. New York: Grove Press, 2009.

DeLillo, Don. *Libra*. New York. Viking, 1988.

———. *White Noise*. New York: Viking Penguin, 1984.

SOURCES | 443

Diano, Giada, and Matthew Gleeson. *Lawrence Ferlinghetti: Writing Across the Landscape; Travel Journals, 1960–2010*. New York: Liveright, 2015.

Didion, Joan. *Play It as It Lays*. New York: Farrar, Straus & Giroux, 1970.

———. *Slouching Towards Bethlehem*. New York: Farrar, Straus & Giroux, 1968.

———. *Where I Was From*. New York: Alfred A. Knopf, 2003.

———. *The White Album*. New York: Simon & Schuster, 1979.

Dodgson, Richard. *Sparks Fly Upward*, a dissertation presented to Ohio University. Included with the Ken Kesey papers, University of Oregon.

Dylan, Bob. *Chronicles*, vol. 1. New York: Simon & Schuster, 2004.

———. *The Philosophy of Modern Song*. New York: Simon & Schuster, 2022.

Ebenkamp, Paul, ed. *The Etiquette of Freedom: Gary Snyder, Jim Harrison, and the Practice of the Wild*. Berkeley: Counterpoint, 2010,

Evans, Mike, and Paul Kingsbury, eds. *Woodstock: Three Days that Rocked the World*. Fiftieth anniversary edition. New York: Sterling, 2019.

Farber, David. *Chicago '68*. Chicago: University of Chicago Press, 1988.

Feenberg, Andrew, and William Leiss, eds. *The Essential Marcuse: Selected Writings of Philosopher and Social Critic Herbert Marcuse*. Boston: Beacon Press, 2007.

Flacks, Richard, and Nelson Lichtenstein. *The Port Huron Statements: Sources and Legacies of the New Left's Founding Manifesto*. Philadelphia: University of Pennsylvania Press, 2015.

Fukuyama, Francis. *The End of History and the Last Man*. New York: Free Press, 1992.

Gaines, Steven. *Heroes and Villains: The True Story of the Beach Boys*. New York: Dutton/Signet, 1986.

Gans, David. *Conversations with the Dead: The Grateful Dead Interview Book*. Cambridge, Mass.: Da Capo Press, 2002.

———. *Talking Heads: The Band and Their Music*. New York: Avon Books, 1985.

Gans, David, and Peter Simon. *Playing in the Band: An Oral and Visual Portrait of the Grateful Dead*. New York: St. Martin's Press, 1985.

Garcia, Carolyn (Mountain Girl). *Harrington Street*. New York: Delacorte Press, 1995.

———. *Jerry Garcia's "Amazing Grace."* New York: HarperCollins, 2002.

———. *Primo Plant: Growing Marijuana Outdoors*. Oakland, Calif.: Quick American Archives, 1998.

Getz, Michael M., and John R. Dwork. *The Deadhead's Taping Compendium*, vols. 1–3. New York: Henry Holt/Owl Books, 1998, 1999, 2000.

Ginsberg, Allen. *Howl and Other Poems*. San Francisco: City Lights Books, 1955.

———. *Planet News, 1961–1967*. San Francisco: City Lights Books, 1968.

Gitlin, Todd. *The Sixties: Years of Hope, Days of Rage*. New York: Bantam Books, 1987.

Goldberg, Danny. *In Search of the Lost Chord: 1967 and the Hippie Idea*. Brooklyn, N.Y.: Akashic Books, 2017.

Gonzales, Rodolfo "Corky." *Message to Aztlán: Selected Writings*. Houston: Arte Público Press, 2001.

Goodman, Mitchell, ed. *The Movement Toward a New America: The Beginnings of a Long Revolution (A Collage) A What?* Philadelphia: Pilgrim Press, 1970.

Graham, Bill, and Robert Greenfield. *Bill Graham Presents: My Life Inside Rock and Out*. New York: Doubleday, 1990.

Graysmith, Robert. *Zodiac: The Shocking True Story of America's Most Elusive Serial Killer*. London: Titan Books, 2007.

Greene, Herb. *Book of the Dead: Celebrating 25 Years with the Grateful Dead*. New York: Delacorte Press/Delta Books, 1990.

444 | SOURCES

Greenfield, Robert. *Bear: The Life and Times of Augustus Owsley Stanley III*. New York: Thomas Dunne Books, 2016.

———. *Dark Star: An Oral Biography of Jerry Garcia*. New York: William Morrow, 1996.

Grogan, Emmett. *Ringolevio*. Boston: Little, Brown, 1972.

Harries-Jones, Peter. *A Recursive Vision: Ecological Understanding and Gregory Bateson*. Toronto: University of Toronto Press, 1995.

Harrison, Hank. *The Dead Book: A Social History of the Haight-Ashbury Experience. San Francisco, Volume One of a Trilogy*. Los Altos, Calif.: Archives Press, 1973.

———. *The Dead: Volume Two of a Trilogy*. Los Altos, Calif.: Archives Press, 1980.

Hart, Mickey, with Jay Stevens. *Drumming at the Edge of Magic: A Journey into the Spirit of Percussion*. New York: HarperCollins, 1990.

Hayden, Tom. *The Port Huron Statement: The Visionary Call of the 1960s Revolution*. New York: Thunder's Mouth Press, 2005.

———. *Reunion: A Memoir*. New York: Random House, 1988.

Heinlein, Robert A. *Stranger in a Strange Land*. New York: Penguin Books, 1961.

Hunter, Robert. *A Box of Rain: Collected Lyrics of Robert Hunter*. New York: Viking, 1990.

———. *Sentinel*. New York: Penguin Poets, 1993.

———. *The Silver Snarling Trumpet*. New York: Hachette, 2024.

Jackson, Blair. *Garcia: An American Life*. New York: Penguin Books, 1999.

———. *Grateful Dead Gear: The Band's Instruments, Sound Systems, and Recording Sessions, 1965–1995*. San Francisco: Backbeat Books, 2006.

Jackson, Blair, and David Gans. *This Is All a Dream We Dreamed: An Oral History of the Grateful Dead*. New York: Flatiron Press, 2015.

Jacobs, Ron. *The Way the Wind Blows: A History of the Weather Underground*. London and New York: Verso, 1997.

Jarnow, Jesse. *Heads: A Biography of Psychedelic America*. Boston: Da Capo Press, 2016.

Kaiser, David. *How the Hippies Saved Physics: Science, Counterculture, and the Quantum Revival*. New York: W. W. Norton, 2011.

Kandel, Lenore. *The Love Book*. San Francisco: Stolen Paper Review, 1966.

Kātz, Barry. *Herbert Marcuse and the Art of Liberation: An Intellectual Biography*. London: Verso, 1982.

Kaukonen, Jorma. *Been So Long: My Life and Music*. New York: St. Martin's Press, 2018.

Kelly, Linda. *Deadheads: Stories from Fellow Artists, Friends and Followers of the Grateful Dead*. New York: Skyhorse, 1975.

Kerouac, Jack. *Big Sur*. New York: Farrar, Straus & Cudahy, 1962.

———. *The Dharma Bums*. New York: Viking Press, 1958.

———. *On the Road*. New York: Viking Press, 1957.

Kesey, Ken. *Demon Box*. New York: Viking Penguin, 1986.

———. *One Flew over the Cuckoo's Nest*. New York: Viking Press, 1962.

———. *Sometimes a Great Notion*. New York: Viking Penguin, 1964.

Kramer, Michael J. *The Republic of Rock: Music and Citizenship in the Sixties Counterculture*. New York: Oxford University Press, 2013.

Kreutzmann, Bill, with Benjy Eisen. *Deal: My Three Decades of Drumming, Dreams, and Drugs with the Grateful Dead*. New York: St. Martin's Press, 2015.

Kubernik, Harvey, and Kenneth Kubernik. *A Perfect Haze: The Illustrated History of the Monterey International Pop Festival*. Solana Beach, Calif.: Santa Monica Press, 2011.

Kusch, Frank. *Battleground Chicago: The Police and the 1968 Democratic National Convention*. Westport, Conn.: Praeger, 2004.

Lake, Dianne, and Deborah Herman. *Member of the Family: My Story of Charles Manson, Life Inside His Cult, And the Darkness that Ended the Sixties*. New York: HarperCollins, 2017.

SOURCES | 445

Lang, Michael, with Holly George-Warren. *The Road to Woodstock from the Man Behind the Legendary Festival.* New York: HarperCollins, 2009.

Lee, Martin A., and Bruce Shlain. *Acid Dreams: The Complete Social History of LSD; the CIA, the Sixties, and Beyond.* New York: Grove Press, 1985.

Lesh, Phil. *Searching for the Sound: My Life with the Grateful Dead.* New York: Little, Brown, 2005.

Lowery, Wesley. *"They Can't Kill Us All": Ferguson, Baltimore, and a New Era in America's Racial Justice Movement.* New York: Little, Brown, 2016.

Lukas, J. Anthony. *Don't Shoot—We Are Your Children!* New York: Random House, 1968.

Mailer, Norman. *The Armies of the Night.* New York: Plume, 1968.

———. *The Naked and the Dead.* New York: Rinehart & Company, 1948.

———. *Why Are We in Vietnam?* New York: G. P. Putnam's Sons, 1967.

Marcus, Greil. *Folk Music: A Bob Dylan Biography in Seven Songs.* New Haven: Yale University Press, 2022.

Marcuse, Herbert. *One-Dimensional Man.* Boston: Beacon Press, 1964.

———. *Reason and Revolution.* London: Woolf Haus, 2020.

Markoff, John. *What the Dormouse Said: How the 60s Counterculture Shaped the Personal Computer Industry.* New York: Viking Penguin, 2005.

———. *Whole Earth: The Many Lives of Stewart Brand.* New York: Penguin Press, 2022.

McClure, Michael. *Scratching the Beat Surface: Essays on New Vision from Blake to Kerouac.* New York: North Point Press, 1982.

McEneaney, Kevin T. *Hunter S. Thompson: Fear, Loathing, and the Birth of Gonzo.* Lanham, Md.: Rowman & Littlefield, 2016.

McGee, Rosie. *Dancing with the Dead: A Photographic Memoir.* Self-published: Produced by TIOLI Press and Bytes, 2013.

———. *My Grateful Dead Photos and How I Came to Take Them.* Self-published: Produced by TIOLI Press and Bytes, 2022.

McNally, Dennis. *Desolate Angel: Jack Kerouac, The Beat Generation, and America.* Cambridge, Mass.: Da Capo Press, 2003.

———. *A Long Strange Trip: The Inside History of the Grateful Dead.* New York: Broadway Books, 2002.

———, ed. *Jerry on Jerry: The Unpublished Jerry Garcia Interviews.* New York: Black Dog and Leventhal Publishers, 2015.

McWilliams, Carey. *Factories in the Field: The Story of Migratory Farm Labor in California.* Berkeley: University of California Press, 1935.

Menand, Louis. *The Free World: Art and Thought in the Cold War.* New York: Farrar, Straus and Giroux, 2021.

Meriwether, Nicholas, ed. *All Graceful Instruments: The Contexts of the Grateful Dead Phenomenon.* Newcastle, U.K.: Cambridge Scholars Publishing, 2007.

———. *Reading the Grateful Dead: A Critical Survey.* Lanham, Md.: Scarecrow Press, 2012.

———. *Studying the Dead: An Informal History of the Grateful Dead Scholars Caucus.* Lanham, Md.: Scarecrow Press, 2013.

Millman, Susana. *Alive with the Dead, or, A Fly on the Wall with a Camera.* Self-published: Produced by Last Gasp Press, 2016.

Moore, Dave, ed. *Neal Cassady Collected Letters, 1944–1967.* New York: Penguin Books, 2004.

Moretta, John Anthony. *The Hippies: A 1960s History.* Jefferson, N.C.: McFarland, 2017.

Morgan, Bill, and David Stanford, eds. *Jack Kerouac, Allen Ginsberg: The Letters.* New York: Penguin, 2010.

Murger, Henri. *Scenes from the Life of Bohemia.* Dhaka, Bangladesh: Adansonia Press, 2023.

446 | SOURCES

Norman, Gurney. *Divine Right's Trip: A Novel of the Counterculture*. Frankfurt, Ky.: Gnomon Press, 1971.

Novoa, Bruce. *Chicano Poetry: A Response to Chaos*. Austin: University of Texas Press, 1982.

Pagels, Elaine. *Why Religion? A Personal Story*. New York: HarperCollins, 2018.

Parker, Scott F., ed. *Conversations with Ken Kesey*. Jackson: University Press of Mississippi, 2014.

Peck, Abe. *Uncovering the Sixties: The Life and Times of the Underground Press*. New York: Pantheon Books, 1985.

Perry, Charles. *The Haight-Ashbury: A History*. New York: Rolling Stone Press, 1984.

Perry, Helen Swick. *The Human Be-In*. New York: Basic Books, 1970.

Pirsig, Robert M. *Zen and the Art of Motorcycle Maintenance: An Inquiry into Values*. New York: William Morrow, 1974.

Poole, Buzz. *Workingman's Dead* (part of the 33⅓ series). New York: Bloomsbury, 2006.

Pynchon, Thomas. *The Crying of Lot 49*. Philadelphia: J. B. Lippincott, 1966.

———. *Gravity's Rainbow*. New York: Viking Press, 1973.

———. *V*. Philadelphia: J. B. Lippincott., 1963.

Rao, Arun. *A History of Silicon Valley: The Greatest Creation of Wealth in the History of the Planet*. 2nd ed. Palo Alto: Omniware Group, 2013.

Reich, Charles. *The Greening of America: How the Youth Revolution Is Trying to Make America Livable*. New York: Random House, 1970.

Reich, Charles, and Jann Wenner. *Garcia: A Signpost to New Space*. San Francisco: Straight Arrow Books, 1972.

Reiterman, Tim, with John Jacobs. *Raven: The Untold Story of the Rev. Jim Jones and His People*. New York: E. P. Dutton, 1982.

Richardson, Peter. *No Simple Highway: A Cultural History of the Grateful Dead*. New York: St. Martin's Press, 2014.

———. *Savage Journey: Hunter S. Thompson and the Weird Road to Gonzo*. Berkeley: University of California Press, 2022.

Rigney, Francis J., and L. Douglas Smith. *The Real Bohemia*. New York: Basic Books, 1961.

Robertson, Ray. *All the Years Combine: The Grateful Dead in Fifty Shows*. Windsor, Ontario: Biblioasis, 2023.

Rodriguez, Mark A. *After All Is Said and Done: Taping the Grateful Dead, 1965–1995*. Brooklyn, N.Y.: Anthology Editions, 2022.

Ronstadt, Linda. *Simple Dreams: A Musical Memoir*. New York: Simon & Schuster, 2013.

Rorabaugh, W. J. *Berkeley at War: The 1960s*. New York: Oxford University Press, 1989.

Rosenfeld, Seth. *Subversives: The FBI's War on Student Radicals, and Reagan's Rise to Power*. New York: Farrar, Straus & Giroux, 2012.

Roszak, Theodore. *The Making of a Counter Culture: Reflections on the Technocratic Society and Its Youthful Opposition*. London: Faber and Faber, 1970.

Rubin, Rick. *The Creative Act: A Way of Being*. New York: Penguin Press, 2023.

Santokh, Sat. *There Is a Way to Create Our Future*. A Limited Private Pre-Publication Printing, satsantokh.com/my-book.html.

Schumacher, E. F. *Small Is Beautiful: Economics as if People Mattered*. London: Blond & Briggs, 1970.

Schumacher, Michael, ed. *Allen Ginsberg: The Fall of America Journals, 1965–1971*. Minneapolis: University of Minnesota Press, 2020.

Scully, Rock, with David Dalton. *Living with the Dead: Twenty Years on the Bus with Garcia and the Grateful Dead*. New York: Little, Brown, 1996.

Selvin, Joel. *Altamont: The Rolling Stones, the Hells Angels, and the Inside Story of Rock's Darkest Day*. New York: HarperCollins/Dey Street, 2016.

SOURCES | 447

———. *Fare Thee Well: The Final Chapters of the Grateful Dead's Long, Strange Trip*. New York: Hachette, 2018.

———. *The Haight: Love, Rock, and Revolution*. Revised and expanded edition. San Rafael, Calif.: Insight Editions, 2020.

———. *Summer of Love: The Inside Story of LSD, Rock and Roll, Free Love and High Times in the Wild West*. New York: Dutton, 1994.

Shane, Stephen, and Bobby Seale. *Power to the People: The World of the Black Panthers*. New York: Abrams, 2016.

Shenk, David, and Steve Silberman. *Skeleton Key: A Dictionary for Deadheads*. New York: Doubleday, 1994.

Shih, Bryan, and Yohuru Williams, eds. *The Black Panthers: Portraits from an Unfinished Revolution*. New York: Nation Books, 2016.

Sims, Norman, ed. *The Literary Journalists: The New Art of Personal Reportage*. New York: Ballantine Books, 1984.

Smith, Cándida. *Utopia and Dissent: Art, Poetry, and Politics in California*. Berkeley: University of California Press, 1995.

Smith, Joe. *Off the Record: An Oral History of Popular Music*. New York: Warner Books, 1988.

Snyder, Gary. *Earth House Hold*. New York: New Directions Books, 1969.

———. *Mountains and Rivers Without End*. Washington, D.C.: Counterpoint, 1996.

Springsteen, Bruce. *Born to Run*. New York: Simon & Schuster, 2016.

Stanley, Rhoney Gissen. *Owsley and Me: My LSD Family*. Rhinebeck, N.Y.: Monkfish Book Publishing Company, 2012.

Stegner, Wallace. *All the Little Live Things*. New York: Viking Press, 1967.

———. *The Big Rock Candy Mountain*. New York: Duell, Sloan and Pearce, 1943.

———. *The Sound of Mountain Water*. Garden City, N.Y.: Doubleday, 1969.

Stone, Robert. *Prime Green: Remembering the Sixties*. New York: HarperCollins, 2007.

Talbot, David. *Season of the Witch*. New York: Free Press, 2012.

Thompson, Hunter S. *Fear and Loathing in Las Vegas*. 50th anniversary edition. New York: Modern Library, 2021.

———. *Fear and Loathing on the Campaign Trail '72*. San Francisco: Straight Arrow Books, 1973.

———. *Hell's Angels: A Strange and Terrible Saga*. New York: Random House, 1967.

Toobin, Jeffrey. *American Heiress: The Wild Saga of the Kidnapping, Crimes and Trial of Patty Hearst*. New York: Doubleday, 2016.

Trager, Oliver. *The American Book of the Dead: The Definitive Grateful Dead Encyclopedia*. New York: Simon & Schuster, 1997.

Trist, Alan. *The Water of Life: A Tale of the Grateful Dead*. Eugene, Ore.: Hulogosi, 1989.

Troy, Sandy. *Captain Trips: A Biography of Jerry Garcia*. New York: Thunder's Mouth Press, 1994.

Turner, Fred. *From Counterculture to Cyberculture: Stewart Brand, the Whole Earth Network, and the Rise of Digital Utopianism*. Chicago: University of Chicago Press, 2008.

Ulrich, Jennifer. *The Timothy Leary Project: Inside the Great Counterculture Experiment*. New York: Abrams Press, 2018.

Vonnegut, Kurt. *The Sirens of Titan*. New York: Dell, 1959.

———. *Slaughterhouse-Five, or, The Children's Crusade, A Duty-Dance with Death*. New York: Dial Press Trade Paperbacks, 1969.

Wade, Simeon. *Foucault in California: [A True Story—Wherein the Great French Philosopher Drops Acid in the Valley of Death]*. Berkeley: Heyday, 2019.

Walton, Bill. *Back from the Dead: Searching for the Sound, Shining the Light, and Throwing It Down*. New York: Simon & Schuster, 2016.

448 | SOURCES

Weather Underground. *Prairie Fire: The Politics of Revolutionary Anti-Imperialism; Political Statement of the Weather Underground.* Underground Press publication, 1974.

Weir, David. *Bohemians: A Very Short Introduction.* New York: Oxford University Press, 2023.

Wenner, Jann S. *Like a Rolling Stone: A Memoir.* New York: Little, Brown, 2022.

White, Curtis. *Living in a World That Can't Be Fixed: Reimagining Counterculture Today.* Brooklyn, N.Y.: Melville House, 2019.

———. *Transcendent: Art and Dharma in a Time of Collapse.* Brooklyn, N.Y.: Melville House, 2023.

Wolfe, Tom. *The Electric Kool-Aid Acid Test.* New York: Picador, 1968.

———, ed. *The New Journalism.* New York: Harper & Row, 1973.

ARCHIVAL MATERIAL

University of California, Santa Cruz (UCSC), Special Collections. Grateful Dead Records, including History, Press, Business and Show Files, all of which are referenced in these pages. Many of the newspaper clippings cited in this book come from the Dead archives at UCSC. The Dead's clipping service saved published references to the band beginning in the late 1960s. Where possible, those are cited to the original publications.

Oral History Project of Bancroft Library, University of California, Berkeley.

Stanford University, Special Collections. Papers of Allen Ginsberg, including correspondence, journals, manuscripts, business records, and other material.

University of Oregon, Eugene, Special Collections, Papers of Ken Kesey, including correspondence, journals, personal papers, and other material.

CIA files on Project MK-ULTRA, (FOIA)/ESDN (CREST): 06760269, created Dec. 28, 2022.

FBI files on Ken Kesey (including his flight to Mexico), Jerome "Jerry" Garcia, the Grateful Dead, Jefferson Airplane, Tom Hayden, and the antiwar movement, obtained through the Freedom of Information Act (FOIA).

U.S. Census Reports

PERIODICALS

This list includes only those mentioned frequently in text or cited frequently in notes.

Berkeley Barb
The Black Panther
Dupree's Diamond News
Evergreen Review
The Golden Road
Lapham's Quarterly
Los Angeles Times
The New York Times
The Oracle
Rolling Stone
San Francisco Chronicle
San Francisco Examiner
Time
The Village Voice
The Washington Post
Whole Earth Catalog

SOURCES | 449

FILMS

Bar-Lev, Amir. *Long Strange Trip* (documentary film about the Grateful Dead), 2017.
Field, Sam. *Sunshine Daydream* (documentary film about the Dead's 1972 concert in Veneta, Oregon), 2013.
Kreutzmann, Justin, and Matt Busch. *Move Me Brightly*, 2013.
Maysles, Albert, and David and Charlotte Zwerin. *Gimme Shelter* (documentary film about the Rolling Stones' 1969 U.S. tour), 1971.
Washington, Edward, and Ron Rakow, *The Grateful Dead Movie*, 1977.

PODCASTS

Good Ol' Grateful Deadcast, hosted by Rich Mahan and Jesse Jarnow
Guess the Year, hosted by Mike McClure
A History of Rock Music in 500 Songs, hosted by Andrew Hickey
Wiser than Me, hosted by Julia Louis-Dreyfus

INTERVIEWS

This book draws on two major sets of interviews, those I conducted myself and those conducted by others. Garcia gave scores of interviews, and those that were published or aired are cited throughout. Recordings of some of those and many other interviews are archived with the Grateful Dead records at UCSC. The UCSC interviews include the following (this is a partial list but represents interviews that I listened to and, in many cases, drew upon):

LCD 11338—Dennis McNally interviews Sam Cutler
LCD 11340—Dennis McNally interviews Jon Riester
LCD 11342—Dennis McNally interviews Lou Gottlieb
LCD 11343—Dennis McNally interviews Joe Smith
LCD 11344—Dennis McNally interviews Carl Scott
LCD 11345—Dennis McNally interviews Allen Gross
LCD 11346—Dennis McNally interviews Freddie Herrera
LCD 11347—Dennis McNally interviews Stan Cornyn
LCD 11348—Dennis McNally interviews Goldie Rush
LCD 11349—Dennis McNally interviews Jon McIntire
LCD 11352—Dennis McNally interviews Danny Rifkin
LCD 11380—Dennis McNally interviews Bill Graham
LCD 11381—Dennis McNally and David Gans interview Candace Brightman
LCD 11382—Dennis McNally interviews Merl Saunders
LCD 11384—Dennis McNally interviews Owsley (Bear) Stanley
LCD 11387—Dennis McNally interviews Cameron Sears
LCD 11388—Dennis McNally interviews Roy Lott
LCD 11389—Dennis McNally interviews Candace Brightman
LCD 11390—Dennis McNally interviews Bruce Hornsby
LCD 11395—Dennis McNally interviews Eileen Law
LCD 11396—Dennis McNally interviews Clive Davis
LCD 11400—Dennis McNally interviews Donna Jean Godchaux MacKay
LCD 11402—Dennis McNally interviews Sue Stephens
LCD 11403—Dennis McNally interviews Tim Scully
LCD 11404—Dennis McNally interviews Barbara Meier

450 | SOURCES

LCD 11408—Dennis McNally interviews John Scher
LCD 11409—Dennis McNally interviews Cliff Garcia
LCD 11428—Dennis McNally interviews Jerry Garcia
LCD 11429—Dennis McNally interviews Phil Lesh
LCD 11430—Dennis McNally interviews Bob Weir and John Perry Barlow
LCD 11469—Dennis McNally interviews Hal Kant
LCD 11471—Dennis McNally interviews Robert Hunter
LCD 11472—Dennis McNally interviews Bob Weir
LCD 11473—Dennis McNally interviews Danny Weiner
LCD 11477—Dennis McNally interviews Jerry Garcia on comics
LCD 11479—A conversation with Jerry Garcia and Nick Spitzer
LCD 11487—Dennis McNally interviews Alan Trist
LCD 11488—Dennis McNally interviews Jerry Garcia
LCD 11489—Dennis McNally interviews Bill Belmont
LCD 11490—Dennis McNally interviews Brian Rohan
LCD 11491—Dennis McNally interviews Chesley Milliken
LCD 11506—Dennis McNally interviews David Grisman
LCD 11507—Dennis McNally interviews Laird Grant
LCD 11517—Dennis McNally interviews John Perry Barlow
LCD 11518—Dennis McNally interviews Nicki Scully
LCD 11565—Dennis McNally interviews Jerry Pompili
LCD 11566—Dennis McNally interviews Jerry Abrams
LCD 11567—Dennis McNally interviews Hillel Resner
LCD 11568—Dennis McNally interviews Lawrence Shurtliff (Ramrod)
LCD 11569—Dennis McNally interviews Gert Chiarito
LCD 11579—Dennis McNally interviews David Nelson
LCD 11581—Dennis McNally interviews Tom Constanten
LCD 11596—Dennis McNally interviews John Kahn
LCD 11597—Dennis McNally interviews John Cipollina
LCD 11599—Dennis McNally interviews Danny Rifkin
LCD 11601—Dennis McNally interviews Phil Lesh
LCD 11603—Dennis McNally interviews Bill Kreutzmann
LCD 11604—Dennis McNally interviews Bill Kreutzmann
LCD 11606—Dennis McNally interviews Frankie Weir
LCD 11607—Dennis McNally interviews Jerry Garcia
LCD 11709—Studs Terkel with Jerry Garcia and Abe Peck
LCD 11713—Grateful Dead interview from "The Hippie Temptation" (Harry Reasoner, CBS News)
LCD 11724—Dennis McNally and Al Aronowitz interview Jerry Garcia
LCD 11725—Dennis McNally interviews Jerry Garcia
LCD 11726—Dennis McNally interviews Luria Castell
LCD 11727—Dennis McNally interviews Carolyn Adams Garcia (Mountain Girl)
LCD 11762—Phil Lesh, Mickey Hart, and Bob Weir interviewed for *In the Studio* radio program about "the Arista years"
LCD 11778—Joel Selvin interviews Dan Healy
LCD 11779—Joel Selvin interviews Grace Slick
LCD 11780—Joel Selvin interviews Darby Slick
LCD 11781—Joel Selvin interviews Jorma Kaukonen
LCD 11786—John Dawson speaks with Ralph Gleason and Bill Graham

SOURCES | 451

LCD 11795—Father Miles Riley interviews Jerry Garcia
LCD 11800—Dennis McNally interviews David Freiberg
LCD 11829—Nicholas G. Meriwether interviews Michael Bowen
LCD 11830—Nicholas G. Meriwether interviews Lt. Arthur Gerrans
LCD 11831—Nicholas G. Meriwether interviews Roger Siegel
LCD 11832—Nicholas G. Meriwether interviews Bill Collins
LCD 11833—Nicholas G. Meriwether interviews Michael Wagner with Michael Goetz

My interviews and other conversations/email exchanges include:

Nicholas Meriwether: Many occasions, 2020–25
Sen. Dianne Feinstein: April 2, 2019
Alan Trist: June 22, 2021
Joel Selvin: Sept. 8, 2021
Peter Richardson: October 2021
John Markoff: Oct. 16, 2021
Dennis McNally: Nov. 5, 2021; March 28, 2023; March 29, 2024
Jesse Jarnow: Jan. 6, 2022, and others
Carolyn Adams Garcia (Mountain Girl): Jan. 15, 2022; March 14, 2022; March 17, 2022;
    July 10, 2022
Sat Santokh: Jan. 29, 2022
Ken Babbs: March 15, 2022
Steve Dunne: May 15, 2022
Susan Klein: June 27, 2022
Sunshine Kesey: July 10, 2022
Rosie McGee: July 11, 2022
Buzz Poole: July 31, 2022
Gov. Jerry Brown: Sept. 19, 2022
Peter Coyote: Sept. 19, 2022
Tom Stephens: Sept. 21, 2022
Steve Silberman: Oct. 5, 2022; Dec. 28, 2022; and follow-up conversations
Bob Bralove: Oct. 22, 2022
Michael Kramer: Dec. 30, 2022
Wavy Gravy: Jan. 10, 2023
Brian Miskis: Jan. 19, 2023
Paul Feldman: Feb. 1, 2023
Sara Ruppenthal Katz: Feb. 11, 2023; March 28–30, 2024
Sandy Rothman: Feb. 11, 2023
Huey Lewis: April 18, 2023
Blair Jackson: June 16, 2023
Bill Walton: Aug. 15, 2023 (email exchange)
Gillian Welch: Sept. 15, 2023
Al Franken: Oct. 4, 2023
Jane Fonda: Nov. 27, 2023
Peter Rowan: March 29, 2024 (backstage at the Bluegrass Hall of Fame)
David Nelson: March 30, 2024
Heather Garcia: March 30, 2024
Dave Stever, CEO of Ben & Jerry's: April 25, 2024
Tom Unterman: April 29, 2024
Cliff Palefsky: May 2, 2024

452 | SOURCES

Cameron Sears: May 2, 2024 (and follow-ups)
David Gans: July 14, 2024
Edward Sweeney: July 16, 2024
Theresa Garcia: Sept. 17, 2024
Justin Kreutzmann: Oct. 1, 2024
Jay Blakesberg: Nov. 6, 2024

NOTES

INTRODUCTION

xv **more than twenty-three hundred ticketed shows:** As with many facts connected to the Grateful Dead, these numbers are imprecise, as are estimates of fans or concert audiences. How many people were at Woodstock? At Watkins Glen? Does an appearance on *Saturday Night Live* constitute a "ticketed" show? These are questions for the community of Grateful Dead scholars in all their deep and admirable dedication.

xvi **"They are their own greatest influence":** Michael Lydon, "Good Old Grateful Dead," *Rolling Stone*, Aug. 23, 1969.

xvii **"This is Dionysus talking through these kids":** Nicholas Meriwether, "Documenting the Dead: Joseph Campbell and the Grateful Dead," Dead.net, Oct. 29, 2015, dead.net /features/blog/documenting-dead-joseph-campbell-and-grateful-dead.

xvii **"We move minds":** Dennis McNally, *A Long Strange Trip*, 538.

xix **"These are the very bonds of social life":** Theodore Roszak, *The Making of a Counter Culture*, 148.

CHAPTER 1: "UTTER LOSS"

4 **when the General Strike shut down the port:** The U.S. Census for 1940.

4 **handy with tools, and sporting:** UCSC, Dennis McNally interview with Cliff Garcia, archived at LCD 11409.

4 **eighty-four hours at Joe Garcia's:** Ruth worked off the books at the bar, so the census does not capture her work, listing her only employment as in the home.

5 **"loose Catholics rather than devout Catholics":** Interviewed by Father Miles Riley for *I Believe*, KPIX broadcast, 1976, youtube.com/watch?v=8odcUvmVWzM.

5 **more impressed by the sound of Latin:** Father Guido Sarducci interview with Jerry Garcia, Dec. 31, 1984, youtube.com/watch?v=igfxUvcu_-I.

6 **on her wind-up Victrola:** UCSC, Dennis McNally interview with Garcia, archived at LCD 11607.

6 **placing the wood to be chopped:** The exact date of this incident is elusive, but Cliff's memory suggests it took place in the summer of 1946. To Robert Greenfield, Cliff Garcia described it as "a year before my father died," which would place it in 1946. And though the family used the Lompico cabin all year, they were there most frequently in the summer.

6 **"Finally, I nailed him":** Luke Wilson interview with Cliff Garcia, date unknown, included on "Move Me Brightly."

7 **the events of that August day:** Author interview with Carolyn Garcia, March 17, 2022.

7 **no mention is made of Jerry's presence at the scene:** No byline, "Bay Man Is Drowned in Trinity River First Day of Vacation," *Sacramento Bee*, Aug. 26, 1947, 8.

454 | NOTES

7 **"an odd couple":** Jerry Garcia, *Harrington Street* (pages are unnumbered).

8 **Cliff knew his grandmother's boyfriend:** UCSC, Dennis McNally interview with Cliff Garcia, archived at LCD 11409.

8 **after they had cooled off:** No byline, "War of Sexes Is Reversed in Police Court," *San Francisco Examiner*, April 16, 1916, 7.

8 **She sued for divorce:** Legal listings, *Recorder*, San Francisco, April 18, 1916, 5.

9 **"loss. Utter loss":** Robert Greenfield, *Dark Star*, 38.

10 **"Inquisitive," he said:** Robert Hunter, diary entry, May 18, 1996, UCSC, Special Collections, GD Records, History, Box 1, Folder: Biographical, Robert Hunter Journal, March–July 1996.

10 **married a merchant mariner:** In an interview with Dennis McNally, Cliff Garcia recalled that his mother married a man named Ben Brown in about 1949. Brown never lived with Cliff and Jerry, however. The marriage lasted only a year or two, and Brown quickly disappeared from the scene. Interview is archived at LCD 11409 at UCSC.

10 **"A new life":** Greenfield, *Dark Star*, 8.

11 **skirted the edges of that culture:** Blair Jackson, *Garcia*, 19.

12 **"full of intense conviction":** Jack Kerouac, "Aftermath: The Philosophy of the Beat Generation," *Esquire*, March 1958, 24.

12 **"continually from early youth":** Clellon Holmes, "This Is the Beat Generation," *New York Times Magazine*, Nov. 16, 1952, 10.

13 **"and certainly no rebel":** Lawrence Ferlinghetti, *Writing Across the Landscape*, 16 (diary entry for April 1, 1960).

13 **"someplace like Aix en Provence":** Kenneth Rexroth, "Letter from San Francisco," *Evergreen Review*, vol. 1, no. 2, 5–6.

14 **The event took place at Six Gallery:** Louis Menand, *The Free World*, 194–95.

15 **"a mad night":** Jack Kerouac, *The Dharma Bums*, 13–15.

15 **the preeminent young writers of the moment:** Luther Nichols, "Local Poets Praised," *San Francisco Examiner*, Oct. 3, 1956, section 2, p. 3, and "Our Literary Heritage," Oct. 19, 1956, section 3, p. 3.

15 **"I greet you at the beginning of a great career":** Menand, *Free World*, 194–95. See also Academy of American Poets, poets.org/book/howl-and-other-poems.

15 **"beyond a point of no return":** Menand, *Free World*, 195.

15 **he thought the work was "dull":** Menand, *Free World*, 196. Trilling's remark included "Howl" as well as the other poems in the small collection.

15 **"a common ancestry whose name is Disgust":** Nancy J. Peters, "The Beat Generation and San Francisco's Culture of Dissent" in "Reclaiming San Francisco: History, Politics, Culture," 1998, foundsf.org/index.php?title=Beat_Generation_and_San_Francisco%27s_Culture_of_Dissent.

16 **"'On the Road' is a major novel":** Gilbert Millstein, "Books of The Times," *New York Times*, Sept. 5, 1957, 27.

16 **a publisher willing to produce the book:** Andrea Shea, "Jack Kerouac's Famous Scroll, 'On the Road' Again," NPR, July 5, 2007, npr.org/templates/story/story.php?storyId=11709924.

17 **"my keenest sense of self":** Peter Richardson, *No Simple Highway*, 25.

17 **"if it weren't for Kerouac opening those doors":** Ibid., 28.

18 **"It's all here":** Ralph J. Gleason, "San Francisco Jazz Scene," *Evergreen Review*, vol. 1, no. 2, 64.

19 **"I definitely do want a guitar":** UCSC, Dennis McNally and Al Aronowitz interview with Jerry Garcia, archived at LCD 11724.

NOTES | **455**

19 **"I went nuts"**: Anthony DeCurtis, "Jerry Garcia: The *Rolling Stone* Interview," *Rolling Stone*, Sept. 2, 1993.

19 **"good old Danelectro"**: David Gans, interview with Garcia, *Conversations with the Dead*, 87.

19 **helping Garcia mold a specific style**: UCSC, Bob Coburn interviews Jerry Garcia, archived at LCD 11768.

19 **"It was just what I wanted"**: Charles Reich and Jann Wenner, "The *Rolling Stone* Interview: Jerry Garcia," *Rolling Stone*, Jan. 20, 1972, 33.

19 **Eager for more**: Greenfield, *Dark Star*, 12–13.

20 **"dressed" as a cookie**: Ibid., 14.

20 **"a last attempt to pull me out of the trip"**: UCSC, Dennis McNally and Al Aronowitz interview with Jerry Garcia, archived at UCSC, LCD 11724.

21 **Grant fixed up a chicken coop**: Al Aronowitz, "*High Times* Greats: Jerry Garcia," *High Times*, Aug. 7, 2020. (This article was published in 2020, but the original interview appeared in 2001, and the interview for it took place in June 1972.)

21 **"It was the time to leave it all"**: Reich and Wenner, "*Rolling Stone* Interview: Jerry Garcia," 34.

CHAPTER 2: THE SLINGSHOT

23 **He was accepted into the Army**: This information and other official records of Garcia's brief military service have been made available through the Freedom of Information Act. Garcia's entire file consists of 99 pages, many of them duplicates, documenting his enlistment, service record, and discharge—all during 1960.

24 **"no desire to improve himself as a soldier"**: Downey memo to Commanding Officer, 30th Artillery Group, Ft. Winfield Scott, Dec. 12, 1960.

24 **a "basic character behavior disorder of lifelong duration"**: Capt. Levin F. Magruder, Consultation Sheet, Dec. 5, 1960.

24 **"getting out of the Army"**: John H. Downey, "Statement," Headquarters Battery, Dec. 12, 1960.

25 **Music wafted from room to room**: Robert Hunter, *The Silver Snarling Trumpet*, 17–19.

26 **crashed through a fence, flipping twice**: No byline, "Paul Speegle's Son Killed," *San Francisco Examiner*, Feb. 21, 1961, 5.

26 **"Wow, this is really beautiful"**: Greenfield, *Dark Star*, 22.

26 **"semi-Edwardian finery"**: Biographical details are from the class notes of the Menlo-Atherton Class of 1962, available online at classcreator.com/Atherton-California-Menlo-Atherton-1962/class_profile.cfm?member_id=4959942.

27 **"like Claude Debussy"**: Hank Harrison, *The Dead Book*, 53.

27 **"That was the slingshot"**: Sandy Troy, *Captain Trips*, 27.

27 **"tell her I love her"**: Dennis McNally interview with Barbara Meier, UCSC, Grateful Dead Records, archived at LCD 11404.

28 **"twenty-four to thirty-eight hours a day"**: Hunter, *Silver Snarling Trumpet*, 22.

28 **"You couldn't get him to stop"**: Author interview with Sandy Rothman, Feb. 11, 2023.

29 **as did Westerns**: UCSC, Dennis McNally interview with Hunter, archived at LCD 11471.

29 **he styled himself an Elvis**: Ibid.

29 **made his way west again**: For the Folk Music Club, see Hunter letter of Nov. 4, 1996, in a discussion of "Uncle John's Band," artsites.ucsc.edu/GDead/AGDL/uncle.html.

30 **They ate pineapple**: UCSC, Dennis McNally interview with Barbara Meier, archived at LCD 11404.

456 | NOTES

30 **"a completely innocent conscience":** Hunter, *Silver Snarling Trumpet*, 22.

30 **celebrating their exciting young friend:** This event was recorded by Dick Meier, and a tape of it survives. It is included in "Before the Dead," a priceless collection of early Garcia recordings released by Round Records.

31 **"It was so fucking boring":** UCSC, Dennis McNally interview with Barbara Meier, archived at LCD 11404.

32 **all the creativity and determination of a driven teenager:** Ibid.

32 **"a legendary figure at the Kepler's scene":** UCSC, Dennis McNally interview with David Nelson, archived at LCD 11579.

33 **a sheriff's deputy hauled him in:** The deputy who arrested Bruce in West Hollywood was Sherman Block, and that arrest would propel Block into a spotlight for the rest of his life, rising to the elected office of Los Angeles County Sheriff and holding that until his death in 1998. So popular was Block that he won 38 percent of the ballots cast in the 1998 campaign, notwithstanding that he had died a few weeks before the election.

33 **"I had an ear for it":** Dennis McNally interview with Garcia, *Jerry on Jerry*, 90–93. Audio at LCD 11607 (UCSC archives).

33 **"bits and pieces of language":** Ibid.

34 **Garcia's post-crash seriousness:** Photographs of Garcia at this event were discovered by Professor Michael J. Kramer, who presented them at a conference on the history of the counterculture in San Francisco in 2022. I'm indebted to him for his careful scrutiny of those images, especially because the Garcia pictured in them is lean and clean-shaven, undoubtedly explaining why previous researchers failed to recognize him.

34 **in its many hidden rooms:** Author interview with Michael Kramer, Dec. 30, 2022.

35 **"Better," he would pronounce, "much better":** Author interview with Steve Dunne, May 15, 2022.

36 **"almost a regular":** David Gans, interview with Phil Lesh, *Conversations with the Dead*, 106.

36 **The engineer was Phil Lesh:** UCSC, Dennis McNally interview with Gert Chiarito, archived at LCD 11569.

36 **"a very bad scene":** UCSC, Dennis McNally interview with Barbara Meier, archived at LCD 11404.

36 **curiously detached from the issues of the day:** Author interviews with Sara Ruppenthal Katz, Feb. 11, 2023, and March 30, 2024.

36 **"Jerry wasn't political":** Author interview with Sara Ruppenthal Katz, Feb. 11, 2023.

37 **They were wed:** Many writers have misstated this date as April 23, 25, or 29. Sara Ruppenthal Katz confirmed to me that the wedding took place on Saturday, April 27, 1963.

37 **"that he was marrying a college girl":** Email from Sara Ruppenthal Katz to the author, Dec. 12, 2024.

37 **had not gotten a haircut beforehand:** UCSC, Dennis McNally interview with David Nelson, archived at LCD 11579.

37 **Roszak was standing nearby:** Phil Lesh attended the wedding too, but he did not make it into this photograph.

38 **"instructor at the Dana Morgan Music Studio":** Unbylined photo caption, *Palo Alto Times* (the photo as reproduced does not include a date).

38 **"Deep Elem Blues":** An early performance of the Garcia/Ruppenthal collaboration, including their rendition of "Deep Elem Blues," came on May 4, 1963, when the two performed at the Tangent in Palo Alto. A recording can be found at youtube.com /watch?v=77fosvhePIU.

NOTES | **457**

39 **"and that thing of fun":** Jerry Garcia, uncut interview with *Rolling Stone*, 1987. This interview was recorded and a tape of it survives, though most of the questions are inaudible. A copy can be found at facebook.com/watch/?v=180530867394705.

40 **"We were searching for something big":** Author interview with Rothman, Feb. 11, 2023.

40 **Their friendship would blossom later:** UCSC, Dennis McNally interview with David Grisman, archived at LCD 11506.

41 **"finding my musical identity":** Jon Sievert, "Jerry Garcia: For More than a Decade the Patriarch of the San Francisco Sound," *Guitar Player*, October 1978, 44.

CHAPTER 3: THE WARLOCKS TO THE DEAD

44 **Lightnin' Hopkins:** Blair Jackson, "Pigpen Forever," oral history collection published in *The Golden Road*, Issue 27, 1993 Annual.

44 **"The hallways would clear":** Ibid., 42.

44 **to find a point of entry into the blues:** Reich and Wenner, *"Rolling Stone* Interview: Jerry Garcia," 35.

45 **"I wouldn't like to, but I will anyway":** This performance, from 1964, can be found at youtube.com/watch?v=gaqa9dNMLUA.

45 **"Ain't It Crazy":** This exchange took place at the Top of the Tangent in Palo Alto. It was captured on tape and presented as part of a radio documentary about the Dead broadcast on San Francisco's KSAN in June 1969. A transcript of that broadcast can be found at deadsources.blogspot.com/2012/02/june-1969-radio-documentary.html.

46 **"I dress like a Republican":** UCSC, Dennis McNally interview with Weir, archived at LCD 11472.

46 **practical jokes and mild vandalism:** John Perry Barlow, *Mother American Night*, 26.

46 **Weir was expelled:** UCSC, Dennis McNally interview with Weir, archived at LCD 11472. Weir returned to Fountain Valley in 2015 and performed for what would have been his fiftieth reunion. Time heals wounds.

46 **"enough half-talent to start a jug band":** Alan Paul, "Bob Weir Recalls How He Met Jerry Garcia, Looks Back at Some of His Greatest Songwriting Moments with the Grateful Dead," originally published in *Revolver* magazine, 2001, reprinted at alan paul.net/2011/11/bob-weir-recalls-how-he-met-jerry-garcia-and-looks-back-at-some-of -his-greatest-songwriting-moments-with-the-grateful-dead/.

47 **"a fine jug band":** Jerry Garcia letter to "Dear Craig," July 11, 1967, UCSC, Grateful Dead Records, Series 1, Box 3, Folder: Lyrics and sound cues, annotated by Garcia.

47 **"I became the first Deadhead":** Bill Kreutzmann, *Deal*, 26.

47 **defend his son's playing:** UCSC, Dennis McNally interview with Bill Kreutzmann, archived at LCD 11603.

47 **worked out dance steps in the living room:** Ibid.

48 **"the first truly joyful moment of my life":** Kreutzmann, *Deal*, 16.

48 **impressing Garcia:** Jerry Garcia letter to "Dear Craig," July 11, 1967, UCSC, Grateful Dead Records, Series 1, Box 3, Folder: Lyrics and sound cues, annotated by Garcia.

48 **"The guy just couldn't play the bass":** Kreutzmann, *Deal*, 29.

49 **"I'll give it a try":** Jackson, "Pigpen Forever," 48.

49 **noting it in his memoirs:** Phil Lesh, *Searching for the Sound*, 7.

49 **"the king of them all: Benny Goodman":** Ibid., 10.

50 **"a limpid stream of melody":** Ibid., 27.

50 **"solid and edgy":** Ibid., 10.

51 **"unless you really *mean* it":** Ibid., 47.

458 | NOTES

51 **"we could have fun, *big fun*"**: Anthony Decurtis, "Jerry Garcia: The Rolling Stone Interview," *Rolling Stone*, Sept. 2, 1993.

51 **"That shaped what they did"**: Author interview with Huey Lewis, April 18, 2023.

52 **"brilliant and very fast"**: Garcia to Craig Corwin, July 7, 1967, UCSC, Grateful Dead Records, Series 1, Box 3, Folder: Lyrics and sound cues, annotated by Garcia.

52 **a "hardworking young musician"**: Ibid.

52 **"certainly not for dancing"**: Blair Jackson and David Gans, *This Is All a Dream We Dreamed*, 18.

52 **"The whole world just went kablooey"**: Reich and Wenner, "*Rolling Stone* Interview: Jerry Garcia," *Rolling Stone*, Jan. 20, 1972, 35.

53 **memorialized as Bicycle Day**: Benjamin Breen, *Tripping on Utopia*, 70–72.

54 **setting out on a mission**: Ibid., 167–75.

54 **"creatively formative for him"**: CIA documents, Project MK-ULTRA, (FOIA)/ESDN (CREST): 06760269, created Dec. 28, 2022, cia.gov/readingroom/document /06760269.

55 **"another release, yet another opening"**: Blair Jackson, *Garcia: An American Life*, 73.

55 **"a wonderful, wonderful, magical day"**: Author interview with Sara Ruppenthal Katz, Feb. 11, 2023.

55 **revealed the word "All"**: David Gans, interview with Garcia, *Conversations with the Dead*, 76.

55 **"back to the roots"**: Author interview with Sara Ruppenthal Katz, Feb. 11, 2023.

56 **hippies had just discovered acid**: Michael Fallon, "New Hip Hangout—the Blue Unicorn," *San Francisco Examiner*, Sept. 6, 1965. Damon Bach relays this story and its significance in "The American Counterculture," 71.

56 **"Bump! Grind!"**: Lesh, *Searching for the Sound*, 61.

56 **took time off to record a demo**: Dennis McNally and Lou Tambakos, liner notes to "Birth of the Dead," Rhino Entertainment, 2001.

56 **Mythical Ethical Icicle Tricycle**: Lesh, *Searching for the Sound*, 61.

57 **Garcia's eye lit upon "Grateful Dead"**: Some sources have identified the dictionary in question as an edition of Funk & Wagnall's. This account comes from Lesh's memoir at p. 62. Since he was there, I'm taking his word for it.

57 **"the gift of the Grateful Dead"**: Lesh, *Searching for the Sound*, 62. See also William Safire, "On Language: Of 'The' I Sing," *New York Times*, March 2, 1986, and Alan Trist, *The Water of Life: A Tale of the Grateful Dead*, 1989.

57 **parents hated it**: Blair Jackson, *Garcia*, 85.

CHAPTER 4: THE ACID TESTS

62 **"he took issue with it"**: Excerpted from a speech by Ken Kesey at Claremont McKenna College on Sept. 17, 1993, printed in the *Los Angeles Times*, latimes.com/archives/la -xpm-1993-09-17-me-36029-story.html.

62 **They eyed each other from a distance**: Jerry Garcia and Ken Kesey, interviewed by Tom Snyder on NBC's *The Tomorrow Show*, May 7, 1981, facebook.com/watch/?v= 184418963586819.

63 **"awful and unique logic"**: Scott F. Parker, ed., *Conversations with Ken Kesey*, 20.

63 **"We were alive and life was us"**: Martin A. Lee and Bruce Shalin, *Acid Dreams*, 120.

63 **"that makes it exceptional"**: Scott F. Parker, ed., *Conversations with Ken Kesey*, 114.

63 **"brilliantly tempered novel"**: Unsigned review, *Kirkus Reviews*, Feb. 1, 1962, kirkus reviews.com/book-reviews/ken-kesey/one-flew-over-cuckoos-nest/.

63 **"the invisible Rulers who enforce them"**: Unsigned review, "Life in a Loony Bin,"

Time, Feb. 16, 1962, web.archive.org/web/20071018004040/http://www.time.com/time/magazine/article/0,9171,829087,00.html.

63 **shrugged that off and was suddenly flush:** Sterling Lord letter to Kesey, Dec. 18, 1963, royalty statement enclosed, University of Oregon, Knight Library, Special Collections, Ken Kesey papers, Box 39, Correspondence, Friends; Folder: Sterling Lord, 1962–1976.

64 **"has not taken off in hardcover":** Sterling Lord letter to Kesey, Sept. 10, 1964, University of Oregon, Knight Library, Special Collections, Ken Kesey papers, Box 39, Correspondence, Friends; Folder: Sterling Lord, 1962–1976.

64 **"insufferably pretentious":** Orville Prescott, "A Tiresome Literary Disaster," *New York Times*, July 27, 1964.

64 **"captures the tenor of post-Korea America":** Conrad Knickerbocker, "Any Dream May Come True," *New York Times Book Review*, Aug. 2, 1964.

65 **when the Pranksters rolled into Manhattan:** Robert Stone, *Prime Green*, 121.

65 **"the world's greatest driver":** Ibid., 120.

66 **"wouldn't speak to Cassady":** Ibid., 122.

66 **"had replaced tournament polo":** Ibid.

66 **"the Huns knocking on the gates of Rome":** Ken Babbs, *Cronies*, 180.

66 **"We can learn from your tribal nature":** Ibid., 185.

67 **Carolyn Adams was easy to notice:** Tom Wolfe writes that Carolyn Adams was waiting for the bus when it pulled in to La Honda, but she disputes that. According to Adams, she met Cassady on the night after the bus returned, and he drove her to La Honda that night for the first time.

67 **"one big loud charge of vitality":** Tom Wolfe, *The Electric Kool-Aid Acid Test*, 130.

67 **fending off advances from the night janitor:** Author interview with Carolyn Garcia, March 14, 2022.

68 **political activity on campus:** Mary Ellen Perry, "Demonstration Leaders, Kerr Reach Agreement," *Berkeley Daily Gazette*, Oct. 3, 1964, 1.

68 **"sorry-looking car":** Ibid.

69 **"you've got to make it stop":** Mario Savio, "Sit-In Address on the Steps of Sproul Hall," Dec. 4, 1964.

69 **"The student movement":** Mitchell Goodman, ed., "The Movement Toward a New America," x.

70 **"that she assumed to be marijuana":** Richard Dodgson, "Sparks Fly Upward," dissertation presented to Ohio University, draft included with Ken Kesey papers, University of Oregon.

70 **"the liaison guy":** Greenfield, *Dark Star*, 71.

70 **caught Wong's attention:** Babbs, *Cronies*, 198.

71 **"Biggest Haul in S.M. County":** Unbylined story, "Top Novelist Kesey, 13 Others Held in La Honda Marijuana Raid," *San Mateo Times and Daily News Leader*, April 24, 1965, 1.

71 **chewed up the evidence:** Babbs, *Cronies*, 195.

71 **"two or three would be on her at once":** Wolfe, *Electric Kool-Aid Acid Test*, 176.

72 **"joyously gang-banged":** Peter Richardson, *Savage Journey*, 62.

72 **a party at Babbs's home:** Author interview with Ken Babbs, March 17, 2022.

72 **instruments that the Pranksters liked to play:** Numerous sources place this party on the night of Nov. 27, 1965. One exception is Babbs himself, who, in his memoir and in our conversation, recalled it being Halloween night. Other evidence suggests his memory is off, mainly because others remember that it was just one week between that party and the San Jose Acid Tests, which all sources agree occurred on Dec. 4. My own guess is that although Babbs's memory of guests being in costume inclines him

460 | NOTES

to associate it with Halloween, it's possible that guests were in costume because it was, after all, a Prankster party.

73 **"but it completely devastated everyone"**: Joe Smith, interview with Jerry Garcia, May 23, 1988, youtube.com/watch?v=gyCooEjfhH8https://soundcloud.com/blank-on-blank/jerry-garcia-on-the-acid-tests.

73 **"was as much performer as audience"**: Ibid.

73 **"everybody has art in them"**: Scott F. Parker, *Conversations with Ken Kesey*, 179.

73 **"one gigantic Animal House party on acid"**: Dodgson, "Sparks Fly Upward," 553.

73 **"to blow away the fog"**: Bob Dylan, *Chronicles*, 46.

73 **"It's hard, what Faulkner does"**: Dylan, *Chronicles*, 56.

74 **"As for what time it was"**: Dylan, *Chronicles*, 35.

74 **"songwriter of exceptional facility and cleverness"**: Stacey Williams, *Bob Dylan* liner notes, March 1962.

75 **the Dead did not make it onto the bill**: A copy of the bill can be found at jerrygarcia.com/show/1965-12-10-fillmore-auditorium-san-francisco-ca-usa/.

76 **"It was dangerously scary"**: Jackson and Gans, *This Is All a Dream*, 33.

76 **coaxed him away from it**: Dodgson, "Sparks Fly Upward," 551.

76 **"making other people uncomfortable"**: Reich and Wenner, "*Rolling Stone* Interview: Jerry Garcia," 38.

76 **struck up a romance**: Author interview with Rosie McGee, July 11, 2022.

76 **disappeared from history**: Dodgson, "Sparks Fly Upward," 568.

77 **"raging success"**: Dodgson, "Sparks Fly Upward," 588.

77 **meeting people and making photographs**: John Markoff, *Whole Earth*, 86.

77 **"As Kesey writes it"**: Ibid.

78 **bonded out for $1,000**: Unbylined story, "Author Kesey Has New Bout with Law," *San Francisco Examiner*, Jan. 19, 1966.

78 **a "beautiful mess and no two ways about it"**: Wolfe, *Electric Kool-Aid Acid Test*, 258.

79 **they were thwarted by events**: Markoff, *Whole Earth*, 130.

79 **"oily swells moving on the vast deep"**: Lesh, *Searching for the Sound*, 74.

79 **"three weekend nights"**: Philip F. Elwood, "Is Trips Festival Really Necessary?" *San Francisco Examiner*, Jan. 24, 1966.

79 **"far-out, beautiful magic"**: Richardson, *No Simple Highway*, 63.

80 **with a few members of his merry band**: Markoff, *Whole Earth*, 131. These details, though not the amounts, were confirmed by Mountain Girl in our interviews in 2021 and 2022.

80 **"and the end of everybody else"**: This remark has been widely quoted, but it appears originally in an interview with David W. Bernstein. See David W. Bernstein, "The San Francisco Tape Center," 244. It also features in Markoff, *Whole Earth*, 130; Richardson, *No Simple Highway*, 60; and Jarnow, *Heads*, 14.

80 **"I don't really remember"**: Lesh, *Searching for the Sound*, 77.

81 **violated his "nutritional" guidelines**: Author interview with Carolyn Garcia, March 15, 2022.

81 **"Frightening, insane, chaotic?"**: Paul Jay Robbins, "Happenings" column, *Los Angeles Free Press*, Feb. 11, 1966.

81 **tremulous about the future**: Author interview with Carolyn Garcia, March 14, 2022.

82 **she was drawn to a member of the Pranksters**: Author interview with Sara Ruppenthal Katz, Feb. 11, 2023.

82 **before dissolving with exhaustion**: Ibid.

82 **She took note**: Author interview with Carolyn Garcia, March 15, 2022.

83 **"That is not it for me"**: Amir Bar-Levi, "Long Strange Trip," Episode 1.

NOTES | **461**

83 **"just have fun?":** Ibid.

83 **"one of the few truly democratic art forms":** Jerry Garcia, uncut version of the *Rolling Stone* interview, 1987, facebook.com/watch/?v=180530867394705.

83 **"playing to the thing that's happening":** Scott F. Parker, *Conversations with Ken Kesey,* 180.

83 **"the prototype for our whole basic trip":** Reich and Wenner, "*Rolling Stone* Interview: Jerry Garcia," 37.

84 **"were the best by far":** Parker, *Conversations with Ken Kesey,* 180.

84 **(but made no mention of Kesey):** The biography can be found at the website for the Wallace Stegner Center, wallacestegner.org/bio.html.

84 **"he found me to be ineducable":** Parker, *Conversations with Ken Kesey,* 148.

85 **"And a copy of *Playboy*":** Wallace Stegner, *All the Little Live Things,* 18.

85 **"my own foolishness made manifest in him":** Ibid., 247.

CHAPTER 5: FORCES COLLIDE

88 **"but we'll settle for nothing less?":** Ronald Reagan, Taped Announcement on Candidacy for California Governor, Jan. 4, 1966, americanrhetoric.com/speeches/ronald reagancalgovcandidacy.htm.

89 **"prelude to Act I of a terrible tragedy":** Charles Davis, "Minor Incident Ignited Violence," *Los Angeles Times,* Aug. 15, 1965.

89 **would find their way to Reagan:** Louis Harris, "Whites Feel Negroes Prefer Non-Violence," *Los Angeles Times,* Aug. 30, 1965.

91 **"they crumbled at a wisecrack":** Stone, *Prime Green,* 160.

91 **"poor and beautiful beyond belief":** Ibid., 153.

91 **"and is a 'beatnik' ":** Report of Francis J. Collopy, Jr., July 29, 1966, Field Office File #88-10038, Bureau File #88-37196, "Ken Elton Kesey."

92 **"a perennial overdose of solicitude":** Wolfe, *Electric Kool-Aid Acid Test,* 307.

92 **the "no rules, good-time sixties":** Interviewed by Tiffany Eckert for KLCC, Feb. 10, 2017.

92 **seven thousand rose to oppose it:** Lynn Ludlow, "Goldberg Talks at Cal—Everybody's Happy!" *San Francisco Examiner,* March 26, 1966, 2.

92 **caskets draped with American flags:** No byline, "Thousands Protest War," *Thousand Oaks Star,* March 27, 1966, 1. See also photo caption from *San Francisco Examiner,* March 26, 1966, 2.

93 **"flicks" and "magic lights":** A copy of the flyer advertising the event can be found at concerts.fandom.com/wiki/March_25,_1966_Harmon_Gymnasium,_University_of _California,_Berkeley,_CA?file=Image-1483967667.jpg.

93 **"The Morality Gap at Berkeley":** KRON TV broadcast, available at the Bay Area Television Archive.

93 **"by the scruff of the neck":** These quotes differ slightly from other accounts of Reagan's address. This transcription comes directly from the videotape made by KRON TV and preserved by the Bay Area Television Archive, batv.quartexcollections.com /Documents/Detail/ronald-reagans-morality-gap-speech-1966/337.

94 **they fell into natural roles:** Scully, *Living with the Dead,* 70.

95 **it was rarely out of rotation:** Analyses of the Dead's setlists are too numerous to include here and range from the curious to the deeply researched. I have relied on *The Deadhead's Taping Compendium,* collected works at the Internet Archive, "The Deadlists Project," and "The Grateful Dead Family Discography," among others.

95 **the role that Lewis's harmonica had long ago occupied:** Garcia was particularly fond

462 | NOTES

of Lewis's work, and the Dead would incorporate three of Lewis's songs into their sets. In addition to "Viola Lee Blues," the Dead also performed "Big Railroad Blues," mostly in the early 1970s and again in the early 1980s, and "New, New Minglewood Blues," versions of which appeared on two albums and in performances in the late 1960s and from 1975 through the end of the band's run.

95 **hinted at what was to come:** No setlist survives of the Jan. 5 performance, but the band played "It's All Over Now, Baby Blue" the following night and closed with it on Jan. 7. See herbibot.com.

95 **"one of the prettiest things I'd ever heard":** Jerry Garcia, interviewed by *Rolling Stone* in 1987. Portions of that conversation were videotaped, and one excerpt survives at youtube.com/watch?v=H_MYXCGXr2w.

96 **a crisp five-minute version:** The Dead performed "It's All Over Now, Baby Blue" at the Fillmore on July 16, 1966, herbibot.com/radio/?song=It%27s+All+Over+Now+Baby +Blue.

96 **"the threshold of her understanding":** Thomas Pynchon, *The Crying of Lot 49*, 13–14.

97 **"students in nose-to-nose dialogue":** Ibid., 90.

97 **They traveled light, played loud:** They traveled light indeed. Visiting Vancouver in 1966, the Dead needed a place to practice, and it was supplied to them by a bunch of teenagers in a band of their own, the United Empire Loyalists. The band arranged for the Dead to borrow some space in the home of their drummer's mother. The Dead practiced there until the neighbors complained, and the police shut them down. UCSC, Grateful Dead Records, Series 3, Box 1, Folder: Vancouver, B.C., Canada, Aug. 5–6, 1966.

98 **"there is no free ride":** Reich and Wenner, "*Rolling Stone* Interview: Jerry Garcia," 39.

99 **"operating in unison with the universe":** Charles Reich, *Stoned Sunday Rap*, 213–14.

100 **the so-called Eleventh Commandment:** Lou Cannon, *Governor Reagan*, 145–48.

100 **"the Grateful Dead, just the opposite":** Michael Kramer, *The Republic of Rock*, 58.

101 **"It's hard to tell which is which":** Scully, *Living with the Dead*, 56.

102 **in the shade of an oak:** Herb Greene, a legendary photographer of the Dead and San Francisco scene, was invited to Olompali and allowed to bring a camera. His images capture the flavor of the place: datebook.sfchronicle.com/art-exhibits/unearthed -grateful-dead-pool-party-photos-debut-at-north-bay-museum-exhibition.

102 **never left little Huey Lewis:** Author interview with Huey Lewis, April 18, 2023.

103 **"time, patience, and practice":** Peter Coyote, *Sleeping Where I Fall*, 140.

103 **Drowning and the fear of it:** Email to the author from Susan Klein, Jan. 23, 2025.

103 **"a tree is a tree":** Ronald Reagan, address to the Western Wood Products Association, March 12, 1966. This comment is often misquoted as "If you've seen one redwood, you've seen them all." The original is bad enough.

104 **"synergy of spontaneity and structure":** Lesh, *Searching for the Sound*, 90.

104 **"A new purity of insight":** John Morgan, "The Rock Is Acid at Party Given by The Grateful Dead," *Redding Record-Searchlight.*, Oct. 19, 1966. UCSC, Special Collections, GD Records, Press, Box 1, Folder 2.

105 **the title was said to have been his idea:** Blair Jackson, *Grateful Dead Gear*, 46.

105 **"Musical and Spiritual Adviser":** Jefferson Airplane, *Surrealistic Pillow*, released Feb. 1, 1967.

105 **"We all play together in various combinations":** The interview is undated, but it is clear from the context that it took place in 1966.

106 **"didn't seem like it would work":** Greenfield, *Dark Star*, 93.

107 **"pioneer of topless entertainment":** Sam Roberts, "Carol Doda, Pioneer of Topless Entertainment, Dies at 78," *New York Times*, Nov. 11, 2015.

NOTES | 463

107 **"beatniks from the neighborhood"**: Miles Ottenheimer, "Still Hot, but Ski Nuts Out," *San Francisco Chronicle*, Oct. 28, 1966. UCSC, Special Collections, GD Records, Press, Box 1, Folder 2.

107 **"surely the equal"**: Ralph J. Gleason, "All That Jazz and Rock Paid Off," *San Francisco Chronicle*, Sept. 11, 1966. UCSC, Special Collections, GD Records, Press, Box 1, Folder 2.

107 **"less of a presence than Pig"**: Nick Meriwether, included in Michael M. Getz and John R. Dwork's *The Deadhead's Taping Compendium*, vol. 1, 110.

107 **potentially dangerous extremism**: Cannon, *Governor Reagan*, 151.

108 **in a joint appearance with Reagan**: Ibid., 158.

108 **perfect for Reagan's playbook**: *San Francisco Examiner* coverage of Sept. 28 and Sept. 29, 1966.

108 **"and rent unpaid"**: Urgent FBI cable, Oct. 7, 1966, from Legat Mexico City, No. 202, to Director, Bureau File #88-37196.

109 **relieved to be home**: Author interview with Carolyn Garcia, March 14, 2022.

109 **burdened with guilt and shame**: Meriwether, in *Deadhead's Taping Compendium*, 106.

109 **"intensive investigation"**: Urgent FBI cable, Oct. 6, 1966, from San Francisco to Director, Bureau File #88-37196.

109 **an "urgent" cable**: Urgent FBI cable, Oct. 6, 1966, from San Francisco to Director, Bureau File #88-37196.

109 **racing for five blocks before giving up**: Report of Francis J. Collopy, Jr., Field Office File #88-10038, Bureau File #88-37196, Oct. 26, 1966, "Ken Elton Kesey." See also Memorandum of A. B. Eddy to Mr. Gale, Oct. 20, 1966.

109 **"and jumped onto Jerry"**: Author interview with Carolyn Garcia, Jan. 15, 2022.

110 **ninety days after the legislature recessed**: Bob Jackson, "Brown Signs LSD Bill, But Nevada Almost Beats Him," *Los Angeles Times*, May 31, 1966.

110 **lawlessness of the type that Reagan was highlighting**: Bill Boyarsky, "Reagan Declares Demos Are Planning Big Smear," *Sacramento Bee*, Oct. 26, 1966.

110 **"this will be one step into adulthood"**: Unbylined story, "Kesey's Second Break," *San Francisco Chronicle*, Oct. 26, 1966 (clipping in FBI file).

111 **"people have a hard time following it"**: Tom Wolfe, "The Fugitive Faces His Acid Test," *New York* magazine, recorded in FBI files on Feb. 12, 1967.

111 **"it must be fought for and defended constantly"**: Ronald Reagan, "First Inaugural Address," delivered on Jan. 5, 1967.

CHAPTER 6: THE GATHERING

113 **no mention of the Human Be-In**: Unbylined pieces, "Today's Highlights," *San Francisco Examiner*, Jan. 14, 1967, 10; "Baha'is To Hear Talk in Golden Gate Park," *San Francisco Examiner*, Jan. 14, 1967, 24.

115 **Victorian top hats, brocade vests**: Peter Conners, *White Hand Society*, 203.

115 **"like priests of some strange religion"**: UPI, "Beatniks, LSD 'Saints' Turn On at SF Rally," *Sacramento Bee*, Jan. 15, 1967, 4.

115 **a daffodil tucked into his breast pocket**: No byline, "They Came . . . Saw . . . Stared," *San Francisco Examiner*, Jan. 15, 1967, 3.

115 **about twenty thousand people**: As is often the case, estimates varied, sometimes revealing the bias of the estimator. The *Examiner*'s grudging coverage put the crowd at 10,000. Others guessed higher, and some estimates grew over time. Conners puts the crowd at "more than 25,000."

115 **"I'd never seen so many people"**: Blair Jackson, *Garcia*, 121.

464 | NOTES

115 **"it was a happening":** Helen Swick Perry, *The Human Be-In*, 86.

115 **"never been anything like it since the Persians":** Ralph Gleason, "The Tribes Gather for a Yea-Saying," *San Francisco Chronicle*, Jan. 16, 1967.

115 **"I was gobsmacked":** Author interview with Peter Coyote, Nov. 2, 2022.

116 **"every angry voice I'd ever heard":** UCSC, Jerry Garcia, interviewed by Studs Terkel and Abe Peck, Dec. 6, 1979, archived at LCD 11709.

116 **the activist "tribe" gathered on the field that afternoon:** Jane Fonda, interviewed by Julia Louis-Dreyfus for her podcast, *Wiser than Me*, April 11, 2023.

117 **"loving spirit of concern for all beings":** Gary Snyder, *Mountains and Rivers Without End*, 155.

117 **"To Fuck with Love":** Lenore Kandel, *The Love Book.*

117 **the crowd sang "Happy Birthday":** Emily Dutton, "Hidden Figures of Drug History: Lenore Kandel, 1932–2009," Points, April 14, 2018, pointshistory.com/2018/08/14 /hidden-figures-of-drug-history-lenore-kandel-1932-2009/.

117 **"Turn on, tune in, and drop out":** Peter Conners, *White Hand Society*, 204. See also: No byline, "They Came . . . Saw . . . Stared."

117 **and the Grateful Dead:** Conners, *White Hand Society*, 203. See also Perry, *Haight-Ashbury*, 126.

118 **"grounded the Jefferson Airplane":** No byline, "They Came . . . Saw . . . Stared."

118 **"has a leadership complex":** No byline, "Changes," *Oracle*, vol. 1, no. 7, 15, archive.org /details/SanFranciscoOracleVol.1No.7D.D.TeoliJr.A.C.1/page/n13/mode/2up.

118 **children who had been separated from their parents:** Larry Freudiger, "The White Revolution," *The Rag* (Austin), Jan. 30, 1967, 7, jstor.org/stable/community.28043033 ?searchText=&searchUri=&ab_segments=&searchKey=&refreqid=fastly-default%3A e80bb3c0c65954b324c61109e61eac5b&seq=6#metadata_info_tab_contents.

118 **"heavenly nursery":** Perry, *Human Be-In*, 87.

119 **"create the condition you describe":** Author interview with Peter Coyote, Sept. 19, 2022.

119 **"physically or spiritually":** Emmett Grogan, *Ringolevio*, 274.

119 **"I was one of the guys handing it out":** Author interview with Peter Coyote, Nov. 2, 2022.

119 **undulations of color across the green grass:** Lesh, *Searching for the Sound*, 97.

119 **"a single ripple of turned heads and eyes":** Perry, *Human Be-In*, 87.

120 **"Was he really the Great Provider?":** Gleason, "Tribes Gather for a Yea-Saying."

120 **"We wanted to believe in magic":** Perry, *Human Be-In*, 88.

120 **Weir strumming almost frantically:** On tape, Garcia can be heard asking Lesh to slow down.

120 **"remarkably exciting":** Gleason, "Tribes Gather for a Yea-Saying."

120 **"mantra of the Buddha of the future":** Conners, *White Hand Society*, 206.

120 **"a promise of good, not of evil":** Gleason, "Tribes Gather for a Yea-Saying."

120 **Peter Coyote departed in wonder:** Author interview with Peter Coyote, Nov. 2, 2022.

121 **"nothing to fear from Ronald Reagan":** Freudiger, "White Revolution."

121 **"I almost didn't believe it":** Jackson, *Garcia*, 121.

CHAPTER 7: SUMMER OF LOVE

123 **"modernizing, up-dating, rationalizing, planning":** Theodore Roszak, *The Making of a Counter Culture*, 5.

124 **"turning over efficiently":** Ibid., 7.

124 **"a wealth of ingenious rationalization":** Ibid., 47.

NOTES | 465

124 valiant attempts to find joy in that work: Ibid., 99.

125 "on this benighted side of liberation": Ibid., 120.

125 "the violence and inequality of Western capitalist culture": Curtis White, *Living in a World That Can't Be Fixed*, xiv.

126 "art itself is a belief": David Weir, *Bohemians*, 7.

126 struggling artists living in the Latin Quarter: Henry Murger, *Life in Bohemia*.

127 "That's the way we live our lives": Garcia with unknown interviewer. Context appears to set the interview in early 1970, possibly as the Dead arrived for shows in England that May. Edited interview can be found at youtube.com/watch?v=gpJUZn_G6og.

127 "Not much": Lisa Robinson, "*Creem* Interview with Grateful Dead," *Creem* magazine, December 1970, 21.

127 "trancelike guitar voyage?": Email to the author, Aug. 13, 2023.

128 the Dead's emphasis on long improvisation: Andrew Hickey, *A History of Rock Music in 500 Songs*, Episode 165, "Dark Star."

128 "So the adventure began!": David Browne, "That Time Joe Smith Sent the Grateful Dead a Letter Complaining About Their Work Ethic," *Rolling Stone*, Dec. 3, 2019.

128 a supply of Mountain Girl's diet pills: Author interview with Carolyn Garcia, March 17, 2022.

129 "the Vehicle Assembly Building at Cape Canaveral": Lesh, *Searching for the Sound*, 99.

129 "What I was after on the album": Blair Jackson, "Dave Hassinger on Producing the Dead, 1967," *Golden Road*, Issue 6, Spring 1985, 32.

130 "sound and fury buried in a cavern": Phil Lesh, *Searching for the Sound*, 99.

130 "It sounds just like us": Jackson, *Grateful Dead Gear*, 49.

130 "hyperactive" and "embarrassing": Charles Reich, *A Signpost to New Space*, 88.

130 In their own way, each was right: Dennis McNally, *Long Strange Trip*, 188.

130 "a learned and highly articulate man": Ralph Gleason, "Dead Like Live Thunder," *San Francisco Chronicle*, March 19, 1967.

131 "Dance music, for dancers, at dances": Ralph Gleason interview with the Dead, April 8, 1967, KPIX, archive.org/details/gd67-04-08.tv.hanno.12623.sbeok.shnf/gd -maze-to3.shn.

131 "We're the Grateful Dead": Ibid.

131 "an art project": Author interview with Peter Coyote, Sept. 19, 2022.

132 "Then act it out": Ibid.

132 "They were the most like a family": Ibid.

133 "real freedom and justice for all the people": Stephen Shames and Bobby Seale, *Power to the People*, 8.

134 They carried rifles, shotguns, and handguns: Ibid, 27.

135 "at least one man with long hair and sunglasses": Hunter Thompson, "The 'Hash-bury' Is the Capital of the Hippies," *New York Times Magazine*, May 14, 1967.

135 messages from worried parents to wandering children: Emmett Grogan, *Ringolevio*, 288–89.

135 freighted by its "pansyness": Emmett Grogan, *Ringolevio*, 238.

136 a skeleton surrounded by blooming flowers: Joel Selvin (notes to accompany the pho-tographs of Jim Marshall), *The Haight*, 61.

136 "They always came through for us": UCSC, Dennis McNally interview with Hillel Resner, UCSC, archived at LCD 11567.

137 "A carnival seemed to be taking place on every block": Joel Selvin, *Summer of Love*, 118.

137 when addressing the city commission: Will Stevens, "The Seekers Tired of Haight Gawkers," *San Francisco Examiner*, March 3, 1967, 4.

466 | NOTES

138 **"beginning to understand police problems"**: George Rhodes, "The Haight Hippies Meet The Fuzz," *San Francisco Examiner*, Feb. 7, 1967, 3.

138 **"the district's 'new community' or 'hippie' elements"**: No byline, "Haight Town Hall Meeting," *San Francisco Examiner*, March 1, 1967, 22. See also June Mullter, "Crusading Cops vs. Hippies Stirs Haight-Ashbury Protest, *San Francisco Examiner*, March 1, 1967, 22.

138 **"She is a dependable"**: No byline, "Mother's Plea for Girl, 13," *San Francisco Examiner*, April 12, 1967, 13.

138 **"the crowded, defiant dope fortress"**: Hunter Thompson, "The 'Hashbury' Is the Capital of the Hippies," *New York Times Magazine*, May 14, 1967.

139 **"was not holding"**: Joan Didion, *Slouching Towards Bethlehem*, 84.

139 **"whoever later entered the brush"**: Joan Didion, *Where I Was From*, 95.

139 **"an army of children"**: Joan Didion, *Slouching Towards Bethlehem*, 123.

139 **"High Kindergarten"**: Joan Didion, *Slouching Towards Bethlehem*, 128.

140 **"very touchy, touchy, touchy"**: Sue Swanson, quoted in Greenfield, *Dark Star*, 97.

141 **"I never thought of it as demeaning"**: Author interview with Rosie McGee, July 11, 2022.

141 **"a lot of energy exchanged"**: Charles Reich and Jann Wenner, "The *Rolling Stone* Interview: Jerry Garcia," *Rolling Stone*, Jan. 20, 1972, 39.

141 **required to sign a loyalty oath**: Dennis McNally, *Long Strange Trip*, 191.

142 **had supported the broader oath**: Seth Rosenfeld, *Subversives*, 135.

142 *Petulia* **features a clip of the Dead**: Garcia also shows up in a brief cameo in the film, part of a small crowd of onlookers gathered around an ambulance.

142 **"getting to be a bore"**: Jerry Garcia, "Cream Puff War," first performed May 19, 1966; appears on *The Grateful Dead*, released in 1967.

142 **"making bullets out of them"**: Unpublished Garcia interview by Randy Groenke and Mike Cramer. March 1967.

143 **"We like it a lot"**: Ibid.

143 **the Monterey International Pop Festival was born**: Ben Sisario, "Monterey Pop, the Rock Festival That Sparked It All, Returns," *New York Times*, April 14, 2017.

145 **"postures that would make Bo Diddley blush"**: Byline and headline missing, *DownBeat* magazine, Aug. 10, 1967.

145 **Lesh taunted him**: York's interruption can be found at 14:12: youtube.com/watch?v=pB1pDbQoMfo.

145 **"a slipshod, lazy way to play music"**: No byline or headline available, but the article appeared in *DownBeat* on Aug. 10, 1967. This clip can be found in the UCSC archives, Press clippings, Folder 5, July–December 1967.

146 **"And then Jimi Hendrix comes out"**: Garcia interview, *Today*, Aug. 7, 1987, youtube.com/watch?v=xg3sDElRLic.

147 **"It turned me right off the whole scene"**: George Harrison, "Anthology," excerpt at beatlesbible.com/1967/08/07/george-harrison-visits-haight-ashbury-san-francisco/2/.

147 **"Topless hippie chicks were abundant"**: Dick Hyer, "Topless Is Going Bust," *San Francisco Examiner*, Aug. 6, 1967, 1.

148 **"an uncluttered life, a simple life"**: CBS, "The Hippie Temptation," *Who, What, Where, When, Why*, aired on Aug. 22, 1967.

148 **"failure of communication and shared responsibility"**: Lesh, *Searching for the Sound*, 108.

149 **"it was like an ecological upset"**: Steve Peacock, "Jerry Garcia in London," *Rock* magazine, December 1972.

NOTES | **467**

CHAPTER 8: "DARK STAR"

151 **"asking me to come out and join the band":** Robert Hunter, *The Complete, Annotated Grateful Dead Lyrics* (foreword by Hunter), xxii.

151 **the band threw in a few kazoos:** Blair Jackson, "Alligator," *Golden Road*, Issue 12, Fall 1986, back page.

152 **"a few things in this world are clear to all of us":** Robert Hunter, *Box of Rain*, 35.

153 **a musical fragment, really:** It was released on Lesh's "Fallout from the Phil Zone."

154 **"It brings up something that you can see":** Jeff Tamarkin, "Behind the Song: The Grateful Dead, 'Dark Star,'" *American Songwriter*, 2020, americansongwriter.com /dark-star-by-the-grateful-dead. See also Tyler Golsen, "The Poem That Inspired the Grateful Dead Song 'Dark Star,'" *Far Out*, Jan. 19, 2023, faroutmagazine.co.uk/the -poem-that-inspired-the-grateful-dead-song-dark-star.

155 **it found its way into the mainstream:** No byline, "Harper's Index," *Harper's* magazine, September 1987.

155 **"'Dark Star' as a playing experiment":** Reich, *Signpost to New Space*, 84–85.

155 **they rebuffed his attempts to pin it down:** Graeme Boone, "Tonal and Expressive Ambiguity in 'Dark Star,'" in *Understanding Rock*, 171.

156 **"I refuse to be inducted":** Edwin Shrake, "Taps for the Champ," *Sports Illustrated*, May 8, 1967.

156 **"No Vietcong ever called me nigger":** Bob Orkand, "I Ain't Got No Quarrel with Them Vietcong," *New York Times*, June 27, 2017.

157 **"were never the same again":** Bill Walton, interviewed by Joe Canzano, date of interview unclear, aired on May 28, 2024, tiktok.com/@johncanzano/video/73742315382 98260779?lang=en.

158 **"in total awe":** Kreutzmann, *Deal*, 77. There is some confusion around this account. Payne left the Count Basie band in 1964, and the night that Kreutzmann records in his memoirs was in August 1967. It is possible, of course, that Kreutzmann misremembered the date, though it seems unlikely that a drummer of his seriousness and caliber would misremember hearing Sonny Payne. Ralph Gleason's piece in the *San Francisco Chronicle* on August 13, 1967, identifies Rufus Jones as playing drums for Basie during the San Francisco gigs. It is also possible that Payne sat in with Basie the night that Kreutzmann and Hart attended.

158 **"didn't know how to do this stuff":** Kreutzmann, *Deal*, 78.

158 **"I became a better player":** Ibid., 79.

158 **to see the Dead at the Straight Theater:** Various accounts place this night as Sept. 24, 28, or 29. Available evidence points to the 29th—participants recall that it was the second of three shows at the Straight, which dovetails with the 29th, since the Dead played there the nights of Sept. 28, 29, and 30.

159 **wisecracks about "Stiff Doctor Dick":** A tape of Cassady's rap can be found at archive.org/details/gd1967-07-23.aud.sorochty.125462.flac16/gd67-07-23d1t1.aud .flac.

159 **ricocheted through time and culture:** Meriwether, in *Deadhead's Taping Compendium*, 139–42.

159 **"dance class":** An image of the poster can be found at dead.net/show/september-30 -1967.

159 **"We can take *this* all over the world":** Lesh, *Searching for the Sound*, 115.

160 **She was speechless for days:** Author interview with Rosie McGee, July 11, 2022.

160 **"long-haired blues singer":** Unbylined piece, "Lots of Grass—Grateful Dead Mowed Down," *San Francisco Examiner*, Oct. 3, 1967.

468 | NOTES

161 **"off the books before Thanksgiving":** Unbylined story, "The Dead Did Get It: Reporters and Cops," *Rolling Stone*, Nov. 9, 1967.

162 **"how this odd notion struck me":** Jann S. Wenner, *Like a Rolling Stone*, 7.

163 **the magazine's interest in the band waxed and waned:** Ibid., 145.

164 **"is really woven into that record":** UCSC, McNally interview with Tom Constanten, archived at LCD 11581.

164 **"I was the white man's keyboard player":** Ibid.

165 **"and people sitting on the floor":** Blair Jackson, "Dave Hassinger on Producing the Dead, 1967," *Golden Road*, Issue 6, Spring 1985, 32.

165 **"heavy air":** Scully, *Living with the Dead*, 125. Versions of this episode abound, and in some, Weir is said to have asked for "thick air."

166 **"the most unreasonable project":** Joe Smith to Danny Rifkin, Dec. 27, 1967. The letter can be viewed at dead.net/archives/1967/clippings/angry-letter-warner-brothers-page -1-2.

166 **"Fuck you":** The handwritten notes on the Smith letter can be viewed at dead.net /archives/1967/clippings/angry-letter-warner-brothers-page-1-2.

167 **ominous shades of a world gone wrong:** Jim Miller, "Anthem of the Sun," *Rolling Stone*, Sept. 28, 1968.

167 **"fraught with hidden meaning":** Lucian Truscott, "Recordings," *Village Voice*, Sept. 27, 1968. Included at UCSC, Special Collection, Grateful Dead Records, Press clippings, Box 1, Folder 5 (July–December 1968).

167 **"essential background music for pot parties":** S.L., "Anthem of the Sun," *High Fidelity*, November 1968, 130.

167 **"summation of our musical direction":** Lesh, *Searching for the Sound*, 130.

169 **"a possible gateway":** Sat Santokh, "There Is a Way—A Summary," unpublished manuscript, 1.

169 **to watch as others performed:** Author interview with Sat Santokh, Jan. 29, 2022.

170 **"a community of energy":** Andy Childs, "Grateful Dead," concert bill, Nassau Coliseum, Sept. 7, 8, and 9, 1973.

170 **"the best hall in San Francisco":** Ralph Gleason, "On the Town," *San Francisco Chronicle*, March 18, 1968.

170 **a highly anticipated show:** There is some confusion about whether this was the Dead's first performance at the Carousel under the band's co-ownership. An official band history contained with its papers at the Santa Cruz archives lists it as such, but a tape exists of the Dead playing the venue on Jan. 17. Neither source is impeccable.

171 **"generalized congestion":** U.S. Department of State, "Report of the Death of an American Citizen," June 27, 1968, wikitree.com/photo.php/2/2e/Cassady-242-1.jpg.

172 **"on the bus to never-ever land":** The line has caused some confusion over the years, leading some listeners to conclude that the Dead was part of Kesey's famous bus trip. Still, "on the bus" came to mean much more than literally riding on that bus trip. Chalk it up to metaphor.

172 **"anarchy at its finest":** Blair Jackson, interview with McIntire, *Golden Road*, Issue 17, Summer 1988, 17.

172 **"the largest assemblage of Hells Angels":** Ibid., 16.

173 **"lots of little scenes and happenings":** No byline, "Free City Convention Free for All," *Berkeley Barb*, May 1968.

173 **"We're all part of it":** Sandy Darlington, "Ambrosia Cake Falstaff Bliss," *San Francisco Express Times*, June 6, 1968.

173 **"The bands could never agree on anything":** UCSC, Dennis McNally interview with Phil Lesh, archived at LCD 11601.

173 **"rotten manager"**: McNally, *Long Strange Trip*, 265.
173 **"stupidest lease in show business"**: No byline, "Fillmore Scene Moves to Carousel Hall," *Rolling Stone*, Aug. 10, 1968.
173 **He met with representatives:** Graham told others that he had flown to Ireland to meet with Fuller, and that was reported as fact in 1968. In later years, however, Graham seemed to retract that assertion. In any event, he certainly secured the lease, whether or not it actually required a trip to Ireland.
174 **it "was a fine dream"**: Ralph Gleason, "Death and Life of the Carousel," *San Francisco Examiner*, July 7, 1968, 23.

CHAPTER 9: ALL FALL DOWN

177 **marshals had arrested 682 demonstrators:** Unbylined entry, "U.S. Marshals and the Pentagon Riot of Oct. 21, 1967," website of the U.S. Marshals Service, usmarshals.gov/who-we-are/history/historical-reading-room/us-marshals-and-pentagon-riot-of-october-21-1967.
177 **"became the official watchword"**: Todd Gitlin, *The Sixties*, 287.
178 **"that time has come for us in relation to Vietnam"**: Martin Luther King, Jr., "Beyond Vietnam," delivered April 4, 1967, at Riverside Church, americanrhetoric.com/speeches/mlkatimetobreaksilence.htm.
178 **"a cyclone in a wind tunnel"**: Todd Gitlin, *The Sixties*, 242.
178 **the Johnson administration claimed victory:** Unbylined story, UPI, "Tet Offensive Backfires, US Government Claims," *Daily Record-Gazette* (Banning, Calif.), newspapers.com/image/688580808/?match=1&terms=%22Tet%20Offensive%20Backfires%22.
178 **"shattered any Pentagon illusions"**: Tom Hayden, *Reunion*, 257.
179 **"I shall not seek, and I will not accept"**: Film and transcript courtesy of the Miller Center at UVA, millercenter.org/the-presidency/presidential-speeches/march-31-1968-remarks-decision-not-seek-re-election.
180 **"a grief that has not healed to this day"**: Hayden, *Reunion*, 270.
180 **"long-haired, unkempt rebels"**: Edward Benes and Arthur Mulligan, "Seal Columbia Campus as Sit-ins Continue," *New York Daily News*, April 25, 1968, 3; and William Travers and Paul Meskil, "Columbia Stays Shut; Rebels Under Siege," *New York Daily News*, April 29, 1968, 3.
180 **"taken power in their own hands"**: Hayden, *Reunion*, 274.
181 **"of prime importance"**: Memo from FBI Director to SAC Newark, May 17, 1968, reprinted in Hayden, *Reunion*, 284.
181 **"brutal bloody show of strength"**: No byline, "University Calls In 1,000 Police to End Demonstration as Nearly 700 Are Arrested and 100 Injured; Violent Solution Follows Failure of Negotiations," *Columbia Daily Spectator*, April 30, 1968, 1. An updated tally of arrests brought the total to 712.
181 **The day's agenda:** Columbia University Libraries, "1968: Columbia in Crisis," "Campus 'Liberated,'" exhibitions.library.columbia.edu/exhibits/show/1968/campus.
182 **the band's equipment arrived:** Jackson and Gans, *This Is All a Dream*, 108.
182 **"crass bourgeois son of a bitch"**: Ibid., 109.
182 **"do-as-you-wish hippies"**: Kreutzmann, *Deal*, 97.
182 **"represented the alternative universe"**: Jackson and Gans, *This Is All a Dream*, 109.
183 **"the terrible real world"**: Ralph Gleason, "On the Town," *San Francisco Chronicle*, June 7, 1968, 49.
184 **"not six as the band is now formed"**: A copy of this tape recording was supplied to the author by a source.

470 | NOTES

188 **"the way I tied my shoes"**: Undated tape (context makes clear it was in August 1968) supplied to the author by a source. This tape is sometimes hard to follow, with cuts and barely audible voices in places.

190 **"We hear sirens in the night"**: Richard Nixon, "Address Accepting the Presidential Nomination," Aug. 8, 1968.

191 **by Richard Nixon, no less**: Nixon for American Youth, 1968.

191 **"slumped to zero"**: Tom Hayden, *Reunion*, 293.

192 **"half-cocked combination"**: David Farber, *Chicago '68*, 3.

192 **Youth International Party**: "Yippie" is not a shorthand for Youth International Party. It was the other way around. Hoffman and Rubin and others came up with "Yippie" first, and then Anita Hoffman observed that the group needed something more serious for when reporters came calling. She suggested Youth International Party, a subversive back-formation that worked on every level. Even "party" meant something different to reporters than it meant to participants.

192 **"not who you vote for or who you support"**: Transcript of Dec. 29, 1967, debate between Fred Halstead and Jerry Rubin, "Halstead, Rubin Debate," *Militant*, Jan. 8, 1968, 4.

193 **"some of them are hippies and yippies"**: George Tagge, "Mayor Daley Denies Bias in Providing Convention Spaces," *Chicago Tribune*, Aug. 17, 1968.

193 **"There will be no trouble in Chicago"**: John O'Brien, "Mayor, Reporters Tour Convention Site," *Chicago Tribune*, Aug. 17, 1968.

193 **"armor in your hair"**: Todd Gitlin, "If You're Going to Chicago, Be Sure to Wear Some Armor in Your Hair," *San Francisco Express Times*, Aug. 21, 1968, 1.

193 **"Cops, Hippies War in Street"**: *Tribune* coverage of Aug. 25–30, 1968.

193 **"Cut it out," some yelled at police**: Unbylined story, "Cops, Hippies War in Street," *Chicago Tribune*, Aug. 29, 1968, 1.

194 **"Go home"**: Daley's comment that night was not captured on any audio recording, but an enterprising underground paper hired a lip reader to review video of the event and produced that quote. Given that provenance, there have been quibbles over the years—some say Daley called Ribicoff a "faker," not a "fucker." Still, there is no doubt that Daley leaped up and yelled at Ribicoff, an event captured on live television, and that he was agitated and furious. See politico.com/magazine/story/2018/09/02/how-fake-news-was-born-at-the-1968-dnc-219627/.

194 **"advice for sale cheap"**: Markoff, *Whole Earth*, 155.

194 **"It's the next thing after acid"**: Ibid., 156.

195 **"A realm of intimate, personal power is developing"**: Stewart Brand, *Whole Earth Catalog*, vol. 1, 1968.

196 **"neat tools and great notions"**: Steven Jobs, Commencement Address to Stanford University, June 12, 2005. A recording can be found at youtube.com/watch?v=D1R-jKKp3NA.

198 **"The Dead are artists"**: Raymond Lang, "The Grateful Dead: Life and Joy," *Daily Californian*, May 29, 1969, 13.

199 **"where one ended and the other began"**: Mat Callahan, *The Explosion of Deferred Dreams*, 171.

199 **"a real slow revolution"**: Unbylined piece, "Jerry Garcia," *Hard Road*, July 20, 1970.

199 **"and I'll build around it"**: Damon Bach, *The American Counterculture*, 141.

200 **"we quietly left the Heartbeats behind"**: Lesh, *Searching for the Sound*, 136.

200 **Weir and Pigpen were reabsorbed**: Pigpen was absent on Oct. 12, but not because he was fired. He was tending to his girlfriend, who had suffered an aneurysm and was in the hospital. He returned shortly thereafter.

NOTES | 471

201 **"warriors for the forces of light and love"**: This remark appears at the Archives.org site as part of the comments accompanying the recording of the Oct. 12, 1968, show. It is attributed to "Dr. Flashback," and is dated June 6, 2013. It can be found at archive .org/details/gd1968-10-12.sbd.miller.115593.flac16/gd68-10-12d1t05.flac.

CHAPTER 10: THE END OF THE BEGINNING

204 **perennial shortage of student housing:** One especially thoughtful and colorful history of People's Park chirpily titled its opening chapter "The Crying of Lot 1875-2." Tom Dalzell, *The Battle for People's Park*, 1.

204 **"whatever our fantasy pleases"**: Robin Hood (Stew Albert), "Hear Ye, Hear Ye," *Berkeley Barb*, Aug. 18–24, 1969, 2.

204 **"socialism in practice"**: Unbylined story, "Berkeley . . . Ronald Reagan Creats [*sic*] The Fascist States," *Black Panther*, May 21, 1969, 7, archive.org/details/03-no-6-1-18-may -31-1969/page/n5/mode/2up.

205 **"no normal Berkeley street battle"**: Ibid.

205 **Berkeley was placed under martial law:** Seth Rosenfeld, *Subversives*, 460.

205 **"hand-to-hand combat"**: Dalzell, *Battle for People's Park*, 222.

206 **"the scum of public life"**: Ibid., 228.

206 **"his own Vietnam"**: Rosenfeld, *Subversives*, 467.

206 **"Jail's a terrible place, man"**: Michael Lydon, full transcript of Garcia interview, which apparently took place soon after the benefit, can be found at deadsources.blogspot .com/2014/06/summer-1969-jerry-garcia-interview.html.

207 **"the timeless experience of constant change"**: Michael Lydon, "Good Old Grateful Dead," *Rolling Stone*, Aug. 23, 1968.

209 **not for lack of enthusiasm on Garcia's part:** In his memoir, Davis gives a hint as to why the project failed to take off. He cites a note from Garcia's papers that sketched out his budget for the project. It listed $100,000 for script development, $20,000 for "salaries, payoffs, etc." and $30,000 a month for drugs. See Tom Davis, *Thirty-Nine Years of Short-Term Memory Loss*, 257.

209 **"Everyone was dosed"**: Kreutzmann, *Deal*, 109. See also UCSC, Grateful Dead Records, Series 3, Box 1, Folder: "Playboy After Dark," Hollywood, Calif., Jan. 18, 1969.

211 **"and the band when he isn't"**: Adele Novelli, "Aoxomoxoa," *Rolling Stone*, July 12, 1969.

212 **"among towering redwoods"**: Scully, *Living with the Dead*, 162.

213 **capturing its sweetness and longing:** Graham Nash, interviewed about Garcia's role, instagram.com/p/CwyrEqWxMnk/#.

214 **the Mescaline Rompers:** "Zig Zag 1974 Genealogy," UCSC Special Collections, GD Records, Series 1, Box 2, Folder: New Riders of the Purple Sage, 1969–1971.

214 **"you were glad to ride with him"**: Robert Christgau, "The Grateful Dead Are Rising Again," *New York Times*, Sunday, July 27, 1969.

215 **nabbing the Dead for just $7,500:** Michael Lang, *The Road to Woodstock*, 55 and 83. Creedence signed for $10,000 and Canned Heat for $12,500.

216 **shuttled the band to a nearby hotel:** Lesh recalls the Dead's arrival differently, writing in his memoir that the band arrived in a "caravan of rented cars." In most other respects, their memories are similar.

216 **"Line up on the left"**: Babbs, *Cronies*, 367.

216 **"they were not in a comfortable place"**: Author interview with Sat Santokh, Jan. 29, 2022.

217 **"great big blue spark"**: Lang, *Road to Woodstock*, 216.

472 | NOTES

217 **"and blow this joint"**: Lesh, *Searching for the Sound*, 156.

217 **"Jeez, we were awful!"**: Steve Sutherland, "Jerry Garcia Interview," *Melody Maker*, March 28, 1981.

217 **"blazing freak flag"**: Paul Grimstad, "Rewinding Jimi Hendrix's National Anthem," *New Yorker*, Jan. 26, 2021.

218 **"so colossal a mess?"**: Unsigned editorial, "Nightmare in the Catskills," *New York Times*, Aug. 18, 1969, 34.

218 **"Christ would have smiled"**: William Abruzzi, "Report of Emergency Medical Services During Fair," included in New York State Department of Health, Albany Regional Office, report on Woodstock, received Sept. 25, 1969.

219 **the blood type matched Tate's**: Douglas E. Kneeland, "Manson Trial Hears Testimony on Bloodstains at Murder Scene," *New York Times*, Aug. 27, 1979, 25.

220 **"Charlie and the girls"**: Vincent Bugliosi, *Helter Skelter*, 250–51.

220 **"Never Learn Not to Love"**: The song is at best a lesser piece in the Beach Boys catalog. Even with the Beach Boys' signature harmonies, it's dark and strange. Wags joke about it, calling it a "killer tune." It can be found at youtube.com/watch?v=Jacm CO7GDR4.

221 **"offing those rich pigs"**: Bugliosi, *Helter Skelter*, 221.

221 **"his gospel of love and Christian submission"**: David Felton and David Dalton, "Charles Manson: The Incredible Story of the Most Dangerous Man Alive," *Rolling Stone*, June 25, 1970. See also *Tuesday's Child*, Feb. 16, 1970, cover image, worthpoint .com/worthopedia/1970-tuesdays-child-underground-520011721.

222 **a free concert in San Francisco**: Scully, *Living with the Dead*, 179.

222 **"a kindred spirit"**: UCSC, Dennis McNally interview with Sam Cutler, archived at LCD 11338.

223 **"free ice and free beer"**: Ralph Gleason, "Stones' Plans for Free S.F. Concert," *San Francisco Chronicle*, Nov. 24, 1969, 46.

223 **First Annual Charlie Manson Death Festival**: Greenfield, *Dark Star*, 117.

223 **"masterfully mismanaged"**: Ralph Gleason, "A Few Guesses on Rolling Stones," *San Francisco Chronicle*, Nov. 28, 1969, 50.

223 **the deal fell through**: UCSC, Dennis McNally interview with Sam Cutler, archived at LCD 11338.

224 **they kept pushing**: John Burks and Lorraine Alterman, "The Rolling Stones' Grand Finale to Their 1969 U.S. Tour," *Rolling Stone*, Dec. 27, 1969.

224 **hosting such an event**: Joel Selvin, *Altamont*, 114–15.

224 **"near freezing temperature"**: Carol Gillan, "Chilly Night Waiting for Concert to Begin," *Tracy Press*, Dec. 8, 1969, 1.

224 **"the cocky, aristocratic British rock star"**: Selvin, *Altamont*, 187.

224 **"garbage and old car wrecks"**: Scully, *Living with the Dead*, 181.

224 **"unfriendly, territorial, selfish"**: Sasha Frere-Jones, "The Chaos of Altamont and the Murder of Meredith Hunter," *New Yorker*, March 28, 2019.

225 **"spiritual panic or something"**: Michael Goodwin, "Jerry Garcia at 700 MPH," *Flash*, April 1971.

226 **"Yeow!"**: Andrew Chamings, "Tragedy at Altamont. Remembering Death and Dust in the Deep East Bay," *SF Gate*, Jan. 31, 2023. Also UPI, "Hell's Angel Freed by Jury in Slaying at a Rock Concert," *New York Times*, Jan. 15, 1971, 10.

226 **"Four Born, Five Die"**: Pat Craig, "The 1-Day City of 300,000 People: Four Born, Five Die at Altamont Rock Fest," *Tracy Press*, Dec. 8, 1969.

226 **"modify the rhythm of events"**: Lesh, *Searching for the Sound*, 165.

226 **"we all felt guilty"**: Greenfield, *Dark Star*, 119.

NOTES | **473**

226 **a "hard, hard lesson":** Michael Lydon, "An Evening with the Grateful Dead," *Rolling Stone*, Sept. 17, 1970.

227 **"a huge number of people and no rules":** Undated Garcia interview with the BBC. The context of the interview suggests that it took place in early 1970, when the Dead were in England on tour that spring.

227 **"What started as a dream on Haight Street":** Ralph Gleason, "The Lesson of the Altamont Disaster," *San Francisco Chronicle and Examiner*, Dec. 28, 1969. Jagger was actually singing "Under My Thumb" at the moment Hunter was killed, but the Stones had performed "Sympathy for the Devil" just before the murder.

CHAPTER 11: AN AMERICAN MUSIC

230 **"a reply to an indictment":** Robert Hunter, *Box of Rain*, 158.

230 **became embarrassed by its directness:** *Good Ol' Grateful Deadcast*, "Workingman's Dead 50: Episode 4, New Speedway Boogie."

230 **"I think in time we will":** In the recording from December 20, Garcia's vocal during the second verse is difficult to decipher. The lyric later was amended to be sung "Things went down we don't understand, but I think in time we will."

231 **"Altamont is but one dark moment":** Ed McClanahan, "From My Vita, If You Will." Written in 1971, McClanahan's piece appeared in various publications.

231 **"It says more than anything":** Hunter Thompson, quoted in Douglas Brinkley, *The Gonzo Letters*, vol. 2, 336.

233 **"ecstasy is their chief calling":** Raymond Lang, "Four Explosions: The Grateful Dead," *Daily Californian*, Jan. 20, 1970.

233 **"gamesmanship and power trips":** Tom Constanten, *Between Rock and Hard Places*, 80–82.

234 **The Dead headlined the event:** Paul Droesch, "Music/The Warehouse," publication unknown. Clip courtesy of the Warehouse: blackstrat.net/warehouse/70-01-30r.jpg.

234 **"smelled the odor of burning marijuana":** General Case Report, Incident R.S. 40 Art. 962, New Orleans Police Department, Jan. 31, 1970, 3:45 A.M. The report was written by reporting officers Louis S. Dabdoub and John O. Evans, Jr.

235 **Garcia straggled in at five forty-five:** Ibid.

235 **"a California rock music group":** No byline, "Drug Raid Nets 19 in French Quarter: Rock Musicians, 'King of Acid' Arrested," New Orleans *Times-Picayune*, Feb. 1, 1970.

237 **"helped [Garrison] make that decision":** David Browne, "That Time Joe Smith Sent the Grateful Dead a Letter Complaining About Their Work Ethic," *Rolling Stone*, Dec. 3, 2019.

237 **"stripped down and simplified":** Blair Jackson, *Grateful Dead Gear*, 99.

238 **"a shock to the system":** Jesse Jarnow, *Good Ol' Grateful Deadcast*, season 1, "Workingman's Dead 50: Uncle John's Band," May 20, 2020.

238 **"the emotional feel of the project":** Jackson and Gans, *This Is All a Dream*, 152–53.

238 **would assume greater importance:** Hat tip here to Jesse Jarnow, whose terrific *Deadcast* series recaps the making of *Workingman's Dead* with Jarnow's characteristic attention to detail.

239 **"It's real satisfying to sing":** Reich and Wenner, *Garcia: A Signpost to New Space*, 121.

239 **"is the most fun I know":** David Gans, *Conversations with the Dead*, 11 (from an interview on Aug. 9, 1977).

239 **"sparkles start coming out of your eyes":** David Dodd, *The Complete Annotated Grateful Dead Lyrics*, 105.

474 | NOTES

240 **Garcia was teaching him to play the song:** Recording session from Aug. 28, 1990, youtube.com/watch?v=BfLzXhYHreg. Comment appears just after 2 minutes.

240 **while he was composing:** The Pennywhistlers' version can be found at youtube.com /watch?v=rjvSvGAsU7g.

240 **"was a *major* effort":** Reich and Wenner, *Garcia: A Signpost to New Space*, 96.

240 **"I really can't do justice":** Ibid., 98.

241 **bears scant resemblance to the film:** UCSC, Grateful Dead Records, History series, Hunter, Robert, journal entry for July 29, 1996; also artsites.ucsc.edu/gdead/agdl /direwolf.html.

241 **"Zodiac Killer's fingerprints":** Buzz Poole, *Workingman's Dead*, 69.

244 **It was Garcia clearing his sinuses:** Ibid., 123.

244 **"expressing thanks to that whole tradition":** Michael Goodwin, "Jerry Garcia at 700 MPH," *Flash*, April 1971.

245 **"a little melody that gets in your head":** Reich and Wenner, *Garcia: A Signpost to New Space*, 96.

247 **"he had stolen our money":** Mickey Hart, *Drumming at the Edge of Magic*, 145.

247 **the end of Lenny Hart's run:** Reich and Wenner, *Garcia: A Signpost to New Space*, 105; Hart, *Drumming at the Edge of Magic*, 145.

247 **in a "crashing finish":** Lesh, *Searching for the Sound*, 176–77.

247 **"*This* is what it's all about":** Ibid., 177.

248 **"had been listening to it for a long time":** Miles Davis, "Sketches in Spain," quoted by Joe Taysom, *Far Out* magazine, Aug. 24, 2020.

248 **"The dam broke":** Todd Gitlin, *The Sixties*, 410.

248 **Almost a third went on strike:** Tom Hayden, *Reunion*, 417.

248 **"to demonstrate in a single spasm":** Gitlin, *Sixties*, 410.

249 **sixty-five shots were fired in thirteen seconds:** Jerry M. Lewis and Thomas R. Hensley, "The May 4 Shootings at Kent State University: The Search for Historical Accuracy," Kent State University, https://www.kent.edu/may-4-historical-accuracy. See also John Anthony Moretta, *The Hippies: A 1960s History*, 344.

249 **"it invites tragedy":** Richard Nixon, "Statement on the Death of Four Students at Kent State University," Kent, Ohio, May 4, 1970.

250 **"brought repression home":** Goodman, *Movement Toward a New America*, 752.

251 **"It just ain't so":** Cameron Crowe, "Grateful Dead Show Off New Bodies," *Creem*, Jan. 1, 1974, 33.

252 **"never-ending transcontinental jam":** Lesh, *Searching for the Sound*, 181.

252 **"I'd like to take that ride again":** Robert Hunter and Jerry Garcia, "Might as Well," first performed by the Dead on June 3, 1976.

253 **his father was genuinely proud of him:** Lesh, *Searching for the Sound*, 187.

253 **"love will see you through":** Robert Hunter and Philip Lesh, "Box of Rain," 1970, first performed on Oct. 9, 1972.

254 **Hunter contributed ideas and phrasing:** James Henke, "Jerry Garcia: The *Rolling Stone* Interview," *Rolling Stone*, Oct. 31, 1991, 38.

254 **"Then it'll be your turn":** Robert Hunter, journal entry, "Dear JG (letter written to Garcia a year after Garcia's death)," UCSC Special Collections, Grateful Dead Records, History, Series 1, Box 1, Biographical: Robert Hunter's letter to Garcia, August 1996.

256 **"were written by Robert Weir":** Robert Hunter, *Box of Rain*, 211.

257 **"nine inches long":** Blair Jackson, *The Golden Road*, artsites.ucsc.edu/GDead/AGDL /candy.html.

258 **"a fantastic craftsman":** Reich and Wenner, *Garcia: A Signpost to New Space*, 81.

NOTES | **475**

258 **"that sort of help you along":** Jerry Garcia, interviewed by Jim Ladd in 1981. The show can be viewed here, with Garcia's comment at 42:30: youtube.com/watch?v=tipvK6lufog.

258 **"I'd love for you to play on our record":** UCSC, Dennis McNally interview with David Grisman, archived at LCD 11506.

259 **"We wrote it from city to city":** Robert Hunter, April 30, 1981. The provenance of this interview is difficult to establish, but the videotape can be viewed at youtube.com /watch?v=DCu7rjbwqK4.

259 **"we really labored over the bastard":** Reich and Wenner, *Garcia: A Signpost,* 81.

261 **"That's not a word":** Appearance on *Late Night with David Letterman,* Sept. 17, 1987.

261 **"the Dead are a swinging dance band":** Bob Dylan, *The Philosophy of Modern Song,* 139.

261 **framed the image and photographed it:** Jackson and Gans, *This Is All a Dream,* 167–68.

261 **"a fucking tire iron":** Hunter Thompson, quoted in Douglas Brinkley, *The Gonzo Letters,* vol. 2, 343.

CHAPTER 12: NOW WHAT?

263 **"a masterpiece":** See reviews from, among others, the Montreal *Gazette, The Philadelphia Inquirer, Rolling Stone,* and *The Boston Globe,* all in December 1970.

263 **"an underlying tone of sadness":** David Shenk and Steve Silberman, *Dictionary for Deadheads,* 7.

264 **"the fuckup":** Correspondence with the author, Dec. 5, 2024.

264 **the mother-in-law connected to that marriage:** Author interview with Sara Ruppenthal Katz, Feb. 11, 2023.

264 **"But he showed up for this":** Greenfield, *Dark Star,* 130.

265 **"She's already dead":** Author interview with Sara Ruppenthal Katz, Feb. 11, 2023.

265 **"they could never be resolved":** Greenfield, *Dark Star,* 131–32.

266 **"Dry your eyes on the wind":** The song title is sometimes styled as "Bird Song." I have gone with "Bird Song," one word, because Hunter styles it that way in his collected lyrics.

266 **"deeper and deeper into drugs":** No byline, "Ex-Grateful Dead Aide Gets 6 Months," *Daily Independent Journal* (San Rafael), March 2, 1972, 3.

266 **"he burned him too!":** Unsigned note, UCSC Grateful Dead Archives, Business Records, Box 137, Folder: "Interoffice memos."

267 **"the thing that counts is what you do":** Jerry Garcia, "Action World," November 1970, interviewed on Oct. 10, 1970, itkowitz.com/itkowitzaoi/interview-with.

267 **"nuclear warfare and TNT this evening":** Charles Bronson, Intercommunal Day of Solidarity, March 5, 1971.

268 **participation in some holy wars:** *Clay v. United States,* 403 U.S. 698 (1971).

268 **American casualties peaked in 1968:** Casualty figures are available at archives.gov /research/military/vietnam-war/casualty-statistics.

269 **smoking a joint and listening to a Grateful Dead tape:** Ron Jacobs, *The Way the Wind Blew,* 118.

269 **"we'll stop the government":** Georgetown University Library online collection. A copy of the poster can be found at library.georgetown.edu/sites/default/files/ex/1%20 img175.jpg.

269 **"re-grouping and re-thinking":** Larry D. Hatfield, "The Peace Movement: Re-grouping and Re-thinking," *San Francisco Chronicle,* May 9, 1971, A12.

270 **the earth had reached a desperation point:** See Jim Newton, *Man of Tomorrow,* 166–76.

476 | NOTES

270 **"ecological carnival":** Joseph Lelyveld, "Mood Is Joyful as City Gives Its Support," *New York Times*, April 23, 1970, A1.

270 **parks and beaches in Los Angeles:** Ed Meagher, "No Smog on LA Earth Day," *Los Angeles Times*, April 23, 1970, 35.

270 **cleaned up its parking lot:** Vaughn Proctor, "Will the Real Diane Stand?" *Lompoc Record*, April 23, 1970, 18.

270 **tidied up a square block near San Diego:** No byline, "Earth Day Grade School Style Is Celebrated Here," *Imperial Beach Star-News*, April 23, 1970, 6.

270 **picked up trash in Parsons:** Jim Davis, "FYI," *Parsons Sun*, April 23, 1970, 1.

270 **deplored the quality of their community's air:** Various stories, *Montgomery Advertiser*, April 23, 1970, 1.

270 **her painful rumination on nihilism and meaning:** Joan Didion, *Play It as It Lays*, 5.

271 **"a man in the depths of an ether binge":** Hunter Thompson, *Fear and Loathing in Las Vegas*, 4.

272 **"bury my head and cry":** Mickey Hart, *Drumming at the Edge of Magic*, 145.

272 **he simply could not go on:** Lesh, *Searching for the Sound*, 193.

273 **"Keith is your next piano player":** Donna Godchaux, interviewed for the Rock and Roll Hall of Fame, July 7, 2012, youtube.com/watch?v=N1RzbN-NBTo.

275 **"I don't think they listen very deeply":** Leslie D. Kippel and Toni A. Brown, "The Man Behind Those Songs: Robert Hunter Interview," *Relix*, October 1981, 15–17.

275 **"pre-feminist, or perhaps prehistoric":** Jon Pareles, "The Grateful Dead, Most Alive on the Stage," *New York Times*, July 26, 1987, Section 2, 24.

275 **largely avoided the subject of romantic love:** The Barlow-Weir number, "Money Money," which was included on *From the Mars Hotel*, contributed another dash of sexism. Meant to be tongue-in-cheek, the song playfully spoke of a woman's rapacious claim to her man's cash, taxing him "to the limit of my revenue." "Lord made a lady out of Adam's rib," one couplet ran, "next thing you know you got women's lib." The Dead played it three times, then dropped it, but not before it got a ration of scorn from Deadheads and critics.

276 **"and they learned things":** Alison Fensterstock, " 'Do You Want To Talk to the Man-In-Charge, or the Woman Who Knows What's Going On?' Stories of the Women of the Grateful Dead," NPR, March 20, 2018.

276 **"an undercurrent of continuous change":** Debi Moen, "Candace Brightman: Lighting the Grateful Dead," publication unknown.

CHAPTER 13: "EYES OF THE WORLD"

279 **still part of the family:** Author interview with Rosie McGee, July 11, 2022.

279 **and on Warner Bros.' dime:** Author interview with Carolyn Garcia, March 17, 2022.

279 **"they carry the magic of San Francisco":** Unbylined article, "A Night with the Grateful Dead in Jersey," appearing in "All You Can Eat," New Brunswick, N.J.

280 **Even the equipment was in prime form:** Blair Jackson, *Grateful Dead Gear*, 117.

280 **"we're at one of those peaks":** Steve Peacock, "Jerry Garcia in London," *Rock* magazine, December 1972, 16.

281 **"but smile, smile, smile":** Evidence of the song's layering came from the band itself. Weir would sometimes dedicate it to a recently departed friend or notable, once doing so for the basketball star Len Bias, who died of a crack overdose in 1986, which focused public and political attention on the dangers of that drug and triggered a criminal justice reaction that took decades to undo.

NOTES | **477**

281 **"It was an indescribable privilege":** Rosie McGee, *Dancing with the Dead,* 274, supplemented by author interview on July 11, 2022.

282 **hippies seemed like a minority, sort of:** Jackson, *Garcia,* 232.

282 **He identified four:** UCSC, Grateful Dead Records, Series 2, Box 51, Folder: Business: Alan Trist, Response to "So What" papers, Oct. 5, 1972, "So What—State of the Changes."

282 **"at the edge of our control":** UCSC, Grateful Dead Records, Series 2, Box 51, Folder: Business: Alan Trist, Response to "So What" papers, Oct. 5, 1972, "So What—State of the Changes."

283 **to help pay ongoing operating expenses:** Blair Jackson, *Garcia,* 233. See also Lesh, *Searching for the Sound,* 212.

283 **"No one could see a downside":** Lesh, *Searching for the Sound,* 212.

283 **"field trip":** Getz and Dwork, *Deadhead's Taping Compendium,* vol. 1, 404.

283 **Deadheads for miles:** UCSC, Grateful Dead Records, Series 3, Box 1, Folder: Old Renaissance Faire Grounds, Veneta, Ore., Aug. 27, 1972.

283 **"a transformational ritual that feeds the soul":** John R. Dwork et al., included in *Deadhead's Taping Compendium,* vol. 1, 411.

284 **the "cowboy space":** Hunter and Garcia both quoted in Jackson and Gans, *This Is All a Dream,* 200.

285 **"Feed the poor. Stop the war":** "Wave That Flag," as performed on Feb. 9, 1973, archive.org/details/gd73-02-09.sbd.bertha-fink.14939.sbeok.shnf/gd73-02-09Berthad3to4.shn.

285 **"Still is," he said:** Author interview with Wavy Gravy, Jan. 10, 2023.

285 **the tweeters blew out in a fizzle:** Jay Harlow, "Despite PA Problems, Dead Brings Audience to Its Feet," *Stanford Daily,* Feb. 13, 1973.

285 **"just like that":** Healy, quoted in Jackson and Gans, *This Is All a Dream,* 201.

286 **He was twenty-seven years old:** AP report, " 'Pig Pen' Rock Player Found Dead," *Palo Alto Times,* March 9, 1973.

286 **"We were all prepared for it emotionally":** Joel Selvin, "Garcia Returns to a First Love," *San Francisco Chronicle,* March 14, 1973.

286 **a short, impersonal service:** Alice Yarish, "Coda for Pig Pen," publication unknown, March 1973.

286 **"in a style akin to his own":** Selvin, "Garcia Returns to a First Love."

287 **being an icon of the counterculture did not pay well:** Robert Greenfield, *Bear,* 141.

287 **the album was in production:** *Good Ol' Grateful Deadcast,* "Bear's Choice 50," March 3, 2023.

288 **"cocaine, heroin, marijuana and other drugs":** No byline, "Rock Star Held on Drug Charge," *Burlington County Times,* March 28, 1973.

289 **looking for easy marks:** See "Grateful Dead Bassist Busted," *San Francisco Examiner,* Jan. 10, 1973; "Judge OKs Videotaping of Concert at CU," *Rocky Mountain News,* May 5, 1973; Ed Ruffing, "19 Arrested at Grateful Dead Concert," *New York Observer,* March 22, 1973; unidentified publication, "75 People Arrested at Dead Shows Inside Nassau Coliseum," March 26, 1973.

289 **eager to redeem himself:** *Good Ol' Grateful Deadcast,* "Watkins Glen Summer Jam '73, Part 1," July 27, 2023.

289 **Russell was dropped and the Band added:** *Good Ol' Grateful Deadcast,* "Watkins Glen Summer Jam '73, Part 1," July 27, 2023.

289 **"another Woodstock won't happen here":** Kathy Kozdemba, "Glen's Big Question: Will Rock Concert Go On?" *Elmira Telegram,* July 1, 1973.

478 | NOTES

289 **"We are sweating this one out":** AP, "N.Y. Town 'Sweating' as Rock Siege Nears," *Baltimore Sun*, July 26, 1973, 3.

290 **"over in the library—reading":** Mark Starr (staff writer for the *Rochester Democrat and Chronicle*), "Thousands Arrive at Watkins Glen 2 Days Before Rock Festival Opens," *Niagara Falls Gazette*, July 27, 1973.

291 **"we can't stop them coming":** UPI, "400,000 Jam Rock Site, More Coming," *Palm Springs Desert Sun*, July 28, 1973.

291 **"veteran parachutist":** Wire report, "600,000 Leave Rock Fest," *San Francisco Examiner*, July 30, 1973.

291 **"I've never gotten called 'sir' so much":** NYTimes News Service, "Police Treated Courteously at Rock Festival," Philadelphia *Bulletin*, July 30, 1973.

292 **"trying to figure it out":** Silberman in Getz and Dwork, *Deadhead's Taping Compendium*, vol. 1, 476.

292 **"Biggest, but Not Woodstock":** Tom Zito, Washington Post News Service, "Biggest, but Not Woodstock," *Des Moines Register*, July 30, 1973, 6.

292 **"the biggest party of all time":** Editorial, " 'Summer Jam'—1973," *New York Times*, Aug. 4, 1973.

293 **expressed happiness and relief:** No byline, "Grateful Dead's Jerry Garcia Gets Probation on Drug Charge," Philadelphia *Bulletin*, July 30, 1973. See also Grateful Dead Tour Schedule, 1973, cs.cmu.edu/~./gdead/setlists/73.html.

294 **"turned sour":** Hunter Thompson, *Fear and Loathing on the Campaign Trail '72*, 224.

294 **"They had to reorganize":** Erin Osmon, "The Grateful Dead Were in a State of Flux. 'Wake of the Flood' Gave Them New Life," *Los Angeles Times*, Oct. 3, 2023.

294 **"ample, full and carefully rendered":** Jim Miller, "Wake of the Flood," *Rolling Stone*, Jan. 3, 1974.

295 **the world's drift into World War II:** Katherine Anne Porter, *Ship of Fools*, mentioned in David Dodd's *The Complete Annotated Grateful Dead Lyrics*, 223.

295 **"Topical song, topical lyrics":** Jesse Jarnow, *Good Ol' Grateful Deadcast*, "From the Mars Hotel: Ship of Fools," season 9, episode 8. The note from Garcia appeared with notes prepared in connection with recording the song.

296 **"the war machine had been attacked":** Ron Jacobs, *The Way the Wind Blew*, 142.

296 **congressional hearings revealed the company's role:** Paul L. Montgomery, "I.T.T. Office Here Damaged by Bomb," September 29, 1973, 1, nytimes.com/1973/09/29 /archives/itt-office-here-damaged-by-bomb-caller-linked-explosion-at.html.

297 **"five large window panels":** Ron Jacobs, *The Way the Wind Blew*, 148.

297 **"Scientology and I were not a very good match":** David Browne, "Robert Hunter on Grateful Dead's Early Days, Wild Tours, 'Sacred' Songs," *Rolling Stone*, March 9, 2015, rollingstone.com/feature/robert-hunter-on-grateful-deads-early-days-wild-tours -sacred-songs-37978/.

298 **"I'm not a crook":** United Press International, "Nixon Says, 'I'm Not a Crook,' Promises to Produce Evidence," *Fort Lauderdale News and Sun-Sentinel*, Nov. 18, 1973.

299 **"just in time to attend Woodstock":** Kreutzmann, *Deal*, 65.

299 **"but no serious relationship":** Lesh, *Searching for the Sound*, 202–203.

299 **"He was game for it all":** Interviewed for "The Other One: The Long, Strange Trip of Bob Weir," 2014.

300 **"I feel for the poor guy":** Jerry Garcia, interviewed by Jim Ladd and Tom Yates in January 1974, clip from *Good Ol' Grateful Deadcast*, March 28, 2024.

300 **"the entire Whitehouse":** Rakow to Nixon, Jan. 23, 1974, UCSC Special Collections, Grateful Dead Business Records, Series 2, Box 40, Folder: "Guerrilla mailings, 1970–75."

NOTES | 479

301 **"a single, big system"**: David Gans, interview with Owsley, *Conversations with the Dead*, 329–30.

302 **to haul it from place to place**: Blair Jackson, *Grateful Dead Gear*, 137.

302 **attended a tech rehearsal**: John L. Wasserman, "Quiet! The Band Is Playing," *San Francisco Chronicle*, March 22, 1974.

302 **"was simply phenomenal"**: Ibid.

302 **crew and equipment costs soared**: UCSC, Grateful Dead Records, Series 3, Boxes 1 and 2, Folders, "Cow Palace, San Francisco, 3/23/1974" and "Europe Tour 1974."

303 **darker, more paranoid**: Jackson and Gans, *This Is All a Dream*, 233–34.

304 **a "grumpy bear" vibe**: Author interview with Trixie Garcia, Sept. 17, 2024.

304 **"rallied behind Mickey"**: Kreutzmann, *Deal*, 196.

CHAPTER 14: "ON THE ROAD AGAIN"

307 **"We haven't broken up"**: Jackson and Gans, *This Is All a Dream*, 236.

307 **"chatty without being friendly"**: Greenfield, *Dark Star*, 164.

308 **to bring Koons onto the Dead's payroll**: UCSC, Grateful Dead Business Records, Series 2. Box 73, Folder: Business: GD Records, Payroll, 1975–1976. See "Deborah Koons 5-2," entries for June 30, 1975, through Jan. 2, 1976.

308 **"started to get to be a problem"**: Greenfield, *Dark Star*, 167.

308 **"We could hear Jerry playing the banjo"**: Peter Rowan, at the opening of the Jerry Garcia exhibition, Owensboro, Kentucky, March 28, 2024.

309 **"just four people who couldn't stop playing"**: Ibid.

309 **lifted by a lightness of spirit**: Ralph Gleason, "This World," *San Francisco Sunday Chronicle and Examiner*, March 9, 1975.

310 **"but there were these tapes"**: UCSC, Dennis McNally interview with David Grisman, archived at LCD 11506b.

310 **"my little piece of the action"**: Ibid.

310 **too personal to be expressed in movements**: Didion, "On the Morning After the Sixties," *The White Album*, 205–208.

311 **"he was addicted"**: Greenfield, *Dark Star*, 184.

312 **one bill from January 1975**: UCSC, GD Business Records, Series 2, Box 72, Folder: Financial: RR Rx-106, purchase orders 1975, "Studio time for 'Seastones.'"

312 **Keith and Donna Godchaux recorded**: UCSC, GD Business Records, Series 2, Box 72, Folder: Financial: RR Rx-104 Godchaux, 8182-3 1975.

313 **an operating loss of $80,198.94**: UCSC, GD Business Records, Series 2, Box 77, Folder: Financial: GDR: Financial statements, accounts, information, 1974-1975, "Financial Statements, March 31, 1975."

313 **"Weir studio"**: UCSC, GD Business Records, Series 2, Box 72, Folder: Financial: RR Bob Weir 8182-B 1975.

313 **"it will never come true"**: UCSC, Grateful Dead Records, Series 1, Box 2, Folder: Biographical: Robert Hunter—lyrics photocopies 1996 and undated. Hunter's original lyric read: "Without love in the dream, which of us can come true?," an alternative formulation that speaks more to the effect of the dream on the one who dreams it. Garcia tweaked it and demonstrated his skill as an editor. The final version is broader, less personal, and more emphatic.

314 **"Keep your fingers crossed"**: Billy Altman, "Blues for Allah," *Rolling Stone*, Oct. 9, 1975.

315 **broadcast on FM stations nationally**: The radio broadcast ended before the Dead's 21-minute version of "Blues for Allah," whose hypnotic meditations were too much for even an open-minded radio programmer.

480 | NOTES

317 **"like a dental extraction":** Barlow, *Mother American Night,* 103.

317 **played hundreds of times:** David Dodd, "Greatest Stories Ever Told—Cassidy," posted on Dead.net, March 7, 2013, dead.net/features/greatest-stories-ever-told/greatest-stories-ever-told-cassidy#:~:text=Furthur%20repertoire%20steadily.-,The%20Grateful%20Dead%20played%20this%20song%20a%20lot%20(334%20times,23%2C%20at%20the%20Cow%20Palace.

319 **"Grateful Dead Endurance Tour '77":** UCSC, Grateful Dead Records, Series 3, Box 3, Folder: East Coast Tour April/May 1977—Receipts.

319 **"a shameless invocation":** Steve Silberman, interview with Robert Hunter, "Standing in the Soul," *Poetry Flash,* December 1992.

320 **"A lot of it is the Muse":** Ibid.

321 **" 'What the *hell* was that?' ":** Betty Cantor-Jackson, interviewed in Getz and Dwork, *Deadhead's Taping Compendium,* vol. 2, 6.

321 **"screwed up the feel":** Weir and Hart and Garcia interviews, featured in Jackson and Gans, *This Is All a Dream,* 259–60.

322 **"really did transcend showbiz":** Robert Christgau, "The Grateful Dead Are Rising Again," *New York Times,* Sunday, July 27, 1969.

322 **"the people never stopped dancing":** Robert Christgau, "They're Grateful for The Dead," *Village Voice,* March 24, 1972.

322 **"the Dead's version of the ultimate reality":** Robert Christgau, "Dropping In on the Grateful Dead," *Village Voice,* May 16, 1977.

324 **Their relationship would continue:** Author interview with Susan Klein, June 27, 2022.

324 **"nonlinear concept of time":** Jackson and Gans, *This Is All a Dream,* 272.

325 **"none of the antisocial posturing":** Malone to H.E. Dr. Ashraf Ghorbal, March 4, 1978, UCSC, Grateful Dead Records, Series 3, Box 4, Folder: "Egypt—Giza Sound and Light Theater, Cairo, Egypt, Sept. 14–16, 1978."

325 **A few hundred enterprising followers:** Author interview with Tom Unterman, March 5, 2024.

325 **" 'What occurs?' ":** University of Oregon, Knight Library, Special Collections, Ken Kesey papers, Box 1, Correspondence, Folder: Outgoing, 1962–1996, Kesey to John Cherry, *Rolling Stone,* Sept. 25, 1978.

325 **The Dead "footed the whole bill":** Ibid.

326 **"in the once-silent desert":** Greg Dobbs, ABC News, date unclear, youtube.com/watch?v=5QYgE631mU8.

326 **"far-out, beautiful magic":** Max Bell, "The incredible story of the Grateful Dead's legendary gigs at the Pyramids of Giza," *Classic Rock,* Oct. 13, 2024.

327 **"driven across the sky":** Kreutzmann, *Deal,* 230, and Lesh, *Searching for the Sound,* 244.

327 **"my life after Egypt":** Jackson and Gans, *This Is All a Dream,* 281.

328 **Michaels eventually relented:** Author interview with Al Franken, Oct. 4, 2023.

328 **Buck Henry slated to host:** It was a banner season for musical guests on the show. The weeks leading up to the Dead's performance included the Rolling Stones, Devo, Frank Zappa, and Van Morrison.

328 **"Not particularly":** Jackson and Gans, *This Is All a Dream,* 285.

328 **they watched cartoons on TV:** Author interview with Susan Klein, June 27, 2022.

331 **remains to this day a mystery:** Tim Reiterman, *Raven,* 571–80.

331 **"White Night":** Author interview with Dianne Feinstein, April 2, 2019.

332 **"There's no mistaking dead":** Ibid.

NOTES | 481

CHAPTER 15: SAFE HARBOR

337 **"its great power to harm us"**: Ronald Reagan, "Address Accepting the Presidential Nomination at the Republican National Convention in Detroit," July 17, 1980.

340 **living "like a badger"**: Sat Santokh, quoted in Greenfield, *Dark Star*, 203.

340 **"a theme and a trigger"**: Email to the author from Susan Klein, January 23, 2025.

340 **lighting a hotel room on fire**: Lesh, *Searching for the Sound*, 248.

340 **Keith sank deeper and deeper**: Scully, *Living with the Dead*, 300.

341 **"began to irritate Jerry no end"**: Lesh, *Searching for the Sound*, 248.

341 **Tom Hayden and Jane Fonda**: David Dodd, "Greatest Stories Ever Told: 'Tons of Steel,'" Dead.net, May 16, 2013.

342 **"really like licorice"**: Nina Blackwood, interviewing Garcia for MTV, aired June 2, 1983. Garcia did not express this observation quite so concisely in his initial interview, at first comparing the Dead to both licorice and buttermilk. He eventually refined the observation, and it became a favorite of Deadheads.

343 **"they have forfeited their jobs and will be terminated"**: Bryan Craig, "Reagan vs. Air Traffic Controllers," UVA Miller Center.

343 **"dance for disarmament"**: Unbylined story, "'Dance for Disarmament' to feature singer Joan Baez," *Peninsula Times Tribune*, Nov. 23, 1981.

343 **American Friends Service Committee**: Unbylined story, "The Dead in Benefits," *San Francisco Examiner*, Jan. 23, 1982.

343 **"He wasn't even a good actor"**: Steve Sutherland, "Grateful Dead, Part One," *Melody Maker*, May 6, 1989.

344 **"not that safe for people like us"**: Jon Carroll, "A Conversation with Jerry Garcia," *Playboy Guide*, March 1982.

344 **"have been pretty much the same"**: Joseph Territo, "The Talk with Jerry Garcia, Part 3," *Funfinder*, June 10–17, 1982.

344 **"It's only a matter of time"**: Joseph Territo, "The Talk with Jerry Garcia, Part 1," *Funfinder*, May 27–June 3, 1982.

344 **"We're like the exception to every rule"**: Blair Jackson and David Gans, "Checking In with Jerry Garcia," Aug. 28, 1981.

345 **"to go out and shoot a politician"**: Ibid.

345 **"I would feel better if we were married"**: Greenfield, *Dark Star*, 199.

345 **"it would have melted a stone"**: Ibid.

346 **"didn't make a damned bit of difference"**: Ibid., 200.

346 **"glad to do anything to help"**: Bill Mandel, "War No; Warriors, Yes," *San Francisco Examiner*, May 13, 1982, 2.

346 **big charity was even worse**: Author interview with Nick Meriwether, Aug. 15, 2024.

347 **"How do you choose between redwoods and blindness?"**: Author interview with Cameron Sears and Cliff Palefsky, May 2, 2024.

349 **not just with the band but with one another**: Author interview with Steve Silberman, Oct. 5, 2022.

349 **"That's Otis"**: Thousands of Deadhead dogs were named Otis as a result. The original Otis was described as "Weir's friendly dog" in *The Golden Road*, solving the mystery for listeners of *Reckoning* puzzled by Garcia's stray comment.

350 **bits of heroin off scraps of foil**: Author interview with Trixie Garcia, Sept. 17, 2024.

350 **payroll and income taxes**: Goldie Love, letter to Garcia, Oct. 25, 1983, UCSC, Grateful Dead Records, Business Records, Series 2, Box 52, Folder: Business-Financial, GDP Personal Records, 1971–86, Jerry Garcia 1 of 2.

482 | NOTES

350 **"doing $700 a day of this stuff"**: Scully, *Living with the Dead*, 315.

350 **"Dope is now our major concern on the road"**: Ibid., 349.

350 **"obliterates everything from our lives"**: Ibid., *Living with the Dead*, 359–60.

350 **the era of the "Desperate Dead"**: Steve (no last name given), appearing on *Guess the Year*, taped on May 7, 2024.

351 **"to glow a dull gray-green"**: Greenfield, *Dark Star*, 212–13.

351 **"listless troll"**: Daniel Gewertz, "Garcia Gives a Dreadful Concert," *Boston Herald*, Nov. 19, 1984.

351 **"You're only a drummer"**: Phil Lesh, in conversation with Jay Blakesberg at Terrapin Crossroads, San Rafael, March 26, 2016.

351 **"brown and white substances"**: Unbylined story, "Dead's Garcia Held for Drugs in GG Park," *San Francisco Examiner*, Jan. 19, 1985.

352 **"this town has always been good to me"**: Unbylined story, "Jerry Garcia Agrees to Drug Diversion Plan," *San Francisco Chronicle*, March 20, 1985.

352 **"a portal into the sublime"**: Sam Cooper, "The Stars Were Set in Spin," presentation to the Grateful Dead Studies Association, Chicago, 2024, attended by the author (no recording available).

353 **accusations of sexual misconduct and abuse**: Mitch Clogg, "Deadhead Church Expels Its Founder," *San Francisco Chronicle*, April 9, 1992. See also Jarnow, *Heads*, 306–308.

353 **the Dead's sound technicians**: Nick Paumgarten, "Deadhead," *New Yorker*, Nov. 18, 2012.

353 **"They've left home"**: Jackson, *Garcia*, 277.

354 **A proposal was "to follow"**: UCSC, Grateful Dead papers, Business Records, Box 137, Folder: "Business Meeting minutes, 1981, 1983–86, n.d." Minutes from July 25, 1984.

354 **soundboard crew's view of the stage**: UCSC, Grateful Dead papers, Business Records, Box 137, Folder: "Business Meeting minutes, 1981, 1983–86, n.d." Minutes from Aug. 28, 1984.

355 **"capturing the moment"**: Rick Monture, presentation at the 2024 meeting of the Grateful Dead Studies Caucus at the Popular Culture Association, March 28, 2024, attended by the author (no recording available).

355 **putting him on the payroll**: Paumgarten, "Deadhead."

355 **"It's analogous to writing nonfiction"**: Ibid.

355 **"we are all the Grateful Dead"**: Paul Krugman, "Bits, Bands and Books," *New York Times*, June 6, 2008.

356 **"out to the back of the hall"**: McNally, *Long Strange Trip*, 217.

357 **"Grateful Janitors"**: *Golden Road*, Issue 1, Winter 1984.

357 **"it wasn't confined then, and isn't now"**: Sally Ansorge, "After All These Years," *Dupree's Diamond News*, Summer 1987, vol. 1, no. 2, 5.

357 **"isn't going anywhere except onward"**: Barbara Meier, "Jerry Garcia Speaks with Barbara Meier," *Tricycle*, Spring 1992.

358 **"takes the prize as the all-around worst"**: Review signed by "Roebuck," archive.org, Oct. 22, 2006, archive.org/details/gd85-08-24.sbd.vernon.13991.sbeok.shnf.

359 **"outspoken intolerance for drug use"**: Nancy Reagan, nationally televised message, Sept. 14, 1986.

360 **"is that they're illegal"**: Jerry Garcia, interviewed by Father Miles Riley on *I Believe*, KPIX, 1976, youtube.com/watch?v=8odcUvmVWzM.

360 **more than $11 million in ticket sales**: Jon Woodhouse, "Musicworld," *Maui News*, Jan. 10, 1986, B6.

360 **where he stayed for more than a decade**: Katie Hafner, "The Saga of The Well," *Wired*, May 1, 1997.

NOTES | 483

361 **"perfect for cyberspace"**: Author interview with David Gans, July 14, 2024.

361 **"It just took off"**: Ibid.

362 **"more lasting, and greater, cultural impact than the Beatles"**: Andrew Hickey, *A History of Rock Music in 500 Songs*, Episode 165, May 19, 2023, 500songs.com/podcast/episode-165-dark-star-by-the-grateful-dead/.

363 **"titles that have such deep cultural roots?"**: William Safire, "On Language: Of 'The' I Sing," *New York Times*, March 2, 1986. A personal note: I had a little something to do with Safire's interest in the Dead. In 1986, I clerked for James Reston at *The New York Times*, and our offices were next door to Safire's. Safire paced and ate peanuts when working on his column, and he passed by my desk one day. He spotted a Grateful Dead songbook on my desk and asked, "Where did they get that name?" I confessed that I didn't know. A few weeks later, the item appeared in his Sunday column.

363 **"the lessons of age and experience"**: Bruce Nixon, "Bob Dylan Reemerging: 'Quasi-mythical' Figure Revising, Recreating His Musical Vision," *Dallas Times Herald* (reprinted in the Greenfield, Mass., *Recorder*), June 26, 1986, 17.

363 **"The thing I really notice now is time"**: Robert Hilburn, "Bob Dylan—Still A-Changin'," *Los Angeles Times*, Nov. 17, 1985.

363 **At a band meeting in November**: UCSC, Grateful Dead Records, Business Records, Box 137, Folder: "Business meeting minutes, 1981, 1983–86, n.d.," minutes of Nov. 26, 1985, meeting.

363 **"see how it works for the remaining three"**: UCSC, Grateful Dead Records, Business Records, Box 137, Folder: "Business meeting minutes, 1981, 1983–86, n.d.," minutes of April 11, 1986, meeting.

364 **performances at RFK Stadium**: UCSC, Grateful Dead Records, Series 3, Box 48, Folder: "Concerts, RFK Stadium, Washington, D.C., July 6–7, 1986."

364 **bouncing amiably between numbers**: Richard Harrington, "Grateful Dead, Dylan, Bringing It All Back," *Washington Post*, July 7, 1986.

364 **high above the sweltering crowd**: There is no overstating the heat of these events. I was present, and my companion on the second night turned to me as the sun fell and announced: "This is like being in the mouth of a volcano." She had a point.

364 **"feared that he would blow a fuse"**: Lesh, *Searching for the Sound*, 278.

365 **"an abscessed tooth and exhaustion"**: Unbylined, "Guitarist Jerry Garcia Checks Into Hospital," *Marin Independent Journal*, July 12, 1986.

365 **"I thought there was no way he would live"**: Author interview with Carolyn Garcia, March 17, 2022.

CHAPTER 16: "THE ANSWER TO THE ATOM BOMB"

367 **"I can hear what you're saying"**: Greenfield, *Dark Star*, 219.

367 **"just like teaching a baby"**: Ibid., 224–25.

368 **He made a quiet appearance**: Michael Conford, "Welcome Back, Uncle Jerry," *San Jose Mercury News*, Oct. 7, 1986.

368 **Garcia picked up a guitar and fell in comfortably**: Joel Selvin, "Starship Checks Up on Old Rival's Performance," *San Francisco Examiner*, Dec. 7, 1986. See also Greenfield, *Dark Star*, 225.

368 **Garcia was thrilled**: Greenfield, *Dark Star*, 226.

368 **"We will survive"**: This audience tape captures the crowd that night: archive.org/details/gd86-12-15.nakcm101-dwonk.25263.sbeok.flacf/gd1986-12-15-dwonk-d1t01.flac. No Deadhead can listen to it without crying.

484 | NOTES

369 **across years and difficulties:** Author interview with Sara Ruppenthal Katz, Feb. 11, 2023.

369 **"move out of the hurricane":** Blair Jackson and Regan McMahon, "Feels like it might be all right . . ." *Golden Road,* Issue 12, Fall 1986.

370 **"I am appalled":** Hamilton Kendall, "The Great 'Touch of Grey' Debate," *Esquire,* July 14, 2020.

370 **"not constantly being reminded of it":** Jerry Garcia, interviewed by Father Miles Riley on *I Believe,* KPIX, 1976, youtube.com/watch?v=8odcUvmVWzM.

371 **"Humans hate it":** Paul Morley, "What a Long, Predictable Trip It's Become," *New Musical Express,* March 28, 1981.

371 **"the blood of Jerry Garcia":** Everett True, "In My Head, I'm So Ugly," *Melody Maker,* July 18, 1992.

371 **"forced to think about yourself all the time":** Jas Obrecht, "Jerry Garcia: The Complete 1985 *Frets* Interview," *Frets,* Jan. 12, 1985.

372 **"come to me with the cross and nails":** David Jay Brown and Rebecca Novick, "Jerry Speaks," *Relix,* August 1995.

372 **"the horror that is modern war":** Ronald Reagan, "War" radio commentary, March 13, 1978.

373 **"the risks of war":** Ronald Reagan, "Address to the Nation on Defense and National Security," March 23, 1983.

373 **"arguably the worst Grateful Dead song ever":** Barlow, *Mother American Night,* 153.

374 **didn't like the song but played it anyway:** Garcia had other issues with the album. "Foolish Heart," a lovely if conventional Hunter lyric, gave the Dead a single and a video, but it never sat well with Garcia. "This is an advice song!" Garcia told Hunter. "I mean, the lyrics are, 'Never give your love, my friend, to a foolish heart.' Is that really good advice? Is that what we want to say? Shouldn't we tell them, 'Hey, brush your teeth twice a day!" Timothy White, "From the Beatles to Bartok," *Goldmine,* Nov. 2, 1990.

374 **nothing could slow the momentum now:** Michael Snyder, "Grateful Dead's 'Built to Last' Isn't," *San Francisco Chronicle,* Nov. 19, 1989.

374 **did not take the pressure off shows:** Steve Morse, "Grateful Dead Live on Cable Tonight," *Boston Globe,* June 21, 1989.

375 **"the number of friends they have lost":** Robert Lindsey, "Where Homosexuals Found a Haven, There's No Haven from AIDS," *New York Times,* July 15, 1987.

375 **"a cowboy version of 'Dark Star' ":** The entire performance can be found at youtube .com/watch?v=ViBJLUJ4fDQ&list=PL4FD1813C7487D7E6&index=5.

376 **one of San Francisco's stricken communities:** Steve Silberman, "AIDS Emergency Fund Benefit: An Evening of Good Intentions," *San Francisco Sentinel,* Dec. 25, 1987.

376 **"it rethinks your life":** Author interview with Gillian Welch, Sept. 15, 2023.

377 **"Not enough":** Bill Walton, interviewed by Joe Canzano, May 28, 2024, tiktok.com/@ johncanzano/video/7374231538298260779?lang=en.

377 **"rhythmic elegance":** Jas Obrecht, Garcia interview, *Frets,* June 1985. *Frets* ran an edited version of this interview. Obrecht later posted the entire transcript online at chrome-extension://efaidnbmnnnibpcajpcglclefindmkaj/https://gdsets.com/extras /jerry1985frets.pdf.

378 **"didn't apply to the kids in California":** UCSC, Jerry Garcia, interviewed by Studs Terkel and Abe Peck, Dec. 6, 1979, archived at LCD 11709.

378 **"what happens while you're doing it":** Bruce Springsteen, *Born to Run,* 453.

378 **"where you make easy things look hard":** Author interview with Huey Lewis, April 18, 2023.

NOTES | 485

379 **"blend into the group as if nothing had happened"**: Jon Pareles, "He Let His Music Do the Talking," *New York Times*, Aug. 20, 1995.

379 **early intellectual fascination with the Dead**: Stanley Krippner, "A Pilot Study in Dream Telepathy with the Grateful Dead," 2007, presented at "Unbroken Chain: The Grateful Dead in Music, Culture and Memory," a symposium held at the University of Massachusetts, Amherst, Nov. 16–18, 2007.

379 **"Deadhead 101"**: Kathy Haight, "Diehard Deadheads as a Subculture," *St. Louis Post-Dispatch*, May 1989; also Steve Silverman, "Deadhead 101" (publication unknown), May 18, 1989, and Tim Gladstone, "A Long, Strange Trip," *Philadelphia Inquirer*, July 7, 1989.

380 **"never struck me as being particularly persuasive"**: Dean Budnick, "Nicholas Meriwether: Innovator and Advocate for Grateful Dead Scholarship," *Relix*, May 22, 2024.

380 **"think about it for the rest of my life"**: Author interview with Nick Meriwether, Jan. 25, 2022.

381 **a "winning combination"**: Author interview with Dave Stever, April 25, 2024.

381 **enough for most people to live on**: Author interview with Dave Stever, April 25, 2024. Other sources have reported that Garcia was receiving roughly $200,000 a year from his ice cream royalties at the time of his death. Stever would not confirm that number, but he did not object to it, either.

382 **"Who's got time?"**: Press conference announcing "So Far" video, Sept. 14, 1997, youtube.com/watch?v=ol3Ghakv8-Y.

383 **"We have no choice really"**: Steve Sutherland, "Grateful Dead, Part One," *Melody Maker*, May 6, 1989.

384 **"is a total idiot"**: Ibid.

386 **Among Campbell's interested readers**: Nicholas Meriwether, "Joseph Campbell and the Grateful Dead," Dead.net, Oct. 29, 2015, dead.net/features/blog/documenting-dead-joseph-campbell-and-grateful-dead.

386 **attended a Dead show in Oakland in early 1986**: Blair Jackson, "Deadline," *Golden Road*, Issue 10, Spring 1986.

386 **Campbell led the discussion**: Joseph Campbell, "From Ritual to Rapture, from Dionysus to the Grateful Dead," Nov. 1, 1986, sirbacon.org/joseph_campbell.htm.

CHAPTER 17: BAD ARCHITECTURE AND OLD WHORES

390 **"carrying a lot of pain"**: Blair Jackson, "Death Don't Have No Mercy in This Land," *Golden Road*, Issue 24, Fall 1990, 2.

390 **"It was a joy to play with him"**: Branford Marsalis, 1996 interview (source unknown), youtube.com/watch?v=GnnoHPFMs3U.

390 **lying on the floor**: Paul Liberatore, "The Dead Mourn 'a Brother,'" *Marin Independent Journal*, July 27, 1990, 1.

391 **"the toughest thing"**: Ken Kesey, reprinted in "Ken Kesey: Furthur," University of Oregon, Knight Library, Special Collections, Ken Kesey papers.

391 **"from the Grateful Dead to our bruised hearts"**: David Dodd, "Greatest Stories Ever Told: Brokedown Palace," Dead.net, Aug. 22, 2013, quoting Kesey from a speech at the University of Virginia in 1998.

392 **he, too, was slipping away**: Author interview with Carolyn Garcia, March 14, 2022.

392 **"the full gamut between spite and irony"**: Barlow, *Mother American Night*, 155.

392 **offered the keyboard job to Bruce Hornsby**: Joel Selvin, "Bruce Hornsby to Replace Dead's Keyboardist for Now," *San Francisco Chronicle*, Aug. 29, 1990.

486 | NOTES

392 **asked for and received the Dead's permission:** UCSC, Dennis McNally interview with Bruce Hornsby, archived at LCD 11390.

393 **the opportunity passed:** Ibid.

393 **"a lot of parts to it":** Jerry Garcia and Vince Welnick rehearsal, Aug. 28, 1990, youtube .com/watch?v=BfLzXhYHreg.

394 **"He has no idea what he's doing":** Dave Becker, "Welnick Can't Keep Pace with the Grateful Dead," *Alameda Times-Star*, Dec. 5, 1990.

394 **"if you don't look down, it'll be okay":** Author unclear, "Grateful Dead, Bone Idols," *Melody Maker*, Oct. 27, 1990.

394 **"Of course he's cool":** Author interview with Steve Silberman, Oct. 5, 2022.

395 **should have been a shoe salesman:** Author interview with Susan Klein, June 27, 2022.

396 **"He knew it!":** "Dark Star" segued into a jam, which Kesey joined at .33, archive.org /details/gd91-10-31.sbd.gardner.2897.sbeok.shnf/gd1991-10-31d2to5.shn.

396 **earnings for the second half of the year:** UCSC, Grateful Dead papers, Business Records, Box 137, Folder: "Business Meeting minutes, 1981, 1983–86, n.d.," minutes from Aug. 6, 1981.

396 **Band members braced for heavy tax bills:** UCSC, Grateful Dead papers, Business Records, Box 137, Folder: "Business Meeting minutes, 1981, 1983–86, n.d.," minutes from Feb. 3, 1987.

396 **top tour of 1993:** 1993 Top 50 Tours, *Pollstar*, Dec. 31, 1993.

397 **pocketed a net profit of $511,390.42:** UCSC, Grateful Dead papers, Business Records, Box 59, Folder: "Financial, Spring 1994 Tour settlements 1994."

397 **"over-abundant numbers of cops":** See, e.g., *Dupree's Diamond News*, April and September 1989 letters, and *Golden Road*, Fall 1990 letters.

397 **the rising number of Deadheads among the prison population:** Letter from Michael Peller; feature by Pam Fischer, *Dupree's Diamond News*, July 1990, 2 and 21.

398 **"led us to some Grateful Dead concerts":** I was the author of these stories, which appeared in the *Los Angeles Times* on July 27, 1992.

399 **"victory of economic and political liberalism":** Francis Fukuyama, "The End of History?" *National Interest*, no. 16, 1989, 3.

399 **The earth brought Fonda home:** Author interview with Jane Fonda, Nov. 27, 2023.

400 **warned against moving too quickly:** Unbylined wire report, "Specter Slow to Back Clinton on Gays in Military," *Daily Item* (Sunbury, Pa.), Nov. 22, 1992, 3.

401 **"We must have both":** Bill Clinton, "State of the Union Address," delivered on Jan. 23, 1996.

401 **"new ideas about liberty":** Barlow, "Crime and Puzzlement," 1990.

402 **"We Owe It All to the Hippies":** "Welcome to Cyberspace," *Time*, Spring 1995.

402 **"the roots of the modern cyberrevolution":** Stewart Brand, "We Owe It All to the Hippies," *Time*, Spring 1995, 54.

403 **he'd taken out a total of $1,200:** UCSC, Grateful Dead Records, Series 1, Box 3, Folder: Garcia and Stephens bank account statements, June–October 1993. The same pattern of ATM withdrawals carried through the summer and fall.

403 **"very much in love with you":** Amir Bar-Levi, "Long Strange Trip," Episode 6.

404 **and went to work:** David Browne, "Grateful Dead's Robert Hunter on Jerry's Final Days," *Rolling Stone*, March 11, 2015.

404 **the last masterpiece of the Grateful Dead:** Conversation with the author, July 12, 2024.

404 **"this isn't going to work":** Amir Bar-Levi, "Long Strange Trip," Episode 6.

405 **"That broke my heart":** Greenfield, *Dark Star*, 290.

NOTES | 487

405 **"express the emotional content of my soul"**: Dave DiMartino, "A Conversation with Jerry Garcia," Yahoo! Entertainment, Feb. 24, 1992, yahoo.com/entertainment/bp/conversation-jerry-garcia-185256815.html.

405 **On Inauguration Night**: "Tennessee Ball at Omni Shorem [sic]," Jan. 21, UCSC, Grateful Dead Records, Series 4, Box 47, Folder: January 1993.

405 **managed to sneak off for a toke**: Author interview with Cameron Sears, May 2, 2024.

406 **"companies with a conscience"**: Mary Barbara Scott and Howard Rothman, *Companies with a Conscience*, 1992.

406 **Bloomingdale's sold fifteen hundred**: Nick Ravo, "Grateful Ties," *New York Times*, July 26, 1992, Section 9, 6.

406 **Lithuanian[s] . . . in tie-dye**: This quirky bit of music and politics is memorialized in the 2012 documentary *The Other Dream Team*, directed by Marius A. Markevicius.

406 **"This is the church's music"**: Scully, *Living with the Dead*, 336.

408 **"someone who doesn't give a shit about the Grateful Dead"**: Author interview with Dennis McNally, May 9, 2024.

408 **"Bonds homers, foghorn blows"**: Marc Sandalow, "Record Crowd Sees Giants Win Home Opener," *San Francisco Chronicle*, April 13, 1993.

408 **"bad architecture and old whores"**: Variations on this quote appear across the internet. This version, which mirrors press clips and McNally's memory, seems the closest to Garcia's actual words.

409 **"made him supremely happy"**: Jackson, *Garcia*, 441.

409 **"Guess Who's Getting Married?"**: Paul Liberatore, "Guess Who's Getting Married?" *Marin Independent Journal*, Feb. 12, 1994, 1.

410 **Grisman performed**: Jackson, *Garcia*, 430.

410 **"There was no tie-dye"**: No byline, "Grateful Wed," *People*, Feb. 28, 1994.

410 **TVs and computer games occupied him**: McNally, *Long Strange Trip*, 607.

411 **"in alarming health"**: Blair Jackson and David Gans, "It Was the Tour from Hell," *Salon*, Dec. 6, 2015.

411 **"not the same this year"**: Carol DeMare, "Deadheads' Mellow Tune Turns Violent," *Times Union* (Albany), June 22, 1995.

412 **"How did we let it get this crazy?"**: Lesh, *Searching for the Sound*, 316.

412 **injuring more than a hundred**: David Bauder, Associated Press, "Bad Trip," *Journal-Courier* (Jacksonville, Ill.), July 13, 1995.

413 **"It was a spiritually challenging time"**: Author interview with Cameron Sears, May 2, 2024.

413 **"to close out the tour"**: Mark Caro and Graeme Zielinski, "Fans of Dead Revel in Usual Weirdness," *Chicago Tribune*, July 10, 1995.

413 **"There's never been a thought to do that"**: Ibid.

CHAPTER 18: "ANY OTHER DAY THAT'S EVER BEEN"

417 **brought him home**: Dr. Randy Baker, quoted in Greenfield, *Dark Star*, 321.

418 **"he knew he didn't have long"**: Greenfield, *Dark Star*, 324.

418 **"something possibly, slightly alarming about it"**: David Browne, "Grateful Dead's Robert Hunter on Jerry's Final Days," *Rolling Stone*, March 11, 2015.

418 **"also had a terrible problem"**: Wire reports, "A Genius and a Junkie," *Washington Post*, Aug. 11, 1995.

418 **"spirit personified of whatever is muddy river country"**: Dylan's statement, which was widely distributed, can be found at visionsofdylan.blogspot.com/2017/08/the-perfect-eulogy-from-dylan-to-jerry.html.

488 | NOTES

418 **"Come on in, says Bill":** Steven A. Chin, "Garcia Tribute Draws Thousands," *San Francisco Examiner,* Aug. 14, 1995.

420 **"I've got something!":** Robert Hunter, Letter to Garcia, August 1996, copy at UCSC Special Collections, Grateful Dead Records, History, Series 1, Box 1, Folder: "Biographical: Robert Hunter's letter to Garcia," August 1996.

420 **"to legions of the dead":** Robert Hunter, "An Elegy for Jerry," Aug. 11, 1995, UCSC Special Collections, Grateful Dead Records, History, Series 1, Box 1.

EPILOGUE

423 **led away in tears:** Joel Selvin, *Fare Thee Well,* 32.

423 **creating a San Francisco museum:** UCSC, Grateful Dead Records, Series 3, Business Records, Box 138, Folders of meeting minutes from 1995 and 1996.

424 **what Mountain Girl called the "rennet":** Author interview with Carolyn Garcia, March 17, 2022.

425 **"May Be the Largest Movement":** Larry Buchanan, Quoctrung Bui, and Jugal K. Patel, "Black Lives Matter May Be the Largest Movement in U.S. History," July 3, 2020.

427 **"justice in all its flavors":** Author interview with Dave Stever, April 25, 2024.

428 **Weir gamely took the torch:** John Mayer and Bob Weir, interviewed on *CBS Sunday Morning,* June 12, 2016.

429 **"made those songs new every time":** Nick Meriwether, email to author, Jan. 9, 2025.

431 **"will be part of that discussion as well":** Bob Weir, remarks upon receiving the Kennedy Center Honors, U.S. Department of State, Dec. 7, 2024.

432 **"to be patient and joyful":** Sara Ruppenthal Katz, remarks at the Bluegrass Hall of Fame, March 30, 2024.

INDEX

Page numbers in *italics* indicate illustrations.

Abbey, Edward, 316
Abruzzi, William, 218
Ace (Weir), 312, 317
"Ace," 76
"acid rock," xvi, 145, 167
Acid Tests, 60, 73, 75, 76–77, 80–81,
    83–84, 87, 90–91, 108, 110–11
Adams, Carolyn "Mountain Girl"
    on Altamont free concert, 226
    on Bear after release from jail, 287
    on Browning, 70
    Cassady and, 67–68
    children of, 92, 216, 236, 304, 349–50,
        409, 419, 425
    drugs and, 71, 92, 311
    in Egypt, 325
    Garcia and, 82, *86*, 109, 140, 212–13,
        298–99, 345–46, 349–50, 367, 369,
        403
    Garcia's addiction and death of father, 7
    Garcia's funeral and, 419
    on Garcia's relationship with mother,
        265
    Kesey and, 77–78
    Koons and, 308, 419, 423
    return to US of, 109
    on touring, 307
Adams, Lee, 25–26
Adams, Rebecca, 379–80
Adler, Lou, 143–44
AIDS, 375–76, 382–83
Alameda Times-Star, 394
Albert, Stew, 204
Alembic, 276, 279, 299, 302

Ali, Muhammad, 156, 268
"Alligator," 151, 152, 163, 166–67, 172, 200
Allman Brothers Band, 247, 289, 291–92
All the Little Live Things (Stegner), 84–85
Altamont free concert, 202, 222–27, 229–
    31
Altman, Billy, 314
American Beauty, 228, 253, 254–60, 261,
    263, 303, 314, 322, 391
Andersen, Lee, 47–48
"And We Bid You Goodnight," 232–33,
    305, 333
Ansorge, Sally, 357
Anthem of the Sun, 163–68, 233
Aoxomoxoa, 211–12, 233, 314
The Aquarian Weekly, 418
"Arabia," 409
Astra, 321
Atlantic Records, 283
"Attics of My Life," 259
Aykroyd, Dan, 333
Azzara, Frankie, 299

Babbs, Ken, 62, 66, 71, 72–73, 109, 283
Bach, Damon, 125
Baez, Joan, 36, 198, 216, 343, 345, 375
Balin, Marty, 95
Barlow, John Perry
    computers and, 401, 402
    on Dead displaying emotions, 392
    on "Victim or the Crime," 373–74
    Weir and, 46, 256, 316–17, 321
Beach, Scott, 375
Beach Boys, 220

490 | INDEX

"Beat It On Down the Line," 129
Beatles, 38–39, 199, 203
Beatniks, 12–13, 14–15
Beats, 11–13
Becker, Dave, 394
Belopolsky, Herman, 293
Benjamin, Walter, 53
Ben & Jerry's Cherry Garcia, 380–81, 427
Berio, Luciano, 50
Berkeley Barb, 113, 172–73, 204
Berkeley Daily Gazette, 69, 204
Berkeley Folk Music Festival (1962),
    xv–xvi, 33–34
Berry, Chuck, 19
"The Berry Feast" (Snyder), 14, 18
"Bertha," 272
"Betty Boards," 276
Bicycle Day, 53
Big Brother and the Holding Company
    in Haight-Ashbury, 137
    at Human Be-In, 117
    at Monterey International Pop Festival,
        144, 145
    New Riders and, 213
    at Olompali, 104
    at Trips Festival, 80
Big Rock Candy Mountain (Stegner), 61
"Birdsong," 265–66, 272, 273, 290, 375,
    390, 418
"Black Muddy River," 418
Black Panther Party for Self-Defense,
    133–34, 176, 205, 206, 266–67
"Black Peter," 242–43, 287, 376, 420
"Black-Throated Wind," 316–17
Blowouts, 178–79
bluegrass music, 32, 40, 41, 308–10
Blues Brothers, 333
Blues for Allah, 313–14
"Blues for Allah," 314, 315
Blues Project, 144
Blue Unicorn, 56
Boarding House club shows, 309–10
Boar's Head Coffeehouse (San Carlos), 31
Bob Dylan, 74
bohemians/bohemianism, 13, 125–27, 133,
    379
Bonner, Robert C., 397–98
Boone, Graeme, 155
"Born Cross-Eyed," 165, 166, 172
"Box of Rain," 253, 255, 263, 418

Brady, Matt, 8
Brand, Stewart, 77, 78, 80, 194–96,
    359–60, 402
Breen, Benjamin, 53
Brightman, Candace, 276
British Columbia Trips Festival, 105
"Brokedown Palace," 258, 263, 391–92,
    396, 418
Bronson, Charles, 267
Brown, Jerry, 328–29
Brown, Pat, 88, 89–90, 107–8, 110
Browning, Page, 70, 72, 78
Bruce, Lenny, 32–33
Bugliosi, Vince, 221
Built to Last, 373–74
Burroughs, William S., 11, 12
Burton, John, 206
Bush, George H. W., 337, 383, 384, 385

Caen, Herb, 12
Cahill, Tom, 147
California School of Fine Arts (later San
    Francisco Art Institute), 11, 17, 20
Callahan, Mat, 198–99
Campbell, Joseph, xvii, 366, 386–87
"Candyman," 257, 274–75
Cantor-Jackson, Betty, 238, 276, 321
Carmichael, Stokley, 276
Carousel Ballroom, 168–70, 171–73
Carr, Lucien, 11–12
Carter, Jimmy, 337–38, 339
"Casey Jones," 210, 244–45, 260, 328
Cassady, Neal
    Carolyn Adams and, 67–68
    at Dead's Straight Theater gig, 158–59
    death of, 170–71
    Kerouac and, 66
    marijuana and, 71
    as Moriarty in *On the Road*, 16
    Pranksters's cross country trip, 65–66
"Cassidy," 317
Cats Under the Stars (JGB), 312
"Caution (Do Not Stop on Tracks)," 167, 172
Chapman, Dorothy, 290
Charlatans, 104
Chateau, 25, 28, 44
Chavez, Cesar, 178
Chicago Tribune, 193
"China Cat Sunflower," 152, 171, 212, 393
"China Doll," 284, 303

INDEX | 491

Chords (band), 20

Christgau, Robert, 214, 295, 321–22

Christopher, George, 100

Church of Unlimited Devotion
("Family"), 353

Ciardi, John, 15

City Lights Bookstore/Booksellers, 14

civil rights movement, 177–80. *See also*
Ali, Muhammad; Black Panther
Party; Jackson State University; King,
Martin Luther, Jr.

Clay v. United States (1971), 268

Clements, Vassar, 309–10

Clemons, Clarence, 406

Cliffords, Bill (grandfather), 5, 7, 8

Cliffords, Tillie "Nan" (grandmother), 5,
7–8, 37

Clinton, Bill, 400–401, 405–6, 418

Cobain, Kurt, 371

Cohen, Ben, 381

"Cold Rain and Snow," 94, 129, 345–46

Coleman, Ornette, 406

Columbia Daily Spectator, 181

Columbia University uprising, 180,
181–82

"Comes a Time," 274

"Coming Back to Me," 105

communes, 102–4

computers, 194, 196, 401, 402

Connolly, John, 137

Connors, Chuck, 93

Constanten, Tom (T.C.), 164, 209, 210,
233–34

counterculture. *See also* Diggers; Haight-
Ashbury; hippies; Thompson,
Hunter S.

Altamont and, 227

basic facts about, xvii–xix, 123, 127–28,
135, 432–33

Berkeley Barb, 113, 172–73, 204

bohemianism and, 125, 126–27, 379

changes in, 292

as consuming self, 296

contemporary, xix, 424, 425–32

Dead as embodiment of, 322

Dead as "rennet" of, 424

Dead during Reagan-Bush era, 341–42,
343–44, 346, 381–82, 385–86

Dead's arrests and, 161

as defined by act, not by product, 155–56

diversity of groups and individuals, xviii

drugs as part of, 310, 424–25

film industry and, 270

Garcia in early phases of, 126–27

health food movement, 283–84

Human Be-In and, 121

literature and, 270–71

in mid-1970s, 315–16

New Journalism and, 140

in 1990s, 398–400

Nixon and, 191

Peoples Temple and Jones, 330–31

politics and, 125–26

Reagan and, 338, 339

Roszak and, xviii–xix, 123–25

Sometimes a Great Notion and, 64

violence and, 297

White Noise, 348

Coyote, Peter
on communal living, 103
on Dead, 132, 168
on Diggers ethos, 131–32
on failure of counterculture, 425
on Human Be-In, 115, 119, 120
Snyder and, 430

Cranston, Alan, 373

"Crazy Fingers," 314

"Cream Puff War," 129

Creedence Clearwater Revival, 206, 215

Crosby, Stills and Nash, 213, 238

The Crying of Lot 49 (Pynchon), 96–97

"Cryptical Envelopment," 166, 171, 182

"Cumberland Blues," 238, 242, 243

Cutler, Sam, 222, 289, 293

cyberspace, 401–2

Daily Californian, 198, 206

Daily News, 180

Daley, Richard, 192–93, 194

Dana Morgan's music store (Palo Alto), 35

"Dancing in the Street," 119, 153, 320

"Dark Hollow," 375

"Dark Star," 153–56, 171, 200–201, 217,
231–32, 233, 237, 247, 283, 333, 393,
395, 396

Davis, Miles, 248

Davis, Tom, 208–9, 327–28

Dawson, John, 213–14, 255

"Days Between," 404

Dead & Company, 427–29, 430

492 | INDEX

Deadheads, *388*
 change in attitude of, 411
 injuries to and deaths of, 410–11, 412
 journalism and, 356–57
 number of, at concerts, 374, 412
 ploys to get tickets, 376
 politics and contemporary, 426
 subgroups of, 352–56
 The Well and, 361
Dead Relix, 357
Dead Set, 349
"Deal," 272
"Death Don't Have No Mercy," 94, 232–33
"Deep Elem Blues," 38
DeLillo, Don, 347–48
The Des Moines Register, 292
"Desolation Row" (Dylan), 364
Didion, Joan, 139–40, 148, 270
Diga, 312
Diggers
 Altamont free concert and, 223
 basic facts about, 118–19
 Dead and, 141
 ethos of, 131–32
 Free Store, 131–32, 134
 politics and, 118, 131
 during Summer of Love, 148
Dillard, Annie, 316
"Dire Wolf," 210, 238, 240, 241, 242, 243, 412
dissent, trajectory and contours of, 124, 125–27
Dog Soldiers (Stone), 316
Dohrn, Bernardine, 221
"Doin' That Rag," 210, 212
DownBeat, 145–46
Downey, John, 24
drugs. *See also* LSD
 arrests at Dead concerts, 397–98
 "Casey Jones" and, 244, 245
 Dead and, 233, 234–37, 303, 307, 311, 411
 Garcia and, 19–20, 311, 324, 340, 350–52, 359–60, 395, 403
 Godchauxes and, 340–41
 in Haight-Ashbury, 136, 139, 140, 146
 Mickey Hart and, 272
 heroin, 311, 324, 340, 350–52, 395
 marijuana, 19, 70–71, 72, 78, 92, 160–61, 310

Mydland and, 389, 390
 as part of counterculture, 310, 424–25
 Reagans and, 359–60
"Drums," 197, 396
Dukakis, Mike, 384
Duncan, Robert, 18
Dunne, Steve, 35
Dupree's Diamond News, 357, 397
Dylan, Bob
 albums by, 74, 363
 American Beauty and, 257
 basic facts about, 73
 Dead and, 95–96
 on Garcia, 418
 place in American music of, 363
 shows with Dead, 363–64
 "Truckin'" and, 261

Eagleton, Thomas, 293–94
Earth Day, 270, 292, 399
"Easy to Love You," 389
"Easy Wind," 243–44
Egypt, 324–27
Eisenhart, Mary, 361
election of 1968, 182–83, 189–94, 203
election of 1972, 293–94
election of 1980, 337–39
election of 1984, 358–59
election of 1988, 383–84
The Electric Kool-Aid Acid Test (Wolfe), 65, 71, 78
"The Eleven," 171, 232
"Elizabeth Cotten style" of playing, 35
Emergency Crew, 56
Empire Burlesque (Dylan), 363
The End of History and the Last Man (Fukuyama), 399
Englishtown, New Jersey, concert, 322–23
environmentalism, 269–70. *See also* Earth Day; Fonda, Jane
"Estimated Prophet," 317, 320–21
Europe, concerts in, 279–81, 303
Evergreen Review, 18
"Eyes of the World," 284, 294, 305

Falk, Bennett, 361
Farber, David, 192
"Far from Me," 389
"The Faster We Go, the Rounder We Get," 166

INDEX | **493**

Fear and Loathing in Las Vegas
(Thompson), 271
"Feel Like a Stranger," 317
Feinstein, Dianne, 332
feminism, 269, 275–76
Ferlinghetti, Lawrence, 12–13, 14, 15, 18
Festival Express, 250–52, 265
Filo, John, 249
Finkel, Shelly, 289
"Fire on the Mountain," 326, 393
Fleetwood Mac, 234, 236
Focus on Sanity (TV series), 54
Folger, Abigail, 219
folk music, 31, 33–34
Fonda, Jane, 116, 341, 399
"Forever Young" (Dylan), 368
Franken, Al, 327, 328, 431
"Franklin's Tower," 313, 315
freedom, 97–99, 111, 127–28, 194–95,
239, 338–39, 344, 384–85, 400,
402
Free Speech Movement, 69, 93, 98
Freudiger, Larry, 121
Frey, John, 177
"Friend of the Devil," 255, 358, 409
"From Egypt with Love" Winterland
show, 327
"From the Heart of Me," 341
From the Mars Hotel, 303
Frye, Marquette, 89
Frye, Rena, 89
Frye, Ronald, 89
Frykowski, Wojciech, 219
Fukuyama, Francis, 399

Gamble, Mark, 351
Gans, David, 361
Garcia, Annabelle, 216, 236, 349–50,
409, 419
Garcia, Carolyn. *See* Adams, Carolyn
"Mountain Girl"
Garcia, Clifford "Tiff" (brother)
drug use by, 20
Garcia's loss of middle finger and, 6
Garcia's music and, 19
living with grandparents, 8, 9
as "loose Catholic," 5
in Marine corporations, 10
mother and, 10, 264
nickname of, 5

Garcia, Heather, 38, 39–40, 82, 106, 213,
368–69
Garcia, Jerry, 2, 306, 366, 422
Acid Tests and, 83
in Army, 23–24
arrests of, 235, 236–37, 262, 288–89,
293, 351–52, 358
art and, 9, 11, 18–19
on Beatles, 39
birth and childhood of, 4–8, 9, 10–11, 20
on Black Panthers, 266–67
Bruce's defense against obscenity
charge and, 33
on George H. W. Bush, 384
Campbell and, 386–87
children of, 38, 39–40, 82, 106, 213,
216, 236, 298, 304, 349–50, 368–69,
403, 405, 409, 419, 425
on Deadheads, 357
in Dead's Haight-Ashbury house, 106,
141
death and funeral, 417, 418–20
on death of Pigpen, 286
drugs and, 359–60, 395, 403
education of, 9, 10–11
fame and, 370–72
finances of, 30, 350, 370, 381
on freedom, 98
The Grateful Dead Movie and, 318
Grisman and, 40, 310, 408–9
health of, 9, 364–65, 367, 395, 411, 417
heroin and, 311, 324, 340, 350–52
on Human Be-In, 115
ice cream named after, 380–81
on importance of Dead, 344, 345
as jabberwocky composer, 30
Klein and, 323–24, 328, 350
Koons and, 307, 405, 410, 417
last call to Hunter, 418
on living in Haight-Ashbury, 141
as "loose Catholic," 5
LSD and, 54–55, 101
marriages of, 22, 36–38, 81–82, 106,
345, 346, 409–10
Matheson and, 369, 403, 405
Meier and, 28, 30, 31–32, 36, 37, 403–5
memoir, 417–18
Mountain Girl and, 82, 86, 109, 140,
212–13, 298–99, 345–46, 349–50,
367, 369, 403

494 | INDEX

Garcia, Jerry (*cont'd*):
  movies and, 340
  Mydland and, 392
  Nixon and, 191, 300–301
  at Olompali, 101, 103
  on "People's Park Bail Ball," 206
  politics and, 98–99, 126–27, 142–43,
      199, 206, 266
  on power of art and of government, 127
  Pranksters' trip across America, 65
  rainforest protection and, 383
  on Reagan, 343, 344
  relationship with mother, 264–65
  On the Road and, 16, 17
  San Francisco Giants and, 407–8
  Speegle's death in car accident and,
      25–27
  on Summer of Love, 148–49
  television appearances of, 147–48, 209,
      260–61, 327–28
  on Vietnam War, 142
  Vonnegut's work and, 208–9
Garcia, Jerry: characteristics of, 6, 130,
      394–95
  charm, 43
  craving for community, 34–35, 105, 267
  inner versus outer self, xvi
  inquisitiveness, 10
  optimism, 344
  self-assurance, 30
  tensions and contradictions of, 28
Garcia, Jerry: and music, *278, 416. See also*
      Grateful Dead; Warlocks
  Acid Tests, 75, 81
  Airplane and, 105
  on Altamont free concert, 225, 226–27
  Anthem of the Sun and, 165, 168
  "Attics of My Life," 259
  banjo playing, 31
  at Berkeley Folk Music Festival (1962),
      xv–xvi, 33–34
  "Black Peter," 242–43
  Bluegrass Music Hall of Fame and
      Museum, 431
  Blues for Allah and, 313–14
  "Brokedown Palace" and, 258
  "Casey Jones" and, 244, 245
  Cassady's death and, 171
  Chords band, 20
  Coleman and, 406

craving for community and, 34–35, 105
"Cumberland Blues" and, 242
on "Dark Star," 155
on Dead at Monterey International Pop
    Festival, 146
Dead shows with Dylan and, 363–64
Dead split and, 185, 186–87, 188–89
duets with Sara, 38
Egypt and, 326, 327
"Eyes of the World" and, 284
Festival Express and, 252
first Dead record contract and, 128–29,
    130
first instrument, 19
first "teachers," 19
folk music and, 31
guitars, 19, 25, 28, 213, 214
Hedrick and, 19
on house band at Babbs's, 73
at Human Be-In, 119
"I Know You Rider" and, 95
imitation of others' styles, 34
on importance of music, 206–7
JGB, 311–12, 368
at Keystone Berkeley, 286
last performance by, 413–15
Leicester and, 31, 34, 35
on length of songs, 52
on *Live/Dead*, 232–33
Maples Pavilion concert songs and,
    284–85
on McKernan, 44
Mother McCree's, 45–47
on naming of Dead, 57
New Riders and, 214
"New Speedway Boogie" and, 230
Old & In the Way, 309–10
at open mic events, 31
opinions about other musicians, 377–78
ownership of music, 251
Playboy After Dark performance, 210
practicing, 28, 31
return to, after coma, 367–68
"Ripple" and, 257–58
road trip with Rothman, 40
on singing, 238–39
songwriting with Hunter, 30–31, 34–35,
    36, 253–54, 256
Springsteen and, 377–79
style of, 40–41

INDEX | **495**

on *Terrapin Station*, 320–321
on touring, 223
on Trips Festival, 79
at Trouper's Hall concert (1966), 94
"Truckin'" and, 259, 260, 261
"Uncle John's Band" and, 240
"Viola Lee Blues" and, 95
on Warlocks' potential, 51
with Wildwood Boys, 40
Winterland final show, 333
at Woodstock, 217
Garcia, Jose "Joe" (father), 2, 4–5, 6–7
Garcia, Keelin Noel, 369, 403, 405
Garcia, Ruth "Bobbie" (mother)
ability to deal with Garcia, 20–21
death of, 263–64, 265
death of Joe and, 7
Garcia's first instrument and, 19
Garcia's loss of middle finger and, 6
marriage of, 4–5
relationship with Jerry, 264
Ruppenthal and, 37
second marriage of, 10–11
Garcia, Theresa "Trixie," 304, 349–50, 425
Garrison, Jim, 236–37
gay rights, 203
Georgia Sea Island Singers, 34
Ginsberg, Allen
basic facts about, 12
Democratic Convention (1968), 192, 193
"First Party at Ken Kesey's with Hell's
   Angels," 72
"Howl," 14–16, 18
at Human Be-In, 112, 114, 117, 118, 120
San Francisco Renaissance and, 13
union of Beats and Renaissance, 14–15
Gitlin, Todd, 193, 248
Gleason, Ralph, 18, 107, 120, 130–31, 162,
   170, 174, 183, 222–23, 227, 229
"Gloria," 52
Godchaux, Donna Jean
departure from Dead of, 341
drugs and, 340–41
in Europe, 280
The Grateful Dead Movie and, 318
Keith and Donna and, 312
Pigpen's health and, 273
on *Saturday Night Live*, 328
Wake of the Flood and, 294
Winterland final show, 333

Godchaux, Keith
departure from Dead of, 341
drugs and, 340–41
in Europe, 280
Keith and Donna and, 312
Pigpen's health and, 273–74
Wake of the Flood and, 294
"Goin' Down the Road Feeling Bad," 252,
   318
Goldberg, Arthur, 92
Golden Gate Park, *xiv*
"The Golden Road (to Ultimate
   Devotion)," 129
The Golden Road (Jackson), 357, 369, 390,
   397
"Good Lovin'," 95, 305, 328, 364
"Good Morning, Little Schoolgirl," 120, 171
Gore, Al, 405
Go to Heaven, 389
Gottlieb, Lou, 102
Graham, Bill
Acid Test Graduation and, 110–11
basic facts about, 168, 173
Dead and, 77, 169, 248, 315
in Egypt, 325
Helms and, 136
Kesey's eulogy of, 395–96
Summer Jam and, 290
Summer of Love concerts, 157–58
Trips Festival and, 79
Winterland final show, 333
Grant, Laird, 19, 20, 21
Grateful Dead, 42, 150. *See also specific
   members; specific songs*
as academic subject, 379–80, 427, 431
Acid Tests, 60, 73, 75, 76–77, 80–81,
   83–84, 108, 111
after Garcia's death, 423
Allman Brothers Band and, 247
Altamont and, 222–27
as alternative to increasing violence
   and inequity of American life, 198
arrests of, 160–61, 235, 236–37, 262,
   288–89, 293, 351–52, 358
attitude toward women of, 140, 275–76,
   277
Bear's return to, 287–88, 301
as bohemians, 127
breakup of, 308–10
Campbell and, 386

496 | INDEX

Grateful Dead (*cont'd*):
charity foundation, 346–47, 429–30
Clinton and, 405–6
Columbia University uprising and, 181–82
as counterculture oasis during Reagan era, 341–42, 343–44, 346, 381–82, 385–86
as counterculture's embodiment, 322
country music and, 237–38
"Dark Star" as signature improvisational vehicle, 153–56
Miles Davis and, 248
as defined by act, not by product, 155
departure from San Francisco of, 174
departure of Godchauxes, 341
development of musical signature of, xvi, 97–98
Diggers and, 132
drugs and, 140, 152, 209, 233, 234–37, 303, 307, 311, 397–98, 411
Dylan interpreted by, 95–96
emotions and, 392
"family" members, 76
finances of, 168, 212, 231, 246, 265, 281, 287–88, 318, 319, 360, 364, 369, 396, 397
firing of Weir and Pigpen, 184–89, 200
first record, 107
first record contract, 128–29
Garcia as leader of, 43–44
Garcia as public face of, 130–31
Garcia on importance of, 344, 345
Garcia's car crash and, 348–49
Garcia's heroin use and performances, 350–51
Keith Godchaux's addition to, 273–74
Graham and, 77, 169, 248, 315
in Haight-Ashbury, 106, 122, 140–41
Lenny Hart and, 246–47
Mickey Hart and, 159
having own record company, 282–83
Headstone Productions and Carousel Ballroom, 168–70, 171–73
during hiatus, 308–10, 311–13
Hunter's hiatus from, 151
Kennedy Center Honors, 430–31
Kreutzmann-Garcia first meeting, 32, 48
machismo sensibility of, 275
managers, 94

MTV and, 370
musical repertoire expansion, 94–95
Mydland's replacement, 392, 393–94
naming of, 56–57, 361–63
New Riders and, 214
at Olompali, 100–102, 103, 104, 106
in *Petula*, 141–42
Pigpen's final appearance with, 286
politics and, 90–91, 103, 104, 126–27, 141, 163, 192, 198, 284–85
poster art and, 136
Reasoner and, 147–48
reassembly of, 200, 209
reinvigoration of, after Garcia's coma, 368, 369–70
Rock and Roll Hall of Fame and, 406
on *Saturday Night Live*, 327–28
as stay-at-home studio group, 307, 308
style of, xvi, 214
Weir-Garcia first meeting, 46–47
Grateful Dead albums
American Beauty, 228, 253, 254–60, 261
Anthem of the Sun, 163–68, 233
Aoxomoxoa, 211–12, 233
Blues for Allah, 313–14
Built to Last, 373–74
In the Dark, 370, 389, 396
Dead Set, 349
Europe '72, 280
Go to Heaven, 389
The Grateful Dead, 129–30
History of the Grateful Dead, Vol. 1 (Bear's Choice), 287–88, 301
Live/Dead, 231–33, 246
From the Mars Hotel, 303
Reckoning, 349
Shakedown Street, 340
Terrapin Station, 240, 320–21, 322
Wake of the Flood, 294–95
Workingman's Dead, 228, 238–45, 255, 263, 303
"Grateful Dead Endurance Tour '77," 319
The Grateful Dead Movie, 318
Grateful Dead Records, 282–83, 313, 321
Grateful Dead shows
barriers between band and audience, 356, 411
benefits, 141, 282–84, 341, 375–76
bond with audience during, 83–84
British Columbia Trips Festival, 105

INDEX | **497**

with Dylan, 363–64
in Egypt, 324–27
in Europe, 279–81, 303
Festival Express, 250–52
first public playing of, 73
Halloween (1991), 395–96
at Human Be-In, 119
in late 1960s, 196–98
law enforcement at, 397–98
Maples Pavilion, 284–85
at Matrix Club, 95
in mid-1970s, 315, 318–19, 356
Monterey International Pop Festival,
    144, 145–46
in New Orleans, 234–37
at North Face opening, 106–7
number of ticketed, xv
as opener for Joplin, 211
"People's Park Bail Ball," 206
Playboy After Dark, 209–10
Revolutionary Intercommunal Day of
    Solidarity and, 267
Rio Nido, 152–53
San Francisco Giants opener (1993),
    407–8
Straight Theater, 158–59
structure of, xvii
Summer Jam, 289–92
taping of, by fans, 353–55
"the tour from hell" (Summer Tour),
    410–15
Trips Festival, 79, 80
Trouper's Hall (1966), 94
Winterland, 304–5, 307, 333
at Woodstock, 215–17
Great American Music Hall show, 314–15
"Greatest Story Ever Told," 272
Greek Theatre, *336*
Greene, Richard, 308–10
Greenfield, Robert, 350–51
GRID (Gay-Related Immune Deficiency),
    374–75
Griffin, Rick, 136, 212, 295
Grisman, David, 40, 258, 286, 308–10,
    408–9, 419
Grogan, Emmett, 136, 223
Gutierrez, Gary, 318, 370

Hagen, Jon, 236
Haggard, Merle, 217

Haight-Ashbury. *See also* Diggers
    "anthem albums" of, 39
    Dead house in, 106, *122*, 141
    drugs in, 136, 139, 140, 146
    hippies in, 137–38
    life in, 134–40, 146–49
Hallinan, Patrick, 110
Halloween show (1991), 395–96
A Hard Day's Night, 39
Hard Road, 199
"Hard to Handle," 287
Harlan, John, 268
Harrington Street (Garcia), 417–18
Harrison, George, 146–47
Hart, Gary, 383
Hart, Lenny, 157, 246–47, 266, 280
Hart, Mickey, *366*
    Anthem of the Sun and, 164
    arrest of, as Summer Wind, 235, 236–37
    basic facts about, 157
    Blues for Allah and, 314
    Campbell and, 386–87
    car accident, 319
    on Dead as more than music, xvii
    Dead split and, 186
    departure from Dead of, 272–73
    Diga and, 312
    as member of Dead, 159, 182
    mental health of, 271–72
    rainforest protection and, 383
    in rehab, 279
    during Summer of Love, 157–58
    on *Terrapin Station*, 321
    Winterland shows and, 304, 305
Hartman, Francis J., 293
Hassinger, Dave, 105, 129, 163, 164–65, 167
Haxby, Faye, 62
Hayden, Casey, 276
Hayden, Tom
    on assassination of King, 180
    election of 1968 and, 191
    FBI and, 180–81
    on New Left, 177
    People's Park, 205
    Port Huron Statement, 116
    on protesting, 269
    Rock for Life benefit, 341
    on Tet Offensive, 178
Headstone Productions, 168–70, 171–73
health food movement, 283–84

498 | INDEX

Healy, Dan, 165, 285, 287, 290
Hearst, Patty, 296
Heart of Gold Band, 341
Hedrick, Wally, 14, 17, 18–19
Hefner, Hugh, 209
Heider, Wally, 254
"Hell in a Bucket," 389
Hells Angels, 71–72, 118, 223, 224–25
Helms, Chet, 136, 138
"Help on the Way," 313, 315
Hendrix, Jimi, 144, 145, 146, 217–18, 265
"Here Comes Sunshine," 284
heroin, 311, 324, 340, 350–52, 395
The Hero with a Thousand Faces
     (Campbell), 386
"He's Gone," 280–81, 285, 295, 319–20,
     358, 393
"Hey Little One," 94
Hickey, Andrew, 361
Hicks, James F., 291
"Highest Grateful Dead Concert in the
     World," 358
High Fidelity, 167
"High Time," 240–41
Hilburn, Robert, 363
Hinton, Sam, xvi, 34
hippies
     described, 56, 98
     in Haight-Ashbury, 137–38
     Human Be-In and, 114
     Manson Family as, 220
     as media construct, 148
     Reagan and, 98
A History of Rock Music (Hickey), 361
*History of the Grateful Dead, Vol. 1 (Bear's
     Choice)*, 287–88, 301
Hoffman, Abbie, 116, 191–92
Hofmann, Albert, 53
Hog Farm, 102
Hollander, John, 15
Hollingworth, Ambrose, 115
homosexuality, 332, 372–75, 400–401
Hornsby, Bruce, 392–93, 394, 395, 411
house bands, 72–73
"How Do You Feel," 105
"Howl" (Ginsberg), 14–16, 18
Howl and Other Poems (Ginsberg), 15–16
Human Be-In, 112, 114–21
Humphrey, Hubert, 193, 194
Huncke, Herbert, 11, 12

Hunter, Meredith, 225–26, 230
Hunter, Robert
     as Acid Test attendee, 76
     on Altamont free concert, 229–30
     on *American Beauty*, 263
     "Attics of My Life" and, 259
     basic facts about, 28–30
     "Black Peter" and, 242–43
     Blues for Allah and, 313–14
     "Box of Rain" and, 253
     on "Candyman" and "Jack Straw," 274–75
     "Casey Jones" and, 245
     characteristics of, 152
     creative process and, 319–20
     "Cumberland Blues" and, 242
     Dylan and, 96
     "Easy Wind" and, 244
     at Garcia-Ruppenthal marriage, 22
     on Garcia's characteristics, 9–10
     Garcia's funeral and, 420
     "He's Gone" and, 280–81, 295
     hiatus from Dead of, 151
     Joplin and, 265–66
     last call from Garcia, 418
     living with Garcia in Palo Alto, 30
     LSD and, 54
     Maples Pavilion concert songs and,
          284, 285
     MK-ULTRA experiments and, 54
     "Ripple" and, 257–58
     Scientology and, 297
     "Ship of Fools" and, 295–96
     songs for Dead by, 151–52, 153–56, 404,
          405
     songwriting with Garcia, 30–31, 34–35,
          36, 253–54, 256
     "Sugar Magnolia" and, 255, 256
     "Truckin'" and, 259, 260
     "Uncle John's Band" and, 239–40

"I Know You Rider," 94–95, 152, 238, 392,
     393
"I'm a Hog for You, Baby," 94
In Concert Against AIDS, 382
individualism, 34, 103, 127–28, 310, 338, 339
"I Need a Miracle," 328
In the Dark, 370, 389, 396
"In the Midnight Hour," 79, 94, 152–53
"It's All Over Now, Baby Blue" (Dylan),
     95–96, 364

INDEX | 499

Jackson, Blair, 237, 357, 369, 390
Jackson, Rex, 236, 346–47
Jackson State University (Mississippi), 249–50
"Jack Straw," 274–75
Jagger, Mick, 222, 223, 227
James, Etta, 406
Jarnow, Jesse, 427
Jefferson Airplane
  Haight-Ashbury home of, 137
  Headstone Productions and Carousel Ballroom, 168–70, 172
  at Human Be-In, 117, 118
  Matrix Club and, 95
  at Monterey International Pop Festival, 144
  in New Orleans, 234
  "People's Park Bail Ball," 206
  San Francisco Sound/Scene and, 104–5
  Vietnam War protests, 93
  at Woodstock, 215
Jennings, Lois, 195–96
Jerry Garcia Band "JGB," 311–12, 368
Jerry Garcia/David Grisman, 409
Jobs, Steve, 196
Joe Garcia's bar, 4, 5
"Johnny B. Goode," 305
Johnson, Alvin, 108
Johnson, Lyndon Baines, 178–79
Johnson, Matthew, 108
Jonathan Livingston Seagull, 270–71
Jonestown and Jim Jones, 330–31
Joplin, Janis, 102, 137, 144, 211, 215, 265–66
jug band music, 41, 45–47

Kahn, John, 286, 308–10, 312
Kandel, Lenore, 14, 114, 117
"Katie Mae," 287
Kaukonen, Jorma, 353
Keith and Donna, 312
Kelley, Alton, 136, 261
Kennedy, Edward, 373
Kennedy, Robert, 182–83, 197
Kent State University, 248–49
Kepler's (Palo Alto), 25, 28, 36
Kerouac, Jack
  basic facts about, 11, 13
  Beatniks and, 12–13
  Cassady and, 66

coining and meaning of "the Beat generation," 12
  in *Evergreen Review*, 18
  return to San Francisco of, 13
  On the Road, 13, 16–18
  subjects written about, 14
  union of Beats and Renaissance, 14, 15
Kerr, Clark, 204
Kesey, Ken
  basic facts about, 61
  on computers, 194
  on Dead's playing, 83, 84
  death of son, 391
  in Egypt, 325, 326
  on everyone as artist, 73
  at Halloween show (1991), 395–96
  LSD and, 63
  marijuana and, 70–71, 72, 78
  Merry Pranksters, 70
  in Mexico, 91–92
  MK-ULTRA experiments and, 54
  Mountain Girl and, 77–78
  novels by, 62–63, 64
  Pranksters and, 64–67, 72
  return to US of, 108–9, 110, 111
  Stegner and, 61–62, 84–85
  as student of writing, 61–62
  Trips Festival and, 78, 79
Khalsa, Sat Santokh Singh, 169, 216
King, Freddie, 19
King, Martin Luther, Jr., 177–78, 179–80, 197, 276
Klein, Susan, 323–24, 328, 350
Kley, Heinrich, 320
Knickerbocker, Conrad, 64
"Knockin' on Heaven's Door," 375
Koons, Deborah, 307–8, 405, 410, 417, 419, 423
Kornfield, Artie. *See* Woodstock Music and Art Fair
Kramer, Michael, 34
Kreutzmann, Bill. *See also* Grateful Dead
  Anthem of the Sun and, 165
  arrest of, 235, 236–37
  basic facts about, 47–48, 299
  characteristics of, 165
  Egypt and, 326
  "Estimated Prophet" and, 321
  Garcia on, as drummer, 52
  Garcia's heroin use and, 351

500 | INDEX

Kreutzmann, Bill (*cont'd*):
Hart and, 158
on Hart at Winterland shows, 304, 305
at Human Be-In, 119
meeting with Garcia, 32, 48
Mother McCree's and, 47
at Olompali, 101
on *Playboy After Dark* performance, 209
with Warlocks, 48
Krippner, Stanley, 379
Krugman, Paul, 355

LaBianca, Leno, 219
LaBianca, Rosemary, 219
Lagin, Ned, 305, 312
Lambert, Gary, 237–38
Lang, Michael. *See* Woodstock Music and
Art Fair
Lang, Raymond, 198, 233
language, use of, 14–16, 18, 32–33
Larkspur, 212–13
"The Last Time," 396
Late Night with David Letterman, 260–61
Latinos, 269
Latvala, Dick, 355
Law, Cassidy, 317
Law, Eileen, 276
"Lazy River Road," 404
Leary, Timothy
Democratic Convention (1968) and, 192
escape from prison of, 269
at Human Be-In, 114, 115, 117, 118
LSD and, 54
Pranksters and, xviii, 66
Le Corsaire, 126
Leicester, Marshall, 31, 34, 35
Lemieux, David, 326, 424
Lennon, John, 199, 203
Lesh, Phil. *See also* Grateful Dead
on Acid Tests, 80
on Altamont free concert, 226
Anthem of the Sun and, 165, 166, 167, 168
arrests of, 235, 236–37, 288
basic facts about, 49–50, 253
"Box of Rain" and, 253
on Carousel Ballroom, 173
on changes in Haight-Ashbury, 148
characteristics of, 165
Constanten and, 233
"Cumberland Blues" and, 242

on Dead being own record company, 283
on Deadheads at concerts, 412
on Dead playing with Allman Brothers
Band, 247
Dead split and, 185, 186, 187, 188
death of, 430–31
Egypt and, 326–27
on Festival Express, 252
first Dead record contract and, 128,
129, 130
Garcia's KPFA interview and, 36
on Hart's departure, 272
at Human Be-In, 119
on "In the Midnight Hour" at Rio Nido,
152
McGee and, 299
naming of Dead, 56–57
at Olompali, 101, 104
Seastones, 312
"Seastones" and, 304–5
Warlocks and, 49, 50–51, 56
Lester, Richard, 141–42
"Let It Grow," 317
"Let Me Sing Your Blues Away," 295
Letterman, David, 260–61
Lewis, Huey, 51, 102, 378
Lewis, Noah, 95
"Liberty," 404
Live/Dead, 231–33, 246
Lloyd, Charles, 120
Loading Zone, 79, 80
"Looks Like Rain," 317
"Loose Lucy," 284
Lord, Sterling, 64
Loren, Richard, 324
Los Angeles Free Press, 81, 222
Los Angeles Times, 89, 397–98, 418
"Loser," 272
Los Lobos, 368
The Love Book (Kandel), 117
"Love Light," 210, 211, 217, 232, 233, 247,
406
LSD
Acid Tests, 60, 73, 75, 76–77, 80–81,
83–84, 87, 90–91, 108, 110–11
basic facts about, 52–54, 56
Dead and, 140, 152, 209, 307, 397–98
Garcia and, 54–55, 101
hippies and, 56
at house band parties, 73

at Human Be-In, 118, 119
Kesey and, 63
legality of, 69, 110

Magoo's Pizza Parlor (Menlo Park), 49
The Making of a Counter Culture (Roszak),
   123, 124
Malone, Joseph, 325
the Mamas and the Papas, 143, 144
"Mama Tried" (Haggard), 217
Manson, Charles, and "Family," 138–39,
   219–21, 223
Maples Pavilion concert, 284–85
Marcus, Greil, 224
Marcuse, Herbert, 124–25
marijuana, 19, 70–71, 72, 78, 92, 160–61,
   310
Marin Independent Journal, 409
Marsalis, Branford, 390, 406
Martin, Peter, 14
Matheson, Manasha, 369, 403, 405
Matrix Club (San Francisco), 95
Matthews, Bob, 45, 238
Matusiewicz, Ruth. *See* Garcia, Ruth
   "Bobbie" (mother)
Matusiewicz, Wally (stepfather), 10–11, 19
Mayer, John, 427–28
Mays, Willie, 407–8
McCartney, Paul, 143
McCarty, Francis, 110
McClanahan, Ed, 62, 230–31
McClure, Matthew, 360–61
McClure, Michael, 14, 15, 18, 114, 117, 427
McGee, Rosie
   arrest of, 160
   Dead European tour and, 279, 281
   entrance into Dead family, 76
   The Grateful Dead Movie and, 318
   in Haight-Ashbury, 140, 141
   Lesh and, 299
   at Olompali, 101
McGovern, George, 194, 293–94
McIntire, Jon, 172, 184, 236
McKee, J. Edwin, 156
McKernan, Phil, 44
McKernan, Ron "Pigpen." *See also*
   Grateful Dead
   Anthem of the Sun and, 164, 168
   Aoxomoxoa and, 211
   basic facts about, 44, 130

Dead split and, 185, 189
death of, 286
"Easy Wind" and, 243
in Europe, 280
final appearance with Dead, 286
firing of, from Dead, 184–89, 200
health of, 271, 273, 283
History of the Grateful Dead, Vol. 1 and,
   287–88, 301
"In the Midnight Hour," 79, 152, 153
Joplin and, 265
"Love Light" and, 232
LSD and, 52
Mother McCree's and, 45–46
at North Face opening, 107
"Operator" and, 257
reassembly of Dead, 200, 209
at Trouper's Hall concert (1966), 94
at Woodstock, 217
with Zodiacs, 45
McMahon, Regan, 357
McNally, Dennis, 275–76, 370, 404, 411,
   412, 413
"Me and My Uncle," 238
Meier, Barbara "Brigid"
   basic facts about, 27
   Garcia and, 28, 31–32, 36, 403–5
   Garcia's funeral and, 419
   Ruppenthal and, 37
   sixteenth birthday party, 30
Melody Maker, 371
Menlo College (Menlo Park), 48–49
Meriwether, Nicholas, 380, 427, 429
Merlis, Bob, 181–82
Merry Pranksters
   Adams as member of, 67–68
   cross-country trip by, 64–67
   Kesey and, 64–67, 70, 72
   Leary and, xviii, 66
   return to US of, 108–9
   Trips Festival and, 78–79
   at Woodstock, 215, 216
"Mexicali Blues," 274
Michaels, Lorne, 327–28
Mickey and the Hartbeats, 200
"Might as Well," 252
Milk, Harvey, 331–32
Miller, Henry, 18
Miller, Jeffrey, 249
Miller, Jim, 167

502 | INDEX

Millstein, Gilbert, 16
Mime Troupe, 77, 118–19
"Mississippi Half-Step Uptown
  Toodleoo," 305
MK-ULTRA, 54
Mondale, Walter, 358
"Money, Money," 303
The Monkey Wrench Gang (Abbey), 316
Monroe, Bill, 40
Monterey International Pop Festival,
  143–46
Monture, Rick, 354–55
"The Morality Gap at Berkeley"
  (Reagan), 93
Morgan, Dana, 48
Morley, Paul, 370–71
"Morning Dew," 119, 120, 130, 171
Morning Star, 102
Moscone, George, 331–32
Moscoso, Victor, 136
Mother McCree's Uptown Jug
  Champions, 45–47
"Mountain Dew," 119
Mountains and Rivers Without End
  (Snyder), 117
"Mountains of the Moon," 210
Mount Vernon Argus, 418
Mouse, Stanley, 113, 136, 245, 261
Mulford, Don, 133
Murger, Henry, 126
Murphy, Anne, 71–72
Murray, Bill, 209
music. *See also specific performers*
  at beginning of 1960s, 38
  folk and bluegrass in Bay Area, 31
  formation process of most bands, 51
  freedom in, 97–98
  Garcia on importance of, 206–7
  in mid-1970s, 316
  ownership of, 251
Mydland, Brent, 341, 343, 389–90, 392, 393

"the naked pole guy," 283
Nathan, Florence. *See* McGee, Rosie
The Nation, 231
Nelson, Dave, 22, 32, 36, 37, 45, 213
New Delhi River Band, 213–14
New Journalism, 139–40, 207
New Orleans, 234–37, *262*
"New Potato Caboose," 165, 166, 172

New Riders of the Purple Sage, 213–14,
  283, 333
"New Speedway Boogie," 229–31, 240,
  242, 320
Newton, Huey, 133, 177
The New Yorker, 355
The New York Times, 16, 64, 74, 214, 218,
  248, 275, 292, 375, 418, 425
The New York Times Book Review, 64
The New York Times Magazine, 12
Niagara Falls Gazette, 290
Nichols, Luther, 15
Nixon, Richard, 189–91, 248–49, 293–94,
  298, 300
"Not Fade Away," 305, 396
Novelli, Adele, 211
nuclear weapons, 372–73
Nugent, Kathy, 70

"Oh, Babe, It Ain't No Lie," 349, 376
Old & In the Way, 309–10
Olompali, 100–102, 103, 104, 106
Olsen, Keith, 321
One Flew Over the Cuckoo's Nest (Kesey),
  62–63, 77
"One More Saturday Night," 274
Ono, Yoko, 203
On the Road (Kerouac), 13, 16–18
"Operator," 257, 271
The Oracle, 113, 136, 147, 177
"The Other One," 163–64, 166, 171–72

Pagels, Elaine, 26
Palo Alto, 24–27, 28, 30, 44
Palo Alto Times, 37–38
"Parchman Farm," 94
Pareles, Jon, 275, 378–79
Parent, Steve, 219
Parish, Steve, 356, 417, 419
Passaro, Alan, 225–26
Paul Butterfield Blues Band, 74
peace movement, 34, 36, 372–73. *See also*
  Fonda, Jane; Hayden, Tom; student
  movement; Vietnam War, opposition
  to; Weatherman
Peace Trip, 93
"Peggy-O," 376
People magazine, 410
People's Park, 204, 205–6
Peoples Temple, 330–31

INDEX | 503

Perry, Helen Swick, 115, 118, 120
Petula, 141–42
Philadelphia Spectrum shows, 318, 356
The Philosophy of Modern Song (Dylan), 261
Pigpen. See McKernan, Ron
Pilgrim at Tinker Creek (Dillard), 316
Pirsig, Robert, 271
Plapowski, Dean, 56
"Plastic Fantastic Lover," 105
Playboy After Dark (television show),
  209–10
Playing in the Band (Gans), 361
"Playing in the Band," 272
politics
  contemporary Deadheads, 426
  counterculture and, 125–26
  Dead and, 90–91, 103, 104, 126–27,
    141, 163, 192, 198, 284–85, 405–6
  Diggers and, 118, 131
  Dylan and, 73
  Garcia and, 98–99, 142–43, 199, 206,
    266
  Port Huron Statement, 116–17
  during presidency of Reagan, 343
  technocracy and, 124
  Yippies and, 192
Poole, Buzz, 241, 244
Port Huron statement, 116–17
Prescott, Orville, 64
"Promised Land," 285, 290, 305
Proposition 13, 329–30
Pyat, Félix, 125–26
Pynchon, Thomas, 96–97, 270

"Quadlibet for Tenderfeet," 166
Quicksilver Messenger Service, 117, 118,
  144, 168, 172

The Rag, 121
Rakow, Ron, 168, 169, 173, 281–82, 283,
  300–301
"Ramble On Rose," 274
Ramrod, 235–36, 246, 272
Rawlings, Dave, 377
Reagan, Nancy, 359, 360
Reagan, Ronald
  Bush and, 384
  California governorship, 87–91, 93, 98,
    100, 107–8, 111, 204–6
  communal living and, 103

legacy of, 384–85
philosophy of, 134, 310, 338–39
presidency, 337–39, 343, 344, 358–60,
  372–73, 375, 385
Reasoner, Harry, 147–48
Reckoning, 349
Rector, James, 205
Reed, Lou, xviii
Reich, Charles, 98
Revolutionary Intercommunal Day of
  Solidarity, 267–68
Rex Foundation, 347, 408, 429–30
Rexroth, Kenneth, 13
Reynolds, Raymond, 351–52
Ribicoff, Abraham, 193–94
Riester, Jonathan, 184
Rifkin, Danny, 94, 106, 160, 161, 347
Rinzler, Ralph, 34
"Ripple," 252, 257–58, 263, 349, 432
Ritchie, Jean, 34
Roberts, John, 215–18
Rock and Roll Hall of Fame, 406
Rock for Life benefit, 341
Rodia, Simon, 82
Rohan, Brian, 160, 168–69
Rolling Stone, xvi, 161, 162–63, 167, 211,
  221, 226, 229, 263, 293, 294, 314, 325
Rolling Stones and Altamont, 222–27, 246
Romney, Hugh "Wavy Gravy," 81, 102,
  215, 218, 285, 418
Rosenman, Joel, 215–18
Roszak, Theodore, xviii–xix, 22, 37, 123,
  124–25, 135
Rothman, Sandy, 28, 40, 353
Round Records, 282–83
Rowan, Peter, 286, 308–10
"Row Jimmy," 284, 295
Royerton, Jack, 25–26
Rubin, Jerry, 114, 191–92, 221
"Rubin and Cherise," 312
Ruppenthal, Sara
  Acid Test Graduation and, 111
  on bluegrass morphing into jug band, 41
  child of, 38, 39–40, 82, 92, 106, 140,
    212–13, 368–69
  duets with Garcia, 38
  first impression of Garcia, 36
  on Garcia's childhood, 9
  Garcia's funeral and, 419
  on Garcia's legacy, 432

504 | INDEX

Ruppenthal, Sara (cont'd):
Garcia's mother and, 264–65
LSD and, 54–55
marriage to Garcia, 22, 36–37, 81–82,
106, 213
Russell, Leon, 289
Ryan, Leo, 330–31

Safire, William, 361–63
Sage, Nora, 364
"Samson and Delilah," 414
Sand, George, 126
Sandperl, Ira, 36
San Francisco. See also Diggers; Haight-
Ashbury
bands of the mid-1960s in, 104–5
bohemian culture in, 13
Bruce in, 32–33
Free City Convention, 172–73
history of, 13, 86, 116
Human Be-In, 112, 114–21
as literary center and subject, 17–18, 62
LSD experiments in, 54, 56
murders of Moscone and Milk, 332
police shooting and riot in, 108
in 1940s, 3–4
Zodiac Killer, 241
San Francisco Chronicle, 106, 109, 120,
130, 229, 269, 302, 351–52, 374, 392
San Francisco Examiner, 15, 56, 79, 113,
117–18, 137, 138, 170
San Francisco Express Times, 193
San Francisco Giants opener (1993), 407–8
San Francisco Mime Troupe, 77, 118–19
San Francisco Renaissance, 13–15
San Francisco Sound/Scene, 104–5
Santa Barbara oil spill, 270
Santokh, Sat, 169, 216
Saturday Night Live, 327–28
Saunders, Merl, 367
Savio, Mario, 69, 205
"Scarlet Begonias," 303, 304, 333
Scher, John, 288, 319
Scientology, 297
Scorpio Single, 107
Scully, Rock
Altamont and, 222, 224
basic facts about, 94, 181
Dead split and firing of Pigpen, 184–85,
186–88

Garcia's drug use and, 101, 350324
heroin use by, 350
at Olompali, 106
Seale, Bobby, 133
Seals, Melvin, 312
Sears, Cameron, 347, 412, 413
Seastones, 312
"Seastones," 304–5
Sebern, Roy, 64
Sebring, Jay, 219
Selvin, Joel, 137, 224, 392
Sgt. Pepper's Lonely Hearts Club Band, 39
Shakedown Street, 340
"Shakedown Street," 356
Shelton, Robert, 74
"Ship of Fools," 295–96, 297–98, 303
Shriver, Sargent, 293–94
Shurtliff, Larry. See Ramrod
"Sick and Tired," 94
Siegel, Dan, 205
Silberman, Steve, 292, 394
Six Gallery in North Beach, 14–15
"skinny pinners," 19
Slaughterhouse-Five or The Children's
Crusade (Vonnegut), 207–8
Slick, Grace, 102
"Slipknot!," 313, 315
Slow Train Coming (Dylan), 363
Smith, Joe, 128, 130, 166, 236–37
"Smokestack Lightning," 287
"Snow," 129
Snyder, Gary, 14, 18, 114, 117, 120, 430
"So Many Roads," 405, 414–15
Sometimes a Great Notion (Kesey), 64
"The Sound Test" show, 302
So What papers, 281–82
"Space," 197, 396, 406
"Spanish Jam," 172, 247
Speegle, Paul, 25–27
Springsteen, Bruce, 377–79
St. Michael's Alley (Palo Alto), 25, 28
"St. Stephen," 151–52, 186, 210, 212, 217, 232
"Standing on the Moon," 396
Stanley, Owsley "Bear"
Acid Tests and, 80–81
basic facts about, 75–76
Constanten and, 234
entrance into Dead family, 76
History of the Grateful Dead, Vol. 1 and,
287

jailing of, 236, 287
New Orleans arrest of, 235
at Olompali, 101
return to Dead of, 287–88, 301
subscription service idea of, 282
Summer Jam and, 290
Wall of Sound and, 301
at Woodstock, 217
Stegner, Wallace, 61, 62, 84–85
"Stella Blue," 96, 294–95, 305, 406, 418
Stever, Dave, 381, 427
Sting, 407
Stone, Robert, 62, 65–66, 91, 109, 316
Straight Theater, 136
Stuart (Florida) *News*, 418
Stubs, Robert, 56
student movement, 68–69. *See also*
Hayden, Tom; peace movement;
Vietnam War, opposition to;
Weatherman
"Sugar Magnolia," 255–56, 263, 305, 333
Sullivan, Edmund Joseph, 136
Summer Jam: A Day in the Country,
289–92
Summer of Love, 138, 146–47, 148–49,
157–58
Sundsten, Paula "Fetchin' Gretchen," 109
Sunshine, 92, 140, 212–13
Surrealistic Pillow (Jefferson Airplane), 105
Swanson, Sue, 276
Symbionese Liberation Army, 296

Tate, Sharon, 219
"Teach Your Children," 213
technocracy, 123–24, 125
"Tennessee Jed," 274
"Terrapin Station," 320, 393
Terrapin Station, 240, 320–21, 322
"That's It for the Other One," 163–64,
166, 171–72
Thomas, Bob, 287–88
Thompson, Bill, 173
Thompson, Hunter S., 71, 135, 138, 231,
261, 271, 293
"Throwing Stones," 396
"Till the Morning Comes," 258–59
Time magazine, 63
Times Union, 411
Tittle, Y. A., 20
"Today," 105

"Tons of Steel," 389
Tork, Peter, 145
"Touch of Grey," 368, 370, 413–14
"tour from hell" (Summer Tour), 410–15
Tracy Press, 226
Trewhitt, Henry, 359
Trilling, Lionel, 12, 15
Tripping on Utopia (Breen), 53
Trips Festival, 77, 78–80
Trist, Alan, 25–26, 30, 282, 417–18
Trouper's Hall concert (1966), 94
"Truckin'," 259–61, 273, 284, 319, 428
Truscott, Lucian K., IV, 167
Tuesday's Child, 221
"Turn on Your Love Light," 159, 171, 210,
211, 217, 232, 233, 247, 286, 406
"Turtle Dove," 375

"Uncle John's Band," 239–40, 393
United Artists, 282–83
United States Army, 23–24
University of California, Berkeley, 68–69,
88, 92–93, 204
"U.S. Blues," 285, 303, 318

Van Houten, Leslie, 138, 139
Vecchio, Mary Ann, 249
"Victim or the Crime," 373–74
Vietnam Veterans Project, 346
Vietnam War, 100, 178, 248–49, 268–69
Vietnam War, opposition to, 176
by Ali, 156, 268
Garcia and, 142
at Kent State University, 248–49
by King, 177–78
mass DC protest, 269
New Journalism and, 140
at Pentagon, 177
at UC Berkeley, 92–93
The Village Voice, 167
"Viola Lee Blues" (Lewis), 95, 120, 130, 145
Vonnegut, Kurt, 207–9

Wagner, Bob, 355
Wake of the Flood, 294–95
Walker, Bill, 167
Walker, George, 92
Walkouts, 178–79
Wallace, George, 194
Wallace, Warren, 147

506 | INDEX

Wall of Sound, 301–3, 304, 318
Walton, Bill, 157, 325, 377
Warlocks
  development of music style of, 51–52
  early performances, 48–49, 51
  as Emergency Crew, 56
  Garcia as leader of, 43–44
  Garcia on Kreutzmann and Weir in, 52
  as house band party, 72–73
  LSD and, 52
  members of, 48, 49, 50–51
  New Riders and, 213
  renaming of, 56–57
Warner Bros., 128, 129–30, 166, 168, 212,
    231, 246, 281, 287–88, 298
War on Drugs, 359
The Washington Post, 418
Watkins Glen concert, 289–92
Watts, Alan, 118
Watts riots, 89–90
"Wave That Flag," 284–85
"Weather Report Suite," 295, 304
Weatherman/Weather Underground,
    269, 296–97
Weinberg, Jack, 68
Weir, Bob. See also Grateful Dead
  Ace and, 312, 317
  Anthem of the Sun and, 165, 168
  arrest of, 235, 236–37
  Azzara and, 299
  Barlow and, 46, 316–17
  basic facts about, 45–46, 130, 165
  Campbell and, 386–87
  "Cumberland Blues" and, 242
  on "Dark Hollow," 375
  Dead & Company and, 428
  Dead split and firing of, 184–89, 200
  Egypt and, 326
  "Estimated Prophet" and, 320–21
  Garcia on, as musician, 52
  Garcia's funeral, 419–20
  on Hart at Winterland shows, 305
  at "Highest Concert," 358
  "I Know You Rider" and, 95
  on marijuana, 310
  meeting with Garcia, 46–47
  Mother McCree's and, 45
  on number of Deadheads at concerts,
    374
  Playboy After Dark performance, 210

rainforest protection and, 383
reassembly of Dead and, 200, 209
San Francisco Giants and, 407–8
on singing, 239
"Sugar Magnolia" and, 255, 256
on Terrapin Station, 321
"Truckin'" and, 259
"Weather Report Suite" and, 295
at Woodstock, 217
Weir, Frankie, 276
Welch, Gillian, 376–77
Welch, Lew, 14
"We Leave the Castle," 166
The Well (Whole Earth 'Lectronic Link,
    WELL), 360–62
Welnick, Vince, 393–94, 407–8, 423
Wenner, Jann S., 161–62
"Werewolves of London," 396
Whalen, Philip, 14
"Wharf Rat," 272, 290
"What's Become of the Baby?," 210, 212
White, Curtis, 125, 127
White, Dan, 331–32
White Noise (DeLillo), 347–48
Whitman, Walt, 126
the Who, 144, 145
Whole Earth Catalog (Brand and
    Jennings), 195–96
Wildwood Boys, 40
Williams, Stacey, 74
Williams, William Carlos, 13, 15
Williamson, Jane, 380–81
Wilson, Bill, 54
Wilson, Dan, 100
Wilson, Dennis, 219–20
Wilson, Wes, 136
Winterland shows, 304–5, 307, 327, 333
Wolfe, Tom, 65, 67, 71, 111
Wong, William, 69, 70
Woodstock Music and Art Fair, 215–18
Workingman's Dead, 228, 238–45, 255, 263,
    303

Yippies (Youth International Party),
    191–92, 193
"You Don't Have to Ask," 94

Zen and the Art of Motorcycle Maintenance
    (Pirsig), 271
Zodiacs, 45

ABOUT THE AUTHOR

JIM NEWTON is a journalist, teacher, and author of *Justice for All, Eisenhower, Worthy Fights,* and *Man of Tomorrow.* He was at the *Los Angeles Times* for twenty-five years as a reporter, bureau chief, editorial page editor, columnist, and editor at large. He lives in Pasadena, California, and teaches at UCLA, where he founded and edits the award-winning public affairs magazine *Blueprint.*

X: @newton_jim